CAMBRIDGE LIBRARY COI

Books of enduring scholarly value

African Studies

This series focuses on Africa during the period of European colonial expansion. It includes anthropological studies, travel accounts from missionaries and explorers (including those searching for the sources of the Nile and the Congo), and works that shed light on colonial concerns such as gold mining, big game hunting, trade, education and political rivalries.

Travels in the Interior of Southern Africa

William John Burchell (1781–1863) is remembered for this outstanding geography of South Africa, published in two volumes in 1822–4 and later taken on Darwin's Beagle voyage. It covers the first year of Burchell's 4,500-mile expedition into southern Africa from 1811 to 1815, while 'botanist to the Cape Colony'. The author returned to England with 500 scientific and ethnographical drawings, many of them used as illustrations in the book, and about 63,000 natural history specimens including 120 animal skins and 265 species of bird. His preface emphasises that his journal is accurate, independent and free from prejudice; he also claims that unlike many travelogues, his contains no 'indelicacies … offensive to decency'. Volume 1 focuses mainly on landscapes, flora and fauna, often giving their indigenous names. It covers Burchell's trek to Klaarwater, which became his base for over a year, and a major side trip to the south-east.

Travels in the Interior of Southern Africa

VOLUME 1

WILLIAM JOHN BURCHELL

CAMBRIDGE
UNIVERSITY PRESS

CAMBRIDGE
UNIVERSITY PRESS

University Printing House, Cambridge, CB2 8BS, United Kingdom

Cambridge University Press is part of the University of Cambridge.
It furthers the University's mission by disseminating knowledge in the pursuit of
education, learning and research at the highest international levels of excellence.

www.cambridge.org
Information on this title: www.cambridge.org/9781108084154

© in this compilation Cambridge University Press 2015

This edition first published 1822
This digitally printed version 2015

ISBN 978-1-108-08415-4 Paperback

The original edition of this book contains a number of colour plates,
which have been reproduced in black and white. Colour versions of these
images can be found online at www.cambridge.org/9781108084154

TRAVELS

IN THE

INTERIOR

OF

SOUTHERN AFRICA.

VOL. I.

TRAVELS

IN THE

INTERIOR

OF

SOUTHERN AFRICA,

BY

WILLIAM J. BURCHELL, Esq.

———◆———

VOLUME I.

WITH AN ENTIRELY NEW MAP, AND NUMEROUS ENGRAVINGS.

LONDON:

PRINTED FOR LONGMAN, HURST, REES, ORME, AND BROWN,

PATERNOSTER-ROW.

1822.

CONTENTS.

		Page
PREFACE		1
CHAPTER I.	Approach to, and arrival at, the Cape of Good Hope	1
II.	Residence in Cape Town, and Rambles in the vicinity	11
III.	A sketch of Cape Town and the Colony	70
IV.	A ride through Hottentot-Holland to the Warm-bath at Zwarteberg	83
V.	Visit to Genadendal	103
VI.	Ride from Genadendal to the hot-spring in Brand Valley, and visit to Tulbagh	116
VII.	Ride from Tulbagh to the Paarl, and thence to Stellenbosch	136
VIII.	Residence at Cape Town, and preparations for the journey	148
IX.	Journey from Cape Town to Tulbagh	172
X.	From Tulbagh, through Hex-river Kloof, to the Karro Poort	189
XI.	Journey over the Karro	210
XII.	Journey through the Roggeveld to the borders of the Colony	253
XIII.	Journey from the borders of the Cape Colony, through the country of the Bushmen, to the river Gariep	285
XIV.	Journey in the country of the Koras, from the Gariep to the Asbetos Mountains. — Stay at the Kloof village. — And arrival at Klaarwater	323
XV.	Residence and transactions at Klaarwater; with some account of the settlement and its inhabitants	350
XVI.	Excursion from Klaarwater to the confluence of the Nu-gariep, and thence to the Ky-gariep	381
XVII.	Occurrences on the banks of the Ky-gariep	403
XVIII.	Return from the Ky-gariep to Klaarwater	446
XIX.	Residence and transactions at Klaarwater, till the end of the year	476
XX.	Residence and transactions at Klaarwater, and preparations for resuming the journey into the Interior	506
XXI.	Arrangements for a journey back into the Colony. — Second visit to the village at the Asbestos Mountains. — And preparations for departure.	529
The Itinerary, and Register of the Weather		555
Remarks on the map, and geographical observations		575

a

PLATES.

Facing Page

1. A view of Cape Town, Table Bay, and Tygerberg.................................... 25
2. Portrait of Speelman, a Hottentot.. 167
3. Crossing the Berg river... 178
4. Caravan of waggons assembled at Zak river on the borders of the country of the
    Bushmen 282
5. The Rock Fountain, in the country of the Bushmen............................. 294
6. Scene on the river Gariep... 316
7. A Hottentot Kraal on the banks of the Gariep..................................... 325
8. A view of Klaarwater, looking towards the north-east.......................... 360
9. Portrait of a Bushman, playing on the Goráh....................................... 459
10. Portrait of a Kóra... 490
The Map... 582

The description of Plate 1. at page 25. having been made from the original drawing, does not in a few places correspond with the plate; because, through the haste of the engraver, the minuter details in the outline of the distant mountains, and some other particulars of less moment, have not been sufficiently attended to. But this, however, does not affect the general correctness of the view.

VIGNETTES.

	Page	Described at Page
1. Distant view of the Cape of Good Hope.....................	1	2
2. The Jutty, or landing place, at Cape Town..............	10	10
3. The Castle-gate, at Cape Town............................	11	11. 73.
4. The Mountain-butterfly....................................	45	45
5. The Kukumakranki	55	55
6. The Silver-tree...	69	17. 54. 61.
7. View of a part of Cape Town.............................	70	71
8. A Boor's waggon and oxen................................	82	76
9. The Bath-house at Zwarteberg...........................	83	85. 97.
10. Tower-of-Babel Mountain	100	100
11. The Rhinoceros-bush	102	101. 102. 176.
12. The church at Genadendal...............................	103	106
13. Huts of the Hottentots at Genadendal...................	115	112
14. The village of Tulbagh..................................	116	128

VIGNETTES.

		Page	Described at Page
15.	The Drostdy at Tulbagh	135	128. 129.
16.	The church at Stellenbosch	136	145
17.	The Cape Misseltoe	147	143
18.	Geometrical drawing of the waggon	148	149
19.	Section of the waggon, with various articles appertaining to it	171	151
20.	Scene by fire-light, on the journey; a station for the night	172	173. 180.
21.	Passing Roodezand Kloof	188	137. 181.
22.	The Karro-thorn, or Cape Acacia	189	195. 429.
23.	Cubic pyrites of iron	203	202
24.	Arrival at the Karro Pass	209	207
25.	Crossing the Karro	210	210
26.	A Bushman chief and his companion on ox-back	228	227
27.	A Boor's house in the Roggeveld-Karro, with sheep going out to pasture	238	237
28.	A tanning-vat	252	243
29.	Hottentots sitting round their fire	253	270
30.	The yellow-fish	284	280
31.	A view of the mountains of the Karreebergen	285	299
32.	A Bushwoman and her child	322	291. 292
33.	View at the Kloof village in the Asbestos Mountains	323	328. 334
34.	Rocks in the Asbestos Mountains	349	333
35.	The church at Klaarwater	550	350. 355
36.	Horns of the Koodoo	380	337. 338
37.	Station on the banks of the Nu-gariep; and making presents to a party of Bushmen	381	389. 390
38.	The Kori, a new species of bustard	402	393
39.	Head of the Hippopotamus or River-horse	403	413
40.	Hottentot utensils	406	406
41.	The Flat-head	445	425
42.	Travelling over a plain abounding in ant-hills	446	299. 342. 448
43.	A piece of an ant-hill, with one of the insects	449	448
44.	The Goráh, a Hottentot musical instrument	475	458
45.	The Bookoo plant	476	479
46.	Rocks at Leeuwenkuil	505	491. 492
47.	Hut of the Hottentot chief at Klaarwater	506	351. 365. 479.
48.	Preparing for departure	528	523
49.	The Grapple-plant	529	536
50.	The party asleep	553	553

ERRATA.

Page 4. line 12. *for* " Œolus" *read* " Æolus."
  15. ...   *for* " dipthong," in the note, *read* "diphthong.
  75. ...   8. from the bottom, *for* "Taska" *read* "Tarka."
  87. ...   2. from the bottom, *for* " Duth" *read* " Dutch."
  131. ...   1. *for* " Riebek's" *read* " Riebeck's."
  150. ... 16. *for* " izer" *read* " yzer."
  151. ... 17. *for* "fits" *read* " fit."
  152. ... 11. *for* " brick-plank" *read* " buikplank."
  179. ...   *for* " viminalis," in the note, *read* "viminale."
  190. ...   7. from the bottom, *for* " desart" *read* " desert."
  243. ...   7. from the bottom, *for* " barks" *read* " bark."
  237. ...   2. *for* " Ancistrum," in the note, *read* " Acæna."
  260. ...   6. *for* " Lappago," in the note, *read* " Selago."
  400. ... 13. of the note, the word " Capsula" should be placed in the
                next line, before the word " linearis."
  414. ...   5. *for* " was" *read* " were."
  516. ...   1. *for* " idea" *read* " ideas."
And perhaps a few others of this description, which may have escaped notice at the
time of correcting the press.

PREFACE.

THE travels, of which the following pages contain the narrative, were undertaken solely for the purpose of acquiring knowlege : and it having been thought possible that the communication of facts observed during these researches might contribute some small portion towards the general stock of information, they are here laid before the Public.   As they were commenced with a mind free from prejudice, and in the purest spirit of independence, so they have been conducted, and so they are now concluded. It is not asserted that they are exempt from the natural chance of error to which all human observations are liable; but that their claim to be, even to the minutest particular, regarded as a faithful picture of occurrences and observations, stands on a basis never to be shaken ; the confirmation of which is readily left to every honest and unprejudiced traveller who may hereafter traverse the same ground.   The motive, the expense, and the accomplishment of these travels having been entirely and individually the author's, he has therefore thought proper to adhere to the same principle in the present work, both in the scientific and in the literary parts of it.   As none but those who have personally beheld the scenes, and witnessed the facts, can be competent to communicate to others the impressions they make on the mind, or to describe them with fidelity, the author has judged it more consistent, and more conducive to correctness, to reject all assistance whatever ; and, although the language of this narrative might have been arranged in smoother periods, and expressed with more fashionable elegance, the reader who looks for information more than amusement, will doubtlessly be better satisfied by a feeling of confidence that he is receiving his information in the traveller's own words. Neither have the drawings been touched by any other hand : from these the plates have been immediately coloured, and may be considered as expressing with fidelity the tints, as well as the outlines, of African scenery. In order to ensure greater correctness in the vignettes, the author has made all these drawings upon the blocks themselves; so that the impressions are the fac-similes of every line of the pencil, a style of outline having been adopted, as being best suited to engravings on wood. Those who can appreciate the art, will not fail to admire the care and abilities of the engraver. Of the map, little need be said in this place, as a sufficient explanation will be found at the end of the Itinerary. The General Index, together with a Zoological and Botanical Index, will be given with the second volume.

In the Dutch names, and in words belonging to the languages of the Hottentots and other native tribes, the accented syllable has been generally marked by an acute accent, and the English translation of them added in parentheses. In the body of the work, words have frequently been printed in Italic characters, with the view of pointing out the subject of the paragraph, and of supplying the place of marginal notes. The General Index will answer the purpose of a glossary for all the foreign words found in this volume, by referring to the given page for the interpretation. The orthography of these words has not been neglected; and where it has been found uncertain or ill-established, the different modes in use in the colony, have been occasionally employed. With respect to those languages which have hitherto been merely oral, a system of orthography, suited to the genius or natural sounds of them, has been adopted, and will be explained hereafter. Where any of these have already been received into the Dutch or English languages, the spelling proper to these has frequently been employed; and precepts for their pronunciation given in various parts of this volume.

In the narrative, the strict form of a journal has been adhered to, as being that which best enables the reader and the author to travel, as it were, the journey over again, and view, in their proper light, the facts in connection, and the impressions made by each event in succession. The object of this journal being to give a natural and faithful picture of passing scenes and transactions, many circumstances of less importance have been allowed their place in it; just as, in a landscape or historical painting, even of the sublimest conception, the weeds of the foreground, or the stones of the pavement, however trifling in themselves, must be represented, in order to complete the whole, and convey the just resemblance of nature.

In these pages modesty may read without fearing to meet with descriptions and allusions which might raise a blush upon her cheek. This is the more necessary to be stated in a preface, as books of travels, though professedly lying open to every class of readers, sometimes contain matter offensive to decency, and which renders them unfit for general perusal. Such indelicacies will never be found in these volumes.

The author, during this expedition, which lasted four years, had no companion or assistant, nor other attendants than a few Hottentots, the number of whom never exceeded ten. Of the party which set out from Cape Town, he was the only one who returned to that place; the rest having quitted him, and been several times replaced by others during the journey. In a course of four thousand five hundred miles, exclusive of numerous smaller excursions, regions never before trodden by European foot, were explored and examined. Besides that general information respecting these countries and their inhabitants which it was his principal object to obtain, and which are communicated by the following narrative, considerable collections in Natural History were made, and a multitude of objects hitherto unknown to science brought to England. Of these a few are occasionally mentioned, and distinguished, either by a reference to the 'Geographical Catalogue,' or by the letter B; and, not to interrupt the text, short descriptions of them are added in the notes. These descriptions, however, are not intended as specific characters, but are given merely as the more obvious or striking features, in order to convey to the zoologist or botanist some idea of the more remarkable objects. Neither was it thought requisite, in the present work at least, to adopt every innovation in nomenclature which, since the travels were commenced, these sciences have from time to time undergone. These collections consist of above sixty three thousand objects, inclusive of the duplicates, in every department of the science. Out of two hundred and eighty nine quadrupeds shot on the journey, a hundred and twenty skins, comprising eighty species, were preserved. The collection of birds contains two hundred and sixty-five different kinds. In addition to these results of the expedition, are about five hundred drawings, the subjects of which are landscapes, portraits, costume, zoology, botany, and a variety of other objects.

The author's views in travelling, were not confined to any particular class of observation. As it was general knowledge which he sought, so he has endeavoured to extend his researches to whatever appeared likely to afford interesting information ; but in a country still in a state of nature, and where art has done so little, the works of the creation, ever delightful to all but those of a corrupt and depraved mind, necessarily present themselves the most frequently to notice. In the second volume, however, the investigation of man in an uncivilized state of society, will be found to offer to the contemplation of the philosopher, a picture not altogether undeserving of attention, if the writer should be able by words to communicate to others those feelings which he himself experienced, and those impressions which his abode among the natives of the interior of Africa, has made upon his own mind.

LONDON,
February, 1822.

CHAPTER I.

APPROACH TO, AND ARRIVAL AT, THE CAPE OF GOOD HOPE.

AT five in the afternoon, (13th November, 1810,) the sailors on deck, who had for some time been anxiously looking out, called to us that land was in sight.   At this pleasing intelligence we hastened up from the cabin, and although nothing could be seen but a small cloud, which seemed fixed on the horizon, and was at first not very easily to be distinguished, the captain, who was well acquainted with the singular appearance of the cloud which rests on the *Table Mountain* during a south-east gale, declared that the land which we had now before us was that of the *Cape of Good Hope.*

It appeared gradually and slowly rising out of the ocean, while our sails, well filled with the gentle gale, bore the gliding vessel over the blue waters of the deep, and forced its foamy prow resistless through the yielding waves.   Every other thought was banished, and our whole attention was now turned towards the distant cloud.   The tedious and protracted length of our voyage was felt no longer ; every coun-tenance became enlivened, and each one with new alacrity assisted in the preparations for bringing the ship into port.   The land was distant nearly one hundred miles in the direction of north-east ; but a pleasant south-easterly breeze was carrying us on rapidly towards it, and every mile we advanced added some agreeable idea to the animating anticipation of my feelings on first setting foot on the land of Africa. I now perceived that all the pictures which imagination previously forms of a country, make but faint impressions in comparison with those presented by the country itself: we indulge the more freely in all the speculations of curiosity, whenever the prospect of its immediate gratification banishes the fear of disappointment: we feel an increased desire to ascertain whether the notions we had previously acquired, correspond with things themselves; and our fancy redoubles its activity in pourtraying a thousand delightful objects, ready to pour fresh knowledge into our mind.

Anticipated ideas continued to interest and amuse me during the remainder of the day; and the dawn of daylight the next morning found us on deck, ready to catch the appearance of the long-wished-for land. Nothing, however, was to be seen: the haziness of the atmosphere was not dissipated till the sun had risen high; when the land again came in view*, presenting

---

* See *the Vignette.* — This represents a first view of the land of the Cape of Good Hope, as seen from a distance of about thirty miles in the direction of E.N.E. Cape Point, or the *Cape* of Good Hope proper, was at this time covered with a thick haze, and therefore could not be distinguished; but on comparing the vignette with the map, it will be easily seen how much farther to the right the land should extend. To the left the *Lion's Head*, appearing as a conical mountain, terminates the view; the mountains of Blauwberg, &c. not having yet risen above the horizon. The Lion Mountain is seen foreshortened, and therefore the Rump appears only as a point of less elevation, and close under the Head on the left. The large flat mountain next following is the celebrated *Table Mountain,* presenting its steep rocky western side to the ocean. Cape Town stands on its northern side, and no part of it can be seen till the voyager has sailed round to the other side of the Lion Mountain. Over the low gorge, or *kloof,* between these two mountains, passes the road from the Town to *Camp's Bay.* Through the next kloof or opening there is a horse-road from Camp's Bay to *Hout Bay,* which lies behind the mountain following next to Table Mountain; and the entrance to this bay is round the small conical rocky point (here shaded more darkly) sometimes called the Hanglip, from its resemblance to a mountain similarly situated at the south-eastern point of False Bay. The next large mountain, less shaded than the others, is called the *Steenbergen* (Stony Mountains); behind which, and constituting a part of it, is *Muisenberg* (Mouse Mountain), and the north-western corner of False Bay. The land which next follows is not in reality so low as it here appears to be, but is a continuation of the same range of mountains, receding below the horizon of the sea. The abrupt termination of the range is where the haze concealed the remaining part of it.

from afar a range of faint blue mountains, at the northern end of which *Table Mountain* and *Lion's Head* were very easy to be recognized by the peculiarity of their form. The weather became fine; and the wind, which had continued to blow from the south-east, increased to a gale; so that by noon we were within two leagues of the shore: and soon after getting under the lee of the mountains, the vessel was nearly becalmed, scarcely making any way through the water. This slow progress gave me a favourable opportunity for making several drawings, and for observing the remarkable cloud which covered the top of Table Mountain, resting upon it with all the appearance of a ponderous substance: every other part of the sky was perfectly clear, and the wind, which was evidently blowing there with great violence, seemed unable to dislodge it from its situation. Its thin misty skirts no sooner rolled over the edge of the precipice, than they were rarefied into air and vanished. The western part of Table Mountain, with its rocky precipitous side cleft in deep ravines, rose majestically out of the ocean. Between this and the mountains, which form the western side of *Hout Bay* (Wood Bay), stands the *False Lion's Head*, a mountain of subordinate elevation. The true Lion's Head is much higher than the False, but considerably lower than Table Mountain.

As we advanced nearer along the shore, the mountains displayed an imposing grandeur, which mocked the littleness of human works: buildings were but white specks; too small to add a feature to the scene; too insignificant either to adorn or to disturb the magnificence of nature. We had left behind us the deep blue waters of the ocean, and, sheltered by the land, were sailing on the calm surface of waters of a greener tinge, from which the seals sometimes raised their dripping heads to view us as we passed. Baffling winds frequently impeded our progress, and put the sailors' patience to trial; but the novelty of the scene, and the interesting objects before me, absorbed the whole of my attention. Eager to become acquainted with the details of what I saw, I long occupied myself in scrutinizing, with a telescope, every rock and ravine; though as yet we were too far off to allow my impatient curiosity to be gratified.

We continued till evening frequently tacking and working our way slowly towards Table Bay, where we hoped to cast anchor in the course of the night. The moon had just risen, glittering on the tops of the waves, and, casting its light on the projecting crags of the mountains, spread a beauty and solemnity over the scene, that heightened the effect of every occurrence. At this time we were abreast of *Green Point* at the entrance of the bay.

The moment we had passed beyond the shelter of the Lion Mountain, a furious wind suddenly and unexpectedly assailed the vessel; pouring out of the clouds, as it seemed, its boisterous fury upon us. A poetic imagination would certainly have fancied that the skins given by Œolus to Ulysses, had been carried to the top of Table Mountain, and there all cut open at once.

The vessel was rapidly driving out to sea again : in the utmost hurry the sailors flew up the rigging, and took in all sail possible. We strove to beat into the bay, but a whole hour's struggling against the storm proved all in vain; and the fore top-sail being split, we were compelled to wear the ship, and retreat to the shelter of the Lion Mountain to bend another sail.

Towards morning we made a second attempt, but were repulsed by a wind more furious than before; so that we considered ourselves fortunate in being able to regain our former shelter. Here we continued the whole of this and the following day, standing off and on within the lee of the Lion Mountain, experiencing alternate calms and gales; at one moment the ship rolling in a dead calm, and at the next, if we happened to exceed the limit of our shelter, running with the gunnel under water, through waves whose tops were blown away in spray by the fury of the south-easter : yet the weather appeared fine and the sky cloudless.

We often approached to within half a mile of the shore, where with a glass we could discern people at work, and dust driven up in clouds. Some spots appeared of a beautiful purple and others of a yellow colour, occasioned most probably by the abundance of flowers. So tantalizing a view, after a protracted and tedious voyage, would have induced me to attempt a landing almost at any rate; but the surf, which lined the whole coast with a fringe of white, plainly showed the danger and even impracticability of the attempt at such a time; I therefore contented myself with making a drawing of the view; which in this bearing, more than in any other, presents a resemblance to a lion quite sufficient to justify the name the mountain has received; and is probably that in which the likeness was first observed. To a ship keeping the Lion's Head and the middle of the northern side of Table Mountain in a line, and being at the distance of about two miles, the mountain exhibits the form of a *lion couchant*, whose fore-paws are extended forward, and form the southern point of *Camp's Bay*, while the tail is very well represented by the flat land of *Green Point*.

The first discoverers of a land presenting such grand features of bold and mountainous outline, must have felt that the occurrence itself was full of interest; but when at the same time they knew that they had thus passed the barrier which had stopped all former navigators, at least of the later ages, and had now opened a way to the Eastern world, the doubling of this celebrated promontory must have been an event which might justify the highest exultation. As I looked upon the mountains and the shore, my imagination carried me back to that period when its peaceable inhabitants, the simple Hottentots, roamed freely over the country, enjoying the liberty of nature, nor dreaming that a day could ever arrive when they must resign all to some unknown race of men, coming upon them from the ocean, an element which no tradition had ever told them could be travelled on by man. Their arms and their watchings had no object besides their inland enemies; the turbulent surface of the " Great Water" and the noisy shore, seemed the only side whence no danger was to be dreaded. But it is not at the extremity of Africa only, where treachery has surprised men from a quarter where it was least expected. I was wishing, for the honor of Europeans, men enjoying the blessings of civilization, and illumined by the superior light of arts and science, that I could have persuaded myself that these natives had been rendered happier by their communication with them : I longed to be amongst them, that I might ascertain so important a fact by my own experience; and my fondest wish was, to be able to bear witness to the truth of it.

The idea, that the land was now before me where I was to become acquainted with my fellow-creatures living in primeval simplicity, caused a pleasing glow in my mind, and I imagined myself already in the midst of their tribes, delighted at the novelty of the scene, and acquiring new views of human nature. Not aware that the ardor of a youthful imagination concealed every difficulty, I could see none which could disappoint my hope of traversing in any direction the unknown regions of Southern Africa; and believed that once safely landed, every obstacle to my progress would vanish. My impatience, therefore, at remaining on the sea so long after coming in sight of the harbour, began to render my confinement to the ship exceedingly irksome.

The whole crew, being but few in number, were obliged to remain constantly on the watch; and as the wind was continually changing, they were nearly exhausted by fatigue. Thus passed the day; and the evening came on without any symptoms of abatement in the storm. At last, about eight o'clock, we suddenly found ourselves within its influence, having unfortunately drifted beyond the shelter of the mountain. The wind roared in the rigging, and drove us before it like a feather on the surface of a lake; it was impossible to regain our shelter, and in this extremity we bore up for *Robben island*, hoping under the lee of it to find some protection. But this we could not accomplish, and the fury of the storm sweeping us past it with awful rapidity, hurried us once more out of sight of land. With great difficulty the sails were furled, and under a close reefed fore-topsail we scudded before the tempest. The vessel rolled in a dreadful manner; every minute we expected to hear the crash of masts falling overboard; the men were thrown from side to side, unable to keep on their feet; and worn out with labor and fatigue, they looked at each other in a desponding manner, which betrayed their fears, and showed the reality of our danger. The storm raged still more furiously, and the peril of our situation increased every moment. It was no longer safe to scud; huge waves pursuing as if bent on our destruction, threatened every instant to break over us, and at once overwhelm our bark in the fathomless deep. The captain, whose judgment was always cool, saw no alternative between certain destruction and what was, in our circumstances, a very perilous experiment; but we happily succeeded in heaving the ship to, under storm-mainsail, fore stay-sail, and close-reefed try-sail. There was still much reason for uneasiness, lest she should not keep her head to the sea; and every one continued watching the danger with the greatest anxiety, dreading that some unforeseen accident would before morning bury us all in the cold grave of the ocean. The vessel became so leaky that it was necessary to keep both pumps going day and night; and it was at one time uncertain whether they gained on the water or not.

The night passed without sleep or rest, and the welcome morning light served in some measure to diminish the gloomy appearance of the scene: the sunshine and cloudless sky exhibited the fallacious semblance of fair weather, but the angry wind still howled in the rigging, and the waves still lifted up their foaming heads around. The hatches carefully closed, and the deadlights bolted in, the cabin dark as a dungeon, and the deck deluged with the waves, were appearances well suited to the solemnity of a storm. Heavy seas frequently rolled on board with overwhelming force, throwing every thing into confusion, breaking the spars and casks from their lashings, and washing away the loose utensils into the sea. The seamen, drenched with water, seemed to go aloft with reluctance, expecting hardly to escape being blown overboard. The captain, whose careful eye was unceasingly surveying every part of his ship, discovered that the try-sail, which was an old one, showed in several parts the first symptoms of splitting, some of the threads having already given way. Knowing that on this sail depended the maintenance of the balance of wind necessary for keeping the vessel's head either from falling off or broaching to, he began, with evident melancholy, to express to me his fears. At such a time as this, and indeed on every occasion, when the safety or right management of the ship is in question, a

passenger (and here I was the only one) will naturally feel as
anxious and watchful as those to whom that safety is entrusted.
I saw that our fate depended on the sail, and we knew that to replace
it by another was impracticable at this time.   After devising various
plans, I proposed that another sail should be hoisted under the lee
of it, so that in the event of its giving way, the pressure of the wind
would then be sustained by the lee sail.   The suggestion was instantly
approved, and no time was lost in carrying it into execution.

After this we felt as if the crisis of our danger were past, and
looked with some hope for a favourable termination to the tempest.
Drifting at the mercy of the elements, we were unable to estimate
our lee-way, or to calculate with any certainty what part of the
ocean we were in.

Thus passed the whole of the day.   In the night the violence of
the wind began to abate a little, and in the course of the forenoon of
the following day (18th) it became sufficiently moderate to allow of
our making sail again.   Every one resumed a cheerful countenance,
and congratulated each other on having thus happily weathered so tremendous a storm.   Our little vessel was in gratitude praised for many
good qualities ; and the captain, who had been very unfortunate in his
ships, several having been wrecked or cast ashore, some foundered at
sea, and one consumed by fire, now confessed that at one time his
hopes of ever reaching land had deserted him.   Every one was busily
employed in repairing damages, and in rectifying the confusion into
which the deck had been thrown.   The unusual and unexpected
length of the voyage reduced us to a short allowance of water, and
our stock of fresh provisions had been exhausted three days before.
We shaped our course once more towards the Cape, and continued
sailing, with variable winds and unsettled weather, for four days ; but
on the 23d and 24th the weather became fair and pleasant, and the
wind blew right in our favour.

On the 25th, in the morning, at a little before eight o'clock,
having a light westerly wind, we again made the Cape land ; and rejoiced to find that the cloud had left the mountain.   Having paid so

dearly for our experience and knowledge of the nature of that cloud, it was with no small satisfaction that we beheld Table Mountain in its true outline, presenting its broad, flat, and horizontal summit, unobscured by mist or haze. Although we approached the land but slowly, we were confident in not meeting at present, on entering Table Bay, so ungracious a reception as we had experienced the first time.

The next day, (26th,) by three in the afternoon, we were close in with the *Lion's Head;* but being nearly becalmed, we made but slow progress round *Green Point,* which, as we sailed along, was very close on our right hand. Various buildings began to make their appearance; the Jutty and Castle came in sight; and, as soon as we had passed the Chavonne and Amsterdam batteries, *Cape Town* itself, backed by the immense precipice of Table Mountain, rising like an enormous wall, opened full to view.

At first no object attracted my notice till I had sufficiently admired the majestic amphitheatre of mountains in which the town reposes. Every thing wore, to *my* eye at least, a pleasing aspect: it was the charm of novelty which cast an agreeable hue over the whole scene; even the smallest object interested me, and whatever I beheld seemed to present itself as a subject for my future investigation. On the first arriving at a foreign country, there is a sensation so delightful and so peculiar to an inquisitive mind, that language can convey but little of it to a reader. To many these sentiments must remain unintelligible; to those, at least, who see no other difference in the countries they may have had the opportunities of visiting, than that which arises from the language or dress of the inhabitants, or from the heat or cold of the climate. The strange features which an attentive observer instantly discovers, in animated as well as in inanimated nature; the various shades of human character and manners; the complexion of the mountains and valleys; the ground we tread upon; all open to us gratuitously an inexhaustible source of knowledge and of ideas, and an infinite variety of amusement of the most rational kind. To that cold mind which can look at Nature with insensibility, nearly the whole of the creation exists in vain,

c

and that heart can be but faintly warmed with love for the Creator, which is ignorant of the stupendous wisdom and countless multitude of his works; works which seem formed expressly to conduce in every way to our happiness, and which fill the world we inhabit with beauty, inviting the mind to study their importance and admire their perfection.

At length the anchor was cast; and the voyage ended.

It was six o'clock before the boat was ready to leave the ship; when Captain Waldo, whose attentions had contributed to render my situation during the passage, as comfortable as circumstances would permit, accompanied me for the purpose of being my guide, as he was well acquainted with the place. In ten minutes we reached the shore, and my foot stepped, for the first time, on the land of Africa.

The Vignette represents a part of the Jutty, the usual and only safe landing-place at Cape Town. It is also the only wharf, and, therefore, at all times a very busy spot. Some interest may be felt in this little representation, when the reader recals to mind the many celebrated or well-known characters who have passed along this same platform, and here first set their foot on the African shore. Eminent navigators and men of science of all nations; crowds of European passengers to or from India and the eastern colonies; all, not less than the weather-beaten sailor or the invalid, have leaped from their boat on to this wooden structure with a pleasure which a long and irksome voyage, and the view of a fine town, have equally contributed to heighten: some looking forward to the refreshments and to the amusements which the place is to afford, and others to the acquirement of knowledge, and the investigation of Nature under new forms.

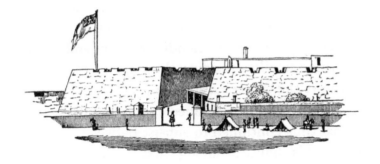

CHAPTER II.

RESIDENCE IN CAPE TOWN, AND RAMBLES IN THE VICINITY.

I HAD brought with me letters of introduction to the Governor, to the Colonial Secretary, and to several English families; and had, above four years and a half before, been so fortunate as to become

---

Explanation of the Vignette, representing a part of the *Castle*, viewed from the west, or on the side towards the town. This subject has been selected chiefly for the purpose of showing the principal outlet from Cape Town. It is through this *Gateway* that most of the waggons from the distant districts of the colony pass and repass. The road turns round under the bastion on the left, on the other side of which it leads through the outer gate; and a little farther on, through the lines, it conducts either to *Rondebosch* and *Simon's Town*, or to *Salt River*, and the rest of the colony. The only other outlet is to the right, by a road without the Castle. The whole fortification is surrounded by a moat: this is not shown in the engraving, because it is seen only on a near approach. A number of tents are pitched by the road-side, for the daily sale of fruit and vegetables, and are kept by free Malays and slaves. About three inches farther on the left of this drawing, and on this side of the castle, commences the *jutty*, part of which is given in the preceding vignette; consequently, the objects here delineated are some of the first which meet the eye of a stranger on his landing.

This subject, and that of the jutty, were drawn in the year 1815, and are taken out of a *panoramic* series of drawings, representing Cape Town and the whole of the surrounding scenery, as viewed from an elevated station at the beginning of Strand Street.

personally known to *General Jansens* the last Dutch governor, and
to several officers of his suite, among whom was *Dr. Lichtenstein,*
the present professor of natural history in the university at Ber-
lin.   On being informed of my intention of visiting the colony, they
voluntarily offered letters and friendly recommendations to many
Dutch and German families residing there.

Among these, the *Reverend Frederick Hesse*, the Lutheran minis-
ter, was more particularly mentioned to me; and a correspondence
having from that time continued to subsist between us, I now decided
on repairing to his house; having first secured a lodging at the
" English Hotel."   The reception which I met with, was such as to
prepossess me with a favourable opinion of the place and of its inhabitants.   He would not allow that I should take up my abode
elsewhere than at his house during my stay in Cape Town; and the
friendly kindness of his manners at last persuaded me to accept his
hospitality.

The lateness of the evening did but just permit me to present
another letter of introduction, and to pay a visit to an old acquaintance: but as I walked along the streets, the remaining twilight was
still sufficient both to excite and to satisfy much of my curiosity;
and I was particularly struck with the elegant style of architecture,
regularity, and cleanness of the town.

Thus passed my first African day.   Gratified by every thing I
had met with, when I retired to rest, a train of pleasing reflections
and anticipations long kept me from sleep.

27th.   The next morning I presented my letters to the Governor
the *Earl of Caledon,* who expressed with much politeness his inclination and readiness to forward my views.

A letter of introduction to the Deputy Colonial Secretary, Major
(now *Colonel*) *Bird,* was the means of my obtaining afterwards much
polite attention from that gentleman.   He was then filling the office
of the Colonial Secretary *Mr. Alexander,* to whom I was already personally known, but who was absent on a mission to England.   To the
friendship of Mr. Alexander, and a voluntary offer of several letters

of introduction, I feel a pleasure in ascribing some of the advantages which I enjoyed.

28th. This, and the greater part of the two following days, were occupied in delivering my letters to such gentlemen as were living in Cape Town; in introductions to others; in receiving the friendly visits of several who now renewed a former acquaintance; in getting my baggage ashore; and in executing several little commissions with which I had been charged.

I had at this time decided on nothing more than the general outlines of the plan for my future travels, agreeable to an intention of exploring the less frequented or unknown parts of Africa, for the purpose of becoming acquainted with its inhabitants, and of increasing my own knowledge by the addition of whatever facts I might have the opportunity of observing. Being accountable to no one for the result of my visit to this country, I felt the more at ease to decide on any arrangement best suited to my views; and determined on delaying my intended journey, until I should have collected some information respecting the country, and acquired some experience and knowledge of its customs and peculiarities.

Besides which, a knowledge and proper pronunciation of the Dutch language, according to the Cape dialect, and even according to the corrupt dialect of the Hottentots, was not among the least important preparations for a journey of research in this part of Africa. For I am convinced that many incorrect and absurd things, which have been written about this Colony, would never have been said, had the writers been sufficiently acquainted with the language to converse with every class of its inhabitants. To be qualified for judging of the character of these inhabitants, it is not enough to have mingled with the better part of society; the Boors must be heard, the Hottentots must be heard, and the slaves must be heard. It is an observation which Hollanders have often made, that on their first arrival they could not readily comprehend the meaning of a Hottentot when he spoke in Dutch; while it was evident to them that the Hottentot had still more difficulty in understanding that language in its pure and grammatical state. The English language may be said to be quite unknown to the natives beyond the colonial boundary, and even within that line it is very little understood, excepting in Cape Town. *

I resolved, therefore, to consider Cape Town as my place of abode for a few months, expecting that a part of this time would be well employed in making collections in Natural History; thus saving myself the labour of bringing from a distance that which might here more easily be procured close at hand. Much of this time would be required for purchasing and collecting together a multitude of things necessary for such a journey, and for finding a number of Hottentots both qualified and willing to accompany me; for it was soon evident that such must be my only companions.

29th. As soon as my baggage was all safely landed, and I had got over the first bustle of introductions and visits, my curiosity to see the environs of the town could not longer be restrained; and Mr. Hesse proposed that we should this afternoon take a walk round the *Lion Mountain.*

As we passed along the western skirts of the town, I continued to admire the cleanness and good appearance of the houses, and the magnificence of the surrounding mountains. Owing to its great height and undivided form, *Table Mountain* does not at first appear to be so distant from the town as it really is; but as we approach, it seems to recede gradually, disclosing to the observer its enormous mass, and apparently, at every step, towering higher and higher above his head.

As soon as we had passed the houses, my attention, in spite of myself, was entirely engrossed by the rich and wonderful variety of plants that grew in every spot. In the bushes, weeds, and herbage by the road-side, at every step I recognised some well-known flower

---

* And at present (1821) in the District of *Albany.*

which I had seen nursed with great care in the green-houses of England. *

A little farther on, we came to some plants of the great American Aloe (*Agave Americana*), in flower. This noble plant is frequently used for forming hedges; and when they stand close together, their thorny leaves present an impregnable barrier to cattle, and even to men. Their leaves, six feet long, and flower-stems of thirty feet in height, present a truly gigantic specimen of the plants commonly termed " flowers." Of these and the surrounding scenery I afterwards made a drawing.

The road, winding up an ascent, leads over a rocky gorge, which joins Lion's Head to Table Mountain. This pass is defended by a block-house, and is called the *Kloof*†, a word of frequent

* Such as, —

Leonotis Leonurus	*Cassine Maurocenia*
Erica cerinthoïdes	*Osteospermum spinescens*
Erica Petiverii	*Atraphaxis undulata*
Erica pubescens	*Kiggelaria Africana*
Athanasia crithmifolia	*Bubon gummiferum*
Athanasia parviflora	*Watsonia alopecuroides*
Royena glabra	*Aristea cyanea*
Myrica quercifolia	*Echium fruticosum*
Myrica serrata	*Polygala (Muraltia) Heisteria*
Cluytia pulchella	*Lightfootia subulata*
Cluytia Alaternoïdes	*Myrsine Africana*
Roella ciliaris	*Montinia acris*
Chironia baccifera	*Brunia nodiflora*
Chironia linoides	*Diosma villosa*
Passerina filiformis	*Psoralea aphylla*
Borbonia lanceolata	*Salvia Africana*
Celastrus pyracanthus	

† As I have endeavoured to preserve the proper orthography of all the Dutch names and words, excepting a very few, it is necessary to apprise such readers as may be unacquainted with that language, that the word *kloof* is pronounced as an Englishman would speak *klofe*, or *kloaf;* the double o having no other sound than that of a long o, or the Greek ω. The dipthong oe sounds exactly the same as the English oo; thus, *boek* in Dutch has the same sound and meaning as *book* in English. *Ou*, in Dutch words, must be pronounced the same as *ow* in the English words *now*, *how*. G is always hard before *e* or *i*, as in *get*, and *give*. Y is always a vowel, having the sound of a long *i*, and *lyk* in Dutch, and *like* in English, have the same sound and meaning. The *j* is pronounced the same as *y* in English when a consonant; as *jong* and *young:* or may be considered as an *i*, forming a dipthong with the vowel which follows it.

occurrence in this colony, and signifying a pass, either over or between mountains, and often a deep ravine down the side of a mountain. Here there is a commanding view of the whole town, looking down the streets, which from this spot exhibit their regularity very remarkably.

In the opposite direction is a view of *Camps Bay* (or, more properly, *Van Camps Bay*); but instead of descending to it, we continued at a considerable elevation, along a road leading round the Lion's Head, having all the way a fine view of the sea on our left, and on our right the rising slope of the mountain, covered with low scattered bushes. All that I had pictured to myself of the riches of the Cape in botany, was far surpassed by what I saw in this day's walk. At every step a different plant appeared; and it is not an exaggerated description, if it should be compared to a botanic garden, neglected and left to grow to a state of nature; so great was the variety every where to be met with.

After having been so long confined to a ship, without taking much exercise, I felt a little fatigued, and we rested at a pleasant cottage belonging to Mr. Beck. We were told that a few days ago a tiger (*Felis Leopardus*) had been shot near this place; but this was mentioned as an extraordinary occurrence, this animal very seldom venturing so near to Cape Town. Continuing our walk homewards, night overtook us, and put an end to further observation; but by the light of the moon, enough could be discovered to raise my curiosity, and excite a strong wish soon to return and examine the road by day-light. We did not reach home till nine o'clock, although the walk had not, perhaps, exceeded nine miles.

Dec. 1st — 4th. I every day became more sensible of my good fortune in having taken up my abode under the hospitable roof of *Mr. Hesse.* A congenial love of the works of nature, added to his learning and acquirements, rendered his society delightful, and ripened my acquaintance with him into a cordial and lasting friendship. He entered into my views in visiting Africa, and was anxious to assist me by advice, the result of long experience at the Cape. Through him I became acquainted with many of the most respectable Dutch families, whose civilities contributed much to render Cape Town so agreeable to me. His friend *Polemann*, who like himself was a lover of natural history, caught the same warmth of friendship, and, by his knowledge of the colony and its customs, greatly facilitated my preparations.

5th. Having determined on taking a day's ramble, with a view to exploring and collecting the productions of the fields and hills, I set out early in the morning, accompanied only by a slave-boy to carry my boxes, and bent my steps southerly through the town, passing the very pleasant villa of *Leeuwenhof*, the residence of *Mr. Zorn*, the Landdrost of the Cape District. Between this place and Table Mountain, I found an excellent field for my researches, the land being but little cultivated, and nearly in a state of nature.

Here the vegetation differed in its character, from that which I had already observed on the sides of the Lion Mountain. As I walked along in the midst of the variety and profusion, I could not for some time divest myself of feelings of regret, that at every step my foot crushed some beautiful plant; for it is not easy, at one's first walks in this country, to lay aside a kind of respect with which one is accustomed, in Europe, to treat the *Proteas*, the *Ericas*, the *Pelargoniums*, the *Chironias*, the *Royenas*, &c. It was now the dry season, and, therefore, not a favourable time for the botanist; most plants having ceased flowering, while many of the bulbous and herbaceous kind, had disappeared altogether.

Coming to a very pleasant spot by the side of a brook of clear water, which ran from Table Mountain, we sat down under some beautiful *Silver-trees* *, which shaded us from a very hot sun : here we opened our basket and took breakfast. After this we bent our course north-westerly, continuing to collect, as it were, with both hands.

The beautiful little *Certhia* (*Nectarinia*) *chalybea*, flying from flower to flower, was frequently seen; and, by its rich and gay

---

* *Leucadendrum argenteum*, the *Protea argentea* of Linnæus. See the Vignette at the end of this Chapter, where it is represented in the proportion of one-third of the natural size.

plumage, and soft and delicate note, often drew my attention. To those who have never before seen any of this tribe of birds alive, their exotic colors and manners will be exceedingly interesting. The delicate Humming-birds (*Trochili*) of South America are, in Southern Africa, represented by the *Nectariniæ*, here called by the Dutch colonists *Suiker-vogels* (sugar-birds), from having been observed, at least in the neighbourhood of Cape Town, to feed principally on the honey of the flowers of the *Suiker-bosch* (sugar-bush). * The loud and clear whistle of the *canari-byter* (canary-biter), a species of *Lanius*†, is heard from afar, its notes being very remarkable.

The weather, which was delightful, though hot, gave a smiling appearance to every object. The novelty of the scenery, the clearness of the atmosphere, and the profuse variety which Flora has strewn over this her favoured country, inspired me with the most agreeable sensations, and created new ardour and activity. By the time we had joined the road leading to Campsbay Kloof, all my boxes were completely filled with what I had already gathered, and having no where room for more, I was obliged to turn my steps homeward.

To give some idea of the botanical riches of the country, I need only state that, in the short distance of one English mile, I collected in four hours and a half, one hundred and five distinct species of plants, even at this unfavourable season; and I believe that more than double that number may, by searching at different times, be found on the same ground.

Descriptions of all the objects of natural history, observed during these travels, are intended to be published in a separate work. A list of the plants, arranged according to the days on which they were collected, and the places where they were found, will be given in a small precursory work, under the title of *Catalogus geographicus plantarum Africæ australis extratropicæ*, with notes of such particulars as may be thought interesting. From this catalogue I shall occasionally extract some names, hoping that even a bare enumeration, exhibiting the *geographical* or *local associations* of plants,

---

* *Protæa mellifera.*   † *Turdus zeylonus* of Linn.

may not be unacceptable to the *philosophical* botanist. To the traveller, or the collector, who shall hereafter visit the places described in these travels, such lists may be useful in directing his attention to some objects that might otherwise escape his notice. *

* Among the plants observed in this day's walk, were, —

Protea acaulis
Royena glabra
Polygala (Muraltia) Heisteria
Scabiosa pumila
Polygala (Muraltia) stipulacea
Andropogon hirtum. Th.
Juncus capensis
Lightfootia subulata
Linum Africanum
Corymbium glabrum
Aspalathus pungens
Aristea spicata. Pers.
Hydrocotyle Asiatica. Th.
Hibiscus Ethiopicus
Polygala Garcini. D.C.
Briza Capensis
Rottböllia dimidiata
Morea bituminosa
Erica imbricata
Cynosurus uniolæ
Atraphaxis undulata
Borbonia crenata
Borbonia lanceolata
Myrica serrata
Erica baccans
Arnica Gerbera
Chironia linoïdes
Cliffortia ruscifolia
Chrysocoma Comaurea
Psoralea aphylla
Myrica quercifolia
Erica cerinthoïdes

Besides, on 28*th February*, —
Plantago hirsuta
Polygala? spinosa, α.
On 16th *March*, —
Hæmanthus coccineus
Aristida Capensis
Lobelia repens.

Cyperus lanceus
Zygophyllum sessilifolium
Scirpus Hottentottus
Senecio longifolius
Selago corymbosa
Cheilanthus Capensis
Anthistiria imberbis
Passerina filiformis
Cheilanthus pteroïdes
Cliffortia trifoliata
Rhus mucronatum
Erica pubescens
Lomaria Capensis
Leysera squarrosa
Salvia aurita?
Hallia imbricata
Commelina Africana
Chironia lychnoïdes?
Psoralea bracteata
Lapeyrousia corymbosa
Thesium strictum?
Lobelia triquetra
Lobelia coronopifolia
Drosera Capensis
Lobelia lutea
Aster tenellus
Euphorbia tuberosa
Briza maxima
Roella ciliata
Serpicula repens
Wachendorfia hirsuta
Antirrhinum aphyllum.

And, on 6*th April*, —
Indigofera coriacea
Cassytha filiformis
Phylica stipularis,
&c.

7th. On the following day we took a walk on the *Lion's Rump,* and added forty-three more species to my Herbarium, although the earth was quite parched up by the sun. Many beautiful flowers, well known in the choicer collections in England, grow wild on this mountain, as the heath and the primrose on the commons and sunny banks of our own country. *

In the afternoon I paid a visit of introduction to the Landdrost, from whom I experienced the same politeness which I had hitherto every where met with. In his garden I noticed a beautiful tree of *Oleander,* above ten feet high, decorated with a profusion of rosy flowers, and a large shrub of *Cassia corymbosa,* loaded with bunches of blossom. This house, delightfully placed in the midst of gardens and plantations, in the country behind the town, towards Table Mountain, commands an extensive view of the Bay and distant mountains, with a great part of the town. In the aviary, I saw the *Touracoo* †, called *Loeri* by the colonists; the *Kaffers Fink*‡; the *Canary* § and the *Paddy-bird.* ||

8th. At this time Cape Town afforded scarcely any public amuse-ments, the theatre being shut up for want of performers. An occa-

---

* Such as —

Phlomis (Leonitis) Leonurus	Together with —
Indigofera psoraloïdes	*Physalis tomentosa*
Gladiolus alopecuroïdes	*Ceanothus Africanus*
Pelargonium pinnatum	*Montinia acris*
Cyanella Capensis	*Alopecurus Capensis*
Pelargonium melananthum	*Cuscuta Africana*
Pelargonium lobatum	*Mohria thurifraga*
Ceropegia tenuifolia	*Stachys Ethiopica*
Echium argenteum	*Pharnaceum incanum*
Aristea cyanea	*Gorteria personata*
Lessertia pulchra. Bot. Mag.	*Lepidium Capense* Th.
Knowltonia hirsuta	*Stobæa atractyloïdes,*
Oxalis monophylla ;	and many others.

† *Corythaix,* Ill. *Cuculus Persa,* Linn.
‡ *Emberiza longicauda,* et *Loxia Caffra.* Linn. Syst. Nat. ed. Gmel.
§ *Fringilla Canaria.* Linn. || *Loxia oryzivora.* Linn.

sional concert was all that the place could offer; and considering that there were but few professed musicians in the orchestra, the perform-ance might be called very good. The leader of the band, a Dane, whose powers on the violin were far above mediocrity, gave us a *con-certo* on that instrument, and, on the same evening, another on the harp. These he played without any assistance whatever from written notes; an example of musical memory not very common. The principal parts were filled by the amateurs, all of whom were of the Dutch part of the community; the French-horns, bassoons, and clarionets being supplied from the regimental bands.

Whenever mention is made of the Dutch in a more general sense, that part of the population of Cape Town, or of the colony, not English, is intended: since by far the greater proportion belongs to that nation; and all those who are born in the colony speak that language, and call themselves *Africaanders*, whether of Dutch, Ger-man, or French origin.

It has been often remarked, whether justly or not, that the English have not that degree of taste and love for music, which several European nations regard as an ornament in their character: and it must be confessed, that, independently of professional persons, more real musicians are to be found among foreigners than among us. This, perhaps, should be attributed, not so much to our want of taste or feeling, as to our viewing music as an inferior kind of study. But we undervalue the importance of it; and do not seem sufficiently aware that it possesses the power of improving the best feelings of the heart, and of calming, and even annihilating, many of the more turbulent passions of men. But to produce this effect, mere execution avails but little, without that expression and speaking intelligence, which can be given to it only by the fingers of sensibility.

The present concert was entirely instrumental; and the greater part of the audience were ladies. They were dressed extremely well, and quite in the English fashion; and it would be thought by many, that, for personal beauty, they ought not easily to yield the prize, even to our own fair countrywomen. As a mark of good sense in the company, it should be noticed, that here was none of that talking and chattering which are too often heard at concerts and music parties, and which serve only to distinguish the tasteless lounger from the lover of music, or, perhaps, sometimes, bad performance from good. It was over soon after nine o'clock, this being the hour at which most of the Dutch parties break up. At this time lanterns are seen moving about in all directions; and as the different parties pass each other, they greet their friends with a *Wel te rusten* (May you rest well). The regulations of the police prohibit all slaves and Hottentots from going about the town after nine o'clock, unless they carry a light. Should any, acting contrary to these orders, be met by the patrole, they are immediately apprehended, and lodged in the jail until the next morning. This is done with a view to the prevention of night robbery.

11th. It may naturally be supposed, that, in a country abounding with the most beautiful flowers and plants, the gardens of the inhabitants contain a great number of its choicest productions; but such is the perverse nature of man's judgment, that whatever is distant, scarce, and difficult to be obtained, is always preferred to that which is within his reach, and is abundant, or may be procured with ease, however beautiful it may be. The common garden-flowers of Europe are here highly valued; and those who wished to show me their taste in horticulture, felt a pride in exhibiting carnations, hollyhocks, balsamines, tulips, and hyacinths; while they viewed all the elegant productions of their hills as mere weeds. It is not uncommon in the gardens at Rondebosch, to see myrtle-hedges twenty feet high. A few exotics have, from time to time, been introduced*; and a small number of the more remark-

---

* Such as —
  Melia Azedirach   *Nerium Oleander*
  Gardenia florida   *Asclepias Curassavica*
  Æschynomene   *Asclepias Syriaca*

able indigenous plants are sometimes admitted to the honor of a place in their gardens * : but in none are any of the elegant tribe of heaths ever seen under cultivation ; and it is a curious fact, that, among the colonists, these have not even a name, but, when spoken of, are indiscriminately called *bosjes* (bushes).　Although the Dutch language has a word to express heath, yet, whenever I made use of it in conversation with the farmers, it seemed always to be unintelligible.　Objects of natural history, such as birds, insects, seeds, and bulbs, the produce of the colony, are collected for sale by an ingenious Frenchman of the name of Villet ; but, besides these, I saw no where any thing of the kind, excepting at the house of Mr. Mack-

Camellia Japonica	*Passiflora cærulea*
Canna Indica	*Phœnix dactylifera*
Casuarina stricta	*Poinciana pulcherrima*
Clitoria Ternatea	*Polianthes tuberosa*
Coffea Arabica	*Rosa,* several kinds
Crinum erubescens ?	*Rosmarinus officinalis*
Daphne Indica	*Sambucus nigra*
Hibiscus mutabilis	*Tabernæmontana*
Embothrium sericeum	*Tropœolum Nasturtium*
Eugenia Jambos	*Vinca rosea*
Heliotropium Peruvianum	*Bambusa arundinacea*
Hydrangea mutabilis	*Pinus Pinaster*
Mangifera Indica	*Pinus Pinea*
Mespilus Japonica	*Populus canescens*
Mirabilis jalapa	*Curcuma longa*
Myrtus communis	*Cassia multiglandulosa*
Parkinsonia aculeata	*Cassia corymbosa.*

This list is given merely from memory ; and the addition of nearly as many more names might possibly render it complete.

The last plant had been introduced by myself, about three years before, into Mr. Hesse's garden, whence it had found its way into almost every other, and was now become a favourite shrub.

---

* Such as —

Calodendrum Capense	*Virgilia Capensis*
Gardenia Thunbergia	*Erythrina Caffra*
Gardenia Rothmannia	*Aloë plicatilis*
Strelitzia reginæ	*Solanum giganteum,*
Amaryllis purpurea	and a few others.
Cyrtanthus obliquus	

rill, a surgeon in Cape Town, who very obligingly allowed me frequent opportunities of inspecting his collection, which, however, was not very numerous.

12th. I took a walk in the Government garden, expecting to see in it many things worth attention; but I was disappointed, as it contained scarcely any thing except vegetables for the table. *

In a walled enclosure, which was made by the Dutch, for containing wild animals, nothing is to be seen but a *Gnu*† and some ostriches. Opposite to this enclosure is the *Menagerie:* its only tenants are, a lion and lioness, and a Bengal tiger. Perhaps no country in the world can boast of possessing so great a variety of wild quadrupeds as Southern Africa; and therefore, with very little trouble or expense, a large and most interesting menagerie might be formed here. And if in the vicinity of Cape Town, a well-ordered *botanic garden* of sufficient extent, were established, for the purpose of receiving plants which might casually, or even expressly, be collected in the more distant parts of the colony, the sum of money required for maintaining it would be but trifling, in comparison with the advantages which science, and the public botanic gardens of England, would derive from it. A *museum* appropriated to the reception of the rarities of the country, would form a proper appendage to the Government House, or might occupy one of the vacant squares of the garden. It might be the means of making the colonists, and perhaps some others, who seldom have any opportunity of knowing much beyond the town and Green Point, better acquainted with the productions of the country; and would, in the end, greatly assist in bringing to light its natural resources.

---

* There is, however, a fine plant of *Strelitzia augusta;* an *Aloë dichotoma;* some large trees of *Erythrina Caffra;* a *Phœnix dactylifera,* about thirty feet high; *Halleria lucida; Gleditsia triacantha; Tabernæmontana;* and *Royena pubescens.* Under some very large trees of *Pinus Pinea,* which are the noblest ornament of the garden, I observed an eatable root growing neglected, *Arum colocasia,* (the St. Helena yam); but it is never cultivated, nor have I any where in the colony seen the root made use of.

† A species of antelope.

A View of Cape Town, Table Bay & Tygerberg

A long broad walk, or avenue, shaded by trees of the common English oak *, divides the garden longitudinally, and leads from the street called the *Heeregragt* † towards an uncultivated plain extending to the foot of Table Mountain, and, in some parts, abounding in low scrubby trees of *Kreupelboom*‡, much used for fire-wood.

From this plain, there is a fine view of the town, Table Bay, and ships at anchor, beyond which, in the distance, are seen the mountains of Tygerberg, Blaauwberg, and the great range near Stellenbosch. In this landscape, the pine trees in the garden present a remarkable feature: the castle, the barracks, and the church, are prominent objects; and, as the open ocean is intercepted from the sight by the Lion's Rump, the bay itself, in a calm day, appears like an extensive lake. §

---

* At the foot of which, in the month of April, the pretty little yellow flowers of *Galaxia graminea* spring up here, not unlike the crocuses in Europe.

† Which may be interpreted as meaning the water-*channel* running by the *governor's* house.

‡ *Leucospermum conocarpum*, (*Protea Conocarpodendron* of Linnæus.)

§ *Plate* I. represents this view. On the left is seen the foot of the *Lion Mountain*, where the houses, which are all white, commence and extend as far as the castle. The roofs being flat and plastered with lime, give to the whole an unvaried whiteness. Beyond the two ships under sail, entering the harbour, is *Blaauwberg* (Blue Mountain), which a long line of white sand-downs divides from the bay. The next mountain, behind the first ship at anchor, is *Koeberg* (Cow Mountain). Behind Blaauwberg the top of *Dassenberg* is visible; and next beyond Koeberg, on the right, is the mountain called *Riebeck's Kasteel* (Riebeck's Castle), which is followed by a very distant serrated range of mountains, whose summits are often whitened with snow; these are the mountains of *Roodezand*. The upper part of *Paardeberg* (Horse Mountain) just appears above the eastern end of Tygerberg, and is only distinguished from the Roodezand mountains by a nearer tint. In the direction of the last ships at anchor, the *Tygerberg*, (Tiger Mountain) commences, and thence extends to the right of the bay. The mountains of *Drakenstein* terminate the distant range. The two female figures are negroes returning home, with linen which they have been washing in the rivulet. Behind these figures, a row of oak-trees and a white wall enclose the garden and the official residence of the admiral commanding on the Cape station. The buildings above the sheep, are those belonging to a water-mill; and over these are seen the trees of the *Government Garden*, in a line extending as far as the large stone-pines (*Pinus Pinea*). The spire of the *Lutheran Church* may just be distinguished as a small speck upon the sea, a little to the right of the ships under sail; and, in this drawing, points out the north. Near the pine-trees, the *Dutch Church*, in which the English service is also performed, is conspicuous; and, close to it, the bell and flag-staff of the naval yard may be perceived.

E

The *26th*, the day on which I made the drawing of this view, was hotter than usual : the thermometer of Fahrenheit was 102° (Reaum. 31.1—Centigrade 38.8), under the shade of my umbrella, while I was drawing ; and even in the thick grove in the government garden, it remained at 92°.   During the night, it did not fall below 77° (20 of Reaum.—25 of the Centigrade).   The sky continued all the day without a cloud ; but there was an unusual haze or hot vapour in the air, yet not very dense, as at night the stars were plainly visible.   At this time not a breath of air disturbed the atmosphere.

In the evening, observing in some persons marks of anxiety and uneasiness, I could not avoid enquiring the cause, and learnt that it was the apprehension of an earthquake being about to happen ; for the atmosphere and the stars had now exactly the same appearance which they were observed to have on the day previous to the earthquake which took place just a year before.   The heat was then equally great ; the wind of the day was also lulled to a dead calm at night ; and this evening, listening to the barking and howling of the dogs, some peculiarity in their tone was noticed to be the same as that which had been remarked at that time.

On many other persons these circumstances made the same impression ; but on the following morning the weather resumed its usual temperature, and this sudden alarm was as suddenly forgotten.

The long regular building, commencing near the last ship at anchor, is the *Cavalry Barracks ;* just above which, and of a dark colour, a part of the *Jutty* appears.   In the foreground, are two *slaves* returning from the mountains with a load of firewood ; and two others are on before, near the sheep.   The *Castle* follows next to the barracks, and is distinguished by a browner colour, and a flag.   The house nearest, towards the foreground, will serve to show the style of architecture in which the generality of farm-houses near the Cape are built : it is thatched with a very durable species of rush, peculiar to this part of the world, and which the Dutch call " Dak-riet" (*Restio tectorum*).   Commencing at Cape Town, and stretching to the foot of Tygerberg, the " *Cape Downs*" are easily distinguished by the pale colour which is given to this part of the *isthmus* by its white sands.   The *waggon* here represented is the usual vehicle for all purposes of business.   The rising ground seen above the oxen, is a part of the foot of the *Duivels-berg,* or *Devil's Mountain.*   Table Mountain is behind the spectator.   The foreground was intended to give some idea of the manner in which the various flowers and low shrubs are scattered over this plain.

It was, however, not without some foundation; for we learned afterwards that a slight trembling of the earth was felt, at the same time,
at Genadendal, a place at the distance of ninety miles eastward.

In the preceding year, on the 4th of December, the inhabitants
of Cape Town were thrown into the greatest consternation by
repeated shocks of an earthquake, the first recorded since this land
has been discovered. They fled from their houses, and pitched
tents in the Boer Plain, in the Market Plain, on the Parade, in their
gardens, and in various other places, to avoid being buried under the
ruins of their houses, many of which were rent from top to bottom,
although none fell in altogether. Some persons lived in that manner
for more than a fortnight, impressed with the idea that the end of
the world was come. Many attended divine service, in the churches
and meeting-houses, for the first time in their lives; and all business
was neglected for a few days. A great number of the urns which
ornamented the parapets of the houses were shaken down; leaving
only the bar of iron to which they had been fixed. No material
damage, however, was occasioned by this event; and all went
off more quietly than was expected: but the alarm which it
inspired continued for a long time; and, with many, its religious
effects are said to have been permanent. It was therefore not to be
wondered at, that the slightest symptom of its recurrence should
be viewed with anxiety: more especially as the time of year coincided so nearly.

27th. Accompanied by my friend Hesse, I made a pedestrian
excursion to *Camps Bay*, attended by a servant to carry my boxes
and our dinner. We took the road round *Green Point*, an extensive
sandy level, which forms the western point of Table Bay; and which,
in the month of September, becomes a complete flower-garden, by
the astonishing variety of the tribe of *Ensatæ*, *Oxalides*, and small
liliaceous plants.

On this level, the races are held twice in the year; at the end of
April and the beginning of October. It is then a gay scene for the
Cape fashionables; vehicles of every description, from the elegant
London-built carriage of the Governor, and the English curricle,

to the antiquated Dutch calash, and the light, but jolting paardewagen*, are seen driving about to enjoy the sport. Horsemen,
without number, fly backwards and forwards to watch the fate of the
day; and exhibit their prancing steeds of half Arab or English
blood; although some, indeed, of their noble animals refuse to
prance without the incitement of the curb or spur. Nor is it
less amusing to watch the motley group on foot: Malays and
Negroes mingled with whites, all crowding and elbowing, eager
to get a sight of the momentous contest. But the patient Hottentot
views it almost with apathy; and, squatted on the ground, seems to
prefer a pipe of tobacco to that which affords such exquisite gratification to his superiors. Together with the art of making horses run
fast, the science and mystery of betting has found its way to the
farthest extremity of Africa; and on Green Point large sums are
said to have been won and lost.

Continuing our walk to a cottage romantically situated under
the Lion's Head, and belonging to Dr. Liesching, we rested a few
minutes. About this spot grow *Mahernia incisa*, *Phylica buxifolia*,
Solanum tomentosum, *Eriocephalus racemosus*, *Euphorbia genistoïdes*.

At a subsequent visit to this place, I followed a narrow path
down to the sea shore, where, it being low water, I saw what might
be called little groves of a very large kind of sea-weed, *Fucus buc-
cinalis*, growing in the sea, under water. Its trunks, or stalks, were
six feet high, hollow within, thin at bottom, but gradually swelling
upwards; having at their top very broad and long leaves floating in
the water. The Dutch call this plant *Zee bambos* (sea-bamboo), and
boys, after cutting its stalk to a convenient length when dry, sometimes amuse themselves in blowing it as a horn or trumpet; but
the sound, thus produced, is very hollow and dull.

---

* *Horse-waggon.* This is so called in contradistinction to the more common waggon
drawn by *oxen*, which travels usually about three English miles in an hour; but the
Paardewagen goes at a trot, estimated at six miles in an hour; although its rate may
vary from five to seven miles, according to the goodness of the road. The *Osse-
wagen*, or Ox-waggon, will, from the same cause, travel from two to four miles.

Leaving Dr. Leisching's, we pursued a road cut along the side of the Lion Mountain, and soon after opened a view of Camps Bay and the western side of Table Mountain, which offered a pleasing subject for a sketch. Here a glittering rock on the side of the road attracted my notice; it was a loose granite, containing abundance of mica. The great mass of rock, in these mountains, is principally sandstone of various degrees of compactness: when red, it is nearly friable; but when white, very hard. Every intermediate kind is occasionally to be met with. Of the latter kind, are generally composed the summits of these mountains, and, as I afterwards found, of the great southern range running from Hottentot Holland to Kromme-river bay. Of granite, the quantity is less than that of sandstone; and of schistus, or slate, less than that of granite.

On our road, we met no one, except a single black man; all the rare productions of these mountains seemed to be our own. We descended to *Camps Bay*, where I soon gathered a rich harvest of interesting plants. This excursion produced* a hundred and nine

---

* Among these, after an examination in the evening, were found,

Cluytia pulchella	*Polygala (Muraltia) stipulacea*
Cissampelos Capensis	*Polycarpum tetraphyllum*
Mesembryanthemum pomeridianum	*Sideroxylum inerme*
Rhus villosum	*Thesium Colpoon (Fusanus compressus)*
Erica pubescens	*Cliffortia strobilifera*
Buchnera Ethiopica	*Periploca Africana*
Tetragonia fruticosa	*Glycine bituminosa*
Rottboellia dimidiata	*Gunnera Perpensum*
Xeranthemum (Elichrysum) sesamoïdes	*Psoralea bracteata*
Stilbe pinastra	*Tanacetum multiflorum*
Berckheya ciliaris	*Antholyza nervosa*
Blairia ericoïdes	*Cassytha filiformis*
Rhus tomentosum	*Erica baccans*
Hebenstreitia cordata	*Erica ramentacea*
Malva Capensis	*Rhus glaucum*
Osteospermum polygaloïdes	*Gnaphalium fœtidum*
Echium glabrum	*Gnaphalium denudatum*
Stachys Æthiopica	*Penæa mucronata*
Erica bruniüdes	*Erica cerinthoïdes*
Heliophila linearis	*Polygala bracteata*
Lobelia coronopifolia	*Euclea racemos .*

additional species for my herbarium; besides seventeen more at subsequent visits. *

In the bay there is only one house, which is government property, but it was in a very neglected and dilapidated state; yet, surrounded by lofty mountains, its situation deserves a better edifice, and might well be the site of an elegant villa. A slave, who had the charge of it, permitted us to spread our dinner in one of the rooms. There we found the swallows † had long had possession; for at the corners under the ceiling were several nests; and these birds had become so familiar, that our presence did not in the least interrupt their constantly flying out, and returning with food for their young. In most countries there are some few birds to which man has allowed the privilege of approaching him without molestation. In England the " Robin Redbreast" and " Jenny Wren," as they are familiarly called, are respected by every one; and at the Cape, the familiarity of this swallow and of the Cape wagtail ‡ is greatly owing to the same cause.

Our meal finished, we ascended the foot of the mountain, where a multitude of new flowers caused me to be always far behind; while my companion continued frequently calling out to me that I must come on, or that otherwise we should be benighted. I hastened my

---

Gethyllis ciliaris	*Bryonia Africana*
Leucospermum Conocarpam	*Phylica buxifolia*
Protæa Lepidocarpon	*Hallia cordata*
Juncus ? serratus. Th.	*Solanum tomentosum*
Selago spuria	*Cyperus lanceus*
Dilatris corymbosa	*Mahernia pinnatifida.*
Diosma rubra	

* *Salicornia fruticosa.* Th.	*Cussonia thyrsiflora*
Statice scabra	*Fucus tomentosus*
Cyperus polystachyos	*Fucus corneus ?* &c.
Myrica cordifolia	

† *Hirundo Capensis*, Linn. Systema Naturæ, editio Gmelini.—*L'Hirondelle rousseline*, Le Vaillant, Oiseaux d'Afrique, planche 245., figure 1.

‡ *Motacilla capensis*, Linn. Syst. Nat. Gmel. — *La Lavandière brune*, Le Vaill. Ois. d'Af. pl. 177. It is called *Kwikstaart* in the colony.

pace with reluctance; but, as both the servant and myself were
nearly overloaded with what I had already collected, and as the
evening began to close in upon us, I was soon obliged to give up all
further search.   By following the ravine upwards, we fell into a
path which conducted us to the Block-house*, whence we descended
by the road over the kloof, and reached home by nine o'clock.
Since this excursion I re-visited Camps Bay several times; and, notwithstanding a careful search, I doubt not that many plants have
escaped my notice.

January 1st, 1811.   This day is generally kept by the Dutch
as the greatest holiday in the year.   The custom of sending to each
other new-year's gifts is still kept up among them; and, in many
families, the slaves are permitted to enjoy the day with their own
friends; on which occasion, they dress in all their best clothes.

---

* Near this Blockhouse, I had already collected sixty-nine species, on the 21st of
of December; and from the corresponding part of my " Catalogue" the following names
are selected ·

Growing on the side towards the town, may be seen,

Diosma villosa	Serissa? capensis. Th. Fl. Cap.
Stobœa atractyloïdes	Burm. Afr. p. 257. tab. 94. (Vulgò)
Aspalathus spinosa	" Schaapdrolletjes"
Chironia baccifera	Cassine maurocenia
Blechnum australe	Lightfootia subulata
Adiantum Æthiopicum	Borbonia lanceolata
Celastrus pyracanthus	Kiggellaria Africana
Myrsine Africana	Arenaria rubra
Juncus punctorius	

And on that side of the Blockhouse, towards Camp's Bay,

Stachys Æthiopica	Celastrus laurinus
Athanasia crithmifolia	Erica Petiverii
Leyscra gnaphalodes	Anthospermum Æthiopicum
Osteospermum spinescens	Chrysocoma Comaurea
Bubon gummiferum	Aristida Capensis
Œnanthe inebrians	Carex clavata?
Rhus angustifolium	Passerina filiformis
Pelargonium tabulare	Diosma rugosa
Salvia Africana	Juncus Capensis.
Athanasia parviflora	

It certainly softens some part of the horrid idea of slavery, to see that slaves possess, notwithstanding their humiliated condition, a mind which allows them to enjoy happiness whenever it may fall within their reach; or whenever their masters are fortunately of so humane and just a disposition as to look upon them as fellow-creatures, and to consider them as entitled to some reasonable share of the comforts of life. It would be unjust not to add, that this disposition in their masters is very common, especially in Cape Town. And though, probably, their humanity may often be attributable to self-interest, which bids them take every care of so valuable a part of their property, yet it is not for us to make a nice distinction in the motives, so long as the benefit which the poor slave enjoys from it, is equal in both cases.

The most valuable slaves are the Malays; especially such as have been born at Cape Town. These are instructed in all the common mechanical arts, and in every useful employment for which they may be found to have suitable capacities. The males are taught to be carpenters, cabinet-makers, masons, shoemakers, tailors, cooks, coachmen, valets, or handicraftsmen of any kind: while the females fill the stations of mantua-maker. cook, nurse, or of various other domestic servants. In dexterity these coachmen excel all our boasted and most accomplished " whips," even of the first rate; for it is a common sight in Cape Town, to see a Malay standing in a long paardewagen, driving six horses at full trot, and turning the corners of the streets with the greatest facility.

The Malays consider themselves superior to all other slaves; and look down on the Hottentots as a very inferior race, who, they say, are descended from orang-outangs. They pride themselves not a little on their fine, long, glossy, black hair; and, notwithstanding their swarthy complexion, their countenances are often handsome. Some of them, whose fathers during several generations have been whites, are quite as fair as any European. They are clever, good, and generally faithful servants; but very sensible of insult, and mindful and revengeful of past injuries.

The value of a Malay slave varies according to his known character and qualifications; the price is sometimes as high as 5000 rix dollars, and appeared to me (in 1815), to be still on the increase; a circumstance which may be attributed both to the abolition of that disgusting trade, and to the increasing demand for servants. For a valet, whom I wished to have hired during my stay in Cape Town, I was to have paid to his owner thirty rix dollars per month; and to have clothed and fed him. And this was considered so reasonable a sum, that another person quickly accepted the bargain before me. Speaking generally, it may be said that no white man is hired as a menial servant; he would consider it a degradation to do, as they term it, the work of a slave: and I believe that whites, in all slave-countries, entertain similar sentiments.

The number of free Malays, the descendants of those who have received manumission, is considerable; and by keeping petty shops, and applying their industry in various ways, either as mechanics or as dealers, they often accumulate property; a thing which the improvident Hottentot, though born free, is scarcely ever known to do.

The Mozambique and Madagascar slaves are at once distinguished from the Malays by their black colour, woolly hair, and negro countenance. These are faithful, patient, and good servants: they are put to various employments; but principally to those which are the most laborious. Slaves of this race are still occasionally brought into the colony, by means of those captured ships which are too often found trading contrary to the Abolition Act, and are condemned here as legal prizes. These vessels have contained each, on an average, about 250 slaves: these are assigned by Government to different masters, for the term of fourteen years, as apprentice-slaves; but it is to be hoped that this source of importation will soon cease altogether. Nothing that the most able and ingenious advocates for slavery have advanced, can stand against that powerful objection, that it is a practice morally wrong, and directly contrary to the best and dearest feelings of human nature.

The ceremony of marriage is seldom or never used among the

slaves, as it would be rendered nugatory by the power which the master unfortunately has, of selling the husband and the wife separately. Since humanity has gone so far, much to the credit of civilized Europe, and of the English nation in particular, as to put an end to the cruel traffic, let it go but a step farther, and forbid the more cruel practice of tearing the poor helpless woman from the man she loves, from the father of her children, or from the children that yet require a mother's care.

The offspring of a slave-woman, whoever the father may be, are the property of her owner. These are often allowed to be the playmates of the children of the family to which they belong; and, as they grow older, they sometimes become their associates also; a fact which shows how very far many inhabitants of this colony are from being cruel and unfeeling slave-masters.

Slaves are often bequeathed by their owner to his children, and constitute, not unfrequently, their whole patrimony. These, increasing in number, are let out on hire to different masters, and ultimately become a sufficient, and, in many instances, the only source of income. Sometimes a slave is permitted to hire himself; that is, to work for whatever master he may choose, or to employ his time in any manner best suited to his inclination, provided he bring home every night, to his master or mistress, a certain stipulated sum of money.

Every slave, or even Hottentot, who is found at a distance from home, without a *pasbrief*, or passport, signed by his master or some responsible person, is liable to be taken into custody as a runaway or vagabond; and this precaution alone is a powerful check to prevent a slave from absconding. Yet it seems hardly fair to place a freeman, as the Hottentot is said to be, under the same restraint; although it must be confessed, that there are some circumstances in which its operation is very salutary.

3rd. This morning, attended only by a good-natured Mozambique slave-boy, named Jak, I made an excursion on foot to a place called *Paradise*, situate on the back of Table Mountain, or, rather, on the eastern side of that range of mountains which runs from the Devil's

Mountain to *Hout-baay* (Wood Bay).   It is between seven and eight miles distant from Cape Town, the road taking first a south-easterly, and then a south-westerly direction.   After passing the castle*, we continued our walk along a broad road of great traffic, it being the only one by which the town is entered from the side of the land. We passed *Roodebloem* (here pronounced Roïbloom), where the great road from Hottentot Holland and the interior of the colony, joins the road from Simon's Bay.   This place is called *Roodebloem*, from a profusion of *red flowers* (probably *Gladioli*,) which annually sprang up there before the land was brought under cultivation.

Rondebosch (Round-wood) is an assemblage of villas and gardens, distributed along the first part of the road; and here many of the inhabitants of Cape Town have their country seats.   A little farther on, we crossed the *Liesbecks river*, a plentiful streamlet, at a place called Westervoort Bridge.   Hereabouts the country becomes extremely beautiful, every where shaded with groves and large trees of luxuriant growth, between which are interspersed vineyards, gardens, and many handsome buildings.   Turning to the right, or westward, out of the Wynberg road, we followed another, equally broad and good, and delightfully shaded by large oaks.   This led us by *Nieuwlands*, (Newlands,) at that time the seat of General Grey; but which has since become the official country residence of the Governor. Near this place is a beautiful spot, called the *Brewery*, where, in the midst of groves and plantations, stands an elegant mansion, built after the designs of Mons. Thibault the government architect and surveyor, to whose taste and talents in architecture, Cape Town is much indebted.

The country between Newlands and Paradise is rich in botany, beyond all that I could have imagined; and, as a European, I might say that we wandered through coppices of green-house plants, and forced our way through thickets of rare exotics.   My sable companion, witnessing the care with which I collected specimens of

---

* See the vignette at page 11.

every thing we passed, caught at last some feelings of botanical pleasure, and good-naturedly plucked for me every showy flower he saw;
and among them some which otherwise might, perhaps, have escaped
my notice. The weather was exceedingly pleasant, and, at this spot,
quite serene, although at Cape Town a disagreeable south-easter continued blowing the whole day. I could have passed many hours in
this charming spot, and the evening would have come on before I
should have strayed a mile from it, or have discovered half the
plants it produced; but Mr. Hesse and part of his family having appointed to meet me at Paradise, I hastened away. I, however, could
scarcely be a loser by doing so, as I found the remaining part of the
way equally rich in variety. The country by degrees assumed a less
cultivated appearance, and the number of whitened villas diminished
in proportion as we advanced.

In approaching the end of our journey, we ascended a considerable way up the foot of the mountains. Here we found *Paradise*, a
very picturesque spot, embosomed in woods. Owing to this elevated
and woody situation, the air felt several degrees cooler than on the
open plains below. Here and there, through the boughs of the
trees, a beautiful and extensive prospect opened over the Cape Flats
(*Kaapsche Vlakte*). The name of this place is derived from its pleasant situation, and abundance of trees. The only building here was
a dilapidated cottage, inhabited by a person placed in charge of the
woods. I intended to have taken my dinner under the shade of some
fine oak-trees; but Jak, supposing that I should prefer a house to the
open air, had asked leave of the mistress of the cottage, that he might
unpack the basket and spread our provisions within doors; and, as
soon as this was done, came running to me in the woods, where I
was busily employed, to tell me that dinner was ready.

The meal was just finished when the expected party arrived.
On foot we were able to advance much higher up the mountain, and
penetrate deeper into the woods, which consisted wholly of indigenous trees in a state of nature, and of which some large pieces of
timber were still standing, having escaped the axe merely by growing
in situations difficult of access. We had no time to examine these

woody ravines, as the evening was fast approaching, and a slave was
sent to let us know that the carriage was ready to take us home.
I quitted this place with the more regret, as I did not expect to have
an opportunity of visiting it again: and I have been since informed
by Mr. Polemann, that the woody kloofs, or ravines in this range,
contain many of the forest trees and other plants which, according
to common opinion, are only to be found in more distant parts of the
colony. *

---

* This day's collection amounted to 104 species; among which were found on the
road near to Cape Town,

Serpicula rubicunda. Cat. Geog. 404. *Folia
linearia opposita integerrima glabra: planta minuta; S. repente multoties minor.*

Osteospermum imbricatum
Chironia frutescens
Lobelia secunda.

Between Newlands and Paradise, the following may be seen, together with a surprising variety of other plants, growing in all their wild beauty; some in heathy places,
some between the shrubs and bushes, and others in the woods and shady places.

In heathy places grow, —
Cyclopia genistoides
Restio tetragonus
Hydrocotyle virgata
Œnanthe inebrians
Thesium strictum
Penaea mucronata
Selago rapunculoides
Polygala Garcini. De C.
Andropogon hirtus. Th.
Arnica piloselloides
Psoralea capitata.

In shrubby and bushy places, —
Borbonia ciliata
Arctotis dentata
Struthiola juniperina?
Cassytha filiformis
Thesium strictum
Cynanchum filiforme
Scabiosa rigida
Phylica plumosa
Montinia acris.

In woods and shady places, —
Schizaea pectinata
Geranium incanum
Passerina filiformis
Gnidia sericea

Lythrum Hyssopifolia! perhaps accident-
ally introduced from Europe.
Brabeïum stellatifolium
Adiantum Ethiopicum
Blechnum australe
Gnaphalium fœtidum.

By the road-side, —
Poa filiformis
Dactylis serrata
Verbena officinalis! perhaps accidentally
introduced from Europe.
Hibiscus gossypinus?
Psoralea decumbens.

At Paradise, in the wood, under the moun-
tain, —
Aspidium Capense
Todea Africana
Halleria lucida
Asparagus scandens
Bryonia punctata?
Alchemilla Capensis
Aspidium aculeatum?
Indigofera filifolia
Knowltonia vesicatoria
Grewia occidentalis
Juncus Capensis.

7th.   At six o'clock in the morning, a shock of an earthquake was felt by many persons, although it was so slight as not to awaken me.   In countries which have for a great length of time been subject to earthquakes, their inhabitants may pass over so slight a shock as this, without any alarm; but to others, to whom this power of nature is known only by description, the smallest symptom of it is really terrifying.   In Cape Town, at this time, the least circumstance resembling it was capable of exciting their fears; and I have known a whole party, in the midst of their conviviality, fly precipitately out of the house on one of the guests happening, in a lively mood, to dance across the room above that in which they were assembled, and cause the floor to shake.

18th.   Yesterday, in honor of the Queen's birth-day, the Governor gave, as usual, a grand dinner to about two hundred persons, Dutch and English.   On this day his levee was well attended; and in the evening a public ball was given at the Government-house. At these parties I had a very favourable opportunity of seeing the *beau monde* of Cape Town.   The ball-room was crowded.   The ladies, who were for the greater part Dutch, were dressed neatly, and to great advantage; and both they and the gentlemen appeared to have adopted the fashions and manners of English society.   Country-dances afforded the chief amusement; neither waltzes nor quadrilles being at that time generally in vogue.   After supper, the dancing was renewed with spirit, and continued until a late hour, the party being apparently much gratified.

23rd.   This night the Devil's Mountain presented a curious sight.   At about two-thirds of its height, it was encircled by an irregular line of fire, which continued slowly advancing towards the summit, varying in direction and in brightness.   It had been constantly burning during the day-time; but was not visible till darkness came on; and, having expended itself, went out before the next morning.   Although it was amusing to watch the progress of this line, I could not view it with the eye of an unconcerned spectator; for, having made arrangements for an excursion to the top of Table

Mountain on the following morning, I feared the fire might spread along the path by which we were to ascend, and, consuming all the vegetation in the way, disappoint my expectation of seeing the multitude of curious and beautiful plants which were said to grow on this celebrated mountain. The slaves who daily frequent its rocky sides, to collect fire-wood for their masters, or for sale, often light a fire to warm themselves, or, perhaps, merely that they may sit round it, and indulge in a pipe and a little idle gossip; and though it be a punishable offence to leave it burning, it sometimes happens that they neglect extinguishing it properly, and thus occasion, almost every year, a conflagration of this kind, which not only destroys the beauty and verdant clothing of the mountain, but, in time, renders fire-wood more scarce than ever. It is a very common practice throughout the colony, at certain seasons of the year, purposely to set fire to the old dry grass and bushes, for the purpose of clearing the land, and allowing the young and fresh pasture to spring up clear from the dry stubble and withered grass, which is found to prevent the cattle feeding with advantage on the new herbage.

24th. As the view from the top of Table Mountain is considered to be most interesting, just at sunrise, we began, at a very early hour, to make every necessary arrangement, that we might reach the summit about that time. The party consisted of Mr. Hesse, Mr. Polemann, Mr. Renou, Mr. Jones chaplain of the Scipion man-of-war, and myself; being all, as we remarked, of a different native language, belonging respectively to Hanover, Denmark, France, Wales, and England; and, to increase this variety of tongues, the slaves whom we took with us happened also to differ from each other.

Our polyglot party being assembled at the hour appointed, we set out at a quarter past three in the morning. As the town is not regularly lighted by lamps, we depended entirely on the light of the stars. Nothing but the sound of our early footsteps disturbed the dead silence of the night; for here no bawling watch tells the townsman the hour, at a time when it can be of no use to know it.

From the town, the ground rises in a regular ascent to the foot

of the mountain, a little below which is the *Water-mill,* the most elevated habitation in Table Valley, and the last house on our road. At
this time the day began to dawn, and the sober light of this early
hour disclosed to our view, with peculiar solemnity, the stupendous
precipice which we were to ascend. It presented a surface apparently flat and perpendicular, leaving me to wonder where it could
be possible for us to find a way up to its summit; but a cleft,
or ravine, was pointed out, and that up this a path would be found;
though, it was confessed, that in some places the ascent was so exceedingly steep as to be but barely practicable.

At a little after four o'clock, we reached *Platte Klip,* (flat rock,)
a large, broad, flat, inclined rock, of granite, lying across the bed of
a ravine, and over which a stream of water was at this time silently
gliding down, in a thin and almost imperceptible sheet, but which, in
the rainy season, becomes a furious torrent. Our path lay over the
upper part of this rock, and some caution is required in crossing it,
as the water renders it very slippery. Notwithstanding this caution,
one of the slaves missed his step, slipped, and was carried part of the
way down the rock, much to the amusement of his fellow-servants.
By good fortune, however, he escaped unhurt; yet he might have
been severely bruised by such an accident.

The path soon became more steep and laborious, and the sun,
from behind the distant mountains of Hottentot Holland, rose upon
us before we had climbed much more than half the height. We had
been told that a sunrise, viewed from the top of this mountain, is
particularly beautiful; but I perceived in it nothing remarkable. I
observed none of those streams of light which, in England, may often
be seen radiating from the sun, just before it appears above the horizon, and which are so trite a feature in pictures of sunrise. Its
horizontal beams illumined, with a reddish tinge, the huge mass of
perpendicular rock which towered in majestic grandeur above our
heads, and, together with the rude wildness of the scene, produced
an effect truly sublime. Still, however, that part of the mountain
above us never appeared so lofty as it really was, its vastness being

intercepted from our view by the nearer and more projecting masses.

The *Devil's Mountain*, which appeared quite close to us on our left, is a part of Table Mountain, and is separated from it only at the top, its elevation being not much inferior. It seemed to accompany us in our ascent, and slowly to rise as we climbed the steep; but, to our right, the *Lion's Head*, on the contrary, seemed to sink as we mounted above the level of its summit. Looking behind us, we watched the hills and distant mountains to the north and east, slowly making their appearance one behind another, till the extensive and grand range of the Hottentot Holland mountains, stood, with its distant blue craggy summits, a barrier to the prospect, being in some parts, loftier even than Table Mountain. These, with the broad, intervening expanse of level country, were the grandest objects which we noticed during the ascent.

On each side of our path was scattered a great variety of shrubs and plants, some growing out of the bare rock. None were of a much greater height than six or seven feet, and the greater part not larger than one year's growth, owing to a fire which happened the year before on the mountain, and which unfortunately spread all the way up this ravine. *Crassula coccinea* had, in many places, escaped the devastation, and its fine scarlet flowers, peeping from between the rocks and herbage, caught the eye much sooner than other beautiful flowers of a less brilliant colour. Towards the top, the path becomes very steep, ascending apparently at an angle of 35 or 40 degrees of elevation; and, in some places, even 45. Still following the same ravine, we entered an enormous fissure which divides the upper edge of the mountain : this opening is called the *Poort*, and, on each side, two lofty natural walls of rock, gradually approaching each other, contract it, towards the top, to a width just sufficient for a pathway. Two of our party, with a couple of the slaves, reached the summit by seven o'clock; but as I had been collecting ever since daylight, and my arms began to ache with the accumulated load, I was obliged to halt with the rest, at the entrance of the Poort, as well for the purpose of taking breath ourselves, as of giving time to the other

G

slaves to come up, who had not been able to keep pace with us.   A
Mozambique negro, one of our servants, was quite exhausted with the
fatigue, and crawled along so slowly, that we began to fear his
strength would not be equal to the task, and that both he and his
load must be left below.   However, with a little more courage and
perseverance, we all reached the summit safely, at a quarter past
seven. *

The view, looking downwards through the Poort, is awful and
singularly grand.   The morning was exceedingly favourable, and not
a cloud intercepted the very distant horizon.   The air on the summit felt cool, and the thermometer, at eight o'clock, was not higher
than 59° of Fahrenheit, (12° of Reamur); and at ten minutes before
nine it rose only to 60° Fahrenheit, although it was now the middle
of the summer season.   We observed a small cloud forming on the
Devil's Mountain, but the increasing heat of the day soon dispersed it.

Our first care, after we were all assembled, was to prepare breakfast; and a place was immediately selected, between some huge
blocks of stone, which formed a commodious room, the ceiling of
which was the azure sky.   The cloth was spread on a flat table of

---

* The following are the names of some of the plants that are to be met with in the
ascent up Table Mountain.

Selago fasciculata	Diosma oppositifolia
Œnanthe ferulacea	Myrica Ethiopica
Holcus asper	Gnaphalium grandiflorum
Cacalia bipinnata	Passerina cephalophora. Th.
Erica coccinea	Indigofera sarmentosa
Erica cerinthoides	Lobelia minuta
Xeranthemum speciosissimum	Roëlla muscosa
Hermas depauperata	Hydrocotyle Asiatica. Th.
Aster taxifolius ?	Orobanche purpurea
Erica planifolia ?	Osteospermum ilicifolium
Phylica stipularis	Aster cymbalariæ
Stilbe ericoïdes	Pelargonium saniculæfolium
Thesium strictum ?	Stoebe prostrata
Erica Petiverii	Crassula coccinea.

stone ; a fire was soon kindled, which blazed with the fuel of *Cliffortia ruscifolia, Mimetes Hartogii,* and *Aulax pinifolia* ; excellent water was found in the cavities of the rocks, and our coffee was in a short time prepared.   Notwithstanding our fatigue, the spirits of our party seemed heightened by the excursion ; and, as I have always since experienced the same agreeable effects on climbing the mountains of Africa, I doubt not that a great share of it was to be attributed to the lightness and purity of the air we breathed ; although certainly the pleasant humour of our companions contributed essentially to the enjoyment which such scenes naturally afford.

Although, in a general sense, the top of this mountain may be called flat and level, yet it is much less so than might be supposed, while viewing it only from below.   Its surface is, in fact, both hilly and rocky, and consists of a hard sand-stone, which, in the bare and more exposed parts, is very compact and flinty.   The weather having worn away the softer parts, leaves the others frequently standing out several inches, and, in some measure, resembling pieces of elks' horns, (Cervus Alces).   The whole summit is covered with plants and bushes ; we observed standing water, and some hollows which had contained extensive ponds, although, at this season, quite dry.

The height of Table Mountain, above the surface of the ocean, has been ascertained to be 3582 English feet, which is only 126 yards less than three quarters of a mile in perpendicular height ; yet La Caille did not calculate it to be more than 3464.   The Devil's Mountain has been found to be 3315 ; the Lion's Head, 2160 ; and the Lion's Rump, 1143, according to Arrowsmith's map.   From the precipice which overlooks the town, a spectator cannot look down the awful depth directly beneath without feeling some dread, or giddiness : and some of our party could not, on that account, venture within several yards of the brink.   The view, as might be expected, is most extensive ; for, calculation proves that the eye ranges over the ocean to the distance of 73 miles ; and that a mountain of equal height, would be within the scope of vision, though distant 146 miles.

The appearance of this view may more easily be imagined than described ; and I shall, therefore, only enumerate the different parts which composed it.   Nothing was to be seen from the south-east to the south and west, but the mountain itself: commencing at the west, on the left hand, was a vast expanse of ocean ; and nearer, in the foreground, but much below us, the *Lion's Head.*   Far in sea, *Dassen Island* was visible; and, beyond this, continuing the view onward towards the right, we could faintly see, in a hazy distance, that part of the western coast of Africa which lies near Saldanha Bay. Nearer, and more to the right, was *Róbben Island ;* north-eastward, on the opposite side of Table Bay, in the distance, *Capócberg* (Cotton Mountain), *Kóeberg* (Cow Mountain), *Dassenberg, Contreberg, Blaaúwberg* (Blue Mountain), *Riébeck's Kasteél* (Riebeck's Castle), *Paárdeberg* (Horse Mountain), *Tygerberg* (Tiger Mountain), and, beyond these, the great range from *Roodezand* to *Hottentot-Holland Kloof,* were all in sight.   On the hither side of the bay, close, as it were, under our feet, and which we look down upon as on a neat, highly-finished map, lay *Cape Town,* and the villas and gardens which are dispersed between it and the mountain.   From this point of view, the regular plan of the town was not so remarkable as from the Kloof leading to Van Camp's Bay. With a glass, we could plainly distinguish people walking along the streets.   The ships at anchor were so diminished, that they scarcely formed a feature in the view. A little farther to the right, *Table Bay* terminates in a bold sweep ; and continuing on still to the right, the eye, passing along the flat sandy isthmus, or *Kaapsche Vlakte,* may distinguish *Rondebosch,* and its little spots of tufted trees, the indication of so many villas.   On the further side of these sand-flats, are seen the mountains of the *Paarl* and *Stellenbosch.*   Just beyond Stellenbosch, in a grand, bold and serrated outline, rise the mountains of *Hottentot-Holland,* which, continuing their range southward, bound the eastern side of *False Bay* ; whose northern shore, being edged by the *Downs,* or ridges of snow-white sand, is remarkable and singular.   The view was terminated by the *Devil's Mountain* on the right.   I employed myself in making a drawing of this interesting and extensive prospect, while the rest of our party walked to the western edge of the mountain, where there is a fine view of *Camps Bay*, and the southern *Atlantic* ocean.

The atmosphere, during the whole day, continued clear; not a cloud interrupted the prospect; the heat, however, caused a thin haze to rise from the plain, but this intercepted only the lower parts of the distant mountains. The spot where we had breakfasted, had been appointed as our rendezvous, and as soon as we were all again assembled, we commenced our walk to the eastern side. A large kind of monkey, with a long greenish-brown fur, (*Cercopithecus ursinus*), called *Baviaan* by the colonists, inhabits this mountain. It is an animal which is found in almost every part of southern Africa which I have visited, and is met with only in the mountains and rocky places. I saw no bird of any kind, and but few insects; a species of butterfly *, which I have never seen but on the tops of the

highest mountains, being all that was collected: but the deficiency in zoology was compensated by a rich harvest in botany. †

---

* *Papilio* (*Hipparchia*) *montana*. B. *P. Hyperbius?* Lin. Sys. Nat. ed. Gmel. p. 2285.
Alæ omnes supra, et anteriores utrinque, fuscæ, areâ rufâ: posteriores subtus canescentes, supra (vix infra) ocellis duobus minutis; anteriores utrinque ocello bipupillato, annulo flavo obsoleto circumdato.

† The following names of a few, out of the great variety of curious plants which grow on the *summit* of Table Mountain, may serve to give some idea of the nature of its vegetable productions.

Cliffortia ruscifolia	*Dilatris viscosa*
Aulax pinifolia	*Leucadendrum salignum ?*
Staavia glutinosa	*Erica empetrifolia*
Staavia radiata	*Erica spumosa*

Having arrived at the eastern edge of the mountain, we rested a while to contemplate the extensive prospect below and around us. On our left, the Devil's Mountain obstructed the view eastward; but commencing from that point, the eye surveys in succession, the *Sand Flats* or *isthmus* curiously marked by the roads leading towards Hottentot Holland, which have the appearance of irregular lines of a lighter color; *Rondebosch, Wynberg, Witteboom* and *Constantia, Zeekoe Valley* and *False Bay.* Beyond these, are seen the important pass of *Hottentot Holland Kloof,* and *False Cape* or *Cape Hanglip.* * Southward are seen the pass and mountain of *Muisenberg* (Mouse-mountain) and *Simon's Bay;* the whole length of the Cape Peninsula, as far as the *Cape of Good Hope* Proper, with *Hout Bay* (Wood Bay), and *Steenbergen* (Stone Mountains), present themselves surrounded by the boundless ocean.

Ehrharta ramosa. Th.
Gleichenia polypodioïdes
Erica tubiflora
Chironia jasminoïdes ?
Erica gelida
Erica Sebana
Erica Pluknetii
Holcus asper. Th.
Gnidia oppositifolia. β. Willd
Pterygodium atratum
Exacum albens
Menyanthes (Villarsia) ovata
Elegia juncea
Selago spuria
Hallia asarina ?
Cluytia alaternoides
Thesium capitatum
Erica tenuifolia ?
Diosma crenata
Stœbe incana ?

Drosera cuneifolia
Chrysitrix Capensis
Erica planifolia ?
Penœa mucronata
Erica comosa
Erica helicacaba
Erica imbricata
Erica glutinosa
Orobanche Capensis
Hermas capitata
Satyrium bracteatum
Disa flexuosa
Disa patens
Hydrocotyle hederæfolia. B. Cat. Geog. 658.—H. decumbens villosa, foliis reniformibus, 3—5 angulatis; angulis acutis.
Protæa cynaroïdes
Mimetes fimbriæfolius. Salisb.

The numbers in my catalogue, previous to this excursion, amounted to 516; all obtained in the vicinity of Cape Town: notwithstanding which, this single day's collection added no less than 148 species, 51 of which were found in the ascent, and 97 on the summit. The number of individual specimens selected and preserved this day, was 1133.

* Corrupted most probably from *Hangklip,* a hanging rock.

In surveying from this high eminence, so great an extent and such a variety of objects, sensations are produced of a very agreeable kind, not at all connected with the idea of picturesque scenery. They seem rather to arise from a feeling of superiority and command, which a great height above all we behold, and an elevation above the inhabited earth, seem to inspire in the spectator, who, at the same time, breathes the freest and purest air.

After some time spent in admiring this scene, we returned by a route nearer to the edge of the precipice facing the town. Such a ramble was, we all confessed, not unattended with fatigue; and, for my part, I had the more reason to complain, as the rugged and sharp rocks we traversed, had literally worn the shoes off my feet. They were, it is true, but an old pair at setting out; and such only, is it advisable to take, on account of the greater ease and safety which they give the wearer in climbing rocky places.

At about three o'clock in the afternoon, we arrived at the top of the ravine, by which we first ascended; and near to it we found a spot very convenient for our dining-place, sheltered from the wind, on one side, by a ledge of rock, of which I brought away a small piece to serve as a specimen of the material of which the whole of the summit of the mountain is formed; and, on another, by a tree of a species of *Protea**, the largest I had seen of this kind ; being between eight and nine feet high, with a bushy.round head, and trunk half a foot in diameter. The leaves which terminated every branch, were of a bright red color, and much more conspicuous than the flowers themselves.

Before our dinner was quite finished, the weather began to change, and soon became very chilly; (at 4 P.M. 58° F.) the wind increased, and misty clouds flying with rapidity past us, threatened soon to envelope, both us and the whole mountain. Those who had visited the summit of this mountain before, were aware of the danger

---

* The *Protæa cucullata* of Linnæus, *Mimetes fimbriæfolius* of Salisbury, and *Mimetes Hartogii* of Brown.

there is in being on it in such weather; and reminded us of a fatal accident which happened there a few months before, when a field-officer of the garrison, who had been dining there with a party of friends, was, in the same manner, overtaken by thick clouds, through which he lost his way, and after wandering about for a long while, at last fell over a deep precipice, and was dashed to pieces. We, therefore, without loss of time, prepared for descending, and ordered the slaves to keep with us, as they only, were well acquainted with every turn of the path; so that, we felt no apprehension of missing our way.

Our French companion, recollecting the circumstance related by *Thunberg* *, of his countryman *Sonnerat*, although equipped with three pair of " French pumps," having returned to the town bare-footed, had taken the precaution of providing himself with a second pair of shoes, strong enough to have lasted four such excursions. But as none of our party had walked over so much ground as myself, these shoes, fortunately for me, were at my service.

At a quarter after five, our whole party commenced the descent, by the same path we climbed in the morning; but now, owing to its steepness, we found it not easy to avoid descending more rapidly than was agreeable. There is, indeed, another path by which we might have descended on the side towards Camps Bay, and one towards Hout Bay; but these were said to be more difficult, and seldom used, except by slaves in search of firewood. At a quarter before seven we halted at Platte Klip, where we rested a quarter of an hour. We reached home by eight o'clock; having made the descent in two hours and a half; whereas the ascent had occupied, at the least, three hours and three quarters.

29th. Not having been able to meet with a map of Southern Africa, exactly suited to the purpose of my journey, I employed part of my time in constructing one, in which I inserted all the particulars that were to be obtained at Cape Town. These, indeed, were very

---

* Thunberg's Travels, vol. i. p. 221. Engl. ed.

few; and in the course of my work I discovered that even the best published maps of the colony were both deficient and inaccurate. Nor were government, it seems, in possession of any general survey which could convey a correct idea of the country. A manuscript map, made during the Dutch government by a surveyor, named *Leiste*, was, at this time, mentioned to me, as the unacknowledged source of much improvement in some maps of the colony; but I had no opportunity of seeing it.

Much of my time also, was spent in arranging and digesting my plans, and in collecting all the particulars that were known relative to the countries and nations beyond the colony. From a missionary of the name of *Anderson*, I had an opportunity of obtaining much satisfactory information, as he had resided for several years at Klaarwater, a Hottentot village on the Orange River or Gariep, lying in the road to a large African town, called *Litákun* (pronounced *Letáhkoon*). I feel much indebted to him for the readiness with which, during his stay at Cape Town, he communicated those particulars which I was desirous of knowing.

In my plan it had long been a fixed point, to make my way through the most inland regions, taking a direction which would ultimately bring me to one of the European settlements on the western coast within the southern tropic; and thence to hire a vessel to St. Helena, where I had no doubt of meeting with every assistance of which I might stand in need. From that island I should not only find a ready opportunity of returning to England, but should also have many chances of soon getting a passage for my Hottentots, in some ship bound for the Cape.

Every published account of the southernmost part of Africa agreed in stating, that, from the Cape Colony northward along the western coast, as far as that country had ever been visited or seen, the land was extremely deficient in water, and consequently barren, and thinly peopled; the few inhabitants living in great poverty. With these accounts, all the reports I heard at the Cape corresponded. On the other hand, the little which was known of the interior regions lying on the eastern side, indicated beautiful, fertile, and

H

populous countries. Of the intermediate parts and their inhabitants, beyond Litakun, nothing was known. All this determined me to avoid the western coast, although that would have been the shortest way, and to adopt a route which should conduct me through the heart of the continent. Litakun, then, was one point to which I resolved to direct my course; and that I might see as much of the Cape Colony as was conveniently possible, I proposed to make Plettenberg's Bay, Algoa Bay, and Graaff Reynet, in my road: having, at the same time, in view, as a desirable object, the investigation of that unexplored and unknown tract of country, lying between Graaff Reynet and Litakun; for, according to the supposed position of these places, Klaarwater would not lie in that track.

I continued thus gleaning information from every quarter within my reach, and familiarising myself with the subject; nor did I, on this account, much regret being obliged to delay the commencement of the journey. The extent of my plan was known to but few of my friends: several reasons induced me to keep it secret; of which, one was the difficulty, and, perhaps, impossibility, which would be found in persuading Hottentots to enter into my service, declaredly for the purpose of going farther into the interior than had been before attempted.

This reluctance to venture far beyond the boundaries of the colony, was occasioned chiefly by the total failure of an expedition sent out by the Governor, under *Dr. Cowan* and *Captain Donovan*, two gentlemen belonging to the Cape garrison. Their party consisted of a Dutch colonist, named *Jacob Krieger;* two Englishmen, private soldiers in the garrison; and about fifteen Hottentots, with four waggons, &c. Their instructions were, to make the best of their way to the Portuguese settlement of Mozambique, on the eastern coast. They departed from Cape Town in September, 1808, and on the 24th of the following December, had reached the river Molappo; since which time, no tidings whatever had been heard of them, and it was generally believed that all must have perished. *

---

* And even at this time, (1821,) nothing certain is known respecting the fate of any one of the party.

This melancholy result of an expedition, the success of which had been regarded as certain, cast a damp on every similar undertaking; and such of my friends as knew my intentions, derived from it an argument to dissuade me from my plan; and they also represented my bodily strength and constitution as unequal to the task. But a project which had been formed so many years, was not easily to be put aside: these well-meant representations made no impression, and I continued·unmoved in my resolution.

31st. This day was dedicated to a ramble over the *Sand Flats,* from Salt River to Munnich's Bridge. Salt River, or *Zout Rivier,* lies eastward from the town; and by this name is commonly understood a small collection of houses, not far from the sea-shore, and situated on the lower part of the Liesbeck's river, by which place, passes the great road into the interior of the colony, branching afterwards northward and eastward. The water here being salt, has given rise to the name, although a river running by *Paarden* (or Horse) Island, is properly the *Zout Rivier.* In this part of the Flats grow various saline plants. *

In the ponds hereabouts, and in many other parts of the colony, there grows a plant called *Water-uyentjes* †, the root of which, when roasted, is much eaten by the slaves and Hottentots. The heads of

---

* Such as, —
Chenolea diffusa. Th.
Frankenia Nothria
Falckia repens
Statice scabra
Scirpus maritimus

Potamogeton marinum
Scirpus Holoschoenus
Triglochin maritimum, and
Salicornia.

Together with which, near Salt River, may be found, —

Cyperus textilis
Campanula procumbens
Cotula coronopifolia
Cotula integrifolia. B. Cat. Geog. 515.
— affinis C. coronopifoliæ sed differt foliis lanceolatis integris.
Clffortia sarmentosa
Polygala (Muraltia) linophylla. B. Cat. Geog. 510.
† Aponogeton distachyum.

Trifolium repens
Cyperus corymbosus
Cyperus lanceus
Juncus punctorius
Cyperus fascicularis.
Clffortia strobilina
Typha latifolia
Scirpus lacustris. Th.
Anthericum (Phalangium) fimbriatum

flowers, boiled, make a dish which may, in taste and appearance, be compared to spinach. The country about this spot is quite level; the bushes and frequent eminences of sand, not interrupting the general flatness of the view. The distance is not more than three English miles from the town, the houses of which continue in sight from every part of the road; Table Mountain, the Devil's Mountain, and Lion's Head forming always the most conspicuous feature of the landscape. This scene afforded me a characteristic, though not a picturesque, subject for a sketch.

On this road, waggons are constantly passing to and from the distant parts of the colony; although the month of March, on account of the rains which then fall, and produce a supply of pasture along the road for the numerous passing teams of oxen, is the time when the greatest number of country waggons arrive in Cape Town. Their appearance, drawn by eight or ten to sixteen oxen, the foremost pair led by a Hottentot, who, if a young boy, is often quite naked, together with the immoderately long whips, and their loud cracking, presents to a stranger a novel and amusing sight. The length of the stock and thong of these whips, is no less than thirty feet, and sometimes even more. A boor considers the driving-seat as a post of honor; but the office of leading the oxen, is thought too degrading for any but Hottentots and slaves, the colonist never performing it but in the greatest necessity, and then only in the more dangerous parts of the road.

As the boors often stop but a single day in Cape Town, though they have, perhaps, come the distance of a twenty days' journey, they very frequently unyoke, or *outspan*, as it is called, at Salt River, to be ready to enter the town by day-break the next morning, or as soon as the barrier gates are opened. By commencing the business of the day at this early hour, they contrive, generally, to sell the produce they may have brought with them, and to purchase all they may be in want of, in the same day, and immediately quit a place where their oxen would soon starve for want of pasture.

This want of pasture around Cape Town is a serious inconvenience; and, in other respects, the situation of the chief town of the colony, could scarcely have been fixed in a spot worse suited for inland traffic. Standing, as it does, at the extreme corner of the country, the number of places within a moderate distance is diminished to one-fourth; while the length of road from one-half of the number of farms is thus doubled, if compared with what their distance would have been, had its situation been more central.   Besides which, the number of miles of incurably heavy sand, by which the town is surrounded, render it still more difficult of access.   Yet, in a country like this, destitute of rivers capable of admitting ships far inland, the capital can flourish no where but on the coast, and therefore can be placed centrally in one way only; that is, either with respect to the length of the colony, or to its breadth.

From Salt River, my walk led me in a south-easterly direction to the last windmill; beyond which, ascending the higher ground, is a heath of pure sand, loose, and exceedingly white.   It was quite covered with *Hæmanthus coccineus* in full bloom, the red flowers of which formed a fine contrast with the snow-white soil, and produced a very singular and curious effect.   Among them was a variety with white flowers. *

The wind, blowing very strong, seemed ill-naturedly disposed to put a stop to all further observations, by leaving no other alternative than walking with my eyes shut, or being blinded with showers of sand.   In many parts of the Isthmus, this sand is carried from place to place by the wind, in such quantities, that, in some spots, the bushes exhibit their roots standing bare, and exposed to the atmosphere; while, in others, they are nearly buried, leaving no part visible but the tops of their branches.   The large mounds, which are here frequently met with, have been formed originally by the sand thus accumulating round either a single bush, or a clump of bushes.

---

* On the Flats, a little beyond the windmills, grow, —

Erica mucosa	*Erica margaritacea ?*
Erica gracilis ?	*Erica verticillata*
Erica concinna	*Blairia ericoïdes ?*
Erica cerinthoïdes	

The scarcity of fire-wood in Cape Town has forced the poorer inhabitants to discover a timely resource in these under-ground stems and roots, which, being in mere loose sand, are dug up with great ease. But, however convenient this source of fuel may be to individuals, the destroying of the bushes, root and branch, will at last become a greater inconvenience to the public, as the Isthmus will then be reduced to a sand-desert, still more difficult for waggons to travel over than it is at present. If an opposite system were pursued, and the growth of shrubs and trees, with sedge and sand-grasses, encouraged, the trees would protect the soil from the action of strong winds; while the sedge would not only fix the loose sand, and form a harder ground, but might, at the same time, afford nourishment for cattle, which would certainly prefer such pasture to the hard reed-like stalks of the different kinds of *Restio* that overspread a great part of these Flats. Few experiments, in the way of agricultural improvement, seem of more importance to Cape Town, or better worth trying, than that of rendering these extensive sands more easily passable, or of converting them to some use, or to some more productive purpose.

From the windmill, I strayed south-easterly, nearly three hours, towards the *Liesbeck* river, over level ground decorated with many pretty heaths; the sand and wind being here less annoying. The Isthmus, in most places, is clothed with bushes in great variety, and hard coarse rushes (*Restiones*); but grass is rarely to be found. *Protea Levisanus* is every where a very common shrub *, and the *Hottentot fig* † grows in many places, spreading over the ground in large patches.

---

* Noticing at this time the very evident diœcious character of this plant, and having already observed the same circumstance in several other species of Protea, I was quite convinced that it was a character separating all the cone-bearing *Proteas* into a very natural and distinct genus; and pointed it out to my friend Hesse. I then gave to it the name of *Strobilaria*, not being aware that the same division had just then been made in England by two different writers, both able botanists, who have each assigned to it names; the one, *Chasme, Euryspermum, Protea,* and *Gissonia ;* and the other, *Leucadendron,* (or *Leucodendron,*) an old name, originally intended as a Greek version of the Dutch word *Witteboom,* the colonial name of the *Protea argentea* of Linnæus, or the *Silver-tree.*

† *Mesembryanthemum edule.*

It produces plentifully, in all seasons of the year, a fruit of the size of a small fig, of a very pleasant acid taste, when perfectly ripe. It must, however, be first divested of the outside pulp or coat, which is at all times saltish; and even the fruit, when unripe, has a disagreeably saline and austere taste. Its name was given by the first colonists, on account of its form bearing some little resemblance to a fig, and because it is every where eaten by the Hottentots. I have frequently seen it in the market; but, by the Dutch, it is used only as a sweet-meat, in which state it still retains the same agreeable acidity.

On Green Point, and on the Flats in the neighbourhood of Cape Town, grows a celebrated little plant*, which still preserves its original Hottentot name, being known by no other than that of *Kúkumakránki*. It has a flower much resembling the common Colchicums of our gardens, and has also a bulbous root, close to which is produced a long, yellow, soft fruit, of the length and size of a lady's finger, its top just appearing above ground. The taste of it is somewhat pleasant, but its smell is delightful, having a perfumed odour of ripe fruit, for which it is chiefly valued. The children of Cape Town

---

* *Gethyllis ciliaris*; the fruit of which, and a longitudinal section, are represented by the above figures, of one-third of the natural size.

sometimes go out in search of kukumakrankies; and as it is difficult
to find them, being very inconspicuous amongst the herbage, they
consider it a little triumph to return home with a few; and the
kukumakranki season (June) never passes unnoticed.

From three o'clock till five, the time was pleasantly spent in
wandering and collecting* in a more southward direction; when,
coming to a hollow spot which appeared sheltered from the wind,
my negro unpacked our basket of provisions.   This solitary situation, in the midst of a wild bushy country, without any traces of
cultivation or of human habitations, might sometimes recall to mind
the romantic tale of Robinson Crusoe; and fancy would assist these
ideas, if one beheld a sable attendant, busily and cheerfully employed
in spreading the frugal meal before us, while seated on the ground,
and delighted with the luxuries of Nature, unalloyed by restraint.
The banquet was soon finished; I rose and left the poor fellow to
take my place, while I rambled to a little distance to explore the
heath in another quarter.

Here, as well as in every other part of the Sand Flats, I observed
innumerable mole-hills; and my foot very often sunk into their
burrows.   For this reason it is very unpleasant, if not dangerous, to
ride on horseback in such places, as persons are liable to be thrown,
by the feet of their horses unexpectedly sinking into these holes.
The animal which makes these hillocks is a very large kind of mole-
rat †, nearly as big as a rabbit, with a very soft downy ash-coloured

---

* In the open sandy country lying eastward from *Rondebosch*, the following were
among the number of plants added to my Herbarium.

Phylica secunda ? Th.	*Anthericum contortum.* Th.
Brunia squarrosa ?	*Aristea cyanea*
Chironia lychnoïdes	*Cliffortia ferruginea*
Roëlla spicata	*Chironia frutescens*
Dianthus	*Chironia linoïdes*
Myrica quercifolia	*Montinia acris*
Gnidia simplex	

† The *Mus maritimus* of Gmelin, Syst. Nat. vol. i. p. 140.

fur, having, in appearance at least, neither eyes, ears, nor tail. It is peculiar to this colony, and is called *Zand Moll* (Sand-mole). From the great softness of the fur and the abundance of skins that might be obtained, it might possibly constitute an article of some value for colonial trade, or for exportation; and it is surprising that no speculating person has hitherto attempted to convert these skins to some useful purpose. There is another kind of mole-rat, much resembling this in color and nature, but in size not exceeding the common mole of Europe: it is also peculiar to this country, and is known by the name of *Bles moll* (White-faced Mole)*. Its haunts may easily be discovered, as it throws up the earth in exactly the same manner as the common mole.

Having already made collections on the Flats in the vicinity of *Rondebosch* †, six weeks before, I did not find many new objects in

---

* The *Mus Capensis* of Gmel. Syst. Nat. i. p. 140. That these two animals belong to a genus quite distinct from *Mus*, will hardly be denied; but to separate them, as a late zoological writer has done, not only into two different genera, but even into two different families, is carrying the modern rage for new genera and new orders a little too far.

† On the 14th of December, 77 species of plants were collected; among which were,

Serpicula repens	*Ehrharta uniflora.* B. Cat. Geog. 182.
Disa barbata	*Ixia erecta*
Cyanella Capensis	*Anthospermum lanceolatum*
Exacum aureum	*Restio tetragonus*
Struthiola virgata	*Schœnus capitellum?* Th.
Penæa fruticulosa	*Athanasia aspera*
Passerina uniflora	*Passerina capitata.*
Hallia imbricata	*Staavia radiata*
Erica calycina	*Passerina uniflora*
Corymbium scabrum	*Watsonia spicata*
Erica margaritacea	*Drosera cuneifolia.*
Cenia turbinata, Juss.	*Andropogon hirtus.* Th.
Polygonum Hydropiper	*Briza Capensis*
Cyperus prolifer	*Lobelia repens*
Diosma oppositifolia	*Pelargonium rapaceum*
Watsonia plantaginea	*Struthiola erecta*
Restio Thamnochortus	*Leucodendron uliginosum*
Hallia flaccida	*Brunia abrotanoïdes*

I

this part of the plain.   Continuing my walk over the heath, (I use this word as expressing a kind of country, like the heaths of England, wild, uncultivated, and open, and partially covered with low bushes.) I directed my course to Munnich's Bridge, and thence, following the high road, reached the town at dark.

The great extent of flat sandy country lying between Cape Town and Hottentot Holland is spoken of by various names, which seem very vaguely applied, and are used in an undefined manner; the Dutch denominate one part, the *Kaapsche Duinen* (Cape Downs), and another, the *Kaapsche Vlakte* (Cape Flats).   Sometimes the term *Zand Vlakte* (Sand Flats) implies the whole.   With some writers it is called the *Isthmus*, and such, in fact, it is; but a single name for so large an extent is very inconvenient for the purpose of pointing out the native places of growth of the great variety of plants which are to be found in every part of it.   The English inhabitants call it merely the *Downs*.

February 6th. This afternoon there was lightning and thunder, the first which had happened since my landing: its effects rendered it the more remarkable, for at this time the flag-staff, which had stood many years on the Lion's Head, was struck down.

8th. During the preceding week, the wind had blown from the north-west, with rain more or less every day, and the air was cold and chilly: but it now shifted to the south-east, and again brought the cloud on Table Mountain.   The south-easter continued for several days, and on the *12th* blew with the greatest violence. The thermometer was 73° (18.2 R.—22.7 C.) in the middle of the day.   During the continuance of this wind, the dust and sand flying about in clouds, render it very unpleasant to be out in the streets,

---

Psoralea pinnata	*Arnica crocea*
Serruria glomerata ?	*Spielmannia Africana*
Leucospermum Hypophylla	*Psoralea aphylla*
Protea purpurea, Linn.	*Cliffortia strobilina*
Athanasia crithmifolia	*Moræa spathacea.*

and at such times, all whose business does not oblige them to do otherwise, keep within doors.

14*th*. I proposed to my friend Hesse to make an excursion to *Constantia*; and although it was a distance of about eleven miles, we agreed to go on foot, that we might with more facility examine the productions of the country as we walked along, and quit the beaten road to wander wherever curiosity might lead us. As we were to dine among the bushes, our negro, Jak, who now had learnt the whole of his duty in these rambles, and seemed to enjoy them as much as his master, was ordered to attend us with a basket of provisions and my boxes.

We set out at seven in the morning. At Roodebloem we felt the symptoms of an approaching hot day; but at Rondebosch, owing, perhaps, to a cooler and more open situation, the thermometer fell to 73°. Between *Rondebosch* and *Wynberg* (Wine-hill), the sandy heath is covered with flowers and bushes, amongst which *Leucadendrum decorum* is a very showy and handsome plant; not on account of its flower, but of the fine bright yellow leaves which surround it. *

At Wynberg a party of the 21st regiment of light dragoons were stationed. The situation of their mess-room, in a grove, or rather avenue, of large trees, appeared to us, more especially on so warm a day, delightful and romantic. Our friend, Lieutenant *Williams*, would not allow us to pass without taking some refreshment. The hospitality and attentions which I frequently received from the officers of

* Here may be found,

Cliffortia sarmentosa	*Epilobium villosum*
Cissampelos Capensis	*Erica concinna*
Kiggelaria Africana	*Erica viscaria*
Aristea cyanea	*Leucodendrum decorum*
Aristea spicata	*Thuïa cupressoïdes*
Cliffortia obcordata	*Protea incompta ?*
Juncus bufonius ?	*Echium verrucosum ?* Th.
Cliffortia falcata	*Chironia baccifera*
Œnothera nocturna	*Asclepias crispa.*

that regiment, in various parts of the colony, during the following years, naturally give rise to pleasant recollections. Those who pass their whole lives without scarcely ever, except by chance, meeting any one but their countrymen, know not the pleasure of falling in unexpectedly, in a foreign land, with one born in their own country and speaking their native language. Such occurrences have often made the word *English* sound more delightful to my ear, but have never been, however, able to make me forget that the good and worthy of every nation on the earth, are equally our country-men in a philanthropic sense, and equally claim our hospitality and friendship.

After resting a quarter of an hour, we resumed our walk, and descending the south side of Wynberg, to an open country, came upon the *Camp*, as it is called, where a part of the Cape regiment was stationed. This regiment is composed entirely of Hottentots, under the command of European officers ; and, as a rifle corps, these men are considered expert and good soldiers. Hottentots have been found very useful as artillery drivers ; and their light weight makes them preferable to Europeans for such service. This camp consists of huts constructed of reeds and plaistered with mud. Those of the officers, although built of the same materials, are not wanting in comfort and neatness within. There is a range of stabling and bar-racks for the cavalry, and the whole forms a little village of singular and interesting appearance.

The view from the camp is very extensive, sweeping over the Flats, to the Hottentot Holland mountains on the east ; while westward is seen the lofty rugged range which continues from Table Mountain to Hout Bay *, and thence to Cape Point. These rocky mountains have a beautiful and grand appearance, and constitute the most prominent feature in every view hereabouts. A large gap or opening seems to separate the southern part of Table Mountain from

---

* Which word an Englishman should pronounce as if it were written *Howt*-bay, otherwise he might convert it, in a Dutch ear, to Hat-bay, instead of *Wood-bay*.

the Steenbergen, and through this gap, or *kloof*, the road descends
to Hout Bay.

Neither of us being acquainted with the proper road to Constantia, we missed it, and wandered till we came to a very pretty
farm-house, where, on enquiring our way of two women whom
we saw at the door, we received an answer in good English. They
informed us that the place belonged to Mr. Duckett, an English
agriculturist, who has for many years resided in the colony, and
whose knowledge of European husbandry has enabled him to manage
a Cape farm with considerable success: he is one of the small number of English colonists who were at this time to be met with in
the country. This place is called *Witteboom*, a name which, with
great propriety, it has received on account of numerous plantations
of large Witteboom, or *Silver trees*, which grow about it. The native
station of this handsome tree, is the sloping ground at the foot of the
eastern side of Table Mountain; and at present very large plantations
occupy the same situation on the northern side, next to the town.
That this space should be the only part in all the colony where it
grows wild, can be no subject of wonder to any person who has the
least knowledge of the character of Cape botany; since the natural
places of growth of a multitude of other plants, are circumscribed by
limits equally contracted.

The soil between Wynberg and Constantia is a pure white sand,
covered with heath, and large bushes*, chiefly of the Proteaceous
tribe, the most abundant of which is the *Suikerbosch* (Sugar-bush). †

---

* On the road between *Wynberg* and *Constantia*, the following plants, with a great
variety of others equally interesting, are found in a wild state:

Erica sebana	*Gnaphalium hirsutum ?* Th.
Rafnia opposita	*Gnaphalium umbellatum,* Lin.
Olea Capensis	*Cliffortia ilicifolia*
Rafnia triflora	*Heliophila linearis*
Protea scolymus	*Polygala ? spinosa,* Lin.
Surruria Burmanni	*Osmites camphorina*

† *Protea mellifera.*

We arrived at *Constantia* about two o'clock, and having received a general invitation from Mr. Cloete, the proprietor, we intended to profit by it this day, and take a view of the vineyards and cellars; after which, to have resumed our ramble over the heath, and dined amongst the bushes. But our intention was partly frustrated; for, the slaves having carried to him the information of our arrival, he came out of the house, and in a friendly manner insisted on our entering, as he was just sitting down to dinner. We therefore took our seat, and although treated with marked hospitality, were more anxious soon to leave the table and pursue the objects of our excursion, than to indulge in the variety of excellent wines which were placed before us. For my part, I had not the gift of distinguishing the relative merits of all these sorts. The red Constantia, as it is called, was of a very agreeable taste; but all were excellent.

After this I was shown the cellar, a long building above ground, and shaded by trees. On each side, a range of large casks, with two of much larger dimensions, contains the valuable wine which has caused the name of this place to be so well known in Europe. We were next conducted to the vineyard, which, however, is managed in a manner not at all different from the other vineyards in the colony; the vines are pruned and kept in the form of dwarf bushes, much resembling currant-bushes; and are planted in rows about six feet apart. At this time they still remained loaded with bunches of fine grapes, and the only peculiarity I could observe, was, that they were allowed to hang on the vine to ripen so long, that they had begun to shrivel, and the juice was become almost a syrup. Whatever may be the cause, or whether there be any cause really

---

Corymbium scabrum
Othonna crassifolia
Gnaphalium nudifolium
Euclea racemosa
Royena glabra
Protea (Leucospermum) Conocarpa
Protea mellifera

Ceropegia (Microloma) tenuifolia
Rubus pinnatus
Cliffortia strobilifera
Rhus mucronatum, Th.
Cliffortia graminea
Erica nudiflora

existing, it is said, and believed, that wine of the quality of Constantia wine cannot be made on any other spot in the colony; a most fortunate circumstance for the proprietor, whose affluence, and that of his family before him, have probably been derived from it. But this is not literally a monopoly; for the adjoining vineyard, called Little Constantia, produces wine scarcely inferior.

Close to the house, stands a beautiful tree of *Wilde Kastanje* (Wild Chesnut), the trunk of which was fifteen inches in diameter, and thirty feet high below the branches. It well merits the generic name it has received *, and the colonial name is equally applicable, as, in the appearance of both the flower and the fruit, it very much resembles a horse-chesnut; but in foliage it is different. This is the largest, and, perhaps, the only tree within a great distance of Cape Town. Close to it, I saw a small tree of *Gardenia Rothmannia*, bearing a profusion of large and very sweet-scented flowers. These were an elegant sample of the trees of the Cape forests.

At half-past four we took our leave, and returned to Wynberg by the high road leading from Simon's Town, which brought us out below the Camp; and at the flag-staff, which stands at a short distance from it, to convey telegraphic signals between Cape Town and Simon's Town, we took a road to the right, which led us again over the wild heath. † Soon after crossing the Liesbeck River, we rejoined the high road. The nearer we approached the town, the stronger we found the wind, which, blowing directly behind us, often forced us to run forward, although we were all exceedingly tired, and much exhausted. We reached home about eight o'clock, after a day's

---

* *Calodendron*, or " beautiful tree."

† On the sandy heath, or Sand Flats, north of Rondebosch, grow —

Erica ramentacea	*Erica racemosa*
Erica margaritacea	*Erica calycina*
Diosma oppositifolia	*Blairia ericoïdes*
Restio tectorum	*Rhinanthus glaber*, Th.
Staavia radiata	*Cyperus fascicularis.*

ramble, which, according to the road we took, could not have been less than twenty-five miles.

On the 18*th*, Mr. Anderson came to tell me that he had just received a letter from the settlement at *Klaarwater*, in which his brother-missionary, residing there, informed him that a party of Hottentots from that place would arrive at Cape Town about the middle of April, bringing with them the oxen necessary for the performance of his journey thither; it being his intention to return and resume his labours at that station, from which he had now been absent two years.   Notice had also been given to him, of a report which had reached the Landdrost of Tulbagh, that five hundred emigrant *Caffres* * had passed along the borders of the district of Graaffreynett, in their way to the Gariep, or Orange River, on the banks of which they had formed a strong and independent settlement, not far from Klaarwater.

Being a warlike set of men, discontented and irritated at the treatment they had received from all quarters, and at variance with the colonists, he was apprehensive that they would make an attack on any party travelling that way, which should not muster strong enough to defend itself against them; and he therefore came to propose, for our mutual safety and defence, as well against these Caffres, as against the *Bushmen* †, that we should travel in company as far as Klaarwater, if I could consent to put off my departure from Cape Town, till the middle of May.

This proposal appearing objectionable, on account of the delay it required, I hesitated in adopting it: but in ten days afterwards,

---

* The word *Caffre*, or *Kaffer*, is generally, at the Cape, applied exclusively to the tribes inhabiting the country beyond the eastern boundary of the colony.

† This is often written *Bosjesman*, and *Boschman*, which being merely Dutch words signifying men living wild among the bushes, and applied generally to several tribes of the Hottentot race, I have preferred using the English orthography, viewing it rather as a descriptive, than as a proper, name.   They call themselves *Sáqua*; those, at least, who inhabit the country southward of the Gariep.   Yet it is difficult to avoid inaccuracy, in the application of one collective name to a race of people who divide themselves into many separate tribes.

having reconsidered all circumstances, I rode to Salt River, where he was then residing, and finally agreed to join his party. I determined, therefore, on giving immediately orders for the building of my waggon. At the same time, it was recommended to me to hire, for my waggon-driver, a Hottentot named *Jan Tamboer*, who, having been as far as Litakun, would be found to be a useful and trustworthy man, and who, as I was informed, was living somewhere in the vicinity of Cape Town.

March 14th. After many enquiries, I at last learnt that this Hottentot had enlisted into the Cape regiment, and was at this time at the camp at *Wynberg.* This gave me another opportunity of enjoying the scenery along that road, certainly the most beautiful ride within that distance of Cape Town. This ride was rendered more than usually pleasant, by the extraordinary clearness of the atmosphere, which had the curious effect of making distant objects appear, comparatively, quite near: the Stellenbosch and Hottentot-Holland mountains, though twenty-seven miles distant, seemed to be not more than three miles from us; and Table Mountain might have been fancied almost close over our heads. The clefts and divisions of the rocks, were as plain and distinct as if viewed through a telescope. This phenomenon was, perhaps, the effect of the south-easter, which had been blowing with great violence during the two preceding days; and, as I have observed a similar kind of effect from a continued heavy rain, succeeded by a cold and cloudless day, it may possibly be explained by the supposition, that these two causes operate in clearing the air of all haze and imperceptible vapors; notwithstanding the contrary opinion, that moisture produces transparency, and that the densest haze is observed in calm hot days. But that opinion is applicable only to solid bodies; and from this it can only be inferred, that the heat of the day extracts the hazy vapour from the earth or sea, at a time when there is no current of air, which, if warmer, would dissipate, or, if colder, condense it.

By the politeness of *Dr. Glaeser,* the surgeon of the regiment,

K

the Hottentot was found, and brought to me.   Even at first sight I
was much pleased with his appearance, and his countenance seemed
expressive of good qualities.   When the object of my enquiries was
explained to him, he answered my questions with unusual alacrity;
and, giving us to understand how much he was rejoiced at the prospect of again leading a life of travelling, he instantly declared his
readiness to engage himself in my service for the whole journey.

Thus much being settled to my wishes, nothing remained but to
obtain his discharge from the regiment; an affair which did not promise to be equally easy of accomplishment, it being feared, that, to
deprive the regiment of a man of so good a character, would be objectionable.   Nothing, however, could be done at present, as it
seemed necessary, for this purpose, to wait till the Governor's return
from a tour through part of the colony.

While waiting till Jan Tamboer could be found, I amused myself in making two drawings of the Camp.   During this employment,
two naked *Hottentot* boys, on my giving them a little encouragement,
came and seated themselves on the ground by my side, though not
without some shyness.   A Hottentot soldier, also, approached from
curiosity; and, not being then on duty, was indulging himself in going
quite undrest, except with a pair of trowsers.   He told me he had
been in the regiment five years, and liked a military life very well;
but added, that many others complained of being thus compelled to be,
as he expressed himself, so exact and regular in all they did, and that
they began to repent of having enlisted themselves.   To me, almost
every thing truly African was interesting; and nothing gratified these
feelings more than an opportunity of observing and conversing with
the Hottentots, a race of men whose character and history, as given
by the romantic pen of *Le Vaillant*, had made on my mind, even in
my earliest days, many pleasing impressions, which now revived with
all their warmth, whenever I chanced to meet any of these men.

From this train of ideas, I was summoned to the hut of one of
the officers, to see a *tame lion*.   This object, instead of interrupting
my reflections, added considerably to the lively feelings they had
created, by reminding me that I was now in the country where these

formidable animals roam at liberty in their native plains; and this circumstance lent a peculiar interest to the sight. As the animal was only nine months old, its tameness might yet be considered as problematical; and it was not unlikely that it would assume its natural ferocity, as soon as it should have attained its full size and strength: for the lion in the Cape Town menagerie, which is now so ferocious, was, when very young, so tame and tractable, that Governor Jansens suffered it to run loose about the house; but, before it was full-grown, several indications of its dangerous nature were observed, and the prudent precaution, of putting it into a place of security, was immediately taken. The present animal allowed any one to play with it, and did not appear to be in the least degree vicious. It was taken, together with a lioness whelp, when but a few days old, from a lioness which had been shot in a distant part of the colony.

Here I also saw a Cape baboon, which was as tame and familiar as such creatures generally are, but not sufficiently so to be trusted without a chain.

On taking leave of Wynberg and its beautiful scenery, Dr. Glaeser and Mr. Stockenstrom accompanied us a short distance, for the purpose of showing us a road from which I might have a view of *Kerstenbosch;* and, that I might take the advantage of this opportunity to botanize over new ground, we went on foot, while two Hottentot soldiers led our horses. This road had been but newly cut through a pleasant coppice, containing a great variety of shrubs, and many large silver-trees. Here I found several plants which I had never met with before. *

---

* These were, —

Penæa acuta. Th.	*Protea grandiflora*
Moræa gladiata	*Anthericum graminifolium,*
	and some others.

On the same spot may be found —

Brunia nodiflora	*Anthospermum Æthiopicum*
Cliffortia ilicifolia	*Aristea bracteata.* Pers.
Rhus villosum	*Cluytia polygonoïdes?*

Our walk conducted us to a high part of the hill of Wynberg, which overlooks Kerstenbosch, a beautiful estate belonging to Government. The view from this spot, and, indeed, all the scenery around, is the most picturesque of any I had seen in the vicinity of Cape Town. The beauties here displayed to the eye could scarcely be represented by the most skilful pencil; for this landscape possessed a character that would require the combined talents of a Claude and a Both : but at this hour, the harmonious effect of light and shade, with the enchanting appearance of the foliage in the foreground, and the tone of the middle distances, were altogether far beyond the painter's art. The objects immediately surrounding us, were purely sylvan; a blue extent of distance terminated the landscape both in front and on the right. To the left, the noble Table Mountain rose in all its grandeur, crowned with rocks, and displaying, in the broad ravines that descended its side, the rich colouring of some inaccessible woods, the growth, perhaps, of centuries. The enormous and lengthened shadow of Table Mountain and Devil's Mountain, stretched far over the Flats, and seemed to touch the foot of Tygerberg. The last beams of the sun, gleaming over the rich, varied, and extensive prospect, laid on the warm finishing lights, in masterly and inimitable touches.

In whatever shape her works appear to us, Nature exhibits nothing defective; whether we view her in the mechanism of animated bodies, in the structure of vegetables, in the laws of the globe we inhabit, or in the combination, beauty, and fitness of all that adorns its surface. Here I beheld her perfection in the sweet harmony of soft colors and tints of every gradation, speaking a language which all may understand, transfusing into the soul a delight which all may enjoy, and which never fails, at least for the time, to smother every uneasy sensation of the mind.

Senecio rigidus ?	*Echium glabrum*
Gnaphalium nudifolium	*Scabiosa rigida*
Rhus rosmarinifolium	*Phylica stipularis*
Roella ciliata	*Gnaphalium ? umbellatum*

After some time spent in admiring the charming scene, I quitted it with regret; but, the setting sun reminding us of home, we took leave of our friends, and, mounting our horses, pursued our ride during the quiet light of evening.

CHAPTER III.

A SKETCH OF CAPE TOWN AND THE COLONY.

It may, perhaps, conduce to the purpose of the narrative, if in this place be drawn the outlines of a view of Cape Town, and of the Colony in general. They may be useful, as giving some general notions which may render the peculiarities of this settlement, and those allusions to local circumstances and customs which frequently recur in the course of this journal more clear and intelligible.

Nothing can be neater, or more pleasant, than the appearance which this town presents, spreading over the valley, from the sea-shore towards the mountains on each side. It contains more than twenty streets, all of which, intersecting at right angles, run, either in a north-westerly direction parallel to the strand, or south-westerly from the sea towards Table Mountain. These streets, though not paved, are kept always in excellent order, and derive an agreeable freshness from trees of oak and pinaster, planted here and there on either side. The houses are built of brick, and faced with a stucco of lime: they are decorated in front with cornices and many architectural ornaments, and frequently with figures both in high and low relief. In front of each house, and of the same length, is a paved platform, usually eight or ten feet wide, and raised, commonly, from two to four feet above the level of the street. It is ascended by steps, and has generally a seat at each end, as may be seen in the engraving * at the head of this chapter. This platform is called the *Stoep* (step); and here the inhabitants frequently walk or sit, in the cool of the evening, and often at other times, to enjoy the air, or to converse with passing friends.

The roofs are flat, and nearly horizontal, having no greater inclination than just sufficient to throw off the rain-water. They form a terrace very commodious for walking on, and are made with strong beams extending from wall to wall; over which stout planks are laid, and upon these, a thin pavement of bricks, well covered with stucco. There is no other lime than that which is made by burning shells, chiefly muscles, which are collected along the sea-shore. The windows are very large; but the panes of glass are small. Beams and floors of the teak-wood of India are not uncommon; but the greatest part of the timber used in building, and, indeed, for every other pur-

---

* This *engraving* represents a small part of *Strand-street*, as viewed from the house adjoining the Lutheran church, looking southward. It may be considered as showing the character of the ordinary buildings of the town; but must not be taken as a specimen of the best houses. On the left are two with thatched roofs; and in these the earlier style of building may be seen. The figure with two baskets suspended from the ends of a pole, exhibits the manner in which the Malays and slaves carry about for sale fruit, fish, vegetables, and various goods. The opening by the side of the highest house, is *Loop-street*. The Devil's Mountain, seen at a great elevation above the tops of the houses, backs this view, but is omitted in the engraving.

pose, is the *Geel-hout**** (Yellow-wood), and the *Stink-hout* † (Stink-wood). The latter is a handsome wood, and resembles mahogany, both in color and quality. Chairs, tables, and other furniture, are made of it: though a preference is given to European goods; and these are to be seen in the houses of the more opulent. The yellow-wood is not unlike deal, but is inferior to it, as possessing no resinous quality.

On account of the mildness of the Cape winters, fire-places are nowhere seen, excepting in the kitchens. Within, the houses have, to an eye accustomed to the elegant decorations and furniture of an English apartment, the appearance of a want of comfort; and, not having a plaistered ceiling, the bare joists and floor above, give them the look of an unfinished building: but the loftiness and size of the rooms render them respectable, and contribute greatly to their coolness in the summer. The houses, even of the poorer class of inhabitants, have, outwardly, a neat and architectural form. Carpets are seldom used; and the reason assigned for this is, that they afford, in this, as in all warm climates, a harbour to insects.

It is remarkable, that one of the finest situations in the town, is occupied by buildings of the most inferior description : the beach, with a full view of the bay and shipping, would seem to be a site worthy of some elegant houses, and of a handsome terrace; which, being the first objects to meet the eye of a stranger on entering the bay, would considerably strengthen the favourable impression of the respectability of the town.

There are two churches; one for the Reformed or Calvinistic

---

* From two species of *Podocarpus*, one of which is the *Taxus elongata* of Linn.

† *Laurus bullata.* B. Catal. Geog. 5409. *Folia longius petiolata ovata acuminata, bullâ in axillis venarum subtus apertâ : racemi florum foliis breviores.*

Our present Under-secretary to the Admiralty, who, it seems, aspires at being thought a botanist, is rather unlucky in the display he makes of his knowledge and learning: he says —

" The stinkhout is the native oak of Africa, and, I believe, the only species found on " that continent. It may, therefore, not improperly be called the *Quercus Africana*." — Barrow's Travels in Southern Africa, p. 134.

He might with equal propriety tell us, that the Walnut is a species of Plum, and that " it might, therefore, not improperly be called" *Prunus Barrowiana.*

congregation, the established church of the Dutch government, and which is also used by the English for the performance of their service; the other was built by the Lutherans, the number of whom is very considerable. Besides these, there is a good-sized meeting-house, which is open to preachers of various denominations. The Malays have also a house dedicated to the Mahometan form of worship, with a regular priest established and supported by themselves. This latter building is nothing more than a private dwelling-house, converted to that use.

The Government-house is situated in the town, surrounded by plantations, in a garden consisting of several acres of ground laid out in avenues crossing each other at right angles, and thickly shaded by oaks. This garden is an exceedingly pleasant promenade during the heat of the day, and is always open to the public. The *Stadhuis*, or Burgher Senate-house, is a large, handsome building, appropriated to the transacting of public business of a civic nature. It stands in the middle of the town, on one side of the square called *Groente Plein*, in which a daily market for vegetables is held. There is, on the northern side of the town, another square, called *Boere Plein* (Farmer's Square), where the farmers used to assemble with their waggons, to dispose of their commodities; but since my arrival in the colony, another boor-market has been established at the southern entrance to the town, and a market-house erected, at which every waggon, bringing a load of country produce, is obliged to halt, while proper officers take an account of every article they may have for sale, and, having ascertained the quantities of each, register them in books kept for that purpose. Here they are generally met by purchasers; if not, they proceed into the town.

The Castle is a large pentagonal fortress on the south-eastern, or inland side of the town, close to the water's edge. It commands the jutty, or landing-place, and part of Table Bay, and completely controls the only road between the town and country. On the north-western side of the castle is the Parade, a large oblong plain, surrounded by a walk shaded by pinasters and stone-pines, and enclosed by a wall and moat. Near the parade are the Barracks for the cavalry,

L

an extensive and ornamental building, begun in the year 1772, originally intended for an hospital; and between this and the Castle is the Custom-house, built in 1813. Close to the entrance to the Government-garden, is a large and handsome building, completed in 1815, which contains the Court of Justice, the Secretary's office, and most of the principal public offices. The Theatre is situated in the Boer Plein; but was seldom used, as it depended chiefly on the performance of amateurs. Cape Town possesses several other buildings appropriated to business of a public nature, such as may easily be supposed requisite for a large town and a considerable population. *

The whole is protected, on the side of the land, by fortified Lines, extending from the Devil's Mountain to the sea-shore. The town is supplied with excellent water, which issues, in several plentiful streams, from Table Mountain; and in 1813, iron pipes, sent from England, were laid down, for the purpose of conducting a supply of it to every street.

On the ' Lion's Rump' is a signal-post and look-out station, where, by hoisting certain numbers of black balls, immediate notice is given of all ships seen in the offing. There is also a telegraphic communication between Cape Town and Simon's Town in False Bay, the place of rendezvous of all ships of war belonging to the Cape station.

Southward of Cape Town, a great number of elegant villas are scattered about between vineyards, plantations, and groves of trees; and the country, as far as Rondebosch, Wynberg, and Constantia, is really delightful, and, more than any other part of the colony, resembles the rich cultivated scenery of England.

That which may be called the *Peninsula* of the Cape of Good Hope, includes Cape Town, Camps Bay, Hout Bay, and Simon's Town, and consists of an irregular range of mountains, commencing at the Lion's Rump, and terminating at Cape Point; which last is the Cape

---

* Other edifices have since been erected; particularly the Exchange, built by the merchants of Cape Town, and founded on 25th August, 1819; and the Butcher's Hall, another building, equally convenient for business, was added in the following year.

of Good Hope Proper, or *Cabo Tormentoso*, discovered by Bartholomeo Diaz, in the year 1487, and doubled by Vasco de Gama, in 1497. This Peninsula is connected with the mainland, by a wide, flat, sandy isthmus, of about twelve or thirteen English miles in breadth, separating False Bay from Table Bay.

The shape and extent of the colony may be more easily known by an inspection of the map, than by description. But, in an agricultural view, great deductions should be made from its size; as many parts of it are barren and uninhabitable from want of water. Such parts are called *karró*, (a Hottentot word signifying *dry*); some of them are of great extent, being not less than 50 miles across in the narrowest part. They are very level, and, though destitute of grass, are generally covered with short stunted bushes and succulent plants. In the rainy season, however, a more luxuriant vegetation springs up; and at this time the neighbouring boors remove with their flocks, and take up a temporary residence in these plains, until drought again obliges them to return home.

The colony, which is intersected in various directions by several ranges of high mountains, is divided into eleven *districts* *, of very unequal sizes: these are the districts of the *Cape*, of *Stellenbosch*, *Caledon*, *Tulbagh*, *Clanwilliam*, *Swellendam*, *George*, *Uitenhage*, *Graaffreynét*, *Albany*, and the *Tarka*; and to give some idea of their situation, they are here enumerated in the order of their distance from Cape Town, the Tarka being the most distant. Each is placed under the superintendance of either a *Landdrost* or a deputy landdrost, who administers the government, in most respects, as the representative of the governor; and it is through him that all laws, proclamations, and inferior regulations, are carried into effect. The districts of Caledon, Clanwilliam, Albany, and the Tarka, are under the deputy-landdrosts of Swellendam, Tulbagh, Uitenhage, and Graaffreynet, respectively. Each district is subdivided into a number of

---

* This is the division which existed at the date of these Travels; but various subdivisions into new districts have since been made by the government.

Veld-cornetcies, in which the duty of the *Veld-cornet,* (or Field-cornet,) is to put in execution all orders from the landdrost, to whom he is more immediately accountable.

The farms are of great extent, especially those in the distant districts; they comprise a circular area of three miles in diameter, and from their great extent are never enclosed. Corn might be produced in great abundance, but the scarcity of labourers, and the want of a market within a moderate journey, are the causes of no more being grown by the farmers, who live beyond a certain distance from the villages, than is found sufficient for the annual consumption of their own families.*

The only mode of travelling is either on horseback, or in waggons drawn by horses or oxen. A representation of the ordinary waggon of the country, with the usual team of oxen and mode of driving, is given in the *vignette* at the end of this chapter. European carriages are used only in Cape Town and its vicinity, nor is there any public conveyance except the *Bolderwagen* (stage-waggon, to Stellenbosch. A regular post conveys letters to each of the villages; Graaffreynet, one of the most distant, receives them from Cape Town in seven or fourteen days, according to the state of the rivers and roads. As there are no inns, the traveller must depend on the uncertain accommodation of farm-houses on the road, unless he carry his provisions and bedding with him, which is the most usual practice.

The only villages in the colony, (1815,) are those of *Stellenbosch,* founded in 1670; *Graaffreynet,* in 1786; *Swellendam,* in 1745; *Tulbagh,* in 1804; *Uitenhage,* in 1804; *Paarl; Simon's Town; Zwartland,* which contains little more than the church, in 1801; *George,* in 1812; *Caledon,* in 1810; and *Grahamstown,* in 1811; here enumerated in the order of their size. And the only churches, (excepting those in Cape Town,) are at Stellenbosch, Swellendam, Paarl, Zwartland, Graaffreynet, Tulbagh, and Caledon, in the order of their date; that of Caledon

---

* A more particular view of the colony, as applicable to the case of new settlers, may be seen in a small pamphlet, entitled " Hints on Emigration to the Cape of Good Hope."

not having been built before the year 1814, at which time the churches at Uitenhage and George town were not yet begun. Once in every year, a deputation of members of the court of justice, called the " Commission of Justice," perform the circuit of the Drostdies, (residences of the landdrosts), for the purpose of hearing and determining all trials or lawsuits which may be brought before them.

The inhabitants of these districts consist principally of Dutch, who first, under Van Riebeck, began to establish themselves at Cape Town, in 1651. A large proportion are of German origin; and between the years 1680 and 1690, a considerable number of French families settled at the Cape of Good Hope, driven thither by the persecutions to which Protestants were, at that time, subjected in France. There are also many of Swedish or Danish origin. As settlers and colonists, the number of British in the different districts was, at this time, extremely small; and might, in a general view, be left out of the account.

The Hottentots of the colony are much less numerous than the Whites; but, if their number be added to that of the slaves, the black population will considerably preponderate. All the inhabitants use the Dutch language, and many slaves and Hottentots speak no other. The nations which border on the colony, are the Namaqua Hottentots, on the north-west; the Bushmen Hottentots, on the north and north-east; and the Kosas or Caffres on the east.

The Cape Settlement was taken by the English, for the first time, in the year 1796; but, on peace being concluded between the two nations, it was restored to the Dutch in February 1803. War soon afterwards breaking out, it was again taken by the English, on the 8th of January, 1806; and by the last treaty of peace, in 1815, has been finally ceded to Great Britain.

Cape Town, as well as the rest of the colony, is inhabited by people of various origins, the chief part of whom are also Dutch, who, in respect to number, are surpassed by the slaves. These latter are, for the greater part, Malays, and natives of Madagascar, and of the country adjoining Mozambique. The Hottentots, preferring a country life, are generally averse from engaging in the service of masters living

in the towns, and consequently but few of that nation are seen there.
In Cape Town the English are numerous, and are principally of the
military and mercantile classes. Many situations of importance are
filled by the native Dutch, in a manner creditable to themselves and
advantageous to government.

Justice continues to be administered according to the Dutch
law, and causes are pleaded in that language in writing. Trials by
jury, and oral pleading, are as yet unknown in these courts; although
the introduction of them, together with the English law modified according to local circumstances, would be no more than a very
natural innovation, in a country now become permanently a British
territory; and would seem a measure justly due to the habits and
feelings of the British portion of its inhabitants, whose numbers are
now likely to become sufficiently important to claim for them the
privilege of being tried by their own laws.

The Fiscal, being the head of the police and the sitting magistrate,
a great variety of business is daily transacted at his office. The Cape
is also the seat of a Vice-admiralty court. Proclamations, and all
orders and regulations of a civil or financial nature, are issued from
the colonial secretary's office, and officially made known in the Cape
Town Gazette, published every Saturday.

This paper rarely contains any information, excepting that which
may be derived from proclamations, official notices, and advertise-
ments of auctions. It might, however, be rendered the vehicle of
valuable knowledge to the colonists; and it is much to be regretted
that so ready an opportunity should have been hitherto neglected, of
conveying to every part of the country, useful information, in the
way of colonial improvement.

The only money in general circulation, is small printed and
countersigned pieces of paper, bearing value from the trifling
sum of one *schelling*, or sixpence currency, upwards to five hundred rix-dollars each. The only current coin, are English penny-
pieces, which here pass for the value of two pence, and are called
dubbeltjes. Spanish dollars are used in Cape Town, rather as bul-
lion than as coin; their value varying according to the rate of ex-

change. Accounts are kept in rix-dollars, schellings, and stivers; although the value of estates and possessions is often rated in guilders, three of which make a rix-dollar. Six stivers are equal to one schelling, and eight schellings to one rix-dollar or four shillings currency; but the value of this currency is excessively reduced by the rate of exchange, which, in 1810, was 33 *per cent.* in favour of England; and has, since that time, gradually risen to above 120. This enormous premium for bills on England, is attributable to the want of exportable colonial produce; wine being the only staple commodity, excepting a few hides, some whale-oil, and an inconsiderable quantity of ivory, ostrich feathers, gum-aloes, argol, and a few other articles of little weight in the scale of general commerce. The islands of St. Helena and Mauritius take from the colony constant and large supplies of live-stock, wine, grain, and various provisions. The consumption at the Cape, of goods of British manufacture, on which there is a duty of 3 *per cent.*, is to a considerable amount; but the high price at which they are sold is the necessary and natural consequence of the high rate of exchange, nor can it be otherwise, till the aggregate value of the exports shall approximate, far more than at present, to that of the imports. The usual mode by which the merchants effect the sale of their investments, is public auction; and in this manner estates also, and property of every description are sold; consequently *vendues* or auctions happen daily, and often several in a day.

The price of provisions is, comparatively with England, exceedingly low; labour, house-rent, and fire-wood, constitute a large proportion of the expenses of living at Cape Town. Coals are here unknown, except by small quantities, sometimes landed from the ships.

The town is plentifully supplied with fish, of which a great variety are caught in the surrounding sea; fresh-water fish, however, is so rare, that I do not recollect having seen at table any, except eels; and these were regarded as a curiosity.

Fruit and vegetables are abundant and cheap; of the former the most common are oranges, lemons, grapes, melons, apples, pears,

peaches, almonds, apricots, figs, walnuts, mulberries, quinces, chesnuts, bananas or plantains, and guavas.   Strawberries, plumbs, rasp-
berries, and cherries, are met with only in the gardens of the curious;
the last has hitherto been found to succeed nowhere but in the division of the Cold Bokkeveld.   For gooseberries and currants, the
climate is considered to be too warm, while, on the other hand, it is
thought too cold for ananas, mangoes, and most tropical fruits.
Nearly all the common vegetables of Europe grow here in perfection.
Wheat and barley are the grain most extensively cultivated; the
latter is the corn usually given to horses.   A small quantity of rice,
scarcely worth mentioning, although of a very good quality, is grown
along the western Elephant's river.

In Snéeuwberg (Sneeberg) and the Roggeveld, innumerable
flocks of sheep are reared; and in these parts of the colony the
greatest number of horses are bred.   Very good soap and butter are
brought from different districts; but cheese is rarely made, the milk
being thought too poor for that purpose.   Tobacco is cultivated in
every part of the colony, and is an article of such universal consumption, that it may here class among the necessaries of life, but has not
yet been raised in quantities sufficient for exportation.   Brandy, which
is made from grapes or peaches, may, in regard to the great request
in which it is held, rank next to tobacco in importance.

The climate of the Cape is not only pleasant but is very favorable to health.   Lying in the southern hemisphere, its seasons
are the reverse of those in Europe; December and January being
the hottest months, and June and July the coldest.   The sun at noon
being always in the north, causes the northern side of the mountains
to be much hotter and dryer than the southern, which differs very
perceptibly also in verdure, and luxuriance of vegetation. The appearance of the starry sky is greatly different from that which it presents
to an observer in Europe; many constellations are here seen in a reversed position.   The well-known stars of *Ursa Major* are never
seen at the Cape; but this loss is well compensated by some constellations and remarkably beautiful stars which must always remain invisible to the inhabitants of England; particularly *Canopus, Achernar,*

two in the feet of the *Centaur*, and the brilliant constellation of the *Cross*.

The winter and spring are the most delightful part of the year ; the summer and autumn in the country along the coast, being constantly dry, and consequently a season when verdure almost disappears. In the districts remote from the sea, the wet season commences in the summer months, the rain falling in heavy showers, accompanied most frequently by lightning and thunder. Cape Town is subject to violent winds, and the dust of the streets, at such times, becomes extremely disagreeable.

The degree of heat and cold varies in different parts of the country ; in Cape Town, the highest degree at which I observed the thermometer, was 102° of Fahrenheit's (31°·1 of Reaumur's: or 38°·8 of the Centigrade) scale in the shade ; but, during the warm season, it ranges between 80° and 90° F., (21° and 26° R., and 27° and 32° C.) In the winter it seldom sinks below 50° F. (8° R., 10° C.): ice is, however, sometimes found on the top of Table Mountain ; and during a few days in every year, the summits of the Stellenbosch and Hottentot-Holland mountains are seen covered with snow. *Cold Bokkeveld*, as its name implies, is a country distinguished by a colder atmosphere ; and the same may be remarked of the *Roggeveld*, where I found the thermometer in August, so low as 26° F. (— 2°·6 R.,— 3·3 C.) But the coldest district is that called *Snéeuwberg*, or the Snow Mountains, in which more particularly, a small and elevated table-land called *Coudveld* (Cold country), is considered by the boors to be the coldest spot in the whole colony : in many farms on Snéeuwberg, the summers are not warm enough to bring grapes and peaches to perfection. At a farm-house on these mountains, I was assured by the owner that snow falls often to the depth of a foot, remaining on the ground two or three days ; and that it has sometimes been seen as deep as two feet. As far as my own experience enables me to decide, it is the coldest region in Southern Africa.

The hottest parts of the colony are to be found in those barren plains which are distinguished by the general appellation of *Karró*, and in the low arid lands situated towards the coast ; but in such places, the heat, being of a dry quality, is not so oppressive to bodily feeling as it would be in England at the same degree.   The western districts are comparatively deficient in trees and water ; while those lying along the southern coast, beyond Zwellendam, to the furthest extent eastward, are, on the contrary, well-wooded, and abound in springs and rivulets ; and it may justly be said that the countries of *Auteniqualand* and the *Zuureveld* are extremely beautiful.

In short, the colony of the Cape of Good Hope, as part of the British dominions, may be considered an important and valuable possession ; not only in a political and commercial point of view, but also in the light of a territorial acquisition ; and, that any writer, who has seen the country, should assert otherwise, proves nothing more than his own want either of observation or of judgment.

CHAPTER IV.

As it was now certain that my final departure from Cape Town could not take place before the middle of May, there was sufficient time for a short excursion into the nearer districts of the colony. This, besides gratifying my curiosity, would be attended with the advantage of giving me, previously to my principal journey, some idea of the nature of the country; and consequently, of enabling me to make my preparatory arrangements more judiciously, and to form a more correct estimate of what provision it would be necessary to make. In the present journey Mr. Polemann was both my companion and my guide, as it was proposed to direct our course through a part of the country with which he was acquainted. One of the objects which we had in view, was to purchase a couple of teams of oxen; because in the immediate vicinity of the town, there was little chance of meeting with any equal to the labor of such an expedition, and wherein so much depended on the good qualities of these animals.

April 8th. Our equipment consisted of a horse and a small portmanteau each, to which I added some requisites for drawing, and a few other instruments of little bulk and weight. Early in the morning we commenced our journey, and, passing Roodebloem and Salt-river, entered upon the *Kaapsche Duinen,* (or Cape Downs) and the Sandy Isthmus, the whole length of which lay in this day's ride. The numberless tracks and roads by which it was traversed in every direction, made us often at a loss to decide which we should take; but as the greater proportion of these lead to Hottentot-Holland Kloof, which we had always in sight, though at a great distance, that beacon was our only guide.

These downs are covered with bushes three or four feet high, and the soil appeared to be everywhere the same as that which has already been noticed *; a loose white sand, of a depth varying from one to five feet, with a substratum of hard clay. Springs of fresh water are very scarce on these flats; but it is probable that by digging through the clay, wells would supply a sufficient quantity to render them habitable. Here and there are scattered a few solitary huts of Hottentots, who earn a living by collecting fire-wood, or by attending such cattle as are kept on this miserable pasture, where they have no other support than browzing on the hard dry shrubs and rushes.

As we approached the *Eerste river* † (the First river) or the Stellenbosch river, as it is sometimes called, several picturesque scenes present themselves. Hillocks of pure, snow-white sand in the foreground, contrasted with, and backed by, the blue of the distant lofty mountains, have a singular and pleasing effect.

Having ridden all the forenoon over nothing but deep sands, and

---

* See 31*st January,* at pages 53 and 54.

† This would be more correctly written *Eerste rivier,* according to Dutch orthography; but in this and in every like case it will, perhaps, be more convenient to use the English word *river.*

our horses beginning to grow weary, we halted about one o'clock at the Eerste river, at the house of an opulent farmer named Meyburg. Here we were immediately invited to take our seat at the family table, where we found several other travellers, who, in the same manner, had halted there merely with the intention of taking their dinner. This house, and many others along the roads most frequented, is seldom free from visitors of this kind, who often have but slight pretensions to any previous acquaintance with their hospitable host.

At the Eerste river the sand downs cease, and are succeeded by a more fertile soil. Here we entered the level tract of country called *Hottentot-Holland* *, in the middle of which is a large grassy mountain called *Schaapenberg* (Sheep-hill). Our road now became very good and hard, and the country assumed a more rural appearance; with houses and farms, at short distances from each other, and several rivulets of good water. It is along these rivulets that the houses are generally situated; most of them being large white buildings of respectable appearance. This country produces good corn, and, with a proportionate increase of labouring population, would probably yield ten times its present produce. As we advanced, False Bay came in view; and as day-light faded away, an atmospherical effect was produced on the mountains, by which they seemed to be nearer to us than they really were. We continued the last hour of our ride by moonlight, and arrived at the place called *Fortuintje*, belonging to a gentleman named *Watermeyer*, where his servant, an Englishman, in consequence of a letter we brought from him, provided us with a supper and good beds. This place is not more than a moderate walk from *Vischer's-hoek* (Fishermen's corner),

---

* In Dutch this word would be more correctly written *Hottentotsch Holland;* but it has been thought unnecessary in this, and in similar cases, to adhere rigidly to the proper orthography; conceiving it to be more convenient to adopt an Anglicised mode of writing such words as do not differ much in the two languages. This name, in English, might be written more strictly *Hottentottish Holland;* but the term *Hottentots' Holland* is an erroneous interpretation of the name.

the north-eastern angle of False Bay, whence it is readily supplied with excellent fish.

9th. After an early breakfast, we mounted our horses, and almost immediately commenced the ascent which leads to the pass called *Hottentot-Holland Kloof.* At the first part of it, the road is not very steep, but as soon as the traveller enters the hollow way of the *Roode Hoogte** (the Red Heights,) the difficulty of the ascent begins. This is a lower hill forming the foot of the mountain, and composed of a hard, barren, reddish, clayey, ferruginous earth, into which the road, towards its summit, is cut down to the depth of, perhaps, twenty feet. After this he has to climb the rocky mountain itself, and will not, without some suprise, behold loaded waggons ascending and descending so steep and frightful a road; nor will he, without a compassionate feeling for the oxen, witness their toil and labor, carried to the very utmost of their strength : sometimes encouraged by good words, at other times terrified into exertion by the blows of the *shambok,* the loud crack of the whip, the smart of its lash, or the whoop and noisy clamour of the boor and his Hottentots. All this cannot be entirely avoided; and it is alone the perilous nature of such passes, which reduces the boor to the necessity of acting with harshness towards these useful animals : in general, the farmer knows too well the value of his oxen, wantonly to illtreat them. The danger in which both oxen and waggon are placed while passing the mountains, renders the utmost care and vigilance indispensable. For, should they become restive, and deviate from the proper road, or obstinately refuse to draw, the waggon would be thrown down the precipice, dragging them, and perhaps the driver also, along with it to inevitable destruction. We met several waggons coming down, all of which were heavily laden.

The *shambok,* here mentioned, is a strip, three feet or more in length, of the hide either of a hippopotamus or of a rhinoceros,

---

* Which words are, according to the Cape dialect, pronounced as an Englishman would read *Roëy Hoaglcter.*

rounded to the thickness of a man's finger, and tapering to the top. This is universally used in the colony for a horsewhip, and is much more durable than the whips of European manufacture. The sham-bok employed by waggon-drivers, and called *Agter-os shambok,* (or the shambok for managing the after pair of oxen) is of the same form as the other, but of double the length, and as much thicker as the hide will admit of. This manufacture is not peculiar to the Cape; it is well known in Northern Africa, and forms an article of trade under the name of *Corbage.*

From the top of the pass there is an extensive and very fine view of the Isthmus, False Bay, and of the whole range of mountains from the Lion's Head to Cape Point. The great number of new and beautiful plants which I saw on this mountain, induced me to collect a bundle of specimens, although I had no means of preserving, nor even of carrying with me, a collection of so much bulk. The most strikingly beautiful then in flower were *Erica taxifolia* and *Erica fascicularis:* many kinds of *Protea,* particularly *Protea spe-ciosa;* together with *Protea cordata,* a very singular species, of a growth nearly herbaceous. At *Steenbraassem* (Stonebream) river, which runs close by the eastern side of the Kloof, finding some wag-gons at *outspan,* we asked the favor of one of the boors * to leave my bundle at Fortuintje, which lay in his road; but received a direct refusal. I applied to one of his Hottentots, offering him some money for his trouble; but having observed his *baas* (master) deny me the same favor, he dared not act contrary to him, and gave me also a refusal. The baas, however, seeing me offer the money, called out to the Hottentot, " *Neem de geld,*"† (take the money). This he immediately did, and promised to deliver the flowers safely, together with a note hastily written, requesting that they might be sent to Cape Town; but nothing after this was heard of my plants, nor were

---

* This word is used for signifying the *Dutch* farmers, and is, on every occasion, to be taken in that sense only; being a substitute for the Duth word *boer* (farmer).

† Written according to the pronunciation and dialect of the country districts.

they ever received at Fortuintje, having, most probably, been thrown away the moment after we rode off. *

Having passed the Kloof, I was surprized to find so little descent on the eastern side: here the country must, therefore, lie at a great elevation above Hottentot-Holland.

The districts situated, with respect to the metropolis, beyond these mountains, and also their inhabitants and produce, are often distinguished in a general way by the word *overbergsch* (tramontane.) Over the whole colony the words *boven* (upper), and *bovenland*, are used to signify those parts of it which are nearer to Cape Town, and often Cape Town itself; while *onder* (under), and *onderveld*, are the terms applied in contradistinction. These are colonial expressions in constant use in a great variety of cases, frequently even for indicating only the situation of a neighbouring farm-house.

This pass, and two or three others farther northward in the same chain of mountains, may be regarded as the great portals by which the interior of Africa may be entered on the side of the Cape of Good Hope; the country on the west of this range being as it were only the vestibule. The *Hottentot-Holland* and *Roodezand Kloofs* are the two principal passes, by which waggons cross these mountains: the former leading to all the districts lying along the southern coast, as Swellendam, George, Uitenhage, and Albany; and the latter to the Tárka, Graaffreynét, the Karró, and Róggeveld. The *Elands Kloof*, *Pikeniérs Kloof*, and *Kardoúws Kloof*, three passes of inferior note, are

---

* This pass was more carefully investigated on a subsequent occasion (March 29. 1815); and among the plants collected at that time, the following, already well known to botanists, may here be noticed:

Olea Capensis	*Protea speciosa*
Phylica buxifolia	*Hydrocotyle tridentata*
Erica taxifolia	*Cliffortia trifoliata*
Aulax umbellata	*Lobelia pinifolia*
Pelargonium angulosum	*Protea sceptrum-Gustavianum*, of Sparrman
Rhus cuneifolium	*Erica glutinosa*
Erica Plukenetii	*Erica fascicularis.*
Brunia nodiflora	

northward of Roodezand ; and besides these, several others divide the great ranges of mountains which separate the southern coast from the regions of the interior.   Of these the principal are, the *Hex river Kloof, Kokman's* or *Kogman's Kloof, Platte Kloof, Attaquas Kloof,* and the *Duivels-Kop;* to which may be added the dangerous and little frequented pass of the *Keurbooms river.* *

As we rode along, the beautiful pink flowers of *Penæa squamosa* caught my eye ; and I once or twice dismounted to pluck *Retzia spicata, Erica Massoni, Erica axillaris,* and *Protea* (*Spatalla* of Salisbury) *incurva.*   *Retzia spicata* is a plant of singular growth, about three or four feet high, with a few upright, undivided branches, thickly clothed with stiff, long, narrow leaves, between which its tubular, orange-colored flowers just appear ; but they are not very conspicuous at a distance.

We soon afterwards crossed the *Palmiet river,* whose waters, like the greatest number of those which take their rise from the southern side of the great southern range of mountains, were of a brown color resembling coffee, but at the same time clear and wholesome.   This is probably to be attributed to the decayed vegetable matter, which is observable in greater quantity on the southern than on the northern side of these mountains ; and which gives to all these waters a color exactly the same as that which is imparted by peat and bog-mould.   After running some distance from the mountains, they lose the brown tincture, and gradually change to a more usual complexion, by the accession of rivulets formed in the plains. The boors believe this brownness to be caused by the great quantity of Palmite (Palmiet), which every where grows in these streams ; but, however much they may assist in producing this effect, they are certainly not the chief cause ; since I have observed them to be thus coloured, before they reach the foot of the mountains, and far above where the Palmite begins to grow.

---

* Since my departure from the Cape, a convenient waggon-road has been made over the mountains near the *Paarl,* at a place called *Du Toit's Kloof,* which till then was merely a foot-path.

N

This greater accumulation of vegetable matter on the southern side, is very easily and naturally accounted for, by the relative position of the sun in this hemisphere; which shining at noon, always in the north, occasions the northern side of these mountains, as far as I have had an opportunity of observing, to be always the more arid, and producing plants and herbage of less luxuriant growth; while, on the contrary, the southern side, being constantly more shaded, and having a cooler aspect, cherishes a rich and verdant vegetation. Numerous rivulets pour down its ravines, and support, in many places, forests of timber trees, whose beautiful verdure is preserved through the whole year by the moist atmosphere which these streamlets, together with shade and shelter, create. From the proximity of these mountains to the sea, the moisture of marine air may perhaps contribute its influence in producing these effects; yet I have remarked the same circumstance in mountains that are distant from the coast a whole degree of latitude, or 90 English miles. * Such a color gives to these streams an unpleasant, forbidding aspect; and the first sight of them recalls to mind the dark waters of one of the infernal rivers: *Cocytus sinu atro.* Although a small quantity in a glass vessel, appear limpid and nearly colourless, yet, at a depth of three feet, the bottom of a river is not visible, and the blackness of the stream gives the appearance of an unfathomable pool. This is a disagreeable, and an inconvenience not merely ideal; for, in fording such rivers, a traveller is hereby prevented from seeing at the bottom the many large stones and holes, which, if not avoided, sometimes occasion serious accidents.

---

* In allowing 90 miles of travelling to a degree, instead of 69½, which is its measure in a straight line, a result will be obtained much nearer to the truth and more applicable to *practical* purposes, than that obtained by the usual measurement over the face of a map; which last seems to be the method resorted to by those who have hitherto given the dimensions and distances of places in this colony. From the experiments and calculations made in the course of four years' travelling in Southern Africa, I have found the irregularity and winding of the roads, and the nature of the surface of this country, to require, on an average, a reduction of two-ninths of the distance travelled, to obtain the real horizontal distance in a straight line.

Most of the rivers which we passed in this excursion, are choked up with the plant called *Palmiet* * by the colonists, and from which this one derives its name.   Some notion of the appearance of these plants, may be gained by imagining a vast number of ananas, or pine-apple plants, without fruit, so thickly crowded together as to cover the sides and even the middle of the stream, standing seldom higher than three or four feet above the surface, but generally under water whenever the river swells above its ordinary height.   The stems which support them are of the thickness of a man's arm ; black, and of a very tough and spongy substance ; generally simple, though not rarely divided into one or two branches.   They rise up from the bottom, not often in an upright posture, but inclined by the force of the current.   They have very much the growth of Dragon-trees, (*Dracæna*), or of some palms, from which latter resemblance they have obtained their name.

A little further on, we came to the house of a man who had formerly been a non-commissioned officer of dragoons in the Dutch service, and who now endeavoured to support himself and his family, by supplying the passing traveller with provisions and the produce of his little garden.   As this might in some respects be considered an inn, we rode up to the door without hesitation, and were met by a man, whose grotesque appearance fixed our attention ; lame in one leg, he hobbled towards us on a crutch, while an enormous broad-brimmed black felt hat overshadowed his whole body, like an umbrella, of which his spare figure might represent the stick.   We dismounted, but soon discovered that we had arrived at an unlucky hour, as our host declared that at that moment he had nothing in the house to eat.   However, after some consultation with them, he desired his daughters to place before us some bread, butter, Spanish

---

* This is the *Juncus serratus* of Thunberg, and with that genus it agrees in fructification ; yet its appearance and habit, together with its gigantic size, would rather refer it to some other family. Hitherto, however, I have not been able to discover any character which might authorize its separation, unless three sessile *stigmata* can be considered as a sufficient generic difference.

N 2

radishes, eggs, and wine.   *Fritje,* his youngest, performed the duties of handmaid, and by her readiness and attention, made us excuse the deficiencies of the meal.   Another visitor, a meagre old man, coming in just at this time, partook with us.   He was on his way to Uiten-hage, a place not less distant than 700 miles.   Such long and laborious journeys are not thought much of by the boors; the nature of their population, thin and widely scattered, has taught them to regard a colonist dwelling at the distance of ten miles, as a near neighbour.

After leaving this house, we came to a short, but rugged range of mountains, where, by an execrable road, we ascended the rocky pass of *Groote Houhoek,* or *Houwhoek.* *   This place is much dreaded by those who have to pass it in waggons: though not so steep, it is more difficult than the Hottentot-Holland Kloof; and, being in the great eastern road, cannot be avoided, unless by the *Kleine* (Little) *Houwhoek,* another pass in the same range, which, how-ever, is said to be even worse than this.

We passed several waggons at *uitspan,* and met others, heavily laden with country produce, proceeding to Cape Town; and, among them, some bringing timber from Auteniqualand.   Were but the same degree of labor and perseverance applied to the repairing and improving of the roads, which is daily wasted in dragging over-land to the Cape these ponderous loads of planks and beams, which in the end yield but a poor return for so much trouble, the boors would be amply repaid by the facility and dispatch with which their journeys would be performed.

These *uitspan,* or *outspan places,* are, in fact, the caravanserays of the Cape; and the varied groups of travellers, with their waggons and oxen, which are frequently seen at such places, taking their meals under shade of the bushes, interest much by the simplicity and novelty of the scene.   These parties appeared often to consist of whole families; and women and children, Hottentots, slaves, and

---

* This word has been spelt in various ways, according to its supposed etymon; *Houwhoek,* implying " Hewing-corner," *Houdhoek,* " Holdfast-corner," or *Houthoek,* " Wood-corner."

dogs, assembled round their fire, presented a curious and amusing sight.

We crossed the *Knóflooks Kraal* (Garlic Kraal) *river*, an inconsiderable stream, and also a branch of the *Bot* (Flounder?) *river*. It was dark when we arrived at the latter, and this rendered it necessary to proceed cautiously in fording it, especially as a late flood had swept away a part of its banks, and covered its bed with large stones. On the left bank stood a farm-house, the residence of *Vaasje* (or *Servaas*) *Kok*, a man with whom my fellow-traveller had some acquaintance. Here, then, we agreed to take up our quarters for the night; and on entering his house, were received in a very friendly and hospitable manner.

10th. In the morning, to amuse us, we were shown the garden, which, for the country districts, might be considered as one of the best, as it produced, besides various fruits, several kinds of culinary vegetables. Turmeric *, under the name of *Bori*, was growing luxuriantly, and in full bloom; but its pale heads of flowers are unobservable, until sought for under the leaves close to the ground. The roots of this, reduced to powder, form an indispensable ingredient in *curry*, a dish much eaten in every part of the colony. I gathered a handful of wild plants which grew about this spot †; and saw abundant reason for regretting my want of convenience for preserving specimens of the numerous kinds which we passed during our ride.

Two light-dragoons of the 21st regiment were stationed here, and, in the same manner, others also, at certain distances along the road, for the purpose of forwarding despatches to and from the Governor, who was at this time on an excursion to Plettenberg's Bay. By such an arrangement, intelligence may be conveyed with a degree of expedition equal to that of an English mail; but,

---

* *Curcuma longa*, Linn.
† Among them were,—

Leucospermum buxifolium	*Aulax umbellata*
Leucodendrum concolor	*Calendula fruticosa*
Mimetes cucullata	*Rhus rosmarinifolium.*

in forwarding letters by the ordinary Cape post, an unnecessary length of time is often lost at the different post-houses on the road; and, in that season when the rivers are suddenly swelled by the rains, the letter-bags, from want of bridges or ferry-boats, are detained two or three days on, what the boors very expressively term, " the wrong side" of the river.

Early in the forenoon we took leave of this hospitable farmer, and set out for the Hot Baths, but were soon overtaken by rain, which continued with little intermission during the whole day. The roads were broad, and in excellent order; a condition for which they are more indebted to the nature of the soil than to the labor of man. The country is hilly, and abounding in low bushes; the *Rhus villosum*, both here and in other parts of the district passed through in this excursion, forming one of the lightest and prettiest little trees that adorn the landscape. The *Chilianthus oleaceus* * grew in the hollows, and, in growth and foliage, bore a resemblance to the European olive-tree. Partridges, of a kind peculiar to the Cape, were frequently seen running between the low bushes, and a greater variety of birds now began to be observable.

At the farm called *Boontjes Kraal* (Bean Kraal), we halted a minute to enquire the way. This gave me an opportunity of noticing a profusion of small black pebbles, of the shape and appearance of, but a little larger than, French beans, lying every where scattered in the road, and which had evidently been washed out of the earth by the rains, and, apparently, were of a ferrugineous quality. These naturally gave a name to the spot, being probably the first place at which they had been observed; although stones of the same

---

* The *Scoparia arborea* of Linnæus. This, together with several other undescribed arboreous species, form a natural genus, quite distinct both in habit, and by a four-seeded capsule, from *Scoparia;* and for which I would propose the name of *Chilianthus*, (à χιλιοι *mille, quasi innumerabiles, et* ἄνθος *flos*,) on account of all the species bearing numerous small white flowers, in large panicles, not unlike those of *Sambucus nigra*, the common elder-tree. From this resemblance, the different species have obtained, among the Dutch colonists, the general name of *Wilde Vlier*, or *Wild Elder*.

kind, and more frequently of a larger size, are pretty common in many parts of the colony.

After passing several farm-houses, we crossed the Bath river at Gildenhuys's, where a road on the right descends into the valley, to a spot which had just been fixed upon by the Cape Government for the site of a village, since named *Caledon*, in honor of the Governor under whom it was founded.   Here also was to be erected the Drostdy of the Deputy Landdrost of Swellendam; it having been found necessary, for the better administration of the executive government, to subdivide that extensive district.   Passing under the western end of Zwarteberg, the *Bath-house* came in view, and had a very pretty effect, being a white, regular, flat-roofed building, pleasantly situated in an elevated part of the southern slope of the mountain.   It was built in the year 1797, and at this time was the property of a medical gentleman of the name of *Hassener*, who resided in the neighbouring house, and under whose superintendence invalids made use of these baths.

The *Zwarteberg* (Black Mountain) is a short mountainous ridge, running east and west, of secondary height, and, in general structure and appearance, as far as I could observe, not differing from the other mountains in its neighbourhood; nor was the blackness, which gave rise to the name, at all remarkable, nor even very evident. From the lower part of its southern front, projects a small flat hill, out of the upper part of which issue, in several places, hot springs, the waters of which raised my thermometer to 118 degrees (38.2 of Reaumur; 47.77 Centig.)   This water deposits, in the channels along which it runs, an orange-coloured ochre; but after a course of two or three hundred yards, ceases to discolour the ground.   It contains iron and sulphur, and has a slightly chalybeate taste. Within three yards of one of these hot springs, there rises another, the water of which is pure and tasteless, without being in the least degree warmer than the usual temperature of spring-water.   The hill is not rocky, but seems to be composed of a loose black earth, having very much of a volcanic appearance, amongst which were pieces of hard, black, scoriated iron ore, of a metallic heaviness.

I discovered nothing that could be fancied to be the remains of a volcanic crater ; nor is there, I am inclined to think, much reason for entertaining the idea that such had ever existed. Excepting just at this spot, all the springs which flow from the Zwarteberg are of the ordinary temperature ; and, although the bath-hill be of a nature different from that of the great mountain to which it is connected, yet, as it also gives rise to a cold spring, it is difficult to avoid the conclusion, that the cause of heat in this water must be very local. *

I shall not here amuse myself in proposing or supporting any hypothesis on the cause of hot springs ; but shall confess myself very much at a loss in attempting to account for the great subterranean operations of Nature, whose dark recesses in the centre of our globe are not less out of the pale of observation, than the wide space beyond the starry system. Is, it may be asked of the lovers of hypothetical philosophy, the solidity or the cavity of this sphere, a fact which will ever admit of proof? or will mortal sagacity ever ascertain, whether the great space within the terrestrial shell be inhabited by animated beings, or occupied by nought but lifeless matter ? The numberless *desiderata* in human knowledge, either shew us the narrow limits of our faculties and mental powers, or teach us that there remains yet more to be known than we have hitherto learnt. The many noble discoveries and deductions which the divine gift of reason has already enabled man to make, give him, indeed, a just hope that, by pursuing an unprejudiced investigation of facts, he may yet arrive at a

---

* Besides the hot spring at *Zwarteberg*, and that in *Brand Valley*, (described hereafter, on 14th April,) some others have been discovered within the colony; particularly one in the valley of the *Western Elephant's River ;* another near the *Eastern Elephant's River*, in Kamnasi-land; and a third in the arid country behind *Kokman's* (or *Kogman's*) *Kloof:* but all are inferior in heat to the two first mentioned. There is also a warm spring on the northern side of the Gariep, in *Great Námaqualand.* Springs of *mineral* waters, of the common temperature, have been noticed in various places; one near *Graaff-Reynett*, another not far from *Uitenhage*, and one also in the *Tarka :* nor is it improbable that several others, equally remarkable, exist in various parts of the colony.

degree of knowledge far beyond that which he now possesses, or
that which by some it may be imagined possible for the human mind
ever to attain.   It is alone by the use of this divine gift, that all
our μάθησις, or *true* knowledge, in matters of science, has been
obtained: but the wisest must admit that there are bounds by
which the universe of ideas is limited; and here, all must stop.   The
wild speculations and unfounded theories of those who go in search of
knowledge without this for their guide, will surely, like the misty
imagery of a dream dispelled by the morning light, vanish at the first
dawn of the light of truth.

No attempts have ever been made to ascertain whether this
mountain, or any part of the surrounding country, produce metals
worth extracting; yet, until the experiment be made, it cannot be
believed that so extensive a colony would not, in some way, repay
its government the expenses of employing a practical mineralogist to
investigate its products, and, by boring or mining in every variety of
situation, to bring to light what may prove worthy of being called,
its sleeping riches.   At least, it is remarkable that the *auri sacra fames*
has not stimulated individuals to search for profit below the surface;
and though their labours should not be rewarded with *gold*, some
other useful substance might be discovered, which could equally well
repay their trouble.

The *Bath-house* stands close under the small flat hill already
mentioned, and the water is conducted down to it by a covered
channel.   The building *, erected in the year 1797, consists only of

---

* See the *Vignette* at the head of this chapter.   This gives a representation of its
front, or southern side, which has a fine view of the range of hills and mountains of
which the *Babylonsche-toren* is the most remarkable.   In the back ground, in the vignette,
is seen a part of the hill from which the hot spring rises.   The foreground consists only
of rough uncultivated ground; the art of ornamental gardening being quite unknown in
the colony, unless a few places in the immediate vicinity of Cape Town, should be allowed
a pretension to it.   The trees are young poplars, of the species already noticed as being
common in this country; and when they shall have attained a size capable of affording
shade and shelter, this spot will certainly have a more picturesque appearance than it can
at present boast of.

a ground-floor, divided lengthwise by a gallery which opens towards the front, into eight small rooms; and, towards the back, into four baths, together with a kitchen and servants' rooms at each end.

Unlike the watering-places of England, the Zwarteberg bath offers no attractions of amusement and society, and can barely accommodate its visitors with the necessary supplies. Consequently it is resorted to only by a few invalids who have faith in the medicinal powers of these waters, which, I was told, are efficacious against rheumatic affections, and possess some tonic properties; but the people of the country use it, without much discrimination, for a variety of other complaints. Their virtues, probably, have never been fairly ascertained; but, under judicious medical direction, these baths may be found beneficial in many cases; and when the neighbouring village shall have attracted a sufficient number of inhabitants, and, with them, the means of accommodating strangers, there is little doubt that this will become a place of considerable resort, as, on account of its greater proximity to the metropolis, it has always been much more frequented than any of the other warm baths of the colony, and, however wide the comparison, may be regarded as the *Baiæ* of the Cape.

Although the government granted a lease of these springs to the present possessor, it retained the privilege of issuing, to all who would apply for it, permission to make use of the original baths; which, however, are merely a few small huts on the eastern side of the springs, and which are kept in repair at public expense. For this permission, each individual pays a trifling sum, but he receives with it no other accommodation; and as this class of bathers consists of

---

* *Sparrman* relates an instance of an injudicious use of these baths, which proved fatal to a slave; he has recorded several chemical experiments on the water, with various tests. (Sparrman's Travels, vol. i. p. 139, 140, 141. English ed. Lond. 1785, 4to.) — *Thunberg* also gives the results of some further trials. (Thunberg's Travels, vol. i. p. 215. English ed. Lond. 8vo.) — The works of these travellers contain much information, and possess a share of *naïveté*, and a character of honesty, which render them useful as a picture of the colony in those days. Sparrman relates many incidents in a very amusing manner, and which bear, at the same time, the stamp of fidelity.

boors, slaves or Hottentots, they generally live in their own waggons or in temporary huts, during the time of their stay.

The water seemed to possess no quality hurtful to vegetation, as *Cliffortia odorata*, which is a shrub frequent in wet places, grew in it, as luxuriantly here as in other rivulets. I gathered *Pelargonium grossularioïdes* on the very edge of the warm rill, which was decorated also with the elegant *Restio verticillatus*, of the height of six feet, together with various *Lobeliæ*, and many other flowers. On the drier ground, *Athanasia trifurca* was a conspicuous shrub, being at this time in bloom. The sides of the Zwarteberg mountain, which my time did not allow me to examine, appeared likely to furnish a good botanical harvest.

The Hot-Bath is about 75 miles distant from Cape Town, and bearing S. E. by E. ½ E. It is not situated on the great eastern road, but stands at a little distance on one side of that branch of it which leads to the spot selected for the intended village; while the great eastern road itself passes along the northern side of Zwarteberg. The name of *Zwarteberg* is applied to several different mountains in the colony; to one near Saldanha Bay; to the lofty range which walls in the southern side of the Great Karro; and perhaps to many others. Numberless instances of one name being given to several different places, may easily be found on the map; but the confusion arising from this inattention, will become more serious in proportion as the country increases in population, and will, in the end, call for the application of some remedy, which, before the colony shall be too far advanced, may not be found impracticable.

The number of mountains and places still undistinguished by any name, continues to be the cause of many mistakes; and the inhabitants have great reason for desiring an authorised, regular, and systematic naming of all such places. As this country, for any thing at present known, will continue attached to the British empire, it seems more natural that the names of the principal places at least, should be English. The transition from Dutch to English names, might be made with little inconvenience to either nation, since translations of the present Dutch names might be used by all speaking or writing in English; while the converse of this, in writing in Dutch, would prevent mistake or confusion with those who are acquainted only with that language. Precisely this has already taken place with some names in daily use, such as *Kaapstad, Tafelberg, Leeuwenkop, Zoute rivier, Zondags rivier, Grootevisch rivier*, for which the English inhabitants have substituted, both in speaking and in writing, *Cape Town, Table-mountain, Lion's-head, Salt-river, Sunday-river*, and *Great Fish-river*. But the aboriginal Hottentot names ought, on no account, to be altered; they should, on the contrary, rather be sought for, and adopted, as being far more appropriate to Southern Africa, than a multitude of foolish names of modern imposition.

11*th.* I spent the forenoon in drawing some views, as memorials of a spot which I might never visit again. The landscape is mountainous and open, and, though it no where presents the desirable feature of wood, it is not deficient in beauty, in the grand, flowing outline of a range of mountains on the opposite side of the valley, and in which the mountain called *Babylonsche Toren* (Tower of Babel) stands conspicuous.* This mountain is, perhaps, the most remarkable of any in the colony, on account of the immense distance at which it is visible. About three years and a half afterwards, I saw it from the spot marked in my map by the words *Mountain Station*, which is distant 120 miles in a straight line; and a peak, which I distinguished when near a place called Helle, near Gaurits river, could hardly be any other than this same mountain, though the distance is not less than 157 miles in a right line. This would seem incredible, if allowance were not made for an extraordinarily re-

---

* The annexed *engraving* is a representation of this mountain, as viewed from the baths.

fractive power which the atmosphere possesses under a peculiar combination of circumstances. The intervening country, being free from high mountains, is favourable to great refraction. By mentioning this curious circumstance, I hope to excite the attention of other travellers, who may pass that way, to ascertain whether or not, I have been mistaken in supposing the mountain which I saw from that spot, to have been Babylonsche Toren.

Not many miles from the Baths, is a small spot, called *Hemel-en-aarde* (Heaven-and-earth), surrounded by high mountains, where there is an hospital (*Ziekenhuis*) for those afflicted with that dreadful and incurable malady the leprosy. This hospital is maintained at public expense; for defraying which, an express tax is levied on the colonists.

Early hours are kept throughout this country, and dinner is really that which its Dutch name implies, a noontide meal (*middag maal*). This enabled us to take our departure from the Baths in good time, as we hoped, to reach the end of our day's journey before dark. We mounted our horses, and took the road to *Genadendal* (Grace vale), the chief establishment of the Moravian missionaries; a place interesting in many respects, and which it was one of our principal objects to visit.

We re-passed the bath river, and, doubling the western point of Zwarteberg, took a northerly track, inclining a little eastward. The earth was generally of a reddish color; in some places, of an argillaceous, and, in others, of a sandy nature. The face of the country was open, and its surface varied with smooth hills, covered almost exclusively with a neat pale bushy shrub, of the height of three or four feet, called *Rhinoster bosch* (Rhinoceros bush)*, and said to have formerly been the food of the huge rhinoceros, till those animals fled before the colonists, as these gradually advanced over the country where the shrub grows. Of European plants, the

---

* *Stoebe rhinocerotis.* The following *Vignette* represents a sprig in its natural size. The leaves are very minute, and like scales, in the manner of the cypress; the flowers are small, and, though very numerous, are neither showy nor ornamental, being of a simple herbaceous color. Several species of Stoebe, which in growth resemble this one, are all, without distinction, called by the colonists, *Rhinoster-bosch,* and perhaps have, in former days, been equally the favourite food of the Rhinoceros.

Tamarisk is that which has the most resemblance to it; but the Rhinoster-bosch is of a hoary complexion, much more close and bushy, and finer in ramification. It abounds in dry hilly lands; and occupying extensive tracts, gives a peculiar character to the landscape. In this day's ride, this monotony became tedious; but as the roads, through what is called a Rhinoceros-bush country, are always very good, travellers regard that convenience as a sufficient recompence for the want of variety in its vegetation.

In this excursion, not a single large tree was any where to be seen, except around the houses of the colonists: these most frequently were either the white poplar, or the common English oak. I soon became accustomed, on observing a distant clump of trees, to view them as the sure indication of a dwelling-house; it being only in the deep ravines of the mountains, that indigenous trees are generally to be found.

CHAPTER V.

VISIT TO GENADENDAL.

THE weather was exceedingly pleasant and fine; but the distant blue lofty mountains of *Baviaan's Kloof* (Baboon's Pass), which now appeared before us, seemed enveloped in rain. The sun, fast sinking to the horizon, induced us to quicken our pace, that we might cross the river *Zondereinde* (Endless River) before dark. As this was a deeper stream than any we had hitherto crossed; and as we judged it would be much swelled with the rain of yesterday, we began to entertain great apprehensions that the ford would be found too deep to be passed safely in the dark. The course of this river is by no means of such a length as to justify the name it bears: not far from the village of Zwellendam, it joins the *Breede* (Broad) *River*. We reached it just before the close of twilight, and forded without accident, the water flowing scarcely so high as our horses' sides, and its width being but a few yards.

As we approached Genadendal, the mountains assumed a grandeur which the dubious light of evening very much increased. We had not long to contemplate the sublimity of this scene, as night soon drew its dark veil over it. The pleasure which it had inspired was succeeded by sensations of a less agreeable kind, when we found ourselves overtaken, on an unknown road, by one of the darkest nights we had witnessed; and were obliged to rely entirely on our horses for keeping us in the beaten road. At last we fortunately caught an uncertain glimpse of a light, which we supposed to proceed from some of the huts of the settlement; and, after groping our way more than a mile further, we arrived at the hut, and engaged its owner, who was a Hottentot, to lead us to the house of the missionaries, where we were received with a cordial welcome.

The name by which the members of this sect distinguish themselves, is, The United Brethren; and, judging from what I witnessed here, no other can be more applicable. On entering their peaceful abode, I seemed to have quitted the stormy world and its turbulent passions: the quiet and unassuming demeanor of the brethren; the order and the cleanliness of every thing I saw, gave me at once a very favorable opinion of the establishment. The missionaries were about four or five in number, and, together with their wives, constituted one family, in the superintendence and management of which each one had his proper department allotted to him; and it was delightful to observe with what tranquillity and regularity every thing was conducted. Their dress was modest and plain, and much resembled that of the sect of Quakers.

After partaking of their supper, we left them to the uninterrupted performance of religious duties peculiar to the day, it being the eve of Good Friday, and retired to a small clean and neat cottage close by, built expressly for the reception of visitors and strangers. At our lodging we were attended by two or three female Hottentot servants, very decently dressed; and I confess that such a specimen of the improvement, in the point of personal cleanliness, in a race of human beings proverbially filthy, was judiciously placed, and did not fail to excite my surprise, at the same time that it was truly gratifying. The walls of our cottage were whitewashed within and without, and the ceilings of the rooms were formed of a reed, called by the colonists *Spaansche riet* (Spanish reed) *, very neatly bound together; but an earthen floor, though swept quite clean, had too unartificial an appearance. Such floors are of very general occurrence, and must long continue so in those parts of the country where timber is scarce; but the force of custom and habit is remarkably exemplified by the fact, that even those boors, who dwell in the vicinity of the forests, still prefer an earthen, to a boarded, floor.

The first mission to the Cape, for propagating the Christian religion, was commenced in the year 1737, by a person named Schmidt, sent out by the Moravian society at Hernhuth. He formed a little settlement at this spot, and had succeeded in collecting round him a few Hottentots; but, finding too many impediments thrown in his way, by the colonists as it is said, he was at last obliged to abandon the undertaking, and finally returned to Europe in 1744. In the latter part of the year 1792, with the permission of the Dutch East India Company, three Moravian missionaries, named Marsveld, Schwinn, and Kühnel, were sent out to renew the mission. They fixed themselves at the same place, where, after a lapse of nearly fifty years, they still found some useful remains of Schmidt's garden and hut.

Such was the commencement of this interesting establishment,

---

* *Arundo Donax*, Lin. This is a strong reed, of the thickness of about an inch at the lower end. It grows to the height of fifteen feet or more, and is cultivated very generally by the boors, and applied to a variety of useful purposes.

which continued for many years to bear the name of Baviaan's Kloof, until it received the more applicable one of *Genadendal* (Grace Vale), while that of Baviaan's Kloof is retained for the adjoining pass over the mountains, being its ancient denomination. Kühnel had died previously to our visit; but other missionaries had at different times been sent out to reinforce the remainder; and a part of these, at the invitation of the Governor, had founded, in the year 1808, a similar settlement at *Groene Kloof* (the Green Pass), a place about midway between Cape Town and Saldanha Bay. *

12th. This morning my curiosity was much gratified, on viewing the place by day-light. Its secluded situation, in a pleasant valley, surrounded by bold and lofty mountains, perfectly accorded with the purpose for which it was chosen. At the head of the valley were erected all the principal buildings. At one end of a small green stood the *Church* †, built in 1797, and which, by its height, was the most conspicuous object in the settlement. It was a plain, oblong, white building, covered with a thatched roof of a very sharp pitch, but without a steeple. On both sides were four large glazed windows, and at each end two. Its interior was plain and neat; the walls were white-washed, and the ceiling was supported by two strong, though rather clumsy, pillars of masonry. The whole area, which was considered by the brethren to be large enough to accommodate an auditory of from eight hundred to a

---

* Of these two institutions, a full and interesting account may be seen in the Rev. C. J. Latrobe's " Journal of a Visit to South Africa, in 1815 and 1816."

† *The Vignette*, at the beginning of this chapter, gives a view of the *Church* on the southern and eastern sides. The hedge, and trees beyond it, form part of the missionaries' *garden*. Some of the lower mountains, which extend from the Baviaan's Kloof westward, are seen in the back-ground; they are covered with bushes and a great variety of plants, and have an appearance of verdure intermingled with rocks. The trees on the right are part of a beautiful grove of oaks, planted soon after the re-establishment of the mission; and the two before the church are chesnuts (*Castanea vesca*). The figures represent *Hottentots* in their ordinary working dress. A little to the right, but out of this picture, are the dwelling-houses and buildings of the mission; above which the mountains of the Kloof appear at a great elevation.

thousand persons, was covered with long benches; one-half of which was appropriated to the women, and the other half to the men. Around three of the sides, a narrow gallery has been constructed; and, at one end of the building, a small portion is partitioned off, for a vestry. The pulpit was merely a desk on a platform raised a little above the floor. Two separate doors admitted the male and the female part of the congregation to their respective benches. Nothing is solicited from visitors; but near the door is a box to receive pecuniary contributions, which, however, are perfectly voluntary. The upper part of this building was converted into a large loft, for containing various stores belonging to the society. All money received, whether from the sale of the articles they manufacture, or of the produce of their vineyard; from visitors for their accommodations; from voluntary donations; or from any other source, is deposited in a common purse, and applied in aid of the expenses of the establishment.

On one side of the green, a shady grove of oaks, regularly planted, surrounded and half concealed the different dwellings of the missionaries, together with the knife-manufactory, the blacksmith's shop, the water-mill and wine-press, the tobacco-house and cellar, the poultry-house, the cow-house, and store-rooms. The whole of these buildings, the work of the missionaries and their Hottentots, is substantially and neatly built in the Dutch style, and covered with thatch. Contiguous to the church and dwelling-houses, was an excellent garden, stocked with a variety of fruits and vegetables; and beyond this a vineyard. In the garden, a large pear-tree, planted by the founder of the establishment, Schmidt, was pointed out to me with all that pleasure and satisfaction, which the respect they bore towards his memory so naturally awakened. Beyond the vineyard, there was a large burying-ground, regularly divided into compartments, in which the graves were dug in a regular and successive order; each being numbered, to correspond with a register of the burials. Two or three graves of the missionaries and their wives were distinguished by broad flat tomb-stones, bearing a plain inscription.

The principal dwelling-house, where the brethren meet at every meal, and at private prayer, had formerly been their church, until the congregation becoming too numerous, they were obliged to build a larger. Every missionary, according to the custom of their society, professes some useful art or trade. One of the above-named, who from their age had now become the fathers of this family, was the constructor of an excellent water-mill, at which, besides the use made of it by the whole settlement, some money is earned towards its expenses, by grinding corn for the neighbouring boors. The second was a carpenter, waggon-maker, &c.; and the third, a smith, who had established a very respectable manufactory for cutlery; the Genadendal knives fetching a higher price among the boors, than those of the same kind imported from Europe. Those Hottentots who are willing to be instructed, are taken as apprentices in the different trades.

A constant stream of water is supplied by a small rivulet, called Baviaan's river, issuing from the mountains of the Kloof, and which, after meandering through the whole length of the valley, joins the river Zondereinde. This valley is divided into a great number of small gardens, portioned out among those Hottentot families who are disposed to submit to all the regulations of the settlement, and take up their abode under its protection. By the rules of the institution, these gardens and advantages become forfeited as soon as they cease to conduct themselves with industry and morality. This simple and just law, is one of the secrets by which the Moravians here have been enabled to maintain that good order and decorum which are among the best practical results of missionary labors. Interspersed between the gardens, but without much regularity, are the huts of the Hottentots; and besides these, a few more are scattered about in the adjoining valleys.

The population of Genadendal, or, more correctly speaking, the number of Hottentots registered as belonging to this institution, amounts, according to the information I received, to about fourteen hundred souls; but the number of actual inhabitants at any one period, falls short of this estimate, in proportion to the demand of the neighbouring farms for Hottentot labourers.

On looking up the valley, a grand scene presents itself: the Baviaan's Kloof exhibits a deep recess, where one mountain shutting in before the other, would lead the spectator to suppose that, along the dark defile, he might find a road through, to the other side of the range; but these mountains can be traversed only by a steep and rugged foot-path, which leads over their summit.   Clouds often envelope their craggy tops, and mist and rain fall more frequently here than in the open country.   This, unfortunately, happened now to be the case; yet, at intervals of fair weather, I found an opportunity of making a sketch of the scene.

At ten o'clock in the morning, the bell summoned the Hottentot congregation to church; and soon were seen coming from all quarters, men and women, who, to the number of about seven hundred, assembled and took their seats in a very orderly manner.   Several of the men still wore the Hottentot sheep-skin cloak, or kaross; but none were without trowsers: the rest were clothed in woollen jackets, with shirts, hats, and shoes.   All the women were remarkably clean, and neatly dressed in European costume; and the majority even wore stockings.   The whole appeared very attentive to the service, performed in the Dutch language, and which consisted in reading that part of the New Testament relating to the Crucifixion and in singing psalms at intervals.   This latter part of the ceremony was exceedingly interesting, and even gratifying, by the exactness with which the whole congregation kept time, and by the perfect unison they preserved throughout.   From amongst the women, I could distinguish some good voices; and the service of the day sufficed to prove to me, that Nature has certainly not denied to Hottentots a musical ear.

To every philanthropist it could not fail to be a treat of the purest kind; to witness a despised and degraded portion of his fellow-creatures taken under the kind protection of those who have had the more fortunate lot of being born to the improvements of European knowledge; to behold them thus reclaimed from disgusting filthiness, to a decent cleanliness; from a wild, irregular life, to order and social rules; from uninstructed stupidity, to a knowledge and practice of morality and the useful arts of civilised man; in fine, from a gross ignorance of the Supreme Being, to a due sense of the superintending goodness of the Great Creator of the universe. When missionary labors produce effects such as these, every well-wisher of mankind will view them with respect. Such, at least, are the professed objects of this institution; and if some instances are to be found, which show that they have not in every case been attained, and that seed sown on a sterile soil has been unproductive, we are not on that account to shut our eyes against the many proofs of the utility of such an establishment as Genadendal. Every one acquainted with human nature, will be ready to acknowledge, that many difficulties must be overcome in the course of such an attempt. To inculcate the necessity of honest industry, as a chief moral duty, is in effect cutting off the root of, at least, half the miseries of the Hottentot race, and tends to make these people a more valuable part of the population of the colony. Their general quiet and harmless character gives them a superior claim to encouragement, and renders them friendly to the existing government. By persuading or compelling them to the observance of the precepts of morality, and by drawing them under the influence of religion, their vices, which commonly are not of the most atrocious kind, may be repressed probably with less difficulty than would be met with in many other uncivilised nations. But such a desirable end is not to be accomplished by the ignorant enthusiast: it is the man of genuine morality and humble piety who, gifted by nature with the talents of a teacher, improved by education, and warmed by the spirit of pure philanthropy, seeks not to gratify his vanity by public approbation, but considers it a sufficient reward for his persevering labors, to behold the temporal and religious improvement of those whom, with affectionate humanity, he has taken under his care and guidance. A solicitude for the welfare of our fellow-creatures, can proceed from nought but the best feelings of the heart; and it is this which constitutes the essence of a true missionary: but a blind desire to infuse his own peculiar religious doctrines, and a disregard to the worldly improvement of his followers, are the distinguishing marks of an opposite character, and can only exist in a mind altogether unfit for the undertaking. The harm such men do in the cause is seldom to be remedied. The savage witnesses the superiority of civilised men, and longs to be taught those arts which have created that superiority; but if, instead of gratifying so natural a wish, his teacher will inform him of nothing but the incomprehensible mysteries of religion, he is disappointed, perhaps disgusted, and resolves to shut his ears to further instruction. Would the missionary content himself, in the onset, with teaching them such useful arts as would add to their daily comfort, he would gain their esteem and respect, most likely their gratitude; and having thus secured their confidence, would find their minds and hearts in a state better fitted to listen to his precepts, and to receive the lessons of religion.

Even the place itself had an air of tranquillity, and the little grove seemed to cast a modest peaceful shade around. The brethren appearing much pleased with the sketch I made of this scene, and lamenting that, though several visitors had promised them a drawing of it, to send to their society in Europe, they had all forgotten their promise, I engaged to fulfil it for them; which I did a few weeks afterwards.

In the afternoon, we were conducted part of the way up the mountains, to a spot whence we had a commanding view of the whole settlement, and of the vale of the Zondereinde; while the numerous huts of the Hottentots, half hid in the midst of gardens, through which the winding rivulet took its course, formed altogether an interesting picture. On the eastern bank, a few huts appeared detached from the rest; these belonged to some *Caffres* (or Kaffers), who had taken up their abode here, and proved worthy members of this community.

From the summit of these mountains, it is said that Table Mountain and the Bay can be distinguished; but the unfavourable state of the weather, and the late hour of the day, obliged us hastily to descend, and the darkness of evening fell upon us before we reached the house. The air became chilly, owing to the rain which had fallen during the day: the thermometer was no higher than 61° (12·8 Reaum.; 16·11 Centig.)

13*th.* The next morning we were attended by *Mr. Küster,* one of the brethren, who conducted us along the valley, through the maze of gardens and fruit-trees, to exhibit the progress which their Hottentots had made in horticulture and domestic order. Warmed with unaffected zeal in the cause in which he was engaged, he displayed their success with a satisfaction and pleasure, in which we fully participated. The huts at Genadendal, unlike those of genuine Hottentot construction, which have an hemispherical shape, and are covered with mats, are merely a rude imitation of the quadrangular buildings of the colonists. Those which we saw, were generally from ten to fifteen feet long, and from eight to ten wide, having an earthen floor, and walls white-washed on their inside, composed of rough unhewn posts, filled up between with reeds and rushes plastered with mud, and the whole covered with a roof of thatch. The eaves being in general not higher from the ground than four or six feet, the doors could not be entered without stooping. A small unglazed window admitted light; but there was neither chimney, nor any other opening in the roof, by which the smoke might escape. *

Some of the huts exhibited superior workmanship, being divided by a partition-wall into two rooms, and were exceedingly neat and clean. A table, two or three chairs, and a box, all manufactured by the Hottentots themselves, made up the principal part of the furniture. A few families, who had been long established here, lived in houses of a much better description, built of square sawn beams, and walls partly of bricks and partly of mud hardened in the sun. One house, situated in a line of huts called *Molen-straat*

---

* *The Vignette* at the end of this chapter is a view of a part of the valley of *Gena-dendal,* showing the ordinary huts of the Hottentots, surrounded by plantations of peach-trees. The mountain there seen is a part of *Zwarteberg.*

(Mill-street), contained a small hand-mill, where three Hottentots were busily employed in grinding their corn.

This mill was remarkable for its very simple construction: the essential parts of its mechanism were merely two horizontal stones, of two feet in diameter, and three handles. The under-stone was fixed, about three feet from the ground, in a circular frame or box of wood, elevated above it high enough to prevent the upper stone, when in motion, from flying off. The inner surface of each stone was channelled in the same manner as we observe in the mill-stones in England; while the upper one was perforated by a funnel-shaped hole of the form of an inverted cone, into which the corn, in small quantities, was continually thrown by hand. In the upper surface of the moving stone was fixed a stout cylindric pin of iron. The handle was a horizontal stick about four feet long, one end of which was fastened by a piece of raw hide to the iron pin; while the other was supported by a long rope attached to the rafters of the roof. In the same manner, two other handles were fixed to the pin, one above the other, and were similarly supported by ropes suspended from different parts of the roof. By alternately pushing forward and pulling back these handles, the upper stone was made to turn round with any desired degree of velocity, and at the same time discharged the flour by a spout in the side of the circular box. The greatest inconvenience of such a mill consists in its having no means for regulating the degree of fineness or coarseness of the meal; but for this country, where regular millwrights are seldom to be found, it possesses a most important advantage, in being so easy of construction, that every farmer may make one for himself. It is, in fact, often to be met with in the houses of the boors, having, most probably, been by them originally introduced into this colony.

As we passed along through their little gardens, under the cool shade of peach-trees, the Hottentots at work touched their hats, and, in a good-natured, respectful manner, accosted each of us with " Dag, Mynheer!" meaning " Good day, Sir!" The women, as we walked by the door of their huts, courtesied with the same salutation; while the boys and girls, half-hidden behind them, seemed also eager to get a peep at the strangers. I could not help noticing the comparatively small proportion of male population that appeared in the settlement: this Mr. Küster accounted for, by the number of men who were absent on service with the boors; some by the week, others by the month, and a few by the year. If a Hottentot have property; that is, provisions, sufficient for the support of his wife and children during his absence, he generally prefers leaving them under the protection of the missionary establishment, to taking them with him to the farmers, where they hardly ever receive any other wages for their work, than their daily food. *

Although their gardens, in neatness and good management, be much below the point at which it would be desirable to see them, it ought to be remembered, that any thing like horticulture in the Hottentot race, should be regarded as an extraordinary improvement on their ancient mode of living. Different vegetables and roots were seen in their gardens; but tobacco and pumkins were to be found in almost every one. The women here, besides all their domestic employments, earn a little money by the sale of mats, which they manufacture from a kind of rush †, very common in the rivers of this district. These rushes are sometimes so long as to admit of being made into mats six feet in width: this is not done in the manner of interweaving, but by placing them parallel to each other, and transversely with respect to the length of the mat, connecting them at every five or six inches by cords, made either of the same material, or of the bark of the Karro thorn tree ‡, run through them the whole length of the mat, by means of a long wooden or bone needle.

We next visited the manufactory of cutlery, where I saw a considerable stock of all those articles for which there is any de-

---

* Some further account of Genadendal; its natural history, &c. will be found under the date of the 13th of February to 7th March, 1815.

† *Cyperus textilis.*

‡ *Acacia Capensis.* B.   See the *Vignette* at the head of Chapter X.

mand in the country. Some Hottentot apprentices were employed in making others; chiefly a sort of pocket sheath-knife much used by the boors. At the blacksmith's shop, other Hottentots were forging the iron-work for a waggon, under the direction of one of the Brethren; and the quiet, steady industry with which these worthy people pursued each their peculiar occupation, was an example which it would be in the highest degree pleasing to see followed every where.

I now made enquiry for Hottentots who would engage themselves in my service for the intended expedition into the interior; but, on account of so many being at this time absent from the settlement, barely one could be found, who was willing to go with me, and that only in case he could persuade some others of his acquaintance to accompany him. But after trying in vain all his friends, who objected to the great length of the proposed journey, he finally declined my offer, although I had acceded to his demand of thirty rix dollars per month, which was at least six times the customary wages of a Hottentot. In this occurrence, an unexpected difficulty disclosed itself; and I began to be fearful that the nature of my undertaking would deter others also from entering my service.

It was with reluctance that we took our departure from this interesting spot: its peaceful character; the tranquillity of the scene; its good order; and especially the benevolent purpose to which it was dedicated, had made a delightful impression on my mind.

CHAPTER VI.

RIDE FROM GENADENDAL TO THE HOT SPRING IN BRAND VALLEY; AND VISIT
TO TULBAGH.

HAVING lingered till the sun had passed the meridian nearly two
hours, we were compelled to hasten our pace. Following, upwards,
the course of the river, along the *Vale of the Zondereinde*, we
forded many little streams. These we found deeper than any
we had hitherto passed; but their waters were clear and limpid;
and I remarked, that none of the rivers which we crossed in the
succeeding part of this excursion, exhibited the brown color noticed
at the Palmiet river. A solitary farm-house was the only dwelling
we saw: the face of the country was shrubby; but not a single tree
of any magnitude was to be seen, although many large and decayed
trunks were observed along the banks of the Zondereinde. Fire-
wood is an article generally very scarce in the vicinity of a Hottentot
settlement; and, in all the grazing parts of the colony, it is rendered
much more so by the wasteful and destructive practice of annually

setting fire to the old withered grass, as the means of clearing the pastures.   The flames, spreading rapidly, scorch and destroy every shrub and plant in their way, and pervade the whole farm, unless stopped by a river, or a beaten road.   In ascending the *Dunkerhoek* (Dark Corner) mountains, part of the Baviaan's Kloof chain, the devastation occasioned by this custom was very striking, in the fatal havoc it had lately made amongst the finest plants of proteas, heaths, and the richest variety of shrubs we had passed in our ride.   That delicate and beautiful heath, *Erica vestita*, with white flowers, grows here, as was discoverable by one large plant which had escaped the conflagration.   *Antholyza lucidor*, and *Aulax umbellata*, were recognised, although quite scorched up.   Every thing was nearly consumed or destroyed, and the black, charcoal-like state of this shrubbery presented a singular, but melancholy appearance. *

We continued our ride for several miles over an elevated mountainous tract, where no signs of a habitation were to be seen ; the sun had set, leaving us under the dismal apprehension of having missed the right road, and of being left to wander all night in a region where deep ravines and precipices occurred on either side. Just as the twilight was drawing to a close, we perceived a house down in the valley below ; and, on arriving at it, had the satisfaction of finding that it was the dwelling of a farmer named *Jacobus Du Toit*, where we had intended taking up our quarters for the night.   We met with a cordial reception ; a Hottentot was instantly called to take our horses, and we were no sooner seated, than the good lady of the house poured us out a cup of tea ; an article which, in most farm-houses, is always kept in readiness, as a beverage that may be taken at any hour of the day.

We took our seat at the family table, and supper was prolonged by a variety of questions from our host and his wife, respecting the nature and object of my intended expedition.   On such topics

---

* The natural productions of this day's journey are noted under the date of the 7th to the 10th of March, 1815.

as travelling in distant parts of the colony; game and wild beasts;
Bushmen and Caffres; oxen, sheep, and pastures, a boor carries
on a conversation with considerable interest, as these are to him
subjects of chief importance. But in respect to the cultivation
of mental capacity, and an extensive variety of ideas, it is unrea-
sonable to expect more in a Dutch peasant of this colony than
we can meet with in the peasantry of Europe. To cast this reproach on the boors of the Cape, as a national character, is an
act of injustice, which, if not to be excused by ignorance, must
be attributed to some worse motive.

At about half an hour after nine, all retired to rest; some to a
mat on the floor in the *voorhuis* (entrance-room, or hall), which
is a large room used for general purposes, and occupying the middle
and principal part of the ground-floor; the master to the bed-
room at one end of the voorhuis, and the guests to a small chamber
at the other.

Those bearing the name of *Du Toit* are said to be the descendants of one of those Protestant French families spoken of in the
third chapter, as having fled to the Cape to avoid religious per-
secution. It is a singular instance of complaisance, that they themselves have relinquished the French pronunciation of their name,
and adopted that of the boors their neighbours, speaking it as
if written in English, Du Towey.

14th. The next morning, we were shown his *kraal,* or cattle-
pound, in which he had not less than a hundred oxen and cows; but of
those which he had for sale, none appeared fit for my purpose. His
income depended chiefly on the produce of his vineyard; and, since
the Cape has been in the hands of the English, it has yielded a much
greater profit than before. In his, as in most of the gardens of these
districts, I noticed all the common culinary vegetables of Europe;
and, of fruit-trees, the peach, apple, pear, apricot, fig, banana or
plantain, guava, orange, lemon, mulberry, and medlar, seemed to
thrive perfectly well.

The quince-tree formed the usual hedges of the gardens in
most parts of the colony; which purpose they answer exceedingly

well, by being treated in the same manner as the quick or haw-
thorn; and, by ' plashing' their long tough and slender twigs,
while young, they produce a very lasting fence, which, at the same
time, possesses the very necessary property of being impenetrable to
cattle. These twigs are very commonly used as horse-whips, when
those made of the hide of the rhinoceros or hippopotamus, are
not to be procured. At this season, every hedge is loaded with
the finest fruit, the flavour of which is excellent; but they are
seldom turned to any other account than that of affording a kind
of brandy: peaches, however, yield a better spirit.

This division of the district, on the northern side of the mountains, is called *Bosjesveld* (Bushland, or the Bushy Country); and,
although that name was probably, at its first imposition, characteristic of the nature of the country, there did not appear at this
time any peculiar feature of that kind, by which it might be considered to differ much from the other divisions of this part of
the colony.

Du Toit's house is beautifully situated in an open country,
surrounded on all sides by distant mountains; and, though it be
wild, and apparently barren, the soil is reckoned productive, as,
indeed, the garden and vineyard clearly proved. A part of the
morning I employed in making two drawings of the scenery, particularly as they might express a certain general character of the
houses and landscape, which most frequently occurs in this settlement. The dwelling itself was a miserable mud-built cottage, with
a ground floor of four or five rooms. It could boast of glazed
windows, but neither of a boarded floor, nor of a plastered ceiling;
in which respect, however, it was not worse than the best farm-
houses in the country. In front was a small garden, of the width
of the house, enclosed by a low mud wall, shaded by two fine trees
of *Melia Azedirach*, twenty feet high, whose horizontal branches
and light foliage gave it an air of much elegance: such trees are
not uncommon. A beautiful bush of *Nerium Oleander*, twelve
feet high, covered with blossom, seemed, by its splendid colors,

to mock the wretched, dirty mien of the house. A large low-spreading tree, of an indigenous species of willow, was the only plant that could afford the house the least shelter from the wind. The out-buildings, of which there were many, were not, in appearance, inferior to the dwelling-house; and, like that, they were built of mud.

The process for making walls of this kind, is extremely simple, though not expeditious; and can only be practicable where earth of a suitable quality is found. This, if too clayey, shrinks and cracks; and, if not sufficiently so, crumbles and moulders away: but, with a good proportion of sand or grit, added to some ferruginous particles, it forms a wall not much less durable than those which are built of bricks. For this purpose, it is made into a mud, which must be well tempered, and sufficiently stiff to remain in layers of about a foot in thickness, without falling out of shape. No kind of mould or form is used in this process; but the earth is merely laid on with a spade, and, when half dry, the sides are pared smooth. When one layer is perfectly dry, but not sooner, another is laid on; and thus, from time to time, repeating the operation, the wall may be carried up, if required, to the height of a second story, while, at the same time, the thickness necessary for supporting that weight need not be greater than one-half more than is generally requisite for a brick wall of the same height. These operations can only be carried on in the dry season of the year. Such materials, it may be remarked, cannot be used with advantage in climates where the thermometer sinks much below the freezing point; as alternate rain, frost, and thaw, would occasion a wall of this sort to crumble away in a little time. When such buildings are white-washed, which I have often observed in other parts of the colony, they look very neat, and are not easily to be distinguished from those which are made of bricks and stuccoed.

This fine valley was but thinly inhabited: not more than two or three other farm-houses were in sight; yet, were the land properly appropriated and well managed, it would, there can be little doubt, support an industrious population of far greater amount than that by which it is at present occupied. The immense tract of land that, in a country such as this where the herbage is never thick enough to cover the ground, is required for a grazing farm, tends to check the progress of agriculture, inasmuch as it prevents the due subdivision of the land. A pastoral district must necessarily be thinly inhabited; and it is only in proportion as it assumes an agricultural character, that it can admit any considerable increase of population. It is not to this valley alone, that these remarks are applicable; they will not be found very incorrect, if applied generally to the whole of the colony.

Our hospitable friends, who had been much pleased by the unreserved and communicative disposition of my companion, would have persuaded us to remain till the next day; for the visits of strangers, from whom any news may be obtained, are almost always welcome in this country: but we took our leave at an early hour, while the whole of the family, standing at the door as we rode off, bade us farewell, and " *aangenaame reis*" (pleasant journey); often repeating, that if we came that way again, we must not fail to take up our quarters at their house.

The weather was delightful, and not a cloud intercepted the brightness of the atmosphere. Nothing could be more pleasant than our ride along this valley: every object glowed with the genial warmth of the air. At the termination of it, we had to ascend a kloof, or gorge, in a range of rocky hills, from the top of which a magnificent scene of mountains burst upon us. At the foot of this kloof, after a considerable descent, commenced a long extended valley, apparently four or five miles broad, and very level, stretching as far as *Brand Valley* (Burning, or Scalding Valley); beyond which we beheld the majestic mountains of *Hex-Riviers Kloof* (the Pass of Witches' River). This country is a continuation of the Bosjesveld; and, at about mid-way, we halted at the dwelling of a boor named *Duplessis*, where we arrived at noon.

Being entirely strangers at this house, we introduced ourselves, according to the custom of the country, by riding up to the door, remaining seated on our horses till the master of the house makes his

R

appearance, when we exchange the word *Dag;* and on being asked if we will not alight, or have the saddles taken off, we dismount and give our hand, saying " *Hoe vaart gy ?*" (How do you do ?) to which the answer is, invariably, " *Gezond*" (In good health). We are then invited into the house, and desired to sit down ; or, if the family happen to be at meals, are expected to make one at the table. A few questions, as to where we come from, and whither we are going, usually follow ; and the meal being finished, we are at liberty to proceed on our journey as soon as we please. Seldom is any direct enquiry made to discover who we are, or even our names. These are the ceremonies and reception most commonly met with throughout the country.

Duplessis seemed desirous of treating us well, and boasted of having as good wine as any in the colony. He poured us out each a glass, and we had already begun to praise its bright color ; but no sooner had it touched our lips, than we discovered by each other's looks, that we perfectly coincided in our judgment, that it was the sourest wine we had ever drank. We sipped again ; but its acidity was intolerable : yet, as it would have been an affront to our good-natured host, to have spoken ill of wine which he called the " best in the colony," I made a sign to Polemann that we must e'en drink it down, let happen what would ; and, to encourage him in a piece of politeness for which he showed but little relish, I set the example, by undauntedly taking another sip. He had scarcely swallowed the half of his, when our host, who had just poured out some for himself, hastily took the glass out of his hand, apologising very warmly for having brought us, by mistake, a bottle of vinegar. But he spoke too late ; and my fellow-traveller, addressing me in English, which was not understood at this house, reproached me for having, by an over-politeness, induced him to drink half a glass of vinegar. Poor Duplessis was much confused at discovering his unfortunate blunder, and immediately fetched a bottle of excellent wine, taking the precaution to drink the first glass himself.

While the horses were feeding, I made use of the short time we stopped here, to take a sketch of the place. A few trees of white poplar near the house, relieved the naked, unsheltered appearance of the situation, which was backed by a low range of mountains, of serrated outline, and composed, probably, of a slaty rock; the nearest summit of which is called *Grootkop* * (Great Head, or Peak.) Several little half-naked Hottentot children, curious to know what I was doing, came round me, and crawled about on the ground before me, amusing themselves in playing with dust and dirt. The boys are most frequently seen with a whip in their hands, proportionably of the same unwieldy length as those which are used by the waggon-drivers; so that, from their very infancy, they begin to acquire a dexterous management of it.

On the road from this place, we passed some large trees of *Wagenboom* (*Protea grandiflora*), so called by the colonists because the wood of it has been found suitable for making the fellies of waggon-wheels. It is reddish, and has a very pretty, reticulated grain, which might, perhaps, render it deserving of being employed for ornamental furniture. It much resembles some of the cabinet-woods brought from New South Wales; which, in fact, are of trees belonging to the same natural order: thus giving to botanists an additional hint, that characters may possibly be discovered in the structure of the wood of plants, that may throw some wished-for light on a natural classification of vegetables. It is the largest growing tree, of the Proteaceous tribe, in this part of Africa. It is found growing in dry, rocky places, with a trunk often a foot or more in diameter; and is remarkable for its exceedingly blue foliage. It is decorated with large handsome flowers of a pale yellow color, which, though four inches wide when fully expanded, are still inferior in size to those of *Protea cynaroïdes.* Another proteaceous tree (*Brabeium stellatifolium*), sometimes exceeds the Wagenboom in the extent of its branches; but is smaller in the trunk. We passed many other species of the same order, and a great variety of shrubby plants

* The word *kop* occurs very frequently in the names of places, and implies either a peak in a range of mountains, or a single hill.

adorning the hills and valleys; but which were over-topped by the *Bezem-riet* (Broom-reed), a large kind of *Restio*, which grew abundantly in several places. An elegant willow-leaved shrub (*Capraria lanceolata*), was common in the beds of small rivulets.

At five o'clock we reached *Brand* (or *Brandt*) *Valley*, and took up our lodging at the farm-house of De Wet. I immediately went to examine the *Hot Spring*, which is at a very short distance from the house, and found it much larger, and more remarkable, than the spring at Zwarteberg. It formed a shallow pond of about fifty feet across, of the most transparent water; in the middle of which several strong springs bubble up through a bottom of loose white sand, and afterwards, flowing in a very copious stream, become a rivulet, which, for at least a mile and a half, continues so hot, that its course along the valley may, at any time of the day, but more particularly early in the morning, be traced by the steam which perpetually arises from it. The pond is sheltered by a small clump of white poplars, which thrive perfectly well, although growing at the very edge of the water, and bedewed with the hot steam, which ascends to their highest branches. No plant, it seems, can grow in the water itself; but the margins of the bank are thickly covered with sedge. *
Royena glabra, a *Rhus*, and a variety of plants, stood within the influence of its heat.

The thermometer, when plunged into the pond, rose only to 144° (49½ Reaum.; 62¼ Centig.); but, to the hand, it felt nearly scalding hot, so that the immersion could scarcely be endured for a couple of seconds; and I have no doubt that the great heat of this spring would cause the death of any animal that should happen to fall in. Where it bubbles up out of the earth, it is, perhaps, a few degrees hotter. This water is pure and tasteless, and is used for all domestic purposes. Nothing resembling a deposition is any where observable; nor are its banks or channel at all discolored. The

---

* Particularly *Cyperus fascicularis* (*C. polystachyos*. Lin. et Th.)

hill, from the foot of which it issues, has no remarkable appearance; at least, there is none of that black, ponderous, earth or iron ore noticed at the Zwarteberg baths.

At the distance of about three hundred yards from the source, two bath-houses have been built over the stream, the heat of which, even here, is almost greater than can be born by a person not gradually inured to it. These little buildings, being public property, were much neglected and dilapidated; and nothing could be in a more wretched, dirty, and ruinous state, than the huts which were meant to accommodate those who use the bath. At this time, a slave and a Hottentot, who had been sent here for the benefit of the water, occupied two of them; but their miserable lodging hardly afforded protection from the weather. I could not learn that this bath has any other medicinal virtues than what it derives from the mere heat of the water.

Between the spring and the bath, where the stream has run a sufficient distance in the open air to allow it time to become a few degrees cooler, the bottom of the rivulet is covered with a beautiful sea-green *Conferva*, waving gracefully beneath the water, like long tresses of hair. In the days of mythology, this circumstance would have furnished the poets with the hint for a history of some lovely nymph metamorphosed into this rivulet, where her flowing locks still remain to attest the truth of the story —

> " Conticuère undæ; quarum Dea sustulit alto
> Fonte caput, viridesque manu siccata capillos,
> ——————— —— veteres narravit amores.

15th. At eight o'clock in the morning, we departed from this remarkable spring, having before us a long ride to the village of Tulbagh. Taking a more westerly course in rounding the mountain which forms the head of Brand Valley, we entered the district or valley of *Roodezand* (Red-sand), formerly called *Waveren*. It is about forty miles long in a direct line, and several miles broad: its surface is flat, and but thinly sprinkled over with houses, although, for this colony, it may be considered a populous tract. Nothing can be more grand than the lofty mountains by which it is enclosed on either side; especially those of *Mostert's Hoek* (Mostert's Corner).

We forded the *Breede* (or Broad) river, which, at this season, is generally shallow, and divided into many little parallel rivulets; but after the rains have fallen, it swells into a broad and impassable stream. It disembogues itself on the southern shore, into St. Sebastian's Bay; and is one of the seven principal rivers of the colony. These are, the *Berg* (Mountain), and the *Oliphants* (Elephants), on the western coast; and along the southern, the *Breede*, the *Gaurits*, the *Camtoos*, the *Zondag* (Sunday), and the *Groote Visch* (Great Fish) rivers.

In several places I remarked a great number of Coloquintida melons (*Cucumis colocynthis*) lying scattered on the ground, but connected together by the dry halm, as by a cord, all the leaves being decayed and entirely withered away. They resembled, in some degree, a common garden-melon; but were perfectly globular and smooth. Should this drug be introduced more generally into medical practice in Europe, it may, perhaps, prove a source of profit not unworthy of notice, especially as the operation of preparing them for exportation is attended with very little trouble or expense. They are to be found in great abundance in many places, growing in the plains; the plant being widely disseminated over the whole of the extratropical part of Southern Africa. Every article of export from this colony, however small at first its amount may be, should be carefully encouraged, and the trade promoted; because it cannot reasonably be expected, that a settlement which should be unable to export a produce of its own, sufficient as a return for the imported articles it consumes, can become rich and prosperous.

At Dantje Hugo's, where we halted to take some refreshment, we met with an Irishman, who had been residing with this boor several months, and who seemed pleased at having an opportunity of entertaining his countryman, and of speaking English. Both here, and at several farms on the road, we made enquiries for draught-oxen, but without success.

Under the mountains westward of us, lay an extensive flat country, called *Goudinie*, (the original Hottentot name,) said to be very fertile; but I had little time for observation, as the day-light, drawing to a close, obliged us to make all haste; and it was not before the evening twilight had ended, that we arrived at Tulbagh. Here we were received with every mark of hospitality, by *The Rev. Mr. Ballot*, the clergyman of the village. This gentleman, before he came to the Cape, had lived several years at Malacca; and, in speaking comparatively of the two countries as a place of residence, decidedly gave the preference to Africa. Indeed, his situation here, appeared to me as one capable of affording every comfort and enjoyment. The parsonage-house was not only large, handsome, and commodious, with a number of suitable offices and out-buildings, and a large garden attached to it; but it stood in the most eligible spot, and commanded the principal view of the village; that, of which a part is represented in the engraving at the head of this chapter.

16th. The village of *Túlbagh* *, so named after a Dutch governor, who died at the Cape in 1771, stands at the northern end of the valley of Roodezand, on a spot which, if pleasantness of situation and beauty of landscape should decide such a choice, has been judiciously selected. But the difficulty of access to it, from any other quarter than the south, is an inconvenience never to be obviated, and which must always continue to operate against its rising prosperity. It seems probable, that the great inducement to erect a town in this place, was the circumstance of its being on the great north-eastern road; a consideration which ought to have its weight, but which should not have had a preponderance: for a town placed in a suitable part of a country, will never fail to draw towards itself a proportionate traffic. The number of houses and inhabitants has increased in a slower proportion here than in most of the other villages; though there is no want of good water or garden-ground,

---

* Pronounced *Túlbak*.

nor of fertile land in the vicinity. The town, at this time, was nothing more than half a score of neat white houses placed in a row, with here and there an intervening space between them; at the back of which were as many more of an inferior size. *   In front, but on the opposite side of the road, and running under the shade of trees, is a strong rill of excellent water, led there, as well for the supply of the inhabitants, as for the irrigation of their gardens, which lie on a gentle declivity immediately below it; but no plan could be more inconvenient than that, which has been here adopted, of separating the gardens from the houses.   At a few hundred yards from the lower, or southern end of the street, stands the church, a neat and respectable edifice, built on the ground plan of a cross; as are, I believe, all the other churches in the colony.   It is white-washed, and covered with a roof of thatch: it has no steeple; but the purpose of one is supplied by a belfry separate from the church, and which consists merely of two large square pillars of masonry, connected at top by an arch, under which hangs the bell.   This is the usual kind of belfry for all the country churches.

At the distance of half an hour's walk northwards from the village, is the *Drostdy,* or official residence of the landdrost, a modern erection, surrounded by the dwellings of the secretary and subordinate civil officers.   In placing the drostdy at so` great a distance from the village, the prosperity of the latter seems to have been unfortunately left out of consideration; for such an arrangement seems calculated to cause rather the desertion of it, than any increase of inhabitants; as experience in similar cases sufficiently

---

* *The Vignette* at the head of this chapter represents the *Village of Tulbagh,* as viewed from the parsonage-house, and looking southward.   The mountains in the distance are those of the *Roodezands Kloof.*   The houses are all white, and covered with thatch: in front of some of them are square pillars, supporting a trellis of vines; and a row of young oaks along the street, with a plantation opposite to them, of larger trees of the same kind, and a few pines, add greatly to the neat and pleasing appearance of this little village. Behind the spectator are the lofty mountains of Winterhoek; on his left, those of Mostertshoek; and on the right, those over which the Oud Kloof (Old Kloof) passes; neither of which are included in this engraving.

shows, that new-comers would prefer that situation which is nearest
to the head buildings of the settlement. Some spot close to the
village, would have been the only proper site; as well on account of
adding to its size and importance, as of the greater convenience it
would possess, on many occasions, for transacting public business.
The two places are now distinguished from each other, by the names
of *Kerk-straat* (Church-street), and the *Drostdy*. This latter is a
large and handsome stuccoed building*, ornamented in front with a
portico of three arches, to which the ascent is by a flight of steps.
It contains several large and lofty rooms; together with a spacious
council-room, in which public meetings, and the sittings of the judges
at the annual circuit, are held.

The mountains, that on each side bound the valley of Waveren,
gradually approach each other as they run northward beyond Tulbagh, increasing in elevation; and at a few miles beyond the Drostdy,
they unite, forming a nook called *Winterhoek* (Winter Corner), on
account of the snow with which the summits here, are more frequently covered than in any other part of the range. The valley
below is exceedingly romantic and secluded; but the surrounding
mountains intercept the sun for some time after it has risen, and
before it has set, to the more open parts of the country; a circumstance which, particularly in summer, is far from being disadvan-
tageous. It contains several pleasant farms, and a number of
streamlets, which, receiving a constant supply from the mountains,
unite their waters to form the *Kleine Berg* (Little Mountain) river.
This, running southward, finds a way, by the Roodezand Kloof,
through the great western chain, and thence, by a north-westerly
course, after joining the *Groote Berg* river, discharges itself into
St. Helena Bay.

17*th*. Mr. Ballot having kindly furnished us with horses, in
order that our own might be left to rest during our stay at Tulbagh,

* A representation of the *Drostdy* is given at the end of the chapter. The distant
mountain there seen is part of the lofty range of *Winterhoek*. At the back of the building, or a little more to the right of the picture, is the Witsenberg range.

S

we started at eight in the morning for an excursion to the top of *Witsenberg*, a mountainous ridge lying eastward of the village, at the distance of about an hour's ride. Over this ridge there is a road, which is frequented by the boors, as it is the only pass from the Bokkeveld to this side of the country. The ascent is so steep, and the road so rocky and dangerous, that any person, unused to Cape travelling, would feel inclined to doubt the possibility of its being practicable for any sort of vehicle; if the track of wheels did not attest to him that waggons had in reality passed that way, and that it was a path in daily use. Huge blocks of hard sand-stone protruded themselves in the very middle of the road; and it is difficult to conceive how a waggon could pass over them, without being either shaken to pieces or overturned. The surface of the Bokkeveld being much higher than the valley of Roodezand, occasions the ascent on the eastern side of the Witsenberg Pass to be so inconsiderable, that farmers with loaded waggons find it practicable to come thence to Tulbagh; but seldom attempt it in the contrary direction, and are therefore obliged to travel by another, and more indirect road.

The inhabitants of this country, led by custom to view it as an ordinary affair, continue, at the hazard of their own lives, and of the destruction of their waggons and oxen, to make use of a road in this state, when, by the contribution of a trifling sum, and a few months' labor, with the assistance of some pounds of gunpowder to blow up the rocks, it might be rendered quite as safe as the pass at Hottentot-Holland. The road-makers of this colony seem to have imagined, that, by carrying their road as directly over the mountain as possible, they are following the best, because the shortest line: but certainly an oblique, although longer ascent, would, on account not only of easier draught, but also of expedition, and even of an ultimate saving of expense, be the wisest mode. In making such roads, particular care should be taken, that no part of the ascent should have an elevation exceeding a certain number of degrees, up which the usual team of the country is able to draw a loaded waggon.

From the top of this kloof, there is an unbounded prospect over the western half of the compass: *Table Mountain, Paardeberg,*

Contreberg, *Riebek's Kasteel*, *Huningberg*, the sea at *Saldanha Bay*, *Piquetberg*, and the district of the *Four-and-twenty-rivers*, are seen in succession on turning the eye from the south-west round to the north-west. *Table Mountain* is seen very clearly and distinctly, though distant seventy miles in a direct line; and *St. Helena Bay*, which is at about an equal distance, is visible when the glitter of the setting sun is reflected from the water. In the north, the high peaks of Winterhoek rise up and intercept the view in that quarter. On the eastern side, a narrow valley, stretching along the foot of Witsenberg, is walled in by a second and parallel range of mountains, called *Schurfdeberg* (Scurfy Mountain), on account of its rocky and rugged appearance. Southward, the view extends over the whole length of the valley of Roodezand, or Waveren.

On the rocky summit of this mountain, I found a great variety of plants, a large proportion of which I had not met with before. The beautiful nodding red flowers of *Protea nana* immediately caught my eye; and a multitude of new and interesting objects seemed as if soliciting me to admire them. I fancied they were crowding round me with complaints against the want of taste, the cold indifference towards them, and the apathy, which they experienced from every body who passed their way. Some, I fancied, represented their having for many years produced blossoms of the most charming hues, and shed the softest perfumes, without any person having deigned even to cast an eye upon them. In this modest assembly of mountaineers were many whose names are well known in Europe*;

---

* *Hermas gigantea*
Liparia lævigata
Protæa speciosa
Liparia umbellifera
Erica comosa
Bupleurum difforme
Dodonea angustifolia
Protæa longifolia
Leucodendrum plumosum
Lobelia pinifolia

Dilatris corymbosa
Erica fastigiata
Cliffortia ilicifolia
Hermas depauperata
Borbonia crenata
Stoebe ericoïdes
Rafnia triflora
Stoebe virgata
Arnica inuloïdes
Othonna tenuissima

and others, who bore so strong a family likeness, that I guessed their names without hesitation. *

The weather was exceedingly favorable to our ramble, and we spent the whole of the day on the mountain top, enjoying the fine prospect and the freshness of the air, and gathering amusement at every step.

Not having any instruments with me, and being desirous of taking the bearings of the distant objects which were in sight, I supplied the deficiency in the following manner. Having found a convenient flat rock, I placed on it a large piece of drawing-paper, and secured it by bits of stone laid on each corner; then, by the help of my compass and a long flat ruler, I drew a line on the paper to represent the magnetic meridian: after which the ruler was brought very exactly to the bearing of the object, by directing the sight along its edge; and a line was then drawn by it, all across the paper, to which was written the name of the object. Though nothing can be more simple than this method, it will be found to be sufficiently correct, and of some use to a traveller who may happen to have with him no mathematical instruments; as it combines all the properties of a theodolite, a protractor, and a field-book, and obviates the possibility of any great mistake in plotting; for, should there be an error in the meridian line, occasioned by the magnetic needle being drawn out of its proper

---

Aulax pinifolia
Xeranthemum canescens
Leucospermum puberum

Brunia nodiflora
Protea amplexicaulis.

* *Protea*
Xeranthemum
Erica
Antholyza
Diosma
Serruria
Restio
Leucospermum
Leucodendrum
Liparia
Arctotis

Hydrocotyle
Brunia
Phylica
Gladiolus
Lightfootia
Mesembryanthemum
Aspalathus
Rhus
Stœbe
Blairia
Cliffortia, &c.

direction by ferruginous rocks, the angular distances of the objects from each other will remain correct. It is not indispensably requisite that all the lines of bearing should pass through one central point in the meridian line, as they may at leisure, any time afterwards, be transferred to a centre by means of a parallel ruler; and, the paper being then properly placed on the map, the bearings may be pricked through, by which the purpose of a protractor is answered very accurately. On this principle, a traveller may construct a simple and portable instrument, by a circular piece of wood, in the centre of which is fixed a short pin with a pointed top. On this, at the time of observation, a piece of paper of the same size is filed; and over it is fixed a moveable limb with sights, having its fiducial line corresponding with the centre of the pin. A magnetic needle may be added to the instrument, if not rendering it too complicated.

Loaded on all sides with flowers and branches of shrubs, we descended to the plain; and those who met us as we were returning to Tulbagh, might have thought, as in Macbeth, that " Birnam-wood was come to Dunsinane." Night overtook us before we reached the parsonage, where hospitality and good humour concluded the day.

18*th*. My first care this morning was to preserve the botanical specimens which I collected yesterday; and, as I had not the means of pressing and drying them in the usual manner between paper, I tied them carefully up in a large bundle, measuring about three feet long and a foot in diameter, binding them round as tightly as possible with twine, and wrapping the whole with strong paper. This I left to be sent after me to Cape Town by the first opportunity, intending afterwards to press and dry them properly.

This bundle, however, did not find its way to Cape Town till more than a twelvemonth afterwards, and remained in the same state for eight years, when, on unpacking it, every specimen was found to be in as good condition as if it had been dried in the regular manner, and to be equally fit for every purpose of scientific investigation. A few, indeed, were the worse for having been left to shrivel up; but many, especially the more hard-leaved plants, preserved a more natural form than they would have done,

had they been pressed.   The chief inconvenience was found to consist in their not lying flat in the herbarium; but, by folding them
up in a wet cloth, they became sufficiently relaxed to admit, with a
little care, of being pressed flat enough for that purpose.

I much regret that I was unacquainted with these facts at
the time when I first travelled from Klaarwater to Graaffreynett.   I
had then no convenience for drying plants, but could, had I been
aware of this method, have preserved, without trouble, any number
of specimens I might have desired.

I have been particular in relating these circumstances, because
a knowledge of the complete success of such an experiment may be
of use to those travellers who would desire to bring home specimens
of the botany of some rarely-visited country, but who might have
neither the means nor the time for the usual method.   I would
recommend for this purpose a pasteboard box, having a good number of large pin-holes pierced in the sides, for the purpose of admitting air till the plants be sufficiently dried; and which, for
safety while on the road, may be enclosed in a box of wood.   It
is unnecessary to give a more detailed explanation, as the above
hints will readily suggest other particulars, and some further advantages of this method: but it should never be resorted to when
the regular mode is practicable.   There are, however, a multitude
of plants which make the best specimens, and preserve the greatest
resemblance to nature, when they are dried without any pressure
at all.

While I was employed in making drawings of the village,
Mr. Polemann attended an auction at a neighbouring farm, at which
some draught-oxen were to be sold; but, as the biddings were as
high as thirty-five rix dollars a-piece, which he considered to be
more than their real value, he purchased none.   Therefore, as
Mr. Mong, the *Boode**, had informed me that proper oxen might
be obtained in the Bokkeveld, at the price of three hundred rix-

* A *Boode* is the official messenger of a *Landdrost*.

dollars for a *span* (a team), he obligingly undertook the commission of selecting and purchasing two teams.　A team of oxen consists of ten; a number which has been found necessary in this country for drawing a loaded waggon; and from this, some judgment may be formed of the general heaviness of the roads; while, in the more difficult passes, sixteen or twenty oxen are often required.

Having thus accomplished one of the principal objects of our present excursion, we prepared for departure on the following morning, under a promise, insisted upon by our kind host, that I should again take up my quarters at his house, when I passed through Tulbagh in my way out of the colony.

CHAPTER VII.

RIDE FROM TULBAGH TO THE PAARL, AND THENCE TO STELLENBOSCH.

April 19*th.* Early this morning we took leave of Mr. Ballot, at whose house we had experienced the most friendly attention. Although strongly urged to remain a day longer, as the weather had every appearance of being rainy, we unfortunately resisted his persuasion, and took our departure; but scarcely had we lost sight of the house, before the rain commenced. It continued to fall without intermission the whole of the day; yet still, under the hope that it might soon clear up, we resolved to keep on our way.

At the entrance of the *Roodezands Kloof* (Red-sand Pass), we stopped to pay a trifling toll, which is levied to defray the expense of keeping this pass in repair. But it will readily be believed, that no more of the money is laid out on that service, than just sufficient to make it passable, when it is stated that these tolls and repairs are farmed out by the government to individuals for a certain annual sum.   Not far from this, over the mountains, there is another pass, now called the *Oude Kloof* (Old Pass), formerly the only road for waggons, although exceedingly steep, and carried over the very summit.   The repairs of this have been quite neglected, and it is now made use of only by those who, to avoid the toll, drive their cattle over that way.

The new pass is by far the best and the easiest, by which the country lying on the eastern side of the great western chain may be entered; and it is very possible to make it still more so.   It is one of the few chasms which completely divide the large ranges of mountains of the colony: though it is probable that there may exist several more than have been hitherto taken notice of.   This is the only cleft of this description in the western range; but in that which branches off from it at Winterhoek, and joins the great southern range at Swellendam, there are two, through which the Breede river at Mostert's Hoek, and the Hex river at the Kloof of that name, flow; and which are both used by the colonists as passes. In the great southern chain, there is a very remarkable gap, through which the waters of the Great Karro escape, and form the Gaurits river; but through this no practicable road has yet been made.

Roodezands Kloof is a narrow winding defile of about three miles in length, just wide enough to allow a passage for the *Little Berg river*, on each side of which the mountains rise up abrupt and lofty.   Their rocky sides are thickly clothed with bushes and trees, from their very summits down to the water, presenting a beautiful and romantic picture, adorned with every variety of foliage.   Along the steep and winding sides, a road * has been cut out, which follows the course of the river, at a height above it generally between fifty and a hundred feet; in one part rising much higher, and in another, descending to the bottom, and leading through the river, which, at this time, was not more than three feet deep, although

---

* See the *Vignette* at the end of the ninth chapter of this volume.

T

often so much swollen by the rains, as to be, for a day or two, quite impassable.

The unfavorable state of the weather prevented our halting for a minute to take a look around us: the rain poured down in such torrents, as frequently to shut out our view entirely. To a traveller, nothing is more vexatious, both to his patience and to his curiosity, than to find himself in the midst of beautiful scenery, without being permitted to contemplate and admire it; or even to catch a glimpse of it but through streams of rain. We rode nearly three quarters of an hour before we cleared the mountains, and entered upon the open road. The course, and frequent falls of the river, prove that the valley of Roodezand lies at a considerably higher level than the country westward of these mountains.

In such weather, we could not enjoy our ride through the division of *Drakenstein*, which is accounted the most cultivated and beautiful part of the colony. It lay on our left, and occupies the fertile flat country, stretching along the foot of the mountains, from Roodezands Kloof to the village of the Paarl.

We halted for a few minutes at the door of a farm-house, to procure a cup of wine, when its owner, Piet Van der Merwe, wished to persuade us to remain under shelter, offering, at the same time, to have a fire lighted in one of the rooms, that we might dry our clothes; but, as it was not possible for the rain to make us more wet than we were, we resolved to proceed. We passed *Paardeberg* (Horse Mountain), which was situated at a little distance on our right, and Wagenmaker's Valley on the left. The former was so named from the *Wilde Paard* (Wild Horse), which, at that time, inhabited it; for, at the present day, not one is to be found there.

This beautiful animal has been hitherto confounded by naturalists with the Zebra *. When these were first described by modern

---

* " Nous ne savons pas comment Buffon a pu dire que le zébre mâle était rayé de " jaune et de noir, et la femelle de blanc et de noir." — Cuvier; ' Menagerie du Muséum National,' article Zébre: which, according to the figure and description there given, is the *Equus montanus.*

writers, the Quakka * was considered to be the female Zebra; while both that and the true Zebra bore in common, among the colonists, the name of Quakka. The *Wilde Paard*, named *Dauw* † by the Hottentots, and a much scarcer animal than the other two, was never suspected to be a different species, although it be far more distinct from the Quakka and Zebra, than these are from each other.

The hoofs of animals destined by nature to inhabit rocky mountains, are, as far as I have observed, of a form very different from those intended for sandy plains; and this form is, in itself, sufficient to point out the *Dauw* as a separate species. The stripes of the skin will answer that purpose equally well, and show, at the same time, the great affinity, and the specific distinction, of the *Ass* (*Equus Asinus*), which may be characterised by a *single stripe* across the shoulders. The *Quakka* has many similar marks on the *head and fore-part of the body*: the Zebra is covered with stripes over the *head and the whole of the body*; but the legs are white: and the *Wilde Paard* is striped over *every part, even down to the feet*. The Zebra and *Wilde Paard* may be further distinguished from each other, by the stripes of the former being *brown and white*, and the brown stripe being *double*; that is, having a paler stripe within it ‡ : while the latter, which may be named *Equus montanus*, is most regularly and beautifully covered with *single black and white* stripes. Added to this, the former is never to be found on the *mountains*, nor the latter on the *plains.* §

The most beautiful part of Drakenstein is *Wagen-makers'* (Waggon-makers') *Valley*; and the *Dal van Josaphat* (Vale of Josaphat) is not less pleasant. The farms lie nearer together, and population and fertility appeared to increase in proportion as we advanced towards the Paarl.

We approached the *Berg river* with some anxiety, lest it should

---

* *Equus Quagga*, of authors.

† Pronounced *Dow*, as in the English word *dower*.

‡ See the *Vignette* at the end of Chapter XI.

§ I have presented all these three animals to the British Museum, where the distinctions here pointed out may readily be seen.

not be fordable; but found it not yet risen higher than four feet.
The ford, which had rather the appearance of a lane, led us through
the tall, thick *Palmite*, with which the river was, in this part, so
choked up, that its waters seemed as if struggling to find a passage
between their stems. It would be very unsafe, without great care,
for a traveller to ford a river of this kind; for should he, by the
force of the stream, be carried into the Palmites, he might find the
greatest difficulty in extricating himself or his horse from amongst
their entangled trunks. This ford, by turning obliquely, and in
different directions, was so lengthened as to occupy us ten minutes
in passing through. Means for crossing this river, when too deep
to be forded, have been provided by building a *Pont* (Ferry-boat), at
a place a little further up the stream. *

At three o'clock we arrived at the village of the *Paarl*, and
alighted at the house of an opulent wine-farmer, named *Vanderbyl*,
with whom my fellow-traveller had a previous acquaintance, and
from whose son-in-law, the landdrost of Tulbagh, he was the bearer
of a letter.

We were met by him at the door, and were received and wel-
comed in the usual form. The pitiless rain had pursued us to the
end of our journey, and our drenched appearance rendering it unnecessary to ask for a room where we might change our clothes, we
were immediately shown into an apartment; but, on opening our
portmanteaus, we discovered that nearly the whole of our linen was
wet. We, however, consoled each other in our disappointment, by
the expectation of dinner; for, having made known that we had
been riding ever since eight o'clock, we did not suppose there would
be any further necessity for hinting that some refreshment would be
acceptable.

We took our seat at one end of the *voorhuis* with the master of
the house, with whom we spent nearly two hours in conversing on
various topics, but chiefly on the subject of my projected journey

---

* See the 24th of June, 1811, and Plate 3.

into the interior.   At last our conversation exhausted itself: our
host rose, and went out of the room, we doubted not, to reprimand
the servants for their unusual delay in bringing in the dinner, it
being now past five o'clock.

In the interim, being alone, we had nothing better to amuse us,
than the view from the window; whence we had only a melancholy
prospect of the rain, which deluged the ground, and left us without
hope of being permitted to take a walk to see the village.

The hour of six passed by without any symptom of dinner appearing: seven also passed, and eight; but still nothing was offered us
to eat.   At intervals we resumed the conversation, in which the lady
of the house and her daughters sometimes joined.   This produced
a more agreeable variety, which, together with the friendly manners
of her son, who spoke English very well, relieved the tedium of so
many hours, but could not repel the imperious craving of hunger,
which, like the Spartan youth with the fox under his cloak, we had
the fortitude to conceal, though we felt it gnawing our vitals.

At last, when nine o'clock arrived, several slaves followed each
other with dishes of hot meat and stews, and as many of vegetables
cooked in different ways.   With these, and other things, a large
table was soon covered, while wine-glasses and bottles occupied the
intermediate spaces.   So plentiful was the display, that my companion was equally surprised at it with myself; and it was now evident, that some pains had been taken to prepare a supper better
than ordinary: and, whatever might have been our thoughts previously to this, we fully acquitted our host of intentional neglect.   All
those attentions which hospitality prompts, were shown to us by
every part of the family, who evinced a real desire to please.

This occurrence served to exemplify, and to teach me, with
most impressive effect, a common feature in colonial manners.   It
has been already mentioned, that in this country no inns are any
where to be found; consequently, the necessity of the case, as well
as common humanity, urges every Christian-like colonist to open his
door to the hungry or benighted traveller.   And, as this hospitality becomes reciprocal, by their occasionally passing each other's

houses, they feel no hesitation either in asking such favors, or in granting them. Thus a boor is never at a loss for a meal on the road; and as the customary time of dinner is about noon, he, without much ceremony, unsaddles his horse at any door where he may happen to come at that hour. If he arrive later, he is supposed to have dined at some other place on the road, and the question whether he may be in want of refreshment, is considered superfluous: but in most parts of the country, a cup of tea is generally presented to him, without any regard to the time of day. It is therefore a boor's own fault if he lose his dinner. Those who travel in waggons, and who most frequently carry their provisions and cooking utensils with them, are looked upon as not standing in need of assistance, though such persons freely make use of those houses where they have any acquaintance with the family.

20th. The weather this day was more favourable; and notwithstanding the ground was still wet from the rain of yesterday, the sunshine tempted us to go out of doors. We were conducted to see the kitchen garden; and in the wine cellar, two casks were pointed out as being reputed the largest in the colony. We were also shown a corn-mill, of very good though simple mechanism, worked by an overshot wheel.

In almost every farmer's garden, a clump of Bamboo-cane may be seen growing; which, though an elegant and ornamental plant, is no where cultivated on that account, but merely for the uses to which its cane is applicable; and principally for whip-stocks, as possessing the desirable qualities of strength and lightness. Of these I now purchased a number for the use of my journey.

In a walk to the foot of the mountains behind the house, I first met with *Cunonia Capensis*, growing wild in the damp rocky places along the banks of a rivulet. This is a handsome tree, with fine shining green foliage, contrasted by numerous dense, elongated bunches of small milk-white flowers, and twigs of a red color; having the habit rather of a tropical, than of a Cape, plant. Its colonial name is *Rood Elze* (Red Alder), although the tree has not, in any point of view, the least resemblance to the Alder of Europe; but the waggon-makers say, there is some similarity in their wood. I am, however, inclined to believe that the name was given rather on account of their growing in similar situations: and this seems the more probable, as the name of *Witte Elze* (White Alder) is applied to another tree (*Weinmannia trifoliata*) which naturally grows in the same kind of places as the common Alder.

In moist places I met with *Erica pubescens* growing luxuriantly, and covered with a profusion of little pink flowers ; this is one of the commonest of the Cape heaths. Growing on the branches of *Cassine Capensis*, I found the *Cape Missleto*, a very curious parasitic plant, bearing small white berries, but without leaves, and exceedingly brittle. • A kind of wild cucumber † spreads itself over the bushes and along the ground, bearing a small yellow oval fruit hardly an inch long, covered with soft prickles, and called *Gift-Appel* (Poison-apple) on account of its extreme bitterness; in which quality it agrees with the Coloquintida, and several of the Cucumber tribe. The ' African Sage' ‡ is an ornamental flowering shrub, of very frequent occurrence. All the *Diosmas* when bruised, give out a strong odor more or less pleasant ; so that, in walking, it is not easy to tread on a plant of this tribe without being made sensible of it by the smell. By this means I discovered a species § which otherwise might have escaped my notice. The baboons‖ which inhabit this mountain in great numbers, are very troublesome by committing depredations on the neighbouring gardens ; and various stories are told both of their ingenuity and of their stupidity, which, not having it in my power to confirm, I shall not here repeat.

Soon after noon we took leave of the family of Vanderbyl, and commenced our ride to Stellenbosch. We passed through the *Paarl Village*, which consists of between forty and fifty very neat houses, placed at a considerable distance from each other, and forming a single street, about the middle of which stands

---

• *The Vignette* at the end of this chapter is a figure of the *Viscum Capense*, or Cape Missleto, of the natural size.

† *Cucumis prophetarum.*   ‡ *Salvia Africana.*
§ *Diosma capitata.*   ‖ *Cercopithecus ursinus.*

the church. This village appeared to be by much the most agreeable and pleasant situation, as a residence, of any I had hitherto seen, and is superior to Stellenbosch in rural beauty. Those who would be desirous of passing a few months from Cape Town, for the sake of the amusements and pleasures of a country life, would not be disappointed by taking up their abode at the Paarl, where, within a short ride or a walk, a great variety of scenery may be found. It takes its name * from the neighbouring mountain, on the summit of which, among others, of the same kind, is an enormous rock called the *Paarl* (the Pearl), having, at the distance at which we viewed it, the rounded form and outward appearance of granite.

Leaving the village, we continued our way along a level sandy country covered with bushes, among which the *Protœa corymbosa* predominated. It may easily be distinguished by its long slender upright stems about four feet high, (having at top a corymbe of short branches) springing from a dense base of suckers and leaves ; a singularity of growth not observed in any other proteaceous plant. Small trees of *Rhus villosum*, ten or twelve feet high, were not unfrequent.

We passed through one end of the division of *Drakenstein*, which, with *Fransche Hoek* (French Corner), may be called the vineyard of the colony. *Fransche Hoek*, which lay on our left in a deep and extensive bosom or bay of the mountains, was the spot where vineyards were first established by the French refugées already mentioned. The mountains which surround it, are lofty and sublime, having their craggy summits divided into rocky masses of the grandest forms.

During a heavy shower, we took shelter, near a farm house, under two very fine oak trees, the largest which I had seen in the colony : their trunks measuring between four and five feet in diameter.

A little further on, we came to a very romantic pass between steep and high mountains, where, in the ravine below the road, the noisy waters of a torrent were hastening down its rocky bed. This

---

* Perhaps more properly written *Paarldorp*.

place, the name of which is *Banghoek*, appeared a most delightful spot; and being in many parts quite woody, the scenery is extremely beautiful and picturesque, and capable of affording some charming studies for the landscape painter; who could not fail to improve in his art by the imitation of those wild beauties, such as nature here presents.

The road leading down a long descent, seemed in most places to consist of pure clay, as we judged from its slipperiness, much increased by the rain which fell during the afternoon. As we rode on, the darkness of night closed over us: we were often doubtful of the way, till occasional flashes of lightning showed us the road. At last, about seven o'clock, we reached Stellenbosch, where we took up our quarters at the house of a gentleman of the name of *Morel*, a particular friend of my companion.

21st. During the intervals between the showers, I walked out to view the town. *Stellenbosch*, so named in 1670 [*], after its founder, Governor Van der Stell, is a place of much greater extent and importance than any of the other villages, and consists of a number of streets intersecting each other at right angles. A great part, however, of the space comprehended in the size of the town, was occupied by gardens, which, with an avenue of trees planted along almost every street, produced a cool and pleasing effect. Many of the houses were not inferior to those of Cape Town; their appearance was neat and clean, and gave altogether the idea of an agreeable and cheerful place of abode. A few years [†] previous to our visit, a great part of the town was destroyed by fire; but from so distressing an occurrence resulted one advantage, that the original thatched cottages were now replaced by buildings of a better style of architecture. At the lower end of the principal street, is a spacious military parade; at the upper end, stands the *church*, built in 1722. [‡] This edifice, is represented by the *vignette* at the head of

---

[*] Thunberg's Travels.   [†] In the year 1803.
[‡] According to Lichtentein.

U

this chapter.   In an open square, near to the church, is the *Drostdy*, or residence of the Landdrost, a large and commodious building. At the back of this, flows the *Eerste* (First) river, having its source in the great mountains rising up immediately behind the town. These mountains are a part of the Great Western chain, already noticed, and constitute an essential feature in the beauty of the situation.   A number of new dwellings are yearly increasing the size of the town, and the accommodations are superior to those of other villages, but the expences of living are said to be nearly the same as in Cape Town ; from which it is distant, due east, not more than thirty miles.   A stage-waggon carries passengers to and from the Cape, and the post arrives and returns twice a week.   From its proximity to the metropolis, it is much better known to foreigners, and to the English, than any of the other villages : a more detailed description of it in this place, is therefore the less necessary. *   The country immediately surrounding the town, offers no beauty of scenery to charm the eye ; but the mountains form a back-ground of the finest kind, and are of so great a height, that, for several days in the winter, their rugged summits are capped with snow.   These I much desired to ascend, in order to examine their productions, but the weather would not allow us to make the attempt.   I have the less reason to regret this disappointment, as it happened that circumstances, four years afterwards, put it in my power to explore a neighbouring part of this range, and to add to my collection several things which are peculiar to these mountains, and which will be more particularly mentioned in another place.

At two o'clock in the afternoon, we left Stellenbosch to return to Cape Town, and were again unfortunate in the day, which, soon after our departure, set in with rain and wind; and, to increase our misfortunes, one of the horses fell lame, while the other stumbled at every

---

* I visited Stellenbosch again in April 1815, when I found a considerable increase in houses had taken place, and the town much improved.   I profited by this opportunity to make several drawings of it: the *Vignette* at page 136 is a part of one of them.

step. It was evidently time that our excursion ended; for this last day's journey being, for nearly the whole way, over the heavy loose sand of the Cape Flats, was excessively fatiguing and painful to the animals.

At sunset, we passed the foot of Tygerberg, and were soon afterwards overtaken by a night of impenetrable darkness, and both wet and chilly. To the fear of losing the way, was added that of finding the sands impassably flooded by the late rains, as, at almost every five minutes, we had to wade through ponds of rain-water. It may seem singular, that plains of sand should be found covered with standing water; but this is easily accounted for, by a stratum of clay lying immediately beneath the sand, at the depth of from one to perhaps six feet or more.

In the midst of our uncertainty, wandering in various directions, a glimmering light at last appeared at a distance, and enabled us to shape our course to Salt river. Here we procured a guide to conduct us safely through the river, which occupied ten minutes in wading through, as it had overflowed its banks and inundated a great part of the adjoining flats; and nearly all the way to Cape Town, we seemed to be travelling in a river rather than a road. So complete was the darkness, that when arrived at the hospital, it was not possible to find our way, even the short distance to the castle without a guide: the atmosphere seemed as if bereft of every particle of light. At length, at eight o'clock, we reached Cape Town.

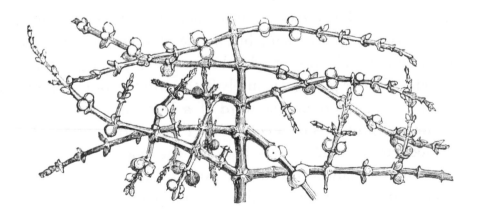

Inches⟨…⟩ 1 4 5 6 7 8 9 10 11 12 13 14 Feet.

CHAPTER VIII.

RESIDENCE AT CAPE TOWN, AND PREPARATIONS FOR THE JOURNEY.

*A*PRIL 23d. The objects principally in view in the foregoing excursion, had all been attained, excepting that of hiring Hottentots for the service of the journey. But I did not doubt, should I succeed in obtaining Jan Tamboer, that he would be able to engage as many of his countrymen as would be required. The petty deceptions which are often practised on this race of people render them in general suspicious of the promises of white men ; but if one of their own tribe should undertake to persuade, they readily listen to every thing he says, and often assent without giving themselves the trouble of examining the proposal ; relying more on the word of a Hottentot than on all the arguments and promises of a colonist. I therefore considered it the better mode to depend on this man for the management of these affairs. Nothing, however, could be done till his discharge from the regiment had been granted : for that purpose I waited on the

Governor, to solicit it; when he very politely and readily promised to do all that depended on him for procuring the man's release.

30th. At the end of the month my waggon was finished and sent home. The price I paid for it, exclusive of the tilt, and all the other separate articles required in travelling, was 585 rix dollars, at that time equal to eighty-eight pounds sterling; in addition to which, the fitting up of the inside with chests and various conveniences, amounted to a considerable sum. The length of it was fifteen feet, and breadth at bottom two feet nine inches. The frame work of the tilt was made of bamboo cane, covered over with Hottentot mats, above which there was a painted canvas; and over all a covering of sail-cloth, having a flap to close up the ends, rendered the whole impervious to rain. * The height, from the bottom of the waggon to the top of the tilt, was five feet and a half. The sides (*leer*) were two feet high in front, gradually rising up to two feet and three quarters at the back, and painted on the outside. The rail that forms the upper and lower edge of the sides, is distinguished by the colonists, by the names of *opper-leer-boom*, and *onder-leer-boom*. The planks of the bottom (*buik plank*) were two inches thick. The axletrees were perfectly horizontal and tapering. A bar of iron an inch and a half wide, called the *scheen*, is let into the underpart of them, to receive the friction of the wheel. Besides a set of linchpins of the common form (*steek-lens*), there is another to be used occasionally, named *platte-lens*, having a broad head, like an umbrella, to shelter the end of the nave and axletree from the mud and sand which might drop from off the upper fellies. The diameter of the hind wheels is five feet, of the fore wheels three feet and a

---

* The *engraving* at the beginning of this chapter, represents the geometrical elevation of the waggon, with the canvas partly rolled back to show the formation of the tilt, drawn from an actual measurement of every part, and proportioned to the scale of English feet marked beneath it. At the *end* of the chapter may be seen a transverse section of it, according to the same scale; together with all the different articles necessary for its equipment. By the help of these two engravings, and the following description the excellent construction, and peculiar advantages of a *Cape Waggon*, will be easily understood.

half, and their distance apart five feet. The tire (*band*) is of one piece, and in width two inches and a half. The whole of the wheels, axletrees, and parts connected with them, constituting what the boors call the *onderstel* or carriage, is well covered with tar. Those parts belonging to, and joined with, the fore pair of wheels, are denominated the *voor-stel* ; and those to the after pair, the *agter-stel*. On the top of each axletree lies a strong piece of timber, called the *skammel*, upon which the *buik plank* or bottom of the waggon rests. Into each end of the *skammels*, is strongly morticed an upright piece named the *rong*, against which the sides rest, and by which they are prevented from spreading outwards. A strong bolt of iron runs through the fore-*skammel*, and connects it with the axletree which turns upon it ; but the after-*skammel* is firmly confined to its axletree by iron bands. The *langwagen* is that beam which connects the two axletrees together, and for safety, in case of its suddenly breaking by any accident, a long separate bar of iron, called the *izer* (iron) *langwagen*, is added. Behind the after axletree is fixed the *trap* (or step), a wooden frame serving both as steps to assist in getting into the waggon, and, usually, as a convenient place for the cooking utensils. Through the middle of the fore axletree, passes a strong piece of timber, called the *tang* ; the fore end of which is shaped into two cheeks between which the pole is bolted, and is free to move vertically only. The pole (*disselboom*) is ten feet long, having at the end a strong iron staple ; the *tang-arms* are two curved (they ought rather to be straight) bars of iron ; one on each side, connecting the end of the *tang* with the ends of the axletree. Their use is to support the *tang* in the act of turning the waggon ; the *tang* is, as it were, a continuation of the *langwagen*, with which it is connected by a horizontal joint. The wheels are of that form, technically called ' dishing' wheels, and stand vertically. The tilt (*tent*) is made shorter than the waggon, for the purpose of leaving an open space in front, of about two feet and a half; where there is a raised seat or box for the driver. The *ligter* (lifter) is a strong lever, about eight or nine feet long, the fulcrum of which is an upright piece of timber, called the *ligter-voet* or lever-foot, about two feet and a half high. This is used for hoisting up the axletrees when the wheels are taken off to be greased. The *teerput* (tar-bucket) is usually suspended from a hook in the *onder le'erboom*. The *drag-chain* is fixed to a ring in the afterpart of the *tang*, behind the fore axletree. The *remschoen* (lock-shoe cr skid), is a log of wood, generally about eight inches square, and nearly two feet long, having a groove in it to receive the felly of the wheel ; and is furnished in front with a stout loop of twisted raw hide. The manner in which the wheels are skidded, may be seen by the preceding engraving : it obviates the great danger which would arise from the skid suddenly flying from under the felly, as, in this mode, the wheel in such case would still remain locked. The *trektouw* (draw-rope or trace), is a long rope made of twisted thongs of raw hide, made fast by a hook to the staple at the end of the pole, and having iron rings attached to it at proper distances, into which rings the yokes are hooked. The yokes are straight, and pierced with two pair of mortices to receive the *juk-schei* which fits in loosely, and answer to what in English husbandry are called the *bows :* but are merely two straight pegs, one on each side of the ox's neck, and having notches on their outer sides to receive the *nek-strop* (neck strap) The *riem* (or halter), is a leathern thong about twelve feet in length, with a noose at one end, by which it is fixed round the ox's horns. It is used for holding and managing the animal, while yoking and unyoking; and afterwards for making it fast, if necessary : it is always left coiled round its horns, except when turned loose to graze. The whip, and the shambok have been already described. †

The principal and very important advantage of a Cape-built waggon consists in its sides, bottom, and carriage, not being joined

---

* The *engraving* at the end of the chapter exhibits in their relative proportion, according to the subjoined scale, the various articles here described : a yoke with its neck-strap, &c., complete; the drag-rope; the pole; the halter; the skid; the lever; the whip, and the shambok; together with a horizontal plan of the fore axletree, and part of the pole; besides a vertical section of the fore wheels, axletree, body of the waggon, and tilt.

† At pages 52 and 86.

together; a construction admirably well adapted for rough and uneven roads, by admitting each part to play freely, so as completely to avoid that straining and cracking to which solid built waggons are subjected, when travelling over irregular ground. The agter stel and voorstel are, in their movement, independent of each other; being held together only by the langwagen, which by its joint, moves either way. The sides resting on the skammels, lean against the rongs, and are united to the tilt, only by the ribs which are elastic and yield to every motion: they are, besides, each kept in their place by a single thong of raw hide, passing under the end of the after skammel through two staples in the lower leerboom. The brick plank simply rests on the skammels, and is confined in its place only by two pieces of iron, which pass, one before, and the other behind the after skammel. The bolt, on which the fore axletree turns, is not rivetted nor pinned through; by which means it is at liberty to draw out a little upwards to relieve the rocking of the waggon, when any one of the wheels is much lifted up by a hillock or other unevenness in the ground.

The preceding description of my waggon, which, although one of the largest dimensions, was made exactly in the manner of the usual ox-waggon of the colony, will not only be found useful for showing how excellently they are constructed for the purpose of travelling over an uncultivated country, but will, as an excuse for its length, enable the reader to comprehend many passages in this journal in which the mention of the different parts of a waggon cannot but frequently occur.

My undertaking was generally looked upon in Cape Town as an imprudent attempt, after the failure of an expedition, in which, previously to its setting out, every precaution had been taken, and provision made, to ensure its success; and whose numbers and strength so much exceeded mine. Notwithstanding this, a person, who had already expressed some desire to accompany me, now came seriously to make the proposal, and very earnestly volunteered his services as my companion and assistant. He possessed, indeed, qualifications which would have rendered him both a useful, and an agreeable associate; yet I sacrificed my inclination to my judgment, and preferred being quite alone. I feared those disagreeable, and often fatal, consequences, which arise from a want of harmony between the members of such an expedition, too much to suffer myself to listen to my natural wish for a companion. Yet I must confess that there were often moments during my subsequent travels in which I severely felt the want of some companion, whose assistance and advice might have relieved my daily fatigues, and the anxieties of my mind.

22nd. At this season the weather is generally rainy at the Cape, although in the present year they set in earlier than usual, having fallen very abundantly in the months of April and May. The thermometer in Cape Town during this time, stood ordinarily about 55° Fahr. (10°2 Reaum; 12°7 Centig.) in the morning, and 64° (14°2 R.; 17°7 C.) in the middle of the day. The winter might be considered as having already commenced; yet, excepting these rainy days, it was the most agreeable time of the year; although, by persons habituated to a warm climate, it might be accounted rather chilly.

The day being sunny and pleasant, tempted me to take a stroll on *Green-Point*. The effect of the late rains was surprising: not six weeks before, the herbage seemed entirely parched up; vegetation had disappeared, and the plain looked like a barren waste; but the sterile plain was now changed to a verdant field, and myriads of gay flowers had started up out of the earth. Those who have seen this spot only in the summer, would never suppose that a soil so arid and bare, contained such an astonishing quantity, and such a great variety of bulbous roots. Blossoms of every color and every hue were at this time expanded to the genial warmth of the sun, and in such profusion that, from a little distance, some particular parts of the plain appeared as if painted red, others white, and others yellow. It is chiefly to the beautiful tribe of *Oxalis* that these enlivening effects are at this season attributable; but not less so to two other extremely small and delicate plants,* which, in countless

---

* *Ixia minuta* and *Strumaria spiralis*. Of the uncertain flowering of many of the bulbous plants of this colony, the former, among a great many others, may be adduced as an example; since, by Thunberg, who for three years was indefatigable in collecting every where near Cape Town, it was considered as a rare plant.

multitudes, whiten the soil.   Later in the season other flowers spring up in their place, and colour the ground with other tints.

Should any botanist allow himself the time, carefully to explore, at all seasons, every part of the Cape peninsula, including a portion of the isthmus, and afterwards publish a list of his collection, the lovers of the science would, I doubt not, be surprised, not only at the unexampled number of species growing in so small an extent of country, but at the number of undescribed plants that were still to be found in a tract, over which so many collectors have rambled.   The importance and practical utility of local catalogues, pointing out the natural stations and circumstances of the native plants, will, it may be supposed, increase in proportion as the science advances, and as the objects it embraces become more multiplied.

25th.   The party of Hottentots which had long been expected from Klaarwater*, arrived at Salt-river with their waggons and oxen.   It consisted of about twenty men, with an equal number of women, and as many children ; besides three waggons and families left behind at Tulbagh.

These people were nearly all of the mixed race of Hottentots. †   Their object, in making this long journey to Cape Town, was principally that of exchanging ivory and cattle for such manufactured articles as their present mode of life leads them to regard as necessaries.   These were chiefly, gunpowder, muskets, lead, flints, porcelain beads, knives, tinder-boxes and steels, tobacco, woollen jackets and trowsers, horses and waggons.   The quantity of ivory which they had now brought to town, was about a thousand pounds weight, which was sold to English merchants at the rate of seven schellings a-pound, Dutch weight: ‡   their cattle had

---

* Mentioned on the 18th of February, at page 64.

† Denominated *Bastaards* by the colonists; which word is intended to signify Hottentots who are not of the genuine race, or who are sprung from parents, of whom one is not a pure Hottentot, whether the descendants of the colonists, or of any neighbouring tribe.   This name is objectionable, as conveying to us a false idea; it will not, therefore, be thought an unnecessary innovation, if I use in its place, the term *Mixed Hottentots*, or, sometimes, that of *Half-Hottentots*.

‡ One hundred pounds, Dutch weight, are equal to one hundred and eight pounds avoirdupois, English weight.

been sold by the way to the boors, as they passed through the colony.

As I had not yet received any decisive answer to the application I had made to the Governor respecting the Hottentot soldier, Mr. Anderson agreed to engage for me some of the Klaarwater Hottentots; but gave me to understand, that they would not be willing to go with me farther than their own homes. This was not, indeed, sufficient for my purpose; yet, as the time appointed for my departure was fast approaching, and considering that there might be some advantage in having with me, even thus far, men who were well acquainted with the country, I judged it advisable to hire two of them.

Two days after this, *Colonel Graham*, who commanded the Cape regiment, obligingly sent to inform me that Jan Tamboer would receive his discharge, agreeably to my request. Still, however, disappointment awaited me; for, on the 30th of the month, when I rode to Wynberg to hasten these arrangements, I found him lying sick in the hospital, although I hoped he was not so unwell as ultimately to be unable to undertake the journey.

31*st*. To-day the two Klaarwater Hottentots, whose names were *Magers* and *Jan Kok*, commenced their service, and came to receive their instructions. *

Not yet habituated to men of this description, I could not survey my future servants without a smile at their grotesque appearance. Their dark African visage seemed at variance with their clothes of European fashion, made, indeed, so bunglingly, that they would not fit in any part. Their leathern trowsers had shrunk up

---

* The Hottentots of the colony have universally adopted Dutch names, of which some are those of the colonists; and others have, probably, been given to them by the boors, as they seem to have been intended originally as characteristic epithets, applicable only to the individual to whom they were given: thus, *Magers* signifies *meagre*, or *lean*. Many of these are ridiculous, and their import was, perhaps, little understood by those who bore them; but they now pass current, and the families of *Thickhead* (Dikkop), and *Rogue* (Platje), and others of this kind, are respectable enough in the estimation of their countrymen.

towards the knee, and left their brown skin exposed; but the blue English jackets, as if to compensate the deficiency, were such as had certainly been intended for men of double the size. Their woolly heads were decorated with the new hats they had just purchased; and shoes of their own making covered their otherwise naked feet.

They introduced themselves with a respectful manner; but the Dutch they spoke was so peculiar, that I required the assistance of an interpreter. I showed them my waggon, which they minutely inspected in every part, and seemed more particularly to examine the wheels, shaking them to ascertain if the vehicle would run lightly; when they gave their decision, that " all was good." They expressed themselves much pleased at having been selected for my service, promising that they would *mooï oppassen* (take good care of every thing), and serve me faithfully. Magers's son, a boy of about twelve years of age, was engaged to act as leader of the team. The whole of their wages was paid in advance, that they might profit by the present opportunity of laying it out to advantage in Cape Town.

I gave them orders to go immediately to the Bokkeveld, to fetch my oxen; and, for their use during their journey thither and back, I provided them with a quantity of tobacco. So large a supply of an article which produces no small portion of their enjoyments, gave them a high opinion of the generosity of their new master, and inspired a cheerful briskness in their talk, and a wonderful alacrity in their motions: wonderful, at least, in a Hottentot. For my part, I was equally well pleased with them, and was not less delighted at the prospect of our departure. They then took leave, perfectly satisfied with the bargain, and hastened away to lay out their money, as the waggons of their countrymen, by which they were to send home their purchases, were, in a day or two, to start from Salt-river, and to proceed slowly on, to wait for us at the borders of the colony.

This morning the thermometer was found to have sunk to 48° (7·1 R.; 8·8 C.). A new sight presented itself: the highest parts of the great western range of mountains appeared covered with *snow*. This remained unmelted for two or three days, although the temperature of the air around the lower part of the mountains is never cold enough to allow snow to fall there. It is, therefore, only by what they see at a distance on these summits, that those who reside always in Cape Town can become acquainted with this phenomenon.

June 2nd. This day the warmth was greater than is usual at this season, the thermometer having risen to 70° (16°8 R.; 21°1 C.) A thick haze filled the atmosphere, yet did not weaken the power of the sun, which shone with the more effect, as the air continued undisturbed by the least breath of wind. This state of the weather brought to mind the earthquake of the preceding year; and it afterwards appeared, that those who thought so were not mistaken in their interpretation of the symptoms.

The weather, during the forenoon, had been warmer than usual; (the thermometer 75°) and the air was calm and perfectly tranquil. At this time I was in my room occupied in preparations for the journey: a part of the garrison, having been exercising on Green-Point, were returning to their barracks, when a sudden and violent explosion shook the whole house, with a noise as loud as that of a cannon fired close at the door. In three or four seconds after this, another report, still more violent and sharp, like the loudest clap of thunder, shook the building more forcibly than the first; and at the same moment I felt a strange and unusual motion. The atmosphere at that instant was agitated by a dreadful concussion.

The whole of this occurrence did not take up more than the time of five or six seconds; the day still continuing very fine and the sky perfectly cloudless. There remained a dead calm, and the air was suffused with a misty vapor, such as may often be seen in hot, damp weather. At the first explosion, it was naturally thought that one of the field-pieces, which were then passing by the house, had by some accident exploded; but the second being too violent for the effect of a cannon, I immediately supposed that one of the powder magazines had blown up; and even imagined that the report might have been occasioned by two of my barrels of gunpowder, which I had received from the magazine the day before.

I hastened out of doors to ascertain what had happened; but when I came into the street, and beheld all the inhabitants rushing out of their houses in wild disorder and fright; some pale and trembling, running up and down, unconscious whither they were going; mothers distracted at not finding their children with them; and every one with terror depicted in his countenance, crowding into the open street; when I beheld this, I instantly guessed that an earthquake had happened, for no answer could be got from those to whom I addressed the question; fright prevented their hearing what was said. As soon as this conviction gains possession of the mind, our sensations, which, till then, may have been only those of surprise, assume a new and peculiar character. To those born in a country where these convulsions of nature happen frequently, such an occurrence as this may perhaps occasion little uneasiness: but to others who, for the first time in their lives, feel that the ground they walk upon is not immoveable, an earthquake, with all the dangers which may possibly accompany it, is an event which cannot fail to excite considerable alarm. Every body stood for a while in dreadful expectation of the catastrophe. Nothing could be more distressing than to witness the terror of the women; some in tears, others trembling and speechless, and none seeming to know what they were about, or where they were. All had fled out of their houses with the utmost precipitation, without hats or bonnets, just as they happened to be dressed at the moment: and I believe that every individual inhabitant of Cape Town, men, women, and children, excepting those who from infirmity were unable to move, was, at that time, out in the street. There, all remained for at least an hour; and many for the whole day. As soon as the second explosion was over, the air immediately resumed its former tranquillity, nor was any other change perceptible, more than that of its becoming shortly afterwards a little cooler. Finding no further shock succeed, the inhabitants gradually recovered from their first alarm, and from the general confusion: the crowds slowly became thinner; yet still the greater number, afraid to trust themselves within their houses, brought out chairs, and remained sitting on the ' stupe,' or in the street, the rest of the day.

Walking afterwards about the town, to make several purchases for my journey, I was told that many houses were exceedingly rent, and some more materially damaged: but none were actually thrown down. At the mill, however, at Salt-river, the dwelling-house, it was said, had received so much injury, that the owner considered it no longer safe or habitable. In the barracks great confusion arose from all the men endeavouring to rush out at the same instant. Many of the ornamental urns which had escaped the earthquake of 1809, were now tumbled from the parapets down into the street: one on the top of the house where I resided, was shivered to pieces; and the wall of my bed-room was in the same instant divided by a crack which extended from the top of the house to the bottom.

The weather continued pleasant during the afternoon, and, before night came on, the apprehensions of the inhabitants were in some measure quieted, as every one ventured to sleep in their houses, excepting four or five tents which were pitched on the Parade and in the *Boer Plain*. As for myself, I followed the example of others, in passing the night with my clothes on, that I might be ready to escape the more quickly out of the house, in case another shock happened before morning.

This precaution was the result of past experience; for the former earthquake, which commenced about nine o'clock in the evening, returned several times in the course of the same night. But it must be concluded, that these convulsions of the earth have no connection either with the time of the day, or with the season of the year, since they now took place at five minutes before noon, and in the middle of winter; whereas the former happened in the middle of summer, and during the night.

All the symptoms attendant on this phenomenon bore so much the character of electricity, that it could not easily be viewed in any other light than as the explosion of electric matter.

But many of the good people of the town had quite another opinion : they coupled the *comet*, which had been seen every night since the 12th of the foregoing month, and the earthquake together, and drew from this two-fold portentous sign, the certain prognostics of the annihilation of the Cape.

This event gave me the first opportunity of knowing, from experience, something of the operation and effects of an effort of nature, regarded by all as formidable, but which, by the superstitious, is viewed as the manifestation of supernatural agency. But its true nature becomes, in every succeeding generation, more generally understood as the result of laws established by the Divine Power at the creation.

The night passed over undisturbed; and on the following day there was no other difference perceptible in the state of the atmosphere, than that of its being much less loaded with hazy vapor. The sun shone bright and pleasant; the universal fear, by degrees, subsided; each one resumed his usual occupation, and business and money-making began, as heretofore, to animate every nerve, and to occupy every thought.

8th.   Jan Tamboer still continued in the hospital very ill; and it was the surgeon's opinion, that there was little likelihood of his being able to undertake the journey.   This was a serious disappointment, and not a trifling derangement of my plans; but it gave to the Colonel an opportunity of proving his readiness to oblige: for, on learning the circumstance, he directed enquiry to be made in the regiment for any other Hottentot who might possess the requisite qualifications; and, by good fortune, one was found, who not only had been used to the management of a waggon and oxen, but who had formerly made a journey beyond the Gariep, into the country of the Bachapins.

This man instantly accepted the offered appointment, overjoyed at exchanging a military life for one so much more congenial to his inclinations. Having neither family nor possessions, nor, indeed, any property at all, which he would be under the necessity of leaving unprotected, he was ready to start at a moment's notice; and, as soon as he had received the trifling arrears of his pay, together with a furlough for twelve months, renewable from time to time, he bade farewell to his comrades, many of whom would gladly have followed him, and hastened away to take possession of his new office.

His name was *Philip Willems*. He was of small and compact figure, not above five feet high, steady and measured in his motions; of a countenance possessing somewhat of a melancholy cast, and of a complexion rather darker than the generality of his nation. He was, however, a genuine Hottentot, and seemed to be about thirty years of age. His nose was very much depressed, so that the mouth or lips projected beyond it; and the chin was narrow, and cheek-bones high, like all of his race; but the forehead had a good elevation. His hair, which had been lately cut, resembled nothing more than very small tufts of black wool, sprinkled over the skull so thinly, that the bare skin might be seen between them. He had scarcely any beard, excepting on the upper lip, where it was short and woolly. His eyes would be considered small, if measured by European proportions, but were rather large for a Hottentot: they exhibited a good deal of animation, the pupils being of a bright black, although the surrounding part of the ball was of a yellowish white. He seemed on this occasion to possess some vivacity and shrewdness; and I readily allowed myself to believe that I had now hired a man on whose qualifications and fidelity I might rely.

I appointed him to be the foreman of the party, as well as the driver of my waggon; a post of dignity with which he appeared much pleased. After examining every particular part of the waggon with the same ceremony and attention as had been done by Magers and Jan Kok, he set himself to work to put the various apparatus in readiness for travelling.

His uniform, musket, and accoutrements having been given up to the regiment, my first care was to clothe him, and furnish him with bedding. Amongst the different articles of his equipment, he was most proud of a large watch-coat, in which, I believe, he fancied that he looked as big and important as a Dutch boor.

I commissioned him to make enquiry among the Hottentots of his acquaintance, for the number of men still wanting to make up the complement of my party. He knew of several who happened to be at that time in Cape Town, and who, he thought, would be willing to go with us. With this view he went every day to the *Pagter's* (the licensed retailer of wine and brandy), where, he said, he had no doubt of meeting with them. He was quite right in his idea of where his countrymen were most likely to be found, when they come up to Cape Town; for these pernicious wine and brandy-houses are commonly filled with these thoughtless creatures, who never leave them till every *stuiver* of their money is spent. Among the number which he saw there in the course of the week, not one could be obtained fit for the service, as all those whom he would have persuaded to join us, were unfortunately bound by legal contract to other masters.

There remained another resource in the Hottentot settlement under the Moravian missionaries at *Groene Kloof*, (Green Pass), and I immediately despatched a letter to *Mr. Schmidt*, one of the Brethren, requesting that, if any men could be found inclined for such a journey, they might be sent to Cape Town as soon as possible.

As, by the laws of the colony, every inhabitant is prohibited going beyond the established boundary, it became necessary that I should be provided with a special permission for that purpose. Accordingly, I received from the Colonial Secretary's office the proper document, and, together with it, another official paper which the Governor, to facilitate my views, ordered to be prepared for me. It was written in duplicate in the English and Dutch languages, and was addressed to " all Landdrosts, Field-cornets, and other inhabitants, requiring them to afford every accommodation in their power, and to provide every necessary I might stand in need of and require; and also to convey back to Cape Town such letters, parcels, &c. as I should have occasion to send." Persons in the employ of government, are, when travelling in their official capacity, usually furnished with papers of this nature. The degree and kind of accommodation and assistance which this procured for me, will appear in the sequel.

13th. In the mean time, constantly occupied in getting all things ready for my departure, I found little leisure for profiting by the various invitations which I received from my friends in Cape Town, and which multiplied as the day of taking leave of them drew nearer. Nor would I allow the thought that I was soon to bid, as I then believed, a final farewell to Cape Town, to seduce me to remain longer; although the hospitality and friendship I had experienced might well admit of excuses for further delay.

It was necessary that I should superintend every preparation, in order to he well acquainted with whatever concerned my outfit; as the future management of every thing was to depend on myself alone. My numerous purchases were not to be completed with that facility and despatch with which they might have been made in a town of greater resources.

On the morning of the 14*th*, the two teams of oxen, which Magers and Jan Kok had been sent to fetch from the Bokkeveld, having arrived safe at Salt-river, I fixed with peculiar pleasure the day on which we were to commence our journey, and gave orders for the waggon to leave Cape Town on the eighteenth.

The following days were employed chiefly in packing all the various articles into the chest. This part of the work I had reserved for myself; because, unless I fixed in my memory the particular place of each article, by putting in every thing with my own hands, and making at the same time lists of the contents of each chest, it would be almost impossible, when on the journey, to find, amidst such a multitude and variety of goods, any thing I sought for. Those articles which were likely to come often into use, were placed uppermost, or where they could readily be got at; and not an inch of space was left unfilled, as well that no room might be lost, as to prevent the damage which the rough motion of the waggon would occasion to any thing which should get loose. I took with me no books of travels whatever; and if on account of this omission, I travelled through the country without the advantage of these to guide me in my observations, and direct my attention to those objects and facts which had been by others thought remarkable; I had, on the other

hand, the greater advantage of carrying with me a judgment unbiassed and unprejudiced by either the opinions or the mistakes, the
ignorance or the misrepresentations of others.   I wished to see things
for myself, and to form my own opinions, independent of every
guide but facts.

   For those who may feel a curiosity to know, more particularly,
the contents of my waggon when it left Cape Town, and in the hope
of its affording some assistance or useful hints to those who may
hereafter undertake a similar journey, a list of some of the articles is
here inserted.

Goods as presents to the chiefs, and for
   bartering with the natives : —
      Black, white, and blue porcelain beads,
      of a small size; these being the
      kinds most admired
      Red porcelain and glass beads. These
      sorts were less acceptable
      Gilt rings, with factitious gems
      Brass rings
      Blue check handkerchiefs
      Blue check cottons
      Plain, gilt, and ornamented buttons
      Tobacco
      Snuff
      Snuff-boxes
      Knives
      Pocket tinder-boxes, and steels
      Looking-glasses
      Brass wire
      Sheets of copper and tin
      Spike nails.
Clothing and blankets for my own Hot-
   tentots.
Arms and ammunition : —
      Six muskets, and powder-horns
      A fowling-piece, and shot-belt
      A large riffle, carrying a ball of the
      weight of two ounces
      Two cases of pistols, and belt
      A cutlass
      Musket balls
      Four barrels of gunpowder

      Bags of shot, of all sizes
      Gun-flints, and bullet-moulds
      Lead and tin, in bars.
Carpenter's tools: such as
      Saws
      Hammers
      Hatchets
      Felling-axe
      Adze
      Sledge-hammer
      And a variety of the more useful sorts
      Spikes and nails
      Spades, pickaxe, and mattock.
Waggon-stores.
      Ropes and lines
      Sacks, and canvas bags
      Spare canvas, and sail-needles
      Prepared ox-hide, and goat-leather
      Spare bamboo whip-stocks, and thongs
      Spare yokes, and halters
      Tar, pitch, grease, and resin
      Spare linch-pins, hooks, and rings.
      A horn lantern
      A dark lantern
      An iron melting-ladle.
The English colors.
Provisions : —
      Rice
      Bread and biscuit
      Flour and wheat
      Wine, rum, and brandy.
Fish-hooks and lines

Water-casks.

A chest of select medicines.

Books: consisting of various works on zoology, mineralogy, natural philosophy, mathematics, medicine, &c.; amounting, all together, to more than fifty volumes, among which were —

    Linné. Systema Naturæ, ed. Gmelini
    ———— Species Plantarum, ed. Willdenovii
    Fabricius, Species Insectorum
    Jussieu, Genera Plantarum, ed. Usteri
    Forster, Enchiridion Historiæ Naturali inserviens
    Portuguese Dictionary

Dutch Dictionary

Nautical Almanacs

    Atlas Céleste de Flamstead; par Fortin, (avec un Planisphère des Etoiles Australes, dressé par M. l'Abbé de la Caille.)

A large assortment of stationary, and every requisite for drawing in water and body-colours; together with prepared canvas, and the articles used for painting in oil.

Spare deal packing-cases.

And a multitude of other things, which are not necessary to be here particularly enumerated.

It may, perhaps, seem difficult to imagine how so many things could be packed into a waggon of these dimensions; and indeed this was not accomplished without much contrivance: but the fact is, that the waggon was greatly overloaded, as the event afterwards proved. Five very large chests, made to fit without any loss of space, occupied nearly all the body of the waggon, leaving but just room enough for one person to sit. To the inside of the tilt, were tied bags filled with a variety of things, such as were expected to come frequently into use: and bottles, muskets, pistols, powder-horns, the cutlass, and a great number of other articles, were made fast with thongs of raw hide to the bamboo frame. The fore half of the waggon, was separated from the other part, by a canvas partition, to form a sleeping-place, where the bedding lay very conveniently along the tops of the chests. The remaining space was quite filled up with reams of paper, a press, the smaller chests, a large tin collecting box, the brandy barrel, the water casks, and other goods. In the bed, during the hours of travelling, were placed the sextant, and such instruments as were liable to be injured by the rough motion of the waggon. In the chest, on which the driver sits, were the tools and implements for repairing the waggon, and such things as more immediately related to the office of waggon-driver. On the outside of the waggon, the spare yokes, lever, tar-bucket, skid, spades, pick-axe, hatchets, and whip-stocks, were fastened. Beneath, on the trap (or step-frame) the cooking utensils, besides the *karosses* (cloaks) and bedding of the Hottentots, were secured.

That no measure of forethought might be omitted, I appointed agents * in Cape Town, to receive and forward to England the packages and collections, which I might have to send back while still within reach of the colony.

All my arrangements were now completed, excepting one, which was not of trifling importance: I was still without the proper complement of men. No answer had yet been received from the missionary at Groene Kloof, although nearly a fortnight had elapsed. The three that were already hired would have been enough, in the ordinary mode of travelling within the colony, that is, one to drive the waggon, another to lead the team, and the third to take charge of the loose oxen ; but for a journey over deserts and through uncivilised nations, so small a number was very insufficient. Philip had been daily employed in making enquiries, but hitherto without success ; and, therefore, seeing little prospect of hiring Hottentots in Cape Town, I resolved to rely on the chances of obtaining them in my way through the colony.

In the afternoon, my two Hottentots were sent to Salt-river to fetch the oxen, and returned with them at sun-set, to be in readiness for the next day.

18th. Early this morning, Philip accidentally met a Hottentot acquaintance of his, who had but just arrived in town, and who, not more than two months before, had received his discharge from the Cape regiment. His old comrade had no sooner mentioned to him the proposed journey, than he expressed the greatest desire to go with us, although he was unfortunately at this time engaged as herdsman in the service of a person of the name of Leibbrandt, who resided in the town.

---

* *Messrs. Ranken & Scott*, English merchants; to whom I am under much obligation, particularly to the latter, during the absence of his partner, for the great care which, during four years, was taken of the different packages that came into their hands.

Pl. 2

Engraved after the original Drawing made by W.. Finch Esq.r in N.r 1814

Portrait of Speelman, a Hottentot

London, Published by Longman & C.o August 1, 1821

The master was immediately applied to, and readily consented to relinquish him. Upon which the Hottentot, highly pleased with the change, got himself ready in less than half an hour, with his wife and his budget, to set off with the rest of our party.

The name of this Hottentot was *Stoffel Speelman* * ; his height was above the common standard, being about five feet seven inches : he was of thin and bony figure, and had a very upright port, acquired, perhaps, during his military service, and possessed a share of activity, which in a Hottentot might be accounted considerable. His age, at a guess, (for a Hottentot scarcely ever knows how old he is) might be about forty ; and though his countenance exhibited no features of beauty, it displayed a look of intelligence and readiness, which soon prepossessed me with the opinion, that he would prove a very useful addition to my little party. His eyebrows were stronger than usual in this nation ; his cheek-bones protuberant ; cheeks hollow ; nose flattened and wide, with large distorted nostrils : his mouth large, and lips thick and projecting ; the chin narrow, having several unusual protuberances ; and the beard very scanty, excepting on the upper lip.

On making enquiry into his character, I learnt that he was an excellent marksman ; an important and valuable qualification, and one which was indispensably required for such an expedition. He was besides, a great traveller, and had visited most parts of the colony. The opportunity of seeing the country beyond the Gariep, and a wish he had long entertained to go to Klaarwater, were the great inducements to add himself to my party.

His wife, *Hannah*, was a genuine Hottentot ; and her com-

---

* His *portrait* is given at *Plate 2.* It was drawn in September 1814, at the time when he quitted my service; in exactly the same dress which he happened then to wear. His cap, which is a fashion of his own, was made of calf-skin prepared with the hair on. A red cotton handkerchief was bound round his head, and a blue one of the same kind, loosely tied about his neck. He wore a pair of leathern trowsers and a blue cloth jacket, over which was buckled a *kogel-tas* (bullet-pouch) made by himself, from the skin of a tiger which he had shot.

plexion, like that of all her race, was of a tawny buff or fawn color ;
such as a painter might imagine that of a Guinea negro would be, if
half washed off, and a light tint of ochre put over the remainder. Her
age was probably about thirty, though she had the appearance of
being much older. Her figure was not quite so small as the general
size of her country-women ; yet the hands and feet were little. Her
manners were heavy and lifeless, with a countenance indicating a
dull and stupid mind ; while her features were as little handsome
as those of her husband. Her eyes unfurnished with eyebrows,
were small and set very obliquely ; that is, instead of the four corners
being in the same horizontal line, imaginary lines, drawn through
both corners of each eye, would intersect as low down as the middle
of the nose. From one cheek bone to the other, the space was
uniformly flat, the ridge of the nose being scarcely elevated enough
to be perceivable. The end of this organ was wide and depressed,
the nostrils seeming as if squeezed out of shape ; but the mouth
and thick lips pouted out much beyond it. The chin was long
and forward, and exceedingly pointed and narrow : this narrowness of the lower part of the face, being one of the distinguishing
features of the Hottentot race. Her short black woolly hair was
entirely concealed by a handkerchief bound tight round her head ;
a custom followed by every one, who is able to procure it, whether
male or female ; but particularly by the women, who, conscious that
their hair is no ornament, seem desirous of concealing a mark by
which they think their inferiority to the colonists is more evidently
pointed out. She wore a coarse linen dress made in the Dutch
fashion, and shoes of raw hide covered her feet.

Fearing that she would be unable to bear the fatigue of so
laborious a journey, or that she might become rather an incumbrance
than a serviceable addition to our number, I at first objected to her
coming with us ; but as her husband begged earnestly that she might
be permitted to go with him, and as she engaged to make herself useful
in cooking and washing, I consented to add a lady to our party.

No sooner was this arrangement made, and Speelman's ragged

appearance improved by a new suit of clothes which I immediately gave him, than, without loss of time, he was set to work to assist in loading up the waggon.   After which, a team of ten oxen having been selected from out of the twenty, he set out with the remainder to Salt-river.

At length, about noon, every thing being ready for starting, Philip mounted his seat, and taking in his hand the great whip, the emblem of his office, made the street echo with one of his loudest claps; at the same moment, with an animated voice, calling out to the oxen, *Loop!** The waggon moved steadily away: I watched its progress till, passing the castle, it turned out of sight; little supposing at that moment, that it would ever pass that castle again; or that, out of the whole party who were now to accompany it, I should be the only person to return with it.

My waggon at this time, with its contents and the oxen which drew it, had already cost me six hundred pounds sterling.

In order to be satisfied of its safe arrival at the first stage, I followed on horseback to Salt-river; and after seeing it properly secured for the night, and leaving farther instructions with the men, I returned to town to take my farewell dinner at the Governor's table.

I had now the honor of taking leave of His Excellency, who, apparently with much sincerity, expressed his wishes for my safety and success; nor ought I here to omit my acknowledgments for the many attentions which I received from His Lordship during my stay in Cape Town.

19*th*.   This morning an event took place, which excited universal alarm, and for a short time interrupted every occupation. At about ten o'clock all the inhabitants were again thrown into terror and consternation, by the shock of an earthquake. The circumstances of this earthquake, differed in several respects, from that which happened on the seventh.   No explosion took place, but a tremulous hollow sound, somewhat resembling a smothered howling,

---

* Signifying, *Go!* It is the usual exclamation of the Cape waggoners, when they wish to put their oxen in motion.

seemed to pass under our feet, in a direction from the north towards the south; occupying a space of time, of about three seconds, and accompanied by a strong trembling of the earth. This was the only shock that occurred: the consequences were the same as before; the same alarm and confusion took place; but on finding no repetition of it, the fears of the inhabitants more easily subsided, and they sooner returned into their houses. Some damage was done to the buildings; but it was not considerable. The *former* earthquake was distinguished by an instantaneous and very loud explosion in the atmosphere, without any trembling movement of the earth: *this* occupied a very sensible duration of time, and the field of its action was very perceptibly subterraneous. Yet it can hardly be doubted that the essential principle was the same, and that in both, electric matter was the great agent.

In taking leave of my esteemed friend, *Mr. Hesse,* I was unable to suppress those painful feelings, which the idea of so long a farewell could not fail to excite. The recollections of my stay at the Cape, will ever remind me of the pleasure I have enjoyed in his society, of the hospitality I experienced in his house, and of the obliging and friendly attentions of his lady and of the different members of her family. *

At a little before noon, I took my final departure from Cape Town; and, accompanied by two of my friends, rode to Salt-river, where I found Mr. Anderson had already given the necessary orders for putting the oxen to the waggons.

The whole party were soon in motion; and, taking the road over the flats, between bushes and hillocks of sand, were presently out of sight. The writing of a letter detained me a short time; we then mounted our horses, and hastened to overtake the waggon. We came up with it in half an hour, and continued following at a slow pace, for some time longer, during which my friends were insensibly increasing their distance from home, led on, both by the desire of

---

* The family of *Bergh* is one of the most respectable in Cape Town: various situations under government, of trust and responsibility, have been filled by them, during three generations.

prolonging a last conversation, and by a reluctance to bid an adieu, that was to be succeeded by an absence of which neither could foresee the duration.

At last, we bade farewell : they turned their horses towards Cape Town, while I mounted my waggon, and threw myself on the mattress, to repose a while, and recover from the bodily fatigue and the exhaustion of spirits, which the exertions of the last two days had occasioned ; as well as to relieve some perturbation of mind, arising from the thoughts of having now taken leave of my family, and all my friends, perhaps for ever.

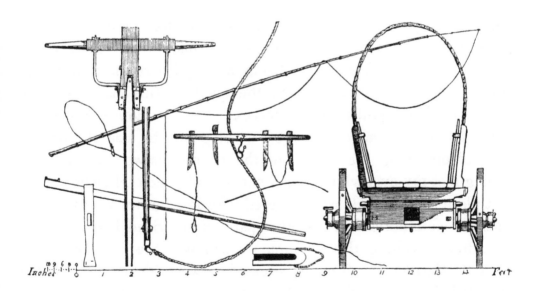

CHAPTER IX.

JOURNEY FROM CAPE TOWN TO TULBAGH.

THE waggon moved slowly and silently on, over deep sands; the whole of our journey this day being over the downs, which embrace the southern side of Table Bay. Being now quite released from all business and bustle of the town, the quiet of this easy travelling soon restored tranquillity to my nerves. After an hour's rest, I felt able to follow the waggons on foot, wishing not to lose the opportunity of observing the nature of the country as we passed. But nothing met my eye, which I had not already seen elsewhere. In most places, these sands were covered with low bushes of the same kinds as before noticed in the other parts of the Sand Flats.

After travelling three hours, we arrived at a pool of water, called *Zand-valléy* (Sand-pond) situated between Tygerberg and the bay. It being one of the regular outspan-places of the boors, we halted here for the night. Our oxen were turned loose among the bushes to graze, or rather to browze, while the Hottentots kindled a fire with wonderful expedition. We were obliged to make coffee with brackish water, no better being to be found at this place.

In the evening, our little caravan, which consisted only of the Missionary's waggon and people, together with my own, had to me, who till now had never passed a night in the open air, a most curious and romantic appearance. *   The novelty of the scene kept my mind continually amused, and the sight of the Hottentots, and all their movements, fixed my attention.   Their number was about a dozen, men and women : they seemed now to have recovered their natural manners, having left behind them the constraints of Cape Town.   It was easy to perceive, that this was the mode of life which suited them, and that they felt quite at home amongst the bushes.   Seated on the ground by a blazing fire, they passed the time in talking and smoking; while the light, thrown against the nearer shrubs, and various parts of the waggons, produced an effect really picturesque.   As soon as their supper was finished, they retired to sleep; some wrapping themselves up in their *karosses*, (sheep-skin cloaks,) lay down under a bush, others by the fire, and others under the waggons, sheltered from the wind by a skreen of mats.

20*th*.   In the morning I arose, refreshed by sleep, and recovered from all indisposition.   The business of the day commenced by examining the state of the waggons and oxen, and giving out orders to the men.   Mrs. Anderson, who was to accompany her husband to Klaarwater, having yesterday remained at Salt-river, joined us this morning at eight o' clock, attended by a party of friends.

We proceeded on our journey at two in the afternoon, and after a few miles, began to ascend *Tygerberg.*   Here the party who had travelled with us from Zand-valley took their leave; and as soon as we were nearly out of sight, they repeatedly saluted us with the reports of their pistols, which they had brought for that purpose; this being an old colonial custom.   They thus bade us their last farewell, while we waved our hats, and returned it by discharging our muskets.   There was something pleasing, though melancholy,

---

* The *engraving* at the beginning of this chapter is a representation of one of these *night-parties.*

in this custom: it was one which certainly owed its origin to no other feeling than that of heartfelt goodwill.   The journey they had left us to pursue, was long and not free from danger: none of us could feel assured of meeting again.   The missionaries were about to take up their residence for several years on the other side of the Gariep, and in that time the ordinary casualties of human life might naturally be expected to lessen our number.   For some time after their friends were lost to our view, we continued to hear the reports of their pistols; to which we as often replied, till, crossing the mountain, we could hear each other no longer.

It had been agreed that we should generally proceed only by easy stages, that the strength of the oxen might not be exhausted before we reached Klaarwater: and this slow progress perfectly accorded with my views of travelling.   We therefore unyoked at an outspan-place, called *Pampoen Kraal*, (Pumpkin Kraal); where, during the stillness of the night, we could plainly hear the noise of the surf on the shore of Table Bay.

21st.   From midnight till two o'clock this afternoon, there was a continuance of rain: this occasioned the wood to be so wet, that we had great difficulty in making fires.   The veld-cornet here, paid a visit to our waggons, merely out of curiosity to know who we were. We purchased from him some wine and bread, and I obtained also a *voortouw* (fore-rope) or short trektouw, which, it was found, would be required occasionally to hook on at the end of the draw-rope, whenever it was necessary to employ a larger team than ten or twelve oxen.   We soon observed that my waggon was so heavily laden, that fewer than fourteen were not enough to draw it; and that, in consequence of so disproportionate a weight resting on these narrow wheels, the waggon had once or twice, in the course of the day before, escaped sinking into the ground, only by whipping the oxen hastily over those parts of the road where the ground happened to be softer than in others.

At this place grows in abundance a small plant * said by the

---

* *Euphorbia tuberosa.*

boors to occasion the strangury, at a certain time of the year, if eaten by the oxen; and this appeared confirmed by the fact that several of our oxen were at this spot actually taken ill of that disorder. It would seem that its acrid milky juice has the quality of inspissating the liquor of the stomach.   The Hottentots have a practice of removing the obstruction, and in most cases succeed in giving relief: such fortunately was the case at this time.   Whether the complaint be caused by this weed alone, or by any other, I could not ascertain; but it is probable that several species of *Euphorbia* have the same deleterious effect, as Thunberg attributes it in like manner to the *Euphorbia genistoïdes,* a plant which I did not observe growing any where hereabouts. *   Stones and veins in the earth, having outwardly some resemblance to volcanic matter, were noticed at this spot.

As soon as the weather began to clear up, we prepared for departing.   Standing attentive to all that was going on, and noticing the manner in which my men yoked the oxen to the waggon, I was surprised to find they all were as well acquainted with the name of every individual ox, and knew the place in the team where each had been trained to draw, as if they had been used to them for several years.   Their quickness and memory, in every thing relating to cattle, is really astonishing; of which numberless proofs have occurred in the course of these travels.   When Magers and his companion were sent into the Bokkeveld to fetch home the oxen, the farmer of whom they were bought, having mustered the whole, merely repeated their names and places in the team.   These he correctly retained in his memory, and afterwards again repeated to Jan Kok, Philip, and Speelman, who now called each ox by his name with the utmost readiness.   This faculty, common to Hottentots, and to all the African tribes that I visited, shows the high degree of

---

* At *Pampoen Kraal* may be found:
    Microloma sagittatum,
    Tetragonia hirsuta, and
    Galaxia ciliata.

perfection to which any particular use of the mind may be brought by constant exercise; for, with these people, tending and managing their cattle is the grand employment of life. For myself, it was a long time before I was able to distinguish my own team, even from those belonging to the other waggons.

The weather prevented our setting out until a late hour, and it became dark before we had advanced more than seven miles and a half; when we unyoked at an outspan-place, in the midst of rhinoceros-bushes, which abound in this part of the country.

22nd. This day proved very fine; and so early as eight o'clock in the morning, the thermometer was not lower than 57 (11·1 R.; 13·8 C.) although it was now the depth of winter; a circumstance from which some estimate may be formed of the general mildness of the winters at the Cape.

Soon after we left this place, Table Mountain was seen very distinctly: its form is too remarkable, in this part of the colony, to be mistaken for any other. During the whole of this day's journey, which was twenty miles, the road was exceedingly even, being over an open, and, in most parts, a rhinoceros-bush country. *

After advancing a couple of hours, we halted to take dinner; while the oxen were left standing in the yoke. I could not but admire the expedition with which the Hottentots made a fire and broiled their meat. The *rhinoceros-bush* is well known for its valuable property of burning while green, as freely as the driest fuel; and whole plants which we threw on the fire, blazed up in an instant, the larger stems giving a very strong heat and flame. Although one may venture to assert that the whole plant contains a considerable quantity of either inflammable oil, or resinous gum, these are not discoverable by the eye.

We continued travelling by moonlight, till a little before nine

---

* A variety of proteaceous plants, decorate the sides of the road: among them were *Protea scolymus* three feet high, and *Mimetes purpurea*. A very pretty *Blairia*, forming a little shrub a foot and a half high, was now covered with blossom.

in the evening, when an accident suddenly put a stop to our further progress this night. Philip, happening unluckily to drive a few yards out of the beaten road, on ground which was sandy and much softened by yesterday's rain, the waggon sunk into the earth up to the axletrees, and defied all our power to move it from the spot. Immediately we set to work with pickaxe and spades to clear away the earth from before the wheels; and four oxen more being then added to the team, we succeeded in releasing the waggon. But before it had advanced a yard forward, it sunk again as deep as before; and with the struggling of the cattle to drag it out, the fore-rope snapped asunder, and the pole broke; nor was it possible to extricate the waggon without unloading a great part of its contents. This dilemma obliged us to wait till the morning.

The place where we happened to be thus detained, was called *Olyvenhout-bosch* (Olive-tree wood), so named from the *Olyf boom* *, a tree so much resembling the European Olive, as to have been mistaken for it by botanists; but few were now growing here. It attains a large size, and the wood, which is exceedingly compact and heavy, is very handsome, and well suited for cabinet work.

23rd. The next morning we bound together the broken pole, unloaded several of the boxes in order to lighten the waggon; and, after again digging away the earth, a layer of bushes was placed in the track, to render the ground firm. With the strength of sixteen oxen it was at last dragged out.

This affair gave me an opportunity of witnessing the helplessness of Hottentots, and their want of contrivance, in occurrences a little out of the common way. They could not imagine any other mode of extricating the vehicle than by main force; and it was in this foolish attempt that the pole was broken. When they discovered that such means would not answer, they stood looking on with a most provoking apathy, silently smoking their pipes; and

---

* *Olea similis,* B; *O. Europœa,* Th. et *O. Europœa,* var. *verrucosa* Pers.

A A

even while I was pointing out how they were to dig the channel, they stood as unmoved as if they had been statues fixed there upon a pedestal.

I was now convinced of the necessity of having a second waggon, not only on account of the great quantity of goods to be carried with us, but also of my own comfort; as, by restricting the Hottentots to the use of the second for carrying their clothes, and by placing in that one our provisions and such things as were dirty or otherwise disagreeable, my own would always remain clean. I resolved, therefore, to purchase another, as soon as we should arrive at Tulbagh, where it was proposed to rest a few days.

We quitted Olyvenhout-bosch at three o'clock, and soon arrived on the left bank of the *Groote Berg-rivier* (Great Mountain-river) at the *Pont*, (or ferry,) where we found people in readiness to convey us over. *

The river, at this place, was deep and rapid, and might, at this time, be about seventy yards across. This stream is sometimes very suddenly and unexpectedly swelled by torrents, which descend from the mountains of *Drakenstein* and *Fransche Hoek;* on which account it is imprudent for travellers, at any time, to remain at outspan immediately on its banks. A melancholy accident of this kind had happened here about a month before, when a boor and his family, not suspecting danger, halted close to the ferry. The floods coming down in the night, swept away the waggon, while all in it were asleep, and three of the party were drowned.

The ferry-boat is of a construction well adapted for conveying

---

* *Plate* 3. represents this view. The level country seen on the left in the distance, is a part of *Wagen-maker's* (Waggon-maker's) *Valley.* The mountains are those of *Klein* (Little) *Drakenstein.* A *farm-house*, with a few large orange-trees in front, is seen on the bushy plain. A few white poplars stand on the opposite bank, and the foreground is shaded by a large many-stemmed tree of *Karree-hout*, some of the branches of which are loaded with grass and rubbish left there by the waters, attesting the great height to which this river occasionally swells. All the figures in the foreground, excepting two, were Hottentots.

Crossing the Berg River

over cattle and heavy carriages. It may be described as a floating platform, with rails at the sides, and having its ends rising on hinges so as to lie at all times flat on the shore. It was sufficiently capacious to carry over my waggon with eight oxen, and six men, at one time. It was hauled to and fro, by means of a strong rope, strained from one bank of the river to the other, and was managed by a couple of men with great ease. The tolls were one rix-dollar for each waggon, with its oxen and men; and one schelling for every single ox, and for each foot passenger. The ferry belongs to government, but was farmed to a neighbouring boor.

The landscape here is rich and fertile: the beautiful flat country of *Wagenmaker's Valley* and *Drakenstein*, enlivened with numerous farm-houses, lay extended before us, bounded by a fine range of mountains, a part of the great western chain. The ground is well covered with vegetation, and abounds with shrubs. Very large bushes of *Karree-hout* *, which, in growth and foliage, have a great resemblance to our common willows, grow along the banks.

After crossing the river, and travelling till dark, we arrived at the house of a wine-boor, named *Marais*, a man of a religious turn, and a friend of my fellow-travellers; where we were well received.

24th.   This house was situated near the Berg-river, and a part of the vineyard was pointed out, where an acre or two of the soil had been completely swept away by the flood; the stream at this place having lately found a new course.

After taking dinner with the family, we departed, directing our way over an open heathy country till evening. † The brightness of moonlight enabled us to proceed with as much safety as by day; yet the necessity of travelling in the night is always to be regretted, because the views of a country, obtained in passing through it under such circumstances, seldom leave a correct impression on

---

* *Rhus viminalis*, L.

† In this day's journey I frequently met with *Tetragonia hirtsuta*, a curious little annual plant with small yellow flowers.

A A 2

the mind; and various objects easily escape notice, in this dubious light. We halted at an outspan-place, in the midst of Rhinoceros-bushes. A pack of jackals * continued howling and barking near us, for some time, in the hope of picking up a stray sheep.

Our people now seemed all in the height of good humour; and, cheered with the blaze of four different fires, they sat up till midnight, talking and smoking, while the sound of my flute at intervals, seemed to increase their satisfaction, and gain all their attention.

25th. I walked to the house of *Piet Van der Merwe*, a neighbouring farmer †, to enquire for a new pole for the waggon, and fortunately obtained one. He told my fellow-traveller, that he had heard there was an Englishman on the road, who had general orders from government, authorizing him to demand such assistance as he might stand in need of, but he candidly confessed that had I made use of it on this occasion, I should not have been able to persuade him to do any thing, as he would in that case have pleaded a hurt in his hand, as an excuse for not lending us any help at the forge; but that, as I had asked it as a favor, he willingly sold me the pole, and would freely give his assistance.

After considerable delay, and some trouble, a new pole was at length fixed in. The old one, from its peculiar fracture, excited my attention: it was made of the wood called *Hassagay-hout* ‡, which possesses the valuable property of extreme toughness, as this accident clearly evinced. Although bent to an angle of about 150 degrees, it exhibited scarcely any transverse fracture, but appeared split into a great number of longitudinal splinters, which still held the two parts strongly together. The pole we had now put in, being of *Yzer-hout* §

---

* *Canis mesomelas,* Linn.

† By the side of a rivulet here, grows *Capraria lanceolata,* Linn. a very neat willow-leaved shrub, decorated with long yellowish flowers: It is peculiar to such situations.

‡ So named by the colonists, on account of its being the wood of which the Kaffers most commonly make the shafts of their hassagays or javelins. It is the *Curtisia faginea.*

§ *Olea undulata.*

(or Iron-wood), was not so tough as the other; but many degrees
harder and heavier. The boors esteem the iron-wood to be, for this
purpose, but little inferior to the hassagay-wood.

This business detained us at Van der Merwe's till within an hour
of sunset. Here we took our last view of Table Mountain, which
appeared distinct and full in sight, although, in a direct line, its
distance was not much less than forty-eight miles.

In a little more than seven hours, we reached the western
entrance of *Roodezand's Kloof* (Red-sand Pass) where we took up
our station for the night. At this place, a furious stream of wind
continued pouring, as it were, through this opening in the mountains,
during the whole time of our stay; and it has been remarked by the
boors, that this spot is always subject to strong winds. The difficulty
of keeping a fire burning, or a candle alight in the waggons, obliged
us to remain in darkness till morning.

26th. We entered the mountains at an early hour in the morning.
This *Kloof* appeared much more terrific while travelling through it in
a waggon, than it did when on horseback. * About the middle of it
we met another waggon; and I could not, without considerable
uneasiness, see how very near to the edge of the precipice the wheels
of mine were obliged to go, while making room for it to pass.

Following on foot, I was enabled to collect a variety of plants
not hitherto met with. These added thirty-six numbers to my
catalogue. † Among them was a shrub more particularly interesting,

---

* *The Engraving* at the end of the chapter is a view of the *Kloof*, taken when the
waggons were about half-way through it. A description of this scene has already been
given on the 19th of April, at page 137.

† They were,

Othonna amplexicaulis	*Leucodendrum plumosum*
———— *denticulata*	*Viscum rotundifolium*
———— *abrotanifolia*	*Cluytia Alaternoïdes*
———— *capillaris*	*Metrosideros angustifolia*
———— *frutescens*	*Aster angustifolius*
Aizoon lanceolatum	*Diosma pectinata*
Berckheya setosa	*Eriocephalus racemosus*
	Rhus incisum,

With

on account of its close resemblance in character to the plants of New Holland. It was in fact a species of *Metrosideros* (M. angustifolia) a genus peculiar to that quarter of the world and the neighbouring islands. There is a certain affinity between the botany of that country and that of the Cape of Good Hope, of which numberless proofs are known; but none perhaps so remarkable as this. Of the boundless study of natural history, no part is more instructive than the comparative view of the productions of different countries. By this, the peculiar features by which each are characterized may be discovered. Reflections of a pleasing nature were always produced when I happened to detect any plant, which, not according with these peculiar features, led me to fancy that, like myself, it had strayed from a different and far distant clime. Of such, I found many in the course of these travels. Some appeared as if they had migrated from India, some from China or Japan, others from North America, the West Indies, South America, the Straits of Magellan, Madagascar, the Mauritius, Barbary, Egypt, Southern Europe, and even the colder countries of the North. Sometimes, the unexpected discovery of a plant whose garb and features were English, changed the whole train of ideas, and filled the mind with other thoughts.

In a couple of hours we were safely through the *Kloof*, and soon afterwards arrived at the widow *De Wet's*, a farm-house of a superior description. Here my fellow-travellers took up their abode, during our stay at Tulbagh.

The mistress, whose respectable appearance and hospitable manners took our attention, immediately prepared dinner expressly for us. She offered me accommodations at her house, but *Mr. Ballot*,

---

With other species of

Othonna	*Oxalis*	*Buchnera*
Serruria	*Gladiolus*	*Erica*
Blairia	*Phylica*	*Periploca*
Cotyledon	*Calendula*	*Salvia*, and
Cassine	*Adiantum*	*Leucospermum.*
Restio		

having been informed of my arrival, renewed very pressingly his former invitation ; and proposed that I should come to his house without delay.   My oxen were therefore again put to, and I reached his hospitable mansion just at dark.

27*th.* This morning I rode to the Drostdy for the purpose of conferring with the landdrost ; but unfortunately he was gone from home, and not expected to return in less than a week.   In the absence of a landdrost, all public business, not requiring the sanction of the *Heemraaden* (the District Council), is transacted by the District Secretary.   Mine being of this nature, I addressed myself to *Mr. Munnik*, the secretary, from whom I experienced a polite and ready attention to my wishes.   A copy of my papers was registered in his office, and orders were immediately issued to the *veld cornets* residing along the northern boundary of the colony, that they should afford me whatever assistance I might need, should I again return into the colony.   This was intended merely as a precautionary measure, so that, in the case of meeting with any unforeseen accident, such as the loss of the waggons, or some misfortune compelling me to retreat, I might secure the aid and authority of the field-cornets, even should these papers be lost.   This gentleman anticipated my wants, by proposing, as the passage of the Hex-river Kloof, and the ascent of the Roggeveld mountain, would greatly exhaust the strength of my own oxen, that he might issue orders for a *voor-span*, (relay of oxen) to meet me at those places.   At the office of the secretary, Speelman was bound in my service, by the usual legal forms ; which consist in each party signing in triplicate a certain prescribed and printed form of agreement, so constructed as to secure to the Hottentot the due payment of his wages, and his liberty at the expiration of the term, and to the master his obedience and services during the time contracted for.   Of these three papers, one is given to each party, and the third is left in the secretary's office.

At the Drostdy I received a small packet, containing vaccine matter, dispatched from Cape Town after my departure.   It was sent by order of the governor, in consequence of a conversation in which it was remarked that, as the small pox had once made its appearance a few years ago in the country beyond the Gariep, it seemed probable that much good might result from introducing, among the natives, the art of vaccination.

In my way back to the village, I met a Hottentot, who, asking me if I was not *de Engelsche heer* (the English gentleman), presented a letter from my friend Poleman, informing me that the name of the bearer was *Gert* (Gerrit, pronounced Ghairt) *Roodezand:* that in consequence of my application to the Moravian missionaries at Groene-Kloof, this Hottentot had been sent to Cape Town, whence he was immediately despatched to Tulbagh.

The circumstance was the more fortunate, as there appeared now but little chance of procuring any men at this village: I therefore gladly took him into my service. This man was a Hottentot of mixed race, as was evident from the greater width of the lower part of the face, and from the hair being a little less woolly. His figure was stouter than that of Hottentots in general, but, excepting in these particulars, he did not vary from the genuine character. His eyes were small and sunken, his nose wide and flattened, and lips large and thick. I thought I could perceive in him, sufficient indications of willingness and of a tolerably active and acute disposition, to make me satisfied with my new servant; and, to ratify our agreement as soon as we got home, I equipped him in a new suit of clothes, consisting of jacket, shirt, trowsers, and watch-coat.

29th. Of a waggon-maker named Jacob de Bruyn, in *Winter-hoek* (Winter Corner), I purchased another waggon. It had been much used, and was in need of some repairs; but I had no choice, as this was the only one for sale to be met with, notwithstanding numberless enquiries had been made every where in the neighbourhood. The repairs were instantly begun, under an assurance that the waggon would be rendered as strong as a new one. It was so much smaller than my own, that it could not carry more than half the load : but I considered that, on many occasions, for the purposes of short journeys, or of fetching home large game shot at a distance from the principal waggon, a light vehicle of this size would be found useful ; and therefore, to increase its lightness, I had the sides enclosed with reeds * instead of boards.

The situation of *Winterhoek* is to be admired for its pleasantness and singularity. A few farm-houses, surrounded by trees, and dispersed here and there over this secluded little tract of country, had a very picturesque sheltered appearance, in the bosom of lofty mountains whose summits were at this time covered with snow.

30th. The weather beginning to assume a rainy aspect, raised our fears that the *Breede river* (Broad river) would soon be impassable. My fellow traveller became impatient to ford it before the torrents from the mountains had reached its bed. This river may, without danger, be crossed, till about twenty four hours after heavy rains : but on the second day, the waters begin to find their way to it, and often detain the traveller a fortnight on its banks. To avoid this, it was arranged that he, and the other missionary whom we expected to join our party at Tulbagh, should set out on the day after the morrow, as I, who was obliged to remain till the waggon was ready, could easily overtake them by the help of *voorspans.*

July 1st. Mr. Anderson came this morning, to apprize me that he had received fresh intelligence respecting the body of hostile *Caffres* lying in our route. They had, it was reported, stationed themselves in the *Karreebergen* (Karee Mountains) for the purpose of intercepting us. Their leaders were the same who, a year or two before, had visited Cape Town for the purpose of petitioning the governor to interfere between them and their own chiefs ; from whom they had revolted, on account, they said, of unredressed grievances. Instead of acceding to their wishes, His Excellency thought it wiser not to intermeddle with their quarrels ;

* *Arundo Donax,* Lin.

B B

and, with instructions that they should be conducted back into their own country, ordered them to be put on board a ship which was just then going to sail to Algoa Bay. Their principal leader was a chief of the name of *Dansa* or *Danser*. He was a man of high spirit; and, feeling indignant at having been sent away from Cape Town against his inclination, openly avowed a hostile disposition against the colonists. We, however, agreed that it would be best to proceed as far as the boundary of the colony, where we should better ascertain the truth of this report; and whether or not, they would be too strong for us: if they were, it was my determination to take the route by Námaqualand.

In the afternoon I took a walk to the waggon-maker's, and on the way collected some plants. * On my return, it being then nearly dusk, the delightful fragrance of the *Avond-bloem* (evening flower), a species of *Ixia* (*Hesperanthera*), began to fill the air, and led to the discovery of the plants. In the day-time their flowers, which, though white within, are of a dusky color on the outside, and, being then quite closed, do not readily catch the eye.

2nd. Speelman, who had been sent out for game, returned in a couple of hours with the first-fruits of his hunting, a kind of antelope called *Duyker* by the colonists; together with a small species of *Otis*, or bustard, called *Korhaan* (or *Knorhaan*), a name which is given also to two or three other kinds of Otis. This bird was about the size of a large domestic fowl, and, for eating, is esteemed one of the best of the feathered game. Its plumage having been plucked off before I

---

* *Stœbe rhinocerotis*   *Lidbeckia turbinata*
  Anthospermum ciliare   *Watsonia plantaginea*
  Anthospermum lanceolatum   *Amaryllis ciliaris*
  Strumaria filifolia
And species of the genera: —

Hermannia	*Oxalis*, 5 *sp.*	*Aspalathus*
Buchnera	*Psoralea*	*Hesperanthera*
Cyperus, 2 *sp.*	*Phylica*	*Glycine*

saw it, prevented my ascertaining to what described species it should be referred.

The *Duyker* (Diver) * is one of the smaller *Antelopes*, being not much above two feet in height; very light and elegantly made, like most of that tribe. Its color is an uniformly dusky grizzled brown; the males have short, upright, and straight horns : the tail is not more than three inches long, black on the upper side, and white beneath. But the mark which distinguishes this animal from all the rest of the genus, and perhaps from all the ruminating tribe, is a singular little black, upright, thin tuft of long hairs, growing on the top of the head, between the ears. The Duyker is found chiefly in bushy places; and, from its mode of eluding its pursuers, by a sudden strong leap over the bushes, instantly plunging down amongst them again out of sight, it has gained the name it bears. The meat is very good eating, but is, at all seasons, like most of the venison at the Cape, rather dry, and much inferior to that of England : the cause of this is a total want of fat; a defect which the Cape cooks endeavour to remedy by larding. This animal is found only in Africa; some authors regarding it as the same with the Guinea antelope †, while others suppose it to be a different species peculiar to the southern point of this continent.

The clouds which had threatened to fill the Breede river and detain us at Tulbagh, disappeared in the course of the forenoon, and the wind shifted round to the south-east, a quarter from which the inhabitants of this village seldom receive rain. This is, doubtlessly, to be attributed to the immense tract of arid Karro, and dry country, which lies in that direction. In the afternoon the two missionaries commenced their journey.

3rd. The waggon being finished, was brought home to day; and by the evening, the loading and arrangement of it were completed. Gert was appointed to be the driver, and Maagers's son

---

* *Antilope mergens.*   † *Antilope Grimmia*, Gmel.

the leader.   This being done, I packed up all I had hitherto collected, and delivered them, together with my letters to Mr. *Van de Graaff*, the son of the landdrost, who, being about to depart on the morrow for Cape Town, obligingly offered to take charge of them.

4*th*.   The lady of Mr. Ballot, who had been thoughtful of whatever could contribute to render my abode at the parsonage agreeable, extending her hospitality beyond the present moment, had prepared a basket of provisions sufficient for my own use, for at least a couple of days.

CHAPTER X.

FROM TULBAGH, THROUGH HEX-RIVER KLOOF, TO THE KARRO POORT.

AT last, all being in readiness, my little caravan began its departure from Tulbagh, early in the forenoon. I took leave of this kind family, under feelings which were heightened by the consideration of their being most probably the last Europeans I should meet with until my arrival at a European colony in some distant part of the African coast. As we passed through the village, many persons who had been waiting for us at their doors, expressed their wishes for the safety of our journey. A blind man hearing this, inquired who was passing, and, on being told that it was people who were going far out of the colony, gave us his blessing in a tone of religious warmth, and earnestly wished me success.

After travelling a distance of about thirteen miles, we reached the *Veld-cornet's* on the Breede river; where, in consequence of orders issued from the Drostdy, two teams of twelve oxen each, were, with drivers and leaders, in readiness, to take my waggons forward. We stopped here no longer than necessary to change the teams, and to give directions for Maagers to take my own oxen through Mosterts Hoek, a shorter road, passable for cattle, but not for loaded waggons; and to meet us at the farm of a boor, named Pieter Jacobs.

The country, about this part of the Breede river, abounds in shrubs; among which, a variety of proteaceous plants are conspicuous. We forded the river safely; and, after a further journey of fifteen miles, partly in the dark, halted at the house of *Piet Hugo*, where my coming was expected, and two fresh teams of oxen were in waiting. The people here were very civil and attentive; and as it happened to be near their supper-time, I was invited to partake of the meal. Hottentots are rarely the objects of hospitality; for, with whatever necessaries a boor may think fit to furnish the passing traveller, his servants, if black men, must shift for themselves. This seems to be, at least, the general custom of the colony; although I have met with many instances to the contrary. At this house, a large family sat down to a table where cleanness and plenty were conspicuous.

The supper consisted of hot meat with various dishes of vegetables, and concluded, as usual in farm-houses, with a large bowl of milk. Among these dishes was a *kool salaade*, (cabbage salad,) made of a large unboiled white cabbage cut into narrow shreds, to which were added a dressing of warmed vinegar and melted butter. Both the master and the mistress of the house, pressed me, very good-naturedly, to eat heartily, saying " This is the last place at which you will find a comfortable meal:" and, as if to hint at the folly of leaving a country where all these comforts were to be had, for the inhospitable regions beyond the colony, added " There is no wine nor food in the desart."

We stopped here but an hour, as I was desirous of taking the advantage of a fine moonlight night to make all possible haste to arrive at the Hex-river Kloof, before the floods could have time to render it impassable; as, at this season of the year, the weather is always very unsettled, or at best, uncertain. The Hex river itself, we luckily found fordable; although, had it been but a few inches deeper, we could not, without danger, have ventured through. After this, we travelled nineteen miles, and, at a quarter past two at night, unyoked at the house of *Cootje Du Toit*, a farmer and a *Heemraad* of the district of Tulbagh. No one being awake to receive us, we slept by the waggons till day-light; glad to rest from the fatigue of a very long day's journey of forty-seven miles.

The colonists are so much accustomed to call each other by the familiar and shortened forms of their Christian names, that I have repeatedly noticed instances of their not immediately comprehending what person was intended when the names were mentioned at full length. I have, therefore, in this journal, generally preferred as a rule to give such as were found in common use. The owner of this place, as an example of the remark, although a respectable and affluent person, was seldom spoken of among his neighbours by the name of *Jacobus* (or James); being better known as *Cootje* (or Jemmy).

5th. The Heemraad not being at home, his brother, who lived at a neighbouring farm, and acted as field-cornet of this division, came to give orders respecting the relays. He told me he had received instructions from the Drostdy to supply us with provisions; but that not knowing what we stood in need of, he had not provided any thing. Pointing to the clouds that were collecting in the mountains, he advised me to commence the day's journey as soon as possible, lest the rain should fall, and, making the passage through the Kloof impracticable, detain me here for several days.

At an early hour, therefore, we drove off, and immediately began to enter the *Hex-river Kloof*. In addition to my own people, our number was increased by two young men, nephews of Cootje Du Toit, and two Hottentot drivers, with their leaders. These young men came for the purpose of driving the waggons through, not wishing to trust their oxen to Hottentots in this part of the road, the most difficult and dangerous of the *skoft* (day's journey).

At the entrance to the pass, I met with a curious shrub *, eight

---

* *Carissa Arduina.* — *Arduina bispinosa.* Lin.

to ten feet high, armed at all points with exceedingly strong branch-
ed thorns.   It produces little bunches of small white flowers, which
have both the form and the scent of the jasmine, and are succeeded
by berries resembling those of the berberry.   The Hottentots call
this shrub '*Num'num* (or Noomnoom, agreeably to English orthography), each syllable preceded by a guttural clap of the tongue.
They eat the berries; but I always found them very insipid.

At the same place, I first saw the *Euphorbia Mauritanica*, growing in bushes, as they might be called, from three to four feet
in height.   The milky juice of its branches forms, when inspissated,
a frequent ingredient in the poisonous composition which the Bushmen (or Bush-Hottentots) apply to their arrows.

The *Hex-river Kloof* is a winding defile through a range of very
lofty mountains.   Through this opening, the *Hex-river* (Witches'
river) forces a passage, and soon after joins its waters with those of
the Breede river.   On each side, the mountains rose in majestic
and bold forms, clothed with numerous plants, among which an
arborescent species of *Cotyledon* was curious and remarkable.   In
growth, it resembled a small tree, having a disproportionately thick
fleshy trunk.   It was called the *Boterboom.* (Butter-tree); probably
from the soft fleshy nature of its trunk and branches.

The strata of these mountains seemed to have been thrown into
confusion, and often appeared inclined at an angle of forty-five degrees.   As our road, if it could be called one, followed the course of
the river, we crossed this frequently, and in many places it was three
feet deep, the greatest depth which we could venture to pass without
the risk of wetting the contents of the chests.   The way was plentifully strewed with large stones, which caused the waggon to jolt so
violently that it was not possible to endure riding in it: I was therefore forced to follow on foot, excepting when we went through the
river.   The huge rounded pieces of rock, rolled down by the mountain torrents, and the depth of the ravines, were marks sufficient to
inform the traveller that this pass is often visited by heavy floods,
sweeping every thing away before them.

The kloof was, throughout, a very picturesque, wild scene.   Its rocky sides re-echoed back the loud rattling noise of the waggons, intermingled, every now and then, with the chattering and scream- ing of baboons *, the numerous parties of which relieved the deserted loneliness of the place.   The rushing of the stream, or the falling of the waters, deadened, at times, the boisterous cries with which the drivers encouraged or excited their oxen.   Frequent large trees of rich foliage adorned the scene, and softened the rough features of the frowning rocks, which here projected in enormous masses, and there retired in deep, solemn, shady recesses. .

To have spent several days in exploring these mountains, appa- rently so interesting and so enticing, as well to the eye of the geolo- gist as of the botanist, would have been a delightful employment; but, orders having been issued for the different *voorspans* to be ready on the appointed days, to take my waggons forward, and having with me at this time no oxen of my own to enable me to proceed without them, I could not stop so long on the road, without causing much confusion and unnecessary trouble to those farmers whose duty it was to furnish the relays.   I now discovered that such a mode, or rather rate, of travelling was quite at variance with the idea I had formed, of the manner in which a country ought to be ex- plored and examined.   To be thus hurried through the land, by night as well as by day, would indeed have brought me very ex- peditiously to the end of my journey; but it would at the same time have left me little wiser, as to the true nature of these regions, than I was at the commencement of it.   I therefore determined on the more reasonable plan, of advancing quietly and steadily with my own oxen, as soon as we joined them, excepting such places where the road was particularly laborious and fatiguing.   This I considered to be a more independent, and, therefore, a more agreeable way of travelling.

As soon as we had got through the kloof, and were clear of the mountains, the two young farmers, wishing us a pleasant journey,

---

* *Cercopithecus ursinus.*

and leaving directions with their Hottentots respecting the road they were to take, and where they should leave us, mounted their horses and returned home. Travelling a mile or two further, we halted in an open plain, to rest the oxen, and give them time to graze.

We had now entered the *Vale of the Hex-river*, a long narrow country, surrounded on all sides by ridges of mountains. The soil was here more arid than on the western side of the kloof, and some change in its botanical features began to be observable: large trees of *Lycium*, some ten feet high, indicated the difference of climate. The road along this vale, though level, is very sandy and toilsome. The passage of the kloof, and the very irregular rate at which we advanced, rendered it difficult to estimate correctly the length of this day's journey; but it could not be less than twenty-seven miles.

At eight o'clock in the evening, we unyoked at a farm-house called *Buffels-Kraal*, where the owner, a widow, whose name was *De Vos*, received us with much civility. Her house, which was the best I had seen since leaving Tulbagh, exhibited signs of affluence and plenty; and its inhabitants, who were probably all of her own family, appeared to be numerous.

I was here told, that the late earthquakes, even at this distance from Cape Town, had been felt, although but in a slight degree.

The parsonage at Tulbagh was the last dwelling in which I had passed the night: henceforward I was destined no more to sleep under a roof; my waggon was to be my shelter, and my only abode, a lodging always preferable to the house of a boor, especially now, since by the purchase of a second waggon, this one had been rendered more convenient. At my declining her offer of a bed-room, the good lady expressed surprise that the *Heer* should think his waggon better than the house.

6th. This dwelling was situated close under the range of mountains which bounds the northern side of the vale. The snow at this time lay on their rugged summits. Large umbrageous oaks, standing around the house, showed this farm to have been esta-

blished many years.   Some fine lemon-trees, at this time both in flower
and fruit, grew before the door.   It produces the two staple commodities of wine and tobacco, and a well-cultivated garden affords abundance of every useful fruit and vegetable.   It yields, also, large
quantities of pumkins, to secure which, a singular kind of storehouse
was formed among the branches of one of the large trees, with poles
and hurdles.   On these the fruit was heaped, and appeared to keep
very well, notwithstanding their being quite exposed to the weather.
Besides the business of farmer, that of waggon-maker was also carried
on ; and I took the opportunity of having some spare articles of iron-
work made here, as a reserve against future wants or accidents.

I now laid in my stock of brandy, flour, and biscuits ; and,
although I had already with me a large quantity of tobacco, I here
doubled my store, as the additional waggon enabled me to carry
more than was at first intended, and as it is a merchandise of which a
traveller in this part of the world can hardly take with him too much.
It was amusing to observe the alacrity with which my men assisted in
loading up the barrel of brandy, and the delight which brightened up
their countenances, when they saw the large stock of tobacco that
was to be taken with us.   At this moment they would have promised almost any thing I should have asked ; but still I dared not,
before experience had given them a confidence in their new master,
make them acquainted with the whole plan of my travels.

A fresh set of oxen and drivers, put in requisition by the Veld-
cornet of this subdivision, met us here punctually at the hour appointed, and we left Buffels Kraal at noon.

In this sheltered and enclosed valley, the weather was very
warm, and various symptoms of a different soil and climate became more observable.   Our road now abounded in trees of the
Cape Acacia*, the colonial name of which is *Doornboom* ('Thorn-
tree).   It is also called *Wittedoorn* (White-thorn), and *Karródoorn*

---

* *Acacia Capensis ;* of which a part of a branch, of the natural size, is represented at
the head of this chapter.

(Karro-thorn). The name of *Acacia* is correctly applicable to this tree, on account of its great affinity and resemblance to the *True Acacia* of the ancients, or gum-arabic tree of Egypt. It is very different from that which in England is commonly, but improperly, called Acacia. This was the first spot in which we met with it; but I was told by the Hottentots, that in the following part of our journey it would be one of the most frequent, and often the only tree we should see for several days. Its height here did not exceed twenty feet. Innumerable straight white thorns, from two to four inches long, cover every branch and twig; and the foliage is so fine and thin, as to afford a remarkable example of a tree furnished with abundance of leaves, being neither dense nor umbrageous. They generally grow in a sandy soil, on the banks of rivers, along the dry beds of periodical streams, or in hollow spots that receive water in the rainy season. It is certainly the most abundant and widely-disseminated tree of the extra-tropical part of Southern Africa.

The road being sandy, we moved but slowly onwards; but, when arrived at the termination of the Vale of the Hex-river, the oxen had to drag the waggons up a long and steep ascent, the only exit from the valley. This road having been made at public expense, a toll is collected from every waggon.

Galenia Africana, a small bush, growing in great abundance here, is a very common plant in hot, dry, karro-like places, and affects the same soil and situations as the Doornboom: a very pretty kind of *Cyphia* was observed twining round its branches. Different species of *Hermannia* and *Selago* grow by the road-side, together with a variety of plants not seen before, and of which I added to my list thirty-two.

We continued the whole day travelling over a level monotonous country, covered generally with the rhinoceros-bush. A little before dark, the drivers wished to *outspan* for the night; but, finding that no water was to be obtained, either for the cattle or for ourselves, I ordered them to push forward till we reached Pieter Jacobs's. This day's journey had been both long and fatiguing, especially for the oxen; but I judged it less distressing to urge them on for a few hours longer, than to rest in a country where they could get neither water nor pasture.

A very remarkable and material difference of character distinguishes the country, on the borders of which we now were, from that which lay behind us. To a certain distance from the sea-coast, the rainy season takes place in the winter months: but beyond that, the soil is watered only by the thunder-showers, which fall during the summer season: consequently, we were now entering upon a country where, at the present time of the year, water and pasture might be expected to be scarce.

Hitherto we had seen none of the large game, which I had understood to be so plentiful in the colony, that we should be enabled to obtain our daily supply of meat by hunting; but it was now said, that this would not be the case until we had crossed the Great Karro.

By moonlight we passed through a singular defile in a ridge of rocky hills. It was very narrow and stony; and the perpendicular wall-like sides which enclosed the road on either hand, favoured by the uncertain light of the moon, gave to the place a considerable degree of resemblance to a large street; and the sound of the wheels rattling over the rocky ground, as on a pavement, and reverberated from these walls, still further assisted the imagination. It is, therefore, not surprising that this defile should have obtained the name of *De Straat* (The Street). It is, perhaps, less than the eighth of a mile in length.

We continued travelling over a level, sandy, and open country; passing close by a lake called *Verkeerde Valley* (Contrary Lake). This is an extensive sheet of water, which, in the rainy season, has a constant outlet; but becomes stagnant during the rest of the year. It is said to owe its name to the circumstance of the rivulet, which issues from it, running in a direction contrary to the other streams of that part of the country. It abounds in water-fowl, chiefly ducks, geese, and coots.

At ten o'clock, after a journey of thirty miles, we arrived at *Pieter Jacobs's*. The family, not expecting us till the next day, had retired to bed: no one was stirring, except a Hottentot, whom the noise of the waggons awoke as they passed his hut.   He pointed out the place where we might unyoke, and assisted my men in their search after fire-wood.   The night having become very cold, a fire was doubly necessary, both for the purpose of warming ourselves, and of cooking our supper.

7th.   The early part of the morning was exceedingly chilling; and the thermometer was, probably, not many degrees above the freezing point; the snow, at the same time, lying on one of the neighbouring mountains.

As soon as the family were up, I delivered to the mistress of the house a letter, which her daughter at Piet Hugo's had requested me to take charge of, and which did me all the service of a letter of introduction.   The old lady and her husband received me with great cordiality and good-nature.   A cup of coffee and a slice of bread and butter were immediately handed to me by one of the daughters, of whom three were then living at home.   The father seemed a plain, honest farmer: the appearance of his dwelling indicated neither affluence nor comfort; yet the family looked contented and happy.

The situation of the house was bleak and exposed, and exhibited but little display of art or cultivation around it.   At the back, extended a wild flat, bounded by high rocky mountains.   One large room, having a mud floor, and a single glazed window, showing, by its broken panes, proofs of the scarcity of glass, constituted the principal part of the house.   At one end were the bed-rooms; and a door through the back wall, opened into the kitchen.   Hanging from the rafters of the thatched roof, were seen a heterogeneous assemblage of domestic utensils and stores.   The other end was filled by a very wide and deep fire-place, exactly resembling that of an English farm-house; and a large iron cauldron of boiling soap was standing over the fire.   A small window near the fire-place was, at this season, kept constantly closed with a wooden shutter, in order to keep out the cold wind, as it had neither sash nor glass.   Against the wall, under the glazed window, stood a small table, partly occupied by a little old-fashioned coffee-urn, an article in continual employ.

On each side of this table, two homely chairs were stationed, with their backs close to the wall: in these sat the master and mistress. A few chairs and benches, with the large family dining-table, were ranged in order round the room. , On a shelf lay a variety of articles, with a large Bible and a few other books.

A black slave-woman and a Hottentot girl, assisted in the domestic duties; while the more laborious work of the farm was performed by a man-slave and a few Hottentots. The daughters, three good-tempered young women, were under the tuition of an itinerant tutor, or *Meester*, as he was called, who had been for several months an inmate of the family. Although a Hollander by birth, he had passed the last twenty-nine years of his life in the colony; but in the younger part of it, had served in the Dutch and English navies. He was a very communicative, amusing, and, to a certain degree, intelligent, person; he could make himself understood both in English and in French; and, in point of learning and acquirements, appeared fully equal to the task of completing the education of a boor's family.

A number of schoolmasters of this description, and who are mostly Europeans, are dispersed every where through the country. In many instances, their qualifications would not enable them to get their living by the same occupation in their native country; but, considering the low salary they receive for their services, it cannot reasonably be expected that men of higher qualifications could be found to lead such a life. In the course of their profession, it may happen that they peregrinate in every district of the colony, as their usual stay at each house, is from six to twelve months; and, in this short time, must they engage to complete the education of their pupils in reading, writing, and arithmetic. They are not always paid in money, the scarcity of which, in the more remote districts, compels them to accept their remuneration in cattle; and thus, by degrees, some become possessed of large flocks and herds, with which, in the end, they often commence the business of farmer.

The *Meester* seemed desirous of recommending himself to my good opinion, by a display of all his learning at once. He entered into disputations on every topic with which he fancied himself to be acquainted; and, not to hurt his vanity, or lower him in the eyes of his scholars and employers, I sometimes confessed myself vanquished by his arguments, because, indeed, they were incomprehensible; and was rewarded for my submission by the complacency and good humour which he showed in return. The three sisters and the good old lady, listened with attention to all that was said, and whenever they gave an opinion, it was in favor of the *Heer*. At last, having exhausted the learned sciences, he began to prove his knowledge of the politer accomplishments, by introducing the subject of dancing. This art he offered to teach the young ladies; whereupon, immediately starting up, he proceeded, in a laughable attitude, to show them the five positions; and, happening to be correct in three of them, looked round with a happy satisfaction, to receive my approbation.

All these harmless vanities excited a great deal of good-humoured mirth, and the coldness and ceremoniousness of strangers very soon wore off. They insisted on my taking all my meals in the house, and omitted nothing in their power to convince me that I was heartily welcome to partake of their homely fare. This offer of hospitality was no empty complimentary pretension to friendship, such as, in more polished society, is too trite to deceive: it was the more sincere for being made under a knowledge of the probability of my remaining here several days; for they had received intelligence that the missionaries, whom I must have passed on the road during the night-time, were far behind, and not likely, from their slow rate of travelling, to come up with me for three or four days.

A boor, who had received orders to furnish the next *voorspans*, sent in the morning to enquire when they would be wanted; but, as I had now determined on proceeding with my own oxen, he was informed that no further services would be required.

A young farmer, living in the neighbourhood, who had heard of my being on my way to the countries beyond the *Gariep*, or *Groote rivier*, as it is called by the colonists, a country where he had spent all the first portion of his life, paid me a visit. IIis name was

Carel Krieger, nephew to the *Jacob Krieger* who unfortunately accompanied the expedition of Dr. Cowan, and son of a person of the same name, who was trampled to death by an elephant in the country of the Bushmen.

These two brothers, having trespassed against the laws, fled from the colony, and, for many years, led a wandering life among the tribes on either side of the Gariep. Their ingenuity, together with their courage, enabled them to procure a subsistence in the deserts, and, in some measure, to gain the good-will of the natives. When the colony fell the second time into the hands of the English, the surviving brother, by an act of amnesty, was permitted to return within the boundary, and was living on a small farm in the Roggeveld at the time when that expedition was set on foot. The knowledge of the country, and the experience which he had gained during his extensive wanderings among the savages, occasioned his being selected, as peculiarly fitted for remedying any want of experience in the others; and he was tempted to join their party, fated never to return.

This young man spoke with evident pleasure of the different countries I was to pass through; and so interwoven with his feelings, was the predilection he had imbibed for the mode of life of his early youth, that he expressed the strongest desire to accompany me, and seemed to regret that he had just purchased a farm. The truth, however, appeared to be, that he was on the point of being married. He still recollected something of the *Sichuána* and *Kóraqua* languages: the former of which he called *Briqua*, and wrote down about twenty words.

The farm of Pieter Jacobs, being employed only for the rearing of cattle, was visited at this time by a *slagter's knegt* (butcher's man), for the purpose of purchasing a large number of sheep. A slagter's knegt is a person commissioned by a butcher in Cape Town to travel into the grazing districts, and buy up the number of sheep or oxen he may require; for which the man pays the grazier, not in money, but in small notes of hand, called *Slagter's brief*, previously signed by his employer, and the validity of which is certified at the Fiscal's office. These are considered as good as cash, into which they are convertible whenever the grazier takes them to town; or they are sometimes negotiated in payment with his neighbours.

Speelman brought home a *Steenbok* (Stone-buck *) he had shot on the rocky plain under the mountains. This is a small antelope, of nearly the same size as the *Duyker* †, but of a lighter and reddish color, having the under part of the body white; a white spot under each eye, and a small mark of the same color on the chin; but there is not, as in the Duyker, any tuft of hair between the ears.

8th. Early this morning the thermometer was very few degrees above the freezing point; and, even at noon, it rose no higher than 52° (8·8 R.; 11·1 C.). The weather, although cold, was invigorating; but finding it too chilly for sitting in the waggon, I took my seat by the fire-side, in the house, where the sight of some of my instruments afforded amusement to the family, and excited considerable curiosity to know their uses. The *Meester*, ready on all occasions to communicate his knowledge, gave them so extraordinary an explanation of the nature and properties of the magnetic needle, that I was no less surprised at it than they were; but my subsequent comments (I was almost sorry at having made them) on the schoolmaster's doctrine, very much reduced their wondering and his vanity; and, I was happy to find, without at all hurting his feelings.

In the evening, as a compliment to the Englishman, he displayed his vocal powers, in singing " *God save the King;*" and his pupils, well acquainted with the air, sometimes joined in chorus, with Dutch words, but of a different import.

9th. Having been shown, at this house, some *cubic pyrites of iron*, got from the neighbouring mountains, I took a walk in the afternoon to the spot, having one of Jacobs's Hottentots as a guide. The mountain is composed of a red, compact sand-stone, in which these cubes are closely embedded. ‡ They are scattered in the stony

---

* *Antilope rupestris.*   † Described at page 187.

‡ As may be seen by the following *engraving*, which represents a specimen of the rock, and the separate cubes, of the natural size. The two cubes on the left show the dimensions of the largest and of the smallest which I met with; and the two on the right may give an idea of the compound cubes.

matrix, at various distances, without any order, and, when first taken out, were of a black hue; but after a few days' exposure to the air, became covered with a bright-red powdery rust. They burn with a blue flame, are very light, and within, porous, like slag; and, on being broken, some of them exhibit a yellow, shining, metallic appearance. Sometimes the cubes are simple, and sometimes compounded of as many as five, growing into each other at various angles. Their sides are slightly striated; the *striæ* of each face being parallel to themselves, but opposite in direction to those of all the adjoining faces.

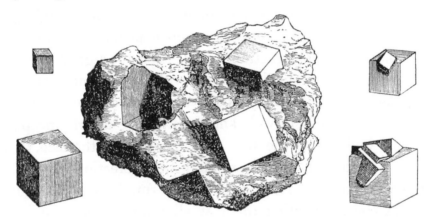

The mountains, generally, may be considered as the repository of the more interesting vegetable productions of the colony; and in this day's excursion I gathered forty-five species, most of which were new to me. * The beautiful *Erica monsoniana* may here be seen growing to the height of six feet, with long straggling branches, covered with paper-white flowers. *Protea nana*, and many other proteaceous plants, inhabit the mountains; and on the plain below, in moist places, grow *Protea glaucophylla* and *repens*.

The *Ostrich*, the largest bird known to man, sometimes frequents this vicinity; and, from the house, I had this morning the pleasure

---

* These, together with all that had been collected since my departure from Tulbagh, were lost; as will be explained in the note appended to the 3d of August following.

of discovering a pair at a distance, running across the plain. With the telescope they could be seen very distinctly; and being the first I had met with in a wild state, I could not but watch, with the greatest gratification, this interesting sight. The bushes intercepted the view of their long legs; but their black bodies were plainly to be seen; and those beautiful plumes, destined, possibly, hereafter to decorate the head of some elegant beauty, and wave in the drawing-room, were now fluttering in the wind, and rudely hurrying over the desert. Their long necks, and comparatively small heads, reared high above the shrubs, like two tall stakes, remained the last in view; but their hasty long strides soon carried them out of sight.

As these birds inhabit only large open plains, and their heads, elevated above every obstruction, enable them, at a great distance, to discover man, from whom they escape with the swiftness of a horse, it is not an easy affair to approach them unperceived, or to *hunt* them down; for, as it is well known, they are utterly incapable of raising their bodies into the air. It is fortunate for the race, that this difficulty of approach affords some little protection against their restless enemy, man. The boors have formerly been so indefatig-able in this chace, shooting them at all times of the year, without regard to the season of breeding and rearing their young, that there are but few now to be found in the inhabited parts of the colony. If a law were enacted to prohibit their eggs from being taken or de-stroyed, and to prevent the hunting of them during that season, or at any other time than that in which their plumes are in per-fection, the exportation of their feathers might become a trade of much more importance than it is likely ever to be, without some such regulations.

11*th.* By observations of the meridional altitude of the sun, both this and the preceding day, I computed the latitude of *Pieter Jacobs's* to be 33° 24′ 2′ south. Notwithstanding the greatest care, it is not impossible that, into some of these computations, a mistake might happen, through inadvertence, to find its way; and therefore, with the view of giving to others an opportunity of verifying my calcu-lations, or of correcting my errors, I shall, throughout this journal, give, as below *, the actual observations on which they are founded. These observations must be understood as cleared only of the error of the instrument; and further, divided by 2, on account of the real angle of altitude being doubled by reflection from the artificial horizon. The corrections for parallax, refraction, sun's semi-diameter, &c., are left to be made by the operator. The longitudes used in correcting the sun's declination, were nearly the same as those which are to be found in the " *Itinerary*" at the end of the volume; but these latter are to be preferred, as being the final result of course, distance, and latitude combined: yet, for the estimation of latitude, they will scarcely produce any material difference from the numbers here given.

A woman seated astride on horseback was to me, as yet, an unusual sight: a female visitor, the wife of one of their neighbours, rode in this manner up to the door, alighted with masculine agility, and, after an hour's visit, mounted her steed and trotted off, without the least sign of timidity. This, I found, was the customary mode of sitting, whenever women, in these distant parts of the country, ride on horseback; which, however, is not very often.

12th. One of the sheep bought at Tulbagh, dropped a lamb this morning; an increase of stock by no means advantageous to me, as there was no chance of either surviving the fatigue of travelling. It was, therefore, exchanged for one of the wethers of Jacobs's flock.

The missionaries remained behind so much longer than was expected, that I began to fear some accident had been the cause of the delay; but in the forenoon their three waggons were descried coming on, and, soon after, they unyoked at the distance of a mile from the house. Mr. Anderson came immediately to give notice of his arrival, and informed me that the pole of his waggon had been broken, and that one of the other waggons had been overturned, but

---

* 11th July, 1811, at Pieter Jacobs's, the observed meridional altitude of the sun's centre was 34° 23′ 26″.

without any other inconvenience than the trouble and delay occasioned by having to rectify its contents. We had appointed the
Karró Poort as the place of rendezvous for to-morrow, intending to
remain there till the next day, to prepare for crossing the Karro
desert.

This being nearly the last place where I could have any opportunity of replenishing my stores, I filled up two of the empty water-
casks with wine, one of my wine-casks having entirely leaked out;
and laid in a stock of potatoes, onions, and dried pears. These,
called the sugar-pear, were of a middling size and very sweet taste;
the manner of preserving which, consisted in merely drying them,
whole and unpeeled, in the sun, and afterwards pressing them flat:
by which simple process they keep in perfection for more than a
twelvemonth, as I afterwards learnt by experience; and therefore can
recommend them as a valuable addition to the stores of a traveller.
The wine made here was very poor and thin, the soil and situation
not being congenial to grapes; but the price of it was certainly in
proportion, for eleven gallons cost no more than four rix-dollars
and a half, equal, at that time, to thirteen shillings and sixpence.

All my Hottentots, excepting Philip, became so idle during our
stay here, that the little work they had to do, was left undone: and
therefore, for the purpose of letting them know what kind of punishment they had to expect for neglect or disobedience, I this day
stopped their rations of brandy and tobacco, and had the pleasure of
finding this privation a powerful stimulus to exertion.

13*th.*   In settling the account with our host for the stores, and
the food with which he had supplied my men, he would not be persuaded to accept any thing in consideration of the meals I had myself taken at his house. His good lady, unknown to me, put into
my waggon a duck ready-roasted, and various other eatables; as if
not satisfied that their hospitality was complete, without my carrying away with me some proofs of it. Our taking leave was like the
parting of old friends: they gave their blessing for my protection

from the dangers of the journey, and for a safe return; and seemed
to regret so soon losing their English acquaintance.

At an hour before noon, I finally quitted their friendly cottage.
After travelling four hours over an uncultivated country, without
seeing a dwelling of any kind, we arrived at the southern entrance of
the *Karró Poort* (or Karró Pass) *, where we unyoked the oxen, and
took up our station under the shelter of two large bushy trees of
Karrée-hout (Karree-wood) †, near a small stream of water.

On the banks of this rivulet grow some large trees of the same
kind, forming, by the peculiar softness of their foliage, very picturesque ornaments to the landscape. The soil was clothed with
low bushes of *Atriplex albicans* and *Galenia Africana*. The latter
produces a remarkable effect on the legs of cattle that graze amongst
it, by staining them of a green color. All our oxen, but more particularly the white ones, exhibited this singular appearance.

A range of mountains, of moderate height, separates the great
Karro from the inhabited parts of the colony, lying to the southward. Another range, of much greater elevation, bounds it on the
northern side; and in this the Pass of the Roggeveld-mountain is
situated. That division lying nearest to the Roggeveld, is distinguished as the *Roggeveld Karro*, and is partly inhabited, during four
or five months in the winter season, by the boors of that country,
who then remove, with their families and cattle, to certain temporary huts, called *Leg-plaats* (which may be translated *Cattle-place*).
From these they remove back again to the Roggeveld at the end of
October. In like manner, the other division is denominated the
Bokkeveld Karro. The *Karro Pass* conducts the traveller, by a
winding defile, through the range of *Witteberg*, or the *Wittebergen*
(White Mountains), and ushers him into the *Great Karro*. The
strata of the mountains here, on each side, are inclined in opposite
positions, and curiously curved in undulating lines. The word *Karró*
belongs to the Hottentot language, and signifies *dry*, or *arid*.

---

* This scene is represented by the *engraving* at the end of the chapter.
† *Rhus viminale;* a species which I now observed to be dioicous.

Before sunset, the two missionaries, with their families, joined us; but the great body of our caravan was not yet assembled: a considerable number of the Klaarwater Hottentots, with their waggons, were waiting for us on the borders of the colony; and, besides these, we expected the accession of others in the course of our journey through the Roggeveld.

14*th.* This morning was misty; a state of weather not very frequently occurring. The whole of the forenoon was exceedingly cold and chilly; and my fingers were so much benumbed, that I found some difficulty in writing.

In order to give our oxen more time for grazing, we remained here till sunset. In the mean time I took a stroll into the Pass, and climbed up the rocks on our right, to examine the productions of the mountains; of which, notwithstanding the earth was excessively dry and parched, there was a great variety. Out of these I selected as many as thirty plants not collected before. * Among these rocks, the *Pelargonium renifolium* was found, growing to the height of two feet; and a frutescent *Othonna*, four feet high †, enlivened the rugged declivity with its large yellow flowers.

The list of *genera* here given may serve to show the botanical character of this spot, as contrasted with the country in the following part of the journey northward. Beyond this, a very remarkable change takes place in its vegetable productions. Four of the strongest and most characteristic features of Cape botany, the *Ericæ,* the *Diosmæ,* and the *Proteaceous* and *Restiaceous* tribes, entirely disappear; nor did I meet with any of them again till two years after-

---

* *Sisymbrium*	*Phylica*	*Atriplex*
Adiantum, and 2 other ferns	*Mahernia,* 2 species	*Erica*
Asparagus, 2 species	*Gnaphalium*	*Malva*
Eriocephalus, 2 species	*Diosma*	*Cliffortia*
Lobelia	*Indigofera*	*Othonna,* 4 species
Aster, 2 species	*Hebenstreitia*	*Oxalis*
Osteospermum	*Psoralea*	*Restiaceæ,* &c.
Pelargonium		
† *Cat. Geog.* 1198.		

wards, when I re-entered the same botanical parallel at *Kommedakka* and *Zwartwater Poort*, lying in the same latitude as the *Karro Pass*, but at six degrees of longitude more to the eastward. The *Heath* mentioned in this list was, I believe, *Erica Plukenetii*. This elegant tribe had attended me the whole way from Cape Town, till now that I was arrived at the very door of the desert; beyond which the scorching heat rendered it impossible for them to exist: and it seemed as if this handsome species had accompanied me till the last moment, to take a long farewell in the name of the whole family.

CHAPTER XI.

JOURNEY OVER THE KARRO.

As soon as the oxen were yoked, we immediately began to enter the Pass. At about midway, we found a party with three waggons at *outspan*, which proved to be the same *Frans Van der Merwe*, of whom my two teams of oxen were bought. We halted a minute, to enquire if we might still expect to find water enough in the Karro for our cattle, and were rejoiced at hearing that this indispensable requisite was not quite dried up. He had been residing at his cattle-station in the Karro during the season of the rains, and was now removing, with all his family, to his dwelling in the Bokkeveld.

The number of *Karrée-trees* growing along the course of the rivulet, give a more pleasing appearance to the Pass. Though the road was generally level, this defile occupied us nearly an hour before we cleared the mountains. The *Bokkeveld-Karró* then opened upon us, and we beheld an immense plain, unbroken by hill or eminence, stretching before us in every direction, as far as the eye could discern. (See the above *Vignette*). Along the northern and eastern horizon, is seen a range of distant blue mountains, probably those of the *Roggeveld* (Rye-land).

Our road was in some parts sandy, and in others stony. We continued travelling long after it became dark; but the dry atmosphere of the Karro was so exceedingly clear from vapors, that an infinite multitude of sparkling stars enabled us easily to see our way, till we reached the *Kleine Doorn* (Little Thorn) river, where we halted for the night. Several graziers were at this time stationed here, with their waggons, cattle, and families.

15th. On the next morning they paid us a visit; and if they derived any news or information from us, it was more than we did from them; so very uninformed, or so little communicative, did this party seem to be. Yet, in these wilds, but little used to converse with strangers, it is possible that their taciturnity might be the effect rather of timidity than of natural dullness.

The *Doorn-rivier* takes its name from the trees of *Doorn-boom* that grow on its banks: a name equally applicable to every other river in the Karro, and, indeed, to the greatest number of the rivers, not only in the colony, but in the whole of Southern Africa, as far as I have been. All the rivers crossed in the following part of my journey, to its farthest extent northward, take a westerly course, and discharge their waters into the Southern Atlantic Ocean.

In the afternoon we departed from *Little Thorn-river*, having warm and exceedingly agreeable weather. The excellence of the roads, in many parts of these plains, cannot be surpassed: a clayey soil, washed level and smooth by frequent thunder-showers, and afterwards hardened and baked by the heat of the sun, forms a strong floor, on which the wheels of a waggon leave little or no impression; and on which eight oxen are found to be a sufficient team. These African roads are, however, nothing more than the space cleared from shrubs and plants, by the passing and repassing of waggons. Those of the Karro are mostly worn a few inches below the general surface of the plain. In one part of this day's journey, the soil was a very deep, loose, yellow sand, in which we were much annoyed by dust.

I now gathered, for the first time, specimens of a very extraordinary grass. * Its panicle of flowers formed a bunch of

---

* *Poa spinosa.*

E E 2

strong, sharp thorns, so rigid and pungent, that no animal could graze near it; nor would the naked-legged Hottentots venture to walk amongst it, although it was not more than a foot and a half high.

My men pointed out to me a small shrub *, the flowers of which they use as a dye for giving a yellow color to the leather of their preparing. By experiment, I found that the *corollæ* of the dried flowers, being infused in a small quantity of warm water, gave out very readily a strong color, approaching to what is called Raw Terra di Sienna, but brighter. Being a vegetable color, it possesses the advantage of flowing freely from the pencil or pen, and might be used as a very pleasing yellow ink. Some trials which I then made, have remained ten years, without fading or losing any of their original brightness. A permanent vegetable color of this quality would, perhaps, be useful in the arts; and the collection of it might be a source of advantage, the more profitable, as being derived from land at present useless to man. Some other plants of the same natural order, which I afterwards met with, afford a dye equally good.

A great variety of succulent plants grow in every part of the Karro; and I exceedingly regret that I had neither opportunity for preserving them, nor time for making drawings. An object very desirable for botany, would be obtained, if a good draughtsman were to pass three or four years in travelling about the Cape colony, with the sole view of drawing, on their native spot, all those plants (excepting such as have already been figured and published) which, from their fleshy nature or delicate substance, cannot well be preserved in an herbarium. He would, by doing this, accomplish a work of great utility, and one which, from the singular forms, or the delicate and beautiful flowers of the objects, could not fail to interest every lover of nature. No one, who has not examined this country, can form any correct idea of the immense number and variety of plants of the succulent tribe, that are dis-

* Catal. Geogr. No. 1208. *Ex ordine Thymelearum.*

persed in every district, and in all situations; but more especially in the hot arid plains which occupy so large a portion of this territory. Of these it may be asserted, that by much the smaller number are known in Europe.

At half-past nine at night, we arrived at the *Groote Doorn-rivier* (Great Thorn-river), after travelling twenty miles, which is accounted a full day's work for oxen. *

16*th.*   Day-light this morning showed us that we had taken up our station near the dry bed of a river, in a very picturesque sheltered spot, surrounded by Acacia-trees (*Doornboom*) twenty feet in height. The soil here is entirely sand.

In the midst of the unvaried and treeless landscape of the Karro, the clumps of Thorn-trees, which occur chiefly by the rivers, were as grateful to the traveller as the *Oases* in the sandy desert. Their light airy foliage gave a cheerfulness to the scene; while the cooing of turtle-doves †, in the heart of an uninhabited waste, was a sound that, being unexpected, was the more soothing and fascinating. I sat on the dry bank for a long time, listening with delight to their gentle, plaintive note. For the sake of a little water, which still remained in a small puddle in the bed of the river, this place was frequented by a few birds; among which were, the *Musch-vogel*

---

* The plants found in this day's journey, were —

Poa spinosa	*Eriocephalus*
Viscum Capense : var. Cat. Geog. 1207.	*Pteronia*
Aphyteïa hydnora ‡	*Chrysocoma*
Androcymbium volutare. B. C. G. 1215.	*Loranthus*
So named from its two leaves being	*Lapeyrousia*
curled back in the manner of the *vo-*	*Arctotis*
lutes in the capital of the Ionic column.	*Crassula*
	Sesamum, &c.

† *Columba risoria.* Lin. Sys. Nat.

‡ *Aphyteïa multiceps,* B., is a new species, found in the more western parts of this Karro, and of which I received a specimen from my friend Hesse, to whom it had been sent from the district of *Clanwilliam* or the *Elephant's River.* It is easily distinguished, by a subterraneous stem, about two inches long, clothed with a few large scales, as in all radical parasitic plants, and producing, in a close head, several flowers, (in my specimen, five,) which had not the appearance of being succeeded by a seed-vessel of a magnitude at all proportionable to that of *A. Hydnora.*

(Sparrow) *, a bird of about the size of the common sparrow, having red feet, a long tail, and a cinereous brown-coloured plumage; the *Capoc-vogel* (Cotton-bird) †, so called on account of its curious bottle-shaped nest, built of the cotton-like down of certain plants; its manners and singing very much resemble those of the common wren : and a kind of finch ‡, of a ferrugineous brown color, having a white collar and black head.

One of the missionaries' oxen, which was much worn out by fatigue and sickness, died at this place. Its flesh, not being considered eatable, was left on the spot where it fell, as food for the crows and vultures; a food with which they are too often supplied by the passage of this dreary Karro, where, from want of water and pasturage, many an ox has fallen a sacrifice in the service of man.

The Hottentots of our party soon took off the hide, which they cut in small pieces, for the purpose of making *velschoen* § (hide-shoes), as every man is his own shoemaker. With this view, these pieces, after their animal juices have been allowed to dry out, are greased, and beaten or hammered, till half tawed, or reduced nearly to the state of leather. The hide of an ox being too thick for any other part than the sole, they use for the upper-leathers the skin of goats, or any other kind equally pliable. They are sewed together with thread made of the sinews ‖, taken from each side of the back-bone of sheep or goats, in such a manner that the stitches are all on the inside, and which, passing but half through the sole, never wear out or break away. There is another mode of making the *hide-shoe*, much more simple, as consisting of a single piece, and formed without any

---

* Perhaps *Muts-vogel* (Cap-bird), from its crest; or, possibly, *Muis-vogel* (Mouse-bird). *Colius erythropus* of Linnæus; *Le Coliou à dos blanc* of that beautiful work by *Le Vaillant,* " *L'Histoire Naturelle des Oiseaux d'Afrique,*" planche 257.

The genus *Colius* appears, in a Natural arrangement, to have some affinity with the *Corythaïx* of Illiger; *Cuculus Persa* of Linnæus.

† *Malurus* of Cuv.; *Motacilla macroura,* Linn. Syst. Nat. ed. Gmel. vol. i. p. 953.; *Le Capocier,* Le Vaill. *Ois. d'Afr.* pl. 130.

‡ *Fringilla ; Loxia,* Linn.

§ Or, as some pronounce it, *Veld-schoen* (Country-shoes).

‖ The *Longissimus dorsi,* and the *Spinalis dorsi.*

sewing: it is, by applying to the foot a piece of fresh hide with the hairy side outwards, and of such a shape as will just wrap round and enclose it.   All along the edge, excepting that part which turns up behind the heel, a number of small holes are made, to receive a narrow thong of leather, by which the hide is drawn tight round the foot, where it must remain till dried sufficiently to retain its form. It is a great objection to hide-shoes, that wet softens them so much, that, in that state, they can scarcely be kept on the feet; and that they become extremely hard and stubborn in dry weather, when the soles are often rendered by use so slippery, as to put the wearer in continual danger of falling.   Hide-shoes are generally worn by the Hottentots; but many of the boors seldom wear any others.

Our oxen having nearly exhausted all the water, leaving only a few muddy draughts for those who might happen to come after us, we resumed our journey in the afternoon, and, the road being very good, travelled at a brisk rate for six hours, without halting.   Each waggon, agreeably to a rule we established, took its turn each day in leading the van, in order that every driver might bear a share in the care and attention required in driving the foremost team, which would be continually swerving from the track, unless restrained by the *ox-leader*.   All the other teams gave scarcely any trouble in guiding them, as each one followed instinctively in the footsteps of the preceding.

The *Bokkeveld Karro* is covered chiefly with various species of Fig-marigolds, of which a shrubby thorny kind *, with purple flowers, was the most abundant, and the most widely diffused.   About the end of the rainy season, the Karro is said to assume a verdant hue, from the vast number of small plants which then make their transitory appearance above ground.

At such times the rivers are filled with water, even enough, sometimes, to stop the passage of waggons.   But all these streams are periodical, and, like the vegetable clothing of the country through

---

* *Mesembryanthemum spinosum*, Linn.

which they flow, totally disappear during a great part of the year, and are then only to be traced by their empty beds. A river of this nature was crossed in this day's journey, almost without our being aware of it. A broad hollow marked the place where some of our Hottentots had, in a former journey, found a large impassable stream, well known to the colonists of this district, who distinguish it by the name of the *Groote-rivier* (Great-river), and consider it as the line of demarcation between the Bokkeveld Karro and the Roggeveld Karro. This must not be confounded with the Gariep, or Orange-river, which they also, and with far greater propriety, call the Great-river.

The *Hottentot women* belonging to our party had marched gaily on for a great part of the day, talking with each other nearly the whole way, and giving to Speelman's wife an account of their village of Klaarwater. They were at last exceedingly fatigued, and were permitted to ride in the waggons after sunset. One of them, the missionary's cook, whose name was *Tryn*, or *Katryn*, was very large and protuberant behind; a peculiarity of shape often to be found among Hottentot women, though seldom before they have reached the middle age of life. The ridiculous appearance she had when walking, often made me smile, at the same time that it attracted no particular notice from the rest of the party, to all of whom the frequency of its occurrence had rendered it indifferent. *

---

* The exhibition of a woman of this description, in the principal countries of Europe, has made the subject well known to all those who are curious in such matters; and I readily take advantage of that circumstance, to excuse myself from further digression. But I ought not to allow this occasion to pass by, without endeavouring to correct some erroneous notions, which the debates of both the learned, and the unlearned, have equally contributed to render current. It is not a fact, that the whole of the Hottentot race are thus formed; neither is there any particular tribe to which this *steütopyga*, as it may be called, is peculiar: nor is it more common to the Bushman (Bosjesman) tribe, than to other Hottentots. It will not greatly mislead, if our idea of its frequency be formed by comparing it with the corpulency of individuals among European nations. It is true, that the Hottentot race affords numerous examples of it; while, on the other hand, I do

At nine o'clock at night we reached the foot of a mountain called the *Hangklip* (Hanging-rock), where we released the oxen from the yoke, and were ourselves glad to rest for the night.   While some were busy in the ceremony of unyoking, others went out in search of fire-wood; which, on arriving at a halting-place, is the very first thing a Hottentot sets himself about.   For this work there is no necessity for the master to give any orders: in this they never forget to perform their duty.   In winter or in summer, a fire seems to be to them equally needful: they cannot sit without it.

The Hottentots assembled in two or three parties round as many blazing fires, now assumed a busy look, each intent on broiling his own steak.   No sooner was it done, or nearly so, than, seizing it in his hand, he began and finished his meal, without seeming much to feel the want of fork, or plate, or table.   The duty of the knife was most frequently performed by his teeth; and his bare legs, arms, and feet supplied the place of a napkin; in which last ceremony, he seemed particularly anxious that no grease might be lost.   This custom, dirty as it must appear, can be defended by a Hottentot with reasonable arguments; for experience has taught this race of people, as it has others in different quarters of the globe, that to anoint or grease their bodies, is the most easy and effectual mode of preserving their skin from the unpleasant and painful effects of a scorching sun.

These fire-light scenes have always a picturesque appearance*; and the oxen, lying by the waggons, increased the social character of the assembly; while the watchful dogs, continually moving about, gave us a security and confidence that no danger would approach us in the night, without being observed in time.   We had hitherto slept unmolested by beasts of prey; and though there was no apprehension of falling in with many, till we approached the borders of the colony, yet it was deemed a proper and prudent precaution, to

---

not recollect to have seen any very remarkable instance of it in the other African tribes which I visited in this journey.

   * Compare with the *Vignette* at page 172 of this volume.

hold ourselves on our guard, and keep watch, that the oxen strayed not too far from our fires. My little terrier lay every night in the waggon, at my feet; a faithful sentinel, under whose care I slept without fear. It was generally midnight before I had finished writing down the various observations, and disposed of the collections of the day.

My health and strength improved daily by the exercise of travelling; and the novelty and interest of the country, and its productions, increasing as we advanced, inspired me with a high degree of alacrity, and surprisingly raised the spirits. My mind glowed with the sanguine expectation of succeeding in all my plans. I began to lose sight of the Cape of Good Hope, and to turn my view forward, often imagining myself already arrived at the termination of my long and laborious journey. These delightful pictures of fancy, which were but dreams by day, frequently became also dreams by night; and the agreeable impressions of objects, on my waking senses, continued to play before me in my sleep.

17*th.* Between the Karro Poort and the Hangklip, not a hill intervenes; but hence, through the Roggeveld Karro, the road is interspersed with elevations and low mountains; and it is only here and there that it wears the appearance of a plain, such as the Bokkeveld Karro. Other large divisions of this Karro are, however, as I was informed, perfectly level.

Immediately after breakfast, I set out on foot, about an hour before the waggons, to explore the ridge of a rocky hill, over which the road passes. Hence the prospect was most extensive; bounded only by the far-distant mountains of the Bokkeveld, softened nearly into blue vapor. The Great *Karro*, stretched out before me, presented, at this distance, no visible object to break the evenness of the plain, or relieve the eye. The rivers and their Thorn-trees, were lost in the vast extent, and were not to be distinguished as a feature in the landscape. The road we had travelled might be traced for a few miles, in an undulating line across the desert, till it gradually lessened and vanished away. The Hangklip, in the second distance, constituted the only object; and, by its projecting and overhanging crag, naturally gave a name to a spot where nothing else presents itself, that could suggest an appellation. In these solitary wilds, no moving being was to be seen, no sound to be heard. Inclining my view to the foot of the hill upon which I was standing, I contemplated our waggons with a species of satisfaction quite peculiar to our circumstances. It was a busy scene; a little society within itself, in every movement of which I was interested: every individual, and every animal composing it, seemed more warmly to participate in my good-will the farther we removed from the rest of the civilized world.

For the purpose of recalling these impressions to mind, when the lapse of future years, and the presence of other scenes, should increase the pleasures of memory, I made a drawing of the view before me; and, as a further memento, collected three new and curious plants *; of which, one was never met with in any other part of the country.

By the time these observations were finished, the waggons had ascended the hill. We soon descended on the other side, and proceeded for a couple of miles over a Karro producing, at this season, not a single flower to enliven the arid soil. After this, nothing

---

* *Aptósimum indivisum*, B. Catal. Geogr. 1217. Folia longissimè petiolantia † pubescentia (sæpè nuda) ovata acuta mucronata, glomerata in caule brevissimâ vix divisâ. Flores sessiles, corollis purpureis, fauce nigro-maculata.

Nomen generis derivatur ab α *privativum* et ϖlώσιμος *caducus*, ob capsulas post seminum delapsionem diù persistentes. Genus hocce in systemate naturali *Caprariæ* proximum est.

Cotyledon parvula, B. Catal. Geogr. 1218. Planta 6—9—pollicaris, erecta. Folia crassa ovalia compressiuscula. Panicula dichotomè ramosa. Pedunculi erecti longissimi capillares.

Euphorbia tenax, B. Catal. Geogr. 1219. Suffruticosa, inermis, glabra, ramosa, aphylla, sub-bipedalis. Rami teretes, virides, vix lactescentes. Ramuli oppositi. Inflorescentia paniculata.

Euphorbia Mauritanica, also, was here a common plant, growing out of the dry rocky soil; and was distinguishable, even at some distance, by its pleasing light-green color.

† Folium *petiolans*, est cujus pagina sensim contrahitur in petiolum. Folium *petiolatum* dicitur, cum petiolus abruptè in basi transversâ paginæ inseritur. — Sic, germen *stylans* et *stylatum*: flores *pedunculantes* et *pedunculati;* cum aliis hujusmodi verbis.

more of the Bokkeveld Karro was seen, the hills intercepting it from our sight.

We travelled no more than four miles and a half this day; but unyoked at *Ongeluks river* (Misfortune river), where the land begins to be hilly. This river is said to have received its name from the circumstance of a boor having formerly been torn to pieces by a lion. I had also. some occasion to call it Misfortune river; for here, the jolting of the waggon broke a pocket compass: a loss which would have been a serious one, had I not provided against such an accident, by having more than one.

The river was quite dry, excepting two or three puddles of bad water. We took up our station in the bed of it, where an abundance of Karro-thorns and large Karree-trees afforded us shelter from a violent south-easterly wind, which came on in the afternoon. We had scarcely released the oxen from the yoke, when we were visited by a boor, lying here with his flocks. We accompanied him to a miserable hut close by, to purchase some sheep. His only food was mutton, without bread, or any kind of vegetables. His sheep were numerous and thriving, though they fed on nothing but bushes: of large cattle, he had none, as the land of the Karro and the Roggeveld does not produce the grassy pasture proper for cows and oxen. Our visitor's place in the scale of civilization, would be nearly at the bottom, if even it should not be below zero: his mental powers appeared to have lowered themselves down to a level with those cattle which were the only concern of his thoughts. He seemed to possess a mere animal existence: he could eat meat, drink a dram, smoke a pipe, spit, and practise some other disgusting vulgarities; which last enjoyments he indulged in without ceremony, and almost without cessation. He seldom spoke, because he had nothing to say; while a lifeless eye betrayed the vacancy of his mind. He was, however, invited to the waggons during our stay, and treated civilly.

A young boor on horseback, having with him two other horses, which he led by a halter, to serve him as relays during his journey to some distant part of the colony, was passing by; but, seeing us, he approached and dismounted; saluted us with " *Dag!*" and gave his hand to each of us in turn, in a cold and unmeaning manner, by merely touching palms.   One might have expected that he would have had a long chat with his brother boor; but he, at that time, not thinking of any thing to say, they stood insensibly looking at each other for about five minutes, without exchanging a single word. The stranger, whom no one seemed to know, then repeated his ' *Dag!*' which we all in like manner returned, mounted his horse, and proceeded on his way.

This ceremony of passing strangers halting to salute each other, has long been a custom, although at present an expiring one, among those colonists who dwell in the more remote corners of the country.   Rarely visiting or visited, they think that a *Christenmensch* (a Christian), so they term all white men, should never be passed without salutation.   This practice doubtlessly took its rise, originally, from that pleasure which the first settlers must have felt on meeting a white man in these distant places of their banishment from the world; a meeting which, in those days, could have been a circumstance only of rare occurrence.   As population encreases, this sentiment wears out, and with it the customs derived from it; no longer the token of that neighbourly and mutual good-will which it formerly implied.

In the evening, the chilliness of the air rendered the warmth of a fire very acceptable.   Abundance of dead and half-decayed stems of the Karro-thorn lay every where scattered along the banks, and enabled us to illuminate our retreat with a constant blaze.   We assembled round it like one large family; and the presence of the missionaries' wives and children, completed the resemblance of a domestic fireside.   Our elegant friend joined the party at coffee-time, and favoured us with a further display of his accomplishments.

18*th.*   Early this morning, with my gun, I left the waggons to go in search of some beautiful birds, which I had observed in the Acacia-woods along the river, fluttering about the flowers of a kind of *Salvia* (Sage), from which, with its long, slender, curved bill, it extracted the honey without settling.   They proved

to be the same kind of *Suiker-vogel* (Sugar-bird) * which I had seen
in the vicinity of Cape Town. Their elegance and beauty, added
to their soft, delicate, warbling notes, engaged my admiration and
attention for a long time; and it was indeed with reluctance that I
permitted my desire of having this bird in my collection, to overcome my natural feelings, and induce me to kill it. With much less
hesitation, I plucked some of the flowers from which they had been
sipping: it was the most showy plant at this time in bloom. I
collected a few others †; but it was not now the *bloemtyd*, as the
boors express it, the flower-season, here.

The rains, contrary to our expectations, had not yet fallen; and,
on that account, we found, wherever we came, only dry channels instead of rivers. This unlooked-for drought had already produced a
melancholy, and a too visible, effect on our oxen. Lean and weary,
they were not in a state for crossing the Bushman country; and
it was intended to have halted at this place for two or three days, to
recruit their strength; but in this plan we were disappointed.

The scarcity of pasture and water, determined us to remove to a
place about three miles further, pointed out on the map by the words
Sugar-bird Station, where our spitting visitor assured us there was
plenty of both. Here we were again disappointed: nothing was to
be found but the dry bed of a rivulet, and a parched country all
around, worse even than at the last station.

No one doubted that the boor had intentionally given us a false
account, in order to get rid of us, that our cattle might not deprive
his flocks of their scanty herbage. It was, at the time, remarked by

---

* *Nectarinia chalybea; Certhia chalybea*, Linn. Syst. ed. Gmel. vol. i. p. 475. —
Le Sucrier à double collier, Le Vaill. *Ois. d'Afr.* tome vi. pl. 178.

† *Convolvulus*   *Hemimeris diffusa ?*
 Gnaphalium   *Heliophila chamæmelifolia*
 Cotula nudicaulis ?   *Festuca*
 Calendula amplexicaulis ? *Salvia*
 Cynoglossum hirsutum, Th. *Medeola asparagoïdes*, Linn.
 Hemimeris montana ?

our party, that this is an artifice very commonly practised by the farmers, who, too often, are desirous of appropriating to the use of their own herds, that which is the common property of all, or, speaking more correctly, of government.

This was an old deserted cattle-place, as appeared by the ruins of a miserable hut, where some of our people took up their quarters. After searching for an hour or two along the bed of the river, some water was at length discovered, at a great distance from the waggons; but as it was barely sufficient for our own drinking, and for the purposes of cooking, our unfortunate oxen were obliged still longer to endure a painful thirst.

Speelman and Philip, during our stay, were employed in making a step-frame for the little waggon, which the waggon-maker, in the hurry at Tulbagh, had omitted. For this work they cut down, without leave or ceremony, as much timber as they required; no one reprimanding them for trespass, or calling them to account. Such is the custom, as I was told, in this part of the colony, that whoever has occasion to appropriate any particular tree, need only put his mark upon it, and his neighbours will respect it as his property.

At Ongeluks river, we received information that the body of hostile *Caffres*, before mentioned*, had separated into four divisions, waiting to attack us, either at the Zak river, or in the *Karreebergen* (Karree-mountains), in the Bushman country; and that they had neither women nor children with them; a certain indication of the party being on some warlike or plundering expedition. In the evening, two of our Hottentots returned from a visit to some of their countrymen, who lived in a hut not far off, and brought a confirmation of the report, as far as regarded their numbers, their hostile intentions, and their lying in wait for us in the Karree-mountains. This intelligence created among all our party much weighty conversation, respecting the most prudent steps to be taken. Our

---

* At pages 64 and 185.

Hottentots, who were well acquainted with the nature of the country, and the habits of these savages, talked with each other very seriously and warmly on the subject, but were unable to come to any determination. Some of my fellow-travellers were exceedingly alarmed, and began to fear the worst; but one of them coincided in opinion with me, that we should not allow mere reports, perhaps greatly exaggerated, to deter us from going forward on our journey. At last, we all agreed to suspend our final decision till we had reached the Roggeveld.

After supper, the night being calm, and the sky serene, all the Hottentots were called together for *prayers*. They assembled around our fire, seating themselves orderly on the ground, and, with well-tuned voices, joined in an evening hymn, in which the missionaries and their wives took the lead. After this, a long extemporaneous prayer was said by one of the missionaries; and, as soon as this was finished, they retired to sleep round their respective fires.

To me, an assemblage of this kind, in the open air, and under such circumstances as the present, was a scene both novel and interesting; to which, the dark hour of night, and the wild loneliness of the spot, gave an effect that was legendary and romantic; and I could easily have thought it a caravan of pilgrims travelling to the Holy Land. But the pleasing spell of fancy was dissipated, and all my warm emotions cooled, when reason reminded me that it was only a party of people who, with, perhaps, a few exceptions, had learnt to sing psalms by rote, and whose motives for admitting missionaries to dwell with them, might probably not proceed from a sentiment purely religious.

I cannot imagine any thing more delightful and gratifying to a good and feeling mind, than the act of returning thanks with devout gratitude to the Great and Good Creator of the universe, for the numerous blessings we are daily permitted to enjoy; and of imploring the aid of His Divine Spirit, in strengthening our hearts in the love and pursuit of virtue. Could but the rude uncultivated savage be converted to sentiments such as these, with what satisfaction would not every philanthropic man view crowds of missionaries pouring over all the uncivilized countries of the globe. But, alas! human nature does not admit of so much perfection; and this scheme, so fascinating to the enthusiast, may, so far as its professed object is concerned, prove at last to have been only an Utopian vision. Yet our benevolence towards our fellow-men, while it is within reasonable limits, has no irremoveable cause for despairing of being able, by judicious means, to convey the blessings of civilized life to nations now lost in the darkness of ignorance; nor ought the failure of those who reject the aid of reason and common sense, to operate in deterring us from the attempt.

19th. Want of water compelling us to quit this place, we removed early in the day to the *Juk rivier* (Yoke river), at the distance of about five miles further. Here our hopes were again disappointed: not a single drop of water could any where be found, even by digging; yet, as the oxen were miserably weak and weary, it was necessary to halt a few hours.

In the interim, I took a botanical ramble, and added forty-eight plants to my collection*, many of which I never met with either

---

* *Anthericum squameum*
Phlomis parvifolia, B. Cat. Geog. 1232.
   Fruticosa. Rami tomentosi. Folia
   nudiuscula ovata lanceolataquè, sub-
   integra. Flores flavi. Calyx valdè
   tomentosus, dentibus subulatis.
Cyphia hastata. B. Catal. Geog. 1234.
   Volubilis. Folia hastata, laciniis
   linearibus.
Codon Royeni
Hyobanche sanguinea ?
Geranium spinosum, Linn.

Pelargonium munitum. B. Cat. Geog.
   1240. Glabrum. Folia bi-pinnati-
   fida. Panicula dichotoma spinoso-
   lignescens.
Atriplex microphylla ?
Aptosimum indivisum. B.
Colutea frutescens, Linn.
Marrubium Africanum
Borago Africana
Lycium Afrum
Heliophila chamamælifolia. B. Cat.
   Geog. 1226.

And species of the genera

Phlomis	*Nemesia*	*Selago*
Calendula, 2 species	*Cotula*	*Plantago*
Othonna	*Aizoon*	*Pappophorum*
Hermannia, 2 species	*Silene*	*Eriocephalus*
Leysera	*Hemimeris*, 2 species	*Ononis*
Indigofera	*Zygophyllum*	*Gazania*
Erinus, 7 species	*Aristida*	*Buchnera*
Senecio		

before or since. Of that very curious flower, *Codon Royeni*, I saw but one plant; and of this I brought away the whole. It is a remarkable coincidence, which, not having in my waggon any books of travels, I was not aware of at the time, that Thunberg should also have met with no more than a single plant, although anxious to procure more. * *Geranium spinosum*, with a fleshy stem and large white flowers, was more abundant, and well deserved its name; and a succulent species of *Pelargonium* was so defended by the old panicles, grown to hard woody thorns, that no cattle could browze upon it.

In this arid country, where every juicy vegetable would soon be eaten up by the wild animals, the Great Creating Power, with all-provident wisdom, has given to such plants either an acrid or poisonous juice, or sharp thorns, to preserve the species from annihilation in those regions, where, for good and wise purposes, they have been placed. The harmony which pervades every part of the universe, is not less wonderful and beautiful in the distribution of animals and vegetables over the face of the globe, than in the planetary system, and in the sublime arrangement of myriads of worlds throughout the inconceivable infinity of space. When we permit ourselves to contemplate the great designs of the creation, all our boasted knowledge of Nature appears only as the ideas and the knowledge of children. Too intent on some little parts of the edifice, we often remain totally ignorant of the proportions and perfect symmetry of the whole. In the wide system of created objects, nothing is wanting, nothing is superfluous: the smallest weed or insect is as indispensably necessary to the general good, as the largest object we behold. Each has its peculiar part to perform, conducive ultimately to the well-being of all. Nothing more bespeaks a littleness of mind, and a narrowness of ideas, than the admiring of a production of Nature, *merely* for its magnitude, or the despising of one, merely for its minuteness: nothing more erroneous than to regard as useless, all that does not visibly tend to the benefit of *man*.

---

* Thunberg's Travels, vol. ii. p. 147.

At about four o'clock we again put the thirsty oxen to the wag-gons; and just as we were moving off, two men, mounted on oxen, rode up to us. They were *Bushmen* belonging to a *kraal* * near the Zak river. The people of this horde being in amity with the boors, were therefore denominated *Makke Boschjesmans* (Tame Bushmen). One of them, who was called their *Captain*, carried in his hand the ensign of his authority, a staff about four feet long, having a large tabular top of brass, on which were inscribed a few words, showing that he had been elevated to that rank by Governor Caledon.

A number of these staves have been given away, as well by the English as by the Dutch government, mostly to Hottentot chiefs. They are, together with the influence pertaining to them, handed down from father to son, conformably to the right of inheritance; and the possessor is always acknowledged as the head, and, with the Cape authorities, the lawful representative of his own particular kraal or tribe; and therefore has, or ought to have, some degree of consider-ation shown to him by the landdrosts and field-cornets. This act of policy in the colonial government has, in most cases, the effect of securing the allegiance and friendly disposition of these kraals, espe-cially as it is often, perhaps always, accompanied by a certain annual stipend or present

These two Bushmen, as they told us, had been employed by the farmers residing on the Zak river, to carry a letter to the landdrost of Tulbagh, requesting assistance and protection against the above-mentioned party of Caffres, whose threats of a hostile attack had induced them to desert their habitations. This captain, whose kraal were also sufferers from the Caffres, was now on his return with the landdrost's answer; but was at this place deviating somewhat from his direct road, in order to fetch a pack-ox, which, in his former journey, being over-fatigued, he had been obliged to leave by the way. After giving us this information, and promising to join us

---

* A Hottentot word, used, properly, for signifying a *village*, or *horde*.

on the morrow, they quickly trotted out of sight, leaving me much pleased at our meeting.

These oxen are generally broken in for riding, when they are not more than a year old. The first ceremony is that of piercing their nose to receive the bridle; for which purpose they are thrown on their back, and a slit is made through the *septum*, or cartilage between the nostrils, large enough to admit a finger. In this hole is thrust a strong stick stripped of its bark, and having at one end a forked branch, to prevent it passing through. To each end of it is fastened a thong of hide, of a length sufficient to reach round the neck and form the reins; and a sheep-skin, with the wool on, placed across the back, together with another folded up, and bound on with a *reim* long enough to pass several times round the body, constitutes the saddle. To this is sometimes added a pair of stirrups, consisting only of a thong with a loop at each end, slung across the saddle. Frequently the loops are distended by a piece of wood, to form an easier rest for the foot. While the animal's nose is still sore, it is mounted, and put in training; and, in a week or two, is generally rendered tolerably obedient to its rider. The facility and adroitness with which Hottentots manage the ox, has often excited my admiration. It is made to walk, trot, or gallop, at the will of its master; and, being longer legged, and rather more lightly made, than the ox of England, travels with greater ease and expedition; walking three or four miles in the hour, trotting five, and gallopping, on an emergency, seven or eight.

Juk-rivier's Hoogte (Yoke-river Heights) is a considerable eminence; and in descending it, we were, for the first time, since leaving Tulbagh, obliged to skid the wheels. After this we continued our journey by night, and at about eight o'clock halted under *Goudsbloem's Hoogte* (Marygold Heights)* at an ' outspan-place' called *Tys-kraal,* by a dry river-course abounding in acacias and karree-trees. Under their spreading branches we kindled a large fire, which the coldness of the night now rendered very necessary. Coffee was immediately prepared, and our Hottentot cooks having soon broiled the mutton *carbonaadtjes* (chops or steaks), it was not long before supper was finished, and all the party were asleep; but the recording of the observations, and the disposing of the collections, of the day, kept me fully employed till midnight.

At Hangklip we quitted what may properly be called the Karro *plains,* and continued travelling between hills of inconsiderable size and elevation, all the strata of which were perfectly horizontal, till we came to *Juk river,* where the country becomes much more hilly.

20th. By an observation of the sun's meridional altitude, I ascertained the latitude of *Tys-kraal,* to be 32° 46′ 52″. † Just as the observation was completed, I had the misfortune, in taking up the artificial horizon, to spill half the quicksilver on the ground. The quantity which remained not being enough to form a reflecting surface of the required size, and knowing that no money could replace the loss, without returning to Cape Town, I could not but

---

* So called from a profusion of flowers, of the class *Compositæ,* observed here at a particular season of the year. The term *Goudsbloem,* like too many of the colonial names, is applied gratuitously to various plants, fancied to have a resemblance to the *Marygold.* Different species of *Arctotis* have generally been pointed out to me for it, and sometimes a kind of *Cotula.*

† 20*th July* 1811, at Tys Kraal under Goudsbloem's Hoogte, observed meridional altitude of the Sun's centre, 36° 24′ 39″.

consider this as the most serious accident which had hitherto happened, as it appeared likely to interfere with the accuracy of my future observations.   For although tar, or even water in a bowl painted black, might have been used as a substitute, yet no surface would reflect the stars so clearly and accurately as quicksilver.   The ground being a loose sand, the mercury would soon have been irrecoverably lost, had I not instantly had the idea of making a small hollow near it, and placing in it a sheep-skin so as to form a basin ; carefully and expeditiously scooping into it all the sand, to the extent and depth to which it was supposed likely that the mercury had penetrated.   Then, by taking in a cup small quantities of this sand, and giving it a circular motion, at the same time blowing away the dust and lighter particles, the quicksilver was found clean at the bottom ; and in this manner, persevering at every leisure moment for three whole days, I had the satisfaction, at last, to recover very nearly all that had been spilled.

Receiving information that the main body of the Klaarwater Hottentots, under a ' captain' whose name was *Berns* (or *Berends*), was not more than one day's journey in advance, one of our Hottentots was sent forward to give them notice of our approach.   The *Bushman* captain joined us in the afternoon, accompanied by four others ; among whom was his father, a little old man possessing quite as much liveliness and vigor as his son.   All were mounted on oxen ; they appeared happy at having fallen in with us, and seemed to have a friendly confidence in our good intentions towards them.

This race of people had been pictured to me in the most wretched colors ; and, having been led to expect only a set of beings without reason or intellect, I was now much pleased at finding that they might be viewed in a more favorable light, and that the first individuals of this nation, whom we fell in with, were men of lively manners and shrewd understandings.   They were all of small stature (about five feet), and dressed partly in the colonial, and partly in their own costume.

The day being cold and windy, and the clouds which were fast gathering in every quarter, threatening a rainy night, we removed for shelter against the storm, to the deserted hut at a cattle-place, discovered by our herdsmen at a distance of about a mile and a half on our right.   One of the missionaries, with the Bushmen for their guides, set out immediately on foot ; and, as soon as the oxen could be brought in from pasture, and put to the waggons, we followed ; but, missing the proper direction, did not arrive there till dark. The hut was in, what might be called in this part of the colony, very decent condition, as the walls and roof were weather-tight, and it was furnished with a door ; for it appeared not to have been many weeks since it was inhabited.   It contained, however, merely a single room, which fortunately was large enough to lodge the whole party, as the missionaries and myself always slept in the waggons, and the Bushmen betook themselves to their own fire, a few yards off, amongst the bushes.

21*st*.   Being Sunday, all our people were assembled in the hut, for divine worship.   This consisted in singing psalms for half an hour ; after which a sermon was read to them, out of a favourite Dutch author, of a very proper and useful tendency.

The Bushman captain and his companions left us, and proceeded on their journey to the Veldcornet's with the letter.

22*nd*.   The Hottentots, who hitherto were seldom observed to be in a hurry to depart, were now very active in getting every thing early in readiness for starting ; and it was quite unusual to find that, instead of requiring to be repeatedly ordered to work, all this was to-day done of their own accord, and without any directions from the missionaries.   The cause, however, was not their sudden reformation, but an anxiety and haste to join the party of their countrymen, which was on before.

We returned to Tys-kraal, and immediately commenced the rather steep ascent of the *Goudsbloem's Hoogte*.   The flowers which gave rise to its name, were not to be found at the present season.

The *Wind-heuvel* (Wind-hill) is a mountain much more difficult to climb, and required all the strength of our oxen, and great care in the drivers, to bring the waggons over it in safety.   The road is very rocky and irregular, and the declivity but thinly clothed with vege-

tation. *   Near the summit of the mountain, we halted a few minutes
at a hut in which a colonist happened at this time to be residing,
and where our caravan was strengthened by the addition of a small
party of the Klaarwater Hottentots.

The waggon which they had with them, was one that formerly
belonged to Dr. Cowan's expedition, and had been taken as far as
the place at which their last letters were written; and not finding
occasion for all their four waggons, this was sent back to the Cape
by one of the missionaries who had accompanied them thus far, and
had been sold to these Hottentots.

This object excited a mournful interest, and filled my mind with
melancholy reflections on the untimely end of those who once rode in
it, now the only vestige of them remaining. Fortunate would it have
been for any of that party, had it been his lot to be the conductor of
it back to the colony, instead of sending it under the care of others.

From the highest point of our road over this mountain, there is
a fine view of the hilly *Roggeveld Karro*, and beyond it, in a blue
distance, of the lofty *Roggeveld Mountains*, or cliffs, as they really are,
with respect to the country beyond them.   Their even summits
appeared one long, unbroken, and horizontal line, trending a great
distance eastward, at the same elevation, and forming the third step
or rise in the surface of Southern Africa, in advancing from the Cape
of Good Hope.   The first step seems to be at the great western
chain of mountains, and the second along the southern side of the
Great Karro.   The high level of the Roggeveld, may be inferred

---

* The collection of this day consisted only of

Eriocephalus purpureus, B. Catal. Geog. 1281. Folia filiformia minuta. Flores spicati, sed sæpiùs in ramulis terminales solitarii, purpureï.	*Septas*
	Sparaxis
	Selago
	Asparagus
Lichtensteinia undulata. Willd. Beob. ges. Berl. 1807.	*Parmelia*. Vegetables of this order are of extremely rare occurrence in the more arid regions of the interior.

An umbelliferous plant, probably a *Seseli*, was called by the Hottentots, *Anýs-wortel*,
(Anise-root) the root of which was said to be eatable: but it is entirely different from the
Anýs-wortel of Zwartland.

from the circumstance of its being for several months in the year, as the boors assured me, subject to storms of snow, although lying under the parallel of only thirty-two degrees and a half from the equinoctial line.

In the course of this day's journey, a small species of bustard (*Otis*) was shot. It is considered a rare bird and difficult to be obtained; and, being only found in the Karro, is distinguished by the name of the *Karro Kóorhaan*. Its flesh is exceedingly good, and, in this respect, it agrees with all of the *Otis* tribe. It is so scarce that we never met with it again during the whole of my travels.

The descent on the northern side of the *Wind-heuvel* is very gradual, continuing for about two miles. Not far on the other side of the mountain, we came to a *leg-plaats*, belonging to *Jasper Cloete*, where we took up our station, near the hut, which was not only deserted, but in ruins.

A colonist, who lived in the neighbourhood, paid us a visit, and was invited to dinner; but as he preserved a most extraordinary taciturnity all the time, we learnt nothing from his company, except that he was a tall man in a great *jas* (watch coat), and ate mutton with a crooked knife.

Our party of Hottentots being now increased by the accession of several of their old friends, together with some shepherds, who chancing to pass by, were invited to take a seat at their fire, the evening and a great part of the night were spent in conviviality, smoking, laughing, and talking.

At one of the fires, an amusement of a very singular, and nearly unintelligible kind, was the source of great merriment, not only to the performers themselves, but to all the bystanders. They called it *Kaartspel* (card-playing), a word, in this instance, strangely misapplied. Two Hottentots seated opposite to each other, on the ground, were vociferating, as if in a rage, some particular expressions in their own language; laughing violently; throwing their bodies on either side; tossing their arms in all directions; at one moment with their hands close together; at another, stretched out wide apart; up in

H H

the air at one time, or in an instant, down on the ground; sometimes with them closed, at others, exhibiting them open to their opponent. Frequently in the heat of their game, they started up on their knees, falling back immediately on the ground again; and all this in such a quick, wild, extraordinary manner, that it was impossible, after watching their motions for a long time, to discover the nature of their game, or to comprehend the principle on which it was founded, any more than a person entirely ignorant of the moves at chess, could learn that by merely looking on.

This is a genuine Hottentot game, as every one would certainly suppose, on seeing the uncouth manner in which it is played. It is, they say, of great antiquity, and at present practised only by such as have preserved some portion of their original customs; and they pretend that it is not every Hottentot who possesses the talents necessary for playing at it in perfection. I found some difficulty in obtaining an intelligible explanation, but learnt, at last, that the principle consists in concealing a small piece of stick in one hand so dexterously, that the opponent shall not be able, when both closed hands are presented to him, to distinguish in which it is held; while, at the same time, he is obliged to decide, by some sign or motion, either on one or the other. As soon as the opponent has gained a certain number of guesses, he is considered to have won a game; and it then becomes his turn to take the stick, and display his ingenuity in concealing it, and in deceiving the other. In this manner the games are continued alternately, often the whole night long, or until the players are exhausted with fatigue. In the course of them, various little incidents, either of ingenuity or of mistake, occur to animate their exertions, and excite the rude harmless mirth of their surrounding friends.

23rd. Having sent one of my men to the farm of *Jasper Cloete*, to purchase a sheep, he returned with a lamb, and the farmer's " compliments to the Englishman, begging his acceptance of it." Being perfectly unknown to him, except by means of my Hottentot who represented his master as a stranger travelling through the country, this disinterested instance of neighbourly kindness was the more pleasing ; but of such, during the five years I was in Africa, many might be recorded.

In addition to the lamb, which constituted the principal dish of the feast, my people received extra rations of tobacco, flour, and potatoes, and also of wine and brandy, with which they regaled themselves ; and, by an extra degree of talkativeness, evinced their exhilarating power.

At noon, an observation of the sun proved that we were in the latitude of 32° 45′ 18″.*

The Hottentot captain, Berends, with all his people, was lying at an outspan-place, only a few miles off, and came to consult with the missionaries respecting the measures to be adopted for our defence against the Caffres in the Karreebergen.　All the Hottentots of his party had manfully come to the decision, rather to take the hazards of fighting their way, than be prevented from returning to their homes and families ; a decision, with which he coincided.　But the missionaries hesitated in adopting Berends's proposal, on account of its exposing their wives and children to danger, or at least to great alarm ; and these, on the matter being referred to them, expressed a disinclination to advance beyond the borders of the colony, if it should then appear that any danger of this kind awaited them.

As to my little band, no such impediments detained them ; and, being well armed, and having plenty of ammunition, there was not much to fear, provided their resolution was to be depended on : for, on sounding their courage, the whole expressed themselves, not only ready, but very desirous of pushing forward ; and boldly declared that every man of them would fight to the last.

It was therefore settled, that captain Berends's party and mine, would advance, notwithstanding these reports, and stand by each other till we reached Klaarwater.　He then left us and returned to his people ; promising to wait for us at the Riet (Reed) River, it being

* 23rd July 1811, at *Wind heuvel station*, the observed meridional altitude of the Sun's centre, was 37′ 0 44″.

H H 2

his intention to make the ascent of the Roggeveld mountain on the morrow, or the day after.

It was late in the afternoon before the oxen were put to the waggons: our company now separated into three divisions, and we took leave of each other for a short time. As in a few days' journey further, we were about to quit the inhabited part of the colony, and the missionaries had some friends in this quarter, with whom they wished to pass a week or two before taking a final departure from the land of Christendom, it was agreed to suspend our journey for that time. During this period, I proposed to take up my station at the *Veldcornet*'s, to whom government-orders to provide *voorspans* at the Roggeveld-berg, had been previously despatched.

None of my people were acquainted with the situation of his place, which lay out of our road at a considerable distance eastward. But Hottentots, in general, possess the valuable faculty of easily finding their way over the country; therefore, a few slight instructions, from a *schaap-wagter* (shepherd) whom we met with, were considered sufficient to enable us to take the proper direction to the Fieldcornet's.

At half-past four o'clock we drove away from the *Wind-heuvel station.* The country was nearly level, abounding in thorn trees, but deficient in water. On the road no new object of natural history was observable. We had been told that the place might be reached by sunset; yet the darkness of night came on, and no appearance of a human habitation having been seen all the way, Philip began to fear he had mistaken the tract; yet, as there was no moon to guide us, we continued travelling on the same course.

The barking of dogs at a distance, gave us hopes that we were approaching the house, and a light being seen in the same direction, put all our fears to rest. But on coming up to it, this proved to be only a boor with his waggon at *outspan*, under some large trees of Karro-thorns, by the side of the dry bed of a rivulet. We learnt that we were still in the right road, and that the Veldcornet's was at the distance of a quarter of an hour's travelling further. Not having taken the precaution to fill our water-cask, we were exceedingly thirsty, and fortunately now procured a supply from the farmer.

Being relieved from anxiety, we continued onwards for a quarter of an hour, without coming to the house; and even after the half-hour, all was dark and silent, without the least sign of any habitation being near. The Hottentots began to suspect that we had been deceived by the boor, and advised halting till morning; but as soon as the waggon stopped, and the oxen were just going to be loosed from the yoke, we fancied, in the silence, that we heard the distant barking of dogs.

These watchful animals, ever attentive to the least noise at night, are enabled, by the openness of the country, to hear the howl of wild beasts, or the sound of a waggon, at a very great distance. We therefore continued on our way, for about two miles further, finding, as we advanced, that the barking became more distinct.

At last we arrived at a hut; but every body was asleep, excepting two Hottentots, from whom we learnt that it was the habitation of *Gerrit Snyman*, the *veldcornet*. They assisted my men in unyoking, and in collecting firewood; and as soon as our supper was finished, we retired to rest, without disturbing the family, who knew nothing of our arrival till the next morning.

24th. When daylight disclosed the place to our view, we beheld a miserable abode, corresponding exactly with the unfavorable description which had already been given me: a small oblong low hut built of rough bits of rock; rudely thatched with reed and sedge; having no window, excepting one small opening covered with white linen, instead of glass; and the doorway but half closed with a clumsy panel of reeds. The inside corresponded with the exterior, and was divided into two apartments, serving for sitting-room and bed-room, which last was also the store-room. No other furniture was to be seen, than a table and three chairs, or rather stools.

Near to this hut were two out-buildings, which at a little distance might be mistaken for hay-cocks; one of them was the storehouse, or barn, as it might be considered, and the other, the kitchen. In this the fire was made in the middle, on the ground; and the smoke escaped either out at the door, or through the ill-thatched roof. Every part of the hut within, was stained like ebony, of a glossy jet-black, the effect of long-continued wood-smoke.   At a little distance from the building, or on the *werf*, as the space immediately surrounding a colonist's dwelling, is termed, was a very large sheep-fold, hedged round with branches of Karro-thorn.   Not a tree was visible, excepting a line of Acacias, marking the meandering course of a rivulet, which ran close by the house, and at this time formed a plentiful rill of excellent water.*

The appearance of its inhabitants accorded with that of the place ; none could harmonize more perfectly with the kitchen, than the squalid Hottentots who were sitting round the fire.   The *veld-cornet* himself was better dressed ; but the style of his clothing, as well as the dwelling, bespoke his moderate ambition.

As soon as he found I was awake, he came to the waggon, to welcome me to his house ; where his wife, a woman whose cleanly

---

* The above *Engraving* is a view of *Snyman's habitation*, looking southward.   It will give a just idea of the dwellings of the boors in the Karro, and also in the Roggeveld, few being there much larger or more convenient.   The mountains are a continuation to the eastward of the same ridge, of which the Wind-heuvel forms a part, and is situated at a little distance to the right, out of the picture.   The scene here represented, is that of the flocks going out to pasture early in the morning.   The *shepherds*, who are seldom of any other race than Hottentots, are always armed with a gun, as a defence against either the wild beasts, or the Bushmen, who, frequently concealing themselves behind the rocks or the bushes, suddenly attack the shepherd, and carry off the flock.

appearance strongly contrasted that of her greasy dirty servants, immediately got breakfast ready.

He had received the landdrost's letter about four days before; but I was exceedingly disappointed that no other letter had arrived by the same conveyance. I therefore now gave up all expectation of hearing again from my friends, as there appeared no chance of their letters reaching us, after we left this place.

He showed, by his conversation, some curiosity respecting the nature and extent of my travels, which, in part, I satisfied; but found it not an easy task to convince him that there was any utility in travelling, when the making of money was not the object. Till he had seen my papers, he continued in the supposition that I was a missionary; but having discovered this mistake, he fell into another, in concluding, as former travellers at the Cape had been sent out at the expense, and by the authority, of Government, or by assistance from other quarters, that my case must be the same; and asked very respectfully if the *heer* was not sent by the *Koning van Engeland.* Although I put him right in this point, I was at last obliged to leave him in an error, as he would not be persuaded that I was not travelling at the expense of the Cape government, since the landdrost had given him orders, in the name of government, to provide the relays of oxen.

The authority which I appeared to derive from my papers, was considered a proof that he might, without hurting his conscience, demand a greater price for what I bought, than was customarily paid by his neighbours. It was my intention to have purchased of him a horse, as the breed of the Roggeveld is much esteemed, and, from the great numbers which are reared there, might be obtained at a reasonable rate; but as he imposed an additional sum of three-fifths of the usual price, I declined the bargain altogether. When one of my men, the next day, remarked to him, that he had asked by much too great a price for the horse, he merely replied, " your master is an Englishman, and can afford to pay it." However, for the eighteen sheep which I had of him, he was so conscientious as to lay on no more than an eighth, as the charge for my being an Englishman : this I thought very moderate for such a privilege.

In common with all the boors of the Roggeveld, Snyman's whole property consisted in sheep and horses. Of the former, he possessed a flock of twenty-five hundred, exclusive of the lambs. This, he told me, was considered a small number; as a boor with five thousand could scarcely be called affluent.

Very little corn being grown in that district, they are accustomed to live almost entirely on mutton. While I remained at Snyman's, they had three meals of mutton every day; at half-past eight in the morning, at half-past one, and at eight o'clock in the evening. During the latter part of this time, they had no bread; yet, as a substitute, and by him regarded as a rarity, he produced some potatoes grown on his farm in the Roggeveld, which were as good as any I had seen in Europe. At this time the family had no other drink than water or coffee.

It seems to be the custom, more particularly in this part of the colony, for every one to use at dinner the knife which he always carries about him. Consequently, the first day, nothing was laid for me but a fork; and as soon as he perceived that I was not equipped with a knife of my own, I was accommodated with a small one not much bigger than a penknife, which he pulled out of his pocket. His fork served for a variety of purposes, and I now had an opportunity of seeing how dexterously it may be used as a tooth-pick.

In the evening the air began to feel cold, and, there being no fire-place in the house, a large iron pot full of wood embers brought in and placed in the middle of the room, soon afforded a comfortable warmth. In conversing on the nature of the *Karro*, he was pleased at finding that my opinion agreed with his, that the soil was of a fertile kind, and that nothing but the great want of water and rain prevented its being a productive district. This is confirmed by the fruitful appearance it assumes during the short continuance of the rains; but he told me, as a proof of the precarious nature of this fertility, that no rain had fallen in the Karro during the last two months.

25th. From two altitudes of the sun, I computed the latitude of this place to be 32° 46′ 45″. *

Gerrit Maritz, the field-cornet of the division next to Snyman's, had also received orders from the Drostdy to render me his official aid in proceeding on the journey; and, having heard of my arrival in the Karro, came to learn what assistance was required. He offered his services with great civility and readiness, and concerted the order for the *voorspans,* with Snyman, who was equally ready to fulfil his duty. I mention this with pleasure, because I experienced on other occasions, afterwards, a very different treatment; and ascertained, to my mortification, that an order from the government will not always procure for an Englishman the necessary assistance from the boors; nor, though they receive a remuneration, ensure even their civility to him, or their respect for a higher authority.

28th. Early this morning, one of my Hottentots was sent with a packet of letters to a farm-house at the distance of eight miles, where the Tulbagh *Boode,* who was to forward them to Cape Town, was expected to arrive in his way from the Hantam.

29th. Having, in the course of travelling, learnt by experience, what alterations in the internal arrangement of my waggon would render it more convenient, I here changed the place of one of the chests; and, by moving it backwards to the extremity of the *buik-plank,* a vacant space of nearly three feet, was left between that and the next, forming a very commodious sitting-room, well enclosed and barricaded by the after-chest. This arrangement proved so convenient in every respect, and so well adapted for personal safety, that it was never afterwards found necessary to make any change in it during the whole of my travels.

30th. A letter, brought by a Hottentot from the missionaries, informed me that no flour was to be purchased any where, as I had requested them to make enquiry for me in the quarter where they

* 25th July, 1811, at 8h. 44m. 30sec. A.M., the observed altitude of the sun's centre was 19° 33′ 29″; and at 10h. 36m. 15sec., 33° 35′ 44″.

were residing, seeing the necessity of replenishing my stock before I quitted the inhabited part of the colony. They proposed resuming their journey on the fifth of the next month; and, as nothing more had been heard respecting the Caffres, they had come to the determination of proceeding to the Zak river, there to await the result of further enquiry, before they decided on the course they were to take.

I was glad to perceive that my men became tired of waiting so long in this arid spot, and that they were anxious to proceed. The oxen did not seem to be gaining either flesh or strength; being obliged to wander every day to a great distance from the house, before they could find pasture, as the sheep of the place consumed, like locusts, every blade of grass and leafy twig within a moderate compass.

It was an amusing and interesting sight to behold, every evening, at sunset, the numerous flocks streaming, like an inundation, over the ridges and low hills, or moving in a compact body, like an army invading the country, and driven forwards only by two or three Hottentots, with a few dogs. At a great distance, the confused sound of their bleating began to be heard; but, as they approached nearer and nearer, the noise gradually increased, till the various cries of the multitude mingled with the whole air, and deadened every other sound. The shepherds seldom returned home without bringing under their arms a lamb or two which had been dropped in the course of the day, and as yet too weak to follow their dam.

————— modò namque gemellos,
Spem gregis, ah! silice in nudâ connixa reliquit.

The faculty which the Hottentots possess, of distinguishing the features, as it were, and characteristic appearance of each sheep, is almost incredible, when the immense number of the flock is considered. They seldom mistake the ewe to which each lambkin belongs; and if they did, such a mistake would immediately be shown by the ewe taking no notice of the lamb offered to her.

From the neighbouring hills, Speelman brought home a short

fleshy plant, well known to the Hottentots by the name of *Guaap,* and to botanists by that of *Stapelia pilifera.* It has an insipid, yet cool and watery, taste, and is much used by them for the purpose of quenching thirst; for which purpose, it would seem, nature has designed it, by placing it only in hot and arid tracts of country. In passing through the Karro, I expected to have seen in large quantities a great variety of plants of that genus, but scarcely half a dozen met my eye. But it appears that no part of the colony is so rich in them, as the dry sandy regions lying along the western coast, and extending over several degrees of latitude. On the other hand, in travelling along the colony to the eastward, they gradually disappear; nor were any discovered as we advanced deeper into the interior of the continent, although their associates, *Aloë, Mesembryanthemum* and *Aizoon,* were now and then fallen in with, almost to our farthest range northward.

My notice was attracted by the beautiful skin of a zebra, that had been formed into a *tanning-vat,* supported by four stakes on a frame to which its edges were bound by thongs in such a manner, that the middle, hanging down, formed a capacious basin: (as may be seen by the figure at the end of this chapter.) It was filled with a liquid, in which lay a quantity of the bark of Karro-thorn, and together with it a number of sheep-skins, first deprived of the hair, were placed to steep. The *Acacia-bark* possesses a large portion of the tanning principle, and imparts a reddish color to the leather; but in other districts, several other sorts of barks are applied to the same purpose. *

The sheep-leather, thus tanned, is made use of in the distant and more unfrequented parts of the colony, for various parts of their clothing, by the Hottentots and the poorer class of boors; but for the making of trowsers, it is every where in general demand. Men's jackets, and even women's gowns and petticoats are made of

* Of which a kind of *Ficus,* C. G. 2487. 3. has been found to have powerful properties: and *Mesembryanthemum coriarium,* B. a new species allied to *M. uncinatum,* has been seen used for this purpose by the Hottentots.

it by those who are unable to buy woollen and linen clothing. Such dresses were, before the English had possession of the land, the common costume of both peasantry and Hottentots; but since that time, the prosperity and riches of the country have increased so much, that by far the greater number of the boors can now afford to wear a dress, entirely of English manufacture.

During the night, the violence of the wind often shook the waggon so much as to disturb my sleep, an inconvenience which custom alone could reconcile, but which, like many others, I acquired in time the habit of bearing with patience; reflecting, that it was at the small price of a few bodily comforts, that the gratification of traversing and exploring so interesting a portion of the globe, was obtained.

31st. The next day continued equally windy, and a change of weather for the worse seemed about to take place. The air became cold and chilly, and those who were acquainted with the climate of the Roggeveld, thought it likely to produce a fall of snow on the mountain; a circumstance by which my progress might be impeded for many days. Not caring to remain longer at this place, where so little was to be done, I gave orders to prepare for departure on the *3rd.* In the afternoon, and during the evening, we had some lightning and thunder, accompanied with the first rain which had fallen here, since two months.

In crossing the Karro, it was remarkable that not a single ostrich had been seen; a fact to be accounted for by the parched state of vegetation, driving them to some other part of the country, where their food, which consists of herbage and vegetables, was more abundant. These plains, where they are sometimes seen in considerable numbers, are their natural domain; and that some were still remaining, was evident from the circumstance of one of the shepherds finding a nest with eggs. On one of these, Snyman, his wife and myself, made the principal part of our dinner this day. A single *ostrich-egg* is reckoned equal to twenty-four eggs of the domestic hen. We had it cooked in the manner of an omelet: it made a very palatable and wholesome dish; and, though coarser than a hen's egg, it possessed no unpleasant, nor otherwise remarkable, taste.

August 1st. Very few plants were at this time to be met with here, and there was little temptation to extend my walks far from the house; especially as I found, in putting the numbered labels to those I had already collected, and in arranging them in the Geographical Catalogue, sufficient employment in the waggon. I here added to it but fourteen numbers *, among which was a Fumitory so exceedingly like an English species, as hardly to be distinguished from it.

A beautiful green *Sugar-bird* † frequented the thorn-trees, and in splendid plumage, surpassed all the other birds of the place. Speelman, who always brought home any thing which appeared to him curious, one day came with a bird ‡ which he had taken out of its hole in the side of a high and abrupt earthy bank. The noise it made, was something like that produced by filing the teeth of a saw. The habits of this bird, in hollowing out for itself, a hole in the earth, instead of one in the trunk of a tree, is a singular anomaly in the *woodpecker* tribe. The *Eland-vogel* § which was procured here, is a handsome bird, and may easily be discovered by its remarkable clear and loud note Its original name was given in the language of the Hottentots, who believe that it is an attendant on the antelope called *Eland* (Antilope Oreas); or at least, that it is an indication of that animal being not far off. For the same reason, they distinguish also a *Rhenoster-vogel* and an *Olifants-vogel*; but whatever might have been believed of these birds formerly, they

---

* *Cysticapnos Africana*
Fumaria capreolata ?
Lepidium subdentatum, B. C. G. 1299.
Stapelia pilifera
Cineraria lobata
Moréa collina

Hemimeris, 3 species
Nemesia
Oxalis .
Bromus
Pteronia.

† *Certhia (Nectarinia) famosa.* L. Syst. Nat.
‡ *Picus terrestris*, B. — Le Pic Laboureur. — Le Vaill. Ois. d'Afr. pl. 254.
§ *Lanius* — *Turdus Zeylonus* of Linné. — LeVaill. Ois. d'Afr. pl. 67. f. 1 & 2. where, in consequence of mistaking its colonial name, it is called " Eyland-vogel" or Island bird.

are not now to be depended upon by the hunter, in search of these quadrupeds. A sparrow called the *Koorn-vreeter*, (Corn-eater) * and an undescribed species of *fly-catcher*, were here added to my collection.

From this spot the lofty and far-extended *Roggevelds-berg* is visible, though distant above twenty miles. The peculiarity of the view, terminated by the blue misty outline of this gigantic precipice, induced me to add this to the number of my drawings. My men, who had scarcely any other work to do at this place, except attending the oxen and sheep, employed some of their time in making a store of *juk-scheis*, as these are continually liable to be broken, whenever the oxen become restive in the yoke. They took advantage also of this leisure, to make a quantity of candles, lest the various other employments in travelling might not again allow them so favorable an opportunity.

One of the oxen having an abscess on the back, Philip, who professed a knowledge of the different disorders of oxen and the modes of curing them, having opened it, filled the cavity with tar ; of which, as a healing application, Hottentots have a high opinion, and make much use, especially for wounds and sores of their cattle.

The day was cold, and towards the afternoon, lightning, thunder, and rain, of which some symptoms had occurred on the preceding day, came on again ; and in consequence, it became the opinion of all, that the season of the thunder-rains had now actually commenced in the Karro. The tilt of the waggon, which, till this storm, had not yet been sufficiently tried, proved, to my great satisfaction, perfectly water-proof; but though I enjoyed the privilege of sleeping dry, the noise of the shower incessantly pelting on the canvass, close above my head, prevented my getting much rest : but custom at last rendered this inconvenience more indifferent.

Early in the morning, Maagers and Speelman set out with the oxen and sheep, in order that they might have time to pro-

---

* *Fringilla arcuata.* Syst. Nat. ed. Gm.

ceed at a slow pace, and wait for us at the house of a colonist named Jan Van der Westhuisen. Gert was despatched with a letter, to give notice to the missionaries, that I should set off on the morrow; and at night he returned with an answer, by which it was arranged that we should all meet at the *Riet* (Reed) *river*, at the distance of five or six days' journey, according to our rate of travelling.

3rd. Having omitted making a legal agreement with Gert while at Tulbagh, we here signed the usual contract before the field-cornet; as, without this, a Hottentot would not consider himself under any obligation to continue his services, if he should feel inclined to desert his master before the expiration of the term for which he had engaged.

A good pack of dogs, of different kinds, was a very necessary part of the equipment; and these we endeavoured to collect at every opportunity. Yet, although every farm-house was apparently overstocked with these animals, the boors, knowing their value, could seldom be persuaded to part with any: Snyman, however, was induced to let me have one.

The field-cornet, also furnished me with a requisition to several colonists residing near the mountain, to supply, on payment, the quantity of flour we stood in need of. He would not receive any pecuniary remuneration for the meals I had taken at his house; but begged to have his brandy-bottles filled. Although there could not possibly be any further opportunity of replenishing this part of my stores, so necessary for keeping my Hottentots in good humour, I did not hesitate to comply; notwithstanding the evident looks of dissatisfaction with which they viewed my giving away this much-valued commodity, as I had found Snyman willing to do all that was in his power to render us assistance.

As soon as every thing was safely repacked, the relays were yoked to, and we started at half-past one in the afternoon. The oxen, being quite fresh, were not easily to be checked in going at a trot; and the road, being at the same time rough and stony, occasioned some of the goods in the chests to be much damaged. Every loss was to us of serious importance; and if the mentioning of such an occurrence may seem·trifling to those who have never travelled in a wild or desert country, they were far from being so to us.   We found it impossible to witness little accidents of this kind, with the same indifference with which they may be viewed by those who journey in countries where, with money, such losses may be immediately rectified.

Snyman overtook us on horseback, and went forward to *Gerrit Vischer's*, to order the relays to be in readiness as soon as we arrived, and where, having travelled eight miles over a dry open country, we halted about two hours afterwards.

This place is a permanent residence, and consequently possesses a better house than the temporary cattle-places we had hitherto seen in the Karro.   An·excellent garden, stocked with fruit trees and vegetables, and a constant supply of water, gladden the eye of the traveller, after passing the dreary waste.

Vischer stood ready at the door, to welcome me into the house, where, as soon as I was seated, coffee was brought in.   There was something in the appearance and manners of this colonist and his family, that pleased me much.   Both the parents, and their thirteen children, were remarkably tall, and one of the daughters was really a giantess, without being unwieldy or clumsy.   The weather being a little chilly, the mother, in the true colonial style, observed that, down in the Karro, it was only a *stuyver* cold, but that we should find it a *ducatoon* cold, up in the Roggeveld.   No rain had fallen at Vischer's place since the last day of May.   I purchased some fine lemons, out of his garden, at the rate of a hundred for a rix dollar.

Field-cornet *Gerrit Maritz*, apprised of my arrival at Vischer's, came for the purpose of giving his assistance, if wanted : having provided *voorspans* to meet us at the foot. of the mountain.   He begged me to take charge of a letter which he had written officially to the missionaries at *Klaarwater*.   The contents, he told me, were a requisition to deliver up and send to Cape Town, certain runaway slaves and Hottentots who had taken refuge at that settlement.   He complained much, that an establishment of that kind, beyond the boundary, composed mostly of men who had once resided in the colony, and consequently had many connections there still, was a temptation to the ill-disposed among the slaves and Hottentots, to be careless of their duty to their masters and desert them, in reliance on finding an asylum beyond the reach of the laws. It was, according to his opinion, nothing but a receptacle for the idle and worthless.

After stopping three quarters of an hour, the waggons proceeded with two fresh teams, driven by one of Vischer's sons and a boor named *Piet Mulder*, the owner of one of them. I had every reason for considering them intelligent and obliging men, and I made use of the opportunity afforded by their conversation, of improving my knowledge of colonial affairs, connected with farming and grazing.

Thus passed the time, till evening came on, and the moon, which was nearly at the full, rose to give a sublimer character to the landscape. The country was open, but varied with hills of flowing outline. As we advanced, the lofty *mountains* of the *Roggeveld* seemed, as it were, growing up rapidly before us, as if menacing to stop the traveller's further progress: they are one of Nature's gigantic walls, with which she has enclosed the Great Karro. The clearness of the sky, the brightness of moonlight, and the novelty of the surrounding scenery, inspired every pleasing sensation.

The agreeable effect of these, was not interrupted by halting a few minutes at Mulder's hut; where his wife, expecting him, had got the coffee ready, and was very solicitous that he should stop to take a regular meal, as he had left home early in the morning. To this, I endeavoured to persuade him, but he preferred seeing the waggons first to Jan Van der Westhuisen's, the end of their day's journey; and whither a Hottentot had been sent off several hours before, to give notice of our coming.

On arriving there we found the house shut, and all the family gone to bed; so that no admittance could be obtained. In this case, as Speelman and Maagers were there in waiting with the oxen and sheep, I resolved to advance as far as the foot of the mountain that night, in order that we might be ready to make the ascent early on the next day. Although the mountain, from its great elevation, appeared to be very near, yet it was not till a quarter before ten that we arrived at the spot where it was proposed to take up our station.

The country, from Snyman's to this place, has a gradual rise, which, in the distance of four-and-twenty miles, must amount to a very considerable increase of elevation.

I now delivered to Mulder a package, containing the botanical specimens collected between Tulbagh and the Karro Pass, and for which Snyman had issued a requisition conformably to the government order, that they should be forwarded from one field-cornet to another, till they reached Cape Town. Mulder promised to take charge of them himself, together with a letter to my agents, as he intended setting out for the Cape in two or three days.

With the view of ensuring their safe arrival, I wrote, by an opportunity which presented itself three weeks afterwards, to the Landdrost of Tulbagh, to apprise him of the circumstance; yet neither these, nor the letter to my agents, ever reached their destination, a fact I was not informed of till my return to Cape Town. Every enquiry was then made, but without discovering them; and, in the mean time, another landdrost was appointed. After I finally left the colony, the enquiry was continued officially by the Deputy Colonial Secretary, who obtained information that the package had been duly delivered to the Field-commandant, Pienaar, residing in the Bokkeveld; by whom they were said to have been left in Cape Town, at the house of a person named Zeyler, who denied its having ever been seen by him. Pienaar, on being further questioned, declared that, as soon as he received it, he gave due notice at the Drostdy. Here the clue was lost, and the affair ended. I mention this circumstance, for the purpose of cautioning future travellers not to trust too much to such a mode of communication. This is the only loss my collection has sustained: it is not altogether inconsiderable, as it amounts to 585 specimens, and must occasion, in the numbers of the Geographical Catalogue, an hiatus that cannot now be filled up.

4th. At this station nothing new was observed: but, expecting the relays, I did not stray far from the waggons; otherwise it is probable that many interesting objects would have rewarded my search. *Euphorbia Mauritanica* was here very abundant; and several other thorny species, resembling in growth the Torch-thistles (*Cacti*) of South America, of which they are in Africa the representatives; assuming, like them, the globular as well as the prismatic form, and occupying the same arid or rocky situations.

As neither oxen nor boors made their appearance this day, though the weather was quite favorable, we were compelled to remain stationary.

5th. It rained during the whole night, and continued all the next day in heavy showers, with now and then only, a short interval of sunshine. At eight in the morning, four boors came with the voorspans; but the rain had rendered the road so slippery, that, it being useless to attempt the ascent, they went with their oxen to wait at Van der Westhuisen's, till the weather cleared up, and the road became dryer and less dangerous.

The field-cornet's requisition produced but a trifling supply of flour; and the whole quantity obtained from three farms was not more than four pecks.

The day passed miserably cold and wet; the thermometer being as low as 43° (6·11 Centig.)* Our station being on a declivity, occasioned a new species of inconvenience: the water washed away our fire, and drove the Hottentots to another spot. Here they contrived to keep one alight, by digging a channel to turn the water off. Under a shelter of mats, they sat patiently the whole day; a patience as much to be attributed to brandy and tobacco, as to their natural disposition to endure hardships without complaining. At night they strewed under the waggons a layer of bushes, that the water

---

* As the whole of the observations on the *weather*, the state of the *thermometer*, and the *distance* travelled each day, are given in the *Itinerary* at the end of the volume, it has not been thought necessary to repeat them in the Journal, unless they were remarkable, or otherwise required by the narrative. Where no particular thermometer is mentioned, that of *Fahrenheit* is always to be understood; and, for its corresponding degree on *Reaumur's* scale, the Itinerary is to be referred to.

might find a passage under their beds, without keeping them from their sleep, as it had done the night before.

While confined to the waggon by the weather, I employed the time in arranging some zoological lists, to assist my researches on the animals that were likely to be met with in this part of Africa.

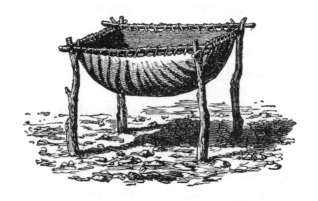

CHAPTER XII.

JOURNEY THROUGH THE ROGGEVELD TO THE BORDERS OF THE COLONY.

AUGUST 6th. The day was occasionally showery, and extremely cold. * The boors came again with their oxen, and at noon we commenced the ascent of the mountain. The road was exceedingly steep, winding in different directions to avoid the deep ravines; but was less rocky than the other kloofs of the colony which I had passed, although the rain had now rendered it slippery and dangerous.

At one spot towards the top of the mountain, where the acclivity was greatest, the oxen slid from side to side, unable to keep on their feet; and the great weight of the waggon began to drag them backwards, in spite of their utmost exertions. The two boors, who were driving, were in the greatest anxiety and alarm, not only for the fate of the waggons, but also for the safety of their own cattle. Witnessing their perilous situation from below, I scrambled hastily out of the road, to save myself among the rocks, expecting to behold every thing hurried headlong down the steep, and for some moments

---

* The thermometer being only 38° (+ 3·33 Cent.)

giving up all for lost. By singular good fortune, the wheel took a direction against a large block of stone, which lay on one side of the road, and thus gave the cattle time to recover their feet, and take breath. The drivers debated whether it would be possible to reach the summit till the ground was become dryer. At length, after allowing the teams to rest a few minutes, they resolved to make the attempt, rather than have the trouble of coming again another day. Accordingly, two Hottentots followed each waggon with large stones, ready to scoat the wheels the moment they began to run backwards; and, by a smart application of the whip, and loud whooping, the oxen made an extraordinary exertion, happily surmounted this dangerous place, and safely gained the summit of the pass.

From this summit, a country, scattered over with hills, extends itself northward, without any very perceptible descent; and it is therefore concluded that the Roggeveld is the most elevated land of the colony, excepting Sneeuwberg and Coudveld, as I have before stated. * The *Hantam-berg*, lying in the direction of north-north-west from the Roggeveld mountain, is said to be also very high land, and is remarkable for being one of the few situations in this part of the country where horses are not liable to the *Paardeziekte* (Horse-distemper), which rages during the summer-season, and annually carries off great numbers.

Climbing this mountain, occupied us an hour and forty minutes, after making allowance for the delays; and on arriving at the top, the thermometer was found to have fallen nine degrees and a half; it standing then at three degrees and a half below the freezing point. (−2°·9 Centig.).   In guessing the height of this part of the Roggeveld above the level of the sea, I am guided only by the frequent ascents in the road from the Cape to this spot; and am aware that, from such vague data, I may be much mistaken in stating the height to be between six and seven thousand feet.   Yet the air

---

* At page 81.

here being throughout the year so much colder than it might be expected in this latitude, is a proof of the very great elevation of surface.

At the upper part of the ascent, in the shade of some large blocks of stone, lay a small quantity of snow still unmelted; and near it, *Acæna latebrosa,* and a pretty undescribed species of *Alyssum,* were found growing.* An opinion that many of the plants of the Roggeveld are sufficiently hardy to bear the winters of England, is not altogether speculative; as some which have been raised in our gardens from seeds taken from my herbarium, have survived the last five winters, without the least care or protection. It is probable that many plants which grow on the snowy tops of great mountains, will endure the cold of the English climate. But the reverse of this is not to be taken as a rule without exceptions, since repeated experiment has ascertained that several species of *Lycium,* the seeds of which were picked from the specimens I gathered in the Karro and in low lands, will endure the severest winters of England, without injury.

It would be an object, in vegetable physiology, worth some attention, the detecting of that principle in the organization of plants, or the discovering of that peculiar structure, or those chemical properties of their juices, from which some genera are naturally hardy, as, for instance, *Mentha* †, and others tender, as may be observed in *Solanum,* without any regard to the climate of which they are natives.

A neat pretty shrub of the order *Thymeleæ* ‡, growing here to the height of two feet, and which was never since met with any where else, was remarkable from having flowers of an azure color. The rhinoceros-bush, which was not seen any where in the Karro,

---

* *Alyssum glomeratum,* B. Catal. Geogr. 1304. Under which name, the description of it has already been given to the public by Professor *De Candolle,* in his *Systema Naturale;* a work which, when completed, will stand as a monument of superior talents combined with great industry.

† *Mentha Capensis,* which has been introduced into England only five years, is as perfectly hardy as the *common Mint.*

‡ *Gnidia? cyanea.* Cat. Geog. 1316. 1.

here makes its appearance again.   But on the mountain itself, I did not observe a single plant deserving the name of tree.

From the edge of the mountain, we had a very extensive view over the Karro bounded by the Bokkeveld mountains to the south; but the weather being cloudy and showery, many other mountains which, under a clearer sky, may be seen from here, could not at this time be distinguished.

Having had the necessary assistance of the *voorspans* in getting the waggons up this toilsome and difficult ascent, I finally dismissed them, intending in future to travel with my own oxen.   We waited no longer than was requisite for changing the teams; after which we proceeded at a brisk pace, the road, or, to speak more correctly, the track worn down by the colonists' waggons, being level and free from every obstruction.

The pack-waggon led the way, and was a good distance in advance, when it was observed suddenly to drop to the ground; surprised at so strange and unexpected an accident, we hastened forward, and discovered that the main bolt, which passes through the iron *langwagen* and connects the fore and after axletrees, not having been properly secured, had fallen out; and the consequence was, as we had seen, that the after axletree with its wheels parted from the rest, and all the contents of the waggon tumbled out upon the road.   At first, we were fearful that some principal part was broken; but, on examination, had the satisfaction to find that it was an accident we could ourselves rectify.   We were detained nearly two hours in reloading and putting every thing in order again.

The country in which we were now travelling, is called the *Middel Roggeveld* (Middle Rye-land); the *Onder* (Further) *Roggeveld*, lies north-north-westward, and joins the Hantam division; and the *Kleine* (Little) *Roggeveld* lying eastward, joins the division of *Nieuwveld* (New-land).   I saw none of the wild rye which has been said to be so abundant as to give the name to this district; but this might be owing to the season of the year.

We had now taken leave of the inhabited part of the colony, and with it all intercourse with white men.   From these no assistance could, in future, be obtained : all now depended upon ourselves, a solitary party roaming over an almost trackless land.

The wind blew cold and boisterous, and clouds obscured the moon, when we discovered the ruins of a hut, of which nothing but the walls remained.* Here we took shelter for the night. Never was there more occasion for a fire than at this time, and seldom have we had more difficulty in finding fuel : the thermometer was six degrees below the freezing point, and the bleak wind scattered the very ashes of our fire as fast as they were burnt. My fingers being too much benumbed to hold the pen, I was compelled to neglect my journal till the next day. †

7th. The common *crow*, or that which is most extensively dispersed over the colony, is one of a shining purple-black color, with a white neck.‡ Great numbers frequent the Roggeveld : they approached us without fear, to pick up the scraps of meat; and would hardly move out of the way of the dogs, till they approached within a few paces.

The road this day was remarkably smooth, and better for travelling, even than those of the Karro. The country was very level, having, here and there, a few eminences; in many places, however, it is rocky. Scarcely a blade of grass is here to be found ; but in its place, the surface is clothed with low bushes, all bearing marks of having been closely browsed upon by the innumerable flocks of sheep which cover the Roggeveld in the summer season. All the strata of the hills were horizontal ; and the geological features appeared quite different from those of the neighbourhood of the Cape of

---

* This spot is pointed out on my map by the words *Freezing Station.*
† The plants noted in my catalogue this day, were—

Ancistrum latebrosum	*Arctotis*
Alyssum glomeratum. C. G. 1304	*Hemimeris*
Oxalis lupinifolia	*Selago*
Gnidia? cyanca. C.G. 1316. 1.	*Pelargonium*
Calendula	*Polygula*
Septas	*Cineraria,* and *Parmelia.*

‡ La Corneille à scapulaire blanc. Le Vaill. Ois. d'Afr. pl. 53.

Good Hope. The predominating rock was a sandstone, and the soil exhibited evident appearances of a ferrugineous nature. The marks of much rain having lately fallen here, were observable: but the thunder showers which water this district, fall very locally, and are uncertain in their course; so that it happens that some spots do not receive the rains till late in the season, while others are very early; and as it is on this circumstance that vegetation entirely depends, the time of its recurrence cannot be known with any precision.*

The Hottentots reported having seen *Quakkas* †; and, expecting soon to fall in with abundance of large game, began to get their muskets and powder-horns in readiness. I saw, with my glass, a solitary female ostrich, as it was feeding amongst the low shrubs, but this bird had not, any where in our journey hitherto, been seen in great numbers.

At sunset, we arrived at *Jakhals Fontein* (Jackals' Fountain), and took up our quarters for the night in an uninhabited farm-house. It has been already mentioned, that the colonists of the Roggeveld quit their houses during the winter to reside in the Karro. On these occasions, they carry with them all their furniture, and every thing that is moveable; giving themselves no concern about the fate of their house, which they entirely desert and leave even unfastened. In these, a traveller may always take shelter, and, whenever we came to one at the end of a day's journey, my men took advantage of it; but for myself, it was thought more prudent to remain in the waggon to watch over the property it contained, and to protect it from the depredation of runaway slaves or vagabond Hottentots.

8th. The next day we crossed the beds of several rivers, now completely dried up, the largest of which was *Rhenoster* (or

---

* On this day were found —
  Heliophila seselifolia. Catal. Geog. 1318.   *Senecio*
  Trichonema. 2 species.   *Pteronia,* and a *genus* allied to *Buch-*
  Arctotis. 3 species.   *nera.*

      † *Equus Quagga.*

Rhinoceros) *river.* The animal from which it takes the name, is becoming every day more scarce in this part of the country, and indeed, is at present rarely to be met with. It is fond of inhabiting an open, dry country, such as this is, abundant in low bushes; but the advances of the colonists, and their destructive huntings, have alarmed, and driven, it more into the interior of the continent.

The inhabitants of this district, when in want of resin, use as a substitute, a gum which exudes from different species of shrubs * ; which they therefore call *Harpuis bosch* (Resin bush). Of this gum, a considerable quantity might be collected.

In the evening we arrived at *Kuilenberg* (Pit Mountain), probably so named from some holes or hollows, where water may generally be found; for, in dry countries, any circumstance relating to water, is of sufficient importance to distinguish that place. Thus it is that the Dutch word *Fontein* is made such liberal use of in every part of the Colony: the Hottentot word *Kamma* (water,) is not less frequently found in the composition of the aboriginal names.

In taking possession of the farm-house here, we disturbed a number of sparrows † which are said to be a troublesome bird to farmers, and well deserving the name they have given it, of *Koornvreeter* (Corn-eater). It has very much the manners of the common domestic sparrow of Europe, and seems also to

---

* Species of *Othonna*, one of which is, perhaps, the *Othonna trifida* of Thunberg. The botany of this day's journey was distinguished by

Relhania paleacea	Hooker in opere suo pulcherrimo
Othonna trifida	de Muscis Exoticis.
Heliophila pubescens. C. G. 1334.	
Mesembryanthemum campestre. C. G.	*Lanipila.* C. G. 1336. Genus *Cotulæ*
1340. Sesquipedale erectum. Flores	affine. Nomen à *lana* et *pila;* ob
rosei. Affine *M.pulchello*, Haworthii.	semina lanâ involuta, et in capitulo
Limosella cœrulea. C. G. 1341. Planta	spherico conglomerata.
pollicaris. Flos cœruleus	*Eriocephalus*
Trichonema tortuosa, B.	*Pteronia*
Grimmia campestris. C. G. 1344. 2.	*Oxalis*
Tortula recurvata. C. G. 1344. 4.	*Androcymbium*
Hujus et precedentis, figuram dedit	*Tillæa*
	Erinus.

† *Fringilla arcuata*

prefer nesting in the habitations of man. Three were caught in the thatch, where they had taken their night's station.

9th. The road continued very level, but the face of the country began to be more thickly scattered over with eminences; and might be considered as a plain studded with a multitude of hills of regular form and horizontal strata, and of various heights from one hundred to three hundred feet. They were clothed with abundance of shrubby bushes, none being more than two feet in height and as much in diameter. The most predominant shrub was a kind of *Lycium* of about four or five feet high, of robust growth and very thorny. * *Mesembryanthemum campestre*, now in bloom, every where decorated the road; and a kind of *Hebenstreitia*, whose flowers smell like mignionette, was not unfrequent. The surface of the land was perfectly destitute of grass; a kind of Fescue-grass being a rare and solitary exception.

Neither men, nor animals of any description, were seen the whole day. Our little party were the only moving objects; amongst these *Speelman*'s grotesque figure often made me smile. He had lately dragged out of his budget, a military full-dress cocked hat, which some of his comrades in Cape Town had given him. And, not satisfied with the fashion of it, he had altered it to his own taste, by letting the brim half down, so as to give it a wider and more formidable appearance: sometimes, for variety's sake, it was let quite down like a parasol. With this strange apparatus on his head, his short blue jacket, sheepskin breeches, naked legs, his gun on his

---

* Very like *L. tetrandrum*, but is probably the *L. horridum* of Thunberg: Growing amongst a variety of low shrubs, I collected—

Hebenstreitia integrifolia?	tentots and Bushmen make their
Aptosimum depressum. C. G. 1354.	mats.
Trichonema spirale, C. G. 1356.	*Medeola angustifolia,* Willd. Sp. Pl.
Planta exigua. Folia spiraliter	*Lappago*
contorta. Flos purpureus.	*Othonna*
Heliophila pectinata, C. G. 1362.	*Leysera*
Alyssum glomeratum	*Relhania*
Scirpus tegetalis, C. G. 1346. (*Schœnus*	*Pteronia*
inanis, Th.?) of which the Hot-	*Hemimeris.*

shoulder and powder-horn by his side, he had little resemblance to the costume of any nation on the globe, and would have raised a smile in any but Hottentots, who seemed much to envy him the possession of that charming hat.   And Hannah, I doubt not, the more she looked at it, the more she admired her husband.

We passed through an opening in one of the ridges of hills, which bore the name of *Poort egaal* (The Equal Pass), on account, most probably, of the road continuing through it, on the same level with the land on either side: I stopped the waggons a few minutes to take a sketch of this view.

After a journey of fourteen miles, we arrived at the *Riet river* (Reed river), the place where it had been agreed to wait for the missionaries.   Captain Berends, we now found, had already left the spot: we therefore concluded that he was waiting for us at the Karree river, the last appointed rendezvous,

The *Reed river*, although at present nothing more than a line of ponds, is, in the rainy season, a considerable stream.   This, the *Sack river* ninety-three miles further, and the *Brakke river*, are all the rivers worth notice, that were met with in the road from the Roggeveld mountains to the Gariep, a distance of 358 miles.   And even these cease to flow during more than six months in the year.   They are said to unite with the Sack river, and afterwards to find their way into the Gariep; but it is most probable that their waters never flow so far, unless in years when there happen to fall an unusual quantity of rain.

The range of the thermometer to-day was remarkable ; being, at a quarter before nine in the forenoon, so low as 33°, and at three in the afternoon, so high as 72°. (0°·55, and 22°·2 Centig.)

The Hottentots chose their abode in the farm-house, and it was fortunate that I had already taken the resolution of always sleeping in the waggon ; for, between one and two o'clock in the night, when I had not long put out the light, and was nearly asleep, I felt by the motion of the waggon that some one was endeavouring to get in. Thinking it might possibly be one of my own people searching for something, I called out, but receiving no answer, I drew a pistol from under my pillow; yet finding that no attack was intended, but rather that they were, it seems, surprised and disappointed at meeting with any one there, I could not suffer my hand to pull the trigger. On calling out again in a louder tone, they instantly scrambled away with the greatest precipitation, tumbling over the yokes which lay spread out on the ground. Having got clear off, I heard them at a distance, talking to the rest of their gang, explaining, most probably, the little chance there was of their expected booty, and rejoicing at their own escape. Of what nation these robbers were, or their number, we never could discover; but had they been less timid, I might have been overpowered and plundered of every thing; for the Hottentots, who were but a few yards off, were all so sound asleep that they heard nothing of the noise, nor were they aware of the occurrence till it was mentioned the next morning. It was henceforward made a standing order that none of them should come to the waggon at night, without first giving notice by calling out their name.

10*th.* The weather this day was remarkably pleasant, and rendered a stroll along the river exceedingly delightful. The scenery possessed, in some points, a character that had not been noticed before. The rushes, which in many places thickly hedged in the sides of the ponds, exhibited a species of the picturesque quite new and peculiar. No trace of man or his works disturbed the more pleasing harmony of Nature. All that was beheld here, was the uncontrolled effect of natural causes.

The *Bonteberg* (Spotted Hill,) seen at a little distance, is remarkable for several large red spots, irregularly disposed upon its side. The bed of the river is not sunk very deep below the surface and consequently its waters must occasionally overflow the surrounding flats, to a considerable extent, of which there was evident proofs. The pools, or ponds, met with at frequent intervals along the bed, being never quite dried up, contain fish, as I was informed by the Hottentots, of the sort mentioned on the 31st of August.* The water was quite clear and fresh.

---

* See the representation of it, at the end of Chapter XII.

These ponds, called *Zeekoe-gatten*, (Sea-cow holes,) are gene-rally supposed to have been made by *Hippopotami*, when that huge animal still held an undisturbed domain in these waters. It appears more probable, that they merely took advantage of these hollows, finding in them a depth of water sufficient to cover their bodies; and where the bottom was not rocky, they might have enlarged them by their continual trampling.

From a kind of *rush* * which here is remarkably abundant, the river may possibly have derived its name, as very little of the true reed is any where to be seen, unless it may be found in some other part of the river. In the thickest masses of this rush, generally lie concealed a large sort of *coot* †, entirely black, and distinguished by two red warts on the forehead. I obtained two for my collection: their flesh, when stewed, was good eating. Of this rush, which is called the *Hard Matjes-goederen*, the Hottentots, in these districts, make all their mats, which are much more durable than those made of *Cyperus textilis*, distinguished by the name of *Sagt* (soft), *Matjes-goederen*, the material of all the mats made near Cape Town. The first forms a thatch that will last for many years; all the huts of the Roggeveld colonists are covered with it.

11*th*. Tempted again by the clearness and serenity of the weather, I equipped myself for a ramble alone, that I might the more freely enjoy my observations; I pursued the course of the river downwards till it conducted me into a narrow winding defile between moderately high rocky mountains, rising abruptly on either hand. Projecting from their sides stood enormous masses of rock of singular appearance, formed of large cubic blocks of sandstone, piled regularly on each other, and richly varied with all the tints of bistre, terra-di-sienna, and the different ochres. The intervening acclivity was composed of loose fragments which had fallen from the upper part of the rocks. A broad horizontal band, or stratum, of

---

* *Scipus tegetalis.* B.   † *Fulica cristata.*

grey rock, formed an appropriate basement to such a superstructure. Close at the foot of this, the river silently crept along, forcing its way between the rushes, which seemed as if endeavouring to smother its stream, or compel it to seek another course. The opposite side of the defile, warmed by a glowing sunshine, and winding round out of sight, gradually receded in aërial perspective. The deserted silence of the spot, was broken only by the noise of wild geese, or the echo of my gun. I climbed the rocks, but found every thing withered or quite parched up, and was able to collect nothing as a memorial of the *Reed-river Pass*, excepting a little plant of *Hermannia*, which appeared quite new and curious.

Having before stated that the Reed river consisted at this season of merely an unconnected line of ponds, it may have appeared contradictory to describe it as *running* through the pass; and I was myself surprised at the fact. On attentively examining the dry parts of the bed, it was found in most places, sufficiently loose and gravelly to admit of a passage for the water *underground*. Without this being the case, it would be difficult to account for the limpid clearness and purity of the water of these pools.

Varying my route, in returning homewards, I came to a part of the river, where the wild beauty and harmonious tints of the landscape detained me till I had taken a sketch. It was nearly sunset; the water was smooth and transparent; the distant hills glowed with a mild warm hue; and there was a certain beautiful appearance in the rushes which grew in the water along the bank, that no painting could express. Their principal color was a fine dark sober green, enlivened by the sun. Towards the bottom, where they were constantly wetted by the gentle rippling of the stream, a dark line, nearly black, marked the division between the real and the reflected stalks, so resembling each other as almost to deceive the eye, and lead the spectator to believe that he saw rushes of a double length. Their tops being dead or half withered, were of every shade between white, Naples-yellow, and light-ochre, but more generally partaking of the white or the ochre. They spread in large extended patches, like a cornfield, often to a great distance from the water side, exhibiting an inimitable delicacy and gradation of keeping. The hills in the back-ground, of a reddish barren hue mellowed by the rich light of the setting sun, contrasted, and rendered more beautiful, the singular pale line formed by the tops of the rushes; whose tall, slender, straight form served to exemplify the assertion that, in a landscape, no shape or uniformity is unpleasing when shadowed and tinted by Nature. The observant artist may discover that the beauty of his picture, depends far less on the choice of subject than on the mode of managing it. If those painters who, having neither taste nor genius, would spend a part of their time in the observation, and confine themselves to the plain copying, of what is before them, their works would possess a certain share of merit; while on the contrary, by attempting to soar above the imitation of Nature, their pictures are entitled only to that of being the production of their own imagination.

12th. At this place my Hottentots went out every day hunting, but without success: their object was that beautiful animal the Mountain-horse or Dauw. * Here I procured, for the first time, the *Das* or *Dasje.* † This is of a brown color, and has much the appearance of a Rabbit: it is found in rocky places, where it takes shelter in the crevices. Its flesh is eatable; but the animal is exceedingly wary and difficult to get. *The Wilde-gans* (Wild-goose) ‡ shot here, is a large well-tasted bird, and was always found in pairs, although very shy, and flying exceedingly well for so heavy a bird: it may often be discovered by its short quacking noise. At this place we met with, for the first time, the *Namaqua Partridge*, a very small species of Grous. §

---

* *Equus montanus:* the description of which has been given at page 138 of this volume.

† *Hyrax Capensis:* the early colonists frequently gave the names of European animals to those of the Cape, without much discrimination, and on no better grounds than a very vague resemblance. Thus it is, that the present bears the name of *Das* or Badger.

‡ *Anas cana.* Sys. Nat. ed. Gmel.

§ *Tetrao Namaquana.* Sys. Nat. ed. Gmel. — *Pterocles.* Temminck, Manuel d'Ornithologie, 2nde ed.

The *Roode-bekje* (Red beak) *, a small finch, seen here in great numbers, is a very common bird, and widely dispersed over the whole country. An ostrich's nest, having only three eggs, was found in the plains.

13*th.* The missionaries arrived in the evening; our party now mustered six waggons with their proportion of people, four horses, a large flock of sheep, and a pack of dogs.

I was here informed of a circumstance which vexed me exceedingly: a Hottentot entrusted with the mail for the Bokkeveld and Karro, had broken it open in expectation of finding money, and thrown all the letters away: some of which had been picked up again and were delivered according to their address. Amongst those which had been thus recovered, was one for the missionaries; and for a long time I continued uneasy at the idea that this mail might have contained letters for me also.

14*th.* The day commenced with a furious wind, and dust flying in all directions; but towards the afternoon these began to abate. Our road led through the *Reed-river Pass,* in which we had to wade through the water three times; and this, with the difficulty of the road, occasioned us to be not less than three quarters of an hour in going through this defile. The country we afterwards travelled over was open, and generally level, though rocky, and apparently very barren. The earth was of a reddish color, scattered over with low stunted bushes, without a single verdant blade of grass in the interstices. Here and there, short compact patches of a singular kind of grass †, of an arid look, were observed, most of which were in part dead; the decay commencing at the centre, and spreading outward.

We halted at *Stink Fontein* (Stinking Spring), where there was no water but what was obtained with difficulty, by digging pits in the bed of a rivulet. It was not found so objectionable as the name of the place would imply.

Here the magnetic variation was observed to be 27°$\frac{1}{2}$ W.

---

* *Loxia Astrild.* Linn.   † *Aristida ? centrifuga,* B. Cat. Geogr. 1392.

15th. The oxen having become leaner from the scarcity of water and pasturage, we removed no further than to *Seldery̆ Fontein* (Celery Spring), a distance of little more than five miles, over a level country thickly covered with small shrubs; amongst which a thorny kind * was most abundant and troublesome.

The latitude of *Celery Spring* was ascertained to be 32° 9′ 23″.†

16th. We moved six miles further, to *Kánna Kraal*, on the Little Reed river, and so named by the Hottentots, from a shrub ‡ which grows there; and, on the next day, seven miles and a half, to the *Karree river.*

Here we found waiting for us, the party of Hottentots under Berends, who were on their way home to Klaarwater, and whom we had expected to make part of our caravan through the wild and desert Bushman country. Our numbers now, with women and children, amounted to ninety-seven persons. They had with them eight waggons, and the usual proportion of oxen, besides sheep and horses. Most of them were armed with muskets, and clad, generally, in jackets and trowsers, either of woollen cloth or of tanned sheep-leather, with shoes of raw hide. Many had cotton shirts and hats of Cape manufacture; yet the kaross, a genuine Hottentot dress, made of sheep-skin prepared with the hair on, was pretty much used by both sexes. Their women and children constituted a third of the number. The younger of the latter were half naked; but the women were decently clothed, some in gowns and aprons of printed calico or leather, neatly made up in the Dutch manner. All had their heads closely bound up with coloured cotton handkerchiefs. There were but very few who did not speak the Dutch

---

* *Mesembryanthemum spinosum.*

† 16th August, 1811, at Seldery Fontein, the observed altitude of the sun's centre, when on the meridian, was 43 51′ 47″.

‡ *Salsola aphylla. Kanna* also signifies the antelope called *Eland.* The *Kanna-bosch* (written *Ganna* by the Dutch) may probably have been considered as the favourite food of the *Kanna;* and in this sense the word *Kannaland,* the name of a part of the Cape colony, may with equal correctness be supposed to intend a country abounding either in the Eland, or in this shrub.

language fluently, being nearly all Hottentots of the mixed race, and in the yearly practice of visiting the colony.

Besides these Hottentots, a party of five *Caffres*, and their wives, were resting here.   These men were not less than six feet in height, strong and finely proportioned ; and, excepting a leathern kaross, wore no covering whatever ; a circumstance, as far as I have since been able to learn, quite peculiar to the *Kosas*, or Caffres on the eastern side of the colony.   Their bodies and cloaks were reddened all over with ochre mixed up with grease.   They accosted us in an easy manly tone, and with manners perfectly free from servile timidity.   These, with seven others left on the Sack River, had come from their kraal on the *Gariep,* for the purpose, as they stated, of bartering in the colony for tobacco ; and begged the missionaries to give them a letter to the Veldcornet Maritz ; which however was very properly refused.   We were rather surprised at so unexpected a rencontre with some of the very men on whose account so much uneasiness had been felt, and could not avoid suspecting them of being sent as spies to discover the strength of our party.   We taxed them with the intention of attacking and robbing us in the Bushman country ; and threatened them on our part with a warm reception, if they thought proper to make the attempt.

But whether the report we had heard to this effect was really unfounded, or whether, seeing our caravan so strong, they thought it prudent to relinquish the plan, or to dissemble, they now affected the greatest submission, and the most friendly disposition. They protested vehemently against the falsity of what had been reported to us, and attributed it to the malice and jealousy of the Bushmen, with whom they had long been on hostile terms, and who, in a recent skirmish, had killed their chief, one of Sambie's brothers ; in consequence of which their whole kraal had meditated a return to their own country, or at least as far as the borders of Bruyntjes Hoogte.

They assumed a canting good-natured tone of voice, and were the most importunate beggars I had ever met with ; soliciting for tobacco, or whatever else they saw which they thought would be useful; complaining also that their wives' heads were uncovered, and much required a handkerchief to protect them from the sun. It was impossible to avoid their importunities, except by granting what they asked for ; and at last we got rid of them, by giving three legs of mutton, a handkerchief for each, and a quantity of tobacco, enough for them and their wives. I purchased of one of these men, for a handkerchief, a very neat basket, wove with rushes so admirably close, that they are always used for holding milk or other liquids. He was careful not to let this opportunity pass, without begging for something ; and first requested to have some brandy, which being refused, he immediately asked for money to buy some ; for these people are shrewd enough to understand very well the nature and use of the Cape money. Two of them could speak Dutch very readily ; and the principal one, with a polite and friendly air, that I little expected in a savage, if such a term could properly be applied to him, gently raised my hand to his lips on taking leave, and expressed at the same time the warmest acknowledgments of gratitude for the presents I had made them. After this they quietly retired to their fire at the other side of a rising ground, about two hundred yards distant, where they passed the night.

18th. Early on the following morning, and before I was up, they departed : but, previously coming to my waggon, said they must see the Englishman before they went, and called out, wishing me to get up. I asked what they had to say, on which they again began to beg for meat and tobacco, not satisfied with having obtained two shoulders of mutton this morning, and another large supply of tobacco. Finding, however, that I was not likely soon to come out to them, each one cried out as he passed the waggon, *Morg manill !* *morg manill !* * which I returned, and they immediately proceeded on their way, and were soon out of sight.

19th, — 23rd. We remained at this place several days on account of the Hottentots, who, not expecting our arrival so soon, and finding here no food for their cattle, had sent them, for the sake of better pasture, to a place at the distance of two days' journey.

---

* Meaning to say, " *Goeden morgen, mynheer,*" Good morning, Sir.

During these days, the weather was remarkably variable: sometimes very hot, the thermometer at 80°, and, at other times, down
to the freezing point.; attended with rain or hail, and violent winds,
generally from the south-west quarter.   The only shelter my men
could find, was a few bushes, against which a mat was placed.   Here
they sat the whole day, their chief employment being smoking, talking, keeping up the fire, or attending their pot.   Each in his *jas*
(great-coat) defied the weather, and sat quite at ease.   The brim of
Speelman's grand hat was now let down, and, during the rain, completely answered the purpose of an umbrella.   *Hannah*, wrapped in
her kaross, seldom stirred from her seat under the bush; while
Philip, to show his greater degree of civilization and polish, seated
himself on one of the water-casks, leaving *Gert* to take advantage of
a small mound of earth near the fire.   As I sat in my waggon,
I made a drawing of this party: it which forms the subject of
the *vignette* at the head of the chapter.

Here I obtained a sort of *Partridge* *, of a uniform ash-brown
color, every where marked with fine white lines, excepting the quill-
feathers and the head.   The feathers of the breast, each with a white
stripe down the middle; the beak and legs of a bright red: but the
ridge of the upper mandible, the nails, and the eyes, were black, and
had two nasal caruncles, of a blackish ash-color.   It was called by
the colonists *Faisánt* (Pheasant), a name, in this instance, quite
misapplied.

The *Schaapwagtertje* (the Little Shepherd), so called from its
familiarity in approaching the Hottentots while tending their sheep,
is a bird common in all the open country of this part of Africa. †

Here we received the information that *Africaander*, a noted
Hottentot freebooter, had forced one of the missionaries in Namaqualand to fly from his station on the Orange river (Gariep), and take
refuge within the colony.   This name has been rendered more formid-

---

* *Perdix Capensis.*
† It is *Le Traquet Pâtre* of Le Vaillant, Ois. d'Afr. pl. 180.; and, perhaps, the
Motacilla aurantia, Sys. Nat. ed. Gm.

able, by its collecting into a single history the deeds of two men equally worthless, the father and son. The former, being at this time too old to commit more mischief, was living peaceably; but one of his sons had proved himself a successor not inferior in villany. The others condemned their brother's conduct, and had as yet shown no symptoms of a similar disposition. This lawless leader, who had associated with him a strong party of marauders of various tribes, and was the terror of all the country around, had advanced upwards along the river, as far as the great waterfall, where, falling in with a party of the Klaarwater Hottentots, he had harassed and attacked them: nor was it known at the time this intelligence came away, whether they had been able to stand against him or not. In addition to this unpleasant news, it was reported that seventy oxen had been driven off from Klaarwater by some of the hostile Bushmen.

A few days before we arrived at the Karree river, four horsemen were despatched to *Klaarwater*, or, as many of the Hottentots called it, *Klaarfontein*, to fetch fresh oxen; those belonging to most of the waggons appearing in a very lean and weak state.

Although every thing exhibited an extremely parched and sterile appearance, there was still plenty of water in different hollows of the river; and in these, every evening, a multitude of frogs commenced their croaking concert, producing an extraordinary loud noise.

The latitude of this place I computed to be $32° 3' 38''$ *; and confirmed my former observation of the magnetic variation being $27\frac{1}{4}°$ W.

24*th*. Yesterday the violence of the wind and inclemency of the weather, with even some snow, prevented our travelling. Early this morning the ground was again covered with snow; and which, although the sun shone the whole morning, was not entirely melted away till noon. The thermometer was, at that hour, only $31°$, and rose no higher during the day than $45°$ ($7°·2$ C.).

---

* 18th August, 1811, at the Karree river, observed meridional altitude of the sun's centre, $44° 35' 42''$.

Leaving on our left the usual track to the Sack river, we were advised by the Hottentots to take a more eastward circuit, through the *Nieuwveld* (New-land, or New-country), in expectation of meeting with better pasture. The waggons, during this day, were dragged over a most rocky, unfrequented, and nearly pathless country, where the wheels of our caravan imprinted a track that would be visible, perhaps, for several years. In one place, an ascent of between eight and ten hundred feet lay over rugged rocks and stones, that seemed, every minute, to threaten destruction to some of the crazy vehicles.

We halted for the night in a rocky situation, near a small river, where the fine scarlet flowers of a new kind of *Aloë* decorated the barren rocks, and gave a certain gay cultivated look to a spot, which, without them, would have appeared a rude neglected waste.* *Crabs*, of nearly two inches in diameter, of an olive-green, variegated with shades of lemon-color, were common in the running water here, and are often to be met with in the rivers of the Roggeveld.

25th. An accident occurred which prevented our travelling this day, and had nearly cost a Hottentot the loss of his life, and

---

* Among the plants found on the road from the Karree river, and at this station, were —

Mesembryanthemum magnipunctatum. B.	*Crassula columnaris*
Mesembryanthemum croceum	*Crassula pyramidalis*
Eriocephalus spinescens. Cat. Geog. 1419. Ramuli apicibus spinescentibus. Flores solitari, laterales.	*Pteronia*, 4 sp.
	Lanipila
	Cotyledon, n. sp.
Eriocephalus decussatus. C. G. 1407. Folia brevissima, sub-fasciculata et quadrifariàm decussata. Flores minuti, in singulo fasciculo solitarii.	*Salsola*, 2 sp.
	Hermannia
	Thesium
	Aster
	Ehrharta
Euphorbia Mauritanica	*Heliophila*
Euphorbia tenax. B.	*Solanum*
Aloë claviflora. C. G. 1425. 2. Acaulis. Folia elongata glauca, marginibus aculeatis. Flores densè spicati. Spica simplex. Corolla clavata, laciniis conniventibus.	*Leysera*
	Gnaphalium
	Eriocephalus
	Pelargonium.

me that of an eye. Observing Speelman busy with the lock of the great rifle-gun, I found that he had put the hair-trigger out of order. As soon as I had rectified and fixed it on again, not supposing the piece loaded, I snapped the cock, on which it went off, although there was no priming in the pan. The ball, by a providential guidance, passed between the people, who were sitting around in all directions, without doing any injury; but the flash from the pan scorched my eye, and rendered me blind for the remainder of the day. The pain and inflammation were at length alleviated by continued bathing with warm water; but it was not ascertained till the next day, that my sight was uninjured, a discovery which, I need hardly say, rejoiced me as much as any event of my journey.

26th. This morning, as soon as the painful operation of picking the grains of powder out of my face had been submitted to, we departed from this rivulet, which, though none of us knew the name of it, would be sufficiently impressed on our memory by the fortunate escape we had all had.

Our intention was to have reached Kleine Quagga Fontein this evening; but half-way, unexpectedly finding a family of colonists, who had taken up this wandering life for the sake of pasture for their flocks and herds, they earnestly persuaded us to tarry till the next day. The spot, though arid, was agreeable: some scattered bushes of considerable size, and low hills on either side, gave it a sheltered and comfortable appearance. * Their abode was merely their two waggons, and a hemispherical hut, made of mats, after the Hottentot manner. They received us with much good will, and were proud of entertaining us in the hut with their best fare; among which was some of the finest wheaten bread, a treat quite unlooked for in this part of the colony. Falling in, at this place, with civilized beings, after we had bid adieu to all society of the kind, was to me a very pleasing

---

* I here met with a remarkable species of *Avond-bloem* (*Hesperanthera*). This genus is very widely dispersed, and occasionally to be found all over the colony, and even beyond it.

occurrence, as it presented once more an opportunity of writing letters.

This man, whose name was *Gaertner*, was a native of Germany, and his wife of Holland : they had been five years servants to a rich Cape boor, and were now beginning the world on their own account. They seemed industrious and active ; but their industry, together with a certain degree of superiority, which European knowledge generally gives, excited, as they said, some jealousy and unkindness in the behaviour of their Africaander neighbours towards them. They possessed a good stud of horses, to the breeding of which they paid much attention. Four or five Hottentot shepherds and herdsmen accompanied them in their migrations from place to place.

A young man, also a native of Germany, followed their fortunes in the capacity of an overseer or bailiff; but seemed to have no relish for such a life, as he complained much of its dull monotony. Day after day, said he, our mouths open for nothing but mutton, and to repeat those remarks that have already been made on the same subjects a thousand times before. Sheep, oxen, waggons, horses, elands, guns, fat and lean, came, he complained, so often into conversation, that he heartily longed to give up this mode of living ; and would, if permitted, gladly follow me. To the latter wish, however, I gave no encouragement. He might, it is very likely, have found his servitude irksome and unprofitable ; but, I doubt not, had these sheep and oxen been his, that he, would have found as much pleasure and satisfaction in talking about them as the honest German, his master.

A new settler cannot expect at first setting out, any other than a life of labor, difficulties, and privations ; from which he will only be relieved gradually, and in proportion to his industry and frugality. The resources of a European mind will help him on rapidly towards comfort and enjoyment ; but it too often happens that, instead of holding fast the advantages of his education, he adopts the rude manners he at first despised, and, step after step, his life degenerates into mere sensual existence. His children follow ; and, for want of better example in their parents, complete the retrogression. But such, it is hoped, will not often be the case should Southern Africa become in future the refuge of *British emigrants;* especially if, occupying some districts by themselves, their numbers be large enough to form an English community and preserve their own customs.

The country we had passed over, since leaving the Karro Poort, offers but few spots that would tempt a European settler. Its aridity and unproductiveness during a great part of the year, would, if viewed at that season, deter almost any one. But, just after the rains have fallen, it puts on quite another face; and, judging from a few instances in our way, in which proper care had been taken in gardening and farming, I believe that many spots might be made to wear a pleasant look throughout the year, and well repay the labor of an industrious settler.

If aridity of soil and atmosphere be unfavorable to vegetation and agriculture, it must not be forgotten that it is highly conducive to health. Beneath the rich luxuriant foliage of a well-watered tropical country, too often lurk the fatal *miasmata* of fever, and the seeds of nervous debility, or of lingering indisposition. Just as the luxurious feast, or the frugal meal, bring either disease or health : the wholesome coarseness of the one too often rejected; while the allurements of the other conduct as frequently to misery as to enjoyment. The almost uninterrupted good health which I enjoyed during these travels, was, I always believed, to be attributed in a great degree to the general dryness of the air.

27th. At about half a mile from Gaertner's station, a boor and his family were, in the same manner, lying with their waggons and cattle. He came to us to beg we would make his quarters in our way, stop to give some advice for his daughter who lay very ill. Accordingly, after taking leave of the hospitable German and his wife, we proceeded, and halted for half an hour at this man's waggons.

Entering a low temporary hut formed of sticks, rushes, and mats, we found the unfortunate patient lying in a bed spread upon the ground. Both she and her mother had been expecting our visit, with hopes of hearing some cheering opinion of her case, or of receiving some beneficial advice. But how was I shocked the moment I beheld her, when obliged to intimate to the father that her disorder was incurable: the mother appeared greatly affected, and shed tears at hearing this. I saw, too plainly to be mistaken, all the symptoms of the loathsome leprosy; and hoped that the melancholy state of the case would not have been mentioned to the poor sufferer herself. But, one of the missionaries, rather ill-timedly, I thought, when he heard my opinion, communicated it to her; and, judging this a proper opportunity for giving some spiritual advice, knelt down by the bed-side, and endeavoured to console her with reflections on the shortness of life, representing to her how little it mattered whether we lived a longer or a shorter time in this world, so as we were but prepared for entering the next. Witnessing how distressing an effect this communication had upon her, and the family who were standing around, I wished that chance had not thrown me in their way to open their eyes to her hopeless situation, since we could offer neither remedy nor mitigation.

The father told me that, about three years ago, at which time her age was only eighteen, she had been vaccinated; but without any subsequent symptom of the inoculation having succeeded. Shortly afterwards she was attacked, as he said, with the measles; and this was followed by an irruption on her arm at the part where she had been vaccinated; after which her hands and face began to put on the deforming swollen appearance which we now beheld. She was said once to have possessed some share of beauty; but every feature was now disgusting; such is the usual effect of this dreadful disease. It is well ascertained that, fortunately, it cannot be communicated but through the blood; and here indeed was a melancholy instance and proof of its being so communicated by the means of inoculation.

What the fate of the poor young woman was after this, I never had an opportunity of knowing. Finding I could be of no service, I left this unhappy family with the most heartfelt commiseration for them, not less than for the ill-fated sufferer.

We travelled over a level country; but which was, in many places, so stony as to occasion such violent jolting that both the screws of the botanical press were broken asunder. This accident detained us three quarters of an hour, to bind them together; which was done with thongs of ox-hide, which, experience teaches, is the only cord strong enough to be used while travelling over a country like this.

We arrived at *Kleine Kwagga Fontein*, (Little Kwakka, or Quakka, fountain,) by moon-light.

28*th*. The next morning, plenty of excellent water was found; but, on the other hand, fire-wood was here exceedingly scarce. The weather, however, was warm enough by day, the thermometer being 76° (24°·4 Centig.). At midnight, it was 44° (6°·6 C.).

To *Dwaal river*, our next station, was a distance of nineteen miles, over a flat country, and a delightfully level, smooth road.* Its name, as I was told, was given by a hunting party of the earlier colonists, who here lost their way, as the name implies. We reached the place by moon-light, and found that all the Hottentot waggons had arrived before us. Their numerous fires had an exceedingly pleasing effect, and, being seen at a considerable distance, were useful in guiding us to the spot.

29*th*. I made a drawing of the scene; and afterwards, with some labor, climbed to the summit of a rocky conical hill, intending to take the magnetic bearings of our road, and of some remarkable mountains seen in the distance; but the great quantity of iron contained in the stone, and with which it was intimately combined in an oxydated state, rendered my compass useless, as the needle varied its position with every change of place. Some large detached masses of rock,

---

* On the road, species of the following genera were collected, many of which were quite new.

Gazania	Gnaphalium	Selago
Lidbeckia	Medicago	Eriocephalus
Arctotis, 4 sp.	Erinus, 2 sp.	Salvia
Senecio, 2 sp.	Ononis	Pteronia
Aira	Malva	Aizoon, &c.
Calendula		

And a curious syngenesious genus, having seeds something resembling those of *Tribulus*.

The *Arctotis*, No. 1451, having large handsome white flowers, and being exceedingly abundant, literally whitened the plains.

which, resting on others, happened to be duly poised, gave, on being struck, a sound as musical as that of a large bell. The whole hill was composed of the same stone; it appeared to be a very hard and compact kind of Primitive Greenstone. The prospect around was very extensive, yet not a tree was to be seen; low scattered bushes were all that covered the naked parched-up soil. *

The old report respecting the evil intentions of the *Caffres*, had been repeated by every body we met, and here it seemed to be confirmed. A baptized Hottentot, who had his abode not far off, paid us a visit for the purpose of letting us know that a countryman of his, who had just come from the Caffre Kraal on the Zak (Sack) river, assured him that they were, most certainly, strong in numbers, and resolved upon attacking us.

The whole caravan was now in commotion; and various were the feelings that agitated the party. A great majority of the Hottentots, recollecting the uneasiness and trouble these Caffres had several times before occasioned them, were determined on making a vigorous attack on their Kraal; and either destroy them altogether, or drive them out of the country. The missionaries again hesitated whether to go on, or to return; and a consultation was held, in which their wives assisted. At last, unable to decide in any other way, they solved the doubt by drawing lots; and, fortunately, the result was that they should continue their journey onwards.

The wife of our Hottentot chief, Berends, being unwell, and in

---

* At *Dwaal river*, I first met with *Hibiscus cucurbitinus*, Cat. Geog. 1481, a very remarkable species. In growth it had, at a short distance, so great a resemblance to plants of the gourd kind, that I was exceedingly surprised, on a nearer approach, to find upon it the flowers of an Hibiscus. It was called *Wilde Kalebás* (Wild Calabash) by our Hottentots. (*Planta valdè tomentosa procumbens. Folia rotundata repanda, suprà minùs tomentosa. Flores conferti in racemis axillaribus. Corolla rufa campanulata, vix calyce major.*)

Mahernia vernicata, Cat. Geog. 1461. grows in abundance between the rocks. (*Fruticulus glaber erectus pedalis, glutinosus. Folia pinnatifida. Flores flavi, petalis conniventibus.*)

On the plain, I picked up a *Pappophorum*, a genus of grass not before recorded as existing in Africa.

expectation of her accouchement, caused us to remain at this station a day longer.   This gave me an opportunity of taking an observation for the latitude, which I here found to be 31° 40′ 0′′.*

30th. The season of spring being now advancing, the days sensibly increased in warmth, though the nights still continued chilly.   At 8 o'clock in the morning, the thermometer was only 44° (6·6 C.) , but rose to 81° (27·2 C.) , in the middle of the day.

After about three hours travelling, we entered an opening in a range of low mountains, and halted for a quarter of an hour, to allow our oxen and sheep to drink at the Dwaal river, which here ran in a stream through a romantic rocky pass, called *Dwaal Riviers Poort·* I, in the meantime, climbed a craggy eminence on our left, whence I brought down some curious plants. †   The plains abounded in hares, of which our dogs caught three.

Speelman, and Maagers, who, in the pursuit of game, had deviated from the waggon-road, fell in with an *ostrich's nest,* containing within it seventeen eggs, and round the outside nine more. This being a number greater than they knew how to carry, and yet not enduring the idea of leaving any behind, they at last hit upon a strange expedient: they took off their shirts, and by tying them up at bottom, converted them into bags.   But these not holding more than half the number, their trowsers were next stripped off, and, in the same manner, the bottom of each leg being closed, they also were crammed full of eggs, and, being then secured at the waistband, were placed upon their shoulders.   The handkerchief which they wore round their head, was taken to supply the place of the trowsers. As they came towards us, nothing could be more grotesque and ridiculous than the figure they cut, with the trowsers thus sitting on

---

* 29th. August 1811, at Dwaal river, the observed meridional altitude of the sun's upper limb 48° 57′ 47″.

† Particularly a *thorny Mahernia,* and a beautiful *Gladiolus (Tritonia)* with orange-coloured flowers of a most delicate odor.   Here, also, between the rocks, grew a fine *Conium* six feet high.

Mahernia spinosa, C. G. 1484.   Fruticulus ramosus erectus glaber.   Folia minuta cuneata, apice sub-tridentata.   Pedunculi demùm spinescentes.

their shoulders, and their head just peeping out between the legs which projected before them.

All the Hottentots confirmed the fact of those nine eggs which were found on the outside of the nest, being intended as food for the young ostriches; and assured me that the eggs in this nest were the produce of two hens.

In the evening we reached the *Zak-rivier* (Sack-river), the northern boundary of the colony, where we remained stationary the four following days.

31st. This is the principal river between the Hex river and the Gariep. The stream was at this time very inconsiderable, though still running. Its banks were clothed with the mat-rush, and here and there with some fresh grass produced by rains, which appeared to have fallen lately. Not a tree was seen, to break the uniformity of the plain through which it meandered, or to mark its course: nor could it even be discovered, till we reached its banks.

In the deepest of its pools I found a beautiful kind of carp, entirely of a yellow-green with a brazen lustre.* The largest we saw was at least two feet long: that from which I made my drawing measured nineteen inches and a half. With a hook and line we caught many without much difficulty; their flesh was white, and of a very delicate taste. It was known by the name of *Geel-visch*, (Yellow-fish.) A *representation* of it is given at the end of the chapter

Although we offered to lend hooks and lines to any of the Hottentots, scarcely one would take the trouble to use them. They appeared to have little relish for such food, and less for that mode of employment; eagerly preferring the more toilsome one of hunting. In this all who had guns, spent their time during our stay. Several quakkas were shot, and the meat shared amongst them; it resembled horseflesh, as might be expected from the nature of the

---

* *Cyprinus aëneus.* B. Totus aënei coloris. Caput parvum, cirris duobus vix ore longioribus. Pinna dorsalis mutica radiis 10: pectoralis 13 vel 14: ventralis 9: analis 6; et caudalis 19: omnes concolores. Irides aëneæ. (Vide iconem Capitulo xii subjunctam.)

animal, and, though much praised, I felt no desire to make a meal of it.

Prudent precaution against future emergencies required that my little flock of sheep should be spared as long as possible, that it might be a resource in greater necessity, and I therefore supplied my men plentifully with powder and ball; but this produced for us at present but little food, owing as much to their want of practice in shooting, as to the scarcity of game. Philip, however, brought home a *Steenbok* *, the meat of which was very good-tasted.

The missionaries also distributed among their people, a large quantity of ammunition, to which I contributed my share, to be used only for the defense of the caravan in case of an attack from the Caffres, or the Bushmen. Every gun was kept ready loaded, and small parties held watch during the night, as we had now reached that part of our road where we might begin to expect some attempt on the part of the natives, to carry off our cattle. The country through which we had now to pass, is inhabited by the wild Hottentots usually called Bushmen; and, as they are almost always in a state of hostility towards the colonists, we were uncertain whether they would treat us as friends or as enemies; although the missionaries had every right to be considered as the former.

Their good intentions towards these savages had been unequivocally shown at a spot a few miles westward of our station; where, about twelve years before, they persevered for a year or two in endeavouring to establish a mission, and to give religious instruction to all who would attend. But, whether owing to the natural difficulties of the undertaking; to want of judgment on one side; or of inclination on the other, the attempt failed altogether.

September 1st. Several more waggons which had been expected, and for which we waited, joined us here; this being the last place appointed as a rendezvous. The number was now increased to eighteen, drawn up together on a wide open plain, where nothing covered the red arid soil, except here and there a scrubby stunted

---

* *Antilope rupestris;* already noticed at page 202.

bush, hardly a foot high. *   It seemed as if a village had suddenly risen up in the desert.   Each waggon had its own fire, around which a little party appeared sitting, generally protected from the wind by a screen of mats.   The oxen, sheep and goats grazing close by; the women going to the river or returning with their calabashes filled with water; the children running about at play: the men, some carrying loads of firewood, others coming home from hunting; together with horses and dogs moving in all directions; constituted a a novel and busy scene that rendered, by contrast, the silent lifeless waste by which we were surrounded, more forlorn and cheerless.

At this place happened the birth of our Hottentot captain's child; and, for the sake of the mother, we delayed our departure: but it did not seem that travelling was afterwards of any inconvenience, either to her or to the infant.

2nd and 3rd.   The signs of advancing into the interior of a dry continent, became gradually more evident: the wood-work of even the best-seasoned waggons, which had stood unaltered during the summers of Cape Town, now began to shrink and crack.   The tires of the wheels, being iron, expanded by the heat of the weather, while the wooden fellies, contracting from the same cause, left a considerable opening, which we were obliged to stop up with wedges of wood, to save the wheels from dropping to pieces.   These effects continued afterwards increasing as we advanced.   The Klaarwater Hottentots assured me, from frequent experience, that all the cracks and openings of this kind close again, as often as they approach the Cape.

---

* *Plate* 4. is a view of our station at the *Sack-river*, looking north-eastward. The rivulet flows from the right of the picture to the left, just beyond the furthest waggons; but is not observable in this situation. The mountains here seen, and which are unnamed, are frequently the lurking-places of Bushmen. The direction of our road onwards, is a little to the right of the two rocky mountains. The foreground will give a correct idea of the little bushes, and the manner and proportion in which they are scattered over the red and naked soil: but it is necessary to notice that the whipstocks which are stuck in the ground to support the skreens of mats by the waggons, are engraved too thick; and that, by mistake, to some of the mats, has been given the appearance of paling.

Caravan of Waggons assembled at Lek. River on the Borders of the Country of the Bushmen

We have thus, though a very unscientific, yet a very true, hygrometer, by which the intense dryness of the inland air may be compared with the atmosphere of Cape Town; which latter exceeds, . probably, in the same proportion, the atmosphere of England.

At this spot the thermometer rose to 84° (28°·8 C.) in the middle of the day, and sunk to 43° (6°·1 C.) in the coldest part of the night.

Here, for the only time during these travels, I met with an elegant bird, differing but little from the *Long-legged Plover* of England *: also the *Egyptian Goose* †, which I have frequently met with in the colony in a domesticated state; the *Crimson-billed Duck* ‡; and a small brown duck §, which, according to Speelman, is called by the colonists *Smi-eendje* (Widgeon). This last is, probably, not a common bird, as I never saw it but this once.

On the surface of the earth, were scattered many remarkable stones, of various sizes, from one to four inches in diameter, of a compressed round form, hard and compact, and of a grey color. These were the first indications of *lime-stone* which had met my notice: they much resembled the Lias of England, and within, were crossed by small *septaria* of a dark color. ‖

The latitude of our station at the Zak river was 31° 33′ 32″. ¶

---

* *Himantopus melanopterus*, Temminck, Manuel d'Ornithologie, p. 528. — *Charadrius Himantopus*, Linn. Syst. Nat. ed. Gmel. i. p. 690. — *Varietas, capite concolore.* B. *Fœmina.* In the intestines a *Tænia*, or Tape-worm, was found, nearly a foot in length, three-tenths of an inch broad, and one-twentieth thick; each joint being no more than one-twentieth of an inch long.

† *Anas Egyptiaca.*

‡ *Anas erythrorhyncha.* It is found in many parts of the Colony.

§ *Anas punctata.* B. Entirely brown, excepting the chin, the cheeks, and a stripe from the eye, which are white. The eyes, bill, legs, and toes, black: the back sprinkled with minute yellow dots; the under part of the body indistinctly marked with darker spots: the tail short and brown, with the tips of the feathers acute.

‖ Here also may be found *Ranunculus pantothrix. var. a.* D. C. Syst. Veg., growing in the river; and a very pretty species of *Colutea* (*Sutherlandia*), with small leaves. Of insects, I picked up an *Anthia*, resembling *A. decemguttata*, but without the white spots.

¶ 31st Aug. 1811, at the Sack river, the observed meridional altitude of the sun's upper limb was 49° 47′ 3″.

The country from the Roggeveld Mountain to the northern border of the colony, may be characterised as a high plain, free from large mountains, but thickly strewed over with moderate hills and elevations; having very few rivers, and all of these nearly dried up in the summer; quite destitute of trees and grass, but every where covered with bushes springing out of a naked red soil deprived of moisture during a great part of the year. These bushes are not more than a foot or two in height, excepting various kinds of Lycium, and almost *exclusively* belong to the Natural Order of *Composite flowers*, or the class *Syngenesia* of Linnæus. One general cast of features, not peculiar, however, to this district, pervades all these vegetables; a minute and arid foliage. Yet on these all the cattle browse, and such wild animals as are herbivorous.

Of game there was but little to be found at this season : neither did we see a single human being, more than those who have been mentioned. Notwithstanding characteristics so apparently unpromising, this district produces some of the best sheep and horses in the colony; and the boors would readily spread themselves farther into the interior, on land of the same nature, if not wisely (for the present, at least,) checked by the regulations of Government. If the occupation of new territory were permitted in the same unrestrained and extensive manner as formerly, it would not be long before the colonists had reached the Gariep ; as much of the intermediate land must, from want of water, necessarily be deemed useless.

CHAPTER XIII.

JOURNEY FROM THE BORDERS OF THE CAPE COLONY, THROUGH THE COUNTRY
OF THE BUSHMEN, TO THE RIVER GARIEP.

SEPTEMBER 4th. Bidding farewell to the Colony, we departed in
the afternoon, and entered upon our journey through the country of
the Bushmen. While the caravan was crossing the Sack river, which
occupied some time, I made two sketches, as a memorial of a spot
always interesting to my recollection, from being the place where,
for the first time, I quitted the jurisdiction and protection of regular
laws, and committed myself to the hostility, or the hospitality, of
savage tribes. My notions of human nature were not so harsh as to
forbid me expecting virtues among savages; and I looked forward
with pleasure and increasing eagerness to that part of my journey
which was hereafter to follow.

We did not advance this day more than ten miles into the
country, but halted for the night in the plain at *Kopjes Fontein,*

so called on account of several low hills in the surrounding distance. *

Why places in the following part of our route, not frequented by the colonists, should bear Dutch names, requires to be explained; and, for that purpose, it is only necessary to repeat that the usual language of the Klaarwater Hottentots, is Dutch, and that these names are frequently the mere translation of the aboriginal names, which latter they never make use of when conversing in the Dutch language. I have, therefore, been too often compelled to use the translation when I ought to have given the original. It is certainly bad taste to substitute, in any country, a modern or a foreign name, for one by which a place has been for ages known to its native inhabitants. I cannot consider myself as falling under this remark when, not having been able to learn the true name, I have been under the necessity of giving a *temporary* one to some of my stations, in order to note afterwards, more precisely, the spot where particular objects of natural history were found.

Having, in the course of the day, observed the foot-marks of lions, we took care to guard against a surprise from those powerful beasts during the night, by placing the waggons in a circle, within

---

* Between Sack river and Kopjes Fontein, sixteen species of plants were added to my catalogue: —

Gorteria diffusa. Th.	*Hermannia*
Grielum sinuatum. Licht. Planta to-	*Sisymbrium*
mentosa prostrata pulchra floribus	*Dais?*
citrinis. Folia pinnatim dissecta.	*Lachenalia*
Pharnaceum salsoloïdes. B. Cat. Geog.	*Nemesia*
1508. Species valdè singularis.	*Lichtensteinia*
Planta depressa ramosa foliosa gla-	*Lycium*
bra. Folia carnosa teretia glauca.	*Calendula*. Lìn.
Umbella pauciflora supra-axillaris	*Chrysocoma*
longè pedunculata.	*Aptosimum*. B. &c.

In the following part of the journey, so many *new* objects were continually met with, that it becomes impossible, without swelling too much the bulk of the present volume, to notice even a small proportion of them. A few of the most remarkable, or such as appeared more interesting, will be occasionally described more particularly; and, in order to give an idea of the botany of a region new to naturalists, the genera of the rest will frequently be added.

which the oxen and sheep were secured. It is fortunate for travellers, that this animal preys on cattle always in preference to man.

5th. Our next stage, owing to a very pleasing circumstance, was only seven miles. Just as a place called *Patrÿs Fontein* (Partridge Fountain) appeared in view, we were agreeably surprised at seeing a party of Hottentots coming towards us, with between fifty and a hundred oxen. These were men with the relays from Klaarwater, and were, it may be imagined, warmly greeted by the rest of the people, who, having been above six months absent from their homes, were eager in making enquiries as to the state of affairs there.

As soon as the four horsemen, despatched from the Karree river, arrived at Klaarwater, the Hottentot captain there immediately collected from the settlement as many oxen as could be spared, and sent them off with remarkable expedition; they having been only nine days on the road, although it was a distance of three hundred miles.

The men with the oxen, reported that the Kraal of *Caffres* on the *Great River,* or Gariep, were peaceable and quiet; nor had any symptoms of evil intention towards the Klaarwater Hottentots been observed. Neither were any of that tribe seen at Schiet Fontein, the place where, we had been so often told, they meant to attack us. Thus were all apprehensions on that head done away. Our prospect, in the state of the country we had to pass through before we reached the river, was less agreeable: beyond Schiet Fontein, the springs were every where very nearly dried up; and the consideration of the little chance there was for so many oxen as we had with us, to obtain water, became a source of serious uneasiness. But, if the unusual drought of the season was, in this view, extremely unfavorable to us, it was, on the other hand, the cause of great convenience, as it rendered the Great-river so shallow, that we might expect to ford it without trouble or danger. Near a place well named *Leeuwe Fontein* (Lion Fountain), the relays had been followed by three lions, one of which, a female, was shot by the Hottentots.

The hunters were very successful to-day, and came home in the

evening with several pack-oxen loaded with the meat of five *Quakkas.*
Immediately there commenced a general broiling and feasting, in
which not only their fellow-travellers, but also their friends from
Klaarwater, lent their most hearty assistance.

By the altitude of the sun when on the meridian, I calculated
the latitude of *Partridge Fountain* to be 31° 23′ 23″ S. *

6th. Our course lay over a hard, even, bare, and open country,
the surface of which was here and there relieved from its monotony,
by a broad, and far-extended undulation. The train of waggons,
steadily following each other at equal distances, drew a lengthened
perspective line over the wide landscape, that presented the only
object on which the eye could fix. While the van was advancing
over the highest swell, the rear was still far out of sight in the
hollow. Waggon behind waggon, slowly rose to view; and oft at
intervals, the loud clapping of the whip, or the jolting of the wheel,
disturbed the silence of the atmosphere, rolling its sound in a half
echo along the surface of the sun-baked earth. Not a green herb
enticed the eye; not a bird winged through the air: the creation
here, was nought but earth and sky; the azure vault of heaven,
expanded into the boundless aërial space, seemed lifted further from
the globe.

There is always a pleasure in novelty; and even the desert may
be found at some times, to afford the traveller both the one and the
other. The painter who viewed these scenes, might, if he knew it
not before, feel a conviction that the truest definition of *Taste,
Beauty,* the *Picturesque,* may be found in that of the word *Nature.*

In one part of this day's journey, the low uniformity of the
horizon, was broken by a distant flat mountain, which, by some of
our party, was called the *Spiónberg* (Spy-mountain.) Of this, and
of the train of waggons, I made two sketches. †

---

* 6th Sept. At *Patrys Fontein,* the observed mer. alt. of the sun's upper limb, was
52° 9′ 27″.

† As we travelled on, I picked up —

Aristida? piligenu, B. Cat. Geog. 1521.
Folia subulata rigida brevia. Culmus spithameus uninodis; geniculo,

pilis verticillatis. Panicula simplex.
Arista intermedia plumosa.

At *Brakke rivier* (Brackish river) in latitude 31° 16′ 14″*, we passed the night.

7th. In the bed of this rivulet we found plenty of water, of good taste, but muddy, and of a yellow colour. The country, here, still continued open, having low flat hills in the distance. The hunters shot a quakka, and wounded a lion. The preceding day, a lioness, with her two cubs, was fallen in with; and, it seems that we had now entered the territory of this " king of the beasts;" a king, however, who preys upon his own subjects. Nor is the title of " king of the forest" very applicable to an animal which, by myself at least, was never met with but on the plains; and, certainly, never in any of the forests where I have been.

A day's journey of twenty-two miles over a surface, for the first part level, but for the last more hilly and uneven, brought us as far as *Leéuwe Fontein.* (Lions' Fountain.) † To me, the fresh relays were only a source of distress, as their speed of four miles in the hour, ill suited the lean and exhausted state of my own oxen; yet, so anxious were the Hottentots to get to their homes, that even those who, like myself, had but single teams, pressed them on to the utmost of their strength.

The method by which, during my travels, I ascertained, to a certain degree of correctness, the measure of each day's journey, was extremely simple; and is, I think, the only practicable one that can be adapted to the circumstances of this mode of travelling. By repeated trials, I obtained the exact length of ground over which

---

Aristida, præcedenti congener.　　　　　*Erinus.*
Hebenstreitia, sp. odore *Resedæ*　　　　*Zygophyllum.* Frutex tripedalis
　　odoratæ.　　　　　　　　　　　　　　　ramosus.
Arctotis, " Goudsbloem" dicta.

　* 7th September. At the *Brakke river,* observed mer. alt. of the sun's upper limb,
52° 38′ 57″.

　† At Lion fountain, I met with a handsome species of—
　　Daïs? Cat. Geog. 1522. which was　　*Pteronia?*
　　　found afterwards in great abun-　　　*Aptosimum.*
　　　dance; even so far as beyond the　　*Senecio.*
　　　Kamhánni Mountains.

the greater wheel passed in a single, or rather in a certain number of, revolutions. This was done by measuring the track, which, for this purpose, gives a truer result than by taking the circumference of the wheel itself. From these data, were constructed two tables. The one showed merely the distance in any number of revolutions; and from this could readily be known the measure of any short space, by counting the number of times the wheel revolved, which were marked by a leathern thong that always remained tied round one of the spokes. The other table was used for showing the rate of travelling per hour, deduced from the observed number of revolutions made in one minute; or, which is preferable, if circumstances would permit, in five. These observations were repeated during the day, as often as it was thought that any change took place in the rate, and immediately pencilled down in a small memorandum book which I always carried in my hand, or in my pocket; and in which short notes were made to assist my recollection in the evening, when I sat down to record in my journal whatever had been thought worthy of notice in the course of the day.

Numbers of that beautiful antelope, the *Springbuck* *, were seen. The dogs caught a young one, and also three hares. To the latter, a swarm of ticks † adhered.

The variety of names by which it has been this antelope's fate to be called by different writers, is rather remarkable. ‡   But *Springbok* by the Dutch, and *Springbuck* by the English, inhabitants of the Cape, is the common appellation; and, therefore, that of *Euchore*, which was intended as a Greek translation of these, is here preferred for its technical name. It is easily distinguished from all the known species, by the very long white hair along the middle of the back, which lying flat, is nearly concealed by the fur on each side, and is expanded only when it takes those extraordinary leaps which first suggested its name.

---

* *Antilope Euchore.*

† In appearance not differing from the *Acarus Ricinus*, Linn.

‡ *A. Euchore.   A. dorsata.   A. saliens.   A. marsupialis.   A. pygarga.   La Gazelle à bourse sur le dos.   La Chèvre sautante.   Gazelle de Parade,* and *Springer Antelope.*

8th. Hitherto, we had not seen a single native; a circumstance occasioned, most probably, by their universal distrust of all strange visitors from out of the Colony. But having, by their spies and observations, satisfied themselves that we were friends, a party of eleven *Bushmen*, with three women, paid us a visit this morning. They were, in stature, all below five feet; and the women still shorter; their skin was of a sallow brown color, much darkened by dirt and grease. Their clothing appeared, in my eyes, wretched in the extreme; but, doubtless, not so to them, as they all seemed contented enough; although, when we first met, I observed in their looks great mistrust, and symptoms of much fear. These gradually wore off; and, after we had confirmed the assurances of our peaceable intentions, by presents of tobacco and beads, they recovered their natural tone, and chattered and clacked with each other in a very lively manner.

Among them, were some young men, whom, with all the remains of ancient prejudices, I could not help viewing as interesting. Though small, and delicately made, they appeared firm and hardy; and my attention was forcibly struck by the proportional smallness, and neatness of their hands and feet. This conformation is common (perhaps in Africa, peculiar,) to all the Hottentot race.

The women were young; their countenances had a cast of prettiness, and, I fancied, too, of innocence: their manners were modest, though unreserved. Their hair was ornamented with small Cowry shells*, and old copper buttons, which were interwoven with it. One of them wore a high cap of leather, the edge of which protected her eyes from the sun: at her back, and entirely hid excepting the head, she carried her infant, whose exceedingly small features presented to me an amusing novelty. The poor little thing bore all the rough jolting motion, with a degree of patience and unconcern which plainly showed it to have been used

---

* *Cypræa moneta.* Linn. These shells are not the natural produce of this part of Africa, but have been passed on from one tribe to another, in the course of barter.

to it from the day of its birth.   While her head was turned aside to talk to her companions, I drew a sketch of her unperceived. *

From the concurrent assertions of all the Hottentots, I now learnt the singular fact, that the teeth of the Bushmen do not, in the course of time, decay, as those of most other nations do; but become, in old age, quite ground down by use, in the same manner as those of sheep.   I have frequently, in corroboration of this, noticed that the front teeth of old people had the appearance of being worn down to mere stumps; but I confess I never had an opportunity of confirming it by a closer examination, and therefore leave the assertion as I found it.

We plentifully feasted these poor creatures, and, I believe, made them happier than they had been for a long while.   Through an interpreter, they asked me my name, and expressed, in artless terms, how much pleasure I had given them by so bountiful a present of tobacco.   Desirous of transfusing into the minds of others those powerful feelings of interest which I myself experienced on beholding and conversing with this little family of Bushmen, heightened by the consideration that I now stood amongst them on their own soil, I never, more than at this moment, longed to possess that command of language, and that talent of descriptive representation, which might enable me to impart all those peculiar sensations with which my first interview with this singular nation, inspired me.

When we departed from Lions' Fountain, the whole of this party left us, excepting three, whom we prevailed upon, by a promise of some sheep and tobacco, to accompany us, for the purpose of guiding us from one spring to another, till we reached the Great

---

* An *engraving* from this drawing is given at the end of the chapter.   The meagre proportions there observed are such as are common to these people.   A description of the Hottentot dress in general, will be found in Chapter XVI., under the date of the 28th of October.   It will suffice, at present, to explain, that in this figure it is entirely of leather, and that the *fore-kaross* or apron, consists of a great number of thin strips of leather, resembling cords; or, to speak more exactly, of two or three leathern aprons cut completely into strips, excepting only the upper edge, by which it is tied round the waist.

river; as we supposed that, by taking a new route, either to the right or the left, we should have a greater chance of falling in with water; for it was known that, in the usual track, it was every where nearly dried up.   There was no doubt that the natives, who daily roam in all directions, were acquainted with every spring; and we even offered them as many live sheep as there were waggons in our caravan, if they would conduct us by a route in which water could be found at all seasons of the year.

In the evening we reached *Klip Fontein* (Rock Fountain), and collected the waggons together on a stony level, just above the spring.

9th.   Daylight the next morning brought to view a desolate, wild, and singular landscape.   From our station on the top of a steep descent, the mountains of the *Karreebergen* (Dry Mountains) appeared before us.   The only color we beheld was a sterile brown, softened into azure or purple in the distance: the eye sought in vain for some tint of verdure; nothing but rocks and stones lay scattered every where around.   But that which rendered the view most remarkable, was the form of the mountains, presenting a multitude of flat, broad, level tops, and creating the idea of a congress of Table mountains.   These were but a small part of the Karreebergen, a range which consists of an innumerable assemblage of mountains, all of this kind without exception, forming a belt across the country of from five to ten miles in breadth, and stretching out of sight on either hand, apparently in a north-westerly and south-easterly direction.   Their extent is quite unknown, as they have never been traversed in any other part than that in which they were now crossed by us.

I made a careful sketch of a portion of this view, including, in the foreground, a part of our caravan; the various groups of which always formed both picturesque and interesting objects.

After this I was obliged to dedicate a couple of hours to the business of putting dry paper to my botanical specimens; which, being a mere mechanical employment, and recurring almost every

day, became already a most irksome task, yet one which was absolutely indispensable. *

By an observation at noon, the latitude of the *Bushman Rock
Fountain* † was ascertained to be 31° 0′ 38″. ‡

I was descending alone to view the spring, the value of which I
had heard our people so much extol, as affording the traveller a
never-failing supply, when one of the Hottentots called out, ad-
vising me to take my gun, lest, seeing me unarmed, some evil-
disposed native might be tempted to attack or rob me. He remarked
very prudently, and, I believed, properly, that it is safe always to
suspect that such men are lurking behind every bush or crag of rock,
ready to let fly a poisoned arrow on the unsuspecting passenger.
I returned for my gun, resolving to keep his advice in memory; and
I now impart it, with serious recommendation, to all who may hereafter find themselves in similar circumstances.

The water lay in a large rocky basin, or reservoir, at the head
of a ravine walled on either side by a precipice of sandstone rocks,
the upper end forming a romantic natural amphitheatre, out of the
sides of which, and from the clefts of the stone, grew a few green
shrubs to decorate this singular scene. At the head of this ravine, a
strong stream, in the rainy season, pours down the precipice into the
basin, and, overflowing the reservoir, runs through the interstices of
large blocks of stone, down into the valley below. In approaching
the spot, I heard a number of voices, the sound of which, reverberat-
ing from the walls, discovered to me two Bushmen and three women :
the latter had their children at their backs. They proved to be of a

---

* At *Klip Fontein*, grow —
    Pteris? calomelanos. Sp. Pl. ed. Willd.
    Ehrharta.
And species of—
    Bromus   *Hermannia*   *Mahernia*
    Zygophyllum   *Buchnera*   *Lachenalia,* &c.

† This is called the Rock Fountain of the Bushmen, to distinguish it from another
spring of the same name, afterwards met with in the country of the Koraquas.

‡ 9th Sept., at *Klip Fontein*, the observed meridional altitude of the sun's upper
limb was 53° 39′ 35″.

The Rock Fountain, on the Country of the Bushmen.

Engraved after the original Drawing made by W.J. Burchell Esq.r 3 September 1811.

London Published by Longman & C.o April 1.t 1822.

A PDF of the colour image originally positioned here can be downloaded
from the web address given on page iv of this book,
by clicking on 'Resources Available'.

friendly tribe, and belonging to a family or party of twelve, who had come from a neighbouring kraal to pay us a visit. What they said to me as I advanced towards them, I was unable to guess, being alone, and understanding nothing of their language. I felt, however, so much confidence in their good intentions, that I sat myself down on one of the large stones, and made a sketch of the spot, in which I inserted them exactly in the attitudes and situation in which they were at the time; and was pleased at finding ready before my pencil such picturesque appendages to the landscape. This scene is represented in the *fifth Plate*.

While thus employed, the time slipped away unperceived: the oxen had all been yoked to, and the waggons were already in motion, before it was known that I was missing. One of the party came in search of me, and we hastened to overtake the caravan.

The country becoming more hilly as we advanced, showed that we had entered the mountainous belt of the *Karreebergen*. The word *Karree*, in the Hottentot language, signifies *dry*, or *arid*, and is, in this case, applied with peculiar propriety. Always winding between the mountains, we had no very steep ascent or descent; sometimes an enclosed plain, of considerable extent, intervened.

In this dry unpromising district, grows one of the most beautiful little shrubs of the Bushman country. It was a *Mahernia**, not more than a foot in height, covered with large scarlet bell-shaped flowers, elegantly turned downwards; the emblem of modesty united

---

* *Mahernia oxalidiflora.* B. Cat. Geog. 1536. Fruticulus pedalis erectus ramosissimus. Folia nuda incisa et inciso-pinnatifida. Calyx, pedunculusque viscosi. Corolla maxima.

It much resembles *M. grandiflora*, which was not found till a year afterwards, and in a very different part of the continent; but from this it may be easily distinguished by its deeply cut, almost *inciso-pinnate*, leaves.

Excepting this, scarcely any thing remarkable was seen this day: the aridity of the soil being so unfavorable to vegetation, that nothing more was added to my list than —

Two *Calendulæ*	A minute *Pelargonium*
A *Chrysocoma*	And a *Leysera*.
Three *Seneciones*	

to beauty : chance having guided my steps to the only spot where it grew; nor was it ever afterwards, during my travels, met with again.

In the middle of a large plain, covered with low arid bushes, and surrounded by moderately high mountains, we found *Schiet Fontein* (Skirmish Fountain *), so named from having been formerly the field of an attack on the Bushmen by the Boors.

As we arrived an hour or two before sunset, I employed the time in making some sketches of the scenery, and in examining the nature of this station. There was abundance of good water. The spring rose in the midst of a thicket of reeds at the head of a ravine, down which it ran for two or three hundred yards, and then was lost in the loose earth. A large quantity of a calcareous deposition from the water, adhered to the base of the reeds. These, which were in their autumnal season, and of a remarkably pale color, were of a greater height than hitherto seen; some being nearly twelve feet long.

The green leaves of a kind of onion, growing here wild, were plucked by many of the Hottentots, and boiled with their meat. Following their example, I found them as good tasted as garden-onions; and made Gert, who acted in capacity of cook, collect a large bundle for use, as the stock of potatoes, our only vegetable, was already exhausted. A great number of Sparrows (*Fringilla arcuata*) frequented the reeds, and kept up a continual noisy chirping. †

One of the distant hills was very remarkable : its summit had some resemblance to a cap or hat; and many others presented nearly the same outline.

10*th.* This morning the sky was clouded, and the thirsty earth was refreshed with a light rain, which, however, ceased before noon.

---

* Literally, ' Shoot Fountain.'
† At *Schiet Fontein* were gathered specimens of—

Pteronia ? of which the numerous flowers, with their long purple pappus, resembled little brushes.	*Tritonia*
	Anthospermum
	Artemisia Afra
Allium, " Wild onions."	*Colutea* (*Sutherlandia*)
Hesperanthera	And a genus allied to *Othonna*.

This little seemed, however, as the promise of more, and indicated the approach of the rainy season. The weather remaining cloudy, prevented my taking any observation for the latitude.

We were visited in a very friendly manner by half a dozen Bushmen, one of whom was well known to the missionaries and Hottentots, by the name of *Goedhart* (Good-heart). His brother, some years ago, going into the colony to beg tobacco, was wantonly shot; in consequence of which this man, naturally enough, conceived a deadly hatred for his brother's murderers; but, unfortunately, classed with them, the whole race of boors, and vowed perpetual vengeance and warfare against them. He was ever on the look-out; and, in his many predatory excursions, had carried off a great number of cattle from the colony. The missionaries and Klaar-water Hottentots were not considered by him as in any way impli-cated with the boors; and it was under this persuasion only, that he came to us in peace: but, had we been a strange party of colonists, he would doubtlessly have visited us in a very different manner; and the first intimation of his approach, would have been a shower of poisoned arrows poured upon us in the middle of the night.

We gave him, and each of his companions, what was considered, a large quantity of tobacco, and they departed well satisfied. In the same mode we dismissed the three who had been engaged at Lion Fountain to guide us to the river by a new track; for, on maturer deliberation, we began to be apprehensive that if, from a natural fickleness, or any other cause, they should desert us by the way, the least misfortune that could befall us, would be the loss of a great part of our oxen, through want of water.

Soon after leaving Schiet Fontein, we began to ascend the barren mountains which form the principal range of the *Karree-bergen*; and for two hours followed a stony road, along a high level between the mountains. In other countries, mountains excite surprise and admiration by their rude, fantastic, and irregular forms, their spiry crags shooting up to the clouds, or their rugged sides crumbled and moulded by time into every variety of surface; but here,

MOUNTAINS OF REMARKABLE SHAPE

in this remarkable Pass, they attract attention, and create wonder, by their *uniformity* and perfectly regular shape. Two on our right, which were too striking to be left unsketched, were of the most exact form of half-truncated cones, and more resembled gigantic artificial mounds, than works of nature. Their horizontal strata of a harder rock, encircling them at intervals with, as it seemed, bands of masonry, gave them very much of an architectural character; and if their general resemblance to all the mountains around, did not clearly indicate what they were, they might, at a little distance, have been easily mistaken for some mighty remains of antiquity. *

On reaching the northern opening of this Pass, which bore the names of the *Schiet Fontein's Poort*, or *Karreebergen Poort*, a wide-extended prospect burst at once upon us. From the foot of the mountains, an immense plain lay spread before us, where the scope of vision was terminated only by far distant hills. The labor of dragging the waggons through this Pass, had exhausted the strength of our oxen, and we were obliged to halt a quarter of an hour, to allow them to recover breath.

In the mean time, I made a couple of sketches, and ascended the nearest mountain. It was composed of a compact hard stone, evidently containing a great proportion of iron. My labor was rewarded by an unexpected harvest of new plants. †

At half-past five the waggons began to descend the northern side of the Karreebergen. For the remainder of this day, our track was over the plain, the soil of which was hard and even. That part of it next to the Karreebergen, abounded in bushes, three and four feet

---

* Near this spot were found *Anchusa Capensis* and *Cheiranthus (Matthiola) torulosus*.
† Among which were species of the genera

Melianthus	*Hermannia*, 2 sp.	*Aptosimum*
Verbena ?	*Thesium*	*Calendula*
Anthospermum	*Tritonia*	*Cissampelos*
Acanthus	*Pelargonium*	*Tetragonia*, &c.
Lidbeckia	*Asparagus*	

high, of that singular shrub *Rhigozum trichotomum**, whose stiff branches, constantly dividing and subdividing, in a most regular manner, into threes, present a very rare and curious ramification, and have obtained for it the name of *Driedoorn* (Three-thorn). A representation of this may be seen in the foreground of the landscape at the head of the eighteenth chapter.

At half-past nine at night, we unyoked at *Elands Valley* (Eland's, or Elk's, Pond), a mere puddle of muddy water in the open plain, produced by the rains, and prevented from soaking into the earth by the clayey nature of the soil. The shrubs about this place were so diminutive, that it was with difficulty the necessary quantity of fuel could be procured.

Here *Old Moses*, one of the Hottentots, got himself into disgrace, by unfairly taking advantage of the night to hasten forwards unperceived, and get to the pond long before us, that *his* oxen, at least, might drink their fill; as it was known that there would be very little water at this place. It was contrary to our rules, to allow any of the cattle to go to the spring before all the casks were filled; and the consequence of Old Moses's selfish conduct was, that his oxen, trampling in the pool, had rendered the water so muddy, that nothing but necessity, and the greatest thirst, could have forced our people to drink it.

11th. Our course on the following day, lay over an immense plain, bounded on the right and on the left, by the level-topped mountains of the *Karreebergen*. The view which we had on our left, forms the subject of the *Vignette* at the head of the chapter. Those on the right were not very distant: amongst them one, remarkable for being in the form of a depressed cone surmounted

---

* *Catalogi Geographici*, 1572. The name of *Rhigozum* is compounded of ῥιγόω and ὄζος; from the *rigid branches* which the species are found to have. It is a true *Bignoniaceous* genus, and distinguished in its Order by five fertile stamens, sometimes varying to seven. In all the species, *simple, trifoliate,* and *fasciculate* leaves are found on the same plant. The flowers are yellow and handsome.

with an additional summit, was distinguished by the name of *Pramberg*.

The soil of this plain is a light clay tempered with sand, apparently well suited for the purposes of agriculture; but, from the want of a more constant supply of rain, producing, in general, no shrub above a foot in height, excepting two or three kinds of *Lycium*. Grass was observed between the bushes; but at this season it was short and very thinly scattered: yet, after the rains have fallen, this plain is said to be covered with verdure.

The oxen being pushed on almost at a trot, we travelled at the rate of four miles and a half in the hour, which brought us to the termination of the plain at half-past five, above seventeen miles from Elands Valley, where we halted at a place called *Carel Krieger's Grave.* * It was intended to unyoke here for the night; but it was found that every drop of water was dried up. No sooner was this ascertained, than a melancholy silence pervaded the whole party, interrupted only by the mournful lowings of the thirsty cattle. From the report of the Hottentots who came with the relays, it was known that, forwards, there was no water within five-and-thirty miles; and the probability of finding none, even there, was a prospect which could not but excite gloomy apprehensions. Deliberation was use-

---

* While waiting at *Carel Krieger's Grave*, I discovered a very curious kind of *Acacia*, which, from its most striking feature, as compared with the other species of Southern Africa, instantly suggested to me the name of

> *Acacia viridiramis.* Cat. Geog. 1586. Frutex 3 – 4-pedalis. Rami virides flexuosi. Spinæ 2 stipulares recurvæ brevissimæ. Gemmæ (sub lente) albo-lanatæ. Folia parva conjugato-pinnata. Pinnæ 6—8-jugæ. Folia ovalia approximata.

Here also was found a new species of

> *Zygophyllum*, of singular robust growth;

And two kinds of

> *Lycium*, species which, a little farther northward, were observed of a larger size than had hitherto been seen in the Bushman country.
> *Crassula*, resembling *C. imbricata*
> *Eriocephalus decussatus.* B.
> *Pteronia?* 2 species
> *Relhania?*

less; there was no choice left, but to travel day and night till we reached some spring.

Without delay, the drivers clap their long whips, and, in a tone of voice half-expressive of ill-temper from their disappointment, loudly call out to the oxen, *Loop!* and instantly the whole of the caravan are again in motion.

As we walked on, I enquired the story of *Carel Krieger's* fate. He was an indefatigable and fearless hunter; and, being also an excellent marksman, often ventured into the most dangerous situations. One day, near this spot, having with his party, pursued an elephant which he had wounded, the irritated animal suddenly turned round, and, singling out from the rest the person by whom he had been wounded, seized him with his trunk, and, lifting his wretched victim high in the air, dashed him with dreadful force to the ground. His companions, struck with horror, fled precipitately from the fatal scene, unable to turn their eyes to behold the rest of the tragedy. But on the following day they repaired to the spot, where they collected the few bones that could be found, and buried them near the spring. The enraged animal had not only trampled his body literally to pieces, but could not feel its vengeance satisfied till it had pounded the very flesh into the dust, so that nothing of this unfortunate man remained, excepting a few of the larger bones. Such is the sad story, as it was related to me on the spot where it happened. *

At Carel Krieger's Grave we passed a narrow chain of low mountains, which divides the *Karreebergen Plain* from a similar and not less extensive, one. Over this unvaried wide expanse, we continued travelling without intermission, or without even once slackening our pace. The hunters no longer cared to pursue the game, which often approached, as if to tempt us to the chace: *water* occupied all our thoughts. The sun at length departed, but no moon succeeded to

---

* Some account of this unfortunate man has already been given under the date of the 7th of July, at page 201.

guide our course. The stars were concealed in a cloudy sky, and flashes of lightning, repeated every minute, and accompanied by distant thunder, dazzled and bewildered our sight, so that even the Hottentots themselves became confused, and lost their way. Not one of the drivers knew with certainty whither to guide us, and the whole caravan were obliged to halt, while they went about from waggon to waggon to consult which way we ought to go. Walking, some out on one side and some on the other, to feel if any beaten track was nigh, they came back as often disappointed. Some drivers were for taking one course, while others resolved on the opposite. Several waggons at last set out, in exactly the wrong direction, and were driving away confident of being in the right. In this dilemma, recollecting the magnetic bearing of the water, as it had been pointed out to me in the day-light, I made Philip strike a light, and, by the help of my compass, I placed my own waggon in the proper direction; but the Klaarwater Hottentots still hesitated to follow, until Mr. Anderson undertook to persuade them that the compass was a thing which never failed to show the right way. Their reluctance to listen to my opinion arose, as they afterwards confessed, from their not being able to conceive how it could be possible for an utter stranger, like myself, to know any thing about the way to Klaarwater.

In the end they suffered themselves to be guided by me, and we all advanced in the best order we could for the darkness of the night. It was then two o clock. We had not travelled more than an hour, before we fortunately fell in with the regular track, which conducted us to the spot we had been desirous of finding, and where we arrived at five o'clock in the morning, just before the twilight began to dawn. When the cry of *Water! water!* relieved all our anxiety, I threw myself down on my bed to alleviate, as much as it was possible by three or four hours' sleep, the excessive fatigue of the last day's journey; which had not been less than fifty-two miles and a half, without resting, and almost without eating, excepting what could be taken as we walked along.

12th. This spring was situated in the middle of a wide open country: it was named *Buffelbout* (Buffalo-leg), after a Hottentot, who bore that name in consequence of having formerly, at this spot, been severely wounded in the thigh by a buffalo. Here, in truth, we had not much to rejoice at; for, although water was indeed found, the quantity was scarcely more than sufficient for our people only. It was merely a little dirty hole in the bed of a periodical rivulet; and the great number of *Namaqua Partridges*, and other small birds, which frequented it notwithstanding our presence, was a proof that no other existed within a great distance. The oxen and sheep, crowding in, trampled what we left, into a thick mud. Thus, unable to assuage their thirst, they stood around us, incessantly making a mournful piteous noise, as if to reproach us for bringing them into a country where thirst and starvation seemed to await them. On mustering our oxen preparatory to selecting the teams for the day, it was discovered that eight were missing, among which were two of the best of mine. It was concluded that, by this time, they must have either fallen into the hands of the Bushmen, by whom they were not very likely to be restored; or that, having been scared in the darkness by the violence of the rain, lightning, and thunder, they had fallen a prey to the lions, which were here very numerous, and during the night actively prowling over the country; as we knew by the symptoms of uneasiness manifested by the cattle, who probably now and then got scent of them whenever these beasts happened to be to windward.

As these two were a serious loss to the team, one being my best ' after-ox,' Philip was desirous of riding back in search of them, provided the other Hottentots, who had in the same manner lost some of their's, would accompany him. But the captain, not thinking it safe to remain longer at this spot, and declaring that he could not wait for their return, the idea was abandoned, and our oxen, not without much regret and distress at their fate, given up as irrecoverably lost.

The soil at this place was more sandy than it had hitherto been, and began to assume a redder hue, which was particularly remarkable in a low, sandy mound close by the water. *

Here, in the dead of the night, I heard the soft warbling of some bird, whose wild notes afforded me the greater delight, and seemed the sweeter, from breaking forth so unexpectedly in the cheerless waste, and recalling to me, in the midst of a scene so different, the plaintive nightingale. At the Karree and Sack rivers, I once or twice heard, also in the middle of the night, the same singing.

The latitude was found to be 30° 20′ 47.″ † The weather now became fair, and the sky cloudless. From nine in the morning, to one in the afternoon, the thermometer rose from 64° (17°·7 C.) to 76° (24°·4 C.).

Having stopped at Buffel-bout no longer than was absolutely necessary for resting the cattle and allowing them time to browse, we commenced another long day's journey, or, rather, two day's journeys in one, over plains of boundless extent, and little variety of surface. For the first three miles the soil was sandy, and of a red color, abounding in a species of grass (*Poa*) eighteen inches high, the stalks and leaves of which were at this time dead and quite withered.

---

* On exploring this, several new and curious plants were found; among which were—

Lessertia annularis. B. Catal. Geog. 1597. Planta erecta palmaris. Legumen, in formam annuli complanati contractum.

Polygala pungens. B. Catal. Geog. 1598. Fruticulus pedalis erectus sub-aphyllus, ramificatione divaricatâ. Ramuli teretes glauci rigidi; omnes in spinam acutam desinentes. Folia linearia acutiuscula ramulo angustiora. Calycis foliola 2 majora albida venis viridibus picta. Crista purpurascens. Legumen obcordatum. Flores in racemulis 2—4-floris.

Sisymbrium
Mahernia
Capraria ?
Chrysocoma, 2 sp.
Convolvulus
Anthericum
Gnaphalium
Poa
Hermannia
Cynoglossum echinatum. Th.
Ferraria undulata. Meeting with this at so great a distance from all those places where it has hitherto been found, is a remarkable circumstance.

† 12th September, at *Buffel-bout*, the observed meridional altitude of the sun's upper limb was 55° 27′ 38″.

The succeeding part of the day we travelled across plains tolerably well scattered over with bushes. The predominating shrubs were *Eriocephalus decussatus*, *Rhigozum trichotomum*, and that already mentioned as a *Daïs* *; each giving the principal feature to its own district. That of the *Eriocephalus* was quite whitened with the abundance of snowy cotton-like seed with which it was covered: the *Rhigozum* was not in blossom, but its brown branches cast a darker tint on the landscape; while a gay enlivening appearance was produced by the profusion of golden flowers which decorated the *Daïs*, in whose presence the arid desert seemed to smile. †

The evening coming on, the party drew closer together, as well for mutual protection, as to avoid losing each other in the darkness of the night. Thus continuing on our dreary way till a late hour, we suddenly heard the cry of *Whoo-ah! Whoo-ah!* from several drivers in the rear. We instantly halted, thinking that some attack had been made by the Bushmen, or that some formidable wild beast had carried off an ox or one of our people. We ran back to their assistance with loaded guns in our hand; but our fears were soon relieved, on being told, as we approached, that it was nothing of this kind: and yet, the *accouchement* of one of the Hottentot ladies, was certainly an occurrence that happened very awkwardly just at this time, and in such a spot.

It was thought not necessary to detain the caravan on this account, considering the great danger of keeping the cattle much longer without water; we therefore left the woman behind, with two waggons, in the care and protection of her relations.

The importance of pushing forward, made us heedless of the risk we ran in separating; yet, for the sake of my oxen, I started while

---

* At page 289.

† A black beetle was very often met with in our road, and seemed fond of crawling along the ground which had been made smooth by the wheels; for which reason, and its proving to be an undescribed species, I have called it

  Moluris vialis. Nigra. Elytra posticè, et ad latera, tuberculata, apicibus productis glabris. Macula abdominalis velutina rufa. Thorax lævis.

In its season it is a very common insect, and, in a geographical view, one of a very wide range, but, I believe, quite extra-colonial.

R R

the rest were still waiting, and, having one Hottentot waggon in company, proceeded at a slow pace in advance, expecting soon to be overtaken. For the purpose of guiding them, a lantern with a light was placed as a beacon at the hinder part of my waggon.

At a little after midnight I passed *Jonker's Water* (Yonker's Water), a place where, excepting in such dry seasons, the traveller may quench his thirst. Beyond here the road became more stony as we advanced. The whole of the party did not overtake me till between two and three o'clock in the morning.

13th. Two Hottentots, with their waggons, were hastening on a-head of us, that they might be the first to get to the water; but we had not missed them long after the first dawn of twilight, before one of them came back in a great hurry for help to drive out of their road a huge lion, which they perceived lying before them just in their road. They had endeavoured to rouse him up, yet were themselves too much alarmed to fire, lest, through the dubious light, they might unfortunately miss their aim, and he should return the compliment by springing upon them. Although the beast would not oblige them by getting out of their way, he favoured them with a roar, which had the effect of making them halt till we came up; when the noise of so many waggons approaching, caused him to move off without molesting us.

By degrees, as the day-light came on, and enabled me to distinguish what kind of country we were passing through, I noticed that about this part the geological nature of it began to assume a very different character. I saw in many places the tops of *Quartz* rocks, peeping out of the ground, and the sharp jagged points of vertical strata of a hard black rock. In one spot I remarked a large mass of cellular stone, having the appearance of ' honeycomb-stone,' yet not volcanic. During the last three hundred and twenty miles, the geological character remained essentially the same; and the daily recurrence of the same substances and forms, occasioned a great want of interest in this department of observation. Through the whole of the *Roggeveld* and *Bushman Country*, I had seen no quartz till now. This was the first indication of a change in the soil, and in

the nature of its mineralogy: consequently, a change in the character of its botanical productions might now begin to be expected;
and this was afterwards found to be the case.

At seven in the morning we reached *Modder-gat*, (Muddy Hole),
a deep hole about fifty feet in diameter, in which there was still some
good clear water remaining. It was with difficulty we could keep
the cattle from rushing into it before we had filled the casks; and
when the draft oxen had once drunk, the Hottentots were obliged to
stand by with their whips and drive them away, that a little might
be left for the loose oxen and sheep which were still on the road
a long way behind: yet, notwithstanding this precaution, the bottom
of the hole being of a strong blue clay, and the oxen naturally
fond of going into the middle of a pond in hot weather, the water
was trampled at last to a thick mud, and none of the cattle could
quench their thirst but those which drank first.

Modder Gat is situated in a very extensive hollow flat, which,
in the rainy season, becomes a lake, as was evident from the want of
vegetation, and the mud which every where covered its surface to the
depth of a foot. This mud is of a clayey nature, and, even at this
time, was so soft that the people could not walk on it without sinking
five or six inches at every step. This periodical lake is nearly half
a mile across; and its two extremities stretched eastward and westward farther than we could see. To the north, a long range of lofty
mountains, through which our road lay, bounded the horizon, and,
to the westward, they join the *Gariep* below a ford named *Brieskap*
by the Hottentots.

During the few hours we remained here, I made a sketch of our
dreary and singular situation: I ascertained the latitude by two
altitudes of the sun to be 29° 59′ 1″ *; and obtained a set of lunar
distances for the computation of the longitude.

On leaving this place, my oxen had the greatest difficulty in

---

* 13th Sept. at *Modder-gat*, at 0 hr. 18 min. 8 sec. P. M. by the watch, the observed
altitude of the sun's upper limb was 55° 42′ 21″; and at 1 hr. 12 min. 54 sec. 51° 17′ 26″.

dragging the waggons through the muddy plain ; but, on quitting it, the land was hard and dry, and plentifully strewed with stones of common white quartz. Low shrubs abounded every where; the soil itself was quite *red*, but covered with fine grass, green only at bottom, while their withered stalks remaining, showed them to be chiefly a kind of *Poa*.

At the distance of about nine miles from the mud-plain, we came to the range of mountains : their formation was quite different from all that had been seen since entering the Roggeveld : their upper outline no longer presented summits with that uniformly horizontal surface which invariably distinguished those we had hitherto passed ; it more resembled that of the mountains near the Cape. In the pass, more particularly, their forms were grand and picturesque. As we wound through the defile, which was called *Modder-gat Poort*, and which occupied us three quarters of an hour, their height appeared to be from six to eight hundred feet ; they were composed of a blackish-brown rock, among which I noticed some that seemed, at the distance at which I viewed them, to have very much of a volcanic character.[*]

After clearing the mountains, darkness soon overtook us, and, having missed the right tract, the whole caravan got into confusion and separated. I kept with two of the Hottentot waggons, whose drivers I believed to be the best acquainted with the country; but they led me through such close thickets of thorny bushes, and which seemed ready every minute to tear away the canvas from the tilts, and our clothes from off our backs, that I had given up all hopes of finding our way out of them till the morning. My guides, however, were resolved to persevere in spite of all the thorns, and, after encountering them for an hour, and getting terribly scratched, and

---

[*] In this pass, nine new plants were added to my Catalogue : —

Galenia	*Justicia*
Lycium	*Barleria*
Aptosimum abictinum. C.G. 1615. Fruticulus prostratus, dense tectus foliis acerosis rigidis.	*Gnaphalium*
	Achyranthes hamosa. C. G. 1621-2.

winding about between them in every direction, we at last discovered
a track which conducted us to the place of rendezvous at half past
ten, where, notwithstanding the darkness of the night, I could distinguish the most delightful object we had beheld for several days:
a large pond in which there was abundance of clear and excellent
water.

Here we found the hunters, who, being on horseback, had
arrived some time before dark; they had started early in the morning, and had been very successful in their chase, having shot four
Elands (Antilope Oreas) which they had left in the middle of the
plain, until the waggons could be sent to fetch them away.

In an hour afterwards, the rest of the waggons, and the loose
cattle, arrived.   All fears for want of water were now at an end, and
past difficulties no longer occupied our thoughts: nothing remained
of our troubles, but great exhaustion from continued travelling
day and night, under such distressing circumstances.

The name of this pool is *Zand Valley* (Sand Pool); and from
a double altitude of the sun, I computed it to be in latitude
29° 48′ 4″. *

14*th.*   The land here is strewed with stones of a siliceous kind,
amongst which were frequently seen white stones of a calcareous
nature.   The largest shrubs were about five feet high, a plant quite
new to me, but well known to the Klaarwater people, by the name
of *Haakedoorn* (Hookthorn), and is the same thorny bush which
gave us so much annoyance the night before, where it was above seven
feet high.   I was preparing to cut some specimens of it; which the
Hottentots observing, warned me to be very careful in doing so,
otherwise I should certainly be caught fast in its branches.   In
consequence of this advice, I proceeded with the utmost caution, but,
with all my care, a small twig caught hold of one sleeve.   While

* 15th Sept. at *Zand Valley*, at 0 hr. 17 min. 0 sec. P. M. by the watch, the observed
altitude of the sun's upper limb, was 57° 6′ 24″; and at 1 hr. 19 min. 0 sec. it was 53° 6′ 52″.

thinking to disengage it quietly with the other hand, both arms were seized by these rapacious thorns, and the more I tried to extricate myself, the more entangled I became; till at last it seized hold of the hat also; and convinced me that there was no possibility for me to free myself, but by main force, and at the expense of tearing all my clothes. I therefore called out for help, and two of my men came and released me by cutting off the branches by which I was held. In revenge for this ill-treatment, I determined to give to the tree a name which should serve to caution future travellers against allowing themselves to venture within its clutches. *

On picking up from the stony ground, what was supposed a curiously shaped pebble, it proved to be a plant, and an additional new species to the numerous tribe of *Mesembryanthemum;* but in color and appearance bore the closest resemblance to the stones, between which it was growing. On the same ground was found a species of the *Gryllus* tribe amongst the stones, and so exactly like them in color and even in shape, that it could never have been discovered, had it not been observed just at a moment when in motion; and as if more completely to elude notice, it seldom stirred, and even then, but slowly. The intention of Nature, in these instances, seems to have been the same as when she gave to the Chameleon the power of accommodating its color, in a certain degree, to that of the object nearest to it, in order to compensate for the deficiency of its locomotive powers. By their form and color, this insect may pass unobserved by those birds, which otherwise would soon extirpate a

---

* *Acacia detinens*, B. Catal. Geog. 1628. Frutex 4 — 8-pedalis. (Vide iconem capitulo xivto adjectam.) Spinæ 2 brevissimæ recurvæ. Folia bipinnata, pinnis unijugis, (sive, conjugato-pinnata). Foliola obovata. Peteoli pubescentes. Flores in capitulis globosis. Legumen ovale complanatum membranaceum oligospermum.

At the *Sand Pool* I found new species of

Zygophyllum	*Mesembryanthemum turbiniforme*, C. G.
Moræa	1630-2 Planta acaulis obconica,
Marsilea	supernè truncata obscurè punctata.
Justicia, 2 species	*Hermannia bipinnata.* C. G. 1627.
Cyanella	Planta palmaris. Folia bipinnati-
Acanthus ?	fida. Flores inter majores.

species so little able to elude its pursuers, and this juicy little Mesembryanthemum may generally escape the notice of cattle and wild animals. *

We agreed to rest a day at this place, as well to refresh our teams, as to give the people an opportunity of hunting *Elands*, of which a considerable number had been seen under the mountains. Those who remained by the waggons, were busily employed in cutting up the meat of the four Elands, brought home the day before, into large slices generally less than an inch in thickness, which they hung on the bushes to dry, as a stock to take home to Klaarwater. All the bushes around us, covered with large flaps of meat, was to me, at this time, a novel sight; but it was one of those to which, in the following years, I became completely habituated; as the nature of the life we led, rendered it a regular business. The firmest and best meat was, in this manner, cured without salt, in two or three days, in proportion as the state of the weather was more or less dry. The entrails, and other parts which had a greater tendency to putrefy, were eaten while fresh.

Of the meat of a young Eland, which happened to be in good case, I made my dinner, and considered it better tasted than the finest beef; with which, in grain and color, it might be compared. It seemed to possess a pure, game-like taste, which rendered it both wholesome and easy of digestion.

Within the colony, this animal is becoming daily more scarce; the boors, as well as the Hottentots, preferring its meat to that of any other antelope, and therefore, on every occasion, hunting it with the greatest eagerness. The principal cause of this preference, and at the same time, a very remarkable circumstance, is, its being the only one of the antelope genus, on which any considerable quantity of fat is ever to be found; no other species yielding a hard fat from which candles may be made. This remark, which probably may be applicable to the whole genus of *Antilope*, and presents

---

* See also the remarks at page 226. of this volume.

another character of distinction between that and *Cervus*, is offered with certainty in respect only to those of Southern Africa, amounting to about twenty-six species, three and twenty of which have occasionally served me as food in the course of my travels.

In the afternoon, I observed, with my telescope, one of the hunters, who was on horseback, following an eland which was coming towards us. It is a practice, whenever it can be done, to drive their game as near home as possible, before it is shot; that they may not have to carry it far: but this cannot easily be done till, by a long chase, the animal begins to flag. This was the case at present, and the Hottentot drove it on before him with as much ease as he might have driven a cow. It had been severely wounded; and this, doubtlessly, occasioned the facility with which it was managed. The animal was brought within twenty yards of the waggons, where it stood still, unable, from fatigue, to move a step further. Before the hunter fired again, he was persuaded to wait till I had made two sketches, one in profile and another in front. During the whole time I was drawing, the animal made no attempt to move, and it was really astonishing that it continued so long in the same attitude, silent and motionless. So far all this was exceedingly interesting and gratifying to my curiosity; but not so the conclusion. This poor creature, to whom I was indebted for so favorable an opportunity of obtaining, without hurry, a careful and correct drawing of the species, appeared so mild and harmless, and had such gentleness, and so much speaking solicitude in its beautiful clear black eye, that I could not witness its fall; but turned away before they fired the fatal shot which brought it to the ground.

This animal was a male, measuring in length from the base of the horns to the insertion of the tail, seven feet seven inches; in height, from the wither, five feet ten inches; and in circumference, seven feet six inches. The tail scarcely reached so low as the knee, and the horns were two and twenty inches long.

The *Eland*, called *Kanna* by the Hottentots, is a handsome animal, of a stouter make than the other antelopes, yet still possessing much elegance; to which its straight spiral horns, pointing backwards, and thin legs, in a great measure contribute. While young, they are fleeter than the generality of Cape horses; but when old, their bulk, especially of the males, renders them heavy and more easily overtaken. Their fur, or more properly hair, is most frequently thin and short; and in color an uniform brown, in some approaching to a blueish ash-color, in others, to sandy hue. From the other antelopes, it is distinguished by a remarkably large dewlap; and is, when at its full size, estimated to be generally larger than an ox, with respect to the quantity of flesh.

All the hunters returned before sunset, having shot a couple more; and two waggons were immediately unloaded and sent to bring the carcases home. But they had paid dearly for their game, by their venturous imprudence in riding into the midst of a large herd; when the animals, in their own defence, turned upon them, and gored two of the horses, one of which received a deep thrust under the shoulder blade, and the other one in the side. The riders fortunately escaped unhurt; but came home with very woful countenances.

Berends's brother, who had been absent two days, to examine the state of the *River*, returned with the pleasing account of its still remaining fordable. In the morning the two waggons which we had left behind on the road, arrived safe with the mother and the new-born child; the former " as well as can be expected," and the latter very likely to make one in an Eland hunt, before twenty years shall have been added to the day on which this stranger joined our caravan.

15th. This being Sunday the greater part of the Hottentots were assembled to prayers; a custom which had been kept up during the whole journey, whenever circumstances permitted: nor was it without practical utility, as it contributed something towards order and decorum, so essential to the safety of a large party of travellers.

It was late in the afternoon, before the whole of the people could get themselves in readiness for starting. Every one appeared in good humour, as this was to be the last day's journey before we reached the *River*, as it was now called; being indeed the only one within several hundred miles, deserving of that appellation. The dogs participated in the general liveliness; but it was from another cause:

they had feasted more plentifully than usual, as the meat of the six elands had enabled the Hottentots to give them, almost for the first time on the journey, as much food as they could eat.

We passed over a country rather flat, and clothed only with bushes, none of which exceeded a foot in height. I know not whether it may be said that the universally diminutive size of the bushes, which had been so often remarked, since leaving the Karro Poort, is a feature peculiar to the southern extremity of Africa; but, certainly, it is one to which nothing in England has the least resemblance. Although so small, they are completely ligneous plants, and more resemble trees in miniature, than shrubs. They seem, in fact, to constitute the character of all the dry hard plains which partake of the nature of Karro. Nothing deserving the name of *tree*, not even an Acacia, is to be seen between the *Roggeveld mountain*, and the *Gariep*,a distance of three hundred and sixty miles.

We had scarcely travelled three miles before the lightning began to flash, and the most tremendous peals of thunder burst over our heads. In an instant, without perhaps more than one minute's notice, a black cloud which had formed suddenly, emptied its contents upon us, pouring down like a torrent, and drenching every thing with water. The parched earth became, in the short time of five minutes, covered with ponds. The rain ceased as suddenly as it came on; leaving me both startled and surprised, at this specimen of an *African thunder shower*. We passed all at once from the deluged, to the arid and dusty ground; the distance of thirty or forty yards being all that intervened between these extremes. Mention had often been made to me while in Cape Town, of the heavy thunder showers of the interior; but their sudden violence far exceeded all that I had imagined.

At a little after eight at night, we found ourselves in the midst of trees much taller than the waggons, a situation we had not been in during the last six weeks of the journey. These indicated our approach to the *Gariep.* * After driving another half hour further,

---

* This word, which is the aboriginal name, and signifies literally *the river*, is pronounced as two syllables with the accent upon the last; the *ie* being a diphthong, and sounding as if written *Gareep* in English, or *Garipe* in French.

between trees, and over hillocks of loose whitish sand deposited by former inundations of the stream, we caught sight of the fires of our Hottentots; who had arrived here, sometime before us, with the sheep and loose oxen. The grove, in which they had taken up their quarters, illuminated all around them, and the busy cheerful look of all the people, seemed like some enchanted scene, or magic change. Every circumstance united to create pleasing sensations. All dangers and difficulties thus far happily surmounted; arrived at length at the long-looked-for stream, incomparably the largest in Southern Africa without the tropic; and our road forward to Klaarwater, pleasant and unobstructed; all contributed to produce a feeling of ease and security, in which, till now, we dared not indulge.

16*th.* Daylight the next morning exhibited to our view, the nature of our station, surrounded by thickets, and large trees of Acacia. Close to the trees, stood a tall scaffolding made of poles ten feet high, on the top of which was constructed a platform of sticks. This had formerly been erected by a hunting party, for the purpose of drying upon it the flesh of their game, out of the reach of dogs and wild beasts. These marks of human labor, appeared to me the more interesting, after traversing so great an extent of country, in which no vestige of art had been seen; for not a trace of the kraals and huts of the Bushmen was observable from our road, as they had been cautiously placed in the most secluded spots, for the purpose of keeping, as much as possible, their situation unknown to all but themselves. Travellers may often pass quite through their country, without seeing a human being: yet it would be erroneous to suppose, therefore, that it was uninhabited; for there are few springs of water, in the vicinity of which a Bushman Kraal may not be found.

Being now arrived within that distance from Klaarwater to which these Hottentots extend their huntings, our people began to feel themselves at home; and, in less than two hours, several temporary huts, or rather tents, constructed in the genuine Hottentot style, with poles bent semicircularly, and covered with mats, gave to the spot the appearance of a Kraal. Although our station was on the very bank of the river, nothing was to be seen of the water, as this flowed at a depth of seventy feet below, hidden by the tall trees which clothe its banks. Yet even at this height, the marks of inundation are evident, and assist the traveller in picturing to himself the magnificence and grandeur of the river *Gariep* at such seasons. But inundations to this extent, happen not often; and seven years, sometimes elapse, without collecting in its channel such an immense volume of water.

Impatient to view the river itself, I descended the steep bank through a tall grove of acacias, karree-trees, and willows, whose cool shade, the burning heat of the day (Therm. 87° — of the Cent. 30°.5) rendered doubly refreshing and delightful: while I felt very sensibly a moisture in the air, to which we had long been unaccustomed. The water glittering under a fervid sun, caught my eye through the leafy screen; and a few steps lower, opened as enchanting a view as it could be possible for fancy to imagine. Whether the feelings of an enthusiastic lover of scenes of nature, may have influenced my judgment, I cannot say; but still I think that, whoever shall visit the banks of the *Gariep*, and not feel both delight and admiration, must be cold indeed, and very deficient in taste or sensibility.

The first view to which I happened to turn myself, in looking up the stream, realized those ideas of elegant and classic scenery, which are created in the minds of poets, those alluring fancies of a fairy tale, or the fascinating imagery of a romance. The waters of the majestic river, flowing in a broad expanse resembling a smooth translucent lake, seemed, with their gentle waves, to kiss the shore and bid it farewell for ever, as they glided past in their way to the restless ocean; bearing on their limpid bosom the image of their wood-clothed banks; while the drooping willows leaned over the tide, as if unwilling to lose them; and the long pendent branches, dipping their leafy twigs in the stream, seemed fain to follow. *

---

    * *Plate* 6. represents this view. The large trees in the foreground, are *Willows* (Salix Gariepina); and, being portraits of those which were actually growing on that spot, will serve to give a correct idea of their growth and ramification: the trees of both banks, in the range next to the water, are of the same species. Above them, higher up on the bank, are seen the *Karree-trees* and *Acacias*, in the second and third tiers. The larger plants in the foreground, were intended to represent a shrub (C. G. 1634), very

Scene on the River Gariep.

Engraved etc. for original drawing made by W. J. Burchell Esq. 16 September 1811

Here I could have rested the whole day; here I could have fixed my abode for months: enjoying the delightful shade, and inhaling the refreshing air. Rapt with the pleasing sensations which the scenery inspired, I sat on the bank a long time contemplating the serenity and beauty of the view. The enormous footsteps of the mighty *River-Horse*, imprinted the sandy shore with numerous large holes, made as he nightly emerges from his watery element, to feed on the grass and foliage along the shore. Lower down, the wreck of large trees which had been swept away by the stream, during some great inundation, and here caught the bottom, leaving their crooked weather-beaten branches, thrust up above the surface, stood a monument of the resistless power of the flood at such times; though now, so smooth and gentle.

The willows (*Wilgan-boom*) which ornamented the banks, bore a great resemblance in their growth to the ' Weeping Willow,' of our gardens, but are botanically different*; they occupied the lower rank close to the water's edge, growing to the height of fifty feet; the next was filled chiefly with *Zwartebast* (Black-bark †), *Karreehout*, and *Buffeldoorn* (Buffalo-thorn) ‡; and the uppermost with the *Doornboom*.

The willow had just put on its new leaves, and their lively yellow-green, and clean vernal freshness, had a cheerful effect on the spirits, and delighted and relieved the eye by a hue the most soothing and grateful. The *Black-bark* and *Buffalo-thorn* had not yet put on their summer dress, but the soft umbrageous foliage of the *Karree-tree* remains equally verdant at all seasons.

---

common on the margins of rivers, but has been engraved too heavily to convey a just notion of its appearance. The figures are a party of *Bushmen*.

* *Salix Gariepina*, C. G .1637. et 2669. Arbor viginti-pedalis. Ramuli glabri penduli. Folia acutè et angustè lanceolata, serrulata, glabra, subtùs glaucescentia. Calyx pubescens. Amenta mascula cylindrica foliis breviora. Stamina 5. Racemi fœminei foliis breviores. Capsulæ glabræ ovatæ pedicellatæ, bivalves.

† *Royena decidua*, C. G. 1750. Frutex 15-pedalis. Cortex nigrescens. Folia anguste-lanceolata, obtusiuscula glabra (juniora pubescentia.) Flores axillares. Pedunculi longissimi filiformes penduli.

The name of *Zwartbaste* is given, in the Cape Colony, to Royena lucida.

‡ *Zizyphus bubalinus*. Licht.

Along the bank I found a poppy * four feet in height, with a showy bright-red flower like that of our common English corn-poppy; an interesting and unexpected discovery, in these southern latitudes, of a genus so decidedly northern.

Birds in great variety inhabit these groves, and the sound of their various notes dispels every feeling of loneliness. Amidst this concert the ear is soothed with the cooing of doves. † The only birds which I could procure, were a little noisy *Barbet* ‡, which the Hottentots called *Hout Kapper* (Wood-cutter), from the noise it makes with its beak against the branches of trees in search of insects: the beautiful *Groene Spreeuw* (Green Thrush) §, with another species ‖, and a small bird ¶, called *Namaquas duif*, (Namaqua Dove) a name which is also given to the *Columba Capensis*.

The Hottentots, glad to shelter from the scorching sun, had thrown aside their karosses, and lay nearly naked in little groups in the shade: others were enjoying a bathe, of whom some swam fearlessly into the middle of the stream. Men and women with their calabashes, were continually ascending and descending the steep pathway to the river, and the dogs, driven by the sultry heat, often came to quench their thirst, while the cattle at the same time, protected from the sun, picked up abundance of fresh grass which grew here and there between the trees.

---

* *Papaver Gariepinum*, C. G. 1633. Planta biennis spinoso-hispida, 4-pedalis. Folia inferiora elongata lobato-pinnatifida dentata. Flores coccineo-aurantiaci biunciales. Petala immaculata.

At this station a new and distinct species of *Lycium* was added to the Catalogue, also a | *Sinapis tripinnata*, C. G. 1640.

Bryonia   Planta facie *Sisymbrii Sophiæ*, tota
Lepidium   pubescens erecta. Folia tripin-
Nemesia   natifida, laciniis inæqualibus ob-
Senecio   tusis. Flores minuti flavi in race-
Gnaphalium and   mis terminalibus. Siliquæ glabræ.

† *Columba risoria.*

‡ *Pogonias* Illig. —— *Bucco, niger*, Gm. Sys. Nat. *Le Barbu à gorge noir.* — Le Vaill. *Ois. de Paradis, &c.* tom. 2. pl. 29 & 30.

§ *Turdus nitens.* Linn. Syst. Nat. —— *Lamprotornis*, Temm.

‖ *Turdus* —— *Varieté de Grivrou.* Le V. Ois. d'Afr. pl. 100., where it is considered to be a variety of *Turdus olivaceus*, Sys. Nat.; but it is certainly a distinct species.

¶ *Columba* —— *La Tourterelle maillée*, Le V. Ois. d'Afr. pl. 270.

I made several drawings of this enchanting scenery; and afterwards, by an observation for the *latitude*, found we were in 29° 40′ 52″ S. *

I ascertained trigonometrically, by a base of four hundred and fifty feet along the shore, and having the trunk of a willow on the opposite side close to the water as an object, that the *breadth* of the river was nine hundred and thirty feet. This spot, as I afterwards observed, was one of the narrowest places, and the average breadth of the *Gariep* in this part of its course, may, perhaps, be more correctly stated at three hundred and fifty yards, during its lowest state; but when overflowing the banks, it may then probably be from a quarter of a mile, to a mile wide, a state in which, in point of fact, I never saw it, but venture this supposition as founded on the indubitable traces of it noticed on the adjoining country.

The banks of this beautiful river are clothed with wood from its mouth upwards as far as it has been explored. This line of trees is sometimes a quarter of a mile in breadth, but is frequently interrupted by short intervals : it would furnish timber sufficient for all the purposes of *colonization* on its banks, and I cannot but believe that at some future period settlers will be tempted, by the advantages of a large river, to form a lengthened colony along its course. Although its frequent falls and rapids would, especially in that part of the year when its waters are low, prevent a continued navigation down to the ocean, yet it still remains to be proved that, at the time of its greatest annual floods, boats or rafts might not with safety convey the produce of the interior down to the sea-shore, without any interruption more than two or three " carrying-places."

The main stem of the *Gariep* is without any constant branch, for at least five hundred miles upwards. It then receives the waters of three great rivers, the *Ky Gariep* or Yellow River, coming from the north-eastward; the *Maap* or Muddy River, whose course and source is unknown; and the *Nu Gariep* or Black River, some branches

---

* 16th Sept. at the *Gariep Station*, the observed meridional altitude of the Sun's upper limb was 57° 39′ 37″.

of which rise in the mountains northward of Caffreland, and others probably near the country of the Tainbu or Tambukis: of these three the *Nu Gariep* is the largest.

Some of the water discharged by the *Gariep* into the ocean, cannot have flowed a distance much less than a *thousand* miles. This fine stream traverses the continent from east to west; thus proving that the highest land of Southern Africa, without the tropic, lies towards the eastern coast.   Among the African rivers, this can hardly claim to be ranked the fourth, as to length; but, for beauty, it probably stands the first, if I may form an opinion of the others, from engraved representations.

17*th*.   The river, at the place where we first reached its banks, not being fordable, search was made, and a practicable ford discovered about nine miles higher up.   A large party of men with spades and pickaxes, had been sent the day before, to make a convenient road down the bank; and every necessary preparation having now been made to ensure a safe passage, we set out at an early hour, that, in case of any unexpected delay, there might still be time enough for all the waggons to get through before the daylight ended.

The new road which we were obliged to take, was very uneven and dusty; often over hillocks and mounds of sand which continually threatened to overturn the waggons; sometimes forcing our way through groves of Acacias; or climbing over the rocky ridges which frequently intervened between the ravines.   The heat was at this time almost too great for travelling in the middle of the day, (Therm. $90\frac{1}{2}°$ — 32°. 6 Centigrade) yet, as it was but a short stage, we thought it adviseable to lose no time, lest the river should suddenly rise, and delay our crossing for a week or a fortnight.

On the way I halted a few minutes, to gather a beautiful parasitic plant *, growing on the branches of a *Haakdoorn*, and now in full flower.   I approached the thorny bush with caution, profiting by past experience, and succeeded in cutting off the plant, without

---

* A species of *Loranthus*.

being detained by the thorns. It grows without a root, out of
the very substance of the branch which supports it, exactly in the
same manner as the mistletoe ; and, like that, is also disseminated
by birds, which after eating the sweet viscous berries, wipe their
beak on the branch of some tree, to which the seed adheres, and
where, if the bark be smooth and full of sap, it soon thrusts out a
large green radicle, which gradually pierces the outer rind, and
fixes itself as firmly as if it were naturally a branch of the tree.   The
flowers grow several together at every leaf ; and their tubular shape,
half split open, red without and white within, might very well cause
it to be compared to the Honey-suckle : but then, it wanted all the
fragrance of our European favorite.   A large shrub, covered with a
cotton-like seed †, was met with for the first time, and occurred in
great abundance.

In three hours we again approached the river, and arrived at
the spot distinguished on my map by the name of *Shallow Ford.*
While the rest were engaged in levelling the road down the bank,
and exploring the safest part of the ford, I made a sketch of the
river, from the top of the high woody bank, whence there was a
broad, and far-extended view up the stream ; the smooth water, like a
polished mirror, appearing divided from the sky, only by a narrow
blue line of distant hills.   Here the southern shore was defined by
naked cliffs ; while, on the opposite side, a continued belt of willows
and acacias extended, gradually diminishing in the distance, till, turning round a low projecting point of land, it entirely disappeared.

The waggons being all assembled, several men, some on horseback, and some on oxen, were the first to enter the river, not only
for the purpose of pointing out where the water was shallowest,
they having been twice across during the morning ; but to give warn-
ing to those who were behind, if by chance a hippopotamus hole
should be found in their way.   They were followed immediately by

---

† A species of *Tarchonanthus.* It was at this time that I first noticed the fact of the
genus being dioicous; a remark afterwards fully confirmed by observing the same
circumstance in some other species.

the train of waggons, each with a steady leader at the head of the team, to restrain the oxen from turning down with the current, which they are very inclined to do, when left to themselves. As one waggon plunged into the stream, another descended headlong down the steep bank, closely followed by another; and as these moved on, others in their turn advanced from the rear, till the line, stretching entirely across the river, seemed like a bridge of waggons. The train at first took a very oblique direction downwards, till they had reached the middle of the river, and from that point, proceeded directly across to the opposite side. The bottom was found to be full of large pebbles, and the greatest depth no more than two feet and eight inches; but the current was therefore very rapid and strong. The water was quite transparent, a proof that no heavy rains had lately fallen in the upper part of its course. At the ford the surface was smooth; but lower down, and in sight, it was broken by a fall of about two feet. Each waggon took a quarter of an hour to perform the passage, which might be estimated at a little more than a quarter of a mile. The oxen were driven through by about a dozen Hottentots; and as many were required to swim the sheep and goats over in safety.

CHAPTER XIV.

JOURNEY IN THE COUNTRY OF THE KORAS, FROM THE GARIEP TO THE
ASBESTOS MOUNTAINS. — STAY AT THE KLOOF VILLAGE. — AND ARRIVAL
AT KLAARWATER.

WE had long been looking forward to the crossing of the Gariep,
as a serious undertaking, and therefore had the greater reason for
congratulating each other on having thus accomplished it without
the least accident, and with so much less difficulty than had been
expected. In less than three hours, every thing belonging to our
caravan, was safely landed on the northern side of this formidable
barrier.

Ascending a beach, covered with large loose stones, we took up
our station by the clumps of acacias, which were everywhere dispersed
over a sandy level, diversified with hillocks. My own waggon was
drawn up under the tempting and refreshing shade of an ancient
Karree tree.

We had now entered upon a new region, as the northern side of the Great River may justly be considered. The traveller may here remark a difference of character in the appearance and nature of the country, and some features peculiar to it; which will be noticed in the course of the journal. The river being impassable to many animals, is a zoological line, marking the southern-most range of some, and the northern-most of others. It is also a botanical limit, in a multitude of instances; and the words *cisgariepine* and *transgariepine* are not mere verbal distinctions.

The Acacia groves were very extensive; and as I was wandering through the maze of stems, admiring the light airy foliage, and listening to the notes of several birds which I had never heard before, I unexpectedly came upon a *Hottentot Kraal* consisting of about half a dozen round mat-huts. A few of its inhabitants were moving about; some putting together the frame work of a hut; some milking the cows; and others, either sauntering in careless ease, or reclining within their humble abodes. One, advancing towards me, wrapped round with a large sheep-skin kaross, the corner of which dragged behind on the ground, saluted me with " *Dag Mynheer ;*" and perceiving by this, that he spoke Dutch, I enquired some particulars respecting the kraal. From him I learnt that it was a detachment of the *Klaarwater Hottentots*, belonging to a village called the " *Kloof*," and who had removed hither with their cattle, for the sake of the herbage, which the banks of the river afford at this season, when, in every other spot, all pasturage is parched up by the summer heat. Some of the huts were empty, their owners being not yet come home with their flock; in others were women and children squatted on the ground, amidst bundles of dirty sheep-skins; some of whom were twisting cord from Acacia bark, or making rush-mats. Their mode of putting the latter together, differed in no particular from that already described at page 114.

The minute leaves of these *acacias* admitted as much sun through them, as they threw shadow; and, although the situation was deep in the grove, there was a lightness of colouring in the scene, as beautiful as it was remarkable; and the ground, undulated

A Hottentot Kraal, on the banks of the Garieb

Engraved after the original Drawing made by R.J.Gamble Esq.r 1798 AD

with hillocks of whitish sand, considerably increased that airy effect. Each tree was composed of a great number of stems; but very rarely of a single trunk. Many were decaying from age, and their dead branches, half cracked off, dropped their tops to the ground. This singular manner of decaying, was almost peculiar to the acacias, and is, perhaps, occasioned by the greater durability of the bark, while the wood is soon destroyed by insects. On examining these dead branches, I found scarcely one that was not bored through, in every direction, by insects, chiefly of the genera *Apate* and *Bostrichus*.

This was the first genuine *Hottentot kraal* which I had seen; and the view not only being on that account interesting, but the scenery extremely picturesque, I made a drawing of it. *

These mats, and the form of hut here represented, more resembling an inverted basket than a building, are the same which have been in use among all the various tribes of Hottentots, from time immemorial; and are, I believe, quite peculiar to this remarkable and distinct race of men. Such huts have their convenience for the Hottentot's mode of life; they may be taken to pieces in an hour, and packed on the back of a couple of oxen, together with all their utensils and young children, and transported with ease and expedition to any part of the country to which they may find it agreeable or necessary to remove, either for water or for pasture for their cattle; or for the purpose of avoiding inimical neighbours. Nor is it likely, so long as they continue to lead a pastoral life, and are free to roam wherever they please, that they will voluntarily

---

* *Plate* 7. is a reduced copy of this drawing. In the fore-ground, a *Hottentot woman* is employed in putting up one of the *mat-houses*. On the left are three *sheep* of the South-African breed, the large tails of which consist of pure fat. Rolls of *matting*, the materials of the house, with various *utensils* are seen on the ground; a *wooden-bowl*, a *bambus*, a *Hottentot hatchet*, and a bundle of tanned *sheep-skin*. On the right, a large *kaross* hangs over a rail; and by it, two *calabashes*. Several *men* are idly sauntering about, indulging in their greatest enjoyment, *smoking*: one is *milking* the cows, while his companion, with a long whip, keeps the herd from straying away. All the trees in this view, are *Acacias*, and the soil is a whitish *sand* thrown into hillocks by the force of the waters of the river, at the time of extraordinary inundations.

exchange their tent of mats, for any dwelling of solid and immoveable construction.

18*th.* We were visited this morning by a party of ten Bushmen, who had been obliged to cross the river to us. I neglected no opportunity of making friends with this nation, and had already discovered that in negotiating a treaty of peace and alliance with them, *tobacco* is a most successful plenipotentiary, or rather a *sine-qua-non.* They were all armed with a hassagay, and a bow and arrows. Their clothing was greasy leather, reddened with ochre, and the apparent color of their skin was the same. In their manners, they were less reserved and timid than the Bushmen whom we saw at the Rock Fountain. They remained with us the greater part of the day, and seemed to consider it no difficulty to have to wade through the river to return home.

I took a ramble with my gun, through the groves a little lower down the river, to a fall, where the water, broken in an easy descent, ran over large pebbles or stones rounded by the force of the current. Just below the fall, a *heron* stood near the shore, patiently watching for fish, and perfectly motionless, except when making a sudden dart at his prey, which, it appeared, never was so fortunate as to escape his aim.

No hippopotami frequent this part of the river, it being too shallow, and the bottom too rocky. The only fish which the Hottentots had seen here, were the *Geelvisch* (Yellow-fish); and one which they called *Plattekop* (Flat-head), which, at this time, I had no opportunity of seeing.

I passed some hours amongst the trees, with the view of encreasing the ornithological part of my collection, and procured a new and beautiful *Hoopoe,* entirely of a deep purple * : a small long-

---

* *Upupa purpurea,* B. — *Fœmina.* Tota purpurea, exceptis corporis parte inferiore nigrâ, et maculâ albâ mediis in remigibus primariis. Cauda elongata utrinque purpurea. Crista nulla. Rostrum, pedes et irides, nigra. Lingua brevissima.

Mas, coloribus iisdem gaudet, exceptis pectore, juguloquè nigro-fuscis: magnitudine fœminam vix æquat.

tailed *pigeon* * seen only in pairs, generally running along the ground as it picks up its food; a very small bird, resembling the golden-crested wren †, and of a yellowish green; a small blackish-brown bird ‡, singing with very soft and sweet notes, frequently met with, and apparently not shy; the *barbet* already mentioned §, now seen in greater number; and a small familiar bird, resembling the Redstart, generally observed hopping under the bushes. ||

The weather being too hot for travelling by day, our departure was delayed till sunset. The air continued very sultry, an effect attributable to the moisture exhaled by the river. At ten in the morning the heat was 79°; at 2 p. m. 89°; and at sunset 81½° (26°·1 —31°·6— and 27°·3. Centig.). But at six on the following morning, it had sunk to 44 (6°·6 Cent.).

Our road, for the first part, was through loose heavy sand, which ceased as soon as we quitted the region of Acacias: after this the ground continued hard during the whole night's journey, and, ex-cepting a solitary one here and there, not a tree was to be seen.

The sands near the river were inhabited by insects of some importance, if we may judge of them by the noise they made. As soon as the sun had set, or within ten minutes afterwards, there commenced a din so loud and continuous, as quite to deafen the ear; and this teazing and stunning sound lasted for about a quarter of an hour, or till the end of twilight. It seemed to proceed out of the earth, and, though I often sought in the very spot whence it came, I was unable, at this time, to get a sight of one of them to satisfy my curiosity; but afterwards ascertained that this remarkable noise was made by a species of *Cricket*¶, much resembling the do-

---

* *Columba Capensis.* Gm. Sys. Nat. — " La Tourterelle à cravatte noir." Le Vaill. Ois. d'Afr. pl. 273, 274. — This is generally called the *Namaqua Dove.*

† Or *Regulus vulgaris.* — *Motacilla Regulus,* Linn.

‡ *Turdus Capensis,* β. Gm. Sys. Nat. — " Le Brunoir." Le Vail. Ois. d'Afr. pl. 106. f. 1.

§ *Pogonias.* — *Bucco niger.* Gm.

|| *Turdus.* — *Le Jan Fredric.* Le Vaill. Ois. d'Afr. pl. 111.

¶ *Acheta.*

mestic kind, but very different in the sound it produces. It is to be met with most frequently in the months of December, January, and February; and it appears that this species has a very wide geographical range, as I afterwards found it far in the Interior, as well as within the Cape Colony.

19th. Having travelled without intermission the whole night, we found ourselves, at sun-rise, at the *Asbestos Mountains.* On entering the defile which leads through them, the Hottentots of our caravan began firing off their muskets, both as a salutation to their friends at the village of *The Kloof,* and to apprise them of our approach. In a few minutes we came in sight of the village. * It stood in a romantic situation, enclosed on all sides by mountains, and consisted of twenty-six round mat-huts, and five little square-built houses, with thatched roofs; while, at the same time, the view of some patches of wheat, of a fresh and delightful verdure, added a wonderful charm and interest to the spot. Its tawny inhabitants, men, women, and children, all ran out of their huts to witness our arrival, and greet their friends and the missionaries, on their safe return.

This settlement had been for a considerable time under the religious care and instruction of my fellow travellers. And, as both *Mr. Anderson,* and *Mr. Kramer,* had been absent from it several years, their return formed an important occurrence to its inhabitants. I could not behold, but with pleasure, the friendly welcome they received; nor witness, without participating in their feelings, their own satisfaction at meeting again, among the number, many Hottentots of their former congregation.

Not far from here, is the spot where these missionaries first established themselves in 1801, at a place called *Aakaap* by the

---

* *The engraving* at page 322 is a view of part of the village of *The Kloof,* looking westward, or towards the opening by which we approached it. The mountain is part of one which forms the northern end of the valley : it is composed of clay-slate (see the vignette at the end of this, and of chapter XIX.) in horizontal strata. In the corner on the left, is seen a part of a cattle-kraal, or pound.

Hottentots, or *Riet fontein* (Reed Fountain) in Dutch. They after-wards removed to *The Kloof*, but finally fixed their head-quarters at *Klaarwater*, as being a situation more central with respect to the different out-posts, or kraals, occupied by this race of Hottentots.

Visiting the different dwellings, making various enquiries, and examining into the state of the settlement, occupied the missionaries the whole of the day. The weather was too hot for attempting the journey in the day-time; but in the cool of the evening, my fellow travellers took leave of me, and proceeded on their way to Klaar-water, accompanied only by that part of our caravan, whose homes were at that station: the rest either remaining at the Kloof, or taking a different road, each to his own kraal. Our Hottentot cap-tain, *Berends*, remained here, being the chief of this village; over which, and a few surrounding outposts, his authority extends.

Wishing to explore, and examine a spot which appeared so interesting, and to gain leisure for putting in order my collections, and the mass of observations which had been daily accumulating, I determined to rest here a few days; and, therefore, selected a con-venient place for my waggons, at a little distance from the kraal, at the mouth of a narrow valley, closed both at the upper end, and on each side, by high rocky mountains. No grass, nor verdure, covered the stony ground; a few scattered bushes contributed scarcely a tint of green to vary the barren brown color which distinguished all the mountains around. My men formed for themselves a low hut, with poles and mats; and, by fixing a skreen of these on the wind-ward side of the smaller waggon, contrived a tolerably comfortable sleeping place. They soon began to feel themselves at home, as they were allowed to visit, or, as they call it, *kuyer*, at the kraal; where, by an introduction from Maagers, it was not long before they made several acquaintances. My Hottentot *Jan Kok*, who had been hired for the journey as far as Klaarwater, here begged to have his discharge; and, as he had all along proved himself to be a lazy fellow, I made no difficulty in granting his request. But his companion and countryman, *Maagers*, was desirous of remaining with me till we arrived at Klaarwater; and afterwards of engaging himself for the journey onwards.

20th. With respect to the long journey before us, none of the men were acquainted with my intentions; and I now thought it time to ascertain the degree of willingness with which they would enter into my plan. Without being directly informed of this, they were told that my object was to penetrate far into the interior of the country, and that we should, most probably, be a long time absent. To this none made the least objection; but, seemingly pleased at the idea of a rambling life, and in high spirits at finding themselves now in the midst of a *kraal* of people of their own nation, they declared that even a twelvemonth's journey would not exhaust either their patience or their strength. This declaration was most agreeable and satisfactory, as I had calculated that it would be possible to reach the Portuguese settlements on the western coast, in nearly that time.

I distributed amongst them various useful articles, and assured them that whatever could be supplied for their comfort should always be freely given, as long as our stores lasted; and that they would never be put forward into hardships which I would not myself participate in. I thought it proper, while we were on such good terms with each other, to state, without reserve, that, although they might confidently depend on my never feeling dissatisfied with any of them, so long as he conducted himself to the best of his ability and judgment; yet, as it was indispensably necessary for the general safety, that each one should zealously do that part of the duty which had been allotted to him, that they might feel equally certain that I should not overlook any wilful neglect.

This mutual declaration created a perfect confidence on both sides; and there appeared to be established betwixt us, a correct understanding, and cordial good-will. To confirm and strengthen this, I permitted them, without restraint, to visit their new friends at the kraal during our stay.

My work confined me the whole day to the waggon, but I received innumerable visits from the Hottentots of the village.

They introduced themselves first by a salutation of *Dag Mynheer*! *
and then proceeded to admire the make and strength of the waggon; which, although I was sitting within, writing, they uncere-
moniously shook, in order to know whether it ran lightly or heavily.
One, having satisfied himself of its good qualities, proposed to exchange waggons with me, and foolishly offered to give ten oxen into
the bargain, although his own was quite new, and just arrived from
the Cape: he was much vexed at his proposal being rejected.
Another offered his services as huntsman during my stay at the
Kloof, for which he wished to have, as a remuneration, the half of
the game he might shoot.   Some experience which I had acquired
on the journey, induced me to suspect that, after supplying him
with a great deal more powder than he would use, I should get only
a share of *my* share of the game.   The value of gunpowder naturally
increases in the proportion of the distance from Cape Town; and it
was already become too valuable, and of too much importance, to
allow us to waste a single charge.   On declining his services, he still
continued, for some time, begging for ammunition.   Many others
solicited, with equal importunity, for the same article, but with no
better success.

Each visitor, as soon as a few minutes had passed after the first
salutation, and a few of my questions answered, began to beg strenu-
ously for some article in the waggon; and, when that was refused,
asked, unabashed, for something else: for it appeared that nothing
would come amiss, and that every thing they saw, seemed, in their

---

* With respect to the *pronunciation* of the various *Dutch names* which occur in these
travels, the following remarks should have been added to those contained in the note at page 15
of this volume.   The *D* at the end of words, or syllables, may be pronounced as a *T*;
and the *G*, in similar situations, as a *K*.   The *G* has a peculiar guttural sound, especially
at the commencement of words; but which there is no necessity, for the present purpose,
to aim at acquiring.   It may be partly represented by imagining such words spelled with
a *Gh*.   The *V* at the beginning of words may be spoken as if it were an *F*; and the *Z* in
like places sounds as an *S*.

By attending to these precepts, together with those for the vowels at page 15, the
English reader may, if not approach to a correct ponunciation, at least avoid a ridiculous
one.

eyes, equally desirable. When, in a good-natured way, I had with-stood almost all their importunities, they left me, and took their seat round the fire, with my men; having noticed that preparations were going forward there, for killing a sheep. As they had no busi-ness of their own to attend to, they stuck close to us, till the evening, when the sheep was killed; and having voluntarily assisted in flaying it, and broiling the meat, they sat feasting till a late hour, when they left us, and returned to their kraal.

21st. Gert, who had undertaken the office of candle-maker, be-gan now to complain greatly against the heat of the weather, the candles made some time ago being all softened into one inseparable mass. He had been patiently labouring all the morning in pouring melted tallow, in the usual mode, over the wicks, without having succeeded in making a single candle; and at last, finding that the fat could not by any contrivance be made to congeal, he was com-pelled to relinquish his job till a cooler day.

The warmth of the weather continued as great as it had been on the preceding day; which might in some degree be occasioned by the nature of our station; where the dry rocky mountains, heated by the sun, increased the temperature of the air enclosed in these narrow valleys, to a degree of heat and dryness which may, without being meant very hyperbolically, be compared to that of an oven.

The sun having now risen in midday altitude, above two thirds of its approach to the zenith, was made use of this day, for the last time, to determine the latitude; which I computed to be 29°. 15′. 32″. *   As the angle of altitude made by any object is doubled by the angle of reflection from an artificial horizon, the traveller provided with no other instrument than a sextant, is pre-cluded from the use of all those celestial bodies which have more than sixty degrees of elevation. On this account, he cannot have the convenience of observing his latitude in the day time, so long as the altitude of the sun may continue above that number of de-

---

* At the *Kloof Village*, 21st of September, the observed meridional altitude of the Sun's upper limb was 60′. 1′. 19″.

grees; nor can he, at any time, make use of more than the half of the number of stars which pass the meridian; those towards the horizon being too low to be observed with convenience, or with certainty, on account of an atmospheric refraction influenced by variable causes.

Little notice as the Hottentots, in general, take of mineralogical objects, their attention has been attracted by a production of these mountains, which, observing to have the singular property of becoming, on being rubbed between the fingers, a soft cotton-like substance, resembling that which they made from their old handkerchiefs for the purpose of tinder, they have named *Doeksteen*, (Handkerchief-stone, or Cloth-stone). They pointed out a particular part of the mountains where it might be found; and I made an excursion for the purpose of examining it, and at the same time to explore the *Kloof-Valley* and its productions.

The *Doeksteen* is a kind of *Asbestos*, of a blue color. Having found the spot, I made a drawing of the remarkable laminated rocks, between the thin horizontal layers of which it is found.* These veins of asbestos are of various thickness, from the tenth to half an inch, and consequently their fibre, which is always transverse, is very short. But, in the mountains, at a place called *Eland's Fountain*, about five and twenty miles north-eastward, some is found, the fibres of which are above two inches long. This is, in fact, another species, and differs not only in the length, but in the more compact, perfectly straight and glossy fibre, and in its deeper color. The more remarkable circumstance is, the existence of Asbestos in mountains of argillaceous schistus. All the rocks at this place are formed of thin plates of this clay-slate, not more than half an inch

---

* An engraving of one of the crags of the *Asbestos rocks*, is given at the end of the chapter. This rock is formed of primitive argillaceous schistus, or clay-slate, and in the crag here represented, the strata are undulated; although in other places they are generally flat. Between these the Asbestos is found in alternate and parallel strata; the fibres of this mineral being perpendicular, or transverse, with respect to the layers. The shrub, represented growing upon it, is the *Acacia detinens*, or *Hook-thorn*, described at pages 309 and 310.

in thickness, and often scarcely the tenth of an inch.   Between these laminæ, a beautiful kind of stone is found, sometimes of a blue and sometimes of a silky golden color, from the twentieth part of an inch to three inches thick.   It is a *species of Asbestos* * in a less mature and flaxen state, with compact fibres of a flinty hardness, either transverse or oblique, straight or wavy.   The fracture of these laminæ is generally according to the direction of the fibres.   When cut and polished, this stone exhibits a very beautiful appearance.   A handsome kind of *jasper*, brown, striped with black, is to be found here; and a green *opal* or *pitch-stone*.   The strata of all these mountains are horizontal, and flat; yet not unfrequently occur undulated.

The *Kraal*, or village, stands on the sloping foot of the mountain (see the engraving at page 323) on the northern side, or rather at the head of a close valley, from which there are three outlets : one on the south-west, by which we came ; another on the north-east, leading to Klaarwater ; and the third opening southward, by which there is a direct road, of about fourteen miles, to the Gariep.

From the village, this valley runs southward; and along the middle of it, a winding brook takes a course between the mountains to the Great River.   By the side of this rivulet, a few acres of wheat are cultivated; and little channels have been made for leading the water out upon the land.   A much greater extent of ground might be ploughed, if the Hottentots could be persuaded to convert the labor they bestow on hunting, to pursuits of agriculture.   In good seasons, a harvest of eighty or ninety bushels of corn is obtained at the *Kloof;* but in the present year, in consequence of a species of mildew, not more than thirty were afterwards reaped, notwithstanding its present promising appearance.   This mildew did the greatest damage in the lowest part of their field ; while, in the higher land, they reaped an abundant produce.

---

* This substance, since my return to Europe, has been by some mineralogists, considered as allied to that which is called *Cat's-eye*.

In a spot so well adapted by nature for the production of fruits, I regretted exceedingly to see no more than one small garden. This belonged, as might be supposed, to the most industrious man of the village, a Hottentot of the mixed race, named *Willem Fortuýn*. He had been brought up in the colony, and learnt the business of a waggon-maker; which he followed, in his present situation, as well as the want of many necessary conveniences would permit. He lived in a better house than the others, and enjoyed more comforts; yet this had no effect in inducing them to imitate his industry. They contented themselves with their mat-huts; the situation of which, on an open, dirty, barren spot, subject to be overwhelmed with dust, they thought, or, their apathy and disinclination to labor, induced them to think, sufficiently agreeable.

In the upper part of this valley, there are no large trees; but at a short distance lower down, are some tall acacias, and large bushes of a new species of *Rhus* (*pyroïdes*); in the habit, ramification, and broad deciduous foliage of which, there was a character which reminded me of the common wild pear tree of Europe. My attention was engaged by flocks of *Colius erythropus*, making a continued harsh chattering noise among its branches.   I observed that, when this bird was silent, the crest was quite depressed; but whenever it uttered a note, or stood on the watch, or was taken by surprise, the crest became considerably elevated; which, with the length of its tail, caused the bird to appear much larger than it really was. I shot a *swallow*, of a species not seen before, whose nests, formed of mud, were built under the crags of the Asbestos rock; and three other birds equally new to me.*

---

* The following birds were added to my collection, during my stay in the *Asbestos Mountains*.

Saxicola leucomelana, B. Mas. Dorsum, gula, pectus, alæ, canda, rostrum et pedes, atra. Vertex et occiput, cana. Humeri, uropygium et abdomen, nivea.

Saxicola —— Le Traquet imitateur. Le Vaill. Ois. d'Afr. pl. 181.

Sylvia flaviventris. B. Mas. Caput, dorsum, cauda et alæ, pallidè murina. Gula et pectus albida. Abdomen citrinum. Remiges fuscæ marginibus albis. Cauda æqualis concolor. Pedes et ungues, nigra. Irides sanguineæ. Avis perpusilla.

Motacilla macroura? Sys. Nat. ed.

The Hook-thorn (*Acacia detinens*) before described, was found growing here; and also a beautiful species of acacia of a hoary complexion, the technical name of which (*Acacia atomiphylla*) is taken from its curious and singular leaves, consisting of very minute leaflets, resembling seeds or atoms, squeezed laterally so close together as to seem united.

The earth was parched up, and, excepting the corn-fields, no spot of green any where met the eye. So pleasing a sight as these fields afford, is a sufficient encouragement for attempting agriculture in almost any situation; and is one proof that man possesses the power of creating the most delightful verdure in the midst of drought and sterility.

22nd. This day the length of twilight, as determined, not by computation, but, by the actual withdrawing of daylight, was observed to be nearly one hour and a quarter.

23rd. The ground on which a Hottentot Kraal stands, being continually trodden by cattle, is always loose; and, in windy weather, produces a troublesome and disagreeable dust. Notwithstanding the wind and dust, which whirled about in clouds, I made a couple of sketches of the village; and had an opportunity of ascertaining how very useful, and indeed indispensable, is a drawing-board in such weather. A traveller will therefore find it well worth the trouble of carrying with him some apparatus of the kind.

From the top of the mountain behind the Kraal, there is a pleasing view of the settlement and the valley; though the prospect is confined on all sides by mountains. On these rocks, I found several interesting and new plants; but was soon forced to descend, by the threatening appearance of thunder clouds, which began suddenly to collect. I had hardly reached my waggon, when a heavy rain and

---

Gmel. (var? *ocellata*, B. Remiges apicibus obscure ocellatis) *Le capocier?* Ois. d'Afr. pl. 129, 130 f. 1.
Le Coriphée, Ois. d'Afr. pl. 120. f. 1.
Muscicapa. — Le Mignard, Ois .d'Af. pl. 154.

L'Hirondelle fauve, Ois.d'Af.pl.246f.1.
Fringilla
Fringilla ———. *Loxia*, Linn.
Muscicapa, Species nova.
Vultur percnopterus, Linn.

hail commenced, attended by lightning and the most tremendous peals of thunder. One explosion, in particular, seemed to have taken place within two hundred yards of us: it sounded like the simultaneous firing of a dozen cannons, the effect of which was even increased by the sound being reiterated in echoes several times repeated, rolling through the mountains. The wind increased to a furious hurricane; and dust, sticks, and fine gravel, filled the air. This storm lasted but a quarter of an hour, and was immediately succeeded by a dead calm, and a cloudless sky. The thermometer, before the commencement of the rain and thunder, stood at $79\frac{1}{2}°$ ($26°$ ·3 C.); during its continuance it fell to $64°$ ($17°$ ·7 .C.), and on the termination rose again to $74°$ ($23°$ ·3 C.) The weather remained undisturbed and pleasant for three hours; but at sun-set the hurricane returned with redoubled fury. Nothing could exceed the violence of the thunder; and the vivid glare of the lightning often blinded us for a whole minute. The rain poured down, as though it would wash us out of the valley; and the wind blew with a force that was near overturning the waggons. This second tempest lasted half an hour, after which the weather continued calm and quiet the whole night.

All the sheep having been sent on to Klaarwater, and Captain Berends, who was to have supplied me with the meat we should require at the Kloof, being gone on a fortnight's hunt, we remained all the day without food. At last, towards evening, a Hottentot was found willing to sell me a sheep. He volunteered his assistance in skinning it, and, with a number of his friends, uninvited, joined our party, and sat till they had consumed the greatest part of it.

24th. Although the thermometer stood at 80° all the middle of the day; yet, owing to the quick evaporation from the wet earth, the air was, to bodily feeling, cool. In the middle of the night, it was only $56\frac{1}{2}°$, and about sunrise not higher than $47\frac{1}{2}$ ($8°$ ·6 C.)

25th. A *Koodoo** was seen, and fired at by my hunters, who

---

* *Antilope strepsiceros*, of modern writers. The Hottentot name is written *Koedoe*, according to Dutch orthography: *Kudu*, in German: and *Koodoo*, or *Coodoo*, in English.

were out the whole day, but without success.   This, which is a handsome animal, is one of the larger antelopes; and is distinguished by long spiral horns, * and several transverse white stripes over the loins.

26th.   At two in the afternoon, the heat was 93° (33° ·8 C.), yet not finding it unpleasant, I was tempted to take a walk up the valley in which we were stationed; but the rays of the sun, reverberated from the rocks, soon forced me home to take shelter from them, in the shade of the waggon.

27th.   At this place I met with a bird exactly the same as the common Kestrel of Europe †; it was called by the Dutch name of *Kleine Roode Valk,* (Little Red Falcon).   Here also I first saw a large white bird which bore the name of *Witte Kraai* (White Crow); and, from its habits and manners, and even its appearance while on the wing, it might merit the name.   Sailing in the air in great numbers, it is seen a constant attendant near the abodes of men, where it descends to feed on carrion and offal.   Nor does it appear to be disturbed by the presence of man or dogs, at least at a certain distance; but, on a nearer approach, they slowly take wing, and mount into the air.   While flying over my head, I several times fired at them with swan-shot, which had no more effect than that of bringing down a few of the smaller feathers.   In an excursion to-day, in which I took Philip with me, we perceived several feeding on a dead sheep, in a spot where the surrounding bushes enabled us to get within musket-shot; and by an excellent aim, he brought one of them down with a bullet.   Till then, I had not discovered that it was a *Vulture;* but on bringing it home to the waggons, and comparing it with the descriptions of the different species, it proved to be the *Vultur percnopterus,* or the Sacred Vulture of Egypt.   Contrary to received opinion, however, I found, depending on their anatomy, that

---

But the Hottentots are much amused at the awkwardness of the boors, in pronouncing it without a strong clap at the beginning.

   * See a representation of them at the end of chapter XV.

   † *Falco Tinnunculus.*

the birds with brown plumage are males, while those with white are females. If, on comparing the South-African with the Egyptian bird it should prove to be the same species, the wide range of it, from one extremity of Africa to the other, is very remarkable.

Few insects were at this season to be seen, or that attracted particular notice. * Loaded with the vulture, and the other birds we had shot, we fell in with a party of boys and girls, bringing home bundles of wood which they had been collecting for the night's fire. It was, they said, one of their daily employments. We walked on to the village together; and as most of them spoke or understood Dutch, we continued in conversation the whole way. In this I derived considerable amusement from their ingenuous and unartificial mode of expression, coupled with some readiness of thought and quickness of answer. But the liveliness which Hottentots possess in their youth, deserts them in general at an early age; and one feels at first a difficulty in imagining the reason why those who take so little heed for the morrow, and whose minds are so little disturbed by the cares of getting riches, or of watching over them when acquired, should so soon lay aside their youthful playfulness. These remarks, however, must be taken only in a general sense, and qualified by frequent exceptions.

Our young walking companions asked me jokingly, if we were taking the vulture home to eat, a thing quite impossible, on account of its abominable carrion-like smell; otherwise, it must be confessed, we should have been glad to have made a meal of it; having taken no other food since yesterday, than a small slice of dry bread. And, to add to our disappointment in this respect, we found, on returning to the waggons, that no meat could be purchased in the village, and that the hunters were returned empty-handed.

Some of the small birds I had shot, were eatable, and of these I made a supper; but the Hottentots preferred sleeping away their hunger.

* Two species of *Pimelia* were found; one of which is probably the *P. inflata* of Olivier.

On such fast days, the inhabitants of the Kraal were careful not to interrupt us; at the same time, perhaps, fearing to give my men an opportunity of inviting themselves to dine at their huts in return for the feastings they had enjoyed at our fire.

In my walk to day I observed, with surprise, how rapidly small annual flowers spring up after the rains. In the cornfield, several European plants seemed quite at home·*; but their presence, at this distance from their own country, is easily accounted for; the seeds having been introduced along with the corn. In this manner many weeds are transported all over the world, and become so completely naturalized in a foreign climate, that, to prevent being misled in supposing them aboriginals, it is necessary first to examine into the possibility of such an emigration having taken place.

The Kloof and its mountains, notwithstanding their apparent sterility, afforded, even at this unfavorable season, many new and remarkable plants. †

---

* *Polygonum aviculare*
Veronica Anagallis
Urtica urens
Lolium temulentum
Hordeum murinum ; and
Phalaris Canariensis.

† *Cleome juncea.* Linn.
Echites succulenta. Thunb.
Cynoglossum echinatum. Th.
Lithospermum papillosum. Th.
Centopodium B. Catal. Geogr. 1687.
(*Rumex spinosus.* Th.) Nomen compositum, a κεντέω *pungo* et πούς, ποδός *pes ;* quia fructus tribuliformes obambulantium pedes pungunt. Genus est monoicum, ex ordine *Polygonearum.*
Pteris calomelanos. Willd. Sp. Pl.
Aitonia Capensis
Celastrus ilicinus. Catal. Geog. 1663.
Frutex pulcher sub-6-pedalis, inermis. Folia subtus glauca, acutè ovata, serraturis pungentibus. Flores solitarii axillares. Pedunculi foliis breviores, infrà medium articulati. Capsulæ flavæ.
Phlomis micrantha. Cat. Geog. 1672.
Frutex 4-pedalis totus tomentosus. Ramuli tomento albo brevissimo denso vestiti. Folia angustè lanceolata, serrulata, subtùs venis reticulatis. Flores folio duplò breviores. Verticilli 6--12-flori. Corolla sulphurea calyce vix longior.
Rhus pyroïdes. Cat. Geog. 1796. Frutex 6—10-pedalis. Ramuli sæpè spinescentes. Foliola ovata-lanceolata integerrima glabra. Racemi axillares folio breviores; terminales longiores.
Rhus tridactyle. Catal. Geog. 1667.
Frutex 4—5-pedalis. Ramuli ri-

29th.   After remaining so many days stationary, the men had become rather dilatory, and were so slow in putting the waggons into travelling order again, that our departure was delayed till between four and five in the afternoon.

In half an hour we cleared the Asbestos mountains, and entered upon an extensive plain, the soil of which was of a red color, varying in places with clay and sand, or a mixture of both, and generally clothed with low bushes. No land could appear better suited for agriculture than this plain, which would, more than probably, produce excellent crops, if sown just before the rains set in ; but, unfortunately, no permanent springs have yet been discovered upon it, which might enable the inhabitants to reside there during the whole year. We passed a grove of *Acacia atomiphylla,* whose soft masses of pale foliage produced an effect extremely beautiful and elegant.

A range of black craggy mountains stretched from the Kloof, and bounded the plain at a distance on our right.   The strata, however, were not horizontal : their huge masses of rock were pro-

---

gidi patentes inermes.   Foliola glabra integerrima linearia obtusissima, versùs apicem latiora.

Cassia arachoïdes. Cat. Geog. 1680. Herbacea humifusa. Folia 4—5-juga. Foliola obovata, apicibus rotundatis vel obcordatis. Racemi simplices axillares foliis longiores. Legumina ovali-orbiculata membranacea complanata.   Planta facie Arachidis hypogææ.

Acacia atomiphylla. Cat. Geog. 1685. Frutex vel arbuscula 8 —16-pedalis. Spinæ gracillimæ rectæ patentes. Folia tomentosa admodùm singularia, (quasì, pectinata simpliciter pinnata 8—19-juga, foliolis linearibus;) sed reverà, bipinnata, pinnis 18 —24-jugis. Foliola minutissima seminiformia arctè compacta, ut

quasi conglutinata.   Flores in capitulis globosis longè pedunculatis. Legumen tomentosum farctum lineare indehiscens.

Justicia
Barleria
Acanthus
Aptosimum
Sida
Convolvulus
Phlomis
Pharnaceum
Melianthus
Nemesia
Calendula ?
Celastrus
Hermannia, 3 sp.
Mahernia
Tarchonanthus
        cum pluribus aliis.

bably *Greenstone* or *Granite*, as they appeared to be of a different formation from the Asbestos rocks. One of these bore a great resemblance in shape to the Lion Mountain at Cape Town.

After travelling seven miles and a half, we halted for ten minutes at *Aakaap*, or *Riet Fontein* (Reed Fountain), situated on a bleak unsheltered flat. Here the stone foundations of a small hut, and the remains of a tank or reservoir for rain-water, dug out of a clayey soil, were still to be seen; but not a reed, as the name of the spot would imply, was now growing here. The spring at this time was only a dirty pond ten feet in diameter, containing little more than water enough for the teams.

I had intended to remain a day at this place, but finding it so miserable and uninteresting a spot, I ordered the drivers to proceed to the next spring. On our road a large herd of *Springbucks* bounded swiftly over the plain, and were soon out of sight. Stones of quartz lay scattered over the surface of the soil, and the points of quartz rocks frequently made their appearance above ground, much to our annoyance in jolting the waggons.

Philip, whose eyes were more employed in looking after the springbucks than in taking notice of the road, had nearly overturned the great waggon by carelessly driving into an *Anteater's**
burrow. *Aardvark* is the colonial name of this animal, and signifies *Earth Hog;* and, indeed, it may, from its appearance and size, be more justly compared to the hog, than to the other Anteaters; but in its mode of life, however, it exactly resembles the latter. With its fore-feet, which are admirably formed for that use, it digs a deep hole, wherein it lies concealed the whole of the day; never venturing out but at night, when it repairs to feed at the ant-hills, which abound in many parts of the country. Scratching a hole on one side of them, (as represented in the engraving at the head of the eighteenth chapter,) it disturbs the little community; on which

---

* The *Oryctero us Capensis*, of later writers; and the *Myrmecophaga Capensis* of Linn. Sys. Nat. ed. Gmel. Of this animal, I have presented a skin to the British Museum.

the insects, running about in confusion, are easily drawn into the animal's mouth, by the long slender tongue with which nature has provided it for this purpose. Without tusks, or any efficient teeth, this animal is quite defenceless, and depends, for its safety, solely on concealment; in which it so completely succeeds, that no animal is less seldom seen; and, from its power of burrowing, with incredible rapidity, away from those who endeavour to dig it out of its retreat, few are more difficult to be obtained. Its flesh is wholesome and well-tasted. Besides the holes of the Aardvark, those of the *Springhaas* (Springhare),* and *Meerkatje* (Weasel),† were very frequent; but we could not, at this time, get a sight of either of these animals ‡.

The moon shone bright, and travelling was exceedingly pleasant; but, from the time the sun went down, the air became chilly; and, increasing in coldness as the night advanced, obliged us to wear our watch-coats.

At eleven oclock, we unyoked at *Wittewater* (Whitewater), called in the Hottentot language *Gattikamma*; a word which has the same meaning. This spring, which, in some seasons, is the source of a rivulet, is situated in an open country, without a single bush near it, excepting a few *Karree-trees*, and some *Olive-trees*, ‖ about twelve feet high, standing close to the water. Our coming disturbed some birds, which immediately began flying round about, and making a great noise; plainly telling me, by their note, to what tribe

---

* *Dipus cafer.* Gm. Sys. Nat.—*Pedetes.* Illiger. Prod. Sys. Mamm.

† Either a species of *Viverra* or *Sciurus;* as there are animals of both genera, which are called by the name of *Meerkat*, or *Meerkatje;* meaning *small monkey.*

‡ In this day's journey were noticed,

    Mesembryanthemum arboriforme. C. G. 2004. Fruticulus 1-2-pedalis ramosus, trunco plerumque simplici. Cymæ octiès dichotomæ. Flores minuti, coloris testacei. Species non longè a *M parvifloro* Haworthii, ordinanda.

    Capparis albitrunca. C. G. 1762. Arbor inermis parva robusta, trunco albo. Folia coriacea elongatè vel lineari-elliptica, apice rotundata vel aliquando emarginata, subtus glaucescentia. Flores minimi. Racemi pauciflori axillares, et etiam ex ramis nudis prodeuntes. Hollandicè *Witgat-boom* dicta.

‖ *Olea similis.* B.

they belonged; continuing to cry *Peevit! Peevit!* the whole night long *.

30th. We were not aware till the morning, that there were any inhabitants at this place: a kraal of *Koras,* or, as they are often called, *Koranas,* were stationed here with their cattle. I was just risen, and employed in putting on my clothes, when several men in leathern karosses and caps, and with a skin coloured with red ochre, lifted up the canvas flap which closed the end of the waggon, and one by one bade me *Dag!* or *Goëi Morg!* (Good day! or Good morning!) the only words which they were able to say in Dutch. Finding that a strange white man was arrived in the country, they were very curious to see me; nor could my people restrain their impatience to interrupt me before I was dressed. They satisfied their curiosity with much good nature and respect; going away as soon as I had returned their salutation: but this visiting, which was a true *levée,* in the strict and original meaning of the word, lasted so long that I believe every individual in the kraal came to have a sight. They were very desirous that I should come out of the waggon and show myself. By this time my shaving and dressing were completed; and just as I was about to make my appearance, another levée commenced. The women, in their turn, must gratify their curiosity also; and jumping up on the step, as many as could stand on it repeated their " *Dag, Mynheer!*" and made room for others. Among the number of faces which peeped in under the canvass, were many that might justly be called pretty. Good humour beamed in every countenance; the girls appeared lively and modest, without timidity. The looking-glass, that often tried and never-failing source of surprise to uncivilized tribes of every quarter of the globe, produced on these also the usual effect. They called to each other to come and see; and presently the end of my waggon looked like a heap of faces, all distorted either with surprize or laughter; and, as it reflected the whole group, they had sufficient

---

* A species of *Charadrius,* or *Plover.*

reason for mirth, in viewing themselves : nor was there, I believe, much more appearance of gravity in my own countenance than in theirs.   This amusing scene would have lasted the whole of the day, for the men were coming back again, had I not closed the box containing the glass, and thus put an end to the exhibition.

The people usually called *Koránas*, are a numerous, and distinct, tribe of the Hottentot race.   In features they possess the common character, but in stature are larger than the *Bushmen*, and equal to the *Hottentots*, properly so called : by which term I would be understood to mean the aborigines of the Colony.   In customs and manners, the *Koránas* are several degrees more civilized than the *Bushmen*, and possess much cattle ; but their dress and arms are the same in kind, though better in quality.   They are considered rather as a peaceable and friendly people : their mode of life is purely pastoral, and, consequently, their places of abode unsettled.   Their language is a dialect of the Hottentot, but differing from it so much, that at first my men could not, without difficulty, catch the sound of any words so clearly as to recognise them.   This difficulty wore off with practice ; yet, from all I could afterwards learn, it appears that the *Kóra language* possesses a great number of words peculiar to itself. It seemed to require a much less frequent use of the clap of the tongue than the Bushman dialect ; but, at the same time, a little more than that of the Cape Hottentots.   The name by which they themselves call their nation, is *Kóra*, or *Kóraqua*.   The adjunct *qua*, signifying man or men in most of the Hottentot dialects, is, in some cases, as in this, used or omitted indifferently.   The word *Kóraqua* means *a man wearing shoes*, as distinguished from *sandals*, which have no upper leather and are in more general use among the other nations and tribes.   This word, like many others, has been *Dutchified* by the colonists ; who, following the forms *Hollander, Afrikaander,* have changed it into *Koraander*, now softened by writers into *Korána*. The word *Kóra*, is, notwithstanding, in frequent use.   This nation is found dispersed widely over the country on the northern side of the Gariep, but not at all on the southern.   They are spread as far northward as Litákun ; and to the eastward have a large and populous kraal called the *Hart*. Along the banks of the Great River, and for several days journey up the Yellow River, or Ky-Gariep, are many of their moveable villages. These do not extend down the river more than two or three days' journey below the spot where we crossed it. It is difficult to define the *boundaries* of the country inhabited by any of these wandering African nations; not only because they are perpetually shifting from one quarter to another, but because the villages of two, and sometimes of three, nations, are often so interlocated, that it can not easily be decided to which of them the territory belongs. In fact, with respect to *territory*, they have none of those ideas which a European would attach to the word. The soil appears never to be considered as property, nor is it hardly ever thought worth claiming or disputing the possession of: the water and pasturage of it, is all that is rated of any value; and when these are exhausted, the soil is abandoned as useless. Wherever they find a spring unoccupied, there they feel themselves at liberty to plant their huts; and, on their removal, others, if they chuse, come and fix their quarters. This last observation, though holding good in many cases with respect to different tribes, is applicable more strictly to different kraals, or families, of the same tribe. On one side, the *Kóra* stations are intermingled with those of the *Bachapins;* on another, with the *Bamuchars;* in the middle, with the settlements of the *Mixed,* or *Klaarwater, Hottentots;* and every where, with the kraals of the *Bushmen.* *

---

* A book, the numerous errors and misrepresentations of which Professor Lichtenstein has, in his " Travels in Southern Africa," taken the trouble fully to expose, tells its readers, that the Koranas are a formidable and cruel tribe of Bosjesmans, and that they dwell " directly east from the Roggeveld," which " for several months in the year " is entirely covered with snow;" (a specimen of the accuracy of that writer's description of the colony;) and concludes its account of that people by stating, with peculiar sagacity, that, " though very good friends among each other while poor, from the moment they " have obtained by plunder a quantity of cattle, they begin to quarrel about the division of " the spoil; and they are said to carry this sometimes to such an excess, that they continue " the fight and massacre, till, like the soldiers of Cadmus, very few remain on the field." Barrow's Travels, page 404. In modern days, I confess, I know of nothing like this, except the story of the two *Kilkenny Cats,* which fought " to such an excess," that they actually devoured each other, and nothing was found remaining on the field, but the tips of their tails.

On coming out of the waggon, a crowd of Kóras gathered round
with an eagerness of curiosity which I did not expect, as a white man
could be no novelty to the greater part of them, who had had the
missionaries so long in their neighbourhood. The report of my
coming had long preceded my arrival; and, as they had been informed that I was neither a missionary nor a colonist, but travelling
only for the purpose of seeing their country, they felt a desire to know
more about the stranger: and that their crowding round me, was
from pure curiosity, was strongly proved by their never once begging,
even for tobacco. This last circumstance appeared to me the more
remarkable, as I had been told that I should find begging an universal practice. Their cloaks and bodies were entirely reddened
with ochre, and almost every one wore a leathern cap. Their huts
here were irregularly placed, and at some distance from the spring,
without even the shelter of a bush.

As far as could be seen in every direction, the tops of huge
masses of a hard blue rock *, appeared above the surface; and among
them some of a beautiful green color, but of exactly the same nature.
The water, issuing from a rocky hollow, did not run, at this season,
many hundred yards; though the wide channel bore marks of having
carried a more plentiful stream. The ground was, in many places,
whitened with a saline efflorescence; and it is to this circumstance
that the spring owes its name. It was frequented by ' Namaqua
partridges' or grous, and a few other birds.

It was nearly sunset before the waggons were in motion. The
Kóras, in a friendly manner, wished us a pleasant journey, as we
drove past their huts; and I departed from their kraal with a favorable impression of the friendly character of the whole tribe.

As this day was to end our travelling for the present, or at least
for three months, according to the plan I had proposed to myself;
a pleasing sensation seemed, with all of us, to attend the idea of
being about to terminate a long journey. For such, with reference

---

* Technically called " Greenstone."

to time, it might justly be denominated, as we had been on the road from Cape Town, three months and a half, although the distance is not more than seven hundred and ninety one miles.

The obdurate rocks of Greenstone annoyed us exceedingly, and, as they were, in many places, too abundant to be avoided, we frequently received the most violent jolts, threatening destruction to our wheels. * For the first six or seven miles, we passed over a plain well covered with dry grass; in a distant part of which, was seen a herd of more than a hundred Springbucks, which at first were mistaken for a flock of sheep.   The surface of the country was varied with gentle risings, and hills of moderate elevation; but night, soon afterwards coming on, put an end to further observation.   The brightness of the moon enabled us to follow the proper track; which, at this short distance from Klaarwater, was much beaten.   In one part, towards the end of our journey, we passed abundance of a handsome shrub, from five to seven feet in height, covered with showy yellow flowers, but quite destitute of leaves; and, even by this light, easily to be distinguished as a plant which had not been any where seen before: it was completely armed at all points; its green leafless branches being terminated by a spine as sharp as a needle. † The coldness of the night air was so great as to oblige us to walk nearly all the way, to keep ourselves warm.

As we drew nearer to the settlement, the road became more rocky, and the noise of the waggons rattling over the stones, announced our approach; but it was at that hour of the night, or rather morning, when all its inhabitants were fast asleep, excepting

---

* A new species of *Royena*, four or five feet high, was remarkable for the smallness of its leaves, its flesh-colored flowers, and the prettiness of its growth.

Royena microphylla. B. Catal. Geogr. 1696.   Frutex ràmosissimus rigidus.   Folia minima tomentosa, elongatè obovata, subtus reticulata, rachide valido.   Flores solitarii axillares deflexi.   Calyx, et corolla externè, hirsuta.   Fructus globosus.

† *Spartium cuspidosum*, B. Catal. Geog. 1697.   Frutex ramosissimus rigidus.   Ramuli divaricati virides teretes, omnes spinâ acutissimâ terminati, aphylli exceptis surculis tenerioribus, quibus sunt folia petiolata simplicia et ternata foliolis ovatis ovalibus vel lanceolatis.   Flores flavi alterni.   Legumen oblongum membranaceum oligospermum.

the watchful dogs. These trusty guardians gave due notice to their masters, by loud and ceaseless barking, which informed us, also, that we were but a short distance from the kraal. Presently, from the top of the ridge, we discovered a light which proceeded from one of the huts; and, at a quarter past one, had the satisfaction of finding ourselves safely arrived at *Klaarwater*. The dogs, in a pack, flew round us; but as many of them knew us again, the fury of their attack was instantly converted into demonstrations of pleasure.

In the mean time, all this noise and clatter had awakened *Mr. Anderson;* who came out to welcome me to the settlement, and point out a convenient spot where the waggons might be stationed. As soon as the oxen were taken out of the yoke, we all gladly preferred sleep to supper; and the men, wrapping their karosses closely round them, laid themselves down under the waggons for the night.

CHAPTER XV.

RESIDENCE AND TRANSACTIONS AT KLAARWATER; WITH SOME ACCOUNT OF
THE SETTLEMENT AND ITS INHABITANTS.

OCTOBER 1st. This morning, as soon as I had risen, I received a visit from *Mr. Jansz*, the missionary, who had been residing at Klaarwater, and had conducted the spiritual affairs of that station, during the long absence of his two brethren. He was a native of Holland, and had been several years in Africa, in the service of the Dissenting Missionary Society of London. The evident cordiality with which he gave me a welcome to the settlement, and the unreserved friendliness of his manners towards those around him, were, I considered, indications of a genuine goodness of heart, which is certainly one of the most valuable qualifications of him whose object is to gain the esteem and good-will of savages.

I accompanied the three missionaries round the village, to take a cursory view of the different parts of it; the huts of the Hottentots; their own dwellings; the house for religious meetings and school instruction *; their storehouse, and their garden. When I

---

* The above *engraving* is a view of the *Church*. The furthest building is the dwelling-house of one of the missionaries; and the intermediate hut is a storehouse.

considered that this little community, and the spot on which I stood, were nearly eight hundred miles deep in the interior of Africa, I could not but look upon every object of their labors with double interest; and received, at that moment, a pleasure, unalloyed by the knowledge of a single untoward circumstance. The Hottentots peeped out of their huts to have a look at me; and I fancied they appeared glad at having one more white man amongst them.

I paid a visit to my fellow-travellers, *Mrs. Anderson* and *Mrs. Kramer*, to whom I was under obligation for much friendly attention during our journey; and found them in their cottages, busily employed in arranging and disposing of the stores they had brought from the Cape. They were assisted in their domestic work by Hottentot women, very cleanly dressed in clothes of European fashion and materials.

We also visited *Captain Dam*, as he is called, the Hottentot chief of Klaarwater, who holds a sort of authority over one-half of this tribe (of *Mixed Hottentots*); while *Captain Berends* is, in like manner, the regulator and commander of the other half. His name was *Adam Kok:* he appeared to be under the middle age, with a countenance indicative of a quiet disposition. My visit to him required no explanations, as the missionaries had already made him acquainted with every thing respecting me. His hut, which was close behind the missionary's, was not better than those of other Hottentots; but was made of mats, in the usual hemispherical form. *

From the moment when 1 decided on making Klaarwater in my

Beyond these is shown a part of the ridge, which is represented at the head of Chapter XX. These same buildings are seen in Plate 8; but are there viewed on the other side.

* The *vignètte* at the head of Chapter XX. is a representation of *Captain Dam's hut*, and of his *waggon*, of which mention is made in the following chapter. Behind them are seen some of the trees of the missionary's garden, enclosed by a hedge of dry bushes. The trunk of a tree is fixed up near the hut, for the purpose of preparing (or, as they call it, *breyen*) leathern *reims*, and for hanging game and various other things upon. Such an apparatus is called by them, and by the colonists, who also make use of it, a *Brey-paal*. On the ridge in the distance may be seen, just above the *Brey-paal*, a part of the road leading to Ongeluk's Fontein.

way to the Interior, I naturally endeavoured to form, in my own mind, some picture of it; and I know not by what mistake it arose, that I should conceive the idea of its being a picturesque spot surrounded by trees and gardens, with a river running through a neat village, where a tall church stood, a distant beacon to mark that Christianity had advanced thus far into the wilds of Africa. But the first glance now convinced me how false may oftentimes be the notions which men form of what they have not seen. The trees of my imagination vanished, leaving nothing in reality but a few which the missionaries themselves had planted; the church sunk to a barn-like building of reeds and mud; the village was merely a row of half a dozen reed cottages; the river was but a rill; and the situation an open, bare, and exposed place, without any appearance of a garden, excepting that of the missionaries.

It would be very unfair towards those who have devoted themselves to a residence in a country, where they are cut off from communication with civilized society, and deprived of all its comforts, to attribute this low state of civilization and outward improvement, to a want of solicitude on their part. Their continual complaint, indeed, was of the laziness of the Hottentots, and of the great difficulty there had always been in persuading them to work, either on the buildings or in the garden; and in this complaint there was too much truth.

My disappointment at the appearance of the place arose from expecting, perhaps, too much. Yet, notwithstanding its discouraging appearance, this colony of Hottentots, and its different outposts, is a field in which the seeds of civilization and religion may be sown with a probability of success; but I will not say that this is to be accomplished without expense, or without the employment of proper and reasonable means, and the adopting of some plan grounded on a knowledge of human nature.

Our whole party being now finally assembled at the termination of our long journey, we all, on this occasion, dined together; and the school-room was found to be the only place large enough for the purpose. A dinner that would have become a table in Cape Town, was served up; and two or three Hottentot women, who formed part of their domestic establishment, waited on us in a very attentive and proper manner. The circumstance of our being the only white people in this part of the world, and all seated round the same table, together with the idea of our being in the heart of a wilderness, and surrounded only by savage nations, created in me some peculiar feelings, and a strange interest in every thing that was passing, and in all that I saw about me.

A small tent, which had been found an unnecessary part of their baggage, and was left here by the travellers sent into the interior by Lord Caledon, was lent me by the missionaries; but the ground by the waggons was so rocky, that it was with difficulty it could be pitched. It was found more convenient to sleep in the waggon than in the tent; which, to those who travel as I did, would prove much more to be an incumbrance than an article of utility.

2nd.   The first affair of importance to be attended to, was that of providing for the recovery of my oxen, which were miserably thin and weak, and quite unable to do any work for at least a couple of months, as their feet were worn tender by the ruggedness of the stony roads, and their strength had been quite exhausted by the labor and hardships of the journey. In the neighbourhood of the village there was, at this season, hardly pasturage enough for a few cows and sheep; and it was, therefore, advised to send them to a place called *Elands Valley*, or *Elands Fountain*, one of the outposts of the settlement, where, it was said, they would find more grass than could any where else be met with at this time. An old friendly Hottentot, named *Hans Lucas*, who had been one of our caravan from the Karree River, and was now residing at Elands Valley, offered, in that case, to befriend and advise my herdsman. I therefore resolved to send the oxen to that place, under the care of *Speelman*, whom I now began to value as a useful, clever, and active servant, and one who might be trusted, as he seemed to take a cordial interest in the business of the journey. His wife, *Hannah*, had not gained so much on my good opinion; and the little work in cooking and washing, that had hitherto fallen to her share, was done with so little cheerfulness or activity, that I began to fear she would be a burthen to us, rather than a help. She had, I observed, always appeared dull and stupid, seldom joining in conversation with the rest of the people, and still more seldom, partaking in their mirth.

Speelman had formed, in the course of the journey, a friendly acquaintance with old Hans; and was therefore highly pleased when I gave him orders to take up his abode at Elands Valley. He quickly rolled up his budget, to which I added a good store of tobacco, both for him and for his wife; for *Hannah* was a most determined smoker. He took also a supply of powder and small shot, with instructions to shoot for me every variety of birds he might chance to see, and which he was immediately to send or bring to Klaarwater.

Although the thermometer stood at 78°, he put on his great watch-coat, to give him an air of importance in the eyes of the Klaarwater people, few of whom could afford this part of dress, though all were desirous of it, as giving them the look of a colonist. His budget, and a bundle of sheep-skins to sleep on, were slung at his back; his gun over his shoulder; a *kéeri* (a short knob-stick)* in his hand; and a short clumsy wooden pipe in his mouth, which every instant sent forth a copious whiff of smoke, indicative of his pleasure and contentment. Thus equipped, and accompanied by *Old Hans* and some other Hottentots, he gaily took leave, and set out for his new abode: et — *ponè subit conjux.*

4th. I soon discovered that my *station* in the middle of the kraal subjected me to the continued interruption of a crowd of visitors, who, not content with satisfying their curiosity by examining every thing belonging to the waggons, felt that their appetite also ought to be satisfied; so that, from the one cause or the other, neither I, nor my men, found any time for attending to the affairs of

---

* The figure of the *Kéeri*, or *Kírri*, may be seen in Plate 10.

the journey. At the distance of a seven minutes' walk north-eastward from the village, there was a much more pleasant situation, having the mead on one side, and on the other a stony rising ground. *   A small channel, conducting from a spring in the upper part of the mead to some huts and corn-land below, supplied us with plenty of good water. The station, like every one in the vicinity, was open and exposed; but it had a pleasant prospect of the whole of the village, to which a narrow path led across the mead.

Hither the waggons and tent were removed by the help of a team of Captain Dam's oxen; and as they were likely to remain on this spot two or three months, large stones were placed under the wheels to keep them dry. A place was formed for our fire, sheltered by a few pieces of rock piled round it. A spot was levelled for the tent; and the little waggon was taken off the wheels, and placed on stone supports. †   The neighbourhood was first reconnoitred, to ascertain where firewood was to be found; but this article had been every where consumed by the inhabitants of the kraal, and was to be procured only at a great distance.

Philip and *Gert* were the only attendants I retained at home; for so, we always termed the spot where my waggons were stationed. The latter showed a disposition to make himself useful in various ways, and undertook the duty of cooking; nor had I any cause of complaint against the former, excepting that he required very often to be reminded of the work to which it was his duty to attend.

6th. This being *Sunday,* I attended the service in the *church,* or *meeting-house.* The building ‡ which they call so was rudely built of rough unhewn timber and reeds, covered with a thatched roof, and having a smooth, hard earthen floor, kept in order by being frequently smeared with cow-dung, in the manner practised by the colonists. Within, the sides were plastered with mud; and, being

---

* Our *station,* during the time I remained at *Klaarwater,* may be seen in Plate 8; at the two waggons in the distance.

† As may be seen in the *vignette* at the end of Chapter XX.

‡ See the *engraving* at page 350.

whitewashed with a kind of clay, which is found near the river, they looked tolerably clean; but the rafters and thatch constituted the only ceiling. The eaves were about six feet from the ground. The upright posts, the beams and rafters, were either of Acacia or Willow, and tied together with strips of Acacia-bark. The space within the building was a long parallelogram, which, when quite filled, might perhaps contain a congregation of three hundred persons, in the way in which the Hottentots squat on the ground; for there were no seats, excepting about a dozen, which some of the more civilized of the auditors had provided themselves with. On one of the longer sides the door-way was placed, and, opposite to it, a pulpit, raised a step above the floor.

On Sundays the service commenced at nine in the morning, and again at four in the afternoon: at each time a bell gave the inhabitants a half-hour's notice, and also tolled when the prayers began. This notice was the more necessary, as some of the huts were scattered a mile from the church; and, from the openness of the situation, the bell could be heard at a great distance. A few people also attend from the nearest outposts; and, occasionally, a marriage takes place; which was the case at this time.

The church was this day, as usual, well filled; and the congregation behaved with great decorum, and, to appearance, listened with attention. In hot weather, the smell of their greasy bodies, and of so many sheepskin karosses, heightened by *Buku* (Bookoo) and other scents, is too strong for a nose unaccustomed to it; and I have often suffered the greatest uneasiness by enduring it till the end of the service: frequently, in such weather, I was compelled to absent myself on that account. My object in attending their Sabbath meetings, was not my own edification; it was, (being an European, whom many of these poor creatures look up to as knowing what is right,) that I might not, by my example, sanction a neglect of divine worship, but rather, by my presence, encourage them, as far as I could have any influence, to listen to, and respect, their teachers. I cannot say that the scope and bearing of the doctrine of these teachers, were altogether such as I myself should have chosen, had

I been in their situation, and desirous of making my hearers lead a more virtuous and religious life. But every man, *sincere* in his religious enthusiasm, and *pure* in his intentions, is entitled to respect, whatever sect or religion he may belong to. Two of the missionaries were of the Dutch *Calvinistic* church, and one of the *Wesleyan* persuasion. The service consisted, both in singing psalms or hymns, and in expounding, and dilating upon, some passage of the Bible, which, on *Sundays*, is interpreted in the *Hottentot language*, for the benefit of those who do not sufficiently understand *Dutch*; but these hearers constitute a very small portion of the congregation. The service concluded always with a long extempore prayer by one of the missionaries, each of whom took his daily or weekly turn in the duty. On stated days, they were in the habit of administering the sacrament to a small number of communicants; and it was only on such occasions that they were dressed in black.

The ceremony of *marriage*, according to Christian rites, had not been introduced at Klaarwater longer than three years; nor, indeed, could the greater part of these people be persuaded to adopt it. The restrictions which it had been endeavoured to lay upon their former customs, had rendered the missionaries rather unpopular; and the law for reducing the number of wives from two, often three, and sometimes four, to one, in a nation consisting of more females than males, did not meet with many advocates in either sex. However, since its first introduction, about a hundred, as I was informed, had submitted to it.

This meeting-house serves also for a *school-room*, where some of the children attend, principally in the evenings, although in a desultory manner, to be instructed in reading, and a few in writing. Once or twice in the week, a greater number are assembled to repeat a catechism, and to have it explained suitably to their capacities. This business, which generally occupies about an hour, concludes with an extempore prayer, and a verse of some psalm or hymn sung by the whole party.

This is the ordinary routine of the business of the mission, as I observed it during the four months which, at different times, I spent at Klaarwater. And, with respect to its effects in forwarding the object of it, I cannot say that they appeared to me very evident: certainly, I saw nothing that would sanction me in making such favorable reports as have been laid before the public.

The enthusiasm which, perhaps, is inseparable from missionary affairs, may create some optical delusion in the mind's eye, that may cause it to see those things which are not visible to a more temperate and unbiassed observer; but still, it is much to be lamented that the community at home are misled by accounts (I speak generally) catching at the most trifling occurrence for their support, and showing none but the favorable circumstances; and even those, unfairly exaggerated. Deception never yet supported any cause for long. Every sensible and reasonable person must be too well aware of the difficulties attending the civilization of wild nations, to expect more than slow and gradual advancement, or to be disappointed or deterred by the untowardness of savages, or by their resistance to novel doctrines. Whatever aversion the African tribes, taken generally, may have to new opinions in religion and morality, they will not, I am sure, reject any proffered instruction in such arts as have for them an evident utility. Why not, therefore, begin with this? As the trial has, I believe, never been made, the objection that such a plan will not succeed, cannot yet be fairly urged against it; while those who have an opportunity of getting at the truth, know that the evangelizing scheme has too often ended in nothing. If there really do exist so much good-will, and such disinterested philanthropy, towards all the untutored savages of the globe; and this has, it cannot be denied, shown itself in a variety of shapes, combined always with religious enthusiasm; why, therefore, has it not shown itself in some endeavour directed exclusively to the object of instructing them in those arts and practices, from which we derive those superior comforts which, in a worldly point of view, distinguish us from them? Why have no missionaries been sent to them with this as their first great object? Because, perhaps, our philanthropy is not strong enough to stand purely by itself, without the enthusiasm of a religious devotee. But I hope not to be misunderstood; for though I well know that nothing can stand without the support of genuine religion, I mean, that as mere men, and having to deal with mere men, there is no absurdity in trying how far worldly means are likely to produce those good effects on our fellow-creatures, which we are so desirous of witnessing.

For the purpose of giving a clearer account of the settlement of Klaarwater and its inhabitants, the same venial anachronism is committed here, as in the second chapter, by bringing together in this place the various particulars which were learnt at different subsequent periods.

The *village* itself is situated close on the eastern side of a low rocky ridge, composed of an argillaceous slate or stone, divisible into thin laminæ like that of the Asbestos mountains*; between which, however, no asbestos has hitherto been observed. On one side is a long grassy *mead* of irregular shape, and containing above a hundred acres. This, being the lowest ground, receives the drainings and springs of the whole valley, and is, in some places, of a boggy nature. It is covered with coarse grass, and, by a little trouble and management, might be converted into gardens for the Hottentots, in the same manner as at Genadendal †; and seems excellently suited for the purpose. The soil is a dark mould; and springs, rising in different parts of it, yield a never-failing stream of water during the whole year. I found this *water* clear and wholesome at all times: it is, however, of a calcareous nature, as is evident by the substance deposited on the roots and stems of the reeds and sedge along its course. All these springs, collected into a small rill, take their course through the mountains southward, by an outpost called *Leeuwcnkuil* (Lion's-den), and passing by *Grootedoorn* (Great-thorn), another outpost, join the *Great River*, after running a distance of forty miles. The whole substratum of this part of the country, for many leagues northward and eastward, is a hard *limestone rock* of

---

* Or that which is represented by the *vignette* at the end of Chapter XIX.
† See pages 110, 112, and 114.

primitive formation; and on this, rest the laminated argillaceous
mountains.   This limestone rock in no place rises into mountains,
but often forms the surface of a great extent of country.   I never
saw in it any marks of extraneous fossils.   The soil on the higher
grounds surrounding the valley, is remarkably red, being a mixture
of sand and clay, which produces bushes and a variety of plants; but
is subject to great drought during the summer.

The number of Hottentot houses immediately round the church,
is not greater than twenty-five*; but at a distance, within the same
valley, nearly as many more are scattered about; and there are three

---

* The *view of Klaarwater*, represented in *Plate* 8, was taken from the rocky ridge
above-mentioned, and shows the whole of the village, and the surrounding country.

The *mat-houses* of the Hottentots may be distinguished by their hemispherical form.
The largest oblong building is the *church*, or *meeting-house;* in a line with which stand
the dwellings of the missionaries, and their storehouses.   In a line just above the church,
are seen the trees of the *garden,* the tallest of which are the Gariepine willow; the rest are
peach-trees.   The waggon on the left, is proceeding on the road towards *Ongeluks Fontein,*
a part of which is seen crossing the ridge in the distance.   Above the waggon is the *willow-
tree,* the history of which is given under the date of the 9th of December following.   Behind the waggon, the foundations of a *new meeting-house* are conspicuous; near which is
the conical thatched hut used as a *storehouse.*   Another round thatched building, in a line
below the fire, is also a storehouse.   Various huts of the Hottentots are scattered in the
distance.   Near the church and dwelling-houses, the missionaries' waggons are, according
to the practice of the Cape colony, stationed in the open air; sheds for such purposes being
very rarely seen among the boors.   The centre of the picture is occupied by the *kraals,* or
pounds, for oxen and sheep, fenced in with large branches of trees.   The *mead* is distinguished by a more verdant colouring.   In the distance, my own *station* is pointed out by
the two waggons, and the party of visitors assembled round our fire.   Behind a low rocky
hill on the right, in the middle distance, the top of a waggon marks the spot of the *sleeping scene* represented in the engraving at the end of this volume; and the waggon a little
further to the left, at the point of the same hill, shows the place where my waggons were
stationed during my absence to *Graaffreynet.*   On both sides of this rocky hill, the waters
collected in the mead find an outlet along the valley to *Leeuwenkuil* (Lion's-den).   The
road from the *Asbestos Mountains* descends just behind the bushy ridge on the left of the
picture.   In the foreground, various groups of *Hottentots* are seen basking in the sun;
some sitting smoking or conversing at the door of their huts; some stretched out upon
sheepskins spread on the ground; one on the left of the picture preparing a skin for
leather; three on the right, beating a large *vel-kombáars* (or sheepskin coverlet), a frequent and very necessary operation.   Of the bushes on the foreground, some are of the
kind described at page 348, under the name of *Spartium cuspidosum,* and others, a new
Rhus, specifically designated by that of *concinnum.*

A View of Kamschatka looking towards the North east.

or four at *Leeuwenkuil*, a place between the mountains, and about a mile and a half distant.   Within fifty miles, in various directions, are nearly a dozen other *out-posts;* but they are not always inhabited : of these, the largest is *the Kloof.*

The aggregate number of *inhabitants* at Klaarwater and the out-stations, amounted in the year 1809, as I was informed, to seven hundred and eighty-four souls; and it was supposed that at this time it had not decreased : for, although some had left them and returned into the Cape colony, others had been added from that quarter in an equal proportion.   The *Koras* and *Bushmen* living within the Klaarwater district, cannot be considered as belonging to the establishment, since they show no desire to receive the least instruction from the missionaries, nor do they attend their meetings, but continue to remove from place to place, a wild independent people.

The tribe of Hottentots now at Klaarwater, had its origin from the two families of the *Mixed Race,* of the name of *Kok* and *Berends,* who, about forty years ago, preferring their freedom on the banks of the *Great River* to a residence within the Cape colony, where they had acquired a few sheep in the service of the farmers, emigrated thither from the *Kamiesberg* with all their cattle and friends.   These were, from time to time, joined by others of the same race, who found their life under the boors not so agreeable as they wished. Thus, their increasing numbers rendered them an object worth the' attention of the missionaries ; whose station amongst the Bushmen at *Zak River,* happened to break up about the year 1800.   These Hottentots appearing to offer an easier and more promising soil for their labors, the missionaries attached themselves to them, and followed them in all their wanderings along the river, till they were at last persuaded to remain stationary at *Aakaap,* and finally at *Klaarwater;* which, at the time they took possession of it, was a Bushman kraal.

The existence of this little community of Hottentots, was well known to the colonists under the name of the *Bastaards,* because the whole of them were at that time, all of the *Mixed Race.* *

See the note at page 154.

They had always professed, among themselves, the Christian religion; and at one time were the dupes of a religious impostor, named *Stephanus.*

This *Stephanus* was a native of Courland, and had been clerk to a merchant in Cape Town: but having been detected in forging the colonial paper money, he contrived to escape from justice, and fled unpursued to the missionaries established at Sack River: where, under another name, he offered them his services; and, being naturally clever and ingenious, he was found extremely useful as an artificer; nor was he, as they assured me, to be considered as an uneducated man.

At last, a letter was received from the Fiscal, describing his person, and requiring the missionaries to detain him if he should happen to make his appearance at their station. The man had, while at Sack River, conducted himself so correctly, that he was not suspected to be the person described, till, having heard of the contents of the letter, and becoming visibly uneasy and melancholy, he eloped from the settlement. He had with him no kind of arms for his defence against the savages, and but a small stock of provisions; yet he succeeded in the hazardous attempt of making his way, alone and unguided, to the Gariep, and joined this Hottentot community at a place called *Kok's Kraal,* where they at that time were stationed.

He had with him a bible, given him at the Zak River; and, with this in his hand, he set up as missionary, and gained an ascendancy over the minds of the kraal, such as, the missionaries have confessed, they have never been able to gain. He persuaded them to attend to agriculture, and also to erect a church.* This he built in a superior style; and, conducting the religious service with much imposing formality and ceremony, made his hearers at length believe that he was expressly sent to them from heaven. He preached such doc-

---

* The situation of this church is placed on the map agreeably to the distance and bearing given me by the Klaarwater Hottentots, who are in the habit of travelling every year from Klaarwater to Namaqualand.

trines as suited his purpose, and was not suspected of imposition, even when, on desiring to take another wife in addition, he declared he had the divine command for selecting such or such a female.   At last, on some occasion he made a journey into the country of the *Great Namaquas*, and was murdered by the natives.

When the missionaries afterwards attached themselves to the *Kok*'s and the *Berends*'s party, they had great difficulty in persuading them that *Stephanus* was nothing but an impostor; so successfully had he managed to secure an authority over their minds, as well as over their conduct.

This little history, among other things, serves to show that there is a mode of treatment by which, even the obstinate and ignorant, may be guided and rendered tractable; an invaluable secret to those who undertake the civilization of a wild people.

Adam Kok and *Berend Berends* are now, at Klaarwater, the representative heads of the two families or parties just mentioned.   The authority, therefore, of these chiefs is of a patriarchal nature, and extends very little beyond a voluntary submission on the part of their people.   It is confined principally to that of ordering out the force of the tribe to attack an enemy, or to take up arms in defence of the settlement.   In cases like this, for the general welfare, they are readily obeyed; and can muster more than two hundred muskets, which are the only weapons they at present make use of.   But, in ordinary cases, their power does not seem to be so strong, as the good of their society requires.   Lately, a man had been accused of a crime for which he was brought before *Captain Dam* and several of the head people, as his council; who, on a formal examination found him guilty, and, agreeably to the Hottentot usage, ordered him to be laid on the ground and severely beaten with sticks; a punishment which, indeed, he well deserved.   During the infliction of the sentence, the friends and relations of the criminal, who were standing by, were bestowing their imprecations on the captain, in the most horrid terms, and behaving in a menacing manner with sticks in their hands.   The other captain seemed to be more resolute, and to possess a spirit better fitted for maintaining his authority.

By a register of *births and deaths* it appears that the former exceed the latter; but I could not learn in what proportion. These Hottentots pretend that their wives are never duly obedient till they have undergone, what they consider, a salutary castigation; and I was assured that it was not easy to find a man who did not occasionally beat his wife.

The number of *cattle* belonging to the Klaarwater Hottentots is guessed at three thousand, including oxen, cows, and calves. The price of an ox is ten or twelve rix dollars; and of a sheep, two. By barter for beads and tobacco, they annually obtain from the *Bachapins* (called *Briquas* or Goat-men, in the Hottentot language), a number of oxen; most of which they sell in the colony at the average rate of twenty rix dollars each. Of sheep and goats they possess a large number; and of horses, between eighty and ninety. Of dogs there is a sufficient proportion, but they have neither cats nor pigs. A little poultry is kept by one or two families only; but the missionaries have a few domestic fowls, ducks, geese, and Guinea hens or Pintadoes, which are called by the quaint name of *Jan Tadentaal*. This bird is found wild in many parts of the country.

These Hottentots have nothing that deserves to be considered as a *garden* producing fruit and esculent vegetables; but those who are not too indolent cultivate tobacco. They are fond of *brandy*, but their distance from the colony prevents their being gratified to the extent of their wishes or means. An attempt at distilling a spirit from the berries of, what they therefore call, the *Brandewyn-bosch* (Brandy-bush*) had succeeded; but the trouble of collecting a sufficient quantity of the berries, was a check to its being too often made. They supply themselves more plentifully, and at an easier rate, with a fermented liquor, which they call " honey-beer," made with honey and water, and which answers sufficiently well for the purpose of intoxication. All are exceedingly fond of *tea*, and when the Chinese kind is not to be procured, they make use of the leaves of various wild plants: next to tobacco and

---

* *Grewia flava.*

brandy, they esteem tea the greatest luxury, as a beverage. Their chief *food* is milk, game, together with mutton, or beef; which latter is rarely killed; their principal dependance being on game, of which they bring home no trifling quantity. Hunting is the only *employ-ment* at which they show any eagerness; and it, therefore, occupies the greatest part of their time. *Adam Kok*, the captain, is reckoned the richest man amongst them; and possesses a thousand sheep, eight hundred goats, and three teams of oxen, besides a number of cows and calves: yet he lives in a miserable mat-house * not better than the rest of his neighbours.

Some of the people cultivate a little *corn;* but so foolish and improvident are they, that as soon as the harvest is gathered in, they eat, I may almost say, night and day, till the little they have is devoured. A Hottentot's motto might very appropriately be " A feast and a fast." This is the reason that, immediately after the harvest, very little work is done. The few individuals amongst them who are more sparing and provident, are beset during the rest of the year by *beggars* and hangers-on, who, under the claims of relationship or friendship, become so heavy a tax on their industry as almost to dissuade them from growing any another season. They frequently are obliged to kill a sheep, as it were, by stealth, that they may save a portion of it for their own families; and elude these beggars, who would seat themselves around the pot without ceremony or waiting for any invitation.

Wheat is the only corn they cultivate; it is sown in June, and reaped in December. The thrashing, or rather treading out, of the grain immediately, as in the colony, follows the harvest, and is per-formed in a similar manner, by horses driven round a circular earthen floor. The corn is ground by a hand-mill of the same construction as that already described. † The land is ploughed by oxen; and both the beam-plough and the wheel-plough are used: the work appeared to me to be performed tolerably well. The quantity of

---

* See the *vignette* at the head of Chapter XX.
† On the 13th of April, at page 113.

land under tillage is much less than it ought to be, considering the facilities of the country and their own necessities; and it can hardly be said that during the preceding six years, the number of cultivated acres has been increased: to justify which, it was complained that in some places the ground has been found on trial, to be of too saline a quality.

The *garden* belonging to the missionaries, contained about an acre, or more, of very good soil; and was enclosed from the edge of the mead, by banks of earth and a hedge of dead bushes. A rill of water was led through it for the purpose of irrigation; and every thing appeared in a thriving state. I saw in it a few trees of peach, almond, fig, vine, and walnut, together with a young orange-tree; all, excepting the two last, were just beginning to yield fruit. The peach trees were in the most luxuriant growth, and seemed to promise a plentiful crop; but a late frost, which happened on the 6th of October while the fruit was just forming, caused the whole to drop off prematurely.

Some seeds of *cotton*, which I had brought with me to Africa, for the purpose of sowing them at different convenient places in the Interior, were planted in this garden. Several plants came up from them, and, as in January 1813, I saw it in flower, I have no doubt that they afterwards produced good seed.

Of *esculent vegetables*, I saw small quantities of potatoes, cabbage, French-beans, peas, lettuce, onions, beet, cucumbers, pumkins, calabash, musk-melons, water-melons, millet, and some others. The common hemp, called *dakka*, was here raised for the purpose of being given as presents to the Bushmen, who smoke it instead of tobacco; as do also many of the Hottentots; but it is considered more deleterious and inebriating.

Maize, or Indian corn, was cultivated for the poultry; but the half-ripe heads, when boiled, made a very agreeable and wholesome dish. When their store of *coffee* became low, the ripe grains, roasted and ground, were mixed with it; but the beverage made from this mixture, though not unpleasant to the taste, had a heating quality which would not agree with every stomach. This corn, sowed in the first week of October, came in flower before the middle of December.

The *dwellings* of the missionaries stand close together in a line with the meeting-house, forming, with two others in a parallel line, a kind of street, in the middle of which stood, at this time, a stuffed *camelopard*, which, being much weather-beaten and decayed, was soon afterwards taken down. This object, reminding me that I was in the country where these animals were to be beheld alive, added a pleasing and very interesting feature to this little village.

The only piece of *masonry* was the foundations of a large building, intended to comprise under one roof a meeting-house and the dwellings of the missionaries; but its only use is to prove that a plan of rendering the mission respectable in its appearance was once entertained. It was commenced, I believe, about seven years before my visit to Klaarwater, and was carried on with spirit by the united labor of the whole community, until the walls reached the height of five or six feet; and in this state it has remained ever since, and still continues, without any prospect of being completed. This neglect is attributed to the temper of the Hottentots, who, like children pleased with a new toy, which is soon thrown aside, at first laboured readily at the work, and would not have deserted it if three or four months could have brought it to a conclusion; but finding, after the novelty of the job had worn off, that nothing was left but hard labor, their little stock of exertion and patience became exhausted, and the thing was given up as an undertaking of too great a magnitude. There was no want of materials; since their mortar was obtained close at hand, being merely mud, and the adjoining hill supplied the stone, which was formed by nature of shapes the best adapted for masonry: while timber might easily be procured from the banks of the Gariep, or even much nearer. The business of sawing planks has not yet been introduced here; but two or three people work as blacksmiths, although in a very bungling manner.

The only means of rendering this mission permanent, is to induce these people to acquire property in immoveable buildings, and in gardens well stocked with fruit-trees. These they would be unwilling to desert, on account of the labor and time that would be required to procure the same advantages on another spot. To persuade them to erect such buildings, had been, as Mr. Anderson informed me, his constant endeavour; and it was not without reason that he complained of the laziness of the people, and of their unwillingness to regulate their conduct by his instructions and advice. It is certainly not an easy task to change the customs and prejudices of any people; but still, however, it may in many cases be done; and, whenever improvements more conducive to their happiness can be substituted in the place of their own rude notions, the attempt may conscientiously be made, and, to a certain extent, persevered in.

The *weather* of this part of the continent, is characterized by an extraordinary clearness in the atmosphere, an extreme dryness of the air (not greater, however, than was afterwards observed further in the interior), a want of rain for the greatest part of the year, and, during the remainder, heavy showers, attended with much lightning and thunder. In January, the *hottest* month, the average mid-day heat was observed to be 89° (31°·6 C.), and in May, 60° (15°·5 C.). In July, the *coldest* month, it would probably be about 56° (13°·3 C.); but this I had no direct opportunity of ascertaining.* In October,

---

* The following compendious Table, showing the range and variations of atmospherical heat at Klaarwater, may be interesting, as affording some idea of the state of the thermometer in a remote part of the interior of Africa, where observations to this extent have never been before made.

At Klaarwater, thermometer in the shade.	1811. Oct.	1811. Dec.	1812. Jan.	1812. Feb.	1812. Mar.	1812. April	1812. May.
Number of days observed	19	16	21	11	8	6	3
Average mid-day heat by Fahrenheit's scale	79	88	89	81½	73	70½	60
Highest mid-day heat observed	90	94	96	86	88	80	70
Lowest mid-day heat observed	68	78	75	79	65	51	51
Lowest degree observed	24	52	65	70	61	50	49

In part of February, March, April, and May, during my absence from Klaarwater, I left my thermometer with one of the missionaries, who obligingly noted down for me several observations in each of these months.

I noted an observation so low as 24° (4°·4 below O. C.), and saw *ice* half an inch thick. One morning in June, the ground was white with *snow*, which, however, was all melted away before night. Thunder-storms not unfrequently bring hailstones half an inch in diameter.

The *lightning*, in its appearance, differs from that of England: the luminous trace formed by it, was not straight, or broken into angles, but moved in a quivering manner, describing a tremulous line, not unlike that by which rivers are represented in maps. The flash was, in general, not instantaneous; but had a duration that was very perceptible: sometimes it continued so long as two seconds; and to the eye it seemed as if liquid fire were rapidly flowing along the luminous line, as along a channel. This phenomenon was more evident when the clouds from which it was produced were more distant; and it may then be observed to take a direction more horizontal than otherwise.

Fatal *accidents from lightning*, though very rarely, have yet sometimes occurred. A few years before, one of the Hottentot huts at Klaarwater was struck by it, and six men killed; but an old woman and a child, who were in it, remained unhurt. Only eighteen months previous to this date, two men, who, during a heavy thunder-shower, took shelter under a tree at Wittewater, were struck dead. But these are the only instances that have come to my knowledge.

One night in the month of January, 1806, the shock of an *earthquake* was felt at Klaarwater, and which one of the missionaries described as producing a movement of the ground like that of a ship at sea in a heavy swell; in which the whole house moved. This motion was repeated three several times, attended with a very hollow deep sound. No mischief was done by it, nor was the earth observed to be rent in any place; as the motion was not of that trembling kind already described as having damaged so many houses in Cape Town.

This place, in common with all countries which I have visited remote from the sea, receives its *rains* in the summer; whereas those within the influence of the maritime air, receive theirs in the opposite season of the year. In the former, the showers are produced by thunder-clouds only, and are very irregular and uncertain as to their season; sometimes falling very early, and at other times continuing unusually late. August and September are considered as the best months in which the journey from Klaarwater to the Cape, can be performed; as, at that time, the weather is cool, and the oxen can arrive there while the grass of the colony is fresh and green.

After the middle of October, no *frost* is expected for seven months; but in the mornings of May it is always found to return, and is the signal for the return of their horses from the *Roggeveld*, whither they are sent in January to avoid the *Paarde-ziekte*, a fatal distemper to which they are liable during the hotter months. Those who object to sending their horses to so great a distance from the settlement, are content to run the risk of keeping them on the *Langberg* (Long Mountain), an elevated mountainous country, lying in a W.N.W. direction, distant about fifty miles. This, however, not being so cold as the Roggeveld, is less safely to be depended on. It does not seem that this distemper acquires its full force till the beginning of February; but after then, the lower districts of the whole of the extra-tropical part of Southern Africa are, as far as my information enables me to speak, subject to its baneful effects. Experience has shown that the first frost, whenever it happens, fortunately puts a stop to its further ravages.

A mild kind of *ophthalmia* is a complaint prevalent amongst the Hottentots in this part of the country. It returns at two opposite seasons of the year; most frequently in November and May, but sometimes in the three following months. I have termed it mild, because I never heard of its having ended in blindness; although it is said to be very painful and troublesome. I performed many speedy and effectual cures by the distribution of small quantities of an eye-water made with a very weak solution of sugar of lead * in plain

---

* *Acetas plumbi.*

water. The missionaries suffered from its attacks; but I had the good fortune always to continue free from even the slightest symptoms.

About two years ago the *measles* found its way here from out of the colony, and made much havoc. It is, perhaps, the first time of its spreading so far into the interior.

The *small-pox* had made its appearance in this part of the Interior, a little more than three years before, and raged from November till June at Klaarwater, where, although every individual was infected, not more than thirteen died under it; while, at the same time, with a more unsparing hand, it thinned the numbers of the Bushmen and Koras. Of the latter it swept off half the inhabitants of a large kraal bordering upon the country of the Bachapins. Amongst these tribes, I saw many individuals whose faces were left deeply pitted by that disease; but this was not the first time it had made itself known to them.

The *vaccine matter* which I brought with me, proved, on trial, to have lost all its power. This was occasioned by the great length of time consumed in the journey, added to the excessive dryness of the weather.

Young children frequently die of *convulsions;* a disorder very general at that age. Cases of *jaundice* sometimes occur; but the most dangerous malady is a kind of cancerous sore or ulcer, called in the colony the *Hottentots Zeer* (Hottentot Sore), which spreads wide, and corrodes so deeply as often to prove fatal. It is said to be communicated by contact, and seems, in most instances, to attack the head and upper parts of the body. The remedy chiefly relied on at Klaarwater, and in some parts of the colony, is onions; the juice of which must be applied to the sore as soon as the existence of it is ascertained. Whenever the patient is so fortunate as to get cured, he bears the marks of it about with him for the rest of his life; a large scar always remaining behind.

The whole catalogue of their disorders, including some ailments too trifling to be enumerated, is not great; and from this it may justly be inferred, that the climate of the Interior is healthy. Judging from my own personal experience, I should characterize it as every where remarkably salubrious.

The preceding account will not only give an idea of the country and people to which it more especially refers, but, in several circumstances of a more general nature, it may be applied to the other tribes also. The meteorological remarks will be found equally applicable to all the country around, within a hundred miles.

7th. The flock of sheep which I bought in the Roggeveld Karro were already consumed, owing to the small quantity of game we had hitherto been able to procure. During my residence at Klaarwater, I obtained occasionally a few sheep or goats from the Hottentots; but it was always attended with some difficulty, as they made a favor of selling them to me. What the missionaries had to spare, they readily supplied me with; but I began to perceive, that if our huntings were not more successful, there would be little prospect of persuading the people here to sell us as much as we required, unless they were paid in gunpowder; a mode of payment which I resolved, if possible, to avoid; for the reason that the quantity demanded for a sheep would be sufficient to procure us ten times as much food in game.

Speelman returned from Elands' Valley, to receive his rations of mutton, flour, tobacco, and brandy; having left the oxen in the care of one of the other herdsmen. From his report of their very emaciated and weak state, I saw that we were likely to be detained here a long time for their recovery. He brought me half a dozen birds, three of which I had not seen before.* One was a Bee-eater, known commonly by the name of *Berg Zwaluw* (Mountain Swallow), which scarcely differed from the European species.

8th. On examining into the state of the *waggons*, it appeared that the one purchased at Tulbagh was not so excellent a bargain as

---

* *Merops Apiaster.*
Sylvia ———. *Le Grivetin?* Le Vaill. Ois. d'Afr. pl. 118.
Saxicola ———. *Le Traquet Fourmilier.* Le V. 186.

the waggon-maker had persuaded me to believe.   Several parts were either decayed, or nearly worn out; and the new fellies proved, by their shrinking so much more than the other wheels, that they had been made of timber not properly seasoned.   We were therefore obliged to drive wedges of wood into the openings, and, as well as we were able, repair what was out of order; and, to preserve the wheels and the carriage part, we covered them over with a double coat of boiled tar.

9th. Having yesterday remained without meat, Philip went out at day-light this morning with his musket, to try his luck in the chace. At noon he returned for some one to assist him in fetching home a large *Springbuck* he had shot; from which, at night, we made our breakfast; but, it being an old animal, the meat bade defiance to all mastication; and what the teeth were unable to accomplish, the digestion was obliged to perform.

We had the misfortune to find the fourth part of our stock of *rice* quite unfit for use.   It had become mouldy from having been wetted by the leaking of the keg of wine.

10th.   When a *Kora* dies without children, it is the custom for his brother to take whatever property he may have left behind him; while the widow is entitled only to that share of it, which has been gained by her own labor and management.   A case of this nature occurred not long before my arrival; in which a *Bushwoman*, wife of a *Korana*, had, by collecting a quantity of certain roots or leaves used for chewing as a substitute for tobacco, acquired about a dozen sheep; which, on the death of her husband, were unjustly taken possession of by his brother.   The woman, remonstrating in vain, and unable to obtain justice, was at this time collecting together her *Bushman* friends; who, exasperated at the unfair treatment she had received, were resolved to seek justice with the aid of the bow and the hassagay.   The *Kora* was taking exactly the same steps to defend himself, and to retain what he had unlawfully seized.   For, among them, as among civilized and polished nations, he who is in the wrong will always find some false argument to prove that he is in the right.   The mode in which this ' trial by battle' was to be decided, consists in plundering each other of their cattle; and some-times, with a more sanguinary intention, in lying in ambush for their adversaries, whom they seldom fail to shoot, if he should unhappily come within their reach; but, as they are well aware of each other's mode of warfare, and are exceedingly cunning and cautious, this does not often happen.   As soon as one party has decidedly proved itself the strongest, the affair is put to rest, and they live as before, without offering each other any further molestation.   So, at least, has this story been related to me.

Speelman, whom I allowed a few days before to take with him the great rifle-piece to Elands' Valley, had made good use of it; and now came home loaded with the hide and meat of a *Koodoo* *, having hired a young *Kora* to assist him in carrying the two legs; the distance being not less than eighteen miles, and under a burning sun.   This was the second koodoo he had shot; the first having been left in the plain till quite spoiled by the heat, as he had not been able either to borrow or hire a pack-ox·to fetch it away.

His companion, who went by the name of Krieger, told me, that he was the son of the unfortunate *Jacob Krieger*, of whom mention has already been made †; and a strong family likeness, which might be discovered in spite of his brown color and woolly hair, confirmed the truth of his assertion.   His mother was a Kora; from her he derived his language and national character; speaking scarcely any Dutch, and having both the manners and dress of the Koras.   He possessed a pleasing and open countenance.

I rejoiced them with an extra ration of tobacco and brandy, with which, and a plentiful feast of koodoo meat, they regaled them-selves at our fire with Philip and Gert, to whom Speelman related

---

* *Antilope strepsiceros* (Twisted-horned Antelope) of zoologists. (See page 337.) At the end of this chapter will be found a representation of the *horns and skull of a Koodoo*, in the proportion of a sixteenth of the natural size.

† At pages 50 and 201.

very minutely every circumstance respecting the oxen, the quantity of game he had seen, and the manner in which he had shot the koodoos; together with a multitude of Hottentot anecdotes.

11*th*. From my waggon-station, the horizon on the east, north, and west was as low, and as level and unbroken, as that of the ocean. The extraordinary clearness and transparency of the air might be remarked in a variety of instances, but in none more evidently than in the distinctness with which the heavenly bodies could be seen. Stars of the first and second magnitudes were visible the moment they rose above the horizon; and some of them shone so much like a light in a distant hut, that I was deceived by their appearance, until they had risen higher than the possible situation of such a light.

By the mean of two very good observations of the meridional altitudes of α and γ *Pegasi*, calculated from the declinations and annual variations given in the ' Requisite Tables,' the *latitude* of my station was found to be 28° 50′ 55·7″; and subsequent observations of α *Oriontis* and the planet *Jupiter* gave the same result. * By the magnetic bearing of β *Cassiopeïæ*, when on the meridian, and the azimuth of α *Herculis*, the *variation* of the compass was found to be 27° westward.

12*th*. The wide range of the thermometer in Southern Africa, in the course of the twenty-four hours, was this day more than usually remarkable. Between the hours of half-past six o'clock in the morning and two in the afternoon, it rose from 24° up to 81½°; a difference, in seven hours and a half, of fifty-seven degrees and a half of Fahrenheit's, twenty-five and a half of Reaumur's, and thirty-two of the Centigrade scale; and on the following morning it was found again as low as 32°.

---

* 11th Oct. 1811, at Klaarwater, the observed meridional altitude of

α *Pegasi* (*Markab*) was	46°	58′	9″
γ *Pegasi* (*Algenib*)	47	1	41
24th Dec. 1811, ... α *Oriontis*	53	47	46
Jupiter	37	54	44

14th. A party of the Klaarwater people, headed by Captain Berends, expecting to be absent two months, set off on an expedition to the northward, to hunt elephants, for the purpose of procuring ivory for their next journey to Cape Town. It consisted of about a dozen men, with two or three waggons and some of their best horses. They were to take the road over Langberg, and, by a circuit, to extend their journey as far as Litakun, to trade with the beads they had lately brought from the Cape. Other bartering expeditions to the same country followed shortly afterwards.

15th. The evening being very warm, and not a breath of air stirring, the canvas flap of my waggon was drawn up for coolness. It was such evenings only, which induced the smaller species of *moths* to make their appearance. They now swarmed round my candle, only to be burnt; and the number of the unfortunate nearly smothered the wick, and put out the light. I caught, almost promiscuously, about five-and-twenty, and was surprised at finding amongst them not less than fifteen different sorts. Besides these, a great number of small beetles * were very troublesome and annoying, entangling themselves in my hair, and flying against the paper upon which I was writing.

17th. My bedding having been left out in the air all day, we found, in the evening, the mattrass taken possession of by a swarm of *bees*, which had taken shelter under it for the night; and, as a favor to these industrious little creatures, we left them undisturbed. They remained there till the next day at noon, when they all departed in quest of some convenient chink in the rock for their hive. Their manner of swarming appeared to me to differ in nothing from that of the common English honey-bee. The same species, or others of the genus (*Apis*), abounds in every part of this continent which

---

* *Aphodius vespertinus.* B. Totus nigro-castaneus; vix 2 lineas longus.

On the same evening I caught a *Notoxus*, and, for the first time, a large *Dorylus*, an insect which I afterwards found, in the months of November and December, within the Cape colony.

has come under my observation, and is every where eagerly robbed of its honey. None of these nations have the least idea of bringing them under domestic management, but are content to take the honey wherever it is found; and this being done oftentimes at an improper season, they make a useless destruction of the larvæ, or young bees still in the comb. It is a circumstance to be wondered at, that in the Cape colony no attempt has yet been made to domesticate this insect.

19th. On the body of a dead ox, I observed several large vultures *, feeding in harmony with a number of crows. This being the first time I had seen this species, I attentively watched its manners for a long while with a telescope. It was of an imposing size; and its solemn, slow, and measured movements, added to its black plumage, possessed something of a funereal cast, well suited to its cadaverous employment. An excellent picture of the manners of a vulture is drawn by Virgil, in the third book of the Æneid, in his story of the harpies; too long to be quoted here, but which the sight of these birds, and their habits, brought immediately to my recollection, and served greatly to increase the interest with which I viewed them. There was a heaviness in their gait and looks, which made one feel half-inclined to consider them rather as beasts of prey, than as feathered inhabitants of the air. When not thus called forth to action, this bird retires to some inaccessible crag, sitting almost motionless in melancholy silence for days together, unless the smell of some distant carrion, or too long an abstinence, draw it from retirement, or force it to ascend into the upper regions of air; where, out of sight, it remains for hours, endeavouring to get scent of its nauseous food. These birds must possess the sense of smelling in a degree of perfection far beyond that of which we have any idea.

---

* *Vultur auricularis ?* —— *L'Oricou ?* Le Vaill. Ois. d'Afr. pl. 9. But the auricular appendage, which suggested this name, was not observable in the birds we shot; neither in the male, nor in the female.

20th. Speelman came to-day for his rations; but his looks instantly announced that something was the matter.   When, with a lengthened piteous visage, he began his narration, his pretensions to beauty were certainly less than ever; and I should perhaps have smiled, had I not feared he was going to tell me that all my oxen were carried off by the savages, or that his wife was dead.   But the case at last proved to be, that in the dead of the night, while he and his faithful Hannah soundly slept, their hut caught fire; and being roused from their slumbers only by the noise of the flames, they barely escaped the fate of his pair of smallclothes and her leathern jacket.   He had too good an opinion, he said, of the people of the kraal, to think it possible that any of them could have done it; although he seemed to wish it were permitted to make such a statement, that he might himself escape some imputation of carelessness.   At last, with a half-stifled confession, he took the blame to himself; or, rather, hinted that the whole conflagration was occasioned by his dear spouse's tobacco-pipe, if even, perchance, she smoked not in her sleep.

He brought with him old *Hans Lucas*, to make me a proposal, that if, on an excursion we were about to make, I would allow the little waggon also to be taken, he would provide a team of oxen, on condition of having half the use of it, to bring home the game he expected to shoot; engaging also to furnish a herdsman to attend them.   I readily agreed to the plan, and we immediately held a consultation respecting its various details.   These, being affairs of high importance in Hottentot economy, cannot be divulged, as I am sure no one else will think them of such magnitude as old Hans considered them to be.

My excursion had for its object to explore the upper part of the course of the *Gariep*, and two or three large branches which were said to join it higher up.   This circumstance had been mentioned to me by *Mr. Jansz;* and on his offering to accompany me, *Adam Kok,* the Klaarwater captain, also proposed joining our party with his waggon, for the sake of hunting the *Hippopotami*, which were said to abound in that part of the river.

As soon as this plan was known, *Willem Berends*, brother to the captain at the Kloof, added himself and his waggon to us with the same view: and a *party of women*, wishing to cut mat-rushes, also took advantage of the opportunity; as our numbers would secure them from all molestation from the Bushmen.

23rd. We struck the tent, and removed the waggons to the village. Here I put into the storehouse my large chests, and so much of the load as we should not have at present any occasion for; by which means the waggons were greatly lightened, and might more easily be dragged over the rugged, uneven, pathless country, which it was expected we should have to travel over.

As it was a district, more especially along the river, known to be inhabited by great numbers of Bushmen, a plentiful stock of tobacco and dakka was taken, as presents to ensure their friendly behaviour. We cast a large supply of bullets, as all joined in the intention of hunting; it being expected by these natives, that, if they on their side allowed us unmolested to kill their game, we on ours, should give them a share of the produce of our chace.

It being necessary that Speelman, as huntsman, should be of the party, another herdsman was engaged to look after my oxen at Elands' Valley, which were still too weak to be used on this occasion; and I therefore hired a team from the captain. A few live sheep were taken with us as a reserve, in case our hunting failed; and, as a preparatory step, one was killed and salted down. Philip and Gert were two days employed in grinding corn; but, in all that time, they were unable to produce more than a bushel of flour, as the hand-mill was very much out of order, and as little calculated for expeditious performance of its duties, as my two millers were for their's; passing half their time in chatting with a party of visitors, who came only for what they could get.

My waggons no sooner arrived at the village, than they were surrounded by a crowd of boys and girls. Most of them came merely out of curiosity; but there were some amongst them only on the look-out to pilfer; and one or two things were missed: but, on application to the captain, he obtained restoration.

In the evening I was present at the catechising of the scholars in the meeting-house, and afterwards took supper with the missionary, who obligingly promised to take into his charge all the chests which it was thought not necessary to take with us ón this excursion.

CHAPTER XVI.

EXCURSION FROM KLAARWATER TO THE CONFLUENCE OF THE NU-GARIEP,
AND THENCE TO THE KY-GARIEP.

OCTOBER 24th. After some bustle and delay in collecting all the party together, we took leave, and commenced our journey at a little after mid-day, directing our course eastward. The number of waggons amounted to ten; of which, besides my own two and Mr. Jansz's, two belonged to Adam Kok, carrying his wife and family; one to Willem Berends; and the other four to different Hottentots, among whom was my late herdsman, Maagers. Women and children of all ages, constituted a third of our numbers; and horses, sheep, goats, and dogs, mingling together, made up the medley of moving objects.

Some of the hunters brought their wives and children, that they might enjoy a plenteous feast of Hippopotamus-fat: besides whom, there were many others, who, with the same view, volunteered their services as drivers, leaders, or herdsmen. The dogs, who had been slyly watching all our movements, were also volunteers, and must, in some sagacious manner, have caught a notion of the carnivorous nature of the expedition; otherwise, so wretchedly thin and emaciated as they were, they never could have felt the animation and strength to produce those rapid vibrations of tail, and to caper round us with such delight, as they exhibited at first setting off.

I took with me but three attendants of this kind; one was the terrier I brought from Tulbagh, who had been my faithful little favorite ever since, and had often served to amuse a few minutes, when fatigue prevented other employment. He had qualities which soon rendered him a favorite with my men also; and no strange foot approached my waggon at night, without being announced by his angry barking. But his barking was destined soon to cease, and the journey, for which he expressed so much pleasure, was to prove for him a fatal one.

The two others were large dogs, both given me by my fellow-traveller, Mr. Kramer: one was of the stag-hound breed; the other, a large white flap-eared dog, having two or three brown spots, wiry hair, and a bearded muzzle. During our journey from the Cape, this one had taken so great a fancy to be friendly with me, that he followed wherever I went, and would no longer attend to the call of his own master, though it was from him that he received all his food. At Klaarwater he took up his quarters at my station, and entirely deserted his former friends; for which reason he was at last very readily given up to me, and as readily accepted.

As he afterwards became, of the canine species, the greatest traveller I am acquainted with, it is a tribute justly due to his memory, to record his history and exploits on these pages, for the imitation of all future dogs who may hereafter accompany any scientific expedition. I have been able to collect very few particulars of his early life, and it is known only that he was born at Tulbagh; but the name which he then received has eluded all the researches of his biographer. From that time little occurred worth notice, until he arrived at the age of doghood, when, from some secret cause, he deserted the family in which he had been brought up, and attached himself to Mr. Kramer's, where, on account of his apparent want of confidence in his first master, the name of *Wantrouw* was bestowed upon him.

Although destiny seemed to have devoted him to a residence with the missionaries at Klaarwater, he soon took a dislike to the monotony of his prospects there; and from that time commenced the new æra of his life.   Having already acquired some knowledge of zoology, (of botany he knew very little, and of entomology nothing at all,) he sighed for an opportunity of improving himself in that science; and in the hope of becoming acquainted with the interior of many rare and nondescript animals, he offered himself to me as comparative anatomist to the expedition.

As I soon began to understand his language, the various conversations which we had together on that subject, evinced so much sagacity, that it is greatly to be regretted that he has never published his observations, which, in justice to myself it is stated, he is at full liberty to do, in any language into which they might be translated; since he was under no bond to deliver up his papers and journals for the use of his employer.   His salary was sufficient for his expenses during the journey, but entirely ceased with his services.

Wantrouw had prepared and cleaned a large collection of bones of rare quadrupeds, which would have been to any museum a valuable present.   Or, to the great extension and benefit of science in England, they might have been deposited in the cellars of the British Museum, to receive the same honors with his master's skins. *   But as they would require no stuffing, and consequently

---

* At my return to England, I brought home 120 skins of quadrupeds, the zoological fruits of my African travels; and in April, 1817, after resisting a flattering invitation from a foreign museum, of the first respectability, and who were desirous of purchasing them, I thought proper, from feelings of patriotism, to present a selection of 43 of the largest and finest skins, to the *British Museum ;* supposing that science would be more benefitted by placing them in our national repository, than in keeping them in my own collection. How far my expectations, and those of the public, have been realized, may be inferred from the fact, that at this time (December, 1821,) not more than seven have been stuffed, and, of these only five placed for public inspection.   The reason assigned for this must appear still more surprising than the fact itself; and the inability of the trustees to furnish out of the funds of the establishment the trifling sum necessary for putting this collection in órder, is exceedingly to be lamented ; not only because the visitors to the

would not put that establishment to any expense, it is very probable that the public would soon be gratified with a sight of them.

His numerous adventures, hair-breadth escapes, and observations on men and manners, would form a pretty thick quarto, if dished up in good language, by some writer acquainted with the art of book-making, and published by a bookseller at the West end of the Town; at the same time taking care to have it properly recommended in the Quarterly Review. Although *Wantrouw* had not the least notion of drawing, yet a few coloured aquatinta plates, or lithographic prints, should, by all means, be inserted; these, his publisher could easily get designed by some artist, who must be told to take especial care that the words *Wantrouw delineavit*, or, *From a sketch, by Wantrouw, Esq.* appear conspicuous at the bottom corner. Such a work, if rightly and humbly dedicated, and well advertised, would be sure to sell.

As, however, there seems at present to be no probability that the learned world will soon be gratified with the perusal of his work, so many books of travels having lately issued from the press, and those authors who are in the habit of making up books, having their hands at this time quite full of work, I have obtained his permission to insert, occasionally, in my own journal, a few of the anecdotes preserved amongst his memoranda, together with some of his principal adventures; because, as he very learnedly and justly remarked,

mea nemo

Scripta legat, vulgo recitare timentis, ob hanc rem,
Quod sunt, quos genus hoc minimè juvat; utpote plures
Culpari dignos.

Museum, are deprived of the gratification and instruction which they might derive from a view of these animals, but because a knowledge of the fact will tend to discourage others from hereafter becoming donors to an establishment where their presents will meet with neglect. At the time when these animals were presented, the Museum exhibited scarcely any thing in this department of Natural History; a circumstance which led me to suppose that forty-three quadrupeds of such magnitude, obtained not without considerable expense and personal danger, nor without a degree of trouble which no one but myself can duly estimate, and among which were many extremely rare, and some never before seen in Europe, were an addition deserving of attention.

How he could become acquainted with the language of
Horace, it is not easy to imagine; since he never had the benefit
of a residence at any of the universities.   But so it was. — Sed ego

Nunc itàque, et versus, et cætera ludicra, pono.

We had travelled not more than a dozen miles, when an accident happening to one of the wheels of the captain's waggon, we
were obliged to halt, and unyoke; while a man on horseback was
sent back to the kraal, for some iron work to replace that which was
broken.

Most of the Hottentots' waggons were in so shattered and
ricketty a state, as to occasion us to entertain serious apprehensions that some of them would drop to pieces in the attempt
at passing the rocky places which traversed our course.   Thongs
of raw hide, bound about various parts, constituted their chief
strength; and on them, the owners placed their principal dependence, for keeping the crazy vehicle together.   One waggon,
however, was quite new, and the same which had been offered
at the Asbestos mountains, in exchange for mine.   Its proprietor often put the strength of it on trial, by driving with surprising heedlessness over rocks and holes and every thing that lay
in his way.

All around us, here, was barren and without water or pasture;
and thus to be delayed above three hours in such a spot, was sufficiently vexatious.   I had not even the amusement of picking up a
few flowers, but as we carried water in the waggons, a fire was
lighted, and the teakettle soon made to boil: the heat of the day
rendering this refreshing drink not only a luxury, but even a
necessary.

The want of water made it impossible to pass the night at this
place; and, though the evening was drawing fast upon us, before the
accident was rectified, we set out again.   The country was exceedingly rocky, but at intervals covered with bushes nearly eight feet
high, with intervening spaces of grass.   The surface, in many places,

was a natural pavement formed of a dark-colored iron-stone rock remarkably pitted with little hollows.

After having travelled above twenty-two miles, without finding any water, we arrived by moonlight at a small spring very pleasantly situated amidst large trees of Karro-thorn.   The herdsmen, with the loose oxen and sheep, had reached the place two hours before the waggons; and, from the abundance of dead branches that lay strewed about, had made several blazing fires: so that on our arrival we found a comfortable home ready prepared.   In these regions, after a very hot day, the night-air, by comparison, frequently feels chilly; and a fire, while the thermometer is at 70°, is sometimes very acceptable, especially if any dew be falling.

25th. This place bore the name of *Spuigslang Fontein* (Spitting-snake Fountain) from a species of snake which is said to spit out at its pursuer a venomous liquid, of which, if a particle enter the eye, blindness may be the consequence, unless it be instantly washed out.   The vicinity of this fountain is inhabited by Bushmen, whose pits for ensnaring game, were every where to be seen.   They had taken a degree of trouble in preparing the country for this purpose, which showed that on some occasions, they could be very laborious. The interval from one to another, was crossed by a line of large branches and limbs of trees, placed so closely together as not to be easily passed by any of the antelopes or kwakkas; the game for which they were intended.   The line extended, in this manner, for a mile or two; and at every convenient place, an opening was left, opposite to which was a deep pit so carefully covered over with thin twigs and grass, that it could not readily be perceived; more especially, when the mould that had been dug out became grown over with herbage.   The pits were generally about six feet in depth, and as much in length.   They were nearly three feet wide at the surface; but contracted gradually to the bottom, where they did not measure much more than one foot.   Or, in other words; these holes were so proportioned to the size of the animal for which they were made, that they just fitted its body and head when fallen into it; while at the same time they so confined the legs, that it was not possible for it to make any use of them in extricating itself. Sometimes a stake, having a very sharp point upwards, is fixed in the bottom, for the cruel purpose of empaling the poor animal; but this is very rarely done, and I can recollect but few instances of having ever found such a stake. Perhaps it is omitted, in order to avoid those dreadful accidents which might otherwise happen to their own people; as it is not easy, even for themselves, as they are running hastily over the country, to discover them in time to escape falling in. The Hottentots when speaking in Dutch, call these pit-falls by the mixed name of 'Kysi-gat, or Tkysi-gat, (Kysi-pit); the first part of which is the aboriginal appellation. *

With the precaution of taking my gun with me, I rambled alone in the grove; and although in general, no new objects were here to be found, I met with a new species of Lanius†, an exceedingly handsome bird having the under part of the body of the brightest scarlet, and all the rest of the finest black, excepting a white stripe down each wing, and a few faint white marks on the back.

Here I saw for the first time, a neat bush of dense foliage like Box, called Guarri‡ by the Hottentots; and which is one of the very few transgariepine shrubs that afford an eatable fruit possessed of any good flavor. It bears a round black berry of the size of a pea, with a proportionally large stone. In taste, it has a little astringency, but is however, perfectly wholesome. Other species resembling myrtles,

---

* This word, as I learn from the Hottentots, is the true etymon of the name of a large river, now forming the eastern boundary of the new English colony beyond Algoa Bay, and which should therefore be written Kysikamma, or Keisikamma.

† Lanius atro-coccineus, B. Totus niger, exceptis corporis partibus inferioribus, a gulâ usque ad crissam, pulchrè coccineis; et lineâ alam percurrente albâ.

It very much resembles the Lanius barbarus of Gmel. Sys. Nat. (the Gonolek of Buffon, and of Le Vaillant, Ois. d'Afr. pl. 69.) but from this it is easily distinguished by a head entirely black, and a white stripe down each wing.

‡ Euclea ovata, Cat. Geog. 1706. Folia acutè ovata rigidia subtùs pubescentia, margine undulatâ sub-crenulatâ. Flores in racemulis nutantibus 3—5-floris. Baccæ globosæ primùm pubescentes, demùm glabræ.

Guarri is the Hottentot name of various species of Euclea, producing eatable berries.

and bearing berries of the same kind, were afterwards found to be plants of frequent occurrence in the regions farther northward.

Philip, judging it not prudent for me to be alone in a place so much frequented by *Bushmen,* very attentively came in search of me. But none ever made their appearance; which, indeed, was the reason why he thought my safety doubtful, as this keeping out of sight is generally considered the sign of a distrustful and unfriendly disposition. Yet it ought often to be attributed rather to fear, and to their not being assured of the peaceable intentions of the strangers.

A small party of *Koras* visited us in a friendly manner, and obtained a few pipes of tobacco. From this tribe we always considered there was nothing to fear: nor did their presence ever excite an apprehension of any thing hostile.

One of the women of our party, having heard that I was an admirer of flowers, good naturedly brought me a large quantity of a very pretty plant which grows here in abundance.* It was quite new, and its fine deep-orange colored flowers induced her to think it worth gathering; for Hottentots, like the generality of Europeans, see no beauty in a plant unless it have a showy flower.

Soon after setting out, the road became so intolerably rocky that it was impossible to endure the jolting of the waggon; I was therefore compelled to walk nearly the whole way, though the heat of the weather, even in the shade, was not less than 88°, and the length of this day's journey, seventeen miles. Under such circumstances, a distant view of the river, which we caught from the top of a ridge, could not fail to be a delightful and refreshing sight.

Some of the waggons, having taken a course which brought them to a rocky place that was found impassable, occasioned a delay of half an hour, which gave me the time for collecting several new plants.†

---

* *Buchnera aurantiaca.* Cat. Geog. 1727. Planta herbacea sub-viscosa, lævitèr pubescens; basi divisa in caulibus pluribus sub-simplicibus. Folia bi-tripinnatifida. Flores aurantiaci alterni.

† *Macromemum junceum,* B. (*Cleome juncea.* Linn.) a μακρον *longum* et μηϱος *femur,* ob germinis et staminum receptaculum elongatum.

A species of *Acacia*, (*A. heteracantha*,) met with here for the first time, was distinguished, by its size and growth, from all which had been hitherto seen.   It was above twenty feet in height; and a tall trunk of eighteen inches in diameter, supported a flat wide-spreading umbrella-like head; forming altogether a picturesque and conspicuous feature in the landscape.

Klaarwater, and the country we had travelled over both this and the preceding day, lies on a much higher level than that through which the river flows; and is distinctly separated from it by a rocky step or cliff, which extends many miles in a north-eastward direction. After descending this step, as it may be called, we travelled a mile or two over a more level and easy road, and just before dark, reached the banks of the *Gariep*, or *Great River*.   Here all the waggons were drawn up, under a grove of Acacias, a little above the confluence of the *Nu-gariep*, or *Black River*.   The latitude of this spot is 29° 4′ 22″. S. *

26th. As I wished to stop at this place a day or two, my first care this morning was to select some pleasant place for my waggon, where I might be retired, and as much as possible, free from interruption.   At a distance of two hundred yards, I found a delightful cool

---

Acacia heteracantha. *Cat. Geog.* 1710. Arbor 20-pedalis. Coma densa depresso-patens. Ramuli pubescentes. Spinæ geminæ brevissimæ recurvæ fuscæ, cum aliis pluriès longioribus rectis albis. Folia bipinnata pubescentia, 4-6-juga; |pinnis 10-14-jugis. Foliola approximata oblonga. Legumen lineare.

Celosia odorata, C. G. 1712. Folia petiloantia linearia obtusa canaliculata. Spicæ densæ terminales. Flores sessiles rosei, odorem melleum spargentes, (Buddleiæ globosæ). Calyci foliola lineari-lanceolata. Stamina

5 insuper tubum. Stigma trifidum. Semina tria.

Rhigozum obovatum, C. G. 1713. Frutex 6-pedalis. Ramuli alterni horizontales. Folia obovata.

Cissampelos angustifolius. C. G. 1717. Volubilis. Folia lato-linearia, apice rotundato, sæpè emarginato.

Anthericum
Messerschmidia ?
Loranthus
Grewia flava
Cacalia
Rhus
Aptosimum
Euphorbia.

* 27th October 1811, at the Confluence of the *Ky-gariep*, and *Nu-gariep*, the observed meridional altitude of β *Andromedæ*, was 26° 20′ 19″.

retreat, between some large trees of *Royena*, on the edge of the *Acacia grove*. Hither I made a dozen of the people drag my waggon, or, as it might now be called, my house, which with some trouble was pushed in under the boughs, and completely concealed from the sun ; whose burning heat (94°) made us feel grateful to the trees for the kind protection they afforded us from his rays. This scene is represented in the *engraving*, at page 381. The distribution of presents to a party of *Bushmen*, forms part of the subject.

On taking a survey of surrounding objects, the first thing which struck me, and with no little astonishment, was, the enormous height to which the water of the river had risen above its ordinary level. Our waggons stood on the top of the lofty bank, in a situation similar to that described on my first arrival at the Gariep*, and yet at this elevation, the water was not two yards below our feet. Nothing of the willows was to be seen but their highest branches ; and many were quite covered by the flood. Even the Acacias in the second tier, appeared as if swimming in the stream, with their heads just above water. On the opposite bank, the summits of the largest willows, seemed like low bushes along the shore ; and, on our side of the river, the inundation had already begun to spread itself over a part of the adjoining country, which lay lower than the rest. Although the natives assured us that they did not expect it would rise any higher, I could not perfectly divest myself of apprehensions of the possibility of our waggons being swept away. Yet it was not the Ky-gariep which thus swelled its own stream, for that river, five miles higher up, was at its natural level; but, on directing my view a little downwards to the opposite side, I beheld the mouth of the *Nu-gariep* rolling into the Great River, a rapid and agitated tide of muddy water, swelled to a terrific height, overwhelming the trees on its banks, and thrown into waves by the force of its own impetuous current; driving back, by a wide extended eddy, the waters of the river near us, to the alarming height that has

---

* See page 316.

been described.   The trees, bent forward by the violence of the torrent, kept bowing their half-sunk heads, in submission to the mighty stream ; while many of their less fortunate brethren, torn by the roots from the bank on which they had stood for half a century, were hurried unresisting down the angry tide.

The name *Gariep*, is applied only to that part of the river below the confluence; while the branch which begins at the place where we were now stationed, is called the *Tky-gariep* or *Ky-gariep*, by the natives, and the *Vaal Rivier* by the Klaarwater Hottentots; which in English may here be rendered by *Yellow River*.   While the *Nu-gariep* is, in the same manner, called *Zwart Rivier*, and *Black River :* and the stream which we intended next to visit, the *Gmaap* or *Maap*, translated by *Modder Rivier* and *Muddy River*.   As the propriety of these three names, has been established by the observation of the natives for many generations, they are, I have no doubt, perfectly just and equally applicable, notwithstanding their distinguishing characters not appearing to me very evident, at the season in which I saw them.

We were visited by half a dozen *Bushmen*, who sold us some honey.   They were paid in tobacco stalks, pounded hemp leaves or dakka, and in tobacco, the true Bushmanic currency, the grand circulating medium, which here suffers no depreciation.   These people were taller and larger than the Bushmen of the Karree Mountains, and appeared wilder or more savage; as would seem to be fully confirmed by an anecdote they related to Mr. Jansz, with visible signs of pleasure in their countenance.   I cannot repeat the horrid circumstance, without surmising that it was probably much exaggerated by the Klaarwater interpreters, who appear on all occasions anxious to prevent the White people from entertaining a good opinion of these savages.

These Bushmen had lately been at war with another kraal, which they completely routed, and unfortunately the chief of it was taken prisoner.   The first thing which they did on getting him into their power, was, to tie him to a stake: they then deliberately proceeded to glut their diabolical vengeance.   But, to make sure of his death, in case he should happen to get loose, they first pricked him in the breast with one of their poisoned arrows. After this they continued, with dreadful barbarity, practising on their miserable victim acts of cruelty too horrible to be related; till at length, the accumulation of pain and torment, terminated the wretched man's existence.

27th. Maagers came to me this forenoon, in much distress, to ask medical advice for his child, of about two years old, who had been bitten by some venomous reptile or insect, supposed to be either a spider, a scorpion or a snake, while playing on a heap of dry reeds. I hastened to the spot, and found the child apparently dying: his body had swelled rapidly; the limbs were growing stiff; and a convulsive blackness had spread over the face. Below the pit of the stomach, I discovered two slight punctures within an inch of each other, which put me out of all doubt as to what might have occasioned the state to which the child was reduced. For these could have been made by nothing else than the two fangs of a snake: but of what species it might be, we were unable to guess. The venom was judged to have pervaded the system, and the symptoms appeared all of the extreme kind; yet although it was looked upon as a hopeless case, I could not omit trying a remedy in which I should have had great confidence, if so much time had not been lost.

I immediately forced the child to swallow ten drops of the solution of ammonia* in two ounces of water; and, having with a penknife scarified the parts around the wound, which operation, however, drew very little blood, I bathed the place with a mixture of the same medicine prepared of four times the strength. In five minutes after this, another draught was administered; and in about ten minutes afterwards, a slight vomiting ensued: but whether occasioned by the medicine, or by the poison, it is uncertain. As I attentively watched the progress of the remedy, I saw within the

---

* *Liquor Ammoniæ* of the London Dispensary.

next quarter of an hour, with no little surprise and pleasure, that the force of the venom was evidently subdued; that the blood began to circulate more freely, and that there was a fair prospect of saving the child's life. The cure was actually completed before the following morning; at which time I found him playing as well as usual; nor did I afterwards hear that this bite left, ultimately, any unpleasant result behind.

We shot a large bird of the bustard kind, which was called *Wilde Paauw* (Wild Peacock). This name is here very wrongly applied, as the bird to which it properly belongs, differs from this in every respect. There are indeed three, or perhaps four, birds to which in different districts, this appellation is given. The present species, which is called *Kori* * in the Sichuana language, measured, in extent of wing, not less than seven feet; and in bulk and weight, was almost greater than some of the people could manage. The under part of the body was white, but the upper part was covered with fine lines of black on a light chesnut-coloured ground. The tail and quill-feathers partook of the general colouring of the back. The shoulders were marked with large blotches of black and white; and the top of the head was black. The feathers of the occiput were elongated into a crest. Those of the neck were also elongated, loose, narrow and pointed, and were of a whitish color marked with numerous transverse lines of black. The irides were of a beautiful, pellucid, changeable, silvery, ferrugineous color. A *representation* of the head of the *Kori Bustard* in the proportion of one-fifth of the natural size, is given at the end of this chapter. Its body was so thickly protected by feathers, that our largest-sized shot made no impression; and, taught by experience, the hunters never fire at it, but with a bullet.

---

* *Otis Kori*, B. Suprà dilutè castanea, plumis nigro lineatis. Abdomen et pectus alba. Cauda èt alæ corpori concolores. Tectrices superiores alarum maculis albis et nigris magnis notatæ. Pileus niger. Cristata ex plumis occipitalibus elongatis. Plumæ colli elongatæ acutæ augustæ, laxæ, albidæ nigro fasciatæ. Pedes et digiti albidi. Irides pellucidæ argenteo-ferrugineæ. — Vide iconem, ad quintam partem magnitudinis naturalis diminutam, capitulo xvi. subjunctam.

It is reckoned the best of the winged game in the country ; not only on account of its size, but because it is always found to abound in fat. The meat of it is not unlike that of a turkey, but is certainly superior, as possessing the flavor of game.*

I took a walk through the grove till I came to a part lower down the stream, where 1 obtained an unobstructed view of the first reach of the *Black River*, by climbing up one of the tallest trees. It was, however, with some difficulty that I could disentangle myself from a species of *Clematis* which, just hereabouts, grows to their very summits, and smothers them with its flowers and foliage ; very much in the same manner as the common English species called ' Traveller's Joy', which, in Europe, indicates a chalky substratum. And it is remarkable, that this African plant, which much resembles it in habit and general appearance, is also an indication of a calcareous quality in the soil. †

The *climate* on the banks of the *Gariep*, and its branches, is at all seasons very sensibly warmer than that of the surrounding country. The heat at this station had daily increased since we arrived : on the 26th it was 94° : this day 98° ; and on the following 101°. (30°·6. R.—38°·3. C.)

28th. Having completed my intended observations, and made

---

* Here I added to my ornithological collection —
  Upupa Epops, or common *Hoopoe,* scarcely differing from our English bird.
  Turdus bicolor. Gm. Sys. Nat. It is called *Witgat Spreuw* in the Cape Colony.
  Falco musicus. Le Faucon chanteur, Le Vaill. Ois. d'Afr. pl. 27.
This species of Falcon appears to inhabit the whole of Southern Africa, as it has since been found amongst a small collection made by the unfortunate expedition lately sent to explore the river Zaire.

† *Galium verum,* or a plant exceedingly like it, grows in plenty on the bank of the river, in grassy places. This is certainly indigenous to the Gariep, and the country beyond.

The outward appearance of another plant so completely deceived me at the moment of gathering it, that I believed I had collected a species of *Thalictrum.* It was not in flower, but probably belongs to some of the *umbelliferous* genera.

Fungi, as well as *Lichens* and *Mosses,* are so very rarely to be met with in the interior of Southern Africa, that, of the *Fungi,* the first which had been seen on the journey, was found at this place.

several sketches of the scenery, I was anxious to quit a station where the fear of being surrounded by the inundation, if the river should rise but a yard higher, prevented me from feeling quite at ease.   I therefore resolved on proceeding to the *Maap;* and in consequence, about the middle of the day, all the party were again in motion.   The waggons drove off, one by one, over the sandy hillocks, and between the clumps of trees, till they gained the higher ground, beyond all marks of former inundations; where they halted a few minutes to give time for all the people to collect themselves together.   We then kept a course as near to the river, as the ravines and uneven ground would permit.

The elder women took their seat in the waggons, but the young rode on oxen ; and a group of these *Hottentot girls* trotting on before formed a sight as curious and picturesque, as it was novel.   They sat astride, and managed the bulky animal with perfect ease and fearlessness.   Their heads were neatly bound round with a cotton, or leathern, handkerchief, and they wore shoes made of the hide of wild animals, but the rest of their body was quite uncovered, except by a bundle of small greasy leathern aprons which, drawn under them, served to render the bony backs of the oxen a less uneasy seat.

These aprons, which they distinguish into fore-kaross and hind-kaross, and which are tied just over the hips, are their only permanent clothing: for the large kaross, or cloak, is only worn, or thrown off, agreeably to the weather or the fancy of the wearer.   The *fore-kaross* is much the smaller, and seldom reaches below the knees : it consists simply of two or three little aprons cut into narrow strips or thongs ; and which by constant wear assume the appearance of a a bundle of strings.   No other kind of covering could less impede the motion of walking, than one of such a make.   These strings are often profusely ornamented with beads of all colors ; and frequently an ostrich-shell girdle of many folds, hangs loosely round the waist. The *hind-kaross* is a single, or sometimes a double, apron, much wider and longer, than the other, and not divided.   This is often made so long as nearly to reach the ground ; though, generally, it does not

3 E 2

hang lower than the calf of the leg.   On this, nothing ornamental is bestowed ; because it is always required as a cushion, when the wearer sits on the ground.

In order to protect themselves from the sun and weather, they carefully anoint their bodies with animal fat ; to which is generally added some sweet-smelling herbs reduced to powder, which they call *Buku* (Bookoo).   This Buku is made of the leaves of various aromatic or scented plants, dried and reduced to a powder, by pounding them on a stone.   The plants most commonly used for this purpose, by the Hottentots in the colony, are chiefly of the tribe of *Diosma*, various species of which are considered equally good.   But in the countries lying beyond the geographical boundary* of that genus, other plants of various genera are, of necessity, made use of ; among which a *Croton* of an undescribed species, hereafter mentioned, always appeared to me to be the most pleasant.

Some wore round their ancles a great number of rings of leather, or neatly-twisted cord, which covered them from the instep, nearly half-way up to the calf.   Rings, of catgut covered with copper wire, or even of simple cord, were worn by many, either above or below the knee ; while several of these, together with bracelets of beads, decorated the wrists, or the arms above the elbow.   These people were also fond of rings on their fingers ; and some had copper ornaments hanging from the ears.

Such is the customary clothing of those Hottentot females who have not yet thought proper to imitate the dress of Europeans ; and this description, with a little variation according to the different tribes and nations, will serve for the whole of Southern Africa which has fallen under my observation.

The *ostrich-shell girdle* is an article of very ingenious manufacture, and is formed of small pieces of the egg-shell, cut exactly circular and of an uniform diameter ; and by a hole bored through the centre of each, a great number are strung close together, enough

---

* See page 208.

to pass several times round the body. This girdle has the appearance of a cord of ivory, of half an inch in thickness; and a very correct idea of it may be given by a long string of small bone button-moulds, such as are sold in the shops. The number of pieces of shell required for such an ornament is very great; and the value of a girdle is therefore considerable: as they are obtained from the more northern nations.

The *aboriginal Hottentot dress* for the men, is still more simple; and it is impossible to reduce decent covering to a smaller compass. A leathern belt is fastened round the waist; and from it, in front, hangs what they call a *Jackal*, because it is usually a piece of the skin of that animal. It is made with the fur outwards, of an oblong convex form, resembling both in size and shape such a covering as might be made with the two hands; from which, one would think, the first idea of it may have originated. From the hinder part of the belt, is suspended a piece of leather, seldom so long as twelve inches, including the strap by which it hangs; and not more than two fingers wide at top; but enlarging toward the lower end, to the breadth of a hand. When speaking in Dutch, they call this a *Staart-riem*, which in English may be expressed by the word *Tail-piece*. Its particular form varies according to the taste of the individual: in some it is nearly circular; in others square; or transversely oblong; or triangular; and in others, shaped like a crescent; or a cross. It is frequently ornamented with large brass or copper buttons, or with other things of that kind. What this ridiculous piece of dress could be intended for, besides mere ornament, I cannot imagine, unless to place under them when they sit down on the ground; for it is impossible it can serve the purpose of a covering, as with every quick movement of the body it shifts from side to side.

This is all the usual and constant covering of the men; besides the *Kaross*, which they have in common with all South Africans, who may literally, if not legitimately according to classic interpretation, be termed the *gentes togatæ*; since the Kaross is, in fact, nothing else than the *toga* in its simplest and rudest, and

perhaps original, form.   The *Jackal* is worn by the Bushmen, and
every tribe of the Hottentot race ; but, by many individuals the Tail-
piece is not considered as indispensable.   In place of the Jackal, the
Bichuana tribes, hereafter mentioned, adopt a different fashion,
which will be described in a future part of this journal.   *Sandals*, or
Shoes, are used by all ; but the difficulty of always procuring the
hide proper for them, obliges the greater part of these people to
reserve them for occasional service, and only when necessity, from
the ruggedness of the ground, requires.

Many of the *Klaarwater people* are clothed in the mode above
described ; but more than half of them imitate the dress of
Europeans.

The river, and its woody banks, attracted all my admiration ;
and in so hot a day, the assurance of having an abundance of pure refreshing water always within reach, mitigated, in idea, the fervid rays
of the sun, smoothed the roughness of our path, and lessened the toil
of our march.

In crossing a small but deep ravine, the pole of my waggon got
by accident between the legs of one of the after-oxen, and nearly
occasioned an overturn ; but we came off with no other misfortune
than the loss of a yoke, broken by the struggling of the ox.   As we
always carried with us several supernumerary yokes, this accident
was soon repaired ; but the number of these dry ravines which
every where crossed our track, occasioned, to one or other of the
waggons, continual mishaps and stoppages ; so that we did not
advance at a faster rate than two miles in the hour.

In the rainy season, the torrent rushing down these hollows in
its way to the river, has laid bare the substratum of rock, and shown
it to be a heterogeneous mass, of more recent formation than the
surrounding mountains.   It is composed of small fragments of other
rocks, such as granite, porphyry, sandstone, limestone, and a few
rounded pebbles ; all firmly conglutinated together by a cement apparently formed of pulverized limestone.   The parts which have been
long exposed to the weather are of a black hue.   Rocks of this

nature are, as far as I have observed, only found in the vicinity of the Gariep. The mystery of their formation is easily explained, by remarking that the neighbouring hills and rocks evidently supply the component fragments, which are brought together by the torrents into the lower places; and the calcareous nature of the waters, together with particles of the limestone rocks collected in their course, form the mortar, by which they are combined into a solid mass.

The heat was so great, that we were unable to proceed; and, after having travelled only six miles and a half, we unyoked by the side of the river, at a place called *Zout-pan's Drift* (Salt-pan Ford), where the stream is very broad, and, consequently, shallow. Many aits, or islets, covered with bushes and rushes, interrupted this breadth of water, and rendered it more easily fordable.

It is from an extensive, and, as it is said, inexhaustible *salt-lake*, situated at about a day's journey to the southward of this ford, that the Hottentots of Klaarwater, and the natives of these regions, are supplied with this necessary article. The fact of ponds or small lakes of salt-water being found so far inland, at a distance from all communication with the sea, is one which must strike every person as remarkable. The cause of it cannot, without absurdity, be supposed to exist in the climate or the atmosphere; since they are found in the vicinity of ponds and springs, the waters of which are perfectly fresh. They afford very good proof of the existence within the earth of a stratum of rock-salt, which, if not at too great a depth, might prove, if worked, to be no inconsiderable treasure to the inhabitants, when civilization shall have taught them its full value, and rendered it indispensable. These salt-lakes exist in various, and very distant, situations, far in the interior of this continent, as well as near the sea-coast. They are often solitary, though sometimes several are found within a short distance of each other. The most northern, of which I have been able to gain any intelligence, is one about the twenty-seventh degree of latitude, eastward of Litakun.

Between the trees and bushes which clothe the bank of the river, a species of *Asparagus* is every where found, climbing and entwining, so that I could not without difficulty force a way through them.   On this plant I found feeding, two handsome insects of the genus *Mylabris;* to one of which I assigned the name of *Mylabris asparagi,* as I never met with it but on that plant.   The other hardly varied from *Mylabris bifasciata,* except in its greater size, and the evenness of its broad yellow bands.

Here, for the first time, I saw a large tree of picturesque growth and thin foliage, called by the Hottentots of Klaarwater, *Roodeblat* (Red-leaf)*, on account of the beautiful crimson color which the leaves assume at the autumnal season, or, rather, season of fading: in which circumstance it remarkably agrees with the Indian Almond (*Terminalia Catappa*), a well-known tree of the same genus.   It grows to the height of forty feet, with several crooked spreading trunks, from one to two feet in diameter, covered with a smooth white or pale greenish bark.   It was met with only on the banks of the Ky-gariep, and was not a tree of very frequent occurrence.

---

* *Terminalia erythrophylla.* Catal. Geogr. 1749.   Folia acutè ovatà integerrima glabra.   Ramuli juniores pubescentes.   Flores omnes hermaphroditi octandri.   Calyx quadridentatus.   Racemi breves ovati.

Here I also added to my herbarium —

Pentzia nana.   Catal. Geogr. 1731.   Fruticulus vix semi-pedalis.   Folia deltoïdea sericea, 2—6-dentata. Flores longissimè pedunculati solitarii terminales.

Corchorus asplenifolius. Cat.Geogr.1737.   Folia elongatè ovata, crenato-serrata, serraturis simplicibus.   Pedunculus oppositifolius. Capsula 4-florus. Alabastra sub-globosa linearis torulosa.

Polygala leptophylla. Cat. Geogr. 1740.   Flores spicati nutantes subherbacei.   Folia linearia obtusa glabra.   Affinis *P. ephedroïdi.*

Asparagus rivalis. B.
Rhigozum
Buchnera
Relhania ?
Uniola
Vahlia
Phlomis
Phyllanthus
Galenia
Pappophorum
Lessertia, &c.

29th. As the oxen appeared much strengthened from having grazed all the forenoon on the delightful fresh grass which grew along the banks, we ventured to resume our journey, though the heat of the weather this day was not less oppressive than it had been on the preceding. Before two in the afternoon, the thermometer had already risen to 98° (36°·6 Centig.) It was 94° at a little after one, the time when we set out. Striking out into the open plain, we quitted the river, and travelled about ten miles over a country covered with dry grass and bushes.

The dogs, to avoid the violent heat of the sun, ran along beneath the shade of the waggon; but my poor unfortunate little *terrier*, through some mismanagement of his own as he ran by the side of the wheel, suffered his foot to be run over, and had scarcely time to utter a cry before his head was crushed. The first notice I received of the accident was the lifeless body of my faithful little dog, brought to me by one of the Hottentots. Although it was but an animal, I could not help feeling a shock, and shall not be ashamed to confess that this sad occurrence prevented all further enjoyment for the rest of the day. Such misfortunes are, from the cause just explained, not unfrequent in hot weather; and during the journey from Cape Town, several dogs of the caravan were lost in this manner.

Our guides, instead of conducting me to the confluence of the Maap, brought me, to suit their own purposes, to a part of the river where the mat-rush grew in great abundance; expecting thus to persuade me to stop here several days, till the rush-gatherers had finished their work. But as they found I would not agree to this, the spot offering, to me at least, no temptations to remain, they left behind the party of women, amounting to about a dozen, with two of the waggons, and some men for their protection.

We continued our way by the side of the river for seven miles, till we arrived opposite to the *Maap*, where, after reconnoitring the spot, we safely brought the waggons down the steep bank, and took up a station on the bank of the *Yellow River* (Ky-gariep), in a delightful shady grove close to the water. Here it was agreed we should fix our abode for some time, and establish our head-quarters during the proposed hunting-parties and excursions, which it was our principal object to make in this vicinity.

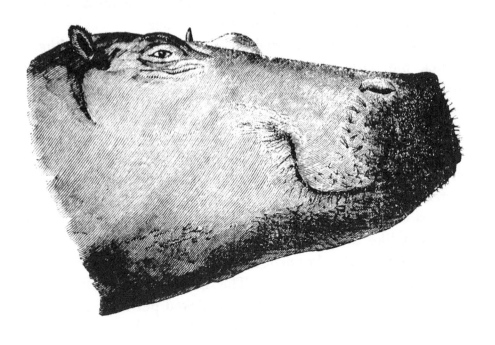

CHAPTER XVII.

OCCURRENCES ON THE BANKS OF THE KY-GARIEP.

Oᴜʀ first care was to uncover the Bushmen's Kysi-pits, and make them visible, in order that our oxen might avoid falling into them. Many of these holes were found every where along the woods which border the river. They were placed lengthwise, and dug exactly in the paths made by the *Hippopotami* in their way out from their watery retreat, to browse on the herbage of the grove. They were, as being intended to entrap this huge animal, several times larger than the game-pits at Spuigslang Fountain, and proportionally deep. By the enormous bones which lay scattered about near one of them, it appeared that a hippopotamus had lately been caught and eaten; and the remains of some Bushman huts close by, and probably erected only for the occasion, showed how determined they were to enjoy the feast; since, not being able to carry the meat to their houses, they had removed their houses to the meat.

These bones, which exceeded in size all that I had hitherto seen, struck me with astonishment, and, for a long while, fixed my attention. On first arriving in the country inhabited by creatures so monstrous, and actually beholding their gigantic remains, the mind cannot avoid surprise and wonder, however familiar the idea of the magnitude and unwieldy bulk of a hippopotamus may have been from the days of one's youth. Yet, until that magnitude be rendered, as it were, tangible, it can never make that forcible and just impression which properly belongs to the object. The thighbone appeared like the stem of a tree just barked; and the skull, which had been much chopped and disfigured, might have been mistaken for a large mass of rock. The Bushmen had left nothing but the bones; and even these had been picked perfectly clean.

30th. The *Yellow River* is much narrower than the Gariep; but it is here apparently very deep, gliding with a smooth and clear stream, between moderately high banks, thickly clothed with woods, consisting of *willows* in the front rank, and behind them *Acacias*, intermixed with the *Black-bark, Red-leaf, Karree-tree,* and *Buffalo-thorn*, entangled and rendered almost impenetrable, with the *Asparagus* already mentioned. At the water's edge, and in the water itself, grew abundance of *reeds*, and a tall species of *Cyperus*.

No situation could be more pleasant than that which we had chosen : in the midst of trees and shade, enlivened by the notes of a variety of birds, with the ever-charming river before us, the opposite banks of which were reflected by a limpid glassy surface; while a fervid cloudless sky rendered the view of the water doubly refreshing. Clumps of Acacias, with a countless multitude of stems, formed vistas and mazes, through which it was delightful to ramble, shielded sufficiently from the mid-day sun by their soft airy foliage. Along the grassy bank, an open path, trodden by the natives or by the river-horse, afforded a pleasant walk by the side of the water, sometimes winding through thickets of green reeds, or over swelling mounds agreeably diversifying the surface. Here and there, short openings conducted down to the water, and tempted the bathers into the stream; who sported about, or swam to the opposite side, with a facility and fearlessness which would have persuaded one that they had never heard of drowning. Their light-brown skin now appeared with its true color, and cleanliness rendered it not unpleasing. With hearts probably devoid of all care, and brow undisturbed by anxiety or reflection, they sported in the cooling element, playfully enjoying their salutary amusement.

Leaving them to their gambols, and striking out of the path into the woods and groves, little parties of Hottentot women and girls were met with, seated in the shade, and busily employed in twisting cord from the Acacia bark, while others were chopping down the branches, or stripping off long pieces of it from the stems. Some were engaged in an occupation of a double nature; for, instead of dividing the fibres by pounding them on a large stone, they performed the operation by chewing, as they fancy the juice to possess an agreeable taste.

Considering the mode in which it is manufactured, this cord is made very expeditiously. The workwoman, for this is a work that forms a part of female duty, being seated on the ground, and having a quantity of prepared bark at hand, spins two yarns at once, by the simple process of rolling them down her thigh with her palm; and then, by bringing them close together, and rolling them upwards with a turn in the contrary way, they are neatly twisted into a strong single cord. A large quantity was made during our stay at this place, and carried home to Klaarwater, where it was used in making the mats, for which the party we had left below the Salt-pan Ford, were collecting the rushes. This process, which can only be performed on the bare thigh, or sometimes down the outside of the calf, if continued for a long time, renders that part so sore, that they are obliged to desist for several days; but after much practice, the skin becomes sufficiently hardened to endure it without inconvenience.

Among the Hottentots an amusing bustle and activity was now

observable.   In one quarter, the hunters, preparing for an excursion
higher up the river, were seen, some cleaning their guns and casting
bullets ; some buckling on their pouch and powder-horn ; and others
saddling their oxen or horses ; mounting with an alacrity, gaily anticipating their success, and promising their wives and children a
plentiful feast at their return : then, whistling their dogs around
them ; briskly trotting off, and calling to their companions to follow
without delay, they brushed through the thicket, and mounting the
high bank, presently rode out of sight.

In another quarter, sitting by the side of their waggons, the
wooden-bowl makers displayed their workmanship and industry,
busily intent on carving out *bowls* and *jugs* *, from the green wood
of the willow ; while at a distance a large willow tree was just
falling to the ground, hacked through by *hatchets*, so weak and
small, that nothing but perseverance and much time could enable
them with such tools, to sever trunks above a foot or eighteen
inches in diameter.   These were cut into convenient lengths, according to the utensil intended to be made ; and the soft, tough
nature of the wood, rendered it peculiarly fit for the purpose.   After
the rough log had been chopped with the hatchet or adze, nearly to

---

* The abovè figures are representations of the *Hottentot hatchet*, the *bowl*, the *jug*
or *bambus*, and the *knife* used for hollowing out the inside.
  These may be considered as some of the aboriginal utensils of the Hottentots.
Hatchets of this form are truly African, and are seen in general use with all the tribes of
the Interior, as far as I penetrated.   Their *adze*, and their *mattock*, differ from this only
by their greater size, and by the position of the edge of the iron being transverse instead
of longitudinal.

the required shape, a common knife was the only tool employed to smooth and complete the outside; and another knife, having its top bent laterally into a semi-circular hook, was used with great dexterity and neatness to hollow out the inside. As soon as this was done, the whole was thoroughly smeared with fat, to prevent it splitting from the heat and dryness of the weather. The *bowls* are of various sizes, but most frequently from twelve to eighteen inches across, shallow and mostly oval. The jug, or jar, which they call a *bambus*, is made in the form of a short cylinder, having the mouth or neck contracted generally to about two-thirds. Their most usual capacity is about a gallon, but they are made of all sizes, from a pint to five gallons.

Some of our party built themselves huts of green boughs, covered with grass and rushes; and a large and safe enclosure for the cattle was made with the thorny branches of Acacia, which, for this purpose, are preferable to every other fence; and, beset in every direction with long sharp thorns, equally well prevent their escape, and keep out invaders, whether men or beasts of prey.

The intelligence of our arrival was, by means of their spies, quickly spread among the natives; and fourteen Bushmen, from a kraal several miles beyond the other side of the river, paid us a visit early this morning. They were nearly all of a mixed race of Bushman, Kora, and Bichuana descent. Their language was quite different from that of the inhabitants of the district of the Karree mountains; and I was assured that the variety of language amongst the Bushman race is so great, that neighbouring kraals often speak dialects so different as not to be understood without difficulty. I cannot, however, assert this from my own knowledge; for depending on Hottentot interpreters, I am rather inclined to believe that the degree of variation in the Bushman language is somewhat exaggerated by them. Yet, as I have found the same remark made by every Hottentot whom I have questioned on the subject, I have no doubt that such is the fact, although not perhaps to so extraordinary a degree as they represent. The language of these men was so abundant in claps, that it seemed as if almost every word was accompanied by this strange noise; and which oft times occurred twice in the same word.   I could not but fancy that talking was with them a troublesome exertion ; for such an enunciation would sound to any European more like an impediment in their speech, than a natural part of the language.

Our *visitors* were all men, and but lightly armed ; their women, being less practised in swimming, were left on the other side of the water.   Their object was as much to express their friendly inclination towards us, as to solicit tobacco and some few presents.   Their chief, or patriarch, was of the number, and through him we engaged them to collect mat-rushes, which they say grow in great plenty along the Maap.   We treated them with kindness, and thus dispelled all mistrust.   Well supplied with food, they seated themselves at ease amongst our people ; began to broil the meat we had given, and soon made themselves quite at home.

By the temptation of a good piece of tobacco, I induced one of them to sit quietly for a quarter of an hour, while I drew his *portrait*.   The whole affair was quite unintelligible to him and his countrymen, none certainly ever having seen a portrait taken before. Observing them look very serious all the while I was drawing, I began to fear that some superstitious notion might lead them to imagine I was practising sorcery, to injure the kraal, or to cause the death of the man ; for tales of this kind had often been related to me.   After it was finished, and the tobacco paid, I explained that in my own country it was esteemed a mark of great friendship and good will, to desire to possess the likeness of another person ; and that this was the reason of my wishing to have his : that my having given him so much tobacco, was a proof of it, and that I should give him a little more, together with the drawing, which he was to keep in his hut, to remind him of his friend, the white man.   On saying which I left them, and retired to my waggon, as if to fetch the tobacco, when I tore the drawing out of my book, and quickly made a copy on the next leaf, and bringing it before the party, tore it out, and gave it to him.   With all this they seemed perfectly satisfied, and went away persuaded that the matter was exactly as it had been explained to them.   In this little affair, it was certainly I who ran the greater risk of incurring harm; for had the man died shortly afterwards, or met with any accident or sickness, my drawing would have been pronounced to be the cause, and myself devoted to the revenge of his relations, and a poisoned arrow have been my fate.

Just after they were gone, intelligence reached us of a *Hippopotamus* having been shot at a little distance up the river, by our Klaarwater captain. Without waiting an instant, away scampered every hungry Hottentot; and presently we were left quite alone, excepting a few who prudently stayed behind to guard the waggons. Mr. Jansz set out on horseback, while I followed on foot with Gert, preferring the walk along the side of the river, to a circuitous ride over the dry plain, where few birds or plants were likely to be met with.

Having quickly armed ourselves, and left Philip in charge of my waggons, we briskly pushed our way between the thickets, winding through the willow grove, and crossing many a deep ravine. Every where the enormous foot of this animal had imprinted the earth with holes. Gert, who had never seen a *Zee-koe* (Sea-cow), as the colonists call the Hippopotamus, enjoyed the trip as much as myself, both equally anxious to gratify our curiosity. He had been less a traveller than the rest of my men; and, therefore, like myself, had the greater novelty to expect. As we hurried on, our conversation was on nothing but the sea-cow; and his animation, excited by the subject to a higher pitch than usual, exceedingly pleased and amused me. Thus beguiling the time, my attention was diverted from the flowers that decked our path, or the birds that enlivened the branches above our heads.

Suddenly he stopped: and, crying out with some emotion, ' Look here! Sir,' I turned my eyes downwards, and saw the recent foot-marks of a *lion* which had been to drink at the river, apparently not more than an hour before. This gave a check to our dialogue on the Hippopotamus, and in a lower and graver tone of voice, he talked now only of lions, and the danger of being alone in a place so covered with wood. That, which a minute before, had been

3 G

praised as a delightful shady path, now was viewed as the lurking place of lions and of every formidable beast of prey. Hitherto, he had always lagged the hindmost; but now, I found some difficulty in keeping pace with him. This acceleration, combined with the heat of the sun, pouring down upon us through the unshaded spaces, which, as we advanced, became more and more frequent, made us feel the latter part of this walk excessively fatiguing; though the distance was probably not more than five miles. In this part no rain could have fallen for several months, as the earth was every where divided by wide gaping cracks occasioned by excessive drought.

Having no other guide than the river itself, we continued walking on, still wondering that we did not reach the place, as we had been told that it was no more than an hour distant, and we had already been an hour and a half on the way. But our apprehensions that we had missed the spot, were relieved by the distant sound of voices, wafted down the stream to us, along the surface of the water. Listening as we advanced, we plainly distinguished the tone of the Bushman language, and were hesitating whether to go on, or to take a circuitous path to avoid them; as they might happen to be some unfriendly kraal, who would be tempted to take advantage of us, thus alone, and beyond the reach of all help. But a few hundred paces more, enabled us to distinguish the less vociferous tongues of our own people; and, quickening our steps, in five minutes we caught sight of them through the stems of the trees.

The busy party were surrounded by the sweetest scenery that landscape can produce. They had floated the animal to the bank, and were labouring hard to get it out of the water; for, although it was but half grown, and only, what they called, a calf, its bulk being equal to two oxen at least, was more than they could manage; till the Bushmen came to their assistance. At last it was rolled on to the grassy bank; and immediately, all who had knives, fell to work in cutting it up.

The monstrous size, and almost shapeless mass, of even a small Hippopotamus, when lying on the ground, and compared with the people who stood about it, appeared enormous. While they were employed in taking off the immoderately thick skin, I judged it would be making the best use of my time, to place the strange groupe in my sketch book; as their haste to cut up and dry the meat before it was spoilt by the heat of the weather, left me little opportunity for examination.   At all times a sketch is a most faithful and comprehensive memorandum, and describes most things much more fully than the pen can ever do.   Whenever time will not admit of using both, there never can be a doubt whether the pencil should be preferred to the pen: it is in fact often the most expeditious mode of making a description.

This animal is entirely of one uniform color, which may be correctly imitated by a light tint of China-ink.   The hide, above an inch in thickness and hardly flexible, was dragged off, as if they had been tearing the planks from a ship's side.   It was carefully divided into such pieces, as would best admit of being cut into shamboks; as these constituted, to the Klaarwater people, the greatest part of the profits.   The ribs are covered with a thick layer of fat, celebrated as the greatest delicacy; and known to the colonists as a rarity by the name of ' *Zeekoe-spek*' (Seacow-pork).   This can only be preserved by salting; as, on attempting to dry it in the sun in the same manner as the other parts of the animal, it melts away.   The rest of the flesh consists entirely of lean; and was, as usual with all other game, cut into large slices, and dried on the bushes; reserving only enough for present use.   This latter portion, however, was no small quantity; as, in addition to a considerable number of self-invited Hottentots, who all of course expected a feast, there was also a party of Bushmen, consisting of six men and five women, whom the report of the muskets had attracted to the spot.

This animal had been killed by only two balls, both of which entered the head.   It is very seldom that they are wounded in any other part; but this does not happen from the impenetrable nature of the rest of the hide, a reason which has often been assigned, and originally invented, like many other such tales, for the purpose of exciting wonder.   The truth is, that, as the Hippopotamus hardly ever quits the river but at night; and by day, seldom ventures more than its head above the surface of the water, there is no other place left for the marksman. For no bullet, owing to its great rapidity, can penetrate that element when fired obliquely, but rebounds from the surface of it, as from a pavement; which is a fact frequently proved by the common experiment called " making ducks and drakes."

The animal, when rendered wary by the suspicion of approaching danger, raises out of the water only his nostrils, eyes, and ears; which, being all placed in the same horizontal plane towards the upper part of the head, it may with probability be concluded that Nature assigned them this position, with a view to ensuring his safety, by enabling him to breathe, see, and hear, without exposing himself much to the observation and attacks of man. On which account, these are not so easily shot, as many other animals. Their great size is nothing in favor of the marksman; and, unless he aim with as much precision as if it were but a hare, he fires in vain.

When no more than the upper part of the head is seen above the water, it appears very much like the head of a horse, and suf-ficiently justifies the name of *Hippopotamus* (River-horse) given to it by the ancients; who, as this circumstance seems to prove, could rarely have had a sight of the entire animal, otherwise they would have discovered that, of all quadrupeds, this one bears, in form and general appearance, the least resemblance to a horse. Nor can any thing be more inapplicable, than the colonial name of *Zeekoe* (Sea-cow), to which animal, I never could perceive that it had, in any respect, the slightest similitude.

In the present animal there was no hair whatever, on any part of the skin, excepting a few scattered short bristles on the muzzle, the edges of the ears, and on the tail. The latter was extremely short, scarcely exceeding a foot. The eyes and ears were dispropor-tionally small, while the mouth was altogether as extraordinarily large. Being not yet full grown, its tusks had not made their appearance. Three bushels, at least, of half-chewed grass were taken out of its stomach and intestines.

Every man was now turned butcher; and so eager were they at this, to them, most pleasing of all work, that it was some time before I could get them to cut off the head, that I might draw it more conveniently. I carefully finished and coloured on the spot, two drawings in front and profile *. Nor was my book closed before some attempt had been made, to represent the beauty of this charming landscape. But its beauty consisted not in the mere outline; the glowing warmth of the atmosphere, diffused a mellow effect over the whole, which the materials I had with me, would never, even in the most skilful hand, be able to exhibit. The placid, noble stream gave to the scene a peaceful, yet animated character, which was strangely contrasted by the spot where our party were so busy at work.

This indeed more resembled a flesh-market, where bushes were converted into shambles, and their branches were bending to the ground, overloaded with meat. Whichever way I turned my head, I beheld men, or women, or dogs, eating; several large fires were crowded with cooks : all around was carving, broiling, gnawing, and chewing. Nor did I myself feel the least inclination to reprobate the practice, for, after a long fatiguing walk, and eight hours fasting, I confess that a *Hippopotamus steak* was not a thing to be rejected ; and, even at this moment, I still remain convinced that, if our English lovers of good eating could but once taste such a steak, they would not rest till they had caused " fine lively Hippopotami" to be an article of regular importation.

All the offal, bones, and head, fell by custom to the Bushmen's share. No sooner was the carcase cut open, than they fell to work upon the entrails ; occasionally wiping the grease from their fingers on to their arms, legs, and thighs ; they were, besides, plentifully bespattered with the blood and filth, each rejoicing at the portion he had obtained.

Among these happy, dirty creatures, was one who, by her airs and dress, showed that she had no mean opinion of her personal accomplishments: she was, in fact, the prettiest young *Bush-girl* I had yet seen ; but her vanity, and too evident consciousness of her superiority, rendered her less pleasing in my eyes, and her extra-

---

* See the *Engraving* at page 403.

vagance in dress made her perhaps a less desirable wife in the eyes of her countrymen; for the immoderate quantity of grease, red ochre, buku, and shining powder * with which her hair was clotted, would ruin any but a very rich husband: herself and every part of her dress, was so well greased, that she must have been, in her nation, a girl of good family; and the number of leathern rings with which her arms and legs were adorned, proclaimed her to be evidently a person of property: round her ancles she carried about a dozen thick rings of this kind, which, added to a pair of sandals, gave her the appearance of wearing buskins.

But the most remarkable piece of affectation with which she adorned herself, was, three small bits of ivory, of the size and shape of sparrow's eggs, loosely pendant from her hair; one in front, as low as the point of the nose, and one on the outer side of each cheek, all hanging at the same length. These dangled from side to side as she moved her head, and, doubtlessly, made full amends for their inconvenience, by the piquancy they were thought to add to the wearer's beauty. The upper part of her head was covered with a small leathern cap, fitted closely, but quite unornamented, and I should have had a pleasure in gratifying her with a present of a string of beads, to render this part of her dress more smart, if I had not been fearful that, by doing this, I should excite in her country-men, an inclination to beg and importune for what I meant to reserve only for the nations further in the interior. Her vanity and affectation, great as it was, did not, as one may sometimes observe, in both sexes, in other countries, seem to choke her, or produce any alteration in the tone of her voice, for the astonishing quantity of meat which she swallowed down, and the readiness with which she called out to her attendants for more, plainly showed her to be resolved that no squeamishness should interfere on this occasion.

---

* Called *Blink-klip* (Shining-rock), by the Klaarwater Hottentots, and *Sibilo* by the Bichuanas. It is a shining, powdery, *iron ore*, feeling greasy to the touch, and soiling the hands exceedingly, and appears to resemble the mineral called *eisenrahm* by the Germans. The *mine* from which it is obtained will be described in the second volume.

With the rest of her female companions, the season of beauty had long passed by, and, if that season with other nations may justly be called shortlived, it may among Bushwomen, with more than equal justice, be termed momentary.   In five or six years after their arrival at womanhood, the fresh plumpness of youth has already given way to the wrinkles of age ; and unless we viewed them with the eye of commiseration and philanthropy, we should be inclined to pronounce them the most disgusting of human beings.   Their early, and it may be said, premature symptoms of age may, perhaps, with much probability, be ascribed to a hard life, an uncertain and irregular supply of food, exposure to every inclemency of weather, and a want of cleanliness which increases with years.   These, rather than the nature of the climate, are the causes of this quick fading, and decay of the bloom and appearance of youth.

The lengthened shadows of the surrounding trees began to remind me of the approach of evening, and of its being time to return to the waggons.   Mounted on Adam Kok's horse, I rode home in company with Mr. Jansz, leaving Gert and some other Hottentots to follow on oxback or on foot, while Kok with his party was to remain at the spot all night to keep watch over the game, and to complete the drying of it on the next day.

Nor were they left without company ; for where there is meat to be had, there of course will Bushmen always fix their quarters. I left the young lady, and my friend *Wantrouw*, who in this instance turned a deaf ear to my call, both eagerly employed in tearing away the remaining flesh from the skull, and from between the joints of the huge backbone.

31*st*.   The next morning we were again visited by the same Bushmen, who brought us about twenty small bundles of green rushes from the opposite side of the river.   Being loaded each with three or four bundles, they would not perhaps have found it practicable to cross the stream without the assistance of what the Klaarwater Hottentots termed a *Houte-paard* (Wooden-horse.)

This *Wooden-horse* is merely a log of dry wood, six or seven feet long, and six inches thick, into which, towards the upper end,

is driven a stout peg of about a foot in length : this log, the chief
utility of which is derived from its buoyancy, is placed under the
body, and there held by one arm, while the other, and both legs, are
used in swimming: the peg resting against the shoulder, keeps the
log in its proper place ; and by directing it obliquely upwards against
the stream, the swimmer generally succeeds in stemming the violence
of the current, so much that he reaches the spot exactly opposite,
or nearly so, to that from which he started.

One is here naturally inclined to wonder that the necessity
under which these people must frequently find themselves, of crossing this broad river, has never yet compelled them to contrive something in the form of a *boat* or *canoe* : but a little consideration on
their wandering, unsettled mode of life, will at once show that, under
their actual circumstances, the present method answers all purposes
sufficiently well.   A log of dry willow wood is to be found without
trouble, at almost every place where the circumstance of the moment,
may require them to cross the stream ; and, on reaching the other
side, they merely draw it a few paces up the bank, out of the reach of
the water, and, without ever giving it a further thought, leave it for
the use of the next person who may chance to come that way.   But
the possession of a canoe would bring on them the care of preserving
it, as well as the necessity of always abiding near the same spot :
both which are, to the highest degree, uncongenial to the inclinations
and habits of these tribes.

Our visitors, whom we had been attentively watching while thus
working their way through the stream, no sooner felt themselves in
shallow water, than they stood up, and warmly greeted us with
salutations in their own language, and advanced toward the shore,
each carrying his log on one shoulder, and dragging the bundles of
rushes with the other hand.   Their horses were left on the bank :
with cheerfulness and good-will expressed in their countenances,
they brought their loads to the waggons, and in the liveliest manner
clacked to us as if we had understood every word they said.   We were
however, not in want of interpreters ; and, having paid them in *dakka*
and tobacco-stems, received a friendly invitation to visit their kraal,

and, at the same time, a present of *uyentjes*. This is a colonial name in very general use, and is applied to several kinds of small eatable bulbs.   None of those in question were larger than a hazle-nut, and were cased in several thin brown husks.   They are usually slightly roasted in the embers; but in taste are inferior, being less sweet than the others, which are chiefly the bulbs of plants of the *Ensatæ* order. The present plant was a species of *Cypérus-grass* hitherto undescribed. *

Our rush-merchants were quite naked, excepting the piece of jackal-skin.   They squatted round the fire to dry and warm themselves; and our kind treatment and good fare induced them to stop with us all night.

In the mean time, our hunting-party had shot an Eland on the other side of the river, and, before dusk, had safely brought the flesh of it over on a raft.   This formed an agreeable change in our food, as it began to appear that otherwise we should have nothing to eat but the fat meat of Hippopotamus.

With this last animal, the river hereabout seemed to abound. In the evening two of them, in their way up the stream, lifted their heads out of water close by our waggons, as if intending to come

---

* *Cyperus usitatus*, B. Cat. Geog. 2082.   Culmus triqueter spithameus.   Umbella contracta, involucris brevior.   Spiculæ purpurascentes angustæ 8–12-floræ.   Valvulæ nervosæ.   Nervi elevati.   Folia plana, culmum subæquantia.   Radix repens bulbifera. Bulbi squamis *magnis ovatis concavis* tecti.

At this station I found growing on the sides of the river and in the water, another species of *Cyperus*, six feet high; a very handsome plant of this class.

On the bank grows abundance of *Vahlia* ; and a *Dracocephalum?*   A species of *Conium* was gathered in the same situations; but owing to the dry state of the ground, very few new plants were here added to my herbarium.

Of *insects*, I found two new species of *Anthia*, to one of which I gave the name of *effugiens*, on account of its very fast running, and of the great difficulty in catching it. This property however is common, but in a degree something less, to all the species of this genus which I saw.   This one is a transgariepine insect.

The only species of *Chironymus* in my collection was caught here.

Lamia virescens was taken out of the wood of the willow, into which it had eaten a deep retreat: this insect is found only on the willow.   I met with it afterwards in the easternmost part of the Cape colony.

3 H

on shore to graze; but quickly discovering us, they plunged beneath the surface, snorting and blowing the water up with their nostrils; nor did they venture to breathe again till far beyond our reach.

November 1st. I here became acquainted with a new species of *Mantis*, whose presence became afterwards sufficiently familiar to me, by its never failing, on calm warm evenings, to pay me a visit as I was writing my journal; and sometimes to interrupt my lucubrations by putting out the lamp. All the Mantis tribe are very remarkable insects; and this one, whose dusky sober coloring well suits the obscurity of night, is certainly so, by the late hours it keeps. It often settled on my book, or on the press where I was writing, and remained still, as if considering some affair of importance, with an appearance of intelligence which had a wonderful effect in withholding my hand from doing it harm. Although hundreds have flown within my power, I never took more than five. I have given to this curious little creature the name of *Mantis lucubrans*; and, having no doubt that he will introduce himself to every traveller who comes into this country in the months of November and December, I beg to recommend him as a harmless little companion, and entreat that kindness and mercy may be shown to him.

2nd. On the day of our arrival at this station, *Willem Berends* had made a proposal to hunt for me, on condition of receiving half the game for himself, and of being supplied with ammunition. As he was reputed an excellent marksman, I agreed to employ him, under a stipulation that *Speelman* should accompany him. They had now been absent more than two days, without our having heard any thing of them; and I was beginning to feel some anxiety, when, very early this morning, a Hottentot arrived from them, desiring that the little waggon might be sent to fetch home a *Hippopotamus* which they had shot, at the distance of a day's journey up the *Ky-gariep*, in a northerly direction.

The men instantly unloaded it, and yoked the oxen to. Intending to go myself, I packed up the requisites for drawing, and the large tin collecting-box; but took, of course, no more meat than would be enough for the day; nor did I encumber myself with any other bedding than my watch-coat. In respect to the latter, I was inclined to try how the customs of a Bushman would suit me; that is, without any other bedding than the clothes on my back, or other shelter than a bush.

Taking Philip as driver, and leaving Gert in charge of the great waggon, I set out a little after seven in the morning, with the Hottentot messenger for our guide, and having in company a waggon which was going on the same business as mine, a little way up the river, to Captain Dam, who had shot another Hippopotamus. The country over which we travelled was a wild trackless level, here and there broken with a few horizontal-topped hills. To the south-south-eastward, a little *table-mountain*, at the distance of a day and a half's journey, is remarkable, and may be seen, as I afterwards remarked, a great way off in different directions. It was said to be situated not more than eight or nine miles eastward from the *Salt-pan* which lies on the eastern side of the Nugariep.

The surface of the land was in general sprinkled over with small scrubby bushes *; and in many places grew abundance of *Kanna-bosch* (Kanna-bush) †, which I had now learnt to consider as an indication of a good soil of some depth, though not always free from a brackish quality. In some parts of the plain the Bushmen had burnt away the old grass, for the purpose of attracting the game by the young herbage which subsequently springs up. At this time it had already begun to sprout, and had given to many extensive patches the beautiful verdure of a field of wheat. In places which had not been in this manner cleared by burning, the green blades were concealed by the old withered grass; a circumstance which ever gives to the plains of Africa a more pale and arid appearance than they would present if the wild animals were able to graze off the yearly crop as closely as the cattle do in the pastures of Europe.

---

* I added to my herbarium a very singular ligneous species of *Aizoon ;* a *Talinum* and another remarkable plant of the same order.

† *Salsola aphylla*, L. or *Caroxylon Salsola*, Th. The ashes of this shrub are much used by the Colonists, as an alkali, in making soap.

At one time we saw a troop of about thirty beautiful *Zebras* *, or, as they were called by the Hottentots, *Quakkas;* and amongst them some ostriches. Eight miles further, we halted the waggon while Philip pursued a small herd of five *Hartebeests* †, but without success.

We were joined by five Bushmen, all armed with hassagays and bows; and, about a mile further, we overtook a party of seven women, among whom was the young beauty already mentioned. They carried in their hands a straight thin walking-stick, taller than themselves; and besides this, a shorter and stronger one, for the purpose of digging up such eatable bulbs as they might chance to meet with in their way. Some were encumbered with a child, which they carried at their back ‡; yet they trudged on as briskly as the rest of their companions, without the least symptom of being fatigued. They all looked contented, and I think I may say they were happy; for they bore the appearance of it in their countenances; and I do not think they are yet so civilized and artificial, as to conceal care and misery under the outside garb of gaiety and contentment. Our hunting seemed to have spread a joy over their kraal, and they viewed us not as intruders among them, but as friends of a most useful kind. Every sentiment of mistrust had vanished: they considered us as acquaintances whose sincerity had been proved; and I now began to feel myself quite at ease in their company.

A bend of the river, which approached us on our right, was the part where Dam's 'Sea-cow' lay; and here his waggon, and all the Bushman party, left us. Two Klaarwater sea-cow-eaters remained with us, and volunteered their professional services, which, in reality, I would rather have refused than accepted; as, by doing

---

* As the word *Zebra* is unknown to the Hottentots, they apply the name of **Quakka** as well to the *Equus Quagga* as to the *Equus Zebra.* — Compare this remark with what has been said at pages 138 and 139.

† *Antilope Bubalis,* Linn., Sparrm., &c.   *A. Caama,* Cuv., Blainv., &c.

‡ In the manner represented at page 322.

so, a larger stock of dried meat might have been saved for my future journey.

Our guide led us along the side of the river, over ground the most rugged and uneven, where thorny bushes, deep ditches and ravines, every minute impeded our progress; and such as in England I believe no person would be venturesome enough to drive a waggon through. The axletrees were strained in opposite directions, so that frequently one or other of the wheels was lifted from the ground; and, but for the peculiar construction of Cape waggons, allowing a free motion to every part, we must most certainly have been several times overturned.

At last we ventured too much, and were on the point of being upset in an exceedingly deep ravine, which proved really impassable. At this moment, conceiving that the waggon was falling over, we fortunately sprang from our seat, and thus preserved the equilibrium, without, in fact, having calculated upon producing so seasonable an effect. To advance was impossible; to retreat seemed nearly so: and as the guide assured us that Speelman could not be beyond hearing, we clapped the whip with all our might, in hopes of calling him to our assistance. But in the mean time, on reconnoitring the ground, it was thought that the waggon might be dragged up the steep bank on our left, although, indeed, there was scarcely room for it to turn. This, however, after a delay of half an hour, was at last effected without accident; but the enormous large stones and rocks that we were afterwards obliged to drive over, threatened destruction to the wheels: and, even on gaining the level above the ravines, we had nothing better than rocks for nearly half a mile. As soon as these difficulties were passed, I reprimanded the guide for bringing us so near to the river, while he knew that, at a proper distance from the banks, we should have found a safe and smooth road over the plain. He had, he confessed, mistaken the spot where he expected to find Speelman; and thought that, by approaching the water at the place where we did, we should the sooner come upon him.

We had not proceeded a mile, before we were met by a Bushman whom Speelman had sent to conduct us; judging, from the clapping of our whip, that we had lost our way.   The distance at which he had heard us, could not have been less than two miles: a proof of the sharp and powerful sound which such a whip is capable of producing.   Innumerable proofs of this kind, and among them some which would be thought almost incredible by those who have never heard a Cape whip, were given during my travels.   The openness of the country is indeed favorable to the wide extension of the sonorific undulations of the air; and, besides this, the river, in the present instance, operated as a conductor, notwithstanding the thick woods by which its banks were covered.

As we rode onwards, I could not cease admiring the beautiful *symmetrical form* of our Bushman guide, who walked, and sometimes ran, before us, with a gait the most easy and free that I had ever beheld. All the limbs, unshackled by clothing, moved with a grace never perhaps seen in Europe.   The contemplation of his well-proportioned, although small and delicate figure; his upright, manly port; his firm and bold step; and the consciousness of liberty, which beamed in his countenance; afforded an indescribable pleasure: and I envied the Bushmen the uncontrouled freedom of their lives, till a thought of the superior mental advantages of civilized society, arose and rendered less irksome the idea of constraint which the formality of laws and a regular government seem, at first sight, to create.   Unfortunate, that *civilization* and this species of *liberty*, cannot, hand in hand, journey through the nations of the world, to make mankind more happy in proportion as they acquire the arts and improvements of social life.   But the Wisdom of Providence scatters its blessings over the globe, with, perhaps, an even hand; yet, if not, that secret influence of Nature, which teaches every nation to view their native soil and customs as superior to all around them, perfectly regulates the balance of worldly enjoyments.

After a journey of twenty miles, we arrived at the place where Speelman and Willem Berends were stationed.   The Hippopotamus was already cut up, and the surrounding bushes were now covered with the meat.   In the waggon a vat had been formed with a large piece of its hide; and in it all the fatter pieces were laid in salt.   This animal was a full-grown female, and proved to be in good condition. It was infested with a very large kind of louse *, which adhered to the outside of its ears.   The hide on the rump and back, was an inch and a half in thickness ; but on the under part of the body, only three quarters of an inch: it may be observed that the tusks of the female are always shorter and smaller than those of the male.   It was killed in the back of the head by a single bullet, supposed to be the one fired by Berends, who, therefore, came in for a half share of it, according to our agreement.

A small party of Bushmen had very readily lent Speelman their assistance in the cutting it up.   The darker color and taller figure of one of the men, showed him to be not of the genuine race; and he informed us, that, although his mother was a Bushwoman, his father was a Briqua, (or Bachapin); but that on their separating, which they did by mutual consent, he had followed his mother, and now classed himself as a Bushman.   Among our number, were two women, and two half-grown-boys: the latter were the first I had seen of that age.   The young lady and her companions, were also here ; having arrived by a shorter path, along the water's edge.

In some places, the willows here bend over the stream, and put out roots from their branches, like the celebrated Banyan tree of India ; but they were too short to reach the ground.   This singularity is occasioned only by local circumstances, and not by any peculiarity in the nature of this tree: these overhanging branches remaining under water during the rise of the stream, push out roots of two or three feet in length, which afterwards, on the subsiding of the flood, are left exposed to the air.   Of this curious scene, I made a drawing ; and another, also, of a beautiful view on the top of the bank, to which the appropriate living appendages, the natives passing to and fro, with red cloaks and glittering hassagays, gave an interesting animation.

---

* Or probably a species of *Ricinus;* but I mention the genus merely from recollection.

In this spot, when evening came on, I prepared, at the distance of a score yards from where Speelman and Philip had their fire, a place on the slope of the grassy bank, where I might conveniently pass the night. The weather was delightfully serene, and without the least dew. A blazing fire of dry acacia wood, enabled me to write my journal and arrange the memoranda of the day. As we had brought neither gridiron nor plates, a forked stick, about two feet long, supplied the place of both. On this fork a steak of our hippopotamus was stuck; while the lower end of it being pointed, was thrust into the ground close to the fire. As soon as the meat was broiled, at what I might call my kitchen fire, Philip brought it to where I was sitting, and stuck it before me in the ground. The luxuries and accommodations of the dining-room, were here reduced to their simplest forms; the grassy bank, the forked stick, and a small pocket-knife, supplied the place of all the costly furniture of a palace. And I might, without inconvenience, have imitated *Diogenes*, by throwing away my cup, although merely an ostrich-egg shell; but he, in return, would have abandoned his tub, as utterly unnecessary, could he have beheld me as I lay on the open bank asleep, housed only by the starry sky.

Our Bushmen friends, wrapped in their karosses, lay down also, within a few yards of us, and took their rest; a proof of the really friendly terms we were upon. For it was not possible to have given a stronger assurance of our confidence in each other's good intentions, than that of lying thus exposed and unprotected, in each other's power, perfectly unsuspicious of treachery, and fearless of harm. I know not whether this degree of confidence ought to be considered as prudent in a solitary European, travelling over the wilds of Africa; nor would I recommend it to be adopted by others, without the most careful circumspection: but I am certain that, in several instances, I am indebted to it for my safety; in many, for a kind treatment; and, in general, for a more friendly reception than, it seems, has hitherto been experienced by European travellers.

3rd. The two boys amused themselves in watching for fish, standing at the water's edge as motionless as herons. After patiently waiting

more than half an hour, one of the fishes came within their reach, and
with unerring aim, was instantly pierced through with their hassagay.
This is the fish which has been already mentioned by the name of
Platte-kop (Flat-head) a species of *Silurus*.* It was nearly three feet
long, entirely of a lead-color; but whitish underneath. The head was
very broad and flat; the eyes pale-yellow and extremely small; and
the mouth was bearded with several very long strings. The skin was
smooth, and, like that of an eel, without scales. The flesh was white,
and in taste very much resembled the conger-eel, being rich and nu-
tritious. It is a remarkable circumstance, and one which is confirmed
by the general observation of the colonists, that it is only those rivers
which run to the western coast, (that is to say, to the northward ofthe
Cape of Good Hope,) in which this fish is found; whilst, on the contrary, eels have never been seen in any but those which fall into the
ocean eastward of that cape. Of this *Silurus* I completed two coloured
drawings on the spot; of one of which, an engraving is given at the
end of the chapter.

I also finished a drawing of a whole tree of the *Red-leaf*; its
growth and appearance being remarkable, and exhibiting a character
very different from that of the other trees of the country. In selecting a position for making this drawing, I was unable to find a single
yard of ground that did not swarm with large black ants. It was,
therefore, impossible to sit down, and nearly so, to stand; for these
troublesome insects, ever on the search for something to eat, soon
found their way over my shoe, and seemed uncommonly delighted
at feasting on a white-man's leg, a treat most likely, till now, quite
unknown to the little tribe, and, in spite of all my endeavours, they
were determined not to let go their prize. Their bite, though not
leaving behind it any inflammation, was yet exceedingly sharp at the
moment, and kept me in continual motion to brush them off. Near

---

* *Silurus (Heterobranchus) Gariepinus* B.—Vide iconem capitulo XVII. adjectam.
Longitudo, pollices (Angl.) 33½. Inter oculos et pinnas pectorales, maxima est latitudo;
poll. 5½. Cirri 8, quorum longissimus, (poll. 7.) in angulo oris situs. Os edentule.
Caput, anticè transverum, planum, plagioplateum. Corporis pars posterior valdè
cathetoplatea. Appendix branchiarum ruberrima arboriformis. Pinnæ omnes inermes:
D.69: A.53: C.18: P.10: V.6: et Br.5.—Reliqua sunt in icone videnda.

this spot were the remains of a Bushman Kraal of seven huts, the inhabitants of which one may almost suppose to have been driven away by these annoying insects.

Amongst the vegetation of the bank, three plants of a most marked European complexion, and as it were almost English*, were found growing together on the same spot. Every thicket was so interwoven and entangled with *Asparagus rivalis*, that the labor and fatigue of tearing a way through it, added to the increasing heat of the day, brought on a degree of lassitude that compelled me to rest during the afternoon. But, in the evening, taking a stroll under the large trees along the river, I observed in a very ancient and picturesque Karree-tree, marks of its being the nightly roosting-place of a considerable number of large birds, and my curiosity induced me to wait in concealment till they came home. They proved to be what are called *Guinea-fowls* or *Pintadoes* (*Numida*): presently the tree became, as it were, a complete poultry-yard; and as I sat watching their movements and manners, each taking its perch, just as tame fowls are seen to do, it was not easy to believe them to be wild birds.

4th. The Bushmen, although I rose early, had all taken their departure before I awoke, carrying with them a large load of dried meat which had been given them as a present to their Kraal.

In the course of the night the river began to swell, and had already risen about three feet : yet not the least appearance of rain had, for a long time, been observable within our horizon. This proved that heavy thunder-showers had fallen in some country very far up the stream, and probably to the eastward. A few Bushmen, who showed themselves in the woods on the opposite bank, called out to us, but seemed not inclined to take the trouble of swimming over. Speelman shot a Hippopotamus in the neck, but not mortally, and it therefore escaped.

The Hottentots having completed the drying of our meat, and

---

* A species of *Potentilla,*
  Polygonum, very much like *P. aviculare.*
  Veronica, like *V. scutellata.*

packed it in the waggon, we prepared for returning to head-quarters ; but the Hottentots were so dilatory in getting every thing in readiness, that, calculating we could not reach the end of our journey before midnight, I deferred setting out till the next morning. This delay soon appeared to have been fortunate ; for, at about three in the afternoon, Berends, who had been absent since an early hour in the morning, returned with the information of his having shot another *Hippopotamus*, which he had left on the side of the bank about six miles higher up.

No time was lost in putting the team to the waggon ; and Speelman and Berends, mounted on oxen, led the way ; a Hottentot was dispatched to head-quarters, to fetch Berends's waggon ; my own being now nearly filled. We advanced in a direct northerly course, over an open plain thinly covered with low bushes. The earth was here also every where gaping with drought : large cracks crossed and divided the sun-dried soil in all directions.

Speelman, who had not, for many years, had an opportunity of hunting the Hippopotamus, was in high spirits at all this success ; and, as he trotted on before, talking with Berends, his animated gestures, and the lively tone of his conversation, interrupted frequently by laughter, afforded me much amusement ; and at the same time, exhibited a curious contrast with Philip's steadiness and natural taciturnity.

At an hour before sunset we reached the place* where the Seacow had been left ; but were surprised to find it not there. At last we discovered it drifted about six hundred yards lower down, but lying, unfortunately, against the opposite bank. The river at this place, was not more than two-thirds as wide as at its confluence with the Gariep ; and was therefore a hundred and sixty-six yards, or thereabouts.

Two men immediately undertook to swim over, and, after great labor, and being in the water a long time, they succeeded in pushing

---

* Distinguished in the map as the *Third Hippopotamus Station*.

the huge carcase over to our side of the river.   But here another difficulty met us : the bank was every where so thickly covered with trees down to the very water's edge, and their branches hung over so far into the stream, that it was not practicable to get it on shore, without felling the trees, and carrying their branches away piece-meal ; a work which we had not time for; neither did the Hotten-tots feel inclined, or able, in such warm weather, to undertake so laborious a task.

The *Hippopotamus* having been all day exposed to the heat of the sun, some degree of putrefaction had taken place ; and the included air had so much swollen the body that it floated with a great part above the surface.   With the thongs used in yoking our oxen, it was fastened by its leg to one of the branches; and in this position they began without loss of time to cut it up.   It was found that a great portion of the meat was spoiled; and the damage was much increased by lying so long in the water.   It was of the full size, and in its stomach were found above six bushels of chewed grass.   The largest intestine, when inflated, measured nearly eight inches in diameter.   The food of the Hippopotamus passes in a very indigested state ; and even then, has more the appearance of mingled grass and straw.

At this place the river was flowing as through a forest; nothing but trees being to be seen on either side ; chiefly the willow, blackbark, and acacia, with abundance of reeds growing in the water.   The still clear smoothness of the stream, indicated consider-able depth, but its magnitude in this place, at less than thirty miles above its confluence with the Gariep, had decreased so much as to convince me that in size and length of course, the *Ky-Gariep* was far inferior to the Nu-Gariep.

Our secluded situation had completely concealed us from the natives who inhabited this part of the country, not one of whom came near us ; which they certainly would have done, had they known that we were there.   In the midst of the woods, wander-ing alone, admiring the scenery, and watching the manners of several beautiful birds, and attending to their various notes, I chanced to follow a narrow path which led me to a Bushman Kraal : but not an inhabitant was there. It was, in fact, deserted ; nothing remaining but a few huts, made of branches, covered with grass and reeds. It was inaccessible, except by two or three small close paths which had been cut through the thicket ; and even these I found obstructed by large limbs of trees, purposely placed there to prevent the intrusion of hippopotami, or other large beasts ; or, at least, to give the inhabitants, at night, timely notice of their approach, by the noise the animals would make in trampling them down, or removing them out of their way. The kraal was surrounded by extensive woods of the largest Acacias I had hitherto met with.

On the branches of these Acacias, which have so great a resemblance to the true *Acacia* of the ancients, or the tree which yields the *Gum-Arabic*, as to have been once considered the same species, I frequently saw large lumps of very good and clear gum. Wherever they had been wounded by the hatchets of the natives, there, most commonly, the gum exuded ; and by some similar operation, it is probable that the trees might, without destroying them, be made to produce annually a large crop. And if a computation could be made of the quantity that might be obtained from those trees only, which line the banks of the Gariep and its branches, amounting to a line of wood (reckoning both sides) of more than two thousand miles, one would feel inclined to suppose that it might be worth while to teach and encourage the natives to collect it. This they certainly would be ready to do, if they knew that tobacco could always be obtained in exchange. But if, to the Acacias of *this* river, are added the myriads which crowd almost every river in extra-tropical Southern Africa, or even between the Cape and the Gariep only, one may feel quite satisfied that there are trees enough to supply a quantity of this drug, more than equal to the whole consumption of Great Britain. Of the productiveness of the *Acacia Capensis*, as compared with that of the *Acacia vera*, I have no information that enables me to give an opinion ; but with respect to the quality, I think one may venture to pronounce it to be, in no point, inferior.*

At a distance on the eastern side of the Yellow River, some large trees were conspicuous by their form ; and were either the *Acacia Giraffæ* or the *Acacia heteracantha* † : but on the western, none of this kind were seen.

Three river-horses passed us, in their way up the stream, and were supposed to have been disturbed by the hunting party below ; for the Hottentots remark that when these animals are molested in their haunts, they generally mover higher up the river ; but are very seldom observed to take their course downwards in such cases. These three followed each other in the middle of the stream, and appeared to swim against the current with ease ; now and then barely putting up their nostrils above the water to breathe. It was therefore evident that they had been rendered extremely suspicious of danger ; as the quantum of their fearfulness may always be measured by the proportion of body under water : never venturing on shore but when they judge themselves in perfect security.

The bank rises up behind the woods, higher than the tops of the trees, and from this there commences an open plain, over which the view reaches without interruption. To the south-eastward is a small table-mountain ; and another long and level mountain appears in the distance ; but northward the country seemed exceedingly flat, and the scope of vision extended immeasureably over the region which adjoins the *Kora* country of the *Hart*. A branch of the Kygariep extends to the *Hart* village, or chief kraal of that tribe, and

---

* The quantity of *Gum* annually imported into England from *Senegal*, for home consumption, is not less than 500 tons, which is purchased in Africa for about one shilling per pound ; and although it sells in London (at present) for no more than 5*l*. per hundred weight ; it still continues to be brought home, as a remittance for English manufactures, on which a counterbalancing profit has been obtained. The present circumstances of the Cape Colony, with respect to mercantile remittances, are such as may be deemed more favorable to the *Gum trade*, considered in this point of view.

† Described at page 389. These two species much resemble each other in the general character of their growth and ramification.

is known at **Klaarwater** by the name of the *Hart river*.   This kraal
has frequently been visited by the Klaarwater Hottentots ; and once
by a Half-Hottentot named *Kok*, who, in the character of missionary,
traversed these countries, and made considerable profit by trading
in ivory ; but was not long afterwards murdered in the country of
the Briquas or Bachapins.

On this open bank, where the ground was perfectly dry, I passed
the night ; and as I lay waiting for sleep, and amusing myself in
observing the constellations above my head, I noticed a faint nebu-
lous star of the third magnitude, which I had not been used to see
in that part of the heavens.   Looking at it more attentively, it appeared plainly to be a *comet*.   Its situation, as well as I could then
determine by the eye, was southward from *α Lyræ*, and near the
tail of *Aquila: α Cygni, α Lyræ*, and the comet, forming a right-
angled triangle.   It was in that part of its orbit approaching the
sun ; and, on the 22d of the month, was so far advanced in its peri-
helium, as to be no longer visible.

5th.   Leaving Speelman and Berends with the two other Hottentots, to finish the business of cutting up and drying, I set out in
the morning at a little after ten, with the loaded waggon, taking
with me only Philip as my driver, and a boy, Berends's son,
as leader of the team.   We struck out into the plain, and now took
good care to keep at a sufficient distance from the river, to avoid
those ravines which had before given us so much trouble.

Here on the plain, we saw a troop of twenty Quakkas grazing, and
with them, on one side, a single *Gnu*, or *Wildebeest*, (*Antilope Gnu*)
which, on observing us, began prancing about, with his mane erect, and
head held very low.   Being blacker than most of the other antelopes
and quadrupeds, it is easily known, even at a great distance ; but on a
nearer approach, its attitude and manners at once distinguish it.
Although it associates in small herds, it is very frequently seen solitary ; and on perceiving a traveller advancing, generally turns towards
him, gazes for a minute, prances about, again stops to look, and if
the person still continue to approach, bounds away with that fleet-
ness which belongs to the antelope tribe.   I never could discover any
thing in this animal to authorise such wonderful and absurd accounts

as have been given of it, and repeated from one book to another :
it is an antelope, and that is all. *

In those parts of the plain where the herbage had been burnt,
the young grass had attracted a great quantity of game. We passed
a large herd of spring-bucks quietly feeding at a distance ; and afterwards saw a *Steinbok* (Stonebuck) ; and a few miles further, some
quakkas. *Haakdoorns* (Hookthorns), abounded in the rocky
places, and greatly annoyed us, in compelling our ox-leader to
make many a circuit, in order to save his ragged kaross from being
torn off his back. †

When we had travelled nearly four hours, we saw before us

---

* From the pen of *Mr. Barrow*, a writer on the Cape, and who says he saw and
actually " hemmed in a troop of about fifty" ! the public has been presented with the following wonderful account of the *Gnu.* " Nature, though regular and systematic in all
" her works, often puzzles and perplexes human systems, of which this animal affords
" an instance. It partakes of the horse, the ox, the stag, and the antelope; the
" shoulders, body, thighs, and mane, are equine; the head completely bovine; the
" tail partly one and partly the other, exactly like that of the quacha; the legs, from
" the knee-joints downwards, and the feet, are slender and elegant like those of the
" stag, and it has the *subocular sinus* that is common to most, though not all of the an-
" telope tribe. Yet from this imperfect character, it has been arranged, on the authority
" of Sparrman, in the *Systema Naturæ*, among the antelopes, to which of the four it
" has certainly the least affinity."—Travels in Southern Africa, page 260.

Sparrman, however, was an anatomist and zoologist, and a man of *real* knowledge,
and consequently of some *modesty*. The preceding description is, as the writer very
sensibly remarks, quite sufficient to " puzzle and perplex" any human system ; although
I suspect that *his* Gnoo, which must be a different animal from that which I have seen,
would be conveniently arranged in the same class with the *Sphinx*, the *Griffin*, the
Chimera, and the *Unicorn*, the last so carefully described by the same author.

† In this day's journey were found—

Boerhaavia pentandra. C. G. 1765.
Caules herbacei teretes procumbentes.
Folia subcordata. Spicæ solitares
elongatæ axillares. Flores maximi
rosei pentandri, verticillati. Verticilli
sub-sexflori.

Asparagus exuvialis. C. G. 1768. Caules
aliquandò volubiles. Rami ramuliquè
inermes, alternatìm divaricatissimi,
tecti epidermide tenui albidâ, citò
exutâ. Folia setacea. Flores axillares bini.

Capparis albitrunca. B.
Cassia arachoïdes. B.
Celosia odorata. B.
Messerschmidia.
Senecio.
Campanula.
Cheiranthus.
Indigofera.

three waggons at *outspan*, two of which were Captain Kok's, carrying home the produce of his hunting, but had been detained at this spot a whole day, by the breaking down of one of the wheels. The other proved to be that which had been sent for, and on its way to Speelman had halted to deliver a wheel brought for the broken-down waggon. Hans Lucas was accompanying it; and, expecting to find me at the river, Mr. Jansz, judging that tea and bread would be very acceptable, had kindly sent some by him, together with the indispensable article of a tea-kettle. Nothing is more refreshing than tea, after a day's travelling in this hot climate; and, I confess that, for myself, I always found it at such times preferable to every thing else.

Old Lucas, or as he was more familiarly called, *Oom Hans* (Uncle Hans), now turned back with us, and I promised them all a treat of their favorite beverage at the next water we came to. It was not long before a turn of the river approaching close to our road, presented for the purpose a delightful spot, where some umbrageous trees offered protection from the burning rays of the sun.

After resting an hour and a half, till the violent heat of the day had a little passed by, we continued our journey; but one of the waggons, which was in a most decrepit state, soon broke down again, and Hans remained behind to help to patch it together. We had not proceeded far by ourselves, when it fell to the turn of my waggon also to get out of order. Suddenly the staple to which the *trecktouw*, or drag-rope, was fastened, broke, and the whole team, excepting the hinder pair, marched on without us, till the boy could overtake and turn them back. With thongs of hide, we made a good substitute for the staple, and once more set forward, quickening our pace, that we might reach head-quarters before dark.

Our view over the country was frequently confined by hills and bushes; and to save ourselves the trouble of considering what course we were to take, we followed the track made by the waggon which we had just passed on its way to Speelman, and unfortunately depended for guidance entirely on these marks. At a quarter before seven, when twilight began to close, the leader found

3 k

that he had missed the track.   We halted and examined the ground in all directions, carefully scrutinizing the bushes to discover if they bore any marks of a wheel having passed over them.   But all our trouble was useless; it grew darker and darker, and, after a half hour's search to no purpose, we gave up all hope of finding our way.   As there was no alternative, we prepared for passing the night on the spot where we happened to halt.   We unyoked the oxen, and made them fast with thongs to the waggon, that they might not stray away, and either fall into the hands of some un-friendly Bushmen, or become a prey to the lions, which, as appeared by their foot-marks, were numerous in this part of the country.

At a great distance in the eastern quarter, we observed, during the whole night, two large fires, kept burning by some kraal of Bushmen as a signal, understood only by those to whom it was made.   These people are always on the look-out; and, wherever a strange fire is seen, send out spies to ascertain what the strangers are.   On this account we durst not make any light, lest we should attract the notice of any hostile party, who, finding us but two men and a boy to defend ten oxen, and that in a dark night, might be tempted, by so favourable an opportunity, to make an attack upon us.

We all suffered so much from thirst, that Philip resolved to make his way to the river, which we knew could not be more than a mile off, and with this view, took the boy with him to assist in carrying the calabashes.

Being in the mean time left alone, I retired to the distance of thirty yards from the waggon, and took my post, with my gun loaded with buck-shot, behind a bush, where, lying flat on the ground, I could the more readily perceive an enemy approaching, as he would thus be rendered visible against the sky; while on the contrary, from the low and dark situation in which I lay, it would not be very easy for any one to observe me.   Had any strangers approached with evil intentions, and their number been small, I could, from my ambush, have fired upon them with effect; but if, on the contrary, they had appeared too numerous, I might then have retreated, probably without being discovered.   This plan gave me also the advantage of avoiding the volley of arrows by which such enemies generally give the first notice of their presence, and which would have been aimed at the waggon, under the supposition that the people belonging to it, must be somewhere near it.

But it was my better fortune to remain unmolested. Philip at last returned : but without water; having found it impossible to get towards the river, on account of the hook-thorns which at every step caught hold of them, and had sadly torn both their clothes and their skin. We therefore laid ourselves down to rest, unable to satisfy either thirst or hunger.

Towards the middle of the night, we heard the sound of waggons at a distance, as they passed over rocky places. Philip sprang up and made a signal of distress, by giving several loud claps with the whip ; which were heard, and answered in a similar manner. They soon approached us, and proved to be what we had expected, the two waggons which we had left behind with Lucas. They had also lost their way, and were glad at falling in with us ; for, having very little ammunition left, they were beginning to be uneasy at the prospect of remaining out in the plain all night without protection.

Our party being now sufficiently strengthened by this reinforcement, we made a fire : while the Hottentots made another attempt to reach the river ; and in this they fortunately succeeded, by taking a different direction, so as to avoid the thorns.

6th. As soon as daylight began to dawn, we resumed the journey, having previously held a short consultation to determine the course most likely to bring us to head-quarters. In less than two hours travelling, we arrived at our station on the Kygariep, where we found all well.

On the preceding day, Mr. Jansz, in consequence of the invitation we had received from our Bushmen friends, crossed the river on a raft conducted by six Hottentot swimmers; and, accompanied by a party of the Klaarwater men, rode on horseback, about a dozen miles to their kraal, where he was received in a very friendly manner. This little village he found pleasantly situated on the banks of the *Maap*, and containing nearly as many dwellings as Klaarwater, ranged in a regular manner, and apparently very orderly. The name of the kraal he understood to be *Karupný*: it seemed to contain a large number of inhabitants, although not more than forty men were seen, the rest happening then to be abroad in the plains in search of game and wild roots. The number of women and children was much more considerable: they flocked around him, begging as usual, for tobacco; some bringing milk. One old woman, with great disinterestedness, requested him to accept a mat, given purely, as she said, as a testimony of good-will. This instance of generosity was the more remarkable, as it is not the character of the nation to give away any thing without receiving an equivalent. It would, therefore, seem illiberal to hint that she had no doubt of Mr. Jansz showing himself equally disinterested; because I believe them not incapable of genuine hospitality, however little they may have in their power to bestow, and however seldom it may happen that they are not themselves in the greater want.

The inhabitants of this kraal appeared to be less wild, and much richer than those which he had hitherto had an opportunity of seeing. They possessed sheep, goats, and cows; which, however, they confessed were part of plunder obtained from the Caffres, already mentioned as having a kraal on the Gariep; and who were here distinguished by the name of *Bloodelyf Kaffers* (Naked Caffres), by the Klaarwater Hottentots. This nation, it is said, are in general, much in dread of the Bushmen, whose insidious mode of warfare and indefatigable activity in expeditions against their enemies, render them, although so diminutive in stature, more than a match for the tall and athletic Caffre.

The *Maap* was found to be of less breadth than the Yellow river; but is deeper, and remarkably meandering. The natives say that it receives, at some distance higher up, a considerable river from the northward; and that both the *Maap* and the *Black River* *,

---

* At a subsequent period of these travels, (February 1813,) I explored a part of the Black-river, never before visited; and ascertained its true course for a considerable distance.

come from a distant country. The former, in one part of its course between Karupny and the Gariep, approaches very near to the Yellow river, or more probably to some branch of it.

Having made presents of dried meat to as many of the Bushmen as the stock he had brought with him would allow, he returned home, accompanied by about a dozen of the natives. They remained that night at our station, and when I arrived, were preparing to depart; as they told us they were going to attack a neighbouring kraal, who had stolen from them two goats. Nor did they think they should be able to pay us another visit for several days, this affair being likely to occupy them during that interval. As Bushmen, they were considered good-looking and rather tall men, and in port like most of their countrymen, very erect.. Besides feeding them plentifully while they remained at our station, we gave each of them, on going away, seven or eight pounds of dried meat, and bargained to pay them in tobacco, for a quantity of rushes which they engaged to cut, and bring over to us.

7th. In the afternoon Speelman, and *Willem Berends*, arrived with the meat of our last hippopotamus; which Berends immediately began to divide, openly taking to himself all the best pieces, and much more than his share. For it seems that I had outwitted him, by sending Speelman on this expedition, and by being also present myself, so that he found himself compelled, sorely against his wish, to divide with me all the game that was shot. I had now for my share, a waggon load of *dried meat;* which was so much more than his greediness could endure to see, that he was unable to conceal his disappointment and ill-will. He laid claim to half the hide of which the vat was made, merely because he knew that by taking it away, he should occasion all my salt-meat to be spoiled: but this I resisted, and thought it advisable to convince the by-standers, that he had already taken more than his due share of the *shamboks.* Those which fell to me, I distributed equally amongst my own men.

From that time we had no more dealings together; and a day or two afterwards, when it became known to Mr. Jansz how large a quantity of powder and ball I had supplied this man with, and his having asserted that it was all expended, although not more than an eighth-part of it had been actually used, he sent for him, and required that he should account for it according to agreement. But this he peremptorily refused to do; and, declaring himself offended at the missionary for asking it, threatened that he would live at Klaarwater no longer; but, as soon as he returned home, would immediately collect together all his cattle, and withdraw to some other spot.

About a week before we left Klaarwater, Mr. Jansz had furnished him with gunpowder and lead, but for which no game at all was ever returned; and for the half of a sea-cow, which, on the same conditions, was soon afterwards due to him from the Klaarwater Captain, Adam Kok, he received a quantity equal only to a fourth of what was retained by Kok. In the same manner, I had, on this excursion, given ammunition to another Hottentot, who satisfied his conscience with giving me the half of a large bird; and on the next day after he had told me that all was expended, he shot a quakka with his *own* powder, although he had no means of getting a grain excepting that which he had received from me. I had given also a large quantity to Hans Lucas, who, in this particular, I found no better than the rest of his associates: this produced nothing for me: yet he, also, with his *own* powder, had managed to procure for himself a tolerably large stock of dried meat. Such is the value of *gunpowder* here, that these people are tempted to obtain it by every, and any, means; which shows, that, if a traveller could be supposed to have any to spare, he might readily purchase with it whatever they possessed.

8th. The weather was at this time excessively hot; and to day the *thermometer* rose to $100\frac{1}{2}$ (30·4 Reaum. 38·3 Centig.) With respect to thermometers, a fatality seemed to have hung over them this day: by an accident, the one I had in use, fell and was broken; and hardly was its place supplied by another, when that also met with a similar fate. Having no other instrument, all further observations were therefore interrupted till I returned to Klaarwater; when I was obliged to request Mr. Anderson to return me the one I had presented to him soon after my first arrival there. And in order to replace this, another was afterwards sent to Klaarwater from Cape Town; as a regular series of meteorological observations, made for several years at a spot so far inland, would be exceedingly interesting.   And it is hoped that missionaries in every country, when their profession calls them to distant regions, seldom frequented by scientific observers, will not think it unnecessary to transmit to Europe the many valuable facts which they must have daily opportunities of learning and verifying.   So that, in the event of their failing to convert the Heathen, some useful information, at least, may result from their labors.

Notwithstanding the great heat of the day, I could not allow so favorable an opportunity to pass by, as the clearness of the sky and stillness of the air offered, for observations for the longitude; and I took a set of nine distances of the sun from the moon, for this purpose.   I had already by the altitude of the star *Algenib* ascertained the latitude to be 29° 0′ 21¼″ South. *

9th. During the last seventeen days, not a drop of rain had fallen ; and, therefore, a thunder shower this evening, after a day hotter even than yesterday, was a delightful refreshing to the animal, as well as vegetable, creation.   Our clothes in such weather felt oppressive ; and, to relieve themselves, many of the Hottentots had been passing the whole day in the water.   But the river itself was quite warm ; and no longer afforded a cooling draught.   In my waggon, by throwing open the canvass at both ends, I had always found a little more air than in other situations ; and this contrivance rendered the overwhelming heat rather more supportable.   While every one around me, yielding to the enervating influence of the weather, and stretched here and there beneath the trees, was indulging in the pleasure of doing nothing ;. the care of preserving, and making notes of, my daily-increasing collections, and the never-ceasing business of recording my observations, kept me at all times more than fully employed.

---

* 1st Nov. 1811, at the confluence of the *Ky-gariep*, and *Maap*, the observed meridional altitude of γ *Pegasi* was 46° 52′ 19″.

and prevented my bodily feelings from giving way to the powers of climate.

At this place my *Ornithological* collection received the addition of several new birds, and I here met with, for the first time, an interesting species of *Reed Sparrow* *, inhabiting the reeds by the river side; where, though its sweet warbling notes betrayed its haunt, it was not always easy to get a sight of it.

I here obtained the only species of *Plotus*, found during my travels. It was called by the Hottentots, *Duyker* (Diver), from a wonderful faculty it possesses, of swimming beneath the water; and this I was assured it can do for the space of fifty yards or more.

That beautiful bird the *Lanius atro-coccineus* was frequently seen here, and the *Turdus nitens* was not rare. A new species of *Finch*, with a scarlet beak, was first procured at this spot; but was afterwards found within the colony. In the males, the four intermediate feathers of the tail were very long, and had their sides folded together, so that one feather sheathed the other.

Lanius forficatus? inhabits the woods; and is altogether a remarkable bird, and easily known by its forked tail and black color. † I have several times witnessed instances of its boldness, which surprized me. Whenever hawks, or ravens, approached its nest, this bird flew out upon them with incredible fury; and, with a harsh angry noise, drove them away, actually attacking in the rear, and pursuing them to a considerable distance. That a bird of this size should have the courage to attack another, so many times larger, and that one even a hawk, the terror of the smaller race, was a singular fact, but not more extraordinary than the evident fear and precipitation with which its enemy hastened to get out of its reach.

10th. Since our arrival at this station, a party of *Koras*, attracted by our provisions, had taken up their abode with us. This morning,

---

* *Curruca (Sylvia)* — *L'Isabelle*, Ois. d'Afr. pl. 121. f. 2.

† This seems to be the *Drongo* of Le Vaill. Oiseaux d'Afrique, pl. 166.; and there would be little doubt of it, if in this bird there could have been found any appearance of a crest: but nothing of the kind was here remarked in either sex.

one of them struck a *Geelvisch*, (Yellow fish)*: and I borrowed it of him to finish the colouring of a drawing made at the Sack river.   As soon as this was done, I called him to the waggon, to take his fish again; when, catching a sight of the drawing, he was in an instant struck with a most laughable degree of astonishment, and for a minute stood literally dumb with wonder ; gazing at it with mouth and eyes wide open.   At last, without taking off his eyes from the object, he called aloud to his companions to come and see.   The astonishment now became general, a crowd gathered round, and their various modes of expressing surprise were highly entertaining.   None having ever imagined the possibility that objects could be so imitated by art as to exhibit the color and appearance of life, they seemed to believe that it had been done by magic ; while others, supposing it to be the fish itself, fastened upon the paper, enquired where was the wound where it had been struck.   Nothing could be more amusing than the curious look of incredulity and amazement exhibited in their countenances, when they beheld the back of the drawing, and felt the thinness of what they had thought to be a solid fish.   There was but one way in which the mystery could be cleared up to them ; and but one mode of explanation which could be rendered at all comprehensible to their simple minds : I showed them the colors and pencils; and in their presence laid some of the same tint on a piece of paper.   After this they all retired satisfied and greatly pleased; and continued for a long while talking with each other on the wonder they had just seen; and possibly in such a manner, the acquisition of ideas perfectly new, might excite in them for the time at least, an encreased activity in the faculty of consideration, and reflection.

11*th*.   By a trigonometrical measurement, I ascertained the mean *breadth* of the *Yellow River* at this spot, which is just below the mouth of the Maap, to be seven hundred and forty-five feet ; being

---

* *Cyprinus aëneus.*

3 L

a hundred and eighty-five feet narrower than it was found to be at the first *Gariep station.* *   This difference is occasioned by the great volume of water which the Nu-Gariep rolls into its channel.

At this time, the river was at its natural and usual height, the water of the stream washing its green banks : but when seen on the 16th September, it did not, at that place, cover the whole of the pebbly bed ; a fact which proved how much it had risen since then, and from which it may be concluded, that in that month the river is at its lowest level. From this remark travellers may take the hint to make their arrangements so as to ford the Gariep about that season of the year. When I forded it in the month of May in the following year, it was with imminent danger, and even at the hazard of the lives of all my party. In the month of January also, that river was found too deep to be passed, except by means of rafts and swimming.

The water within a few days had gradually risen eighteen inches ; but on the day on which we left this station, and just when some heavy rains had fallen, it began to sink again. It is not meant that the falling of the water was connected with these rains ; but the fact is noticed merely to show the probability, that the extraordinary floods and inundations of the Gariep are not occasioned by the showers which fall over the countries lying between this part of it, and its mouth, the greatest portion of the rain-waters, being, in ordinary cases, absorbed by the thirsty soil : and that it can be only when the earth is saturated with moisture, that the supply from showers in the adjoining country contributes its full effect in swelling the stream.

That this does sometimes take place, although perhaps not annually, the ravines, which, in many places, furrow the surface and intersect the banks, plainly bear witness. But the chief cause is more distant, and must be sought in the country at the head of the Black-river. This being, by indisputable reasoning, the highest part of the

---

* See page 319.

southernmost quarter of Africa, one may, judging from effects, sur-
mise that it is also a cold, rugged, mountainous region, attracting
and condensing the vapors of the atmosphere; cherishing in its
deep valleys the innumerable springs which supply the first rivulets
of this beautiful river; and that it is for the greatest part of the year
visited by abundant rains.

There is, it must be acknowledged, some presumption in thus
pronouncing the nature of a country never yet visited by any traveller; but as we are living in the age for hypotheses in geography
and natural philosophy, the presumption will appear the less remarkable; nor indeed do I much care whether this hypothesis be hereafter proved or disproved, if it do but excite the curiosity of some
properly qualified traveller to explore that region.

12th.   We were visited by a party of fourteen Bushmen, who
remained with us till the following morning.   They were nearly all
strangers; and, although we discovered that many of them belonged
to the gang of robbers who a few months ago had carried off from
Klaarwater a herd of cattle belonging to the missionaries, we
thought it prudent to treat them friendly, and with the same hospitality with which the other Bushmen had been entertained.   So
little discredit do they attach to transactions of this kind, that they
openly avowed to us their having been participators in the theft.
As it was difficult to discover their real sentiments, we could
not comprehend why they thus shamelessly owned an act which
could not be deemed, even by themselves, any other than an act of
unprovoked enmity.   For, with respect to the injustice and immo-
rality of it in their eyes, there may be some doubt whether robbery
of this nature may not be considered by them in the same glorious
light as that in which the great civilized nations of Europe view the
capture or destruction of a convoy of enemy's merchant-ships.   But
these savages have one forcible argument in their favor; that they are
urged to it by a pressing want of the first necessaries of life.

It cannot be said that these men were quite averse to getting,
in an honest way, what they wished to possess; for, having heard

3 L 2

that we were in want of rushes, they had immediately set to work, and cut a quantity, which it was the object of their present visit to barter for tobacco.

Several of them wore two or three *cowries*, (*Cypræa moneta*) interwoven with their hair. On enquiring whence these shells had been procured, I could get no further information than that of their having been obtained from their neighbours by barter. It is, however, very probable that these shells, which pass as money in many negro countries, and are not of a nature easily to wear away, have passed through the hands of many a tribe of Negroes and Caffres, as unknown to European geographers as Europe is to them. Many a year may have elapsed since they were first brought to Africa; and, in that time, they may have travelled over the Black Continent, from one end of it to the other. They may have been often paid as tribute, or duty, to some despotic African prince; or given for the hire of a camel, or for a drop of water, in the deserts of the north; or, bestowed as alms on some pitiable enthusiast, toiling on his long pilgrimage to Mecca; or even as the ransom of threatened slavery. They may have visited cities whose existence is still unknown to us, even by name; or they may have been for years current at Timbuctoo. Or who can assert that these identical cowries have not passed through every village with which the banks of the Niger are peopled; or, alas! that they have not been once in the hand of our unfortunate countryman, Park, or of some of his ill-fated companions; or, perhaps, of some earlier, or some later sacrifice to African discovery.

To a solitary European, who may find himself eight hundred miles in the interior of Africa, some little circumstance will often excite a train of reflections, which his imagination, aided by the objects and scenes before him, will carry on through all the wanderings of thought. In such strange and distant regions, the mind naturally draws comparisons between things present, and things absent; and the ready association of ideas, leading it forward over the wide fields of hope, or again returning with it along the varied paths of memory, often constitutes its only solace, or its most pleasing relaxation. To an individual so situated, reflections and comparisons constitute the salt, without which travelling would be insipid, and little better than fatigue and drudgery.

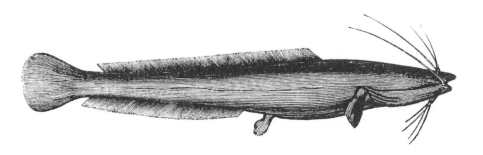

CHAPTER XVIII.

RETURN FROM THE KY-GARIEP TO KLAARWATER.

November 13th. Our stay at the *Yellow River* having been continued till the objects I had in view were attained, orders were yesterday given to prepare for returning to Klaarwater; and early this morning, all the waggons were drawn out of the grove up to the top of the bank, in order to be there loaded; as it would not have been an easy task for the teams to drag them, and their loads, up the steep sandy ascent which backed the woods. Very heavy rains had fallen during the night, and most of the people were thoroughly drenched with water. As there was every appearance of these showers being followed by a continuance of wet weather, none of the Hottentots objected to turn homewards; especially as they had now procured a large stock of dried game, and felt a desire to lie in their huts, and eat it at their ease.

I had determined on returning by a new route, in order to explore a different part of the country, and Mr. Jansz very readily agreed to accompany me; but the Klaarwater Hottentots showed no such disposition to oblige. They talked of nothing but the difficulties and dangers of the course I wished to take; there was, they said, no beaten road; a certain steep, rocky ascent, would be found impassable; the hook-thorns would tear our clothes to pieces; the lions would eat up half our oxen; and, finally, the Bushmen, who in that direction were uncommonly savage, would murder us all. In this manner they are too often in the habit of inventing any tales that may answer their own views; for, the truth was, they wished to join the party of women whom we had left behind cutting rushes; and, finding that Mr. Jansz and I were not to be dissuaded from our purpose, they left us, and drove off, taking the road to the rush-cutters.

With some persuasion, Kok, the Klaarwater chief, was at last induced to accompany us, as the missionary stated to him that the principal object which he had in view, was to ascertain whether a settlement might not be formed at a certain place known by the name of *Groote Fontein* (Great Fountain) which lay in a north-westward direction.

Our party, therefore, consisted of Dam's two waggons, with his wife and family, and another Hottentot waggon, besides the missionaries and my own two; mustering, with the women and children, above twenty persons, with about half that number of dogs. These faithful animals might now be looked at, without exciting that painful compassion for their wretched lean bodies which one could not help feeling when they first left Klaarwater. Their sleek and improved appearance, their contented looks, declared them to have been living in plenty and enjoyment, heightened at the same time by perfect freedom.

I now took my final view of the *Yellow River*, and of the pleasant woods which mark its winding course. I had derived so much pleasure from its scenery, that I left it with regret; and while I still surveyed its glittering surface, my imagination personified its ever-flowing stream, and warmly apostrophized it with a last farewell.

We travelled over a plain of boundless extent, producing much grass, in some places, and a few bushes of *Tarchonanthus* and *Rhigozum*. The soil seemed excellent, and capable of producing abundance of corn, if managed with due attention to the rainy season : it had the appearance of good loam, but was rather a mixture of clay and sand. At this time, all the grass, though still standing, was completely dried up like hay ; and if it had been set on fire, the conflagration would have spread with the greatest rapidity over the plain.

Innumerable *ant-hills*, of large dimensions, interrupted the evenness of the surface. * They were of an obtuse conical form, and so hard and firm, as to bear the weight of a man, yet the wheels of a loaded waggon easily cut through them. Sometimes, however, they are found to resist even this weight, and, in such cases, are carefully avoided to prevent an overturn. This hardness is, perhaps, owing rather to the nature of the soil than to a different species of insect. The height of the hillocks was generally from two to three feet, but higher were not unfrequently seen. Their structure was irregularly cellular, and not unlike a volcanic honeycomb-stone ; or rather consisted of perforations, or passages, opening into each other, without any apparently methodical plan. I brought away a piece of the hillock, and some of its laborious little architects. † In this en-

---

* The *engraving* at page 446, may give an idea of these *ant-hills*, and of the appearance of the country. These hillocks are not unfrequently met with of larger dimensions than are here represented ; but extraordinary as they may appear to a European eye, care has been taken to avoid exaggerating their magnitude, and they may be regarded as not exceeding the average dimensions. The bush on the left in the foreground, is intended to show the singular ramification of the *Driedoorn.* (*Rhigozum trichotomum.*) The larger bush on the right, is a *Tarchonanthus*, and near to it, two hillocks exhibit the manner in which the *ant-eater* (see page 342) scratches holes in them in order to disturb and get at the ants. It has also been attempted, as well as this style of engraving admits of, to represent the picturesque effect of journeying over a country without roads, and the deep track of the waggon wheels over an untravelled soil.

† A species of the genus *Formica* of Linnæus, and of the sub-genus *Polyergus* of Latreille.

Nigrescens. Abdomen rufo-pilosum, maculis tribus nudis nigris. Maxillæ septemdentatæ, dente ultimo acuto reliquis duplò longiore.

graving, both these objects are represented of their natural size; although the ant here delineated (a neuter) must be considered as one of the largest of the species: many others, much smaller, are always found in the same hillock, which, from analogy with European ants, may be supposed to be the males.

We were now met by a thunder storm, so violent that the oxen were hardly able to advance against it; and we found it necessary to halt a few minutes till the force of it abated. Rain fell in torrents, and along with it a great deal of hail, of the size of large peas. Every hollow became almost instantly a pond; and the heat of the weather, which, before the storm came on, was of a dry quality, and not unpleasant, was now rendered sultry and oppressive.

Large worms, above six inches long, and nearly three quarters of an inch thick, were observed crawling along the ground, drawn out of their holes by the rain. This insect never makes its appearance but just after a shower; at no other time, is it any where to be seen. The Hottentots call it the *Regenwerm* (Rain-worm); a name so perfectly appropriate, that I have adopted it in the specific name of *pluvialis*. It is nearly the largest species of the genus *Iulus*.

It being not possible to reach the Groote Fontein this day, without travelling in the dark, a practice I objected to on account of its preventing my examining the country as we passed along, we halted at an early hour of the afternoon, at a small pond just formed by the rain, and capable of affording us and our cattle a sufficiency of water till the next day. As our bleak and exposed situation, in the midst of an open plain, without the shelter of a tree, or scarcely a bush, made it difficult to restrain the oxen from straying away in the night, we placed the waggons in a circle, and connected them together by the *trektouws*; to which, and to the wheels, our cattle were made fast with *reims*.

Towards evening, thunder-clouds collected in every quarter, and the night became excessively dark; until some black; formidable, and massy clouds, which seemed to have the solidity of rocks, burst open all at once, and, with very little thunder, emitted every instant the most vivid flashes of lightning; which, although they rendered for the moment every object as light and visible as by day, left us in the intervals blinded by impenetrable darkness. In addition to this, torrents of the heaviest rain poured down upon us; and, if it did not throw us, as it did our cattle, into confusion, it impeded, however, the work which was necessary to be done, and left us supperless, through the difficulty of keeping up a fire for cooking.

Such nights I already knew, by dear-bought experience, favour the prowling lion, and seem to give him a spirit of daringness which he seldom evinces at other times. Taking advantage of the disorder and confusion into which the other animals are thrown by the conflicting elements, which make no impression upon him, he appears to advance upon them with less caution than usual. This, at least, was now found to be the case; for at a little after nine, while all of us were lying in the waggons, the dogs commenced a barking and howling; the whole of the oxen suddenly made efforts to get loose, and began to express that peculiar kind of uneasiness which, in a very intelligible manner, told us that a lion was not far off. There is probably something in the smell of this beast quite different from that of others, by which, at a great distance, especially if to windward, his prey perceive his approach, and are warned to escape their danger, by instant flight. It was this natural or instinctive propensity to fly, which occasioned our oxen to struggle and endeavour to get loose; but fortunately for them, the strength of the *reims* prevented their doing this. Yet their efforts to disengage themselves were so violent, that my waggon was in great risk of being overturned; and for some time it was unsafe to remain in it. A fire is generally sufficient to hold the lion at a distance; but ours was at this time extinguished by the rain; on which account he pressed closer upon us. Fortunately, some muskets fired at random, or aimed only by guess, had the effect not only of keeping him off, but of quieting, in a great degree, the restlessness of the cattle. The Hottentots say that the oxen have sagacity enough to know that the discharge of muskets, under such circumstances, is for the purpose of driving away their dreaded enemy; and, whatever may be the notions of these poor animals on the subject, such is certainly the effect commonly produced on them, as I often myself witnessed on subsequent occasions. Perhaps it is, that a certain instinct they may possess, enables them to discover that the beast does actually retreat when muskets are fired off. We could discover, from an unusual and peculiar barking of the dogs, that he continued prowling round us till midnight; but his fears to encounter man, were the only obstacle to prevent his carrying off his prey; and finding it thus too strongly protected, he at last withdrew. All then became quiet, and we again lay ourselves down to rest till morning.

14*th*. Speelman, who had been out hunting very early, returned after four hours' absence, to inform us that he had shot two quakkas, a male and a female, which he had left in the plain about four miles off, at a considerable distance out of our road. I therefore altered my course, while the other waggons continued on in the direct road.

The weather, the whole day, was remarkably fine, yet very hot; and the moisture of the air, from the rain of the day before, caused a great sensation of lassitude, and rendered the ordinary business of travelling very fatiguing.

I again took the bearing of the *Table Mountain* near the *Salt-pans*, which still appeared in sight to the southward, though at such a distance that a journey of forty miles would not have brought us to it.   The clearness of the air, and the enormous extent of intermediate plains, were not, perhaps, the sole causes of our seeing this mountain: the atmosphere, now charged with moisture, might, by an increased power of refraction, enable us to behold those distant objects which, at another time, might not be visible above the horizon.   In subsequent parts of this journal, will be found many instances of the singular and curious effects of that power.

Further onwards we had from a rising ground a fine view to the northward, of a high, flat, wall-like mountain stretching out to the right and to the left, and to which we could see no termination.   It had much the appearance of the Roggeveld Mountains, as viewed from the Karro *; but it was not quite so high.   Like those mountains, it had no very perceptible descent on the northern side.   This is a continuation of the same terrace or elevated platform, but far exceeding it in height, from which we descended in travelling from Klaarwater to the Black River †, whence, as I learnt, it extends downwards along the northern side of the Gariep, though in a less regular form, for the distance of several days journey; but of its extent towards the north-east, no one was able to inform me.   It is close under this mountain where *Groote Fontein* is situated.   Several of these gigantic steps, as they may be called, divide the surface in various parts of the southernmost quarter of Africa; but beyond this I never afterwards, when advancing more into the Interior, met with any other.   It is this range which apparently directs the general course of the river, and restrains it from flowing more northerly: and certainly by this the Black River is turned, and prevented from continuing its course to the northward.

On arriving at the spot where the two quakkas lay, we halted to take off the hide.   This being the first large quadruped of which I preserved the skin, it was necessary to show my Hottentots in what manner it ought to be cut, so that, if it should hereafter be stuffed,

* Page 246.   † Page 389.

it might appear as little injured as possible; otherwise their mode of going to work would soon have made it useless for this purpose.

One of the animals was a full-grown male; the other, which was much smaller, was a young female. They were in all respects alike, excepting that the abdominal, longitudinal stripe of the female was the darker, and its light stripes whiter, and dark stripes fainter, of a browner color, and not so well defined as in the male. This latter had much the form of a small, strong, and well-made poney. The skin of this, and the meat of both, were loaded upon the two waggons.

The rocks in this part, are of the same species of primitive lime-rock as that which had been noticed in the neighbourhood of Klaar-water. As we approached *Groote Fontein* (Great Fountain), we passed many trees, which we observed more numerous and crowded the nearer we advanced to the spring. They consisted chiefly of the Cape Acacias, with many *Hookthorn* trees twelve or fourteen feet high. The *Rhus tridactyle* also was remarkable by its delicate foliage. *

The sun was still an hour and a half above the horizon, when we reached the foot of the pass over these mountains, and unyoked at *Groote Fontein*, near the spring, in a pleasant grove, in the midst of which the water is situated. A large solitary tree of *Kameel-doorn* † (Camel-thorn, or the tree on which, generally, the Camelopardalis browses), the first I had seen of the species, was standing here.

Close under the mountain, three springs of good water issue from the earth, and, uniting, form a rill, which at this time lost itself, or was dried up, after running a course of three or four hundred

---

* In this day's journey, six new insects of the *Grylline* tribe were found in the plain; and eight new plants were added to the herbarium.

Aptosimum, species 2	*Mahernia*
Sida	*Aizoon*. Catal. Geogr. 1790. Species
Phyllanthus	notabilis, lignosa sesquipedalis.

† *Acacia Giraffæ*. Of this remarkable tree a more particular account will be found in the second volume.

yards.   It was sheltered by reeds and a large sedge *, intermingled
with a tall and beautiful species of grass †; on the roots of which,
and every where on the ground, the water had deposited a calcareous
incrustation, similar to that which I first observed at Schiet Fontein,
and afterward at Klaarwater and the neighbouring springs. A *Statice*,
growing plentifully about the rivulet, would seem to indicate some
brackish quality in the earth, and, consequently, in the water also;
which, at a distance from the fountain-head, it was found actually
to possess, though not in a very unpleasant degree.

All the species of the genus *Statice* grow, with few exceptions,
either on the sea-shore or on saline ground. Many plants are excellent indicators of the nature of the soil; and the agriculturist
would do well, in bringing new land under culture, to allow himself
to be guided by the hints they offer. So unaccommodating in this
respect are a great number of the vegetable creation, that in vain are
their seeds dispersed by the winds or the waters, unless they happen
to fall in such situations as afford them that terrestrial food, and
aërial nourishment, to which their peculiar structure has been by
Nature adapted. Observers of vegetable physiology have not yet
been enabled to offer any satisfactory explanation of the causes
of those properties of plants which may be termed their instinct, and
which are shown by their affecting particular soils; or situations; or
climates; or cold or heat; or dryness or moisture. Knowledge of this
kind is a desideratum, the practical utility of which, and its application
to numberless and various purposes, might render it worthy of the attention of those who pursue the investigation of physical science.

15*th*. At this place the *Kloof*, or *Pass* up the mountain, is
more even and less steep than any other passage that the Hottentots have hitherto discovered in this range. We were, however,
obliged to keep six men employed for two days, with spades and
pickaxes, in filling up the holes and ravines made by the torrents,

---

* Of the same genus as the *Palmite*, described at page 91.
† A species of *Saccharum*.   Catal. Geogr. 1810.

and in removing out of the way large blocks of stone, which otherwise would have rendered the passage extremely dangerous. This
work, though performed under an almost broiling sun, was not much
objected to, either by the Hottentots or by their captain, since what
was now done would make the kloof safely passable for all who
should hereafter travel that road. Yet, because the work was one
for general advantage, no one had cared even to roll a stone out of
the way; each one preferred the risk of overturning his waggon,
and breaking his own neck, to a day's labour, by which the whole
community were always in future to be benefitted. Had we not insisted on returning by this road to Klaarwater, the pass would long
have remained in its dangerous state; and without our persuasion
and encouragement, no one, perhaps, would ever have bestowed his
time and labour upon it. This circumstance is mentioned with a
view to exemplify a disposition very common, not only among Hottentots, but equally frequent in the Cape colony, where the roads,
with very few exceptions, though daily made use of, are allowed
to remain from year to year in a state of the greatest neglect, each
boor getting his waggon over them in the best manner he may be
able, nor caring for his own risk, or for the neighbour who may be
obliged to follow his track.

Early this morning it was discovered that all our sheep had
strayed away in the course of the night. Without loss of time,
Speelman, with two other Hottentots, was sent on the search, by
following their footmarks from out of the fold.

When evening came, without either returning, we began to feel
much uneasiness on account of the men, and which continued increasing all the following day. In these wild, desert, and lawless
countries, the mind, always ready to feel mistrustful and suspicious
of treachery, easily takes alarm at every occurrence which may
wear a dubious look. The Bushmen are immediately suspected; the
lions, with all the other ferocious animals together, share not a
tenth of the imputation which falls on these necessitous savages.

16th. At noon, while we were still expressing great fears that
the natives had carried off the sheep and murdered our men, Speel-

man and his companions made their appearance, driving before them
the whole of our little flock.   We had thus a double cause for rejoicing ; but when we found that the sheep had been followed by
means of their *track*, as far as our station at the confluence of the
Black River, every one was surprised that they had not been scattered and destroyed, at least by the wild beasts ; among which the
Wilde Hond (Wild Dog), a new and distinct species of *Hyena* *, is
here the most destructive to the flocks.   The Hottentots had fallen
in with some straggling Bushmen, whose behaviour towards them
was perfectly friendly.

In this vicinity we discovered a kraal of *Bushmen*.   Their numbers did not exceed twenty, and their abode was merely a cavern in
the side of the mountain, sheltered by huge impending crags.   They
had no earthly possessions whatever, excepting the miserable bit of
dirty skin which hung round them ; their bows and arrows, a few
hassagays, a knife, and two or three ostrich egg-shells.   They had
not even a hut, or a few mats, like most of their countrymen.
Neither beads, nor any thing intended as ornament, were to be seen
upon them : their persons, meagre and filthy, too plainly bespoke
that hunger had often been their lot.   Except when any game was
caught in their pitfalls, which, they complained, seldom happened,
the only procurable support of life, was the wild roots which they
daily dug up in the plains ; and these, not found but by long and
wearisome search : the eggs of ants, the bodies of snakes or lizards,
a tortoise, or an ostrich egg, met with accidentally, formed the only
variety in their wretched food.   Their life, and that of the wild
beasts, their fellow inhabitants of the land, were the same.   Of both,
the only care seemed to be that of feeding themselves, and of bringing
up their young.   The four men who visited us to-day, exhibited
their lank, shrivelled bodies, and dry parched arms and legs, to
convince us how much they needed provisions, and how long they

---

* *Hyena venatica.* B. Fusca, undiquè maculis irregularibus nigris, cum paucis
albis, variegata. Linea nigra faciem percurrens. Auriculæ maximæ lato-ovatæ nigræ sub-
nudæ. Cauda villosa, extremâ parte albâ, annulo unico nigro. Metacarpi longissimi.
  A more particular account of this animal will be given in another place.

had been without grease or animal food. They looked first wish-
fully at our pots which stood on the fire, and then submissively at
us. Truly, these were the most destitute of beings, and the lowest
in the scale of man. Their miserable poverty-stricken appearance
excited the greatest compassion; and as they stood before me, this
wretched picture of human nature created a train of reflections perfectly new to my mind. What I had as yet seen of man in a wild
state, had amused while it interested and instructed me; but this
sad resemblance, in outward shape, to those great, intellectual and
elevated characters, whose genius and talents have made their names
immortal among us, distressed me to melancholy; and while my
eyes were fixed in painful observation on their vacant countenances,
I asked myself, What is man? and had almost said; Surely all the
inhabitants of the globe never sprang from the same origin! These
men seemed, indeed, the outcast of the Bushman race. Yet, not to
be unjust to them, I must own that I have seen many like them; but
not, however, till a later period of my travels. I have now, I think,
beheld and known the lowest of the human species; and it has
taught me a lesson of humility and gratitude; it has rendered still
greater, my admiration and respect for men of intellect and cultivated minds; it has also taught me to be thankful to the industrious
workman; to feel kind compassion for the uneducated and the uncivilized; and to despise the idle, the arrogant, and vain.

To feed the hungry, is one of the pleasures of the philanthropist;
but that pleasure was here somewhat alloyed by the dog-like voracity
with which they ate the meat we gave them, and their selfishness in
not saving any of it to take home to their families. To this repast
we added some pipes of tobacco, which raised their enjoyment to its
highest. They squatted on the ground by the fire, with the rest of
our people; and remained till late in the evening before they thought
of returning home to their kraal. I took my seat also amongst them,
that I might the better watch their manners; but finding at last that
their smoking absorbed all their thoughts, and created an incapacity,
as well as a disinclination, for conversation, I retired to my waggon,
to try if the sound of my flute would have any effect upon them.

With this they expressed themselves pleased; and even took the trouble of coming to the waggon, to see by what means, and in what manner, the music was produced: but the airs, though some of the liveliest, inspired no visible gaiety; nor was the least demonstration of keeping time, by any motion of the body, observable. Yet they certainly felt some gratification; especially an old man, their chief, who was considered a good performer on the *Goráh*, an instrument of the greatest antiquity of all those which are now to be found in the hands of any tribe of the Hottentot race. Curious to see and to hear a genuine Hottentot musical instrument, I gave him to understand that I wished him to bring it on the morrow, and give me a specimen of his playing; to which he readily agreed.

17th. On the morrow he returned; bringing with him, not only his Goráh, but several women, and all his family; who, till now, had not ventured to approach us, or, more probably, had been restrained by the men from coming. All his companions, whom we had entertained the day before, together with his two sons, repeated their visit, and were again well feasted.

The *Goráh*, as to its appearance and form, may be more aptly compared to the bow of a violin, than to any other thing; but, in its principle and use, it is quite different; being, in fact, that of a stringed, and a wind instrument combined: and thus it agrees with the Æolian harp. But with respect to the principle on which its different *tones* are produced, it may be classed with the trumpet, or French horn; while in the nature and quality of the sound which it gives, at least in the hands of one who is master of it, this strange instrument approaches to the violin.

It consists merely of a slender stick, or bow, on which a string of catgut is strained. But to the lower end of this string, a flat piece, of about an inch and a half long, of the quill of an ostrich, is attached, so as to constitute a part of the length of the string. *

---

* See the *representation* of this part of the *Goráh* of the natural size, at the end of the present chapter

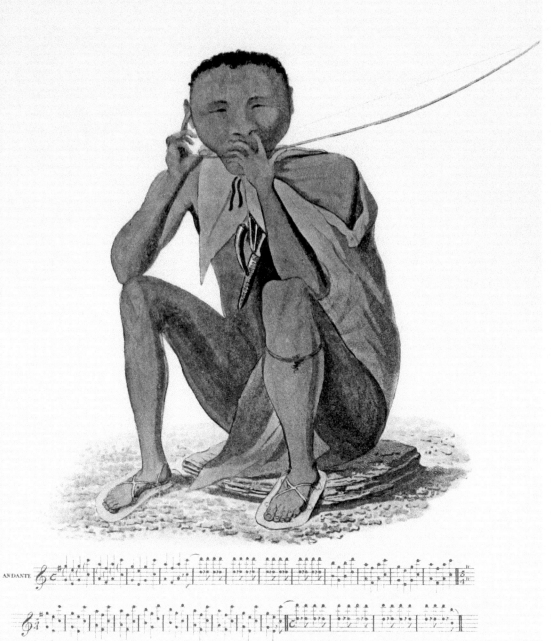

Portrait of a Bushman, playing on the Goráh

This quill, being applied to the lips, is made to vibrate by strong inspirations, and expirations, of the breath; each of which ending with an increased degree of strength, had always the effect of forcing out the upper octave; exactly in the same way as produced on the flute, an instrument, therefore, which may be made to imitate the gorah sufficiently near to give some idea of it.

The old musician, seating himself down on a flat piece of rock, and resting his elbows on his knees, putting one fore-finger into his ear, and the other into his wide nostril, either as it so happened, or for the purpose, it might be, of keeping the head steady, commenced his solo, and continued it with great earnestness, over and over again. The exertion which it required to bring out the tones loudly, was very evident; and, in his anxious haste to draw breath at every note, our *Orpheus* gave us into the bargain, intermingled with his music, certain grunting sounds which would have highly pleased the pigs; and, if any had been in the country, would indubitably have drawn them all round him, if only out of curiosity to know what was the matter.

In the mean time, I was not less employed than he, being obliged to exercise two faculties at the same time; one to listen to, and learn the notes he was playing, so as to enable me to write them down correctly; the other to draw his figure and portrait. The accompanying plate* presents a likeness of him, and is a copy of the

---

* *Plate* 9. His dress, reddened by an ochraceous earth, consists only of a leathern *kaross*, which is of smaller dimensions than those customarily worn. Suspended from his neck, is a knife of African manufacture, such as are worn, in a similar manner, by all the tribes in the Interior. The horn of one of the smaller antelopes, hanging from the same place, serves the purpose of a snuff-box, or receptacle for powdered dakka, or hemp-leaves. Below the knee, a cord of acacia-bark was worn as an ornament. The sandals are such as form part of the aboriginal dress of all the natives of Southern Africa, with no other variation than in the mode of their being bound to the foot. In Bushmen who are a little advanced in life, the eye-lids are often so much closed as to conceal the whole of the eye-ball, and to leave an aperture but just sufficient for the sight, a circumstance which gives to such individuals, as in the present, the appearance of having their eyes shut; this they probably are obliged to do, to protect them from the glare of sunshine. The piece of rock on which he sits, will show the geological character of the neighbouring

drawing made on the spot. Beneath are added the *notes* expressed in the manner in which they were played; or, at least, as they sounded to my ear: although I find a difficulty in conceiving how an instrument, giving its tones on the principle above described, can produce either the *tonum majus* or the *heptachordon*. The crotchets, of that part which is in triple time, were exactly of the same length as those in the common time preceding and following; consequently, the time, reckoning by bars, was there accelerated. The whole piece, played once through, occupied just seventy seconds, and was repeated without variation. There is sufficient in these few notes, to show that he possessed an ear capable of distinguishing musical intervals; and they are besides remarkable, under all circumstances, as a specimen of natural modulation. In the following year, I had an opportunity of noting down other pieces of Bushman music, which were in a style much differing from that which is here given.

Our female visitors, who were past the middle age, were extremely filthy and ugly; their small blinking eyes seemed as if nearly closed, or sunk into their head; wrinkles, filled with dirt, covered their faces and body; their hair was clotted together in large lumps, with the accumulated grease and dust of years, perhaps of their whole lives; and the odor with which they tainted the air, kept me at the distance of a couple of yards, the nearest at which a person having any delicacy of smell, could endure their presence. A wooden bowl, in which was left a quantity of liquid Hippopotamus grease, was eagerly seized upon, and its contents drunk off, with an avidity most nauseous and disgusting to behold; while that which still adhered to the bowl, they carefully scraped out with their hands, and smeared upon their bodies.

Curious to know what degree of *intellect* these beings possessed, I endeavoured, by means of an interpreter, to question them on a

---

mountain: but the ground has been engraved in too spotted a manner. By a mistake of the engraver, the hair is represented too much like curls, instead of wool, as described at page 161.; but this has, in some measure, been rectified by the colouring.

few moral points; but he declared they were so stupid that it was not in his power to make them comprehend at all. The principal question, and to which I was most desirous of having their answer, was, one would think, so intelligible, that their not understanding it must have been either pretended stupidity, or a wilful misrepresentation by the interpreter: I asked what they considered to be *good* actions, and what, *bad*; but to this they made no reply, nor could they at all conceive its meaning. I showed them a looking-glass: at this they laughed, and stared with vacant surprize and wonder, to see their own faces; but expressed not the least curiosity about it; nor do I believe it excited in their minds one single idea; and I may not, perhaps, be doing them an injustice by asserting that, whether capable of reflection or not, these individuals never exerted it. When asked what were their thoughts respecting the glass; what were their notions respecting white men; their senseless looks seemed to say, they made an effort to think, but found themselves utterly unable: their only answer was; I don't know.

They related to us, without the least emotion, and with apparent indifference, a horrid occurrence which had lately taken place in their kraal. This old man had three sons, one of whom had been married several years to a woman by whom he had two children. One of the brothers had conceived a liking for the woman, and she on her part was not averse to change her husband; it was therefore agreed between them, that he should be put out of their way. This (I shudder in relating it) was accomplished by the atrocious demon beating out his brother's brains as he lay asleep. This inhuman act appears to have excited no feelings of horror in the horde: the pair were at this time living together contented, and, seemingly, undismayed by their own reflections on the nefarious deed they had committed. Conscience herself seemed to have neglected her duty, and bestial ignorance to have usurped her place. Instead of chasing him for ever out of their kraal, the father and the remaining brother allowed him to continue in their society on the same terms as if nothing of the kind had happened. I saw the murderer; he was a youth of apparently seventeen or eighteen years of age, and of not an unpleasing countenance. Nothing, I must confess, was discoverable in the behaviour of either him, his father, brother or companions, which could be thought to corroborate the tale we had heard; and I felt a strong suspicion that our Klaarwater interpreter had acted a treacherous part towards them in the version he gave us of their story.

But if it was, in fact, such as we were told, I would, were it not repugnant to reason and our belief in the existence of such knowledge in every individual of the human race, say; Here are men who know not right from wrong. Without fearing to be classed with the approvers of those self-deluded enthusiasts, who believe their own unfitness for the task to be compensated by a special and supernatural assistance from the Deity; who go forth under the presumptuous idea of being selected by Divine will to be the instrument of converting the heathen nations to Christianity, and who too frequently exaggerate the little they accomplish; without being an approver of their system and principles, I cannot but emphatically say; How worthy of the talents of a great and good man, would be the task of teaching savages such as these, to acknowledge a Deity, and guide themselves by the unchanging, eternal laws of right and wrong!

This being *Sunday*, Mr. Jansz caused all the Hottentots to assemble under the trees, and the customary divine service, consisting of singing psalms, and expounding a part of the Scriptures, was performed. That part of Ezekiel *, containing the prophecy of the valley of dry bones, was selected for explanation; and was interpreted to signify the future conversion of all heathens to Christianity. The Bushmen, whose deplorable ignorance we had just witnessed, and who were, perhaps, the occasion of that passage being selected, were present at the service, which, however, being in the Dutch language, was, of course, not understood by them; and if it had been, I should doubt that they would be the better for it.

---

* Chap. xxxvii. ver. 1—10.

18th. After a due examination of the place, *Groote Fontein* was pronounced to be an eligible spot for a new station, or out-post, for the Klaarwater people; and it was decided that Adam Kok, on his return home, should make the necessary arrangements, and appoint a fit person as overseer of the new settlement, which, I proposed to Mr. Anderson, that the missionaries should call by the name of *Jansz's Fountain*, after the artless, honest missionary who first set it on foot. Its latitude, as determined by the meridian-altitude of a star, is 28° 49′ 23″ S.* On the top of the mountain an excellent spot was found, which might easily be converted into corn-land. It abounded in water; and not fewer than ten different springs were discovered within a very short distance of each other, the waters of which uniting, formed a rill that trickled down the Kloof and joined the springs below.

The Bushmen, to whom in some degree the place belonged, as they were the inhabitants of the spot, or at least reside almost constantly in the vicinity, professed themselves glad at having the Klaarwater people for neighbours; and were perfectly ready to admit them and their cattle to the free use of the water and surrounding pasture; promising, at the same time, to conduct themselves as good friends towards the new comers. They felt, indeed, in the abundance of provisions which they had received from us during our stay, a persuasive argument, and powerful inducement, for being sincere in this promise.

They all exhibited, but the old man more remarkably, a proof of the good effects of our hospitality; and gave me the opportunity of witnessing how wonderfully and rapidly their appearance is improved by a plentiful supply of food. I should, without such proof, have thought it incredible, that so great an alteration could possibly take place in four days. On their first visit to us, the skin of their bodies hung in large wrinkles; and the meagre emaciated state in which we found them, excited our greatest commiseration. But

---

* November.15. 1811, at *Groote Fontein*, the observed altitude of γ *Pegasi*, when on the meridian, was 47° 3′ 17″.

now the old man's wrinkles had quite disappeared ; his body was smooth and ridiculously plump ; his skin now seemed to have a flow of blood beneath it, and his sleek, well-anointed limbs, seemed to have grown larger. I found that I had been mistaken, at least ten years, in his age ; and when we parted, he was but a middle-aged man.

At this station I added several new birds to my collection *, and amongst them a cuckoo of exceedingly beautiful plumage, with a glossy metallic lustre of green and gold ; a bee-eater, very much like the European species ; and a handsome oriole, which weaves a globular nest of grass, and attaches it between two reeds, overhanging the water. Besides these birds, I saw a variety of others with which I was already acquainted. †

Sometimes at night the *jackals* came within a little distance, and repeated at short intervals a loud yelping noise, which our dogs as often answered by a sharp barking, though not in so angry a tone as had been observable, whenever a more formidable animal approached us. The Hottentots say the jackal is a fool, because he never goes out by night to steal, without betraying himself by his own barking. After amusing us in this manner for an hour or two, they went away, without making any attempt to come nearer, or without being pursued by the dogs, who contented themselves with answering bark for bark. This animal, as I judged from its voice, was the *Canis mesomelas*.

Very few insects met my eye ; two nondescript species were caught here ‡, one a handsome green beetle *(Cetonia Bachapinica)*,

---

* *Cuculus auratus.* Lin. Syst. Nat.— *Le Coucou Didric.* Le Vaill. Ois. d'Afr. pl. 210 et 211.

Turdus ———- L'Espionneur. Ois. d'Afr. pl. 103.

Muscicapa —— affinis *Le Mignard.* Ois. d'Afr. pl. 154.

Oriolus arundinarius, B.— Mas.— Citrinus. Facies atra. Alæ fuscæ, remigibus et tegminibus flavo marginatis. Dorsum et cauda fusco-virescentia. Uropygium flavum. Nidus globosus, ex graminum foliis contextus, inter arundinum culmos suspensus.

† *Upupa purpurea,* B. was met with at this place.

‡ *Cetonia Bachapinica,* B.— Fulva. Thorax rufescente (aliquando æruginoso-) fuscus, fulvo marginatus. Caput lineis duabus albis striatum. Corpus subtus album, lineis transversis rufis. Longa 8—11 lineas.

which I found afterwards much more numerous in the country of the Bachapins. My little friend, *Mantis lucubrans* *, always paid me an evening visit, whenever the weather was fine.

At this place thirty-three species of plants were added to my catalogue †, among which was a small *asclepiadeous* plant called " *Tky*," by our Hottentots, who value it on account of the root, which is of the size of a round flat turnip; and being full of a watery juice, it is often used by the natives to relieve their thirst, when traversing these arid regions. Southern Africa produces many plants of this order, with a large bulbous eatable root, all of which are well known to the native inhabitants, who, not always distinguishing their differences, apply the same name to various species. A sort

---

Anthia fimbriata. This I adopt for the *Carabus fimbriatus* of Th. and Olivier, on the authority of *Dr. Leach*, whose character as an entomologist is too well known to stand in need of my praise.

Anthia ———-. Atra. Thorax posticè productus bilobus; ad latera dilatatus, areis humeralibus ovatis fulvis hirsutis. Elytrorum margines albæ hirsutæ. Maxillæ longitudine capitis. Longitudo, duo ferè pollices. Affinis *Carabo thoracico*, Th : An eadem?

* *Mantis lucubrans*, B. Tota cinereo-fusca. Alæ venis nigris reticulatæ. Corpus subtùs incarnatum. Longitudo, 17 lineæ.

† *Polygala ephedroïdes*, B. Catal. Geogr. 1793. Fruticulus, 2 - pedalis et ultra, ferè aphyllus. Rami teretes erecti. Folia minima, linearia. Flores in apicibus ramulorum spicati nutantes majusculi.

Rhus pyroïdes. B.
Rhus tridactyle. B.
Salvia ethiopis
Clematis brachiata
Polygala rigens. B. Catal. Geogr. 1821. Fruticulus spithameus ramosus rigidus pubescens. Folia linearia obtusa canaliculata, marginibus apicequè reflexis. Flores minuti sparsi.
Cynanchum viminale ?
Euclea n. s.
Samolus Valerandi. Th.

Celastrus, a remarkable species, with a profusion of slender horizontal thorns, twice or thrice as long as the leaves.
Mentha
Cissampelos
Scabiosa
Tanacetum ?
Gomphocarpus
Andropogon
Festuca
Saccharum
Juncus 3 sp.
Scirpus? 2 sp.
Cyperus
Statice
Convolvulus
Phlomis
Sanseviera, &c.

3 o

of mint, having a very pleasant smell, grows here by the water, and is a plant frequently met with in similar situations, both on this, and on the southern side of the Gariep ; and it deserves remark, that it has been found to endure the hardest winters of England equally well with any of the British species.

At noon our waggons began to ascend the mountain, and safely reached the top of the pass, without any of the difficulty which had been expected. From the summit, the view to the southward was most extensive, and much resembling the prospect from the top of the Roggeveld mountain, looking over the Karro. The country beyond the Yellow River, appeared at this elevation and distance to be flat ; but hills of moderate height could not have been distinguished through the blue vapor of so great a depth of atmosphere. From such situations, a country may appear level to the eye of the spectator, which, in reality, is far otherwise, but a little experience will be sufficient to caution the traveller against forming his opinion under such circumstances.

Having gained the summit of the mountain, the country was found level and open, and without any descent on that side. Just above the pass, are the springs already mentioned ; copious rills of clear water were flowing in every direction ; and one of them, issuing from out of a rock, was colder than the others. The surrounding soil abounded in *Wilde Knoflook* (Wild Garlick) *, the smell of which, as we walked over it, was strong and disagreeable, and remarkably like garlick ; but towards evening the flowers give out a sweet and pleasant odor.

Knowing from my observations, that the latitude of this place was nearly the same as that of Klaarwater, I had now an opportunity of convincing the Hottentots of the value and utility of my compass, of which, I recollected, they had a few months ago some doubts. By the aid of this instrument, I placed a long stick on the ground, exactly in the direction of west ; and told them

---

* *Tulbaghia alliacea.*

that, although, as they knew, I was not in the least acquainted with the road we were about to take, that little box showed that Klaarwater lay just where that stick pointed to. On this they set themselves to consider very attentively where the village was situated. Some pointed in one direction, some in another; and it was amusing to observe how much each prided himself upon being correct; this kind of knowledge being, among Hottentots, held as an accomplishment, and one which they all endeavour to acquire. Those who differed widely from the general bearing, were much laughed at, and made the subject of some Hottentot jokes, but every thing was said in perfect good humour.

This little trial of skill afforded us a short diversion, and as the most experienced amongst them pointed to the same quarter as my stick, the compass was viewed as a most wonderful thing, and gained the greatest attention and respect; while at the same time, I came in myself for a share.

This incident was not forgotten, when some time afterwards I had occasion to propose an expedition through an unknown part of the country, in which I engaged to show the way.

The country we passed over this day presented no new or remarkable feature; it was flat and open; the surface very rocky, although covered with grass and shrubs, few of which were new to me *. Below the mountain the superstratum every where is a deep fertile mould; but above, and in general all the way to Klaarwater, the ground is a hard rock, quite bare in many places, or but thinly covered with earth. It would seem, therefore, that the soil of the lower country is strictly alluvial, and has been washed down from the plains above.

After travelling two and twenty miles, till a quarter before eight, when it began to grow dark, and the rain, which had been

---

* *Olea*
Reseda dipetala. var ? Cat. Geogr. 1828.
Mentha, 2 sp.
Carex flavescens. B. Cat. Geogr. 1831.

Chrysocoma
Gomphocarpus
Bryonia

encreasing for the last hour, became so heavy that we could not proceed, we unyoked in an open plain, without shelter for ourselves, or water for the cattle. But as the night was wet, and the grass and bushes hanging with drops of rain, the oxen did not suffer much from thirst; and our own wants were supplied from the rocky hollows.

19*th*. The inconvenience of our halting place caused every one to be desirous of departing, and at sun-rise we began to yoke the teams; but it was not till half-past six that all the waggons were in motion. The day promised to be fair, and the expectation of reaching home this afternoon, inspired the party with a cheerful activity. But, as if to check their unusual haste and exercise them in patience, a virtue which no one knows better than a Hottentot, but which even he will sometimes forget, we had scarcely proceeded three miles, when the Captain's old rickety waggon got out of repair, and detained us three quarters of an hour before it could be put in a condition to bear moving. This being done, they started once more; and, to make up for lost time, encreased their bustling heedlessness and doubled their haste; a haste without an object. Hardly had the crazy vehicle been dragged on a quarter of a mile further, when again the shattered wheel refused to perform its functions. Another half hour was spent in cobbling and bungling; patching and binding up with leathern thongs, and knocking the diseased part with stones, as though they expected that was to make it sound again. Still, as I stood by, amused at their awkwardness, I doubted whether the dying waggon would ever see its home again, till the Captain, with a determination which evinced his courage, resolved that the oxen should draw, whether the waggon would follow or not. And it was to the great joy of us all, that at last we beheld it tottering on before us, ever and anon giving a sudden drop as the wheel revolved; which, to the chief's lady and family, who sat within, was a motion productive of as many involuntary nods of the head.

We passed a spot, containing about an acre, remarkable from the circumstance of the grass, with which it was covered, being eaten down as smooth as a lawn, and as verdant. What there might be in this particular spot, so different from all the surrounding country, to occasion the peculiarity, I had not time to examine ; although it was evident, by the quantity of manure from various animals, principally quakkas, that it was their favourite grazing place.

One of the Hottentots who was in advance, surprized a large adder of most extraordinary thickness, and, by means of a long stick, killed it before I could come up with him in time to see it alive. All the people shuddered as they viewed it, and some would not venture to approach it, even though dead, so greatly is this particular species dreaded.

It is well known in the Colony, and at Klaarwater, by the name of the *Pof-Adder* (Puff Adder.)* Its venom is said to be most fatal, taking effect so rapidly as to leave the person who has the misfortune to be bitten, no chance of saving his life, but by instantly cutting out the flesh surrounding the wound. Although I have often met with this serpent, yet, happily, no opportunity occurred of witnessing the consequences of its bite : but, from the universal dread in which it is held, I have no doubt of its being one of the most venomous of Southern Africa. There is a peculiarity which renders it more dangerous, and which ought to be known by every person liable to fall in with it. Unlike the generality of snakes, which make a spring, or dart forwards, when irritated, the Puff Adder, it is said, throws itself backwards ; so that those who should be ignorant of this fact would place themselves in the very direction of death, while imagining that by so doing they were escaping the danger. The natives, by keeping always in front, are enabled to destroy it without much risk. The snakes of Africa, as of Europe, lie concealed in their holes, in a torpid state, during the colder part of the year. It is, therefore, only in the hottest summer months

---

* *Vipera inflata,* B. Fusca, undiquè fasciis transversis angulosis vel undulatis albis nigrisquè, variegata. Corpus crassissimum, 2—3-pollicare. Longitudo usquè ad 4½ pedes.

that the traveller is exposed to the danger of being bitten : that season was now just commencing.

This adder measured in the thickest part, seven inches in circumference, and three feet seven inches in length ; and, by its disproportionate thickness, may easily be distinguished from all the others of this country. I have seen one about four feet and a half long, which, probably, is the greatest size it ever attains. The general color is a dusky brown, but varied with black and cream-coloured transverse stripes, in shapes of which it is not easy to convey an idea by mere description.

The mode of travelling, and want of room in my waggon, did not admit of carrying with me all that was necessary for preserving in spirits, objects of Natural History. The bulk, the weight, the breaking of bottles, or the leaking or evaporation of kegs, had deterred me in Cape Town from making any provision for this purpose. Resolved, however, to neglect no object which my time, or circumstances, might present an opportunity of collecting, and bringing home, I found myself, in many instances, taught by necessity, methods and contrivances which I might not otherwise have discovered ; not only in the department of Natural History, but in many other affairs belonging to an expedition of this nature. These methods, whenever they occur, will be disclosed without reserve, in the hope that, to persons under similar circumstances, they may prove useful hints.

For some time at a loss how it would be possible to preserve this Puff-adder, the idea was at last imagined of drying the skin, on the same principle, and in the same manner, as would have been done with a large leaf : but then it was to be feared that by removing the flesh, all its colors would be lost; I, however, determined to try the experiment. The whole process was extremely simple ; and consisted merely in cutting it open, along the under part, entirely from the head to the point of the tail, and stripping off the skin, which was found to separate with the greatest facility. All the flesh was cut away as closely as possible to the head, which was left entire. The skin was then spread flat on a sheet of large strong paper, and placed between a number of other sheets to absorb the moisture. It was put into the press, leaving the head out so as not to be crushed, and kept there till perfectly dry; taking care every day, or every other day, to remove the sheets that had become damp, and replace them by an equal quantity of dry paper; but the skin itself was never separated from that sheet to which its inner side had adhered.

The success of this first experiment, pleased me exceedingly; for not only was the skin dried as well as could be desired, but the colors, and more delicate markings, were preserved with all the clearness and beauty of the living animal. The principle thus discovered, the practice became considerably improved in the course of my travels : and, for the convenience of bringing the whole of the subject in one point of view, I shall in this place communicate the latest results.

The skin requires no antiseptic preparation, nor any varnish to be applied to it: nor is any gum, or paste, at all necessary for making it adhere to the paper; a certain glutinous property of its own being sufficient for that purpose. No danger whatever is to be feared from handling the body; nor will any of its juices, even if adhering to the fingers, produce unpleasant consequences, since even the venom itself may be, and frequently is, swallowed without harm. On this subject some information is reserved for a future period of the Journal; and is alluded to here, merely to show how little cause there is for apprehensions on this head, provided there be no recent wound or scratch in the operator's skin through which any particle of venom can get in contact with the blood. This would be attended with consequences, dangerous in proportion as the species of snake should be more or less poisonous. As the fangs are moveable, and may easily be turned inwards, great care should be taken that they do not stand out of the mouth; for death may yet lurk in them, though all life may have left the serpent : nor would I give an assurance that even after the lapse of years, the fatal power may not still reside in the desiccated venom.

In most serpents, the skin may be cut open along the middle of the under part, and thus avoid interfering with the markings, as that part is generally of a plain pale color.   This method has the advantage of giving to the specimen the most pleasing appearance, because the most uniform.   But if there be any particular pattern on this part, the incision should be made along the side; and, perhaps, the latter method may, for the purpose of science and examination, be preferable; although it give a one-sided, less agreeable form to the specimen.   The paper used for this purpose was a strong white cartridge-paper, cut of the necessary width, and joined together, to the required length.   The most convenient mode of applying the skin to the paper, is by the assistance of a short roller, or cylinder, held in the hand, and on which the skin and paper are gradually rolled.   By these means, only one part of the skin coming on to the paper at one time, the due stretching and placing of it is managed with the greater exactness: but it should not be so much stretched as to leave a space between the scales, as this would very much derange the natural pattern of its colouring.   For safety, the head may be covered by merely turning the end of the paper over it.

The peculiar advantages of this method of preserving serpents are; that their natural colors are perfectly preserved; by being quite flat, a large collection may be put in a small compass, or they may be kept in a portfolio with all the ease of drawings, which they in some respects resemble; but with an infinite superiority in exhibiting their marks with a correctness not to be imitated by the pencil; of whatever length, they may be all folded like a map to one size; their lightness renders them so portable as entirely to do away the great objection to which bottles of spirits have always been liable with travellers; the only provision required to be made for such a collection being merely that of paper; the facility with which they may be examined and compared; by lying flat upon white paper, they no longer have that alarming and forbidding appearance which a serpent in its natural form presents to most people, but are, on the contrary, pleasing objects.   If that revolting sensation, which seems a common feeling, can be once overcome, every person will readily acknowledge that the hand of Nature has not painted the skins of snakes with less beauty than the plumage of birds.

No part of Natural History is less studied, or more in want of regulation, than the Order of Serpents, and if travellers could be persuaded to try the method I have now described, the combined results of their collections would, most probably, very soon dispel this confusion, and raise the study of *Ophiology* to a level with that of Quadrupeds, or Birds. For naturalists cannot fail to have remarked that the different branches of the science are more studied and better understood, in proportion to the facility with which the objects of each branch are collected and preserved.

I ought not in this place to omit mentioning, that, on an occasion, about a year later, when one of my Hottentots brought me a large *caterpillar*, the colors of which were exceedingly beautiful, and its delicate marks beyond the power of imitation, I was induced to try the experiment of preserving it in the manner I had adopted for the serpents. In this I met with exactly the same success; and which was afterwards fully confirmed by several other trials. But as the time required for making a collection of these, must have been taken from other affairs of more importance, and as the possession of insects in the caterpillar state only, would have been of little use to science, and merely amusing curiosities, I collected very few objects of that kind. This hint may, perhaps, be the more valuable, as many difficulties have been found hitherto in the art of preserving the larvæ with their natural colors; a desideratum which this method will accomplish, if ten years be considered sufficient for proving their permanency.

But, to return to our travelling. The country, for many miles, abounded in thick bushy olive-trees, which, by their pleasing, soft appearance, greatly relieved the uniformity of the landscape. Many of these clumps were twenty feet in diameter, and nearly as much in height.

In one of them, a Hottentot found a *Vulture's nest*, with a single young one not yet fledged, and which he brought to me. It was covered only with down, which gave it the appearance of being wrapped up in white wool. As the old bird was not seen, it is not quite certain to what species it belonged, but it was very probably the *Percnopterus.* I took this ill-fated bird home, with the intention of bringing it up tame, and for a few weeks it seemed to thrive; but depending on Philip, whom I appointed to feed it, I was often deceived, and told that it had been fed, when it had eaten nothing for a day or two. At length, after keeping it a month, it died; and I then discovered, too evidently, the proofs of its having been starved. I reproached the Hottentot, not so much for his neglect of the task he had undertaken, as for his want of feeling for the bird; but he stood unmoved at all I could say on his cruelty; and I saw that all the eloquence of man would not have touched his sensibility, for he had none. I might have done as much good by talking to one of the wheels of my waggon, and should have felt much less irritated.

Hares were now and then started from the bushes by our dogs. This animal is here as timid and as fleet as in Europe; and the dogs seem as much its natural enemies, coursing it down with a determined eagerness, as if only for the pleasure of killing it.

We passed a spot of small extent, where the rock, that here and there protruded through the grass, had much appearance of being volcanic, and was accompanied by a quantity of what seemed, as we drove past, to be lava and slag. The country in the vicinity presented no other rocks of the same complexion, nor bore any marks of the action of fire: neither was there at the spot any remarkable rising or mound resembling such as are thrown up by volcanic eruptions. Not far from this place, there are, as I was informed, three small conical hills standing in the plain, which are regarded as a singularity, on account of the rock-crystals found there in great abundance.

After a day's journey of six-and-twenty miles, we arrived at Klaarwater; when our party separated, each betaking himself to his own abode. But to me, every spot on which my waggon stood, was home: there was my resting-place; there was my abode. Few as were the comforts of such a dwelling, and though they might be such as the luxurious would think very little deserving of that name, they were accompanied by health and contentment, and have often afforded greater enjoyment than more splendid accommodations. Whenever I view my drawing of its interior, a thousand agreeable recollections are brought to mind: in an instant a crowd of pleasing reflections surround me; and, while indulging in the various, and often opposite, sensations which they create, I am transported back again to African scenes, unconscious of being in a better land. In the contemplation of past dangers, there is a pleasure and satisfaction, not inferior to any which the remembrance of propitious incidents can inspire.

I again took up my old station beyond the mead, and made the necessary arrangements, according to my original plan, for resting at Klaarwater three months; of which six weeks were yet remaining.

CHAPTER XIX.

November 20*th.* The excursion from which I had just returned although it had not occupied more than twenty-six days, had added very considerably to my knowledge, both of the manners of the natives, and of the nature and productions of the country. From the experience in dealings and converse with wild people, which had been gained in this trip, I thought myself now to be, in some measure, qualified for a journey further into the continent; and was anxious for the arrival of the day of my departure from Klaarwater.

In the arrangement of my observations and notes; in the ordering and packing up of my collections; and in the regulating and disposing of the mass of objects which had accumulated during my last excursion, I found work sufficient to keep me fully employed during the greater part of my stay: and the want of some intelligent assistant, to relieve me from the more laborious department of it, was now very sensibly felt.

This day was occupied in replacing the great chests into the waggon, and in duly adjusting all domestic affairs; a part of a traveller's business too important to be neglected, although very far from being an interesting or agreeable occupation in the midst of pursuits of science: but it was soon discovered to be, in my present situation, a duty of the first importance, and one which consumed a large and valuable portion of my time.

Speelman and Philip went with the little waggon to Eland's Valley, to carry home Hans Lucas's game; and, as we were in want of yokes, Philip had orders to remain there with the waggon till he had cut a quantity of wood for that purpose. As Speelman was to resume his charge of my oxen, Gert was therefore the only one left at home; and where his services were indispensable in keeping watch over the dried meat, which, until the waggon returned, we were obliged to keep in the open air, with no other security than a covering of dry hides.

21st. I was suddenly awoke this morning by the report of a gun, and immediately heard Gert's voice by the side of my waggon. It being in his usual tone, and myself but just roused from sleep, I at first did not clearly understand what was said; but judging from the firing of a gun that he had shot some bird, which he brought to show me, I hastily put on part of my clothes, and came out of the waggon. What I suffered at the moment I saw him, and the acute and distressing sensation which overwhelmed me, has made an impression which, even now, is not effaced. His words were, " Help! help, sir! the gun is burst: my hand's in pieces!"

So unprepared as my mind was at the time, for any thing of this kind, it could not withstand the mournful shock which the sight of poor Gert occasioned; and I would that this unhappy moment never again presented itself before my imagination. It is one, and perhaps the only one during my journey, which I have to reflect on, with the painful feeling of my travels in Africa having

caused harm, or personal injury, to any of my fellow-creatures.   It
was my peculiar situation which rendered this accident more than
ordinarily unfortunate and distressing.   I knew not whether, in
so hot a climate, fatal consequences might not in a few hours ensue
from the wound; or whether mortification could be prevented, or
life saved, only by amputation of part of the arm: an operation
which no one in this part of the globe was competent to perform.
Little, indeed, as I knew of surgery, I may even say that nobody
in these regions knew more.   The secondary, though not unim-
portant, considerations which encreased my distress, were the loss of
his services; the unfavorable gloom which it cast over my affairs,
not very inviting to those Hottentots whom I expected to join my
party; and, added to these, the loss of time and delay which must
unavoidably be occasioned by giving him all that attention which
was requisite, and by waiting at this place till his cure was effected.

He was sitting on the ground, and with his left hand supported
his right, which presented a shocking sight; literally blown to pieces.
The fore-finger and thumb were remaining, although torn apart;
but the other fingers, with part of the palm, and the two outer
metacarpal bones, were quite separated, and adhered, or rather hung,
only by a small piece of the flesh.   A multitude of painful ideas
pressed upon me; but Gert himself appeared quite unchanged and
unmoved; and it was some consolation to perceive that he felt, in
mind, at least, not a tenth part of what I suffered on his account.

I took him instantly to the missionary's house, where I obtained
Mr. Anderson's assistance in cleansing the wound of gunpowder and
particles of dirt.   I bathed it with the preparation called Friar's
Balsam, and closed it with bandages: for, as it did not bleed, I conceived the balsam useful in the absence of blood, to form, as it were,
an artificial skin, to protect it from the effects of the air.   In a
couple of hours after this, it first began to bleed; and having allowed
it to continue doing so for such time as I thought sufficient for the
purpose of preventing inflammation, I washed it frequently with a
solution of alum in plain water, which, before night, gradually
stopped the flow of blood.

Dam, to whom Gert was, as I now found, in some degree
related, very humanely offered to take the poor fellow into his hut,
where his wife could nurse him. This was immediately done; and
I agreed to make them a compensation for their trouble. Twenty
drops of laudanum were given him in the course of the evening; by
the assistance of which he enjoyed his usual sleep. But with me it
was far otherwise: I passed a night of distressing wakefulness, dreading that in the morning I should be told of some fatal symptoms
having shown themselves, or of a lock-jaw having supervened. But,
thanks to the little sensibility of his nerves, nothing untoward of this
kind, nor any inflammatory appearance, occurred to check my hopes
that all would go on properly.

22nd. As the bursting of a gun is an accident too likely to
happen, future travellers in these warm regions, who may unhappily
be placed in such a situation will not think the details here given
of the management by which the cure was effected, a useless part of
my narrative, although others may find it uninteresting.

The Hottentots expressed so much faith in the powers of
Boekoe-azyn (Bookoo vinegar) as a wash to cleanse and heal the
wound, that I allowed it to be used, as I knew of nothing in the
nature of it which could be hurtful; but, on the contrary, had long
believed the leaves of the Diosmas to contain virtues which would at
some future period obtain for them a place in the materia medica of
Europe, as they have long done in that of the Hottentots and Boors.
This Boekoe (or Buku) azyn is made by simply putting the leaves of
some kind of diosma * into a bottle of cold vinegar, in which they
are left to steep. The longer they have been infused, the more
efficacious the vinegar is esteemed; becoming at length almost a
mucilage.

When the small stock which could be procured of old Buku-
vinegar was consumed, a succedaneum was made by a similar infusion

---

* In the present instance, those of Diosma serratifolia; of which the figure of a
sprig in seed of its natural size, is given at page 476.

in brandy; which, being not unpleasant to the palate of a Hottentot, disappeared much faster than could be accounted for by the wants of my patient. With this the wound was washed night and morning, for the first ten days, and occasionally for a fortnight afterwards. But as soon as it began to heal, I employed a wash made of a strong decoction of the leaves of *Wilde-alsem* (Wild Wormwood.) *

The fore-arm, and the remaining part of the hand, rested in a splint supported by a sling from the neck. He had very little fever; and the wound in a few days began to assume a healing appearance. The fungous flesh, which was beginning to form on the fourth day, was reduced by frequently powdering it with burnt alum. A deep wound near the wrist-bone continued for five weeks to cleanse itself, but would have closed much sooner, if I had not judged it prudent to keep it open. A healing plaster was made by melting together a wax-candle with a quantity of sheep's tallow, sufficient to give it the proper softness. There appeared no necessity for opiates after the fourth night, when the dose of laudanum had been gradually lessened to ten drops. All food of a heating quality was denied him; and it was, with much reluctance, that he submitted for three weeks to the privation of his usual rations of brandy. On the sixth day he was allowed a small quantity of vinegar with his food, and his diet was then changed to one of a more solid kind: it had previously consisted only of mutton broth, rice, and bread, with either sweet, or sour, milk. Till the twelfth day he was confined to the hut; but afterwards frequently took a walk from the village to the waggons, remaining with us till the sun began to decline. In the progress of the cure, constant attention was paid to keeping the wound clean, and protecting it from the air: to these, and the regulation of his diet, the successful result of our nursing, is to be attributed; unless perhaps, a dulness of nerve, and a tardy circulation of blood, may not greatly have assisted the remedies. He was never deprived of the consolation of his tobacco-pipe, which, besides its powers as an

---

* *Artemisia Afra.*

opiate, had probably no small share in diverting his thoughts from his irreparable loss, and in keeping him in generally good spirits.

In six weeks from the day when the accident happened, I considered the cure complete: the wound was covered over with a new skin, and the thumb and finger were reunited. The power and use of these returned but slowly; yet ultimately they acquired their full strength, and were of so much service, that, in many instances, the loss of the rest seemed to be of no inconvenience. Here, then, I saw reason for rejoicing that I possessed neither the instruments nor the skill of a surgeon; for, otherwise, my poor Hottentot would have been all the remainder of his life with a useless stump, instead of half a hand.

On that unfortunate morning, the crows flocked round us in great numbers, attracted by our stock of dried meat; pieces of which they carried off with astonishing audacity, though Gert was in sight, sitting within a dozen yards of them. It was for the purpose of driving these birds away that he fired off the gun.

Being thus left without a servant, or any one to attend on Gert, I immediately despatched a Hottentot to Eland's Valley for Philip. This messenger made such good haste, that Philip returned with the waggon on the same day.

23rd. During the night Captain Berends and the *elephant hunters* came home from their expedition. They had shot twelve elephants, which, however, produced no more than two hundred pounds weight of ivory, as all the animals, excepting one, happened to be females, the tusks of which are much smaller than those of the males. They afterwards went to the *Briquas* (Bachapins,) to dispose of their beads; but that nation would not receive them, nor enter into any trading at that season of the year, as they adhere scrupulously to the belief, that bartering while their corn was in the ear, which, just at that time was the case, would occasion a bad harvest: and besides this, the Klaarwater people had thoughtlessly done that which rendered it still more impossible to have any dealings with them as long as the corn was standing: they had shot elephants. In consequence of this mistake, the Hottentots were obliged to

3 Q

return home, without accomplishing a principal object of their journey. Many *superstitious beliefs* of this sort among the Briquas are connected with the growth of their corn, one of which I unwittingly offended against, during my residence at Litakun, and should have incurred heavy displeasure, but for some management in appeasing their apprehensions, a circumstance which will be related hereafter.

24th. The water at Eland's Valley being nearly dried up, Speelman was obliged to remove with my oxen to the Kraal at *Groote-Doorn* (Great Thorn), so called, from a few trees of *Acacia giraffæ* which grow there.

The whole waggon-load of meat which we brought to Klaarwater as a stock for our future journey, was totally eaten up in four days, although I had nobody but Philip to feed. It was not consumed by the crows, nor by the vultures, but by the Klaarwater Hottentots, who are by no means inferior to them in the power of smelling out meat, wherever it may be concealed. From an early hour in the morning, till late at night, my waggons were constantly visited by men, women, and children, whose only object was to eat. But, from the moment the last of the stock was gone, from that moment not one visitor more came near me. Yet still it was impossible to account for this rapid disappearing of the meat, without supposing that they came secretly and stole it by night, as there was nothing to prevent them but their own sense of honesty; nobody sleeping at the waggons but myself, and Philip remaining every night at the village to be in attendance on Gert. Nothing could be more vexatious than this loss, or, more correctly speaking, robbery, as provisions were not easily to be purchased, and a large supply not by any solicitations to be obtained from the inhabitants of this place.

25th. Berends's party, besides elephants, had shot a variety of other animals, some of the meat of which they brought home salted; and in dining to day with the missionaries, I partook of *Eland, Buffalo*, Hippopotamus,* and *Camelopard,* of all of which the meat was

---

* *Bos Caffer.*

excellent, but, being salted, and all boiled in one pot, the peculiar taste of each was not very distinctly to be perceived.

At Mr. Kramer's, I saw a *Briqua* (or Bachapin) *boy*, of about ten years of age, whom Berends, by desire of the missionary, had brought with him from that country, by the consent of the parents, who readily gave him up to be kept, and brought up, at Klaarwater, as one of its inhabitants, under the missionaries' particular care. He was quite naked, like all children of his age, and seemed happy and contented with his new situation, especially at being told that Mr. and Mrs. Kramer were in future to be his father and mother: he belonged to poor parents, who were, probably, glad at having him so well provided for, intending to fetch him home after the lapse of a few years. The poor little fellow was captivated with the good living he now enjoyed, and this contrast with many a hungry day in his own country, operated most effectually to make him pleased with the change, and soon rendered him unmindful of the loss of his former playmates, which, indeed, he soon here replaced by several little Hottentots, as naked and free from care as himself.

This mode of cultivating the minds of the *natives*, could it be followed to a sufficient extent, would, in time, effect much in their *civilization*; the notions and ideas, and even customs of early youth, are not so easily thrown aside and forgotten, as those which are acquired in maturer years. It may seem unnecessary to repeat an axiom so well known, and so universally admitted; but this, like too many others, is acknowledged in theory and forgotten in practice; while, too often, the cunning adult, though attending patiently to the preaching of missionaries, and confessing his belief in all they teach, as long as it suits his worldly convenience and advantage, secretly, in his own mind, feels as ready to abandon his professions, and return to his ignorance, as he did to adopt a creed, and listen to instruction. If I am reprovable for thus judging the hearts of men, I plead in exculpation, those appearances and facts which have so often presented themselves to my observation.

27th. Happening, almost accidentally, to be looking one evening at the planet *Jupiter* through a small pocket telescope, I was exceedingly surprised at beholding all the *Satellites*, as clearly as they would have appeared in England through an instrument of many times greater optical power; although this one was not more than twenty inches in length, and of the common refracting sort.   So unexpected a circumstance afforded me much pleasure, because it raised a hope that I might be enabled to observe an *eclipse* of one of these moons, for the accurate determination of my longitude, and accordingly I prepared for watching the eclipse of the first satellite, which was calculated to happen this night.   For some time I had the fullest expectation of success, but when the satellite approached near to the body of the planet, it gradually lost itself in the confused rays of light emitted from its primary, so it appeared through my telescope, and became invisible several minutes before the eclipse would have taken place.

This disappointment, there was now no means of remedying; and I felt how much reason there was for regretting that, in the absence of an astronomical telescope, it had not occurred to me as advisable to take a common one of the strongest power that could be purchased in Cape Town; but I was not then aware of the extraordinary clearness of the atmosphere in the interior regions of this country, so favourable to *celestial observations*.   This, and many other circumstances propitious to the practical astronomer, render peculiarly suitable to his residence, a country least of all likely ever to possess such an inhabitant; while, on the other hand, strangely enough, this noble science is pursued with the greatest earnestness in countries where the atmosphere is perpetually thwarting and disappointing his patient watchings.

28th.   As it was my intention to visit the *Bachapins* after I had taken my final departure from Klaarwater, it would be absolutely necessary to have with me some person capable of acting as *interpreter* to that nation.   Although there were many Hottentots at this place well enough qualified for that duty, I found it not possible to persuade such to accompany me; and whatever difficulties at Klaarwater may have opposed my endeavours to hire men for the further prosecution of my journey, I owe it in justice to *Mr. Jansz,* to say, that it was entirely by his friendly assistance that I succeeded in engaging a Briqua interpreter to enter my service. During our late excursion to the rivers, he had mentioned to me, and recommended for that purpose, a certain Half-Briqua by the name of *Kees*, who, being born at Litakun (Litaakoon,) a Bachapin on the father's, and a Kora on the mother's, side, was equally well acquainted with both languages; and, by having long resided at Klaarwater, and even visited Cape Town, had acquired a tolerable knowledge of Dutch.

Mr. Jansz having sent a message to one of the out-stations under the Langberg, where Kees was living, to desire him to come to Klaarwater, he arrived this morning at the village, and came to us at Mr. Jansz's hut, where, after much preliminary and explanatory conversation with him, it was at last settled that he should go no farther than Litakoon, there to leave me, and be at liberty to return home.

His real name was *Muchunka*, which in the Sichuana language signifies *poor*. His mother was living at the Kora village of the Hart; but both his brothers had died a few years before of the small-pox, by which disease he also lost his eldest child. His wife was a Hottentot woman. His property consisted in one cow, which being the first he ever possessed, he talked of with no small pleasure, as a proof of his riches and consequence; for it seems that his name had originally been justly bestowed upon him. He was living in society with a Hottentot named Willem Casper, under whose protection it was planned that he was to leave his wife and child, and his cow.

He frequently expressed fears that I meant to take him farther than Litakoon, and these fears occasioned him for some time to hesitate whether to go or not. But after repeating the strongest assurances that he should be quite at liberty to leave me at that town, I at length effaced those impressions, which had evidently been made on his mind by the representations of the Klaarwater Hottentots, with respect to the dangerous nature of the expedition he was about to join.

All these apprehensions being quieted, he took up his abode at my waggons, and seemed as much pleased in his new service, as I was at my new servant; whose liveliness of manners and conversation appeared to much advantage, by the side of the slow phlegmatic movements and apparent apathy of the generality of Hottentots. A spirited tone of voice, and animated gestures while talking, were what I had been long unused to, during the journey: but there were certain things which at this moment contributed greatly to his animation; tobacco and meat in abundance. He brought with him two of his countrymen, who also passed the night at our fire, and partook of the conviviality. With them, he kept up an almost incessant, vociferous conversation, till a late hour of the night, varying it, however, at intervals with a more moderate tone, while speaking in Dutch to Philip, who, having formerly been in *Briqualand,* as it is sometimes called, appeared pleased at the opportunity of talking with him about places with which they were both acquainted.

29th. As one of the people was returning home on horseback, a young *Quakka* (Zebra) *foal,* whose mother had probably just died, or been shot, ran towards the horse, and followed it to Klaarwater; where I saw it in a cattle-pound, standing very quietly, allowing itself to be touched with the hand, and, to all appearance, quite as tame as a common foal; the presence of men, seemingly, giving it not the least uneasiness. It being a handsome animal, it was intended to bring it up tame; with which view it was put to a mare to be suckled. However, it unfortunately died in about ten days afterwards, and thus exceedingly disappointed my expectation of witnessing the success of the experiment. From the Hottentots who had the management of it, I could not learn the real cause of the failure, as one said it pined away for the loss of its mother; the other that the mare would not let it suck enough; and another that her milk did not agree with it. Notwithstanding all this, I am much inclined to believe, and in fact have since seen sufficient to confirm my belief, that many of the wild animals, if taken very young, may be reared by suckling them under such domestic animals as belong to the same genus, or even to the same order. And although the natural wildness, or ferocity, of their nature, cannot be subdued by such nurture; yet they would be thus accustomed to

confinement and the presence of man : by which means an opportunity would be afforded for discovering many particulars of their
history, which can never be known by merely viewing them in their
wild state.   On the other hand, it must be admitted, some of the
most interesting and characteristic particulars are only to be learnt
by him who observes them on their native plains : while the mere
library-naturalist is very liable to commit strange blunders, which,
being communicated to the public, obtain a degree of currency, which
it is afterwards very difficult to check.   It is a trite expression, that
" travellers see strange things ;" but much the strangest are seen,
or rather imagined, by those who never go far from home : and it is,
therefore, the duty of every honest traveller to cut these down to
their proper standard.

A Hottentot brought me a *Spring-haas* * which he had shot.
Great complaints were made against these animals for the mischief
they do to the corn, eating it both green and ripe.   It was of nearly
the size of a hare, with long soft fur of a sandy color, a long tail,
black at the extremity, and hinder legs of twice the length of the
fore pair.   Its very remarkable gait is occasioned by this dispropor-
tion of legs ; as it moves, at least when in haste, only by long leaps
or bounds.   From this circumstance, and its resemblance in several
particulars to a hare, it has obtained from the Dutch colonists a
name signifying *Leaping Hare.*   Its ears, however, have more resemblance to those of a cat than of a hare ; but the two long front
teeth in each jaw, and its leaping motion, plainly prove its close
affinity to the latter.   Its fore feet, which are little more than two
inches in length, are provided with very long hooked claws, better
adapted for holding its food, than for burrowing in the ground ; and
have every appearance of not being used for the latter purpose.
On the contrary, the hinder legs, which are nearly ten inches long,
are furnished with extraordinarily large and strong nails, which might

---

* *Pedetes Caffer.* — *Dipus Caffer.* Linn. Gmel. Sys. Nat. 1. p. 159. — *Cape Jerboa.*
Pennant. Quad. vol. ii. p. 170.

almost be called hoofs ; and which seem to be used only for scratching away the earth, for which office they are well suited; although such an application of the hind legs is a singular anomaly, and not easily to be explained, without having had a more favorable opportunity of watching their mode of life. In this manner, it does, in fact, use them dexterously and expeditiously ; making deep burrows, in which it lies concealed all day.   As it comes out to feed only by night, it is an animal not so well known from its form and appearance, as from its operations.   It inhabits the neighbourhood of mountains, whose rocky sides afford them a greater protection than the plains, where they may be easily overtaken by dogs, or other carnivorous animals.   No construction can be better suited for ascending, nor any worse for descending, a steep.   There must, therefore, one would imagine, be some singular management on the part of an animal so formed, and at the same time inhabiting such places.   It is sometimes, though less frequently, called the *Berg-haas* (Mountain Hare).

A violent west wind continuing the whole day, rendered the air extremely chilly ; and in the evening, soon after sunset, it became so cold, that our thickest clothing could not keep us warm.   The summer being now far advanced, such weather was not to be expected ; but it is, however, not unusual.

December 7th. While sitting employed in the waggon, a sudden crack excited my attention ; and on turning to the spot whence it proceeded, I perceived the upper joint of the flute split from one end to the other.   At the moment, I could not but view this as an accident particularly unfortunate, supposing myself deprived, for the rest of my travels, of the amusement, and, I might say, the consolation, of that instrument ; but the metal tube within, saved it from being rendered useless.   It was, however, this tube which occasioned the accident, by expanding from the heat and dryness of the air, while the woodwork on the outside contracted from the same cause.

It is the wind, more especially, which produces this effect on wood ; and in this climate care should be taken that nothing be left exposed to its influence.   It was, on this account, highly necessary to keep the wheels and various parts of the waggons covered with tar; a work which had been completed only the day before.   It would be difficult for a person, accustomed only to the air of England, to conceive a just idea of the excessive dryness of the atmosphere thus far in the interior of the most arid continent of the globe.   The effects of it were visible in every thing around us: the dry grass crackled under our feet; and even my finger-nails were at such times rendered exceedingly brittle.   In many cases this state of the air had its advantages; and in one, it was particularly useful: in the drying of my plants.   But here it rather exceeeded my wishes, and caused my specimens sometimes to be so brittle, that they required the greatest care in handling.

8th.   I was requested to visit one of the huts of the village, to see an infant whose foot had been scalded in our journey from the Cape.   From bad management, it was now in a deplorable state; much swelled, and covered up with dirt and grease.   It had already lost its great toe, and it appeared as if the rest would soon share the same fate.   From ignorance or carelessness, the wound had been much neglected, though the mother seemed naturally distressed at the child's situation; but she, like many others, imagined that any thing in the shape of medicine would effect the cure, without the necessity for thought or common sense.   The missionaries had supplied her with a plaster, to which her neglect had added filth and dirt.   Wherever I was called upon to act the part of a medical adviser, I never failed strongly to preach to these poor creatures the doctrine of cleanliness; and this, in fact, was the whole of my advice in the present case: merely recommending her to leave off all the grease, and wash it with a decoction of *Artemisia afra.*   The consequence was, that in a fortnight afterwards the foot began to heal.

9th.   Excepting in the missionaries' garden, there was but one tree * in the whole village; and that one was sufficiently thriving and ornamental to have encouraged any but the indolent Hottentot to

---

* This may be seen in the eighth plate, just above the waggon and oxen.

plant hundreds more.   Nor would this have been now growing here, but for the listless laziness of its owner; who, having a few years before cut a block of willow-wood, and brought it from the river, with the intention of converting it into a bowl, or a *bambus*, laid it in the water-run to preserve it from cracking; but could never find himself sufficiently in the mood for work, to commence the long-meditated job.   In the mean time the log of wood, more active than the man, took root, and rapidly pushing up shoots, a stem, and branches, stood before him a flourishing tree, a growing reproach to his idleness and dilatory spirit.

At the request of the missionaries I drew their portraits, as they expressed a wish to send a remembrance to their friends in Europe; and added also a duplicate for themselves.   I was far from regretting the time employed in this work; as it could not but be a pleasure to gratify the feelings of persons banished, as it may be said, not only from the society to which they naturally belonged, but cut off even from all communication with their friends.

10th.   Four *Koras* paid me a visit; and I purchased of them a fresh ostrich-egg for a small piece of tobacco.   They belonged to a neighbouring kraal, and of which one of them was the chief.   Of this man I drew the portrait represented at Plate 10. After making the bargain to give him a large piece of tobacco, he stood patiently and still, till I had finished my drawing; which, however, being done only with a black-lead pencil, excited little wonder or admiration, compared to that which he and his companions expressed at my drawing of the Yellow-fish.   It is by the imitation of the lively colors of nature, far more than by exactness of forms, that drawings afford delight to the far greater number of those who view them: correctness and fidelity of outline being more seldom duly appreciated, although the more valuable part of the art.

This *Kora* wore on his head a piece of leather, bound round in the form of a cap, and in the manner of a turban; and was clothed with a leathern cloak or kaross, which, together with his whole body, were so covered with red ochre and grease, that the part of my waggon against which he leaned was painted, or rather

Pl. 10

Engraved from the original Drawing made by W. J. Burchell Esq.r Oct.r 1st 1817

Portrait of a Kora

London Publ.d Oct.r by Longman & Co. June 1 1822

soiled, with a red stain, which was found not easy to be extracted. From his neck hung a number of bead necklaces of various colors, to which were appended a Bichuana knife, and the shell of a small tortoise to hold snuff or tobacco. His wrist and fore-arm were ornamented with bracelets of beads, cords of acacia-bark, and a broad ivory ring. Although perfectly friendly in all their intentions, these men were each armed with a hassagay and *kirri*, and some with a bow. The countenance and manners of this chief were expressive of a good-natured quiet disposition: his behaviour was even respectful, and less troublesome in the way of begging, than that of the generality of his countrymen.

The heat of the summer season now began to be oppressive; and the thermometer, even in the shade, stood generally as high as 90° of Fahrenheit's, 25°·7 of Reaumur's, or 32°·2 of the Centigrade scale. The herbage of all the country around was parched up: owing to the long absence of the expected rains, the greatest drought prevailed every where, and seemed to have locked up the earth, and put a stop to all vegetation.

12th. At this time some little appearance of business might be observed going on at Klaarwater: a few of the Hottentots were occupied in getting in the *harvest.* The wheat, when cut, was trodden out of the ear by horses, on a hard earthen floor in the open air, precisely in the same mode as practised in the Cape colony. The hand-mills were now in constant work; and one seldom passed by a hut without seeing women or girls pounding corn. If I looked into the pot which stood on the fire, it was always found filled with wheat; or if I met a Hottentot, either man or boy, his mouth, like the mill, was incessantly at work, grinding corn; while his hands were not idle, as they performed the duty of the hopper, in keeping it constantly supplied.

14th. I took a solitary ramble to explore the valley of *Leeuwenkuil* (Lion's-den), along which the Klaarwater rivulet takes its course towards the Gariep. It obtained its name from the circumstance of a lion having been dispossessed of his den when this spot was first taken possession of. Its average width was between three and four hundred feet, and was, on either side, shut in by brown, perpendicular, laminated rocks, of a hundred feet in height *. This was the spot where the missionaries first fixed their abode, when they and the Hottentots settled in this part of the country, about eight years before. There were still at this time three or four mat huts, whose inhabitants cultivated about a couple of acres of wheat ; yet no kind of garden nor fruit-tree marked an appearance of industry, although a large space of ground, and a plentiful rill of delightful water, seemed sufficient to tempt Indolence herself to take the spade in hand. In excuse for this, it was asserted that the soil in many places is of a brackish quality ; but of this I saw no very evident proofs.

Against the rocks, a handsome shrub of a broader foliage than is generally met with in these regions, spread its branches, and, in places, concealed the brown stone by its beautiful dark green laurel-like leaves. Its smooth, pale, tortuous trunk sprung out of the clefts of the hard rock, and clung to its surface in the manner of ivy, but without putting forth any roots. It was a species of *Ficus* (or Fig-tree), whose fruit, not larger than a pea, was first yellow, and afterwards, when quite ripe, of a purple colour, yet not worth eating. Its fresh green appearance against the barren precipice, tempted me to make a sketch of it. †

I found in this valley, *Aristida ? fruticans* ‡, a very remarkable grass, of a hard, shrubby, branching growth.

Here, under the inaccessible crags of the precipice, the great vultures (mentioned at page 377.) hold their abode, perfectly secure from all molestation ; and their retreat would ever remain undiscovered, were it not betrayed by the white stains from their dirt.

This valley has several outlets on either side, and presents a

---

* This scene is represented by the *engraving* at the end of the chapter.

† Out of the fissures of the rock grew some large bushes of *Macromerum junceum*, and *Capparis punctata*, Cat. Geogr. 1891. Frutex inermis 4—6-pedalis, ramificatione subpatente. Folia angustè lanceolata obtusissima. Racemuli brevissimi solitarii, vel bini, axillares. Fructus globosus lævis reticulato-punctatus.

‡ Cat. Geogr. 1885.

wild romantic appearance. Remarkably sheltered and warm, it seems especially adapted for a fruit-garden, and undoubtedly would produce abundance of figs and peaches.

Looking into the huts, I found their inhabitants, with very few exceptions, stretched on the ground, asleep; for which the great heat of the day was almost an excuse. In a Hottentot hut, there is no separate sleeping place for the different members of the family; all are huddled together, each rolled up in his kaross.

15th. At this time the *twilight*, in the absence of the moon, gave light enough for reading till fifty minutes after the sun had gone down; but travelling could not safely be continued longer than an hour after sun-set. These facts were ascertained practically by repeated observations.

17th. I discovered in the mead a species of *peppermint*, growing wild, and pointing it out to the missionaries, recommended a trial of distilling it. Some sheets of tin, which I brought from the Cape, afforded the means of making a still-head, which could be adapted to a common boiling pot, and Mr. Anderson, who understood something of this kind of work, succeeded in making one which answered the purpose. The result of our experiment created universal satisfaction, as some excellent spirit of peppermint was obtained. In this satisfaction, I mean to include the Hottentots; for those who attended the fire at the still, were delighted to find that a liquor of a strong and spirituous taste might be so easily made. Whenever they supposed themselves unobserved, they caught into their hands the spirit as it dropped, and sipped and tasted over again, highly approving the flavour, and much pleased at the discovery. And indeed it was surprising, that with so clumsy an apparatus, the process should succeed so well; a reed, about a yard long, constantly moistened on the outside with wet cloths, performed the office of a refrigeratory; and, with the thermometer standing at 90°, the condensation of the steam could never have been effected, had not the evaporation from the cloths been proportionally quick to produce a sufficient chill.

18th. A Hottentot, as I was informed, had just arrived from a kraal situated several days journeys lower down the river, to solicit his family and friends here to assist them in removing to Klaarwater; the villain *Africaander* having robbed them of every thing, and reduced them to the necessity, through want of food, of eating leathern thongs and the halters of their oxen. At the time when this Hottentot came away, Africaander was stationed a little below the great Waterfall, his party consisting of sixteen Hottentots, besides Bushmen. He was possessed of twenty-seven muskets, with a small quantity of ammunition; and it was now reported that he had lately attacked two kraals of Namaquas, many of whom he had murdered. This lawless wretch had, by caution and cunning, contrived hitherto to escape the revenge of those whom he had injured, and to elude even a *commando* (an armed party of boors), which had been a few weeks before ordered out by the Landdrost, in pursuit of him, but which had returned into the colony without accomplishing the service upon which it had been sent.

This occurrence created a sensation at Klaarwater, and seemed to excite, in some degree, the fears of my own people, who had been industriously told that the great quantity of gunpowder which I had in my waggons, would strongly tempt Africaander to attack us, in the hope of being able to get possession of it; for without a supply of ammunition, his freebooting schemes could not be carried on, as he had no means of recruiting his stock but by plunder. Tales of this kind, most frequently unfounded, were continually being related to my men, who, indeed, too readily listened to them; while I had thus a constant business in endeavouring to do away the impression they generally made.

Fortunately the kraal of Caffres had for a long time been so quiet and peaceable, that we heard nothing of them; but this was accounted for by the season of the year, as they always prefer the long nights of winter, as more favourable for their marauding expeditions. It has been remarked that they more frequently make their attack about an hour before day-light; or, as they express themselves, as soon as they can just see the horns of the oxen; for they know that at this hour it is most likely that all the enemy will be fast asleep.

But another circumstance concurs to induce them to defer the attack till that late hour of the night; they are careful to avoid approaching, during the day-light, so near as to run any risk of being observed; but in most cases halt at the distance of a night's journey; and as soon as evening comes on, advance with great rapidity, so calculating their time that they may arrive at the place of attack just before the commencement of the morning twilight.

I considered every piece of information of this sort, as part of the lesson I had to learn, before I could be qualified for conducting my little party safely through all the dangers and treachery of the various tribes through which I expected I should have to make my way. My protracted stay at Klaarwater was not to be regarded as time lost, as it gave an opportunity of acquiring a species of knowledge, which was of essential necessity in my dealings with the natives; and without which, to have ventured amongst them alone, and defenceless as I was, would certainly not have been a proof of wisdom.

19th. During the preceding night, a heavy rain had fallen, and the country this morning no longer exhibited that arid colorless appearance which, for several months past, had almost persuaded me to believe that it could never be visited by verdure. The moistened earth looked now as if vegetation were every where possible, although its bare surface presented nothing but scattered bushes, almost dried up.

25th. The day of the month is the only circumstance which, in these far-distant wilds, can remind the traveller of that season which the customs of Europe dedicate more especially to conviviality and social enjoyment; among those, at least, who preserve a respect for ancient usages. Here the fur-clad skaiter, rapidly circling round in graceful sweeps, is never seen. Over these hills and plains, no thick snowy mantle of dazzling white, spreading a new beauty over the leafless landscape, conceals the herbage, or clothes the bending bush; here no unrelenting frost locks up the soil, and denies entrance to the plough or spade. Here, in these unknown solitary regions, no fog descends to hide the mountain, or each neighbouring hut or tree, while the peasant doubtful wanders over the moor. No long, chilling wintry nights, and numbing cold, drive the inhabitant into his well-warmed cot, to seek the comforts and the pleasures of a fire-side.   Here the task of sweeping the snow from the door, or the icicles from the eaves, of breaking the ice from the pond, laying in a store of winter fuel, and providing against the inclement season, or of preparing fodder for the cattle, is never known.   Here, at Christmas, if we take shelter in a hut, it is to fly from the rays of a burning sun, and there, for coolness, throw aside our clothing.   Here the bright source of light and warmth revolves in ever-shining splendor, rarely unseen while above the horizon.   Here our winter is excess of heat; this it is which puts a stop to vegetation, and causes verdure to disappear; this locks up the soil, and renders it not less hard than the power of frost; this deprives the flocks and herds of their pasture, and, in the valley, scorches every tuft of grass.   It is at the cooler season of the year only, that these wide-extended plains look like a habitable country.   Here, instead of chilblains, the swarthy native, who ventures to walk barefoot on the burning sands, is rendered lame with blisters.   While the inhabitant of Northern Europe, freezing and shivering, draws nearer and nearer to his fire, here, at that same hour, languid and oppressed with the sultry heat, we lie reclining in the shade, longing for some breath of cooling air. There the thermometer has sunk to 20°, to 10°, or even to 0; while with us it is 88°.

And these surprising contrasts have but one single cause: it is alone the difference of obliquity with which the sun's rays fall upon the different parts of our globe; or, in other words, the greater or less noon-day height of the sun, which occasions all the diversity of heat and cold, from the burning sands under the equator, to the eternal, never-thawing ice of the poles.   How transcendant and ever-wonderful is the Great Wisdom which planned the universe! How stupendous and noble the scheme; how simple, yet efficient, the laws which govern it!   That nothing more complicated than the direction of the sun's beams, should produce all the various climates of the world, and that merely the parallelism and inclination of the earth's axis to its orbit, should give us all the seasons of the year; how admirable! how beautiful!

It can be no argument against this theory, that, within the tropics, perpetual snow covers the summits of the loftiest mountains, and that local circumstances occasion some variation in the regular heat of the climate. These depend on other causes, more complicated, and less satisfactorily explained; unless it be, that the capacity for heat, which the atmosphere possesses, may be in proportion to its density; and, consequently, as its rarity increases generally in the ratio of its elevation above the level of the sea, its power of retaining the heat of the sun's rays will in the same ratio decrease. This principle seems to offer an explanation of some anomalies in atmospheric heat; and, supposing it universal, it is easy to conceive how the heat of our planets may be equalized, by atmospheres of increased density, suited proportionally to their distance from the sun. From this principle it would also follow, that the great immensity of space, in which our solar spheres revolve, is subjected to the extreme of cold.

28th. A strange *Hottentot* from the *Cape colony,* arrived at Klaarwater, having found his way alone, on foot, unarmed, and without any other guide than the track of our waggons. The account he gave of himself was, that he had been in the service of Piet Mulder, a boor in the Roggeveld; but that latterly he had been living in a kraal, of which a Bushman, known by the name of Ruyter, was captain or chief; and that the reason of his coming to Klaarwater was to see his sister, the wife of old Moses. Yet he was here, by almost every one, strongly suspected of being a runaway; and, from his manners and conversation, he appeared to me to be half a simpleton. He was not aware, he said, that Klaarwater was so far from the colony, although he was only nine days on the road from the Sack river to the settlement at the Kloof in the Asbestos Mountains, including two days at the Karree Mountains, which he spent at the kraal of the Bushman captain *Goedhart,* by whom he was treated in a friendly manner. Near Carel Krieger's Grave he was met by two Bushmen, whom, from their manners, he suspected of having

3 s

some evil design against him ; but six *Caffres* happening most pro-
videntially to come up just at that instant, frustrated their intentions,
and occasioned them to make off with all haste.   On representing
his situation to the Caffres, they kindly took him under their protection, turned back, and honorably conducted him safe to the
Gariep, where, having pointed out a fordable place, and given him
proper directions for passing it, they left him to find his way to the
Kloof settlement, where he arrived without accident, and remained a
day or two to rest.

In this hazardous attempt, there were so many chances against
his traversing that part of the country in safety, that we should have
doubted the truth of his story, had we not known that it was still
more improbable that he could have come from any other place than
the Roggeveld.   The rate at which he travelled would seem incredible ; nor could it have been supposed possible in that hot weather,
to have walked two hundred and sixty five miles in seven following
days, or at the average of thirty eight miles each day, had I not already
known several proofs of the extraordinary travelling powers which the
Hottentots and Bushmen possess.   It was the opinion of every one,
that he had met with unusual good fortune, in having escaped being
murdered by the way : but his not having about him either a gun,
or any thing worth taking, nor even a kaross, was a circumstance to
which, doubtlessly, his safety was principally to be attributed.

Not equally fortunate was a *deserter* from the Cape garrison.
This man having made his escape from the colony, had taken refuge
at Klaarwater ; where an offer of pardon was made to him about a
year before my visit to this place, by the missionary on the part of
the governor, on the condition that he undertook to go in search of
Dr. Cowan and his party, and brought back some intelligence respecting their fate.   He, however, went no farther than the country
of the Briquas, or Bachapins, being afraid to venture amongst the nations who live beyond them.   At that town he obtained an account of
their having all been murdered by the second nation beyond Litaakoon : a story fabricated by the natives, without any foundation ; and

which will be fully explained in another part of this journal. *   A
short time after his return to Klaarwater, he set out alone, intending
to find his way back into the Colony; conceiving that by what he
had done he had earned his pardon: but this ill-fated man had
scarcely passed Modder-gat, when he was met by a party of Bushmen, and barbarously murdered.

Speelman came from Groote-doorn, for a fresh supply of provisions, tobacco, and brandy, and communicated the pleasing intelligence that my oxen were fast recovering their strength; but threw
in with it some alloy, by surmising that unless the rains fell before
long, they would soon begin to lose what they had gained; as the
herbage was now every where entirely parched up.   The idle life
of a herdsman, together with plenty of milk, and occasionally some
boiled wheat, had, in some measure, fattened him also.   He was in
high spirits, and by his account appeared to be living happily
enough, amongst his new-formed acquaintances; one of whom,
named Hendrick Abrams, he had engaged to go with us on our
journey into the Interior.   As he called him his cousin, I for some
time supposed him to be really a relation, whom he had unexpectedly
discovered in this distant part of the country; but, with a Hottentot,
as with a Boor, every one towards whom they feel friendly disposed,
is either cousin, uncle, or nephew; according as it happen that the
age may be equal, or greater, or less.

He brought with him a curious proof of his ingenuity; a *fiddle*
of his own making.   I could not be otherwise than exceedingly
amused, for the rudeness of its appearance was really laughable.
Yet it gave, every thing considered, an excellent tone, and proved,
during our travels, a most valuable article.   This mirth-inspiring
utensil was a kind of oblong bowl, carved out of willow-wood, and
covered over with sheep-skin or parchment.   A finger-board, with
screws, bridge, and tail-piece, together with a bow, were all formed in
imitation of a European violin, and nearly in the proper proportion.

---

* Under the date of the 3d of August 1812.

3 s 2

The strings, twisted of their due thickness, were made from sheep's entrails, and the horse's tail supplied the hair for the bow.

When I had examined the various parts of it, and pronounced it a clever piece of workmanship, the maker, who was not without a moderate share of vanity on some occasions, seemed quite happy, and not a little proud of my approbation. But my own pleasure and surprise were heightened still more, when, on desiring to hear a specimen of his playing, he clapped his *Cremona* to his shoulder, handled his bow with all the grace of a Hottentot, and fiddled away a dance, in so lively a manner, that my men and myself were all in the highest degree delighted. Philip, in spite of all his gravity, such is the power of fiddles, now looked smiling; and declared that Speelman should teach him how to move his fingers and play that *mooi liedje* (pretty song).

But to poor *Gert*, this could only serve to remind him, in a most sensible manner, of the distressing loss of that hand with which he had, as he then told us, often used that bow and enlivened his companions: yet with the calmness of a philosopher he expressed his hope that he might still be able to play again, when his thumb and finger were quite healed, and sufficiently strengthened. This was a hope in which, I am happy to say, the poor fellow was not disappointed; and he afterwards proved to us, that he could play so much better than Speelman, that he was soon acknowledged to be the best musician of our party.

As *Speelman*, when he came for his rations, always begged hard, for a larger portion for his *lieve vrouw* (dear wife), as he called her, I had entertained a high opinion of their conjugal affection; but Philip privately came to tell me that this *dear wife* often gets a sound beating, and that her husband appeared to be seeking an excuse for a separation *a mensâ et thoro*. Some time afterwards, when Hannah came to Klaarwater to wash the linen, I discovered that she received but a very small part of her rations of tobacco, and hardly ever got a taste of the brandy. But Speelman, as if to divert me from reproaching him with this unfair conduct, seldom came home without bringing some curious bird or insect; and I confess that I found it difficult to praise and to reprimand, with the same breath.

Once, when I desired him to bring me a specimen from the large thorn trees at *Groote-doorn,* and the blossom of the common acacia, he came loaded with two branches as large as he could carry. On this occasion, my reluctance to throw so fine a plant away, induced me to put into the press a greater number of specimens than my own herbarium required. Among the number of interesting birds procured here, was that singular one the *Spoonbill.* This is said by the natives to be a bird of very rare occurrence; and indeed it was never, during the whole of my travels, met with but this once.

29th. During the time we were stationed at Klaarwater, I obtained in the neighbourhood a variety of *birds* not seen before; and some which proved perfectly new to the science*. We often

---

* The following birds were met with at Klaarwater, and in the vicinity:—

Charadrius armatus, B. *Fœm.* — *Nigra* sunt, rostrum, occiput, genæ, gula, pectus, dorsum, remiges, pedes, ungues, et apices rectricum. *Alba* (vel nivea) sunt, pileus, nucha, abdomen, crissum, alarum tegmina inferiora, uropygium, et rectricum bases. *Cinereæ* sunt alarum tegmina superiora omnia. Margines remigum, duobus extimis exceptis, ferrugineo tinctæ. Irides pulchrè sanguineæ. Cauda æqualis vel subforficata remigibus brevior. Alulæ *spina* acuta recurvata nigra brevis. Caput ne minimè quidem cristatus. Longitudo undecim pollices. Avis gregarius, habitans in uliginosis.

Saxicola ——— *Le Traquet Fourmilier.* Le V. pl. 186.

Saxicola ——— *Le Traquet Montagnard.* Le V. pl. 184.

Saxiçola ———. *Le Traquet Pâtre.* Le V. pl. 180. f. 1.

Sylvia ———. *Le Grivetin?* Le Vaill. Ois. d'Afr. pl. 118.

Turdus ———. *Le Nabouroup.* Le V. pl. 91.

Oriolus arundinarius, B.

Merops Apiaster. (*Berg Zwaluw*)

Corvus albicollis (*Witte-hals Kraai*)

Corvus scapularis

Platalea nivea

Milvus parasiticus (*Kuikendief*)

Falco Tinnunculus (*Kleine Roode Valk*)

Lanius Collurio

Lanius atrococcineus, B.

Lanius forficatus, Linn. *Edolius,* Cuv.

Hirundo Capensis

Motacilla Capensis (*Kwikstaart*)

Cuculus auratus

Caprimulgus pectoralis

Columba Capensis

Columba risoria (*Tortel Duif*)

Columba Guineënsis (*Bosch Duif*)

Upupa Epops

Vultur Percnopterus (*Witte Kraai*)

Vultur auricularis? (*Zwart Aasvogel*)

Alauda (*Anthus*) *Capensis* (*Wilde Kalkoentje*)

enjoyed the delightful notes of a little bird which bore the greatest resemblance to the Canary bird, not only in size and color, but in its singing also ; and it had, therefore, gained from the Klaarwater people the name of *Kanari vogel.* It is not easy to suppress that natural reluctance we feel at taking away the life of any thing so innocent and pleasing as the bird that entertains us by its happy war- bling. On this account I never shot but one individual of that spe- cies, nor did any of my men happen ever to meet with another. In the mead we often started a very remarkable sort of plover, distin- guished by a short thorn or spur at the flexure, or metacarpal joint of the wing. A kite, which in size, manners, and appearance, much resembled the common kite of Europe, now and then occurred in different districts of the interior, but seldom more than two or three were seen at the same time. It is known by the name of *Kúikendief* (Chicken-thief). A Kestrel was frequently met with, and also the common. Butcher-bird or Shrike, the common Hoopoe, and Bee- eater ; all four so much resembling the English bird, that a doubt may be admitted whether they can be considered as forming distinct species. A goat-sucker, first shot at this place, but found in various other parts of Africa, differs very little in general appearance from the European kind. The Green-and-gold Cuckoo was found in abundance ; as were Crows of two species ; the little Cape Pigeon, or *Namaqua duif;* the Guinea Dove, called *Boschduif* (Wood Pigeon) ; the Turtle Dove ; the Cape Lark, called, I know not for what reason, *Wilde Kalkóentje,* (Little Wild Turkey); and the Sacred Vulture, or *Witte Kraai.* Besides these we shot specimens of new species of Snipe, Rail, Orioles, Shrikes, Swallow, Thrush, Barbets, Plovers, Flycatchers, Sparro, Grosbeak, &c. To which list may be added a considerable number of the birds already mentioned in the preceding part of this journal.

30th. Gert, by residing in Captain Kok's hut, and thus passing several weeks entirely among the Klaarwater Hottentots, had an

---

Rallus, species 3

Scolopax

Oriolus

Lanius

Charadrius

Grus ⸺. *(Groote blauwe Kraan- vogel)*

Loxia (Linn.) species 3

opportunity of hearing a great deal of village talk, and sometimes reported whatever he thought important for me to know. Through him I now began to learn that the general feeling of these people was unfavourable to my expedition; for it had been by some means told and circulated amongst them, that I intended to take the same journey as those unfortunate travellers already alluded to. This was, indeed, the same, in effect, as telling them that all who joined me would be murdered by the savages. Hitherto I had not been able actually to hire any men, although three or four had half-promised to go. Still I perceived every where a disposition to avoid any positive engagement; and, until I heard it from Gert, I was at a loss to guess the cause. For not having disclosed to any person, excepting the missionaries, that I had a positive intention of travelling far beyond Litaakoon, the reluctance which the Hottentots seemed to have against my undertaking, appeared unaccountable; especially as these people feel so much pleasure in hunting, and in a constant change of abode, that travelling and our mode of life must have presented some temptation, as being more congenial to their habits, than any other employment. Offers of high wages had been made to them, yet hitherto without effect.

As soon as I became aware of the real cause of this disinclination to enter my service, I immediately endeavoured to counteract it, by frequently repeating an assurance that no idea of following the track of those travellers was ever entertained; and that I had certainly no intention of running into obvious danger; but would give them my promise to turn back, the moment we should discover that there was, by advancing further into the interior, any evident risk of our safety; that as I was perfectly independent, and accountable to no one for the course I was to take, or for the time of my return, I was perfectly at liberty to regulate my travels, just as it might be thought safe and agreeable; and as it was, undoubtedly, quite as much my wish as theirs to return again in safety to my home and to my friends, I should of course never be so senseless or so mad, as to venture into countries which presented no prospect or chance of our safe retreat; that I had much more at stake than they had, and consequently should be proportionally more watchful of danger;

that there would be no want of arms and ammunition, which they well knew would, if rightly used, enable us to make a whole nation of wild men fly before us.

These, and many similar arguments, were urged with the most impressive declarations of sincerity and unreserve ; yet, whether it might be owing to that almost universal prevalence of deceit and falsehood, which teaches these people, as a matter of course, to regard no man's words as expressing his real thoughts and intentions ; or whether some dissuasive advice and misrepresentations had pre-occupied their minds, I had the mortification to find that all I could say appeared to have very little effect. Therefore, after convincing my own men that it was not my intention to lead them into danger, I engaged them privately, and as it were on their own parts, to talk with these people, and use their persuasion to induce some of them to enlist for the expedition. The smallest number that would suffice for the bare purposes of travelling and conducting my waggons, was six in addition to my own ; and I had resolved to proceed on my journey the moment these were engaged. As I could not hope to obtain a body of men strong enough to render our safety from attacks of the natives certain, I contented myself with a number which would answer all my views in other respects, and be sufficient for our protection and defence in ordinary cases, trusting to prudence and watchfulness in circumstances of greater danger, and relying on the Providence of that Great Being whose works and whose wisdom in this remote corner of the creation, I was desirous of studying and making the objects of my meditation.

To view the admirable perfection of *Nature* in a new light, and not less beautiful in the wilds of Africa, was the irresistible motive which led me on : while the charms which novelty of scenery, heightened by the interesting consideration of Human Nature under forms perfectly new to me, and a philosophical contemplation of the various objects which in these untrodden regions incessantly present themselves, have for a mind constituted to feel them, inspire an enthusiasm which none can know but those who have been placed under these circumstances. How pitiable are those cold-hearted beings, whose amusements and views, whose whole life, and even thoughts, are artificial.

Doomed to breathe the thick air of Insensibility; to feed on the gross food, and wallow in the mire, of Sensuality and Selfishness; greedy of every thing which, among men, passes by the name of enjoyment, they never dream of the genuine pleasure which Nature bestows only on those who view, with a broad admiring eye, the beauty and perfection of all her works, equally stupendous in the smallest insect, and the glorious picture of the starry heavens.

It must not be supposed that these charms are produced by the mere discovery of new objects: it is the harmony with which they have been adapted by the Creator to each other, and to the situations in which they are found, which delights the observer in countries where Art has not yet introduced her discords. To him who is satisfied with amassing collections of curious objects, simply for the pleasure of possessing them, such objects can afford, at best, but a childish gratification, faint and fleeting; while he who extends his view beyond the narrow field of nomenclature, beholds a boundless expanse, the exploring of which is worthy of the philosopher, and of the best talents of a reasonable being.

CHAPTER XX.

RESIDENCE AND TRANSACTIONS AT KLAARWATER; AND PREPARATIONS FOR
RESUMING THE JOURNEY INTO THE INTERIOR.

JANUARY 1*st*, 1812.   The commencement of a new year seldom fails
to occasion reflections on the lapse of time; and when, in the evening, this day was recorded in my journal, I felt what any person
similarly situated would, I believe, naturally feel, somewhat anxious to
look into the Book of Futurity; so far in it, at least, as the termination
of my present journey.   But now that this period is past, I clearly
see and confess the wisdom of the dispensation by which that book
has been so inscrutably closed.   Anticipation would have weakened
the impression of every agreeable occurrence, and have strengthened
that of all my troubles and difficulties.   Than to possess such knowledge as this, better is it to remain from day to day in ignorance of
what shall happen on the morrow.   How many times may I have
exclaimed to myself, with peculiar aptness, ' Sufficient unto the day
is the evil thereof.'   Frequently, when surrounded by difficulties,
have I long continued struggling through them, supported only by
the hope and expectation that the morrow, or the morrow, would end
them.   Draw but the picture of one solitary European, wandering,
unsheltered, over the vast plains of Africa, deep in the interior eleven

hundred miles; without a friend or companion from whom to ask advice, or to whom to communicate his thoughts; surrounded by savages, men of another color, of a strange and almost unintelligible language, often of hostile inclinations, or of suspicious manners, awakening every day some new anxiety for his personal safety; unprotected from the caprice of lawless tribes, whom no visible restraint withheld from making his property their own, and to whose power his life, either sleeping or waking, lay at all moments exposed; daily vexed and thwarted by those men on whom he had placed his only dependence for assistance; exhausted by corporal and mental labor without respite; and, through want of suitable food, reduced even to the lowest degree of bodily weakness; draw but this picture, and it will then present no more than the outlines of the history of the following year. Yet, in the midst of all these troubles and dangers, the highest enjoyments may be found by all who are not insensible to those charms, the powers of which have just been faithfully portrayed. The events which succeeded my departure from Klaarwater were marked by a new character; and the vicissitudes and incidents which chequered my way, assumed, not unfrequently, a character of the romantic.

3rd. The heat of the weather was at this time daily increasing, and the summer had nearly attained its greatest height. During the nights the air was exceedingly warm, and at seven in the morning the thermometer was generally found to be about 76° Fahrenheit (19°·5 Reaum.; 24°·4 Centig.); and frequently 96° (28°·4 Reaum; 35°·5 Centig.), at four in the afternoon. The hottest days were often the most calm; and at such times the stillness of the atmosphere was sometimes suddenly disturbed in an extraordinary manner: *whirlwinds* raising up columns of dust to a great height in the air, and sweeping over the plain with momentary fury, were no unusual occurrence. As they were always harmless, it was an amusing sight to watch these tall pillars of dust, as they rapidly passed by, carrying up every light substance to the height of from one to even three and four hundred feet. The rate at which they travelled varied from five to ten miles in the hour: their form was seldom straight, nor were they quite perpendicular; but uncertain and changing. Whenever they happened to pass over our fire, all the ashes were scattered in an instant, and nothing remained but the heavier sticks and logs. Sometimes they were observed to disappear, and, in a minute or two afterwards, to make their re-appearance at a distance further on. This occurred whenever they passed over rocky ground, or a surface on which there was no dust, nor other substances sufficiently light to be carried up in the vortex. Sometimes they changed their color, according to that of the soil or dust which lay in their march; and when they crossed a track of country where the grass had lately been burnt, they assumed a corresponding blackness.

But to-day the calm and heat of the air was only the prelude to a violent wind; which commenced as soon as the sun had sunk, and continued during the greater part of the night. The great heat, and long-protracted drought of the season, had evaporated all moisture from the earth, and rendered the sandy soil excessively light and dusty. Astonishing quantities of the finer particles of this sand were carried up by the wind, and filled the whole atmosphere; where, at a great height, they were borne along by the tempest, and seemed to be real clouds, although of a reddish hue; while the heavier particles, descending again, presented, at a distance, the appearance of mist or driving rain.

During the day, I had been employed in preparing the skin of the large blue crane; but the scorching beams of a nearly vertical sun caused a violent head-ache and throbbing at the temples. The remedy which was always found efficacious in such cases was strong tea taken very warm; the power of which, assisted by wrapping up, particularly the head, caused an active perspiration, that, in the course of the evening, relieved the pain and removed all symptoms. But by degrees, as I became more inured to exposure to the sun, I rarely suffered any serious attack of this kind.

8th. The heat of this day also was intense, and almost insupportable. The thermometer, however, did not rise above 96°; but there was not a breath of air stirring. In the rainy climate of

England, the *umbrella* is seldom, or never, used for the purpose which its name implies; but now I restored to this article its original functions; and from the essential service it rendered in this capacity, I learnt to value it as an important part of an African traveller's equipment.

All herbage was at this time parched up, and no verdure of any kind was to be seen. Many of the inhabitants of the village had removed, with all their cattle, to the Gariep, where some scanty pasture might still be picked up along its banks.

Every pool and pond was completely dried up; even the *frogs* had disappeared and crept into holes in the ground, there to lie, in silence and sleep, till the rains again called them forth. No sooner does the delightful element moisten the earth, and replenish the hollows, than every pool becomes a concert-room, in which frogs of all sizes, old and young, seem contending with each other for a musical prize. Some in deep tones perform their croaking bass, while the young ones, or some of a different species, lead in higher notes of a whistling kind. Tenors and trebles, counter-tenors, sopranos, and altos, may be distinguished in this singular orchestra; while, at intervals, some ancient toad, as double-bass, joins in with a hollow croak, the lowest in the vocal scale. The noise thus produced, particularly in the evenings, is truly astonishing, and nearly stunning: but, to a traveller, the most surprising circumstance attending these musicians, is their sudden appearance after the rains, where, from the excessive aridity of the country, he could, but a few days before, have hardly supposed that such animals had ever existed.

13th. As the season for the *Paarde-ziekte*, or *horse-distemper*, was expected to begin, generally, about the beginning of February, a party of people set out this day for the Colony, taking with them a great number of horses, with which they were to remain till the first of May, at a farm in the Roggeveld, belonging to a boor named Franz Maritz. Many of these people had, this year, sent no more than half their horses into the colony: the other half, in order to be nearer at hand in case of hostilities with any of the neighbouring tribes, were sent off, at the same time, for the Langberg, under the

care of a stronger party.   In a former year, when they preferred running the risk of keeping them at the village in the Asbestos mountains, out of eighty horses, there died of this distemper not fewer
than seventy.

14*th*.   So favorable an opportunity for sending letters to my
friends in Cape Town and England, was not allowed to pass unheeded;
but the pleasure of so delightful a task, was considerably diminished
by not having it in my power to inform them, at the same time,
that every thing here succeeded equal to my expectations.   For
I now began clearly to foresee some part of the difficulties in obtaining men for the journey.   These difficulties I could not refrain
from expressing ; although, at that time, little aware of the turn they
were soon afterwards to give to all my movements.

My situation and sentiments, at this time, are best expressed
in the words of my *letters*, which, though written in haste, are
preferable, as being penned under the impression of present
circumstances.   To my esteemed friend, Mr. Hesse, I wrote,

‘ My dear friend,—An opportunity now suddenly presents
‘ itself, for sending a letter to Cape Town, by some men
‘ who are going on horseback as far as the Roggeveld ; and
‘ although I mean to reserve my principal and final communication
‘ till Mr. Jansz goes, which will be in about March or April, yet I
‘ cannot lose this opportunity of letting you know that I am in very
‘ good health, and have found the journey pleasant and not too
‘ fatiguing, though very laborious in the scientific part of it, as so
‘ much new work every day claims my attention.   We arrived at this
‘ place, (Mr. A., &c. on the 20th of September, and I on the 30th,)
‘ without any other unpleasant occurrence than the want of water
‘ between the Karreebergen and the Orange river (Gariep) and the
‘ loss of two of my oxen, strayed away in the night.   Since I have
‘ been at Klaarwater, I have made a month’s excursion, accompanied
‘ by Mr. Jansz, to explore the Zwart, the Vaal, and Modder rivers,
‘ three large branches of the Orange river ; where my party shot two
‘ Hippopotami.   The tongue of one of them is preserved for you,
‘ but the other, intended for our friend Polemann, was spoiled by

' the heat of the weather; together with more than the half of the
' meat. Here I had an opportunity of making some observations
' on the wild Bushmen; and really, what I saw has considerably
' cleared my ideas respecting human nature in an uncivilized state.
' In the light in which I view every thing that presents itself to me,
' I have derived the greatest gratification from this beginning of my
' journey. What pleasure, therefore, may I not promise myself, in
' proceeding to examine and study those tribes and nations which lie
' more northward! I feel, indeed, that my means and abilities are
' not competent to so great a task; yet I shall certainly make the
' attempt: although, from the state in which affairs are at pre-
' sent, (having only two effective men), I do not consider it very
' probable that I shall accomplish the task I had assigned to myself;
' that of exploring the country as far as Benguela, or St. Paul de
' Loando. The chief obstacle to this is the want of men; for since
' the two that Dr. Cowan took with him from here, are not returned,
' there is not one individual who will venture on a similar journey;
' and, though I have been making incessant enquiries for men, none
' offered themselves till I assured them that I was not going on
' such an expedition as the late one, but would travel no farther
' than I found it safe; upon which two have agreed to accompany
' me. One was persuaded by Speelman, who is his cousin: and if
' I cannot procure more men at any other rate, I must give up the
' idea of proceeding so far, unless I can hereafter, by promising some
' great reward, induce them to go forward. Thus there is a proba-
' bility of my having the pleasure of seeing you, and my Cape
' friends, once more. I do not believe any one has witnessed much
' idleness in me since I left Cape Town; and it is not without
' inconceivable labor that my collections in Natural History have
' been made, and are daily increasing. They at this time amount to
' 163 birds of 29 different genera; about 400 insects; a few small
' quadrupeds, not having at present room in my waggons for the
' larger skins; about 1,000 species of plants; with mineralogical
' specimens, &c.; and 110 drawings of a variety of subjects. I have
' not been fortunate in the botanical part, as the weather has been

‘ constantly so dry that every thing is parched up, excepting the
‘ shrubs and trees.   I find, unless I should decide on proceeding
‘ with pack-oxen only, that it is best to take both my waggons on
‘ with me.   I shall avoid saying much respecting my intended plans,
‘ as experience teaches me that the execution of them depends
‘ entirely on the unforeseen events which each ensuing day may
‘ bring with it.   What I propose to myself to perform may be very
‘ different from that which circumstances may ultimately lead me
‘ to: yet thus much I feel certain of, that should Providence allow
‘ me to return safe, my journey will be productive of great increase
‘ of knowledge to myself, and of the utmost gratification in furnish-
‘ ing my mind with matter for contemplation for the future part of my
‘ life.   As to its being of any benefit to society in general, I at pre-
‘ sent give up that idea; but should be happy indeed, should circum-
‘ stances put it in the power of my individual labors, to add any
‘ thing to the present stock of true knowledge; but I fear I shall not
‘ be able to penetrate far enough to ascertain those facts which I had
‘ supposed to exist.   The chief obstacle, as I have already said, is
‘ the want of proper men, and the manifest reluctance of those I
‘ have with me, to trust themselves to unknown nations.   I shall,
‘ however, journey onwards, till I shall have ascertained the truth of
‘ those difficulties I am told of, and which I suspect to be greatly
‘ exaggerated.   My course, after leaving Letaako, will be northerly,
‘ or north-westerly, as circumstances shall render most advisable.
‘ Respecting the country to the N. E., I have obtained the same
‘ encouraging account which the late travellers received; but
‘ respecting that to the N. and N. W., there seems to hang an
‘ obscurity over it, which I wish to clear away: no one can give me
‘ the least information in that quarter.   Yet I shall always persist
‘ in endeavouring to accomplish so much of my original plan, that
‘ at a future period, I, or some other person, may not find it a diffi-
‘ cult undertaking to set out from St. Paul de Loando and join my
‘ present route: by which a very large portion of the unknown part
‘ of Southern Africa would be explored.   And should I, after my
‘ return to England, feel a desire to attempt this second journey, the

‘ experience I am now acquiring, would prove to be of the greatest
‘ advantage.’

To *Mr. Polemann*, I wrote in these words : ‘ My dear Friend, I
‘ take the opportunity of some people going to the Roggeveld, on
‘ horseback, to remain there till the first of May, to let you know
‘ how it fares with me. I have enjoyed very good health ever since
‘ leaving Cape Town : and have felt no other fatigue than that which
‘ arises from my anxiety not to let any thing escape my notice; but
‘ still I fear I shall pass by many things unobserved; yet have no
‘ doubt that I shall bring home a large collection. I am situated
‘ very unpleasantly, owing to want of men ; having only two besides
‘ the man from Groene Kloof, whom you sent to me at Tulbagh;
‘ who having met with an unfortunate accident, cannot now be of
‘ so much service to me as heretofore. The people of Klaarwater are,
‘ I believe, the laziest men in the world ; yet I am reduced to the
‘ necessity of soliciting some of them to accompany me ; which, I
‘ fear, I shall find great difficulty in doing, as the two men taken from
‘ here by the late travellers, are not returned, and it is suspected
‘ that I am not coming back this way again. Yet, if I cannot get
‘ men at any other rate, I must promise them that they may come
‘ back, as I have some slight hopes that I may supply their place by
‘ Bichuanas. If this last resource should fail, then must I make up
‘ my mind to see Cape Town again; and, indeed, think that the
‘ pleasure of again meeting my Cape friends, will greatly compensate
‘ for my disappointment. I mean first to visit Letaako, and then to
‘ turn off to the N. or N. W., to a country of which no one here
‘ knows even the name or the nature. The climate is here very hot
‘ and dry ; the thermometer being, in the coolest place, at an average,
‘ 95°. The oxen, which were purchased of Van der Merwe, have
‘ proved to be very good ; though I have lost two of the best. The
‘ remainder are now sufficiently recovered to proceed on the journey,
‘ as soon as Gerrit is well enough; which I think will be in a fort-
‘ night. I am quite tired of being here so long, and am anxious to
‘ behold new scenes. I am going to apply myself to hard study, to
‘ obtain a knowledge of the Sichuana language, which, I have reason

' to believe is spoken over a very large extent of country.   I have
' engaged a native for this purpose alone.   I have not yet seen a
' camelopardalis, though I have made two or three meals from one.
' Did any one in Cape Town observe a comet which I first perceived
' on the 30th of October, near the constellation Lyra ? By the 20th
' of November it was so near to the sun that it was no longer
' visible.   When I first saw it, I was high up the Vaal river, away
' from the rest of my party, with one of my waggons, on a hippo-
' potamus hunt, when we shot two of those animals, and saw many
' more.   During this part of my excursion, I had no other bed than
' the bank of the river, nor other covering at night than the sky,
' yet I experienced not the least inconvenience from it.   My only
' food was ' karbonadjes' of hippopotamus, without bread or salt.
' The scenery here was picturesque, the river a very fine stream; and
' it will be long before I forget the contemplative solitary rambles
' I often took along its banks.   The Bushmen slept on the ground
' every night close by us, and were happy at the rencontre, as we
' loaded each of them with as much meat as he could carry away.
' I should have been happy then, at having a companion by me to
' participate in the pleasure these scenes gave me.   The smooth
' glassy surface of the river, which reflected like a mirror the beau-
' tiful thick trees that clothed each bank ; the notes of a multitude
' of strange birds among their branches; the Bushmen busy in dry-
' ing their share of the meat; and the serenity of the atmosphere,
' added to the tranquillity that reigned around us ; made a delight-
' ful impression on my mind.   I look forward to much enjoyment in
' the future part of my journey ; and am convinced that, for a mind
' susceptible of that pleasure which the contemplation of Nature
' affords, nothing can give greater gratification than such an expedi-
' tion as this.   And if it must be so, that I am to return to Cape
' Town, I shall then renew these pleasures by relating to you more
' fully what I have seen.'

My packet, which, besides seven letters of my own, contained
four belonging to the missionaries, was addressed to the Landdrost
of Tulbagh, to be forwarded by the Field-cornet Gerrit Maritz ; and

was now given in charge to a Hottentot, named Titus. Having in a former part of my journal (page 250), noticed the shameful neglect and loss of a package which I sent from the Roggeveld, it is but just that I should record the due arrival of this, and my thanks to every one by whose hands it was forwarded. The degree of sanctity in which packages committed to their charge, and sealed letters, are held, is often no bad criterion of men's probity.

15th. The *rainy season* had at length commenced, and, within the preceding six days a great quantity of water had fallen. The surprising change of the atmosphere, from the utmost degree of dryness to the opposite extreme of moisture, may be easily estimated from the fact, that common salt left standing in a plate in the waggon, entirely deliquesced in the course of the night.

I had never experienced any thing more refreshing than this alteration of weather, after so long a drought. That constant languor which I had lately suffered from intense heat, vanished at once, and was succeeded by the most agreeable sensations, inspiring an unusual cheerfulness. I know not how to account for the great change it produced, not only in my bodily feelings, but even in those of my mind. My nerves and muscles thus braced and invigorated, I fancied that I possessed the strength to walk the whole length of Africa. Impatient of inactivity, I longed again to roam over boundless plains, or climb the lofty mountain ; all my troubles and difficulties retired to the furthest distance, where I viewed them diminished almost to nothing. Rapt in this musing, delightful mood, methought a beneficent deity of refulgent lustre, and countenance of inexpressible benignity, advanced towards me, and whispered softly in my ear, that sweet word LIBERTY : which repeating, till it thrilled in every nerve, the celestial being seemed to say ; *Follow me.* And where, indeed, could I have obeyed the enticing summons, so easily and uncontrolled as in the wild regions before me? For some time I allowed myself full indulgence in these pleasing reflections. By subsequent experience, I have learnt that the delightful sensation of unshackled existence could never be recalled, after I had re-entered the colonial boundary. Here the idea of restraint began to usurp its place; and at Cape Town they became completely annihilated. But if society smothered and extinguished them, I became, on the other hand, like one of society, adopting its mode of thinking, and enjoying its refinements, and its reasonable pleasures, as a compensation for those which I had lost.

The picture here given of the remarkable effects of the freshness of the atmosphere on my feelings, is neither overdrawn nor over-coloured; and though not easily accounted for, is not, therefore, the less exact and faithful.

These reviving showers produce a change in the face of the country, more like the sudden operation of magic, than of the gradual progress of *vegetation*. As if touched by a fairy wand, the dreary surface is transmuted to a verdant flower-garden, and innumerable little flowers, before invisible, spring up into existence, and hasten to cover the ground. In less than a fortnight the earth begins to reanimate, and the complexion of the country assumes so different an appearance, that it no longer could be imagined to be that same sterile region which, for so great a part of the year, presents to the eye of the traveller nought but desolate and unproductive plains. All now looks fair and smiling, and no longer can they be termed the arid deserts and frowning wastes of Africa.

19th. Speelman had informed me that our expectation of having *Hendrik Abrams* with us, had been counteracted by an order from the Klaarwater captain, appointing him to the duty of superintendant, or, as they call it, corporal, of one of the out-posts; and that he had actually been sent in that capacity to investigate the truth of a report of the Koras at Wittewater, having in some quarrel killed a Bushman. Whenever Hendrik came to Klaarwater, he was now afraid to be seen at my waggons, lest the captain should construe into an act of opposition to his orders, the idea of deserting his post to accompany us.

I therefore represented the case to one of the missionaries, and requested him to send for the captain to his house. Here we had some explanation, by which it plainly appeared, that both he and the missionary had a stronger wish to retain the man at Klaarwater, than to persuade him to go with us. Dam, however, said, that he had never positively forbidden his going, but was merely of opinion that it would be better for him to stay at home to take care of his own business, and look after the people of his kraal, as he was one of the few on whose steadiness of conduct he could place any dependence. At last he promised, but without the cordiality I wished, that he would not oppose his accompanying me.

On the part of the missionary, not a word was said to back my request; nothing proposed to forward my plans. His authority and persuasion, if exerted in my behalf, would, I have reason for believing, have smoothed away all these difficulties, and have obtained for me the men I wanted; but from him, and, consequently, from the others, I received, on the contrary, nothing but the most disheartening representations; nor do I recollect their ever once having allowed an encouraging remark to escape their lips. I own that this coldness and backwardness to promote the extension of my journey was not what I had calculated upon; nor did it accord with the civilities which, in other matters of less importance, I frequently received from them. There might possibly be some reason why they might not wish these regions to be known to any but themselves and their people, at least this was the interpretation which I put upon it at the time.

That men whose business is solely that of preaching the Gospel, should view the pursuits of science and every other species of knowledge in a light very inferior to that of their own calling, I have reason for believing; but that they should be able to resist those feelings of sympathy which it seems but natural to entertain in so remote a region, for a person in my situation, an European and a countryman, beset by difficulties on every side, can be explained only by the supposition of a constitutional coldness of nature. I could not but feel disappointed; for having, when in Cape Town been advised by a friend to take with me to Klaarwater some official letter specially requiring the persons of that institution to afford me all possible aid, I rejected the advice, because I was then confident, from the friendly assistance Mr. Anderson had already given me on several occasions, that such a letter would be unnecessary. It must, however, be admitted, that being merely a private individual, I was not entitled to that attention and ready assistance which all who had visited that settlement before me had received, they having been sent vested with the authority of government; and, indeed, when I once slightly hinted that it might be useful if the missionaries would represent to the captain and the people that I was the bearer of papers from government, calling upon the inhabitants of the colony to give me all the aid I might stand in need of, they declined doing this; saying, that the settlement was independent of the colony, which, having refused to afford it protection when they once applied to the Landdrost for that purpose, was, consequently, not entitled to make demands upon it.

Being thus made sensible that neither I, nor my papers, had any power at this place, I begged them to co-operate with me in making inquiries after a few men for my service. They, however, decidedly declined using any persuasion with the Hottentots, or even representing the journey as desirable, since they beheld it as fraught only with danger; and stated further, that having some years before permitted two people of the settlement to accompany Dr. Cowan and Captain Donnovan, they could not, as a matter of conscience, take any steps to induce others to risk the same untimely end; but that all they could do would be, not to prevent him, if any man should think proper to accompany me. From this declaration I clearly discovered the extent of the difficulties that opposed me. I was inclined to suppose that among the missionaries there was some difference of opinion on the subject, although it never was expressed; and I am willing to believe that all three were not, in sentiment at least, equally decided against affording me their assistance in this business.

20th. The next morning Speelman came from Groote-doorn, to stop here a few days to help Philip to grind corn, a small quantity of

which I had just purchased.   As soon as he had, as usual, saluted me
with ' Dag Mynheer,' he gave me to understand that he had some
good news to tell, and, drawing me aside, proceeded to inform me,
that, having been privately talking with *Hans Lucas* on the subject,
he found him willing to go with us.   This I was indeed glad to
hear, as I had always regarded that Hottentot as a useful and
intelligent man, and one whom I believed to have some good-will
towards me.

22nd. About nine o'clock in the evening, as I was crossing the
*valléy**, or mead, in returning home from a visit to the missionaries,
I witnessed an *electrical phenomenon*, which never presented itself to
me but this once : lightning appeared as if emitted from every
quarter of the compass, the flashes following each other in quick
succession, but unaccompanied by thunder ; all was still and silent,
excepting a few heavy drops of rain which escaped from some clouds
which were exceedingly dense and black.   On a sudden I was almost
blinded by a glaring flash of light, which seemed to have descended
from the zenith, and, for a moment, every blade of grass around me,
to the distance of fifteen feet, seemed ignited by the electric matter.
There was no explosion, no kind of noise was heard, nor was any
effect whatever experienced from it ; all was still and quiet, and I
continued my walk, in alternate darkness and flashes of lightning,
without any repetition of this singular phenomenon.   The grass,
being of a coarse sort, was, just at that spot, about a foot high ; each
stalk and blade was strongly illuminated, or rather, as it seemed,
ignited ; but beyond the distance of about fifteen feet, I saw none of
this remarkable illumination.

---

* This word *Valléy* is a Dutch word of most extensive use in the Cape Colony, and
can seldom be translated by the English word *Válley*, as it is sometimes used to signify
a *pond* or *pool ;* sometimes a low *swampy place ;* or, at other times, a *lake*, a *spring*, a
rivulet, a *grassy hollow* containing water in the rainy season, a *meadow*, or, in general,
any low grassy spot which receives the drainings of the surrounding country.   It should,
therefore, be considered, not as an English, but as a colonial, term, its proper pronunciation
being as if written *faly*, with the *a* sounded very faintly and indistinctly, and a strong
accent on the *y*.

23rd.   A melancholy event, and one which caused considerable distress, and was deplored with an universal feeling of sorrow and regret throughout the settlement, took place this day at the village, in the *death of Mrs. Kramer,* the wife of one of the missionaries : an inflammatory attack, which took place about eleven days before, was at last succeeded by those cruel symptoms which thus, in the fair morning of youth, terminated the life of a worthy and amiable woman. About a week previous to this, serious apprehensions began to be entertained, and I was first informed of her danger by a messenger sent to my waggons to request some laudanum.   The distress which this unexpected information occasioned, prevented my attending to my own affairs ; nor could I forbear my unavailing anxiety and assistance to avert the catastrophe, till death put a stop to further hope.   In the alarm and distress which the missionaries and Mrs. Anderson, her only female companion, felt at the too evident prospect of a fatal result, they flew to me for advice, as well as medicine ; and, would that I possessed the knowledge and the power to save my poor fellow-traveller !   I interpreted to them the opinions of the medical books which I had by me, and added all that my own judgment could suggest.   This they hastened to adopt ; and, at my representation, cleared the room of a crowd of sorrowful, but useless Hottentots, who, distressed and anxious for her whom they appeared much to esteem, created a suffocating heat, which considerably increased the danger.   To mitigate this, I recommended a small opening, or window, to be cut through the reeds and plastering to admit fresh air : this also was immediately done ; but, alas ! all was in vain ; and her pain and delirium left her only to make way for the last symptoms of dissolution.

With a mind already rendered susceptible by the disappointments which I had met with at this place, I felt deeply affected at this mournful occurrence.   From her, equally with Mrs. Anderson, I had experienced many marks of good-will, in their kind attentions to supply those deficiencies in the comforts of food, and those privations of many little luxuries, which they imagined a person unaccustomed to them, must find, at first, particularly inconvenient.

I remained entirely at the village, giving whatever assistance was in my power, especially in administering the needful consolation.

24th. Klaas Berends, one of the Hottentots, a relation of captain Berends was engaged to set out as soon as he could get ready for the journey, to carry letters into the colony, for the purpose of giving information of Mrs. Kramer's death to her relations.

25th. The second after the death, was the day appointed for *the funeral.* A great number of people assembled on the occasion, many of whom came from the out-posts at a considerable distance, in order to pay their last duties of respect by following the body to the grave. All the preparations and arrangements were managed with greater propriety than could have been expected here. A sufficient quantity of black linen was found for a pall, with which the coffin was covered, and black crape hat-bands were worn by the missionaries. The corpse born by six Hottentots, was preceded by the same number of people, and followed in procession by the four Europeans and her son; after whom walked the two captains, Kok and Berends. A long train of their people, about fifty in number then succeeded two by two, all cleanly and decently dressed, the greater part in European clothes. Every one conducted himself with a degree of decorum which was truly gratifying, from a tribe of people who in many other respects had made but little progress in civilization.

On arriving at the burying-ground, which is situated between the rocks near Leeuwenkuil, an extempore discourse or address was pronounced by the missionary; after which, the body was deposited in a *grave* seven feet deep, and covered in with mould to the thickness of a foot; then, experience having taught them the necessity, the Hottentots covered it over with large, broad, flat pieces of rock, to secure it against the

3 x

depredations of wild beasts, which, otherwise, would scratch it out of the earth during the night. The hole was then filled up, and afterwards many large stones of the same kind were placed over the grave.

These precautions are noticed on account of their being an ancient Hottentot custom, which still continues to be followed. This race of people, here, as well as in every other part of the country, use no coffins, but commit their dead to the earth, wrapped up merely in their clothes or karosses.

We had now witnessed, most probably, the first burial of a white woman which had ever taken place beyond the Gariep, and a knowledge of this fact rendered the ceremonies and transactions of the day doubly impressive and mournful. The Hottentots themselves were not insensible to that impression, and many of them noticed the circumstance.

26*th.* The following day being Sunday, I attended, according to my custom, the usual service in the church. After it was over I generally paid a visit to each of the missionaries; but this was a mournful Sunday, and the reflection of having just laid one of our party in the grave cast a gloom over all, and threw the affairs of the mission into a very unsettled state. Each beheld his prospects, on one side or the other, deranged by the occurrence: the widower had, in consequence, already resolved on a journey back to the Cape, to dissipate his melancholy; and he, whose turn it would now have been to take the recreation of a visit to the colony, shortly after this reversed his former arrangements, and agreed to remain till some future opportunity; while the third, viewed it as a circumstance particularly affecting his wife, whose residence at Klaarwater, without one white person as a female companion, in the country, was now rendered lonely and friendless. For my own part, I had no stronger wish than that of leaving Klaarwater as soon as possible; as I was now become impatient to pursue my journey, having been delayed at this spot so much longer than had been originally intended: besides which, I could not feel myself altogether at ease in a place where almost every day brought forth some disappointment, or some disagreeable occurrence.

I therefore lost no time in making preparations for my departure, as soon as a sufficient number of men should have been engaged; which I now began to hope, would, by means of my own people, soon be accomplished.

I packed up all my *collections and drawings*, in expectation of being able to send them to Cape Town by some of the waggons which were to accompany the missionary. I put in order all my notes and memoranda, my lists and catalogues, my sketches and *journals:* and at last reduced into an intelligible form, the mass of observations which had up to this date been accumulating. So that, in case of my death during the journey, they would, for the greater part, be found sufficiently clear to explain themselves. Thus, if my labors should prove of any value, I had now the satisfaction of knowing that they would not be entirely lost; though I might never live to explain them myself.

28th. My *waggons*, which during our stay had been partly dismantled, were again put upon their wheels, and placed in order for travelling: the chests were fetched from the store-house at the village, and loaded up and properly secured: the little waggon was repaired, and the wheels rectified: the yokes, straps, and thongs, and, in short, our whole equipage, were examined, and got in readiness. *

29th. *Gert* was now quite recovered from his accident, and declared himself perfectly able to bear the fatigues of the journey; and, to convince me of this, he walked with Speelman to Groote-doorn, to see my oxen, and make a report of the state they were in.

30th. He returned on the following day with a very satisfactory account of my cattle. This decided me in thinking seriously of

---

* The *vignette* at the end of this chapter represents the Hottentots employed in putting the little waggon in order for our departure into the Interior.

commencing the journey in a few days ; as the most important affair, that of the men, was just at the same time brought to a favorable conclusion ; several Hottentots having agreed to accompany us, and promised to be ready in a day or two.   Among these were three of approved character, and on whose services and steadiness I placed much reliance ; Hans Lucas, Hendrik Abrams, and Maagers, my former herdsman : the other was also well recommended. Yet these, together with Kees, and my own three, made my party to consist of no more than eight.   I found, however, that I must content myself with a less number than had been at first fixed upon : but, as it was believed that we could, as we advanced, pick up some Koras, or some Bachapins, who would be able to render us much service in the laborious part of our daily employments, I resolved that this deficiency should not be an obstacle. to our immediate departure.

Accordingly, we set about completing all further arrangements without delay, and began to load the other waggon and fasten every thing in its proper place. Some trifling stores which could be spared, were added to the stock of the mission ; we cast a large quantity of bullets ; and attended to. all the necessary repairs.

Besides other things which I presented to the Klaarwater captain in consideration of the assistance which he had occasionally lent me, and especially on account of his trouble in nursing Gert, and for allowing him the shelter of his hut (vignette, page 506), he stated that half a dozen pounds of gunpowder would perfectly satisfy him as a recompence for every thing he had done. Desirous of gaining his good will by the strongest proof of generosity that it was in my power to show, and of which the invaluable article gunpowder was of all things the most convincing, I presented him with nine pounds, instead of the six he asked for, and to these, over and above, I added a proportionate quantity of gun-flints, and of lead and tin for bullets. To his wife I made presents of a piece of chintz cotton, a quantity of needles, thread, tape, buttons, brandy, pepper, &c., with which she expressed herself highly pleased.

In order to convince him, and the settlement, by obliging acts on my part, how much more ready I was to meet their wishes than they mine, I, in two instances, at his and the missionaries' request, gave up a bargain I had made, one with a Kora, and the other with a Briqua, for the exchange of one of my guns, for oxen to replace those which had been lost in the Bushman country, near Buffelbout; and which were much needed to complete my teams. Their objections were founded on a wish to prevent, as much as possible, any person possessing fire-arms excepting themselves. My compliance with their request on this head, was a sacrifice made to complaisance.

31st. Inspired with alacrity at the near prospect of departure, we gaily continued the necessary preparations; little suspecting that my troubles were still lurking in ambush close at hand, and had not, as I flattered myself, retired to a distance.

February 1st. They first made their re-appearance in the form of reports, which reached Klaarwater this afternoon, through some of the people who had just arrived from a Hottentot kraal, situated at a distance down the river. Some stated that *Africaander,* whose mischievous character has already been mentioned, had advanced a considerable way above the Waterfall, with the intention of taking up his abode among the Briquas; while others assured us that he was actually lying on our road with all his gang, apparently having my waggons and property for his object. It was, besides, ascertained to be true that the three men who were on their way from Klaarwater to visit Captain Kok's father a Half-Hottentot boor in the Kamiesberg in Namaqualand, had been robbed of their guns by this freebooter.

This unlucky report had a very visible effect upon my party, and raised all their fears, while it threw a sudden damp on my own spirits. Not that I had myself any apprehensions on account of this vagabond, against whom we should still be more thau strong enough, provided we stood by each other; but that the terror of his name, rendered every one afraid to encounter him, and unwilling to proceed.

2nd. The effect of these reports was not a little increased by the opinion of the three missionaries, who laid great stress upon them, and apparently were not less alarmed than the Hottentots themselves. Still I continued to forward the arrangements for departing: I ordered Muchunka (Kees) to remain constantly at the waggons, and hold himself in readiness for the journey; and sent the same orders to the other men whom I had engaged.

The next morning the missionary, who had the chief direction of the affairs of the settlement, and the leading voice with his two companions, paid me a visit at my waggons, for the purpose, formally and in the name also of the others, of dissuading me from attempting to proceed on my journey with so few men. They had, he said, been consulting on the affair, and had agreed on the propriety of opposing it by every means of dissuasion; alledging for this, two reasons: the first, my own personal risk, and that of my men; and the second, the very serious consequences to them, and to the settlement, which would result from Africaander's getting possession of my guns and ammunition; and concluded with a clinching argument,—he had ascertained that none of the men I had lately engaged, had any intention of going beyond Litakun; and that the one named Manell, had no other view in going with me than that of suiting his own convenience in bartering with the natives of that town, and then to return home.

The latter part of this unexpected communication, for which I was not at all prepared, was deserving of some attention, as I foresaw in it, if true, the total subversion of my present plans. There was, however, a certain incongruity in his arguments which puzzled me, and held my mind undecided. During our former casual conversations on the subject of Dr. Cowan's failure, it had been his opinion that the exploring of the interior of this part of Africa could perhaps only be accomplished by means of the missionaries; and I therefore could not but naturally conclude that he really believed that a journey, such as I had planned, was neither so perilous, nor so impracticable, as it was now represented to be.

In the afternoon, the other missionaries called on me, for the purpose of adding arguments to the same effect as those which I had heard in the morning.

4th. On examining deeper into this affair, and coming to a fuller explanation with the people lately hired, I found it too true, that they were not by any inducement to be persuaded to go beyond the country of the Bachapins; and that the understanding they had had with my own men, was, that it was not my intention to venture farther into the interior.

I confess that, at first, I could not help giving way to some depression of spirits, the effect rather of anxiety, when I felt myself assailed on all sides by teazing obstructions, and my plans defeated in every quarter.

5th. As the missionaries had told me that Klaas Berends was to set out, in the course of the week, for the Roggeveld, it struck me as practicable that Gert might be sent, under the protection of that party, back to *Cape Town*, with a commission to my friends there to hire men, and dispatch them with the utmost expedition to the Roggeveld, in order that they might be in time to cross the Bushman country in company with the men and horses which were to leave the colony on the first of May; which, with the assistance of horses, and using all diligence, there would have been sufficient time for accomplishing.

Satisfied with the practicability of this plan, I repaired directly to the village to communicate it to Mr. Anderson, and consult with him, in order to make the arrangements for carrying it into effect. But in an instant he threw cold water upon it, by informing me that Klaas would not take his departure within three weeks; from which delay it followed, that there could not be time for my men to reach the Roggeveld by the day appointed. He, however, as it proved, did depart at the expiration of the week ; but, as I relied on what the missionary said, the plan was immediately given up as not to be accomplished, and I returned to my waggons, again to ruminate on this disappointment, and to devise some means for extricating my affairs from the unpleasant situation in which they now appeared to stand.

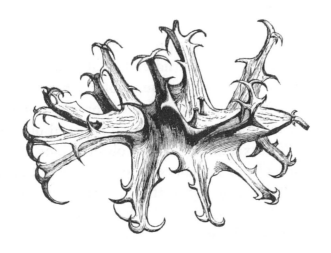

CHAPTER XXI.

THE greater part of the day was passed in the utmost uncertainty as to my future movements. In melancholy mood, I paced backwards and forwards, at a little distance from my waggons; where, alone and uninterrupted, I could muse on the plan that should now be adopted. The idea of going myself to Cape Town, several times presented itself, but the distance, and consequent loss of so much of my own time, appeared a great objection; although I afterwards had reason to believe that such would have been the most advantageous step: as, in that case, I should have accompanied, as far as the Colonial boundary, the waggon of the missionary who was about to return to the Cape, and then, on horseback, have made the best of my way alone. At Cape Town I could have purchased another waggon and oxen, which eventually would have been exceedingly serviceable; and, immediately, with fresh stores, and every deficiency again supplied, have hastened with my new men to join my waggons at Klaarwater, which would have been left in the care of my three Hottentots.

At last, while lamenting the great distance between Cape Town and the place where I was, I considered that Klaarwater might be much nearer to some other part of the colony, where I might equally well obtain the object of my visit. I therefore returned to my waggon, to look over my map: and immediately fixed on the village of *Graaffreynet.** The examining of my observations, together with a rough computation from the course and distance out of the Colony, satisfied me that that village lay in the direction of nearly south, at a distance of only three degrees and a half of latitude ; and that the Colonial boundary at Plettenberg's Baaken was consequently considerably nearer to us than Sack river or the Roggeveld. This, therefore, I perceived, was the quarter where assistance ought to be sought ; especially as the Landdrost of that district, *Mr. Stockenström*, was a particular friend of Mr. Hesse's ; and bore the character of being a man of liberal mind, which, added to the weight and authority of the papers with which I had been furnished by the Cape government, gave me every reasonable assurance of meeting with the best reception.

I again walked over to the village, to communicate this second plan to the missionary, and ask his assistance in obtaining men for this purpose; which, being a journey into the Colony, I concluded was not liable to those objections which had hitherto foiled my endeavours to go forwards.

But here again I was met with nothing but the most disheartening accounts :—that country through which I would pass was, as he had always been told, inhabited by tribes of Bushmen the most savage in Africa : it was, he had every reason to believe, so mountainous as to be quite impassable : he knew that the Klaarwater people

---

* This name is often written *Graaf Reinet* ; but the above orthography is more conformable to its origin. Both, however, are used in the official writings of the Colony.

people were decidedly averse to any road being discovered in that direction, lest the Caffres should take advantage of it, or the Dutch farmers be tempted to come and take possession of their land; in fine, he did not think that I should get any body to go with me. Thus, to every thing that was said, nothing but difficulties were started in reply; and that this, as he candidly remarked, was a scheme, of which, for many reasons, he could not approve.

What some of these reasons were, I afterwards learnt, both from himself, and from his fellow missionaries: they apprehended, that, by opening a new road to another part of the Colony, there would be a more frequent communication and traffic with the boors, to whom the Hottentots would be constantly selling their cattle; that it was a disadvantage to the mission and their people to be too dependant on the Colony, and to make such journeys often; which would, it was feared, be the case, if they found their way to any nearer town than the Cape or Tulbagh; and that their connection with the Colony ought, for their own welfare, to be as slight as possible. As far as these reasons might be meant for the advantage and civilization of the people whom they had undertaken to instruct, this line of policy, I am convinced, is more likely to produce a contrary result.

But these representations, in which I did not place entire confidence, had by no means the intended effect of discouraging me; and I returned to my waggons, there to devise the best mode of carrying this plan into execution. My own men were of the same opinion as myself, that we had better undertake the journey without the incumbrance of a waggon, which, at first, I had some idea of taking with us; and that we should mount ourselves on pack-oxen, as being much more expeditious. This plan, therefore, I resolved to adopt; as the country, which was utterly unknown to every body at Klaarwater, might, as had been hinted, be found impassable, at least for waggons.

6th. By supposing that we should travel all the way in nearly the same course by the compass, and allowing ninety miles by the road, to one degree of latitude*, and thirty miles travelled each day, I calculated that we could arrive at *Graaffreynét* in eleven or twelve days, provided every thing went on aright. Under a conscientious conviction of this, I assured every one that we could reach the borders of the Colony, meaning *Plettenberg's Baaken,* in a week. Although, from unexpected delays, and other unforeseen causes, the length of this journey proved very different from my calculations ; yet I succeeded, by these assurances, in gaining the confidence of *Speelman* and *Philip,* who were, moreover, exceedingly pleased at the expectation of re-visiting a place with which they were well acquainted ; particularly the former, who had made a journey from Cape Town to Graaffreynet but twelve months before. *Gert* and *Hannah* were to remain at *Klaarwater,* to take care of my waggons and oxen. The remarkably pleasant weather which we had just at this time, had certainly a favorable influence, by giving us the prospect of plenty of water and pasture by the way.

7*th*. Philip and Gert were sent off to Groote-doorn, to recruit for men ; or rather, it might be said, they went vested with full powers to explain my plan, and treat in my name with the inhabitants of that place.

8*th*. On the next day these plenipotentiaries returned ; having signed the preliminaries of a treaty with their *Uncle Hans* and *Cousin Hendrik.*

In the meantime I had engaged at Klaarwater several others ; and had nearly obtained the full complement. Those fears which operated so strongly against a journey into the unknown parts of the interior, were now not in the least excited by the proposal of a trip to the Colony, as this seemed to accord exactly with their wishes.

9*th*. Hans Lucas and Hendrik Abrams came to make further arrangements, and appeared not only willing to go, but were even pleased at, and desirous of, the journey. The former agreed to

---

* See the note at page 90.

furnish three pack-oxen, and to supply me, for my own use, with a quiet riding-ox and one that could be easily managed, as I was completely a novice in the art of riding on ox-back.   He was also to bring with him a Bushman whom he had retained several years in his service, and who would be found very useful for driving the loaded oxen. He was one of that class which they called *Makke Bosch-jesman* (Tame Bushman); by which denomination are distinguished such of that race as have either been brought up among the colonists, or are living habitually on good terms with them.   The people of this settlement, therefore, apply the name to all those Bushmen who are under similar circumstances, as respects themselves.

I was now reaping the advantage of the character which I had gained among them *, of being able to find out the true bearing of distant places ; for, although there was not an individual at Klaarwater who was able even to attempt a guess at the direction of Graaff-reynet, or had been aware that it lay in the quarter which I pointed out, yet my own men, and all those whom I hired on this occasion, placed entire confidence in my guidance, and never once expressed the least doubt of my being acquainted with the proper direction.

After church, when I paid my usual visit to the missionaries, my patience was a little exercised in listening to the medley of contradictory argument with which they endeavoured to deter me from the attempt and convince me that, should I escape being murdered by the Bushmen, I should still find myself unable to bear the hardships and fatigue of such a mode of travelling, and should never succeed in any part of my plan.   One even thought I ought to be careful how I enticed the men away, by representing the affair in a less difficult and dangerous light than it really was, and intimated that, when I had got myself and my people into danger, I might not feel so courageous as I expected.   And, that no stone might be left unturned in search for some bugbear, he did not hesitate to give the Klaarwater people the character of being a set of men on whose

---

* See pages 302 and 467.

fidelity no reliance was to be placed; remarking that they once threatened to shoot him for interfering with their practices. As soon as one had exhausted his argument, another began with a fresh one; and it seemed as if they thought it a duty to say any thing that could discourage me. All which served only to convince me that, if they really felt, and believed, their own reasoning, they were the most timid of mortals.

All this jumble of advice was quite lost upon me, who, considering that I had overcome the greatest difficulty by mustering a sufficient party, was too strongly bent on proceeding, to be thus frightened out of my determination. They were, however, perfectly right in one of their predictions; and, in foretelling that I should get no men at Klaarwater, they, on all such occasions, showed a prescience which was unfortunately correct.

10*th*. The next day, I learnt from my own men, that all, excepting Hans and Hendrik, had withdrawn their agreement to go with us. Manell, who had volunteered for this second expedition, now came to say that his wife would not consent to his going away.

11*th*. The last reports respecting *Africaander*, proved to be wholly a fabrication; and appear to have been generally disbelieved, as two waggons, we now heard, set out on a journey directly afterwards, taking the same road that we should have done. A son-in-law of that man, told Gert that his father was still stationed on the Gariep; and not any where near the Briquas, as it had been rumoured.

Being thus once more deserted, it was clearly to be perceived, that at this village my object would never be attained; and I therefore resolved, without previously making my intention known to any one, to go myself to the village of the Kloof, where I had some expectation that Captain Berends might be induced to second my request. But the very rainy weather of the two preceding days prevented our taking any steps for that purpose.

Having received a message that Klaas Berends would set out this day for the Roggeveld, I hastily wrote a letter to my friend

Hesse, in order that it might be known at Cape Town how I was circumstanced. This letter, together with the former two, were the cause of some endeavours by those friends to afford me relief by engaging a party of Hottentots for my service; endeavours indicative of the most genuine friendship, but of which, as they did not succeed, I was never informed till after my return to Cape Town.

Klaas Berends took his departure in the evening, his party consisting of twelve men; which number, but not less, is considered sufficient to secure themselves against any open attack from the Bushmen, yet is not strong enough as a defence against the Caffres. They were obliged to undertake the journey with oxen only, as the river was at this time impassable for waggons, and would continue in that state until the next dry season.

I was careful to conceal from this party my intended visit to the Kloof settlement, so that no information or message might, by their means, arrive there before me, to counteract or obstruct the business which took me to that place.

In the afternoon, Philip was despatched to Groote-doorn, to fetch one of my teams of oxen; and with these he arrived at Klaarwater about eight o'clock in the evening, when they were made fast to the waggons, in order to be ready at hand early in the morning.

During the afternoon, there fell the heaviest shower that had been witnessed this season; yet so partial was its effect that Leeuwen-kuil received only a few drops, while at Klaarwater it poured down in such torrents, that almost instantly every hollow or flat place became a pond. It was mingled with *hail-stones* half an inch in diameter.

14*th.* That there might be nothing to delay us on the road, two sheep were killed and salted for this journey. Gert and Hannah were left at home, in charge of the little waggon and our remaining goods. I set out before noon, taking with me Philip and Speelman; with Kees as ox-leader.

Till we had passed the ridge, and got out of sight of the village, my men had been kept in total ignorance, not only of the object of this journey, but of the place to which we were going: they were,

however, greatly pleased at my management ; and declared that now
they had no doubt of my succeeding. The same country, which, at
the end of September presented an arid, unproductive appearance,
now smiled in charming verdant clothing, variegated with a profusion of beautiful flowers and curious plants, which the late rains had
awaken from out of their subterranean retreat. A handsome and
entirely new species of *Amaryllis** profusely covered a space of ground
of half a mile in extent, and the beautiful *Uncaria procumbens* † (or,
Grapple Plant) was not less abundant. It was just now in full bloom,
spreading on the ground ; some plants having already formed the
grapple-like seed-vessels ‡ ; while others were only beginning to
expand their large purple flowers. The fineness of the day rendered travelling exceedingly pleasant, and imparted an additional
grace to every object.

The incomplete list which a botanist would form from travelling
but once over the dry plains of Africa, may be well exemplified by
the collection made between Klaarwater and the Kloof settlement
in the preceding month of September, as compared with that which
was made during this excursion. At that time, only six numbers
were added to my catalogue ; but at this, fifty-eight. Some allowance, however, must be made for having, at the former time, passed
over a portion of the road in the night. A comparison of that
part of my catalogue now made at the Asbestos mountains in a
single day, with that of my first visit, which was the result of several
days, may perhaps be instructive, as showing these vegetable pro-

* *Amaryllis lucida,* B. Catal. Geogr. 1969. Folia lucida decumbentia. Scapus sub-17-
florus complanatus brevis, pedunculique scabro-pubescentes. Affinis *A. flexuosæ,*
undulatæ, et *humili* ; at, eis quamvis humilior, umbellâ gaudet multò majore.

† *Uncaria,* B. genus est *Martyniæ* affine ; a quo capsulæ formâ, (vide iconem magnitudine naturali; in pag. 529.) satis differt.

Uncaria procumbens, B. Catal. Geogr. 1970. Caules plures prostrati parùm ramosi.
Folia palmato-divisa et lobata, glaucescentia. Flores magni purpurei axillares solitarii.
Calycis foliola 5 linearia acuta. Corolla infundibuliformis, tubo basi angustato, limbi laciniis
rotundatis æqualibus. Stamina 4 didynama, pistillumque corollâ duplò breviora. Capsula bilocularis lignosa, angulis lobato-alatis, lobis uncinatis. Semina numerosa oblonga
angulata rugosa. Tota planta, sub lente visa, punctulis numerosis albis conspersa est.

‡ A figure of one, of the natural size, is given at page 529.

ductions which are met with only at different seasons. Such catalogues are not uninteresting; they are, to a certain extent, the Floras (in the Linnæan use of the word) of each separate spot. And if they indicate concisely the state with respect to flowering, seeding, or leafing, in which plants are at that season, and give briefly some of the more remarkable particulars, their utility in various points of view, will, it is hoped, be sufficiently obvious, to induce future travellers to bestow a small portion of their time on the forming of them.

The whole country was covered with verdure produced by an abundance of tall, fresh *grass*, of a variety of sorts, most of which happened to be now in flower. Of these, I collected in this short journey six and twenty species, plucked merely as I walked along: and it is very probable that many more might have been discovered, had there been time for a more careful search.*

---

* The botanical collection of this day consisted of —

Corchorus serræfolius, B. Catal. Geogr. 1962. Caules elongati procumbentes villosi. Folia linearia grossè serrata. Pedunculus, in medio internodii, triflorus. Alabastra acuta. Capsulæ lineares teretes scabræ sæpiùs tortuosæ sexvalves.

Ornithogalum nervosum, B. Cat. Geog. 1968. Folia erecta marginata nervosa rigida. Scapus foliis paulò altior, sursùm sensim incrassatus. Bracteæ setaceæ. Flores parvi virentes. Pedunculi longissimi horizontales. Filamenta omnia subulata.

Asparagus laricinus, B. C. G. 1971. Fruticosus erectus 4-6-pedalis. Rami ramulique albidi. Spina brevis subrecurva. Folia subulata subpollicaria fasciculata; floribus 1-5 in singulo fasciculo.

Briza nigra, B. C. G. 1978. Gramen erectum annuum. Folia pilis raris conspersa. Ligula pilosa. Panicula nigrescentè vel obscurè viridis. Lo-

custæ cordatæ, 14-18-floræ. Glumæ subcarinatæ.

Cleome heterotricha. B. C. G. 2011. Caules et petioli pubescentes, pilis longioribus interspersis. Folia quinata; foliolis obovatis subintegerrimis. Petala alba. Stamina 6. Maximè affinis *C. pentaphyllæ*, sed huic sunt folia vix serrata.

Celosia odorata, B.
Uncaria procumbens, B.
Cassia arachoïdes, B.
Cyperus usitatus, B.
Amaryllis lucida, B.
Indigofera
Achyranthes
Lappago. 2 sp.
Digitaria
Selago. 2 sp.
Ruellia
Panicum
Poa. 2 sp.
Aristida
Tripsacum

We reached *Wittewater* before sunset, and unyoked there for the night; but at this time it was without inhabitants. Our oxen were made fast to the Olive trees, an emblem of peace which we found here, but not at the place we had come from; and after a couple of hours occupied in cooking and taking our supper, we lay ourselves down early to rest.

15th. The next morning we went on to Aakaap, where we halted during the hottest part of the day, to allow the oxen time to graze, as the plains here abounded in the most beautiful grass I had hitherto seen during the whole journey. About midway we found a kraal of Koras, not very numerous, yet having with them large herds of cattle; on which account they had pitched their huts in the midst of these delightful, but short-lived pastures.*

At a little after four in the afternoon, we left Aakaap; and soon came to a large and very long *valley*,† or lake, in a part of the road where, in September, no traces of any thing of the kind were to be seen. It was frequented by wild ducks; at a flock of which

---

Commelina	*Cyperus*
Hermannia	*Eriospermum*
Barleria	*Tournefortia, &c.*

* Between Wittewater and Aakaap, the following were the genera found on this day:

Kyllingia	*Panicum*
Bryonia	*Aristida*
Commelina	*Convolvulus*
Poa	*Eriospermum*
Anthericum	*Cleome*
Mesembryanthemum	*Reseda dipetala*, (var: *ramosa*.)

Campanula ? denticulata, B. Catal. Geogr. 2000. Planta palmaris erecta. Caules plures paniculati. Folia linearia denticulata, denticulis oppositis. Flores albi oppositifolii. Calyx 5-fidus, divisionibus linearibus denticulatis. Corolla sub-campanulata, laciniis oblongis magnis. Stigma trifidum. Capsula trilocularis subrotunda, intrà calycem dehiscens, apice trivalvi. Semina plura nitida subrotunda spadicea.

This is, for the present, placed in the genus *Campanula*, but can scarcely with propriety stand in the same with *C. Medium*. Although differing in other respects, it agrees in capsule with the unpublished genus *Aikinia* (*C. hederacea* L.) of my friend *R. A. Salisbury*, Esq.; whose superior talents as a botanist, and whose judgment as an acute observer of the natural affinities of plants, have long been well known to the scientific world.

† For an explanation of this word, see the note at page 519.

we fired; but as none were killed, it could not be ascertained to what species they belonged. This temporary lake was formed by the late rains; and the surface of the ground, for a great extent, exhibited the clearest proofs that a prodigious quantity of water had fallen this season; occasioning, literally, a partial deluge. The whole country had been under water, to the depth of two and three feet; as was evident from all the bushes, which, excepting just their tops, were covered with mud.

Our road, for a considerable distance, obliged us to travel through water; and the soil being thus softened almost to mud, the waggon was with difficulty dragged along, and, in one or two places, narrowly escaped sinking in, or being stuck fast.

A little further, the hoary appearance, and soft tufted shapes, of the small grove of *Acacia atomiphylla*, were extremely picturesque, and presented to the eye a pleasing contrast with the lively green of all the surrounding vegetation.

Plants of *Amaryllis toxicaria* were in many places very abundant, their blueish, undulated leaves, rising out of the ground, and spreading in the form of a fan, rendered them remarkable and conspicuous; but their flowers had long since passed away, and here and there only could now be seen the short dried stalks. This plant is well known to the Bushmen, on account of the virulent poison contained in its bulb. It is also known to the Colonists and Hottentots, by the name of *Gift-bol* (Poison-bulb.)

This *poison* is obtained by inspissating the milky juice, either by the heat of the sun, or, as I was told, by boiling. It is mingled with the venom of snakes, or a large black species of spider of the genus *Mygale*, and forms a half-viscous, gummy compound. In this state it is spread upon the heads of their arrows; and the direful and fatal effects of a wound made by them are the chief, and almost only, cause of that dread in which the *Bushmen* are held by every other inhabitant of Southern Africa.

The ingredients of their *arrow-poison* vary according to the part of the country inhabited by them; as the same plants, or substances, are not to be found in every place: but the venom of serpents always constitutes an essential part.   This shows how attentively the nation have studied the horrid art, and how well they understand the effect of their combinations : for they must have perceived that the poison of serpents operates in a manner different from that of vegetables ; the former attacking the blood, while the latter corrupts the flesh.

From such a wound, if the poison be fresh, there is little hope of surviving, unless it happen to have been made in some part of the body where all the surrounding flesh can be instantly cut out. Yet examples of a *cure* are sufficiently numerous to encourage every unfortunate sufferer to try all the remedies within his reach ; for it may be possible, that the poison have, by age, lost much of its strength, or that the manufacturers of it, not having the most dangerous materials at hand, may have been obliged to employ a less fatal kind.

As the Bushmen endeavour to conceal from strangers a knowledge of the different substances which they use, it is not easy to find out exactly what they are.   Of serpents, they select several kinds as preferable ; but, on necessity, often take others.   Of *vegetables*, they occasionally make use of various sorts, which are all endowed with an acrid thick juice, capable of being inspissated, such as *Euphorbias*, several species of different genera of *Amaryllideæ*, and *Apocyneæ ;* with many others.   To these, are to be attributed, the great pain and heat of the wound ; and all the inflammatory symptoms.   On lightly touching the arrow-poison with my tongue, I have, in most cases, experienced a highly acrimonious taste.

Medical men, especially those of the Cape Colony, could not dedicate their time and study to a more important object than the discovery of an antidote to this poison, and of some certain mode of treating such wounds.   This would in effect be nothing less than to disarm these dangerous tribes of their most formidable weapon, and to relieve the bordering colonists of the greatest portion of those fears which render their abode in such parts of the colony exceedingly uneasy.   From what has been stated above respecting the component parts of the arrow-poison, it naturally follows that the

antidote must be of a two-fold nature : one to counteract the ser-
pent-venom, such as the *Liquor Ammoniæ,* * or a similar preparation ;
the other to resist the power of the vegetable poison, yet at the
same time not of such properties as to impede the action of the
former. It would perhaps be advisable to administer these remedies
both internally and externally as a topical application ; for which
latter purpose they might be prepared of greater strength.

He who should discover such a remedy, would receive, in the
consciousness of having been the means of saving the lives of many
of his fellow creatures, the highest reward which a philanthropic
mind can desire. Nor would he, I think, be less entitled to a public
recompense, than those who invent new means of warlike destruction.

When we had passed through the region of the *Poison-bulb,* we
drove over an extensive field of thousands of the beautiful *Amaryllis
lucida* in full bloom ; which gave to the whole plain within view, the
delightful appearance of a gay flower-garden. †

We arrived at the *Kloof village* at a little after sunset, and were
immediately visited by the chief and some of the head people of the
kraal ; to whom I explained the motive of my coming. *Berends,*
who seemed not averse to lending me his aid, promised to make search
for men ; but regretted that all those people of the Kloof who were
best qualified for my purpose, were absent either with the horses in the
Roggeveld, or had just departed with his relation Klaas Berends for
the colony. In the meantime my own men and myself, made all
possible enquiry ; and endeavoured to explain our journey to Graaffreynét, as one of short duration, and easy to be accomplished.

---

* An instance of the efficacy of this medicine, has already been related at page 392.
† At *Aakaap,* I found new species of
    Heliotropium and
    Capraria ?
Between *Aakaap* and the *Kloof,* new species of
    Cucumis
    Bryonia
    Talinum
    Verbena.

16th. Early in the morning, I sent Philip with a message to the Captain, promising him a pound of gunpowder, if he succeeded in procuring the men, well knowing that a pound of powder would prove an irresistible fee to a Hottentot hunter, and sufficient to engage him warmly to plead my cause.

The first man who offered himself, was old *Cobus Berends*, the Captain's uncle. He appeared to be about seventy years old : the feebleness of age had bent him a little forwards, but at the same time gave him an air that excited respect. I was surprised to find so old a man willing to undertake an expedition which seemed fitted only for the strength and hardy activity of youth ; but the motive which induced him to brave the difficulties and perils of an unknown journey was honorable to his feelings, and I could not but admire him on that account ; although so feeble a person seemed very little likely to constitute any addition to the effective number of our party. He had a daughter whom he had not heard of for many years, and having always understood that she was living at Graaffreynet, he expressed himself very desirous of joining us, that he might see her once more before he died. But, notwithstanding the feebleness of his body, he was still to us a desirable companion, on account of his experience, and the calm, assured manner in which he spoke of the practicability of crossing the country lying between us and the colony. He might be considered a person of property, as he had a waggon and oxen and some cattle of his own.

At noon, Captain Berends reported that no men could be found at the Kraal who were fit to accompany me, all such as could leave their homes having been taken away by Klaas ; but he offered to allow his servant *Ruiter* (or *Ruter*) to go with us ; and promised that, if in the mean time, before our departure, he should be able to procure some others, he would send them to me at Klaarwater.

This *Ruiter* was a Briqua or Bachapin, of about the middle age and stature, and of black complexion ; and bore the character of being a lively, active, and useful man. He had lived many years among the Klaarwater people, in whose service he found a more easy life than in his own country ; whither, however, he occasionally made journeys along with his Hottentot masters.   He was no richer than his countryman Muchunka, but had acquired a good knowledge of the Dutch language.

As to *Muchunka,* he had all along expressed so much timidity and reluctance to the journey to Graaffreynet, that I was forced to relinquish the idea of having him as one of the number.

Finding that, at present, nothing more could be done by any further enquiries at this place, I employed the rest of the day in a ramble up the mountains, where an astonishing number of flowers had sprung up since my former visit to this place, and enabled me now to add above forty new plants to my herbarium, nearly the whole of which have been hitherto unknown to the science. *

Gomphocarpus tomentosus, B. Catal. Geogr. 2024.   Fruticosus erectus 4-pedalis albo-tomentosus.   Folia angustissimè linearia, marginibus revolutis.   Flores albi. Affinis *G.frutescenti.*

Cleome rubella, Cat. Geog. 2025.   Caulis pubescens. Foliola septena lanceolato-linearia integerrima.   Petala rosea.   Filamenta sex.

Polygala Asbestina, Cat. Geog. 2030.   Fruticulus subpedalis, ramificatione patente.   Folia obovata, supremis lanceolatis mucronulatis.   Flores axillares solitarii foliis breviores albi.   Calycis foliola duo majora lanceolata viridia.   Capsula ovalis, apice bifido.

Paschanthus repandus, Cat. Geog. 2036, et 2486, 2.   Planta frutescens bipedalis.   Rami simpliciusculi declinati.   Folia oleracea * subglauca elongatè lanceolata semi-collapsa † marginibus repandis rubicundis; glandulis duobus subtùs ad petiolum sitis, cum aliis in paginâ inferiore sparsis.   Pedunculi axillares cirrati.   Flores polygami ochracei. Calyx tubulosus 5-fidus. Petala 5 parva lanceolata, inter divisiones calycis inserta.   Filamenta 5 in parte inferiore calycis inserta.   Antheræ lineares. Germen pedicellatum. Stylus brevissimus.   Stigma lacero-capitatum.   Capsula unilocularis ovata cava, 3—6-sperma trivalvis, purpureo-rosea.   Semina ovata, arillo coccineo involuta.

An hi duo sint specie diversi, ulteriore examinatione determinandum est.

Genus ex Ordine *Passiflorearum;* quarè *Paschanthus* dicitur, ad affinitatem indigitandam.

Celosia odorata, B.

Lichtensteinia lævigata, Willd.

Portulacca oleracea

---

* Folium *oleraceum* dicitur cujus substantia nec carnosa nec membranacea : sed, ut in plantis *oleraceis,* (e. g. *Brassica oleracea,*) tenera et crassiuscula ; et desiccatione plerumque tenuissima evadens.

† Folium *collapsum* est cùm pagina superior longitudinalitèr complicatur, aut latera mutuò sibi sursùm applicantur. Sic verbo *semi-collapsum* designatur folium cujus latera includunt angulum 90°, *subcollapsum* 140°; uti *planum* est 180°.

Amongst them was a very remarkable plant, not more than two feet in height, particularly interesting to the botanist, as being the only one of the natural order of the Passion-flowers hitherto discovered in this part of the globe ; and, notwithstanding its blossoms being very unlike those well-known flowers, I have ventured to name it *Paschanthus*, (a Greek version of the word Passion-flower,) in order to mark its affinity to that order, although the name be not quite unobjectionable. Yet though it was furnished with tendrils, it had not the growth of a climbing plant.

A new kind of *Phyllanthus*, (C. G. 2041,) a very delicate little plant, appeared at first sight to have the pinnated leaves of some East-Indian *Æschynomene*. It sprang up between the brown stones ; and, though not a foot high, attracted notice by the delicacy of its leaves.

A small fern, not yet in fructification, but apparently allied to *Ceterach*, grew in a situation similar to that in which I had found it in England. Such associations of ideas recalling, in scenes so different, the memory of my native land and of those it contained, were never to be resisted, and for a few moments always made me forget that I was in Africa. At that instant, a *Lantana* before me in full bloom, brought our English hot-houses to recollection, and excited an amusing comparison of its situation there, reared with difficulty, and preserved only by the daily care of man, with that in which

---

Pennisetum
Hermannia
Phyllanthus. 2 sp.
Pharnaceum
Hibiscus
Celastrus
Bryonia
Pteris
Kyllingia
Mahernia
Aristida, L.
Glycine
Indigofera

Solanum
Uropetalum, B.
Melhania
Carphalea ?
Pappophorum
Achyranthes. 2 sp.
Telephium ?
Lantana
Rottböllia
Sida
Talinum
Thesium
Nemesia, &c.

I here saw it, growing unheeded and exposed on a wild rocky mountain, and pruned only by the goats who cropped its leaves and blossoms, thus constantly restrained from acquiring its proper size.

Abundance of common *Purslane* grew every where on these
mountains, and I ordered a quantity to be picked and boiled for my
dinner. It very rarely happened during my travels, that I could
convert the wild vegetables to culinary use, as, from the heat and
dryness of the climate, they were too tough and juiceless to be rendered eatable by boiling. The purslane is one of those few plants,
the seeds of which have been scattered by the hand of nature in
various and very distant parts of the earth. In the Island of St.
Helena, at the rainy season of the year, the rocky hills are covered
with it, and are in a few weeks rendered verdant by this plant alone.
Just in the same situation, and under the same circumstances, it
grows on the Asbestos mountains, and, I believe, in most other parts
of the world where it has been observed. This was the only time,
during my travels in Africa, that it was noticed in a truly wild state;
but as it is a plant which entirely vanishes for the greatest part of
the year, it is possible that it may be indigenous to many other spots
which were passed over in the dry season.

17th. At my former visit to this village, the number of mat-
huts was twenty, it was now twenty-five. This increase of population
was occasioned by the return home of those families who had been
residing with their cattle on the banks of the Gariep during the dry
season.

Observing the appearance of heavy rain in the direction of
Wittewater, I delayed our departure till the sky became clear in that
quarter; and, after being detained still longer by the loss of one of
my oxen, which was at last found to have strayed to a great distance
up between the mountains, we commenced our return to Klaarwater
at half past four in the afternoon.

Old Cobus, mounted on one of his own oxen, accompanied us;
and I was glad at perceiving, that, notwithstanding his age, he bore
the rough motion of the animal as well as any of the younger Hottentots. This old man, as well as Hans Lucas and Captain Berends,

in reply to my enquiries respecting the nature of the country on the other side of the river, agreed in their information, that on the southern side of the Gariep there was *a river* which appeared to come a considerable distance from the southward. I therefore decided on following the course of this river, as far as it should be found to follow the direction in which I intended to travel. This plan, therefore, would oblige me once more to return to the Kloof, as this village lay in our road towards that river; and it was, in consequence, arranged that the party should there assemble in order to make the final preparations for the journey.

When we came to that part of the road where the morning's rain had fallen, the red clayey and loamy ground, which in dry weather has all the hardness of rock, was found to be a complete *mud*, and so deep, that for the space of six miles, the oxen had the greatest difficulty in dragging the waggon over it. This mud adhered so firmly to the wheels, that when it had become perfectly dry it was not easy to scrape it away, but remained like a coating of hard red stucco, and required several days travelling to wear it off. We passed innumerable ponds of rain-water which had been formed within the last two days.

The night being fine, we continued our way till the moon had nearly set; and at about half past nine, unyoked for the night at a rain-water pond, in a spot where the oxen stood up to their knees in the midst of abundance of the most delightful grass.

18th. Close to my waggon, in the morning, I remarked a plant growing over the bushes, which, at a little distance might, from its growth, and the color and shape of its flowers, be mistaken for an *Aristolochia*; but which, on nearer examination, proving to be an *Apocyneous* plant of a new and singular genus *, I made a drawing

---

* *Systrepha filiforme*, B. Cat. Geog. 2092. Radix fasciculata, tuberis fusiformibus succulentis albis. Caulis volubilis filiformis. Folia linearia. Pedunculus axillaris biflorus. Calyx 5-phyllus, foliolis subulatis. Corolla tubulosa basi globoso-inflata, apice 5-fida, laciniis longissimis, erectis elegantissimè in formâ coronæ imperialis, contortis. Tubus cylindricus nigro-purpureo punctatus. Nectaria 5 bifida, erecta linearia obtusa.

of it on the spot.   A species of Bryony *, remarkable for its neatly divided leaves, and beautiful scarlet berries, was growing abundantly in this district, and is not uncommon in the country adjoining the Gariep.

We departed hence at ten in the forenoon, having the most beautiful weather imaginable, with the air fresh and reviving, though rather hot; the sky remaining unclouded the whole day.   Old Cobus soon afterwards parted company, and struck off to the left, across the country to Gert Kok's kraal, to ascertain if any one there were willing to go with us.   He rejoined us on the road in the evening, but had met with no success in his enquiries.

We travelled over wide plains of tall verdant *grass*, that might truly be called the finest hay-fields; and where, with very little trouble or labor, the inhabitants might supply themselves with abundance of excellent hay for the support of all their cattle, during that season of the year when every blade of grass is withered up, and their half-starved herds are obliged to live by browsing on any plant which may fall in their way.   But unfortunately, every nation, from the most savage to the most polished, is guided too blindly by custom and fashion: and the advantages of laying up a stock of fodder for the dry season, is therefore not likely soon to become evident to the inhabitants of Southern Africa, although hundreds of their cattle die yearly from want of it.   But the ease of an indolent life, with all its losses, is so much more agreeable to them than the labor of an industrious one with all its advantages, that the minds of such men must be entirely new-modelled before they can be capable of receiving the improvements of other countries.

Not far out of our road, four gigantic *ostriches*, decorated with

---

Filamenta 5 nectariis longiora, apice conniventia et germen orbiculatum depressum tegentia.   Antheræ 5 ad basin filamentorum.   Stylus et stigma inconspicua.

Nomen a συϛρέφω, *contorqueo*, ob apices laciniarum corollæ in funiculo contortos. Genus ex ordine *Apocynearum*.

* *Bryonia pinnatifida*, B. Cat. Geog. 2098.   Folia ternato-pedata, lobis pinnatifidis; laciniis linearibus oblongisque obtusis aveniis

the most beautiful plumes, were quietly feeding, without having noticed our approach. Speelman crept very near to them; but missing his shot, the birds took the alarm, and, moving off with a stately gait, were soon out of sight, though their pace appeared to be but little more than that of walking.

At a little before noon, we halted for three hours at *Gattikamma*, or *Wittewater*. The spring yielded now much less water than at the end of September; but was frequented by the same plovers, who may be considered as the only permanent inhabitants of the spot. Two of these I ate for my dinner, and found them of a delicate taste, and the more acceptable, after having been without meat for two days, as all our salted mutton was soon spoiled by the heat of the weather.

Between the Asbestos Mountains and Gattikamma, even at the third time of passing over the same ground, thirty-six numbers were added to my botanical catalogue. *

Amongst them were, —

Uropetalum glaucum, B. Cat. Geog. 2066. Bulbus subglobosus. Folia glauca, erecta, lanceolata, basi latiora et subcucullata, scapo multò breviora. Scapus erectus 2 - 3-pedalis. Flores virides, intus ochracei, nutantes, alterni. Pedunculi longissimi patentes. Corolla semisexfida. Laciniæ 3 exteriores reflexæ, externè ad apicem auctæ appendice caudiforme; 3 interiores approximatæ apicibus simplicibus. Germen stylans. Capsula brevis trisulcata trilocularis. Semina plura, horizontalia discoidea nitida atra.

Nomen ab οὐρὰ, *cauda*, et πεταλον, *petalum*, ob appendicem caudiformem ad apices petalorum. Genus est propè *Lachenaliam*, cujus species *L. viridis* huic adjicienda.

Oxygonum alatum, B. Cat. Geog. 2074. Planta annua monoica. Folia lanceolata, incisa, et integra. Flores spicati pedunculati; plures in spicæ articulis. Flores masculi incarnati quadrifidi, laciniis patentibus, obovatis petaloideis. Filamenta elongata octo. Antheræ ovatæ. Fructus oblongus, angulis 3 membranaceo-alatis.

Nomen ab ὀξὺς *acutus*, et γωνία *angulus*, ob fructum acutè angulatum; et verbum *Polygono* consonum. Genus ex ordine *Polygonearum*.

Sisymbrium Gariepinum. B. Cat. Geog. 2080.

Cyperus usitatus, B. " *Boschman's uyentjes*."

Cleome diandra, B. Cat. Geog. 2103. Caulis bipedalis, brevissimè spinulosus. Foliola septena filiformia. Stamina 8, quorum duo elongata fertilia, sex brevissima sterilia.

Barleria
Physalis
Tetragonia
Justicia

On our road this afternoon, we met a party of men, women, and children, with their huts and all their goods, removing from Klaarwater to the Asbestos mountains. The whole family, with mats, sticks, utensils, and skins, packed all together on the backs of the oxen, and moving along with a steady pace, presented a curious group, which might have been fancied to bear some resemblance to the journeyings of the people of patriarchal days, notwithstanding the dignity, and splendid robes, with which modern painters have thought proper to invest them. At least, their bringing to recollection, a party of *Gypsies* in England, removing from one county to another, is an idea less fanciful and speculative. We stopped a few minutes to answer each other's questions as to the whence, the whither, the when, and the wherefore, of our journeys; nor did I forget to ask the men if they would like a trip to Graaffreynet.

It was past nine at night, before we arrived at Klaarwater; where nothing remarkable had occurred during our absence, except that the eight oxen we had left at Groote-doorn were all missing.

19*th*. The next day, Philip and Muchunka were sent to take the team to Groote-doorn, and make search after the others. They were absent the whole of the following day, and I was rendered exceedingly uneasy by the circumstance of the two dogs, which they took with them, returning in the evening alone. On the next morning, I sent off Speelman and Gert to follow the track of the lost oxen. In the meantime, Philip returned, after having sought in every direction; and while doing this, the other team strayed away, and were at last found about half way towards Groote Fontein, a distance of above forty miles.

Lactuca	*Anthericum.* 2 sp.
Desmochaeta	*Rottböllia*
Uniola	*Lappago*
Aptosimum	*Chloris*
Pappophorum	*Selago*
Indigofera ?	*Bryonia*
Cyperus	*Leptochloa,* Pal.
Aristida, L. 2 sp.	*Uropetalum.*

As the 24th was the day fixed for commencing the journey to Graaffreynet, each one was busily employed in making, on his own account, such preparations as he thought necessary. I packed all my goods into the chests, and took particular care to secure them from the possibility of getting wet. Hans Lucas came to have a final consultation, and promised to be ready on the day appointed; as I was resolved to take my departure with whatever number of men I might be able to procure by that time.

In the course of this and the following day, Speelman shot four Springbucks; which were dried as a part of the stock to be left with *Gert* and *Hannah*; who were to remain at Klaarwater.

20th. I completed my ornithological, and botanical catalogues, up to the present day. The numbers of the former were 169, and contained 81 species of *birds*, all shot since leaving the Groote-Doorn river in the Bokkeveld Karro. The latter was numbered up to 2102, and contained almost as many species of *plants*. Of these numbers, 964 belonged to Cape Town and its vicinity; while the remaining 1138 were collected on the journey; since the commencement of which, I had dried 5051 specimens. My *insects* were not proportionally numerous; and this is to be accounted for, partly by the season of the year, and partly by the want of time for looking after them; these objects not being easily discovered without especial search and much patience. I however never omitted to preserve all that fell in my way; and, even at this rate, the collection was far from being a small one. My *minerals* were as yet but few, their weight in my waggon having hitherto deterred me from collecting as much as I otherwise would have done; and from the same reason I had not yet ventured to preserve the skins of the larger *quadrupeds*. In the original plan of my travels, I did not propose returning again into the Cape Colony; and it was on this account that 1 thought it absolutely necessary to abstain from loading my waggons with collections of objects of great bulk or weight.

It was in vain that we still endeavoured to persuade some of the Klaarwater people to go with us; there evidently remained no hope of adding more strength to our expedition, and we began to argue ourselves into a belief, that our little party would be quite strong enough.

22nd. The *missionaries* remained mere lookers-on to my preparations, but not silent ones. They ceased not till the last moment to discourage me from the attempt, and Mr. Anderson seriously asked me to give him a written paper, in which it should be stated that they had used their utmost endeavours to dissuade me from so perilous an undertaking; so that in case of a fatal termination, they might stand cleared from the imputation of having contributed to it by any encouragement or advice of theirs.

While engaged in this conversation, a message arrived from Captain Berends, to inform me that he could not find any men for me, nor even a driver and leader to bring back my waggon from the river, as I had intended to take the convenience of it thus far on our road.

Mr. Jansz, who had a horse which had been given him by the late unfortunate expedition into the Interior, offered me the use of it when he saw I was determined on going; and for this friendly act, I feel under considerable obligation, as it certainly saved me all the inconvenience, and the greater fatigue, of riding so long a journey on the back of an ox.

I hired a saddle of Captain Kok, and also a pack ox, and made him some further presents. I gave his uncle, Cupido Kok, a pound of gunpowder, for which in return he engaged to supply Gert with a due portion of the game he might shoot; and I made an arrangement with the Captain, by which he undertook, when necessity required, to furnish Gert and Speelman's wife with food during my absence. I finally satisfied all those who had any claims upon me, and, among them, a woman who demanded two handkerchiefs as payment for sitting up with Gert three nights during his illness. This was calculated to be, under all circumstances, equivalent to paying twenty shillings in England for the same piece of service. I settled my account with Mr. Anderson for some provisions with which I had been supplied, and who obliged me by taking my bill payable in Cape Town.

23rd. This being the last day of my remaining at Klaarwater, a number of people came about my waggons to try what could be obtained by begging. To some I gave a trifle; for, my own wants, and the uncertainty of any supply to my stores, together with the belief, that if I should be in need, they would forget to be grateful in return, forbade my being more generous.

I agreed with *Abraham Abrams*, Hendrik's brother, who resided at Groote-doorn, to take care of my oxen; subject, however, to Gert's superintendence and directions, and to the condition of my making a deduction from the promised remuneration, in case any were lost, or came to accident, through any want of proper attention on his part.

I gave the most strict injunctions to *Gert* and *Hannah*, never to leave my waggons unprotected, but that they should be constantly watched either by the one or the other. I left with them such a stock of tobacco and brandy, as was judged enough, at a reasonable rate, to last till my return; and cautioned them to conceal their having so large a quantity, lest it might be all begged, or stolen from them. Their assurances of fidelity to my service, and promises of obeying my orders in every thing to their utmost, appeared so faithful and warm, that I felt no apprehensions at leaving all my property in their care; more especially as both the waggons were to be stationed in a spot where every movement could be seen from the village and the huts of the missionaries, of whom I asked the favor of their now and then casting an eye that way.

All our preparations being completed, Philip was sent to Groote-doorn for ten of my oxen, and to apprise *Lucas* and *Hendrik* that all was ready for starting early on the following morning. These arrived punctually at my waggons in the evening, with their pack-oxen, and the Bushman *Nieuwveld;* whose appearance, together with the character Lucas gave of him, made me consider him as a very useful addition to our number. Old Hans had engaged a Half-Hottentot, named *Daniel Kaffer*, and his son, to be the driver and leader of my waggon from the river back to Klaarwater: but, in the course of the evening, as they all sat round the fire, talking in high spirits over the prospects of their intended journey, they at last persuaded old Daniel to make one of our party, and Hendrik immediately gave up one of his pack-oxen for his use.

I had not, for several months, experienced so much pleasure and satisfaction as I did this evening, in beholding all my little party assembled, and, in such a cheerful mood, anticipating nothing but pleasure from the journey before us. In the most perfect harmony and good humour, and in a zealous attention to every circumstance which could be thought likely to ensure our success, they now showed themselves to be exactly the men that were to be desired on such an expedition. Nor was this happy situation of affairs without its effect upon myself: my difficulties and disappointments vanished entirely; I felt all my enthusiasm for travelling revived in its greatest ardor; and beheld the prospect open before me, painted with all the glowing colors of a warm imagination.

Thus pleasantly passed the eve of our departure; and, occupied with the enlivening anticipations of new scenes, and of the prosperous result of our journey, all retired to rest, impatient for the arrival of the next morning.

THE

ITINERARY

AND

REGISTER OF THE WEATHER.

1811.	DISTANCES. In Time; by Oxen and Waggons. H. M.	In English Miles	STATIONS AND PLACES ON THE ROAD; With their Latitudes, calculated from Astronomical Observations made on the Journey : to which are added their English names and intermediate Distances.	Time of Observation. H. M.	By Fahrenheit's Scale.	By Reaumur's Scale.	WEATHER.
June 19	3 54	11	Cape Town *, at the Lutheran Church. Latitude 33° 55' 40" S. † 1 hour, or 3 miles ‡ Zoute Rivier (Salt River §) 2 h. 54 m. 8 miles Zand Valléy (Sand Pond) 2 hours 5¼ miles	-	-	-	Fair.
20	3 —	8½	Tygerberg (Tiger Mountain) 1 hour 3 miles	-	-	-	Fair during the day-time.
21	2 30	7½	Pampóen Kraal (Pumkin Kraal) - - · - - Station amongst Rhinoceros-bushes	-	-	-	Rainy at night. Very rainy the whole of the forenoon.
22	6 45	20	- - - - - Olývenhout Bosch (Olive-tree Wood)	8 — a	57	11·1	A fine day.
23	2 45	8½	Berg Rivier (Mountain River) - at the Pont (Ferry) Maráïs's farm on the Berg River		-		Fair weather.
24	4 30	13½	- - - - - Station near Piet Van der Merwe's farm. Vogel Valley (Bird Lake) on the right.		-	-	Air rather chilly in the early part of the mornings. A fine day.
25	7 10	21½	- - - - Western entrance of Roodezands Kloof (Red-sand Pass)	-		-	Cloudless sky, and very pleasant wea-ther.
26	3 45	7	- - - - - Túlbagh; about 97½ miles distant from Cape Town	-		-	The same as the pre-ceding day.

* The mean of the latitudes and longitudes of Cape Town, as observed by different astronomers, is 33° 55' 39½" S. and 18° 23' 11" E. from the Observatory at Greenwich.
† 2nd July, 1815, at the Lutheran Church, the observed meridional altitude of *Arcturus* was 35° 57' 46".
‡ The distances between Cape Town and the Karro Poort, were not so carefully attended to as those of the following part of the Itinerary ; but they will, notwithstanding, be found, perhaps, sufficiently correct for the traveller's use.
§ The words enclosed by parentheses, are the translations of the preceding name.

4 B 2

1811.	Distances.		STATIONS AND PLACES ON THE ROAD; With their Latitudes, calculated from Astronomical Observations made on the Journey: to which are added their English names and intermediate Distances.	Thermometer in the Shade.			WEATHER.
	In Time; by Oxen and Waggons.	In English Miles.		Time of Observation.	By Fahrenheit's Scale.	By Reaumur's Scale.	
June 27	H. M. -	-	At Túlbagh - - - - -	H. M. -	-	-	Snow at this time lying on the summits of the Winter-hoek's bergen (Winter-corner Mountains).
28 29 30 July 1	.		. . . . .			.	Cloudy during these days, but no rain.
2	.	-	. . . .	.	.	.	The wind changed to S.E., which at this place is considered a dry quarter; and the clouds cleared away.
3 4	4 20	13	. . . . . .	.	.	.	
	4 35	15	Veld-cornet Maráis's farm on the Breede Rivier (Broad River) Mostert's Hoek (Mostert's Corner) on the left				Fair.
	6 15	19	Piet Hugo's farm, called De Liefde Hex Rivier (Witch River) Hex Rivier's Kloof (Witch River Pass), at the south entrance	.	.	.	
5	9 —	27	. . . . Buffel's Kraal (Buffalo's Kraal) De Straat (The Street)	.	.	.	Cloudy. Snow at this time lying on the summits of the mountains at Buffel's Kraal.
6	10 —	30	. . . . . Verkéerde Valléy (Contrary Lake) 1 h. 20 m. 4 miles Pieter Jacobs's farm. Latitude 33° 24′ 2″ S. * Longitude 19 59 30 E.	.	.	.	Sunny and warm during the day, but very chilly at night.
7 8	.	.	. . . .	8 30 a 12 — a	40 52	3·5 8·8	Rain in the morning.
9 10 11	.	.	. . . .	9 — p 1 — p 10 — p	40½ 52 36½	3·7 8·8 2·0	Clear sunny weather.
12 13	4 —	11	. . . . Karró Poort (The Karró Pass), at the southern entrance -	7 — p	47	6·6	

* The longitudes given in this Itinerary have been obtained by deduction from the daily course and distance, corrected by the observed latitudes; assuming the longitude of Cape Town as 18° 23′ 11″. They are preferred to the results of my lunar observations, for reasons which are explained in another place.

1811.	DISTANCES. In Time; by Oxen and Waggons.	In English Miles.	STATIONS AND PLACES ON THE ROAD; With their Latitudes, calculated from Astronomical Observations made on the Journey: to which are added their English names and intermediate Distances.	THERMOMETER in the Shade. Time of Observation.	By Fahrenheit's Scale.	By Reaumur's Scale.	WEATHER.
July	H. M.		Karró Poort. Distance from Cape Town, about 213 miles, and from Túlbagh, 115½.	H. M.			
14	2 40	8	Kleine Doorn-riv.(LittleThorn R.) in the Bokkeveld Karro	9 — a / 12 — a	40½ / 47½	3·7 / 6.9	The morning misty and cold.
15	6 45	20	Groote Doorn-rivier (Great Thorn-river)	-	-	-	The whole day very fine and warm. The air cold at night.
16	6 —	20	Groote Rivier (Great River) Hangklip (Hanging-rock), in the Roggeveld Karro	3 — p	69	16·4	A very fine day.
17	1 30	4½	Ongeluks Rivier (Misfortune River)	-	-	-	A very fine day. A very strong S. E. wind during the whole afternoon, and which ceased in the evening, soon after nine o'clock.
18	1 —	3	Sugar-bird Station *.	-	-	-	Fine weather.
19	1 45	5½	Juk Rivier (Yoke River)				
	3 40	11	Juk-rivier's Hoogte (Yoke-river Hill) Tys Kraal. Latitude 32° 46' 52" S. Longitude 20 42 20 E.				A warm sunny day; but the air felt very cold at night.
20	-	-		10 — a	49	7·5	Very cold and windy. Cloudy in the afternoon, with much appearance of rain; but none fell.
21	-	-	Goudbloem's Hoogte (Marygold Heights)	-	-	-	Sunny and fine weather.
22	6 —	18	Wind-Heuvel (Wind Hill) 1 h. 20 m. 4 miles. Wind heuvel Station. Latitude 32° 45' 18" S. Longitude 20 53 30 E.	8 — a / 9 — a	40 / 58	3·5 / 11·5	A very fine and warm day.
23	4 —	12	Veld-cornet Gerrit Snyman's Place Latitude 32° 46' 45" S. Longitude 21 1 10 E.	1 — p	73	18·2	The whole day very serene and cloudless. No rain had fallen at this place during the last two months.

* The names of places in *Italics* are the temporary names alluded to at page 286.

1811.	In Time; by Oxen and Waggons.	In English Miles.	STATIONS AND PLACES ON THE ROAD; With their Latitudes, calculated from Astronomical Observations made on the Journey: to which are added their English names and intermediate Distances.	Time of Observation.	By Fahrenheit's Scale.	By Reaumur's Scale.	WEATHER.
	H. M.	.		H. M.	.	.	
July 24	.	.	At Gerrit Snyman's Place.				
25	.	.	- - - - - - -				} Fair weather.
26	.	.	- - - - - - -				
27	.	.	- - - - - .				
28	.	.	- - - - - - -	2 — p	78	20·4	The whole day cloud-
				6 — p	54	9·7	less and very hot.
29	.	.	- - - - - - -	3 — p	75	19·1	Fair.
30	.	.	- - - - - - -	.	-	-	A violent S. wind dur- ing the afternoon, and the whole night.
31	.	.			-	-	A strong wind all day, and the air very cold.
							In the afternoon, light- ning and thunder, with rain.
Aug. 1	.	.	- - - - - - -	.	.	-	Cold and showery, with much lightning and thunder in the evening.
2	.	.	- - - - - - -	12 — a	55	10·2	Light rain during the
				3 — p	57	11·1	whole of the day.
3	7 25	24	2 h. — 8 miles. Gerrit Fischer's farm. 5 25 16 Foot of the Middel-Roggevelds- berg (Middle-Ryeland moun- tains), or the northern bound- ary of the Karro. The distance travelled from the Karro Pass, or southern boundary, is about 126 miles; and from Cape Town, 339.				The day fine and cloudless.
4	.	.	- - - - - - -	1 — p	58	11 5	Fine weather during the day; but rainy all night.
5	.	.	- - - - - - -	10 — a	43	4·8	Heavy showers all
				2 — p	46	6·2	day.
6		.	- - - - - - -	11 50 a	38	2·6	At the Foot of the Mountain.
			1 h. 40 m. 1½ mile. The top of the mountain				
	6 10	16	- - - -	1 30 p	28½	−1·5	On the Top of the Mountain, and a little snow found re- maining unmelted between the rocks.
			4 h. 30 m. 14½ miles.				Showery all day, and the wind boisterous and cold.
			Freezing Station - - -	9 30 p	26	−2·6	

1811.	DISTANCES.		STATIONS AND PLACES ON THE ROAD; With their Latitudes, calculated from Astronomical Observations made on the Journey: to which are added their English names and intermediate Distances.	THERMOMETER in the Shade.			WEATHER.
	In Time; by Oxen and Waggons.	In English Miles.		Time of Observation.	By Fahrenheit's Scale.	By Rheaumur's Scale.	
Aug. 7	H. M.		*Freezing Station.* - - - - - -	H. M. 2 30 p	42	4·4	A sunny day.
	3 25	8	Jakhal's Fonteín (Jackal's Fountain)	11 — p	37	2·2	Cloudless at night.
8			- - - - -	2 30 p	58	11·5	A very fine, calm, and cloudless day.
	4 5	12	Rhenóster Rivier (Rhinoceros River)				
9			Kuilenberg (Tank Mountain) - - - - - - -	11 15 p 8 45 a	41½ 33	4·2 0·4	Calm.
	4 30	14	De Poort Egaal (Equal Pass)	12 — a 3 — p	65 72	14·6 17·7	
			Riet Rivier (Reed River)	11 — p	37	2·2	
10			- - - - - - -				A fine day.
11			- - - - - - -				A very fine day.
12			- - - - - - -	9 — a 1 — p 10 30 p	57 66 57	11·1 15·1 11·1	⎫
13			- - - - - - -	1 — p 11 — p	65 57	14·6 11·1	⎬ Fair. ⎭
14	4 —	11	- - - - - - - Riet Rivier's Kloof (Reed River Pass) Stink Fontein (Stinking Spring)				A most violent wind, raising clouds of dust.
15	1 45	5½	Selderý Fontein (Celery Spring) Latitude 32° 9' 23" S. Longitude 21 41 20 E.				⎫
16			- - - - - -	10 30 a	55	10·2	⎬
	2 —	6	Kánna Kraal.				
17	2 30	7½	Karrée River. Latitude 32° 3' 38" S. Longitude 21 50 20 E.				⎬ Fair and pleasant weather.
18			- - - - - - '	1 — p	76	19·5	
19							
20			Magnetic Var. 27°¼ W.				
21			- - - -				⎭
22			- - - - - - -	12 — a	80	21·3	Very hot during the day time, but after sun-set the air became almost chilly.
23			- - - - - - -				Very cloudy. In the forenoon rain and hail, accompanied by a most violent W.S.W. wind.
				8 30 p	35	1·3	
24				8 30 a	31	−0.4	The ground lightly sprinkled with snow, which by noon was all melted away.

1811.	In Time; by Oxen and Waggons.	In English Miles.	STATIONS AND PLACES ON THE ROAD; With their Latitudes, calculated from Astronomical Observations made on the Journey: to which are added their English names and intermediate Distances.	Time of Observation.	By Fahrenheit's Scale.	By Reaumur's Scale.	WEATHER.
	DISTANCES.			THERMOMETER in the Shade.			
Aug. 24	H. M. -	-	At the Karree River.	H. M. 1 —p	45	5·7	The day sunny, and the wind not so strong as yesterday. At night cloudless.
	3 30	9	A nameless River.	11 —p	36½	1·9	Fair.
25	-	-		-	-	-	Fine and pleasant.
26	3 40	11½	*Gaértner's Station.*	-	-	-	
27	-	-		1 —p	71	17·3	⎫
	4 —	12	Kleíne Quákka's-Fonteín (Little Quakka-Fountain)	12 —p	44	5·3	
28	-	-		2 —p	76	19·5	
	5 5	19	Dwaal Riviér(Lost-the-way River) Latitude 31° 40' 0" S. Longitude 22 12 0 E.				
29	-	-					
30	-	-	Dwaal Riviers Poort (Dwaal River Pass)	8 —a	44	5·3	Fair and dry weather.
	4 —	12		11 —a	77½	20·2	
			Zak Riviér (Sack River) Latitude 31° 33' 32" S. Longitude 22 14 40 E. The northern boundary of the Colony; distant from Cape Town about 482½ miles.	1 —p	81	21·7	
31	-	-		2 —p	84	23.1	
Sept. 1	-	-		2 30 a	43	4·8	⎭
2	-	-		1 —p	83	22·6	Fair during the day-time, but rather cloudy at night.
				10 —p	59	12·0	
3	-	-		12 —a	59	12·0	Sky overcast. Windy.
4	2 55	10		-	-	-	⎫
			Kopjes Fonteín (Hill Fountain)	6 —p	44	5·3	
5	-	-		1 —a	38	2·6	
	2 10	7	Patrys Fonteín (Partridge Fountain) Latitude 31° 23' 23" Longitude 22 17 40				Fine weather.
6	3 35	11		8 —a	55	10·2	
				1 —p	64	14·2	⎭
			Brakke Rivier (Brackish River) Latitude 31° 16' 14" Longitude 22 19 30				
7	-	-		0 40 a	48½	7·3	
				10 —a	60	12·4	A fine day, with some wind.
	6 35	22		2 —p	76	19·5	
			Leéuwe Fontein (Lions' Fountain)	12 —p	51	8·4	

1811.	DISTANCES. In Time; by Oxen and Waggons.	In English Miles.	STATIONS AND PLACES ON THE ROAD; With their Latitudes, calculated from Astronomical Observations made on the Journey : to which are added their English names and intermediate Distances.	THERMOMETER in the Shade. Time of Observation.	By Fahrenheit's Scale.	By Reaumur's Scale.	WEATHER.
	H. M.			H. M.			
Sept. 8	3 25	13	Leéuwe Fontein. - - - - - -	-	-	-	Fair and dry.
			Klip Fontein (Bushman Rock Fountain) Latitude 31° 0′ 38″ S. Longitude 22 37 40 E.				
9	2 5	6½	- - - - -	10 — a	70	16·8	Fine warm weather.
			Schiet Fontein (Skirmish Fountain) - - - -	4 20 p	83½	22·8	
10			- - - 0 h. 15 min. ¾ mile.	8 — a	58	11·5	Rainy till 11 a. m.
			Karrée-bergen (Dry Mountains) 2 h. — 4¼ miles.	11 30 a	60½	12·6	
	6 10	19½	Northern exit of the Karrée-mountains Pass 3 h. 55 min. 14½ m.	-	-	-	Cloudy the whole day.
11			Eland's Valley (Elk's Pond) - - - 3 h. 50 min. 17½ m.	12 — p	55	10·2	Sky equally overcast.
				8 — a	58	11·5	
			Carel Krieger's Graf (Carel Krieger's Grave) 11 h. — min. 35 m.	1 — p	58	11·5	A light rain began at 9½ a.m., and continued falling the whole day. Incessant lightning from twilight until midnight; with distant thunder.
	14 50	52½					
			Búffel-bout (Buffalo-leg) Latitude 30° 20′ 47″ S. Longitude 23 1 50 E.				Showery weather in the night.
12			- - - - - -	9 — a	64	14·2	The forenoon fair, though overcast.
	13 40	41	7 h. 40 min. 23 miles.	1 — p	76	19·5	The afternoon cloudless.
			Jónker's Water (Yonker's Water) 6 h. —. 18 miles.		-	-	} Serene and cloudless during the night.
			Módder-gat (Muddy Hole). Latitude 29° 59′ 1″ S. Longitude 23 16 50 E.				
13			- - - 3 h. 45 min. 11 miles.	11 — a	65	14·6	
	8 —	21	Modder-gat Poort; the middle. (The Defile through the mountains near Muddy Hole) 4 h. 15 min. 10 miles.				A fine day.
			Zand Valléy (Sand Pool) Latitude 29° 48′ 2″ S. Longitude 23 23 0 E.	10 30 p	57	11·1	
14			- - - - -	2 — p	83	22·6	A fair and cloudless day.
				11 30 p	59	12·0	
				12 30 p	58	11·5	
15			- - - - -	8 — a	54	9·7	
				11 15 a	69½	16·6	

4 c

1811.	DISTANCES.		STATIONS AND PLACES ON THE ROAD; With their Latitudes, calculated from Astronomical Observations made on the Journey : to which are added their English names and intermediate Distances.	THERMOMETER in the Shade.			WEATHER.
	In Time; by Oxen and Waggons.	In English Miles.		Time of Observation.	By Fahrenheit's Scale.	By Reaumur's Scale.	
Sept. 15	H. M.		Zand Valléy.	H. M.			
	4 20	13		2 22 p	82½	22·4	At 4½ p.m. thunder, with much lightning; and during the short time it lasted, rain fell in torrents.
			Gariép Station, on the banks of the " Gariep," or " Groote Rivier" (Great River), or " Oranje Rivier." Latitude 29° 40′ 52″ S. Longitude 23 27 20 E. Distance from the boundary of the Colony, about 218½ ; and from Cape Town, 701.				
16	-	-	- - - - - - -	7 20 a	58½	11·7	
				12 — a	87	24·4	Much lightning and thunder.
17	3 15	9½	- - - -	12 — a	90½	25·9	
			Shallow Ford - - • -	6 45 p	77	20·0	A cloudless day.
				12 30 p	67½	15·7	
18	-		- - - - - - -	10 30 a	79	20·8	
				2 — p	89	25·3	Too hot for travelling by day.
				5 50 p	81½	21·9	Very sultry after sunset. Calm.
19	12 15	37	- - - - - - -	6 — a	44	5·3	
			The Hottentot village of the Kloof (The Defile) in the Asbestos Mountains. Latitude 29° 15′ 32″ S. Longitude 23 46 10 E.				Too hot for travelling by day.
20	-	-	- - - - - - -	5 45 a	41	4·0	⎫ These three days ⎬ were excessively ⎭ hot and sultry.
21	-	-	- - - - - - -	7 — a	48	7·1	
22	-	-	- - - - - - -	12 — a	71	17·3	
				11 20 p	59½	12·2	Sky lightly overcast.
23	-		- - - - - - -	8 15 a	67½	15·7	Very windy, with most violent gusts.
				1 — p	79½	21·0	Sky rather overcast.
				3 — p	64	14·2	Rain and hail, accompanied with lightning and thunder, and the most violent wind, which
				3 15 p	74	18·6	lasted a quarter of an hour; after which it became a dead calm, with fine weather. But at 6 in the evening it began again to lighten and thunder more vivid and loud than before, bringing on

1811.	DISTANCES.		STATIONS AND PLACES ON THE ROAD; With their Latitudes, calculated from Astronomical Observations made on the Journey: to which are added their English names and intermediate Distances.	THERMOMETER in the Shade.			WEATHER.
	In Time; by Oxen and Waggons.	In English Miles.		Time of Observation.	By Fahrenheit's Scale.	By Rheaumur's Scale.	
Sept.	H. M.		At the village of the Kloof.	H. M.			rain, with a boisterous wind, for half an hour; after which it continued calm during the whole night.
24	-	-	- - - - -	1 — p	80	21·3	Fair. But owing to the rain which fell yesterday, the air felt cool.
25	-	-	- - - - -	1 15 a	56½	10·8	All day a fine cloudless sky, with a pleasant breeze.
				6 30 a	47½	6·8	
				12 — a	84	23·1	
				6 30 p	77	20·0	
26	-	-	- - - - -	2 — p	93	27·1	Calm during the daytime; but at night a light breeze sprang up, which rendered the warmth more bearable.
				7 — p	82	22·2	
				12 — p	76	19·5	
27	-	-	- - - - -	-	-	-	Wind from the N.W. in violent gusts, and sky overcast.
				10 — a	66	15·1	
				12 — a	80	21·3	
				6 — p	61	12·8	In the afternoon the wind ceased. In the evening lightning, thunder, rain, and wind.
				12 — p	58	11·5	
28	-	-	- - - - " -	2 — p	60	12·4	The air felt unpleasantly cold all day.
				11 — p	58	11·5	
29	-	-	- - - = - -	9 — a	48	7·1	Cloudy.
				6 — p	61	12·8	
			2 h. 15 min. 7½ miles. Aákaap, or Riet Fontein (Reed Fountain)				
	6 25	21½					
			4 h. 10 min. 14 miles. Wíttewater, or Gáttikamma (Whitewater)	-	-		Very chilly after sunset.
30	-	-	- - - -	7 — a	49	7·5	
				11 — a	77	20·0	
				4 — p	70	16·8	
	7 25	22	Kláarwater, or Kárrikamma (Clearwater) Latitude 28° 50′ 56″ S. Longitude 24 3 0 E from Greenwich; estimated from course and distance. Longitude computed from several sets of lunar observations, gives 23½° E. Magnetic variation 27° W.				

1811.	In Time; by Oxen and Waggons.	In English Miles.	STATIONS AND PLACES ON THE ROAD; With their Latitudes, calculated from Astronomical Observations made on the Journey: to which are added their English names and intermediate Distances.	Time of Observation.	By Fahrenheit's Scale.	By Reaumur's Scale.	WEATHER.
Oct.	H. M.		Kláarwater.	H. M.			
			Distance from miles.				
			Cape Town, about - 791				
			Sack River - - 308½				
			Pléttenberg's Baaken,				
			the nearest part of				
			the Cape colony - 259				
			Graaff-reynet - - 418				
			Litáakoon (or Litá-				
			kun) - - 180				
1	-	-	- - - - -	2 — a	51½	8·6	
2	-	-	- - - - -	12 — a	78	20 4	A very hot day.
				8 30 p	60	12·4	
3	-	-	- - - - -	12 — a	84	23·1	Very hot.
4	-	-	- - - - -	12 — a	82	22·2	All day a very strong N.W. wind.
5	-	-	- - - - -	12 — a	77	20·0	
				10 — p	54	9·7	
6	-	-	- - - - -	8 45 a	49	7·5	Very cold, owing to
				12 — a	70	16·8	a N.E. wind, which
				7 — p	52	8·8	is here observed
				8 35 p	49	7·5	always to produce
				10 — p	45	5·7	cold, but never brings rain. During the night it froze sufficiently hard to cause all the young fruit on the peach-trees to drop off.
7	-	-	- - - - -	12 — a	70	16·8	
				10 — p	46	6·2	
8	-	-	- - - - -	10 — p	45	5·7	A very cold day.
9	-	-	- - - - -	8 30 a	41	4·0	
				12 — a	68	16·0	Cloudy. Wind N.W.
10	-	-	- - - - -	8 30 a	51	8·4	
				10 — a	59	12·0	
				12 — a	68	16·0	The atmosphere so clear, that at night stars of the second magnitude were visible the instant they rose above the horizon.
11	-	·	- - - -	12 — a	70	16·8	Wind easterly and
				6 — p	58	11·5	cold.
12	-	·	- - - -	1 — a	35½	1·5	
				6 30 a	24	−3·5	Ice half an inch thick on the surface of
				2 — p	81½	21·9	the water.
				6 — p	60	12·4	

1811.	DISTANCES.		STATIONS AND PLACES ON THE ROAD; With their Latitudes, calculated from Astronomical Observations made on the Journey : to which are added their English names and intermediate Distances.	THERMOMETER in the Shade.			WEATHER.
	In Time; by Oxen and Waggons.	In English Miles.		Time of Observation.	By Fahrenheit's Scale.	By Reaumur's Scale.	
Oct.	H. M.		At Kláarwater.	H. M.			
				1 — a	40	3·5	
				3 30 a	32	0·0	
13	-	-	- - - - - -	9 — a	62	13·3	Sky cloudless; with a
				1 — p	82	22·2	pleasant easterly
				3 — p	84	23·1	breeze.
				11 — p	46	6·2	
14	-	-	- - - - - -	9 — a	71	17·3	A strong wind from
				11 — a	79	20·8	the north.
				1 45 p	87	24·4	
				2 15 p	90	25·7	The wind continuing strong from the N. Just after sunset the clouds collected in the west; and there was much lightning
				7 — p	79	20·8	from every quarter, except the east.
				12 — p	68	16·0	Wind in violent gusts from the west, and which continued all night, but was not accompanied by much rain.
15	-	-	- - - -	9 — a	70	16·8	Weather fair, with a
				1 40 p	78½	20·6	N. wind.
				4 45 p	83	22·6	At night calm, with much lightning and a little rain.
16	·	-	- - - - - -	2 — p	82	22·2	
				12 — p	62	13·3	Distant lightning during the whole night.
17	-	-	- - - - - -	-	-		Wind N.W.
18	-	-	- - - - -	9 — a	62	13·3	
				12 — a	79	20·8	In the afternoon the wind shifted round to the S. E., and the cold produced by this change was very sensible.
				11 — p	52	8·8	Much lightning in the north-east quarter, very distant.
19	-	-	·· - - - - -	10 — a	76	19·5	
				1 — p	90	25·7	
				3 — p	90	25·7	
				11 — p	69	16·4	A strong N. wind, and distant lightning in the N.
20			- - - - -	10 15 a	80	21·3	A strong N. wind.
				3 30 p	82	22·2	

1811.	Distances. In Time; by Oxen and Waggons. H. M.	Distances. In English Miles.	STATIONS AND PLACES ON THE ROAD; With their Latitudes, calculated from Astronomical Observations made on the Journey : to which are added their English names and intermediate Distances.	Thermometer in the Shade. Time of Observation.	By Fahrenheit's Scale.	By Reaumur's Scale.	WEATHER.
Oct.			At Kláarwater.	9 40 p	71	17·3	Violent gusts of wind. Distant lightning in the quarter from the S.E. to the S.W.
21	-	-	- - - - -	2 — p	82	22·2	
							Lightning, thunder, and rain at night.
22	-	-		12 — a	79	20·8	
				4 30 p	83	22·6	Fair weather, though cloudy. Wind westerly.
							Thunder, lightning, and rain at night.
23							
24	6 30	22½	- - - - - Spúigslang Fonteín (Spitting-snake Fountain)	2 — p	82	22·2	Fair weather, which continued without any alteration or rain till 9th Nov.
25	5 30	17	- - - - - Confluence of the Nu-garíep Black River) with the Ky-garíep (Yellow River). Latitude 29° 4' 22' S. Longitude 24 26 50 E.	2 — p	88	24·8	
26	-	-	- - - - -	2 — p	94	27·5	
27	-	-	- - - - -	12 — a	96	28·4	
				3 — p	98	29·3	
28	-	-	- - - - -	1 30 a	67	15·5	
				11 — a	91	26·2	
	2 —	6½		2 — p	101	30·6	
			Zóutpan's Drift (Salt-pan Ford)				
29	-	-	- - - - -	8 30 a	82	22·2	
				1 15 p	94	27·5	
	5 —	17	- - - - -	1 45 p	98	29·3	
			Confluence of the Maap (Muddy River) with the Ky-garíep (Yellow River) Latitude 29° 0' 22" S Longitude 24 43 40 E.				
30	-	-	- - - - =	-	-	-	
31	-	-	- - - - -	-	-	-	
Nov.							
1	-	-	- - - - -	-	-	-	During this interval the heat of the weather was as great as in the preceding week.
2	6 30	20	- - - - - Second Hippopotamus Station.	-	-	-	
3	-	-	- - - - -	-	-	-	
4	1 45	6	- - - - - Third Hippopotamus Station.	-	-	-	
5	6 30	20	- - - - - Fireless Station.	-	-	-	

1811.	DISTANCES.		STATIONS AND PLACES ON THE ROAD; With their Latitudes, calculated from Astronomical Observations made on the Journey: to which are added their English names and intermediate Distances.	THERMOMETER in the Shade.			WEATHER.
	In Time; by Oxen and Waggons.	In English Miles.		Time of Observation.	By Fahrenheit's Scale.	By Reaumur's Scale.	
Nov.	H. M.		*Fireless Station.*	H. M.			
6	1 45	6					
			Confluence of the 'Maap and the 'Ky-garíep Rivers - -	1 — p	98	29·3	⎫ Very little wind in
7	-	-	- - - - - -	2 — p	89	25·3	⎬ the day-time; and
8	-	-	- - - - - -	2 — p	98½	29·5	⎪ at night the air
				3 30 p	100½	30·4	⎭ perfectly calm.
							In the evening thunder-clouds began to collect, and there was some lightning and thunder.
9		-	- - - -	-		-	The weather hotter than on the preceding day.
							In the evening lightning, thunder, and rain.
10	-	-	- - - -	-		-	The sky cloudless, and the air very hot.
11	-	-	- - - -	-		-	At noon a thundershower.
12	-	-	- - - -	-		-	Showers in the afternoon, and very heavy rains all night.
13	2 25	7	-	2 10 p		-	A heavy thundershower, with hail four-tenths of an inch in diameter.
			Station in the open plain.				Cloudy. The weather hot and close.
							At night the most vivid incessant lightning; with very heavy rain.
14	4 36	15	- - - -	-		-	The weather fine, but very sultry.
			Groote Fontein (Kora Great Fountain) Latitude 28° 49′ 23″ S. Longitude 24 33 18 E.				
15	-	-	- - - -	-			⎫ Fair and very hot weather.
16	-	-	- - - -	-		-	⎬
17	-	-	- - -	-		-	⎭
18	7 30	22	- - - - -	7 45 p		-	Very heavy rain.
			Station without water.				
19	7 38	26	- - - -	-		-	A fine day.
			Kláarwater.				
20	-	-	- - - -				⎫
21	-	-	- - - -			-	⎬ Fair.
22	-	-	- - - -				⎭

1811.	Distances.		STATIONS AND PLACES ON THE ROAD; With their Latitudes, calculated from Astronomical Observations made on the Journey : to which are added their English names and intermediate Distances.	Thermometer in the Shade.			WEATHER.
	In Time; by Oxen and Waggons.	In English Miles.		Time of Observation.	By Fahrenheit's Scale.	By Reaumur's Scale.	
Nov.	H. M.		Kláarwater.	H. M.			
23	-	-			-	-	
24	-	-	- -. - - - -	-	-	-	} Fair.
25	-	-	- - - - - -	-	-	-	
26	-	-	- - - - - -	-	-	··	Wind N. E.
27	-	-	- - - - - -	-	-	-	Much rain fell in the foregoing night and this morning ; but unaccompanied by thunder.
28	-	-	- - - - - -	-	-	-	} Fair.
29	-	-	- - - - - -	-	-	-	
30	-	-	- - - - - -	-	-	-	During the whole day a violent westerly wind; which caused the air to feel very chilly in the evening.
Dec. 1	-	-	- - - - -	4 — p	55	10·2	
2	-	-	- - - - -	-	-	-	A very strong westerly wind continued to blow the whole of this time; but without rain.
3	-	-	- - - - -	-	-	-	
4	-	-	- - - - -	-	-	-	
5	-	-	- - - - -	-	-	-	
6	-	-	- - - - -	-	-	`	The wind abated.
7	-	-	- - - - -	-	-	-	An extraordinary dryness in the air was remarkable about this time.
8							
9	-	-	- - - - -	-	-	-	Wind southerly.
10	-	-	- - - - -	-	-	-	Wind as yesterday. This year the rainy season is much later than usual. At this time all the surrounding country is excessively dry; and the herbage quite parched up.
11	-	-	- - - - -	4 — p	86½	24·2	
12	-	-	- - - - -	9 — p	82	22·2	
				6 — a	73	18·2	
13	-	-	- - - - -	2 — p	90	25·7	} Fair and cloudless.
				6 — a	73½	18·4	
				2 — p	90	25·7	
14	-	-	- - - - -	-	-	-	
15	-	-	- - - - -	3 — p	89	25·3	A strong wind all day from the N.W. or the W.
16	-	-		-	-	-	Fair.

1811.	DISTANCES.		STATIONS AND PLACES ON THE ROAD; With their Latitudes, calculated from Astronomical Observations made on the Journey: to which are added their English Names and intermediate Distances.	THERMOMETER in the Shade.			WEATHER.
	In Time; by Oxen and Waggons.	In English Miles.		Time of Observation.	By Fahrenheit's Scale.	By Reaumur's Scale.	
Dec.	H. M.		At Klaarwater.	H. M.			
17	-	-	-	2 — p	90	25·7	} Fair.
18	-	-	-	-	-	-	
19	-	-	-	-	-	-	A very heavy rain in the preceding night. The wind S.W. The weather now became chilly.
20	-	-	-	7 — a	52	8·8	Wind southerly and cold.
				10 — p	67	15·5	
21	-	-	-	6 — a	59	12·0	
				4 — p	80	21·3	
22	-	-	-	7 — a	63	13·7	
				4 — p	78	20·4	
23	-	-	-	7 — a	69	15·1	
				4 — p	88	24·8	} Fair.
24	-	-	-	7 — a	67	15·5	
				2 — p	87	24·4	
25	-	-	-	2 — p	88	24·8	
26	-	-	-	2 — p	89	25·3	
27	-	-	-	7 — a	80	21·3	
				2 — p	91	26 2	
28	-	-	-	7 — a	80	21·3	
				2 — p	88	24·8	The weather at this time more settled, and the difference in heat between night and day not so astonishingly great as it had been during the last three months.
29	-	-	-	7 — a	76	19·5	
				4 — p	91	26·2	
30	-	-	-	7 — a	75	19·1	The weather clear and very dry, with several whirlwinds.
				4 — p	89	25.3	
31	-	-	-	7 — a	78	20·4	Sky cloudless during the last three days.
				2 — p	94	27·5	
1812 Jan.							
1	-	-	-	7 — a	76	19·5	
				4 — p	94	27·5	} Fair.
2	-	-	-	7 — a	76	19·5	
				4 — p	95	28·0	
3	-	-	-	7 — a	75	19·1	Very hot all day.
				2 — p	93	27·1	Just after sunset a most violent west-wind, which carried so much dust up in the air, where it remained the greatest

1812.	DISTANCES.		STATIONS AND PLACES ON THE ROAD; With their Latitudes, calculated from Astronomical Observations made on the Journey: to which are added their English Names and intermediate Distances.	THERMOMETER in the Shade.			WEATHER.
	In Time; by Oxen and Waggons.	In English Miles.		Time of Observation.	By Fahrenheit's Scale.	By Reaumur's Scale.	
Jan.	H. M.		At Klaarwater.	H. M.			part of the night, that it had the appearance of a mist, or distant driving rain.
4	-	-	- - - - - - -	7 — a	79	20·8	
				2 — p	95	28·0	A strong N. W. wind. A light shower at night.
5	-	-	- - - - -	6 — a	80	21·3	
				2 — p	94	27·5	
6	-	-	- - - - - -	7 — a	75	19·1	Hot, sunny, dry weather.
				4 — p	95	28·0	
7	-	-	- - - - - -	7 — a	76	19·5	
				4 — p	88	24·8	
8	-		- - - - - - -	7 — a	75	19·1	This day calm, and almost insupportably hot. Sky cloudless.
				2 — p	96	28·4	
9	-	-	- - - - - - -	7 — a	84	23 1	
				2 — p	96	28·4	
10		-	- - - - - - -	7 — a	75	19·1	A heavy shower in the foregoing night, and the wind N. W.
				2 — p	96	28·4	
11	-	-	- - - - - - -	7 — a	80	21·3	The last night and all this day the sky was overcast. Wind South. The wind quite round through every point of the compass, twice in the course of the evening; and while it was in the East, there was a shower which lasted from 9 till 11 p.m.; after which it veered to the N.
				4 — p	89	25·3	
12	-	-	- - - -	7 — a	78	20·4	
				2 — p	88	24·8	
13		-	- - - - - -	7 — a	76	19·5	
				2 — p	95	28·0	The evening set in with lightning, thunder, and the heaviest rain that had fallen at Klaarwater this season. It rained the whole night.
14	-	-	- - - - - - -	7 — a	76	19·5	All day many thunder-clouds passing.
				2 — p	85	23·5	

1812.	DISTANCES.		STATIONS AND PLACES ON THE ROAD; With their Latitudes, calculated from Astronomical Observations made on the Journey: to which are added their English Names, and intermediate Distances.	THERMOMETER in the Shade.			WEATHER.
	In Time; by Oxen and Waggons.	In English Miles.		Time of Observation.	By Fahrenheit's Scale.	By Reaumur's Scale.	
Jan. 14	H. M.		At Klaarwater.	H. M.			In the evening, vivid lightning and loud thunder, with rain all night.
15							Sky overcast, and a constant, light and steady rain. The present state of the atmosphere so moist, that culinary salt diliquesces.
				4 30 p			A heavy thunder-shower, with hailstones nearly half an inch in diameter. At night observed a halo round the moon, about 50 degrees in diameter. A halo is a phenomenon of very rare occurrence in the interior regions of Southern Africa.
16							No rain this day.
17				7 — a	76	19·5	No rain.
				2 — p	84	23·1	
18				7 — a	74	18·6	
				4 — p	86	24·0	
19				7 — a	76	19·5	It rained all the preceding night.
				2 — p	84	23·1	
20				7 — a	74	18·6	
				4 — p	85	23·5	Two very heavy showers this day.
21							Heavy rain.
22							Much lightning.
23							Rain at night.
24							The sky overcast all day, and some heavy showers.
25							During the last night and this morning it rained very hard, without the smallest intermission for 13 hours.
26							
27				7 — a	75	19·1	No rain during these days, and weather very pleasant.
				2 — p	80	21·3	
28				7 — a	74	18·6	
				2 — p	75	19·1	

1812.	DISTANCES. In Time; by Oxen and Waggons.	In English Miles.	STATIONS AND PLACES ON THE ROAD; With their Latitudes, calculated from Astronomical Observations made on the Journey: to which are added their English Names and intermediate Distances.	THERMOMETER in the Shade. Time of Observation.	By Fahrenheit's Scale.	By Reaumur's Scale.	WEATHER.
Jan.	H. M.		At Klaarwater.	H. M.			
29	-	-	- - - - -	7 — a 2 — p	65 77	14·6 20·0	{ No rain during these days, and weather very pleasant.
30	-	-	- - - - - -	-		-	The last three mornings were very cold just before sun-rise.
31	-	-	- - - - - -	-	-	-	Fine weather.
Feb.							
1	-	-	- - - - - - -	7 — a 2 — p	74 81	18·6 21·7	A hail-storm.
2	-	-	- - - - -	-	-	-	
3	-	-	- - - - - - -	7 — a 2 — p	74 80	18·6 21·3	} Fair.
4		-	- - - - -	7 — a 2 — p	75 86	19·1 24·0	
5	-	-	- - - - - -	-	-	-	{ Not a cloud was to be seen during these days. The weather very pleasant.
6	-	-	- - - - - -	-	-	-	
7	-	-	- - - - - -	7 — a	74	18·6	
8	-	-	- - - - - -	-	-	-	
9	-	-	- - - - - -	7 — a 2 — p	73 81	18·2 21·7	} Fair, and mostly sunny.
10	-	-	- - - - -	-	-	-	
11	-	-	- - - - - -			-	Scarcely any rain since the 25th last; but the whole of this day was very rainy.
12	-	-	- - - - - -	-	-	-	A heavy rain all the preceding night, and some showers this day.
13	-	-	- - - - - - -	7 — a 4 — p	76 -	19·5 -	Fair, a. m. A most violent thunder-shower, with hail-stones half an inch in diameter.
14	6 45	22	- - - - - -	-	-	-	
			Wittewater, or Gattikamma (Whitewater) 4 h. 15 m. 14 miles.				
15	6 30	21½	Aakaap, or Riet Fontein (Reed Fountain) 2 h. 15 m. 7½ miles.				} Weather very fine and pleasant.
			The Kloof village - - -	-	-	-	It rained at night.
16	-	-	- - - -	-	-	-	Fine weather.
17	-	-	- - = - - - -	-	-	-	Fair, with distant rain.
	5 30	17					
			A pond of rain-water.				

1812.	DISTANCES.		STATIONS AND PLACES ON THE ROAD; With their Latitudes, calculated from Astronomical Observations made on the Journey; to which are added their English Names and intermediate Distances.	THERMOMETER in the Shade.			WEATHER.
	In Time; by Oxen and Waggons.	In English Miles.		Time of Observation.	By Fahrenheit's Scale.	By Reaumur's Scale.	
Feb. 18	H. M. -		A pond of rain-water	H. M. -	-		All day the sky was cloudless. The air fresh and reviving, though rather hot.
	8 30	26½	1 h. 30 m. 4½ miles. Wittewater. 7 h. — m. 22 miles. Klaarwater.				
19	-	-	- - - - - -	7 — a 2 — p	70 80	16·8 21·3	
20		-	- - - - - -	-	-	-	Fair weather.
21	-		- - - - -	7 — a 2 — p	71 79	17·3 20·8	
22		-	- - - - -	-	-	-	
23	-	-	- - - - -	-	-	-	

REMARKS ON THE MAP;

AND

GEOGRAPHICAL OBSERVATIONS.

———————

THE Map which accompanies this Work, differs in so many particulars from those which have hitherto been published of the Southern point of Africa, that it becomes necessary to show from what materials it has been constructed, and on what grounds the alterations have been made; especially as these alterations extend to districts which I have not personally visited.

It must, in the first place, be stated that *my own track* is laid down *entirely* and *solely* from my own observations, made during the journey. These observations consist of the daily distances travelled; the courses from station to station; the bearings and trigonometrical intersections of distant and remarkable mountains; the bearings of various places remote from the track, and their distance, according to the concurrent information of the native inhabitants; very frequent astronomical observations for the latitude; and many sets of lunar distances for the longitude. These, whenever my time permitted, were laid down during the journey, from day to day, on a large scale; and various details added from ocular observation.

After my return to England, I carefully protracted, by a scale of nine inches to one degree of latitude, these observations, independently of my longitudes; and had the satisfaction of finding, notwithstanding the immense distance, that the great triangle formed by Cape Town, Klaarwater, and the mouth of the Great Fish River, guided only by the bearings, distances, and latitudes, closed to within forty miles.

This, I again laid down for the third time, on the same scale; distributing the deficiency of the forty miles equally over the whole triangle. The original map thus formed, measures seven feet and a half by eight and a half; and from this the present map has been reduced and engraved. Having superintended this, as well as every other part of this work myself,

I am enabled to say that the *Engraver* is entitled to the greatest credit for accuracy and fidelity to the original; of which, even to the proportional sizes and forms of the letters, this is a close *fac-simile ;* and with respect to the engraving itself, it is not necessary for me to make any remark, as that will sufficiently prove the talents and care that have been employed upon it.

The explanations on the face of the map will render every part of it easy to be understood; and by having added to every one of my *stations,* the *date* of my arrival there, it may be used with very great convenience as a *Geographical Index* to the journal, by referring to the heads of the pages for the corresponding date. It has for the Naturalist, the advantage of showing, by the name of the place, the season of the year at which the various objects have been met with. Some further explanation of the names which are here underlined, may be found at page 286; and for the rule by which the different *scales* are formed, the note at page 90 may be consulted. The days' journeys are of the usual length; but are too great to be practicable with the same cattle many days in succession. The mode in which I ascertained the daily *distances,* is fully described at pages 289 and 290; and with respect to the *astronomical observations,* and the longitudes given in the Itinerary, pages 332, 204, and 556 contain some remarks.

Nearly all the *latitude*s were determined by observations of the meridional altitude of stars; and this was done from a conviction that they admit of greater accuracy than the sun; at least such whose annual variation in declination have been well ascertained. For, being mere luminous points when viewed through the telescope of the sextant, the reflected image may be brought to coincide with the real, with less risk of any error of sight in the observer, than the edges of the sun's disk. The latter requiring the intervention of darkening glasses, have this source of error more than the stars; and in addition to which may be placed the more rapid change of daily declination, requiring a knowledge of the longitude for its correction.

The use of the *stars* is particularly convenient for a traveller; as, in the usual practice of obtaining the latitude from the sun's altitude at noon, it more frequently happens that, at that time of the day, he is on his journey; and even if at rest, unless at that very moment that part of the sky be free from clouds, he is liable to lose his only opportunity of knowing the latitude of the spot; whereas, stars coming on the meridian at all hours of the night, he seldom can be disappointed, if from any cause he should miss the moment for any particular one; and may obtain the greatest certainty by taking the mean result of several stars on the same night. Or, should other occupations prevent his observing at any particular hour, he may suit his convenience by making use of any star, not less however than the third magnitude, which he may at that time find on the meridian. And a further recommendation of this method, not to be overlooked by him who travels among the barbarous tribes of Africa, or even among the more civilized, but more jealous nations of the other quarters of the globe, is the opportunity which the hour and the darkness of night afford him for concealing his operations and his instruments ; the glittering appearance of which might excite in savages the desire of possessing them, and his imprudence tempt them even to murder.

From my own experience of the great advantages of this practice, I can, without hesitation, recommend it to the adoption of others who may be in similar circumstances. The sextant, which was on the new construction, an excellent instrument made by Troughton of London, and with which all my observations were made, was one of eight inches in radius, and having the limb subdivided by the nonius to every ten seconds ; but virtually to every five, in consequence of the real angle being doubled by reflection from the artificial horizon.

With respect to those parts of the map not comprised in my personal observations, more particularly the western side of the Colony, I must confess that they have cost me considerable trouble, and have exercised the whole of my patience ; for on examining and comparing together those maps which had previously been published, I found them, to an almost incredible degree, at variance with each other ; and had nearly despaired of the possibility of combining such materials together. I undertook the task of forming sketches of the routes, from their own narratives, of such preceding travellers as I judged worthy of confidence, particularly Thunberg, Sparrman, Paterson, and Lichtenstein. Although to Thunberg's Travels no map whatever is annexed, I was enabled by laying down his route on a large scale, to derive from it the greatest portion of the materials obtained by this method of making sketches.

As to the miserable thing called a map, * which has been prefixed to

---

* Its geographical deficiencies are so numerous, that in order to give it some appearance of a map, by covering the blank paper with writing, the compiler of it has been reduced to the necessity of spreading it over with scraps of information taken from the text, and with lists of wild animals. If, in constructing this elegant map, the *Showmen* at Exeter 'Change had been consulted and advised with, they would certainly have recommended it to be written at the edge of it, as an invitation to the readers, " Walk in, ladies and gentlemen, and view the wild

4 E

Mr. Barrow's quarto, I perfectly agree with Professor Lichtenstein, * that it is so defective that it can seldom be found of any use.   That which is given in Lichtenstein's work, is certainly the best general map of the Colony that has hitherto appeared, and is, as it is stated, indebted for its superiority to the use of a manuscript map, made under the late Dutch Government.   This, I conclude to be the same as one made by order of the Dutch Governor, Vandegraaff, of which I have seen a copy, the title purporting that the sea-coast and soundings from Algoa bay to St. Helena bay, were surveyed by Captain Duminy, and the maritime districts, or a narrow tract of land along the same length of coast, by Lieutenants Frederici and Jones ; excepting however, the country from Simon's bay to Zwellendam, which was a blank.   From this source combined with some others, and the sketches above mentioned, I have drawn materials for filling up the parts lying at a distance from my own track.

I have taken a few names out of those published by Arrowsmith, and have made some use of one compiled by De la Rochette, probably from the observations of the Abbé de la Caille.   But in this, great caution was required, as it contains some extraordinary inaccuracies.   From Lichtenstein's map I have adopted some names in the *Great Karro*, and in like manner, about thirteen, chiefly the names of boors, along the *Sunday River*, southward of Graaffreynet, from a small manuscript copy of a military sketch by Colonel Arbuthnot, in which however, the variation of the compass had not been attended to.   Along the coast I have inserted, out of different sea-charts, various names not in use among the inhabitants ; these are enclosed by crochets.   Neither from Sparrman's map, or Paterson's, which is only a copy of it, nor from Le Vaillant's, could I venture to appropriate any thing more than the mere names.

But here it must be owned, that with respect to the situations of places, I did not rely upon any one map, even the best.   The positions I have assigned to these names, are the mean result of all the maps and journals combined ; and which have occasioned me the most troublesome part of my labor, and are a sufficient excuse for mistakes, should any be found in this part of my work.

Many places at a considerable distance out of my track, have been

---

beasts ; here you will see the Buffalo, the Hyena, and the wonderful Secretary-bird †, with his pen stuck behind his ear."

* " Travels in Southern Africa."   Engl. ed. vol. 1. p. 36. — Dutch ed. deel 1. bl. 70.

† Barrow's Travels, page 139.

laid down on my own responsibility, either from the reported bearings and distances given me by the natives, such as all the country *beyond the Gariep*, or by the Hottentots or the boors, for a number of places within the *Colony* ; others from a distant view of them, such as mountains or the *sea-coast*, particularly that extending from the *Great Fish River* to *Gaurits River*.

It will easily be comprehended how I have been able to convert faulty and inaccurate materials to my use, so as to produce a more correct map than the originals from which they were taken, if it be considered that my own observations being first laid down, I had the frame-work of an entirely new construction ; to which I fitted and forced into shape, this heterogeneous collection of pieces. I believe, therefore, it will not be found to be claiming too much for this map, if it should be asserted that, in addition to a large and entirely new contribution to the geography of the southernmost part of Africa, it contains the sum of all that was previously laid before the public, or, at least, that could be thought useful or authentic; while, at the same time, the blank spaces exhibit to view the large proportion of unexplored country, still left within its limits.

The whole of the *western coast*, northward from St. Helena bay, may be regarded as a mere sketch ; and the course of the *Gariep*, from the twenty-third degree of longitude to its mouth, is laid down on the authority only of the Klaarwater Hottentots ; from whose report, also, I have obtained a confirmation of the existence of Le Vaillant's *Fish River*. But of the country of the *Great Namaquas* and *Dammaras*, I have not been able to gain any geographical particulars which could be deemed sufficiently defined for the purposes of a map. Of the names in the country of the *Little Namaquas*, the greater number have been adopted from the journals of Paterson and Le Vaillant ; while the former, with Thunberg and Lichtenstein, have been consulted for the *Further Bokkeveld*, the *Hantam*, and the *Further Roggeveld*. The course along the *Karro*, from Verkeerde Valley to Sneeuwberg, is obtained from the journals of Lichtenstein, Le Vaillant, and Paterson ; and *Kannaland* and *Kamnasiland*, from Thunberg and Sparrman. From the strange confusion and contradictions which are to be found in the pretended maps of that part of the Colony northward of *Zwartland*, I will not be answerable for the entire correctness of that district. For a sketch of the country eastward of the *Great Fish River*, there does not at present exist any materials which can be depended on.

The names of the different *Colonial districts* have been omitted, not only because their boundaries are ill defined and little known, even to the

4 E 2

inhabitants themselves, but principally because they have lately been so much altered, or subdivided into new districts, and will probably undergo still greater changes, that in the course of a few years the divisions of this map would only serve, as those of former maps now do, to mislead. A proof of it has occurred during the engraving of this; for scarcely was the word *Albany* put upon the copper, when I received information that the boundaries of that district had been altered by proclamation of the Cape Government. As however the different *districts* (see page 75), bear in most instances the same name as the principal village (see page 76), their situation and extent may be known well enough for the general purpose of gaining an idea of their relative position. More particular explanations, where they are required, will be found in the correspondent parts of the journal.

The want of proper names for the *natural divisions* of this part of Africa, is, in a geographical point of view, an inconvenience which seems to demand some remedy. The name of *Cape of Good Hope*, which belongs only to a particular promontory, cannot without evident absurdity be applied to the whole of the southern point of Africa; yet this absurdity continues to be tolerated, and even rendered greater, by thus denominating the whole of the country which happens to have been visited or discovered by the way of Cape Town. If it be necessary in a political view of the subject, to call by this name the whole of the Colonial territory, however extensive and distant, it certainly cannot be correct to say that the *Gariep* is a river at the *Cape of Good Hope*, or that the countries of the *Namaquas*, *Bushmen*, *Koras*, *Caffres*, and *Bichuanas*, are comprised geographically under that denomination.

Confining the following remarks to that portion of Southern Africa which is contained within the limits of the present map, it will appear that ten *natural divisions* present themselves to the geographer.

1. The *Peninsula* of the Cape of Good Hope; or the Cape of Good Hope proper. This consists of the mountainous tract extending from Cape Town to Cape Point (see page 74).

2. The *Western Districts*, or country lying between the Great Western Range of mountains and the sea, and stretching in length from False Bay to the Western Elephants River.

3. The *Maritime Districts*, from Hottentot-Holland Kloof to Sitsikamma. To these might be added, but with doubtful propriety, being in general of a different nature, the districts included between the Great Southern Range and the Zwarteberg Range, comprising Kannaland, Kamnasiland, and the maritime districts as far eastward as the Sunday River.

4. The *Intramontane;* comprising Roodezand, the Bokkevelds, Elephants River, Boschjesveld (Boshesveld,) and other districts included within the great ranges of mountains. To this division more strictly belong Kannaland, Kamnasiland, and the Lange Kloof, which might be denominated the *Southern Intramontane.*

5. The *Karro ;* bounded on the south by the Great Zwarteberg Range; on the east by the Sunday River; on the west by the Bokkeveld mountains; and on the north by the mountains of Sneeuwberg, Nieuwveld, Roggeveld, Hantam, and Kamiesberg. To the Karro belongs the westernmost part of the Colony, from the Elephants River to the northern boundary.

6. The *Eastern Districts;* or country extending eastward of the Sunday River, as far as the Caffre boundary, and terminated northward by the mountains of Sneeuwberg, Rhinosterberg, Zuureberg, and Bambosberg, including the Tarka.

7. The *Cisgariepine ;* lying between the Gariep and the Great Inland Range formed by Stormberg, Rhinosterberg, Sneeuwbergen, Nieuwvelds-bergen, Roggeveldsbergen, and continued by the Hantamberg, Kamies-berg, and Koperberg; its eastern limits being the Nugariep.

8. *Caffraria,* Proper; or the territory of the Caffre tribes; the northern boundary of which appears to be the Stormberg and the Great Inland Range, which probably continues for many degrees, to run along the eastern side of the Continent, in a direction parallel to the sea-coast.

9. The *North-eastern;* or unknown country, lying eastward of the Black and the Yellow Rivers.

10. The *Transgariepine ;* in which are comprised all regions situated on the north of the River Gariep. The eastern and western sides of this large division differing very considerably in fertility, will probably, when the intermediate country shall have been better explored, be found to be naturally divisible into the country of the Great Namaquas, and that of the Bichuanas.

The political divisions of the same regions are five, and consist of

1. The *Colony* of the Cape of Good Hope.

2. *Caffraria,* Proper.

3. The *Cisgariepine.*

4. The *Transgariepine ;* the Bushmen inhabitants of which speak dialects different from those which are used on the southern side of the river.

5. *Bichuánia ;* or the country of the Bichuana (Bitjuána) nations, who speak various dialects of a peculiar language.

Besides the preceding geographical and political divisions, a very remarkable distinction may be made in the extratropical part of Southern
Africa, with respect to its aboriginal inhabitants. It is peopled by nations
evidently of two widely distinct origins. The *Hottentot Race* is separated
from all the nations of the globe, by their extraordinary language, instantly
known from every other, by the frequent and peculiar clapping noise in its
pronunciation. From all their neighbours they are distinguished by a less
swarthy skin, a very different cast of features, a smaller stature, and more
delicate limbs and figure. The *Caffre Race*, whose language is free from
the clapping of the tongue, are characterised by a taller figure, and limbs
more robust, by a darker color, and features more round and large ; and
who, although approaching more to the Negro, are as distinct from these,
as from the Hottentots. To the *Hottentot Race* are referable the tribes denominated Bushmen, the Namaquas, and Koras or Koraquas, as well as the
Hottentots proper who at this day, as before the discovery of the land by
Europeans, inhabit the Cape Colony. That part of Africa which they
occupy, may therefore, in its most extended sense, be denominated the
Country of the Hottentots, or *Hottentotaria* if so long a name were admissible,
or the abridged one of *Hottentaria* not be more convenient. To the *Caffre
Race* belong the Bichuanas, and the Dammaras, together with the Kosas or
Caffres Proper, the Tambookis, and probably all the tribes on the eastern
side of the Continent, as far as Delagoa Bay.

LONDON :
Printed by A. & R. Spottiswoode,
New-Street-Square.

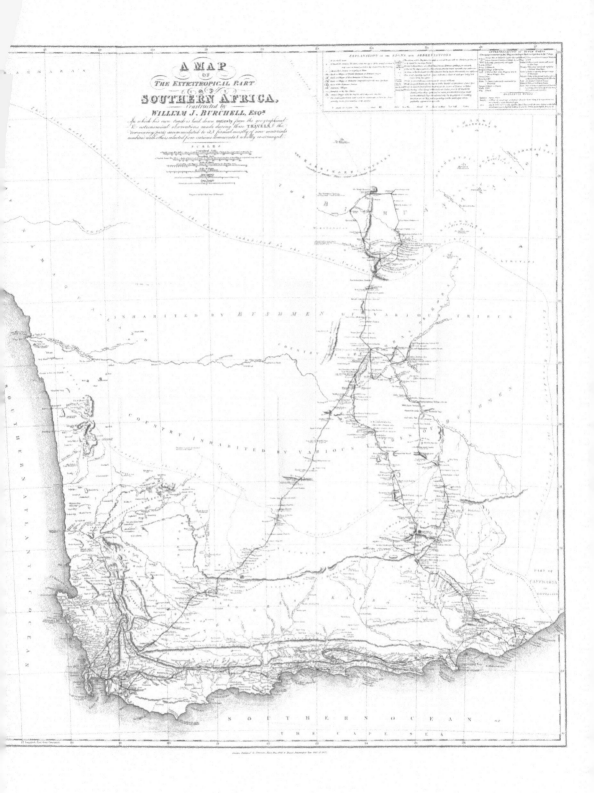

A MAP OF THE EXTRATROPICAL PART OF SOUTHERN AFRICA, Constructed by WILLIAM J. BURCHELL, ESQ.